THE MOST TRUSTED NAME IN TRAVEL

Frommer's®

IRELAND 2026

31st Edition

By Yvonne Gordon

Frommer's Ireland 2026, 31st Edition

Published by:
FrommerMedia LLC

ISBN 978-1-62887-651-2 (paper), 978-1-62887-652-9 (e-book)

Editorial Director: Pauline Frommer
Editor: Alexis Lipsitz Flippin
Production Editor: Cheryl Lenser
Cartographer: Andrew Dolan
Photo Editor: Alyssa Mattei
Indexer: Cheryl Lenser
Compositor: Lissa Auciello-Brogan
Cover Design: Dave Riedy

Front cover: Rock of Cashel.
Title page: Sliabh Liag.

For information on our other products or services, see www.frommers.com.

Frommer Media LLC also publishes its books in a variety of electronic formats. Some content that appears in print may not be available in electronic formats.

Manufactured in Malaysia

5 4 3 2 1

HOW TO CONTACT US

In researching this book, we discovered many wonderful places—hotels, restaurants, shops, and more. We're sure you'll find others. Please tell us about them, so we can share the information with your fellow travelers in upcoming editions. If you were disappointed with a recommendation, we'd love to know that, too. Please write to: Support@FrommerMedia.com

FROMMER'S RATINGS SYSTEM

Every hotel, restaurant and attraction listed in this guide has been ranked for quality and value. Here's what the hearts mean:

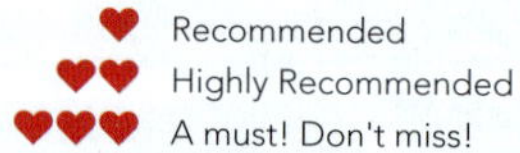

Recommended
Highly Recommended
A must! Don't miss!

AN IMPORTANT NOTE

The world is a dynamic place. Hotels change ownership, restaurants hike their prices, museums alter their opening hours, and buses and trains change their routings. And all of this can occur in the several months after our authors have visited, inspected, and written about these hotels, restaurants, museums, and transportation services. Though we have made valiant efforts to keep all our information fresh and up-to-date, some few changes can inevitably occur in the periods before a revised edition of this guidebook is published. So please bear with us if a tiny number of the details in this book have changed. Please also note that we have no responsibility or liability for any inaccuracy or errors or omissions, or for inconvenience, loss, damage, or expenses suffered by anyone as a result of assertions in this guide.

CONTENTS

LIST OF MAPS v

1 THE BEST OF IRELAND 1

2 IRELAND IN CONTEXT 22

Ireland Today 23

The Making of Ireland 24

Ireland in Culture 41

Eating & Drinking in Ireland 48

Tips on Accommodations 49

When to Go 51

Ireland Calendar of Events 52

3 SUGGESTED IRELAND ITINERARIES 56

The Regions in Brief 57

A Week from the East to Southwest 61

Two Weeks in Ireland 64

The Best Adventures in Ireland 66

The Best of Ireland for Families 70

Exploring Ancient Ireland 73

The Best of the North & Northwest 76

4 DUBLIN 80

Essentials 81

Getting Around 89

Fast Facts: Dublin 92

Exploring Dublin 92

Where to Stay in Dublin 125

Where to Eat in Dublin 141

Shopping 157

Sports & Outdoor Pursuits 165

Spectator Sports 167

Dublin After Dark 168

5 DAY TRIPS FROM DUBLIN 177

Essentials 178

North of Dublin: Counties Meath & Louth 180

West of Dublin: County Kildare 192

South of Dublin: Counties Wicklow & Carlow 199

6 THE SOUTHEAST 211

Essentials 212

County Waterford 215

County Wexford 227

County Kilkenny 239

7 COUNTY CORK 249

Essentials 250

Cork City 251

East Cork 268

Kinsale 274

West Cork 284

8 COUNTY KERRY 295

Essentials 296

The Ring of Kerry 298

Tralee 334

The Dingle Peninsula 338

9 THE BURREN & BEYOND 351

Essentials 352

County Clare 354

County Limerick 370

County Tipperary 378

10 COUNTY GALWAY & CONNEMARA 387

Essentials 388

Galway City 389

Connemara 410

11 THE MIDLANDS 423
Essentials 424
Exploring the Midlands 425
Where to Stay in the Midlands 435
Where to Eat in the Midlands 437

12 COUNTIES MAYO & SLIGO 441
Essentials 442
County Mayo 443
County Sligo 458

13 COUNTY DONEGAL 474
Essentials 475
Donegal Town & Donegal Bay 476
Around County Donegal 486
The Inishowen Peninsula 493

14 BELFAST 499
Essentials 500
Fast Facts: Belfast 501
Exploring Belfast 503
Where to Stay in Belfast 517
Where to Eat in Belfast 523
Shopping 527
Belfast After Dark 528

15 DAY TRIPS FROM BELFAST 531
Essentials 532
The Causeway Coast 533
The Ards Peninsula & Mourne Mountains 544
County Armagh 554

16 DERRY & THE LAKELANDS 561
Essentials 562
Derry City 563
Day Trip to the Sperrin Mountains 574
The Fermanagh Lakelands 578

17 PLANNING YOUR TRIP TO IRELAND 587
Getting There 588
Trips & Tours 589
Getting Around 591
Fast Facts: Ireland 597

INDEX 602

LIST OF MAPS

Ireland 18
A Week from the East to Southwest & Two Weeks in Ireland 63
The Best Adventures in Ireland 67
The Best of Ireland for Families 71
Ancient Ireland 75
The Best of the North & Northwest 77
Dublin Orientation 82
Dublin Attractions 94
Trinity College 105
Where to Stay in Central Dublin 126
Where to Stay in Ballsbridge & the Southern Suburbs 139
Where to Eat in Dublin 142
Temple Bar Restaurants 145
Day Trips from Dublin 179
Kilkenny, Wexford & Waterford 213
Waterford City 217
Wexford Town 229
The Ring of Hook 231
Kilkenny City 241
Cork City 253
County Cork 269
County Kerry 297
Killarney 301
Killarney National Park 303
The Ring of Kerry 325
The Dingle Peninsula 339
Counties Clare, Limerick & Tipperary 353
County Clare 355
County Tipperary 379
Galway City 391
County Galway 407
The Midlands 425
County Mayo 445
County Sligo 459
Sligo Town 461
Donegal Town 477
County Donegal 479
Belfast Attractions 505
Where to Stay & Eat in Belfast 519
Day Trips from Belfast 535
Derry City 565
Derry, Tyrone & Fermanagh 575
Irish Rail Routes 594
Major Irish Bus Routes 596

ABOUT THE AUTHOR

Yvonne Gordon is an award-winning travel writer who writes about Ireland for publications around the globe, including *National Geographic, The Washington Post*, AFAR.com, *BBC Travel, The Guardian, The Irish Independent*, and *Wanderlust* magazine. Her awards include Irish Travel Writer of the Year. She is from Dublin and spends as much time as possible exploring Ireland north and south, hiking coastal and mountain trails, learning about traditions, hearing local stories, and finding atmospheric places to stay.

ABOUT THE FROMMER TRAVEL GUIDES

For most of the past 65 years, Frommer's has been the leading series of travel guides in North America, accounting for as many as 24% of all guidebooks sold. I think I know why.

Though we hope our books are entertaining, we nevertheless deal with travel in a serious fashion. Our guidebooks have never looked on such journeys as a mere recreation, but as a far more important human function, a time of learning and introspection, an essential part of a civilized life. We stress the culture, lifestyle, history, and beliefs of the destinations we cover, and urge our readers to seek out people and new ideas as the chief rewards of travel.

We have never shied from controversy. We have, from the beginning, encouraged our authors to be intensely judgmental, critical—both pro and con—in their comments, and wholly independent. Our only clients are our readers, and we have triggered the ire of countless prominent sorts, from a tourist newspaper we called "practically worthless" (it unsuccessfully sued us) to the many rip-offs we've condemned.

And because we believe that travel should be available to everyone regardless of their incomes, we have always been cost-conscious at every level of expenditure. Though we have broadened our recommendations beyond the budget category, we insist that every lodging we include be sensibly priced. We use every form of media to assist our readers and are particularly proud of our feisty daily website, the award-winning Frommers.com.

I have high hopes for the future of Frommer's. May these guidebooks, in all the years ahead, continue to reflect the joy of travel and the freedom that travel represents. May they always pursue a cost-conscious path, so that people of all incomes can enjoy the rewards of travel. And may they create, for both the traveler and the persons among whom we travel, a community of friends, where all human beings live in harmony and peace.

Arthur Frommer
(1929–2024)

1

THE BEST OF IRELAND

Ireland is a captivating place to explore. Within a few miles, you can travel from plunging cliffs and flat pastureland to towering mountains and gloomy peat bogs. You can spend the night in an ancient castle or state-of-the-art spa hotel, dine on fine Irish cuisine or snack on crispy fish and chips served in a paper bag. Ireland is tiny, but its scenery is ever-changing, and the sheer number of sights, little villages, charming pubs, and adorable restaurants and shops can be overwhelming—you always feel that you might be missing something. So, it's nice to have someone to help you focus, and that's why we've put together this list of some of our favorite places and things to do in Ireland. We hope that while you're exploring this magical country, you'll discover a few favorites of your own.

THE best NATURAL WONDERS

- **The Burren** (County Clare): We can guarantee this: The Burren is one of the strangest landscapes you're likely to see anywhere in the world. Its stark limestone grassland is spread with a quilt of wildflowers from as far afield as the Alps, and its inhabitants include nearly every species of butterfly found in Ireland. See p. 354.
- **Mizen Head** (County Cork): While most travelers flock to the better-known Cliffs of Moher (p. 360), you won't find crowds at these majestic sea cliffs at Ireland's southwest tip. Watch the waves crash against the 210m-high (689-ft.) cliffs from the excellent visitor center. See p. 288.
- **Sliabh Liag** (County Donegal): As the Sliabh Liag (or Slieve League) coastline stretches along Donegal Bay, its pigmented bluffs rise to 600m-high (1,968-ft.) sea cliffs. You can walk along them, if you dare. See p. 482.
- **MacGillycuddy's Reeks** (County Kerry): Cresting grandly over the Iveragh Peninsula, MacGillycuddy's Reeks not only has the best name of any mountain range in Ireland, it also has the highest peak on the island, Carrantuohill (1,041m/3,414 ft.). See p. 304.
- **Malin Head** (County Donegal): From one extreme to the other—literally! The Malin Head promontory, in the remotest part of Ireland's remotest county, looks out over a seemingly unending sea. Next stop: Iceland. See p. 495.

PREVIOUS PAGE: Visitors exploring EPIC The Irish Emigration Museum, in Dublin City.

Epic rock climbing at Malin Head.

- **The Twelve Bens** (County Galway): Amid Connemara's central mountains, bogs, and lakes, the rugged Twelve Bens range crowns a spectacular landscape. The loftiest, Benbaun, in Connemara National Park, reaches a height of 729m (2,392 ft.). See p. 412.
- **Giant's Causeway** (County Antrim): At the foot of a cliff by the sea, this mysterious mass of tightly packed, naturally occurring hexagonal basalt columns is nothing short of astonishing. Formed 60 million years ago, this volcanic wonder looks even better when negotiated (cautiously) on foot. See p. 537.

THE best MUSEUMS

- **Chester Beatty Library** (Dublin City, County Dublin): Not just a library, this is one of Ireland's best museums, with a wealth of books, illuminated texts, and small art objects. Its collection of rare religious manuscripts is among the most unique in the world. See p. 96.
- **Waterford Treasures** (Waterford City, County Waterford): Small but vibrant Waterford City has a superb collection of museums, including the Medieval Museum, Bishop's Palace, Irish Silver Museum, Reginald's Tower, and our favorite, the Irish Museum of Time. See p. 215.
- **Titanic Belfast** (Belfast, County Antrim): Belfast is incredibly proud of having built the most famous ocean liner in history, despite its ultimate fate—though, as they're fond of saying, "She was alright when

The five-story, 20,000-square-foot central atrium in the Titanic Belfast museum.

she left here." This gleaming, high-tech museum is the best of several *Titanic*-related attractions in Belfast. See p. 510.

- **EPIC The Irish Emigration Museum** (Dublin City, County Dublin): This fully digital museum tells the stories of the Irish characters who have made their mark around the world in everything from politics and sports to music and movies, plus the stories of those forced to emigrate during hard times. See p. 114.
- **National Museum of Ireland: Archaeology** (Dublin City, County Dublin): Ireland's National Museum is split into four separate sites, of which this is far and away the best. The collection dates back to the earliest settlers, but it's the relics from the Viking invasion and the early Christian period that dazzle the most. See p. 100.

THE best CASTLES & HISTORIC HOUSES

- **King John's Castle** (Limerick City, County Limerick): This impressive castle was built for King John around 1200. It's fun to explore the towers and courtyard, and a fantastic exhibition in the castle interior will take you right through Irish history. See p. 371.
- **Kilkenny Castle** (Kilkenny City, County Kilkenny): Although parts of this stout, towered castle date from the 13th century, the existing

structure looks more like a 19th-century palace. Beautifully restored, it also has extensive gardens; the old stables now hold art galleries and shops. See p. 240.

- **Bantry House** (Bantry, County Cork): Surrounded by beautiful gardens, this magnificent Georgian house in West Cork offers an extra delight: the breathtaking views of Bantry Bay from the gardens. See p. 284.
- **Bunratty Castle & Folk Park** (Bunratty, County Clare): This grand old castle has been well restored and filled with a curious assortment of medieval furnishings, offering a glimpse into the life of its past inhabitants. It's the first stop for many arrivals from Shannon, so expect crowds. See p. 359.
- **Ross Castle** (Killarney National Park, County Kerry): This tower house is worth seeing for its setting, standing guard over the edge of the Lower Lake in Killarney National Park. See p. 304.
- **Dunluce Castle** (County Antrim): Set atop a razor-sharp promontory jutting into the sea, these castle ruins are picturesque and evocative. Unlike other ruined castles, it wasn't demolished by human enemies, but had to be abandoned after a large section collapsed and fell into the breakers below. See p. 537.

The glorious gardens of Bantry House have been restored to their 19th-century splendor.

THE most beautiful PICTURE-POSTCARD TOWNS

- **Kinsale** (County Cork): Kinsale's narrow streets all lead to the sea, dropping steeply from the hills around the harbor. The walk from Kinsale through Scilly to Charles Fort and Frower Point is breathtaking. ***Bonus:*** It's a gourmet hot spot, full of good restaurants. See p. 274.
- **Dingle—*Daingean Uí Chúis*** (County Kerry): In this charming and vibrant town, stone buildings ramble up and down hills, and the small population is relaxed about visitors. You'll find lots of little diners and picturesque pubs, plus a lovely historic church. See p. 338.
- **Adare** (County Limerick): Literally a picture-postcard town, Adare is hardly a secret, but if you manage to visit when the roads aren't clogged with tour buses, you'll leave with a memory card full of photos. See p. 370.
- **Kenmare** (County Kerry): It's easy to fall in love with Kenmare, with its stone cottages, colorful gardens, and flowers overflowing from window boxes. Home to several elegant hotels, it makes an enchanting base when exploring the Ring of Kerry. See p. 316.
- **Dalkey** (County Dublin): The cutest of a string of upscale seaside towns unfurling south from Dublin, Dalkey is both a short drive and a million miles away from the busy city. With a castle, two tiny

Thatched-roof cottages pillowed in flower gardens make Adare, in County Limerick, one of Ireland's most picturesque towns.

harbors, and some fine restaurants, it tempts you into its affluent embrace. See p. 124.

- **Ardara** (County Donegal): On the southwest coast of Donegal, tiny Ardara looks as if it were carved out of a solid block of granite. Its hilly streets are lined with boutiques and charming arts shops, many selling clothes crafted from the famed Donegal wool. See p. 487.

THE best FOR LOVERS OF LITERATURE

- **MoLI, Museum of Literature Ireland** (Dublin City, County Dublin): Newman House is filled with exciting exhibits about the world of Irish writing, including film, sound, and books, with rare items from the James Joyce archive. See p. 118.
- **Seamus Heaney HomePlace** (Bellaghy, County Derry): Even as his literary fame took him around the world, the poetry of Seamus Heaney (1939–2013) remained rooted in the boglands, fields, and farms of the land here where he grew up. This literary center is dedicated to the Nobel Prize–winning poet. See p. 577.
- **The Seanchaí: Kerry Writers' Museum** (Listowel, County Kerry): Imaginative displays enliven this vibrant museum dedicated to the life and work of some of County Kerry's best writers. See p. 335.
- **Davy Byrnes pub** (Dublin City, County Dublin): After a stop at the **James Joyce Centre** (p. 116), make a pilgrimage to this venerable pub, which crops up in Joyce's masterpiece *Ulysses:* The hero, Leopold Bloom, famously orders a lunch of burgundy and a Gorgonzola sandwich. The pub is acutely aware of its heritage but knows better than to ruin the appeal by being too touristy. See p. 173.
- **County Sligo:** With its many connections to the beloved poet W. B. Yeats, this county is a pilgrimage destination for poetry fans. The landscape shaped the poet's writing, and many of its landmarks—Lough Gill, Glencar Lake, Ben Bulben Mountain, Maeve's tomb—appear in his verse. Be sure to visit Yeats's somber grave in Drumcliffe. See p. 458.

Yeats's grave at Drumcliffe, in County Sligo.

- **The Aran Islands:** Though playwright John Millington Synge was born in County Dublin, as a leading figure in the Irish literary revival of the late 19th century he became passionately interested in these brooding islands off the Galway coast—the setting for his most famous play, *The Playboy of the Western World.* See p. 395.

THE best PREHISTORIC SITES

- **Newgrange** (County Meath): One of the archaeological wonders of Western Europe, Newgrange is the centerpiece of a megalithic cemetery dating back 5,000 years. Its massive mound and passage tomb are amazing feats of engineering. Still, the question remains: What was it all for? See p. 181.
- **Knowth** (County Meath): Another impressive passage tomb, Knowth's awesome presence is matched only by its inscrutability. Hundreds of prehistoric carvings were discovered here when the site was first excavated in the 1960s, and yet nobody seems to quite understand it to this day. See p. 181.
- **Carrowmore & Carrowkeel** (County Sligo): These two megalithic cities of the dead (Europe's largest) may have once contained more than 200 passage tombs. The two together—one in the valley and the other atop a nearby mountain—convey an unequaled sense of the ancient peoples' reverence for the departed. Carrowmore is well presented and interpreted, while Carrowkeel quietly awaits those who seek it out. See p. 463.
- **Céide Fields** (County Mayo): The amazing thing about these stone walls, the remains of farming settlements, hidden under the bog, is simply how unbelievably old they are—people were herding cows in the fields here 5,000 years ago. See p. 450.
- **Dún Aengus** (Aran Islands, County Galway): The eminent archaeologist George Petrie called Dún Aengus "the most magnificent barbaric monument in Europe." No one knows who built this massive stone fort or what year it was constructed. Facing the sea, where its three stone rings meet steep 90m (295-ft.) cliffs, Dún Aengus still stands guard today over the southern coast of Inishmore, the largest of the Aran Islands. See p. 395.
- **Hill of Tara** (County Meath): Of ritual significance from the Stone Age to the early Christian period, Tara has seen it all and kept it a secret. This mostly unexcavated site was the traditional center and seat of Ireland's high kings; it's a place to be walked slowly. Although the hill is only 154m (512 ft.) above sea level, on a clear day you can see each of Ireland's four Celtic provinces from here. See p. 183.

Families at play at the Hill of Tara, ancient seat of Irish kings.

THE best EARLY CHRISTIAN RUINS

- **Skellig Michael** (County Kerry): Early Irish monks built this hermitage dedicated to the archangel Michael on a remote, rocky crag rising sharply 214m (702 ft.) out of the Atlantic, some 13km (8 miles) offshore of the Iveragh Peninsula. The experience of journeying out to Skellig across choppy seas by boat and the arduous climb to its summit are challenging—and equally unforgettable. See p. 326.
- **Glendalough** (County Wicklow): Nestled in "the glen of the two lakes," this remote monastic settlement was founded by St. Kevin in the 6th century. Today its atmospheric ruins preside over an endlessly scenic setting with lakes and forests surrounding it. It's quite simply one of the loveliest spots in Ireland. See p. 201.
- **Jerpoint Abbey** (County Kilkenny): Jerpoint is the finest of many Cistercian abbeys whose ruins dot the Irish landscape. Somehow, hundreds of years of rain and wind have failed to completely wipe away its medieval carvings, leaving us a rare chance to glimpse how magnificent these abbeys once were. Don't miss the splendid, richly carved cloister. See p. 243.
- **The Rock of Cashel** (County Tipperary): In name and appearance, "the Rock" suggests a citadel, a place designed more for power than

prayer. In fact, Cashel (or *Caiseal*) means "fortress." The rock is a huge outcropping—or an *up*cropping—of limestone topped with beautiful ruins, including what was once Ireland's finest Romanesque chapel. The seat of clerics and kings, it was a power center to rival the Hill of Tara; now the two sites vie for the attention of tourists. See p. 381.

- **Clonmacnoise** (County Offaly): The old Irish high kings came to this place to find spiritual solace, and it's still a profound and thought-provoking place to visit. Don't leave without checking out the monumental ancient slabs, inscribed with personal messages in Celtic script. See p. 428.
- **Inishmurray** (County Sligo): This uninhabited island off the Sligo coast holds another striking monastic ruin, this one surrounded by what appears to be the walls of an even more ancient stone fort. Vikings sought out this remote outpost of peace-seeking monks and destroyed it in A.D. 807. Today its circular walls and the surrounding sea create a stunning view, well worth the effort required to reach it. See p. 465.

Carvings decorate the arches of the cloister at Jerpoint Abbey.

THE best FAMILY ACTIVITIES

- **Fota Island & Wildlife Park** (Carrigtwohill, County Cork): In this wildlife park, rare and endangered animals roam freely. You'll see everything from giraffes and zebras to kangaroos, flamingos, penguins, and monkeys wandering the grassland. Add in a tour train, picnic tables, a playground, and a gift shop, and you have the makings of a wonderful family outing. See p. 272.
- **Dolphin & Whale-Watching Tour** (Ventry, County Kerry): While Fungie the dolphin is no longer in Dingle Bay, you might still see wild dolphins, whales, puffins, seals, and lots of other wildlife (depending on the season) on a guided tour with Blasket Island Eco Marine Tours from Ventry Pier, 7km (4.3 miles) from Dingle, which also takes in a stop on Great Blasket Island. See p. 340.

- **Irish National Heritage Park** (Ferrycarrig, County Wexford): Millennia of history are made painlessly educational for children and adults at this engaging "living history" museum. It's a fascinating, informative way to while away a couple of hours or more. See p. 228.
- **Great Western Greenway** (Westport to Achill Island, County Mayo): Pack a picnic, rent some bicycles, and cycle all or part of this gorgeous 42km (26-mile) route to Achill Island, with bog, mountain, and sea views along the way. See p. 456.
- **Muckross House & Gardens** (Killarney, County Kerry): Today the gateway to Killarney National Park, this impressive mansion has been preserved in all its Victorian splendor. Nearby, at Muckross Traditional Farms, workers engage in traditional farm activities while dressed in authentic period clothing. See p. 302.
- **Bunratty Castle & Folk Park** (Bunratty, County Clare): Kids love Bunratty, which looks every bit as satisfyingly medieval as an old castle should. The grounds have been turned over to a replica 19th-century village, complete with actors playing Victorian residents going about their daily lives. It's great fun to wander through. See p. 359.
- **Beyond the Trees** (Avondale House, County Wicklow): This family-friendly Treetop Walk features interactive learning elements along the way. Younger members will love the giant slide at the end. See p. 200.

Rise above the forest canopy on a stroll along the Treetop Walk at the Avondale House.

THE best DRIVING TOURS

- **The Wild Atlantic Way** (County Cork to County Donegal): Stretching 2,500km (1,553 miles) along Ireland's West Coast, between Kinsale in County Cork and Inishowen in Donegal, this drive takes in some of Ireland's wildest and most beautiful coastal scenery. While it's better to do a small section of the drive on one trip (don't even attempt the entire drive in one visit), you will see lots of Wild Atlantic Way road signs and various "discovery points" along the way. See p. 275.
- **The Ring of Kerry** (County Kerry): It's by far the most well-traveled of Ireland's great routes, but there's no denying the Ring of Kerry's

appeal. It's a seductive combination of stunning countryside, charming villages, and inspiring historical sites. The road gets quite busy in summer, but come in the spring or autumn and it's a much more peaceful experience. See p. 323.

Dunquin Pier is a spectacularly scenic viewpoint along Slea Head Drive.

- **Slea Head Drive** (County Kerry): This drive, starting from Dingle Town and heading down the Ventry road, follows the sparkling sea past a series of ancient sites such as the Dunbeg Fort and the beehive-shaped Gallarus Oratory. At Dunquin, you can embark on boats to the mysterious abandoned Blasket Islands. See p. 341.
- **Horn Head** (County Donegal): Drive pretty much anywhere in County Donegal, and before long you'll be in beautiful, wild, unspoiled countryside—that's one reason why we never mind getting lost here. One of the best drives is around Horn Head, near Dunfanaghy, where quartzite sea cliffs glisten like glass when the sun hits them just right. See p. 488.
- **Inishowen Peninsula** (County Donegal): This far-flung promontory in Ireland's northern end stretches out from Lough Foyle to the east and Lough Swilly to the west toward Malin Head, its farthest point. Driving the perimeter, you'll pass ancient sites, pretty villages, and fine sandy beaches in fierce rocky coves. If you are looking to get lost, this is a great place to do it. See p. 493.
- **Causeway Coastal Route** (County Antrim): Sweeping views of midnight-blue sea against gray, unforgiving cliffs and deep-green hillsides make this 97km-long (60-mile) coastal route unforgettable. Start in gorgeous Glenarm with its castle walls and barbican gate, then head north along the coast past Bushmills and the Giant's Causeway to Portrush. Best of all, you often have the road quite to yourself. See p. 534.

THE best HOTELS

- **Adare Manor** (Adare, County Limerick): A haven for the sporty and non-sporty alike, Adare Manor has vast grounds, including a championship golf course, if that's your thing. If not, well, you only have the run of a beautiful Victorian Gothic manor and three outstanding restaurants as compensation. Bummer! See p. 373.
- **Ashford Castle** (Cong, County Mayo): Live like royalty with a stay at this fairy-tale castle in County Mayo. The great and the good have been coming here for decades to see what the fuss is about. The fuss, it turns out, is justified. See p. 452.
- **Cashel Palace Hotel** (Cashel, County Tipperary): The interior of this Palladian manor is about all things luxury, with original features, antiques, and open fires, plus views across to the Rock of Cashel. See p. 383.
- **The Westbury** (Dublin City, County Dublin): What the Shelbourne is to old Dublin, so this place is to new Dublin: a top-class hotel for fashionistas and sophisticates to rest their well-heeled feet. See p. 129.
- **Cliff House Hotel** (Ardmore, County Waterford): This luxury boutique hotel is known as much for its amazing views as for the awards

The Gallery at Adare Manor.

Rooms overlooking the gardens at the Merrion hotel.

it has received—including a Michelin star for its restaurant. See p. 222.

- **The Merrion** (Dublin City, County Dublin): Here you'll find a row of stylish Georgian town houses with original features, open fires, a garden, spa, and luxury dining. There's almost no reason to go out. See p. 129.
- **The Europe** (Killarney, County Kerry): Lake views, sumptuous beds, a wonderful spa . . . what's not to like? Well, very little apparently: The Europe is widely seen as one of the best hotels in Ireland. See p. 307.
- **Sheen Falls Lodge** (Kenmare, County Kerry): This lovely retreat on Kenmare Bay has 300 acres of grounds, including woodlands and a waterfall. See p. 319.
- **Dromoland Castle** (Newmarket on Fergus, County Clare): Another ancient Irish castle that has been converted to a luxury hotel, Dromoland is a grand estate with 500 acres of grounds and even its own golf course. See p. 365.
- **The Merchant** (Belfast, County Antrim): Set in a former bank, with ornate columns and ceilings, this is one of the most beautiful hotels in the city. Choose between a heritage or modern Art Deco–style room. See p. 518.

THE best RESTAURANTS

- **Dede at the Customs House** (Baltimore, County Cork): The food here by chef Ahmet Dede is an exquisite and delicate balance of fine ingredients and delicate spicing, making it one of Ireland's best restaurants (it has two Michelin stars). See p. 291.
- **Terre** (Castlemartyr, County Cork): Prepare to be wowed. The best of land and sea are curated into a series of thoughtful and original dishes, which won it a Michelin star just 6 months after opening. See p. 274.
- **Artis** (Derry, County Derry): At this relaxed space in the city's Craft Village, chef Phelim O'Hagan serves up creative cuisine with the best local produce. See p. 572.
- **Roam** (Belfast, County Antrim): Young chef Ryan Jenkins has scoured the landscape for the best local ingredients, to create a fine dining experience in a casual setting. See p. 526.
- **Goldie** (Cork City, County Cork): In this cozy space, the best of Cork's seafood, including the catch of the day, is served in exciting combinations. See p. 264.
- **Chapter One** (Dublin City, County Dublin): In the vaulted basement of the Dublin Writers Museum, this is one of Dublin's very best

The Dromoland Castle hotel comes with its own golf course.

Beets harvested straight from the garden at the Cook & Gardener in County Donegal.

Flavorful seasonal dishes are only matched by the artful presentations at Ox, in Belfast.

restaurants. It's quite a splurge, but come at lunchtime and you can enjoy the same wonderful food at almost half the price. See p. 150.

- **The Black Pig** (Kinsale, County Cork): Think every place on this list is fancy fine dining? This simple wine bar with heaps of atmosphere is one of our favorite spots in Ireland's "foodie capital," Kinsale. See p. 279.
- **Wild Honey Inn** (Lisdoonvarna, County Clare): Another unique dining experience in the surroundings of a historic inn, the Wild Honey brings in diners from all over the world. See p. 368.
- **The Cook & Gardener** (Rathmullan, County Donegal): Ingredients don't get much fresher, picked straight from the garden. The results are simply sensational. See p. 491.

What's the Score?

In this book, we award listings up to three hearts based on the overall experience of a place. Just because a hotel has all the best facilities, or a restaurant is supertrendy, doesn't necessarily mean it'll score a full house from us. But please remember, our view is subjective! Your own favorites will be based on *your* experience of Ireland, and that may be different from anyone else's. That's one of the joys of travel. So if you have a favorite Ireland discovery that we've left out, please write and tell us. We can't wait to discover it too. ***Note:*** We thoroughly update this guide for every edition, checking on any closures, but it's always a good idea to call ahead to confirm that an establishment is open before you go.

- **Ox** (Belfast, County Antrim): Cool and contemporary, this Michelin-starred restaurant is one of Belfast's most sought-after dining hotspots. See p. 523.

IRELAND'S best SHOPPING

- **Brown Thomas** (Grafton St., Dublin): Among the most quintessential of Dublin's grand old department stores, Brown Thomas has the works, from top-hatted doormen to the latest in designer fashions. See p. 161.
- **Kilkenny** (Nassau St., Dublin): Everything here is Irish, from fashion and jewelry to homewares and crafts. It's a great place to pick up Irish pottery and prints—and they ship internationally. See p. 160.
- **Belleek China** (Belleek, County Fermanagh): The world-famous Belleek brand of fine china has been furnishing the tables of the upper crust since 1864. The visitor center, near Donegal, has a magnificent collection for sale—and will ship internationally if you're worried about getting your delicate selection home in one piece. See p. 579.
- **Louis Mulcahy Pottery** (Ballyferriter, County Kerry): Exquisite fine porcelain and Irish stoneware pottery pieces are all crafted here at the workshop. They also ship internationally. See p. 348.
- **St. George's Market** (East Bridge St., Belfast): There's plenty to browse at this weekend market with food, antiques, and crafts, plus live music, too. See p. 509.

Shoppers enjoy live music on weekends at St. George's Market in Belfast.

THE best AUTHENTIC EXPERIENCES

- **Seeing a traditional music session at a proper Irish pub:** While there are plenty of shows for the tourist crowd, nothing beats the energy, atmosphere, and authenticity of a genuine small-town traditional music session. The instructions for getting the most out of a session are simple: Buy a pint, grab a seat (preferably one near a

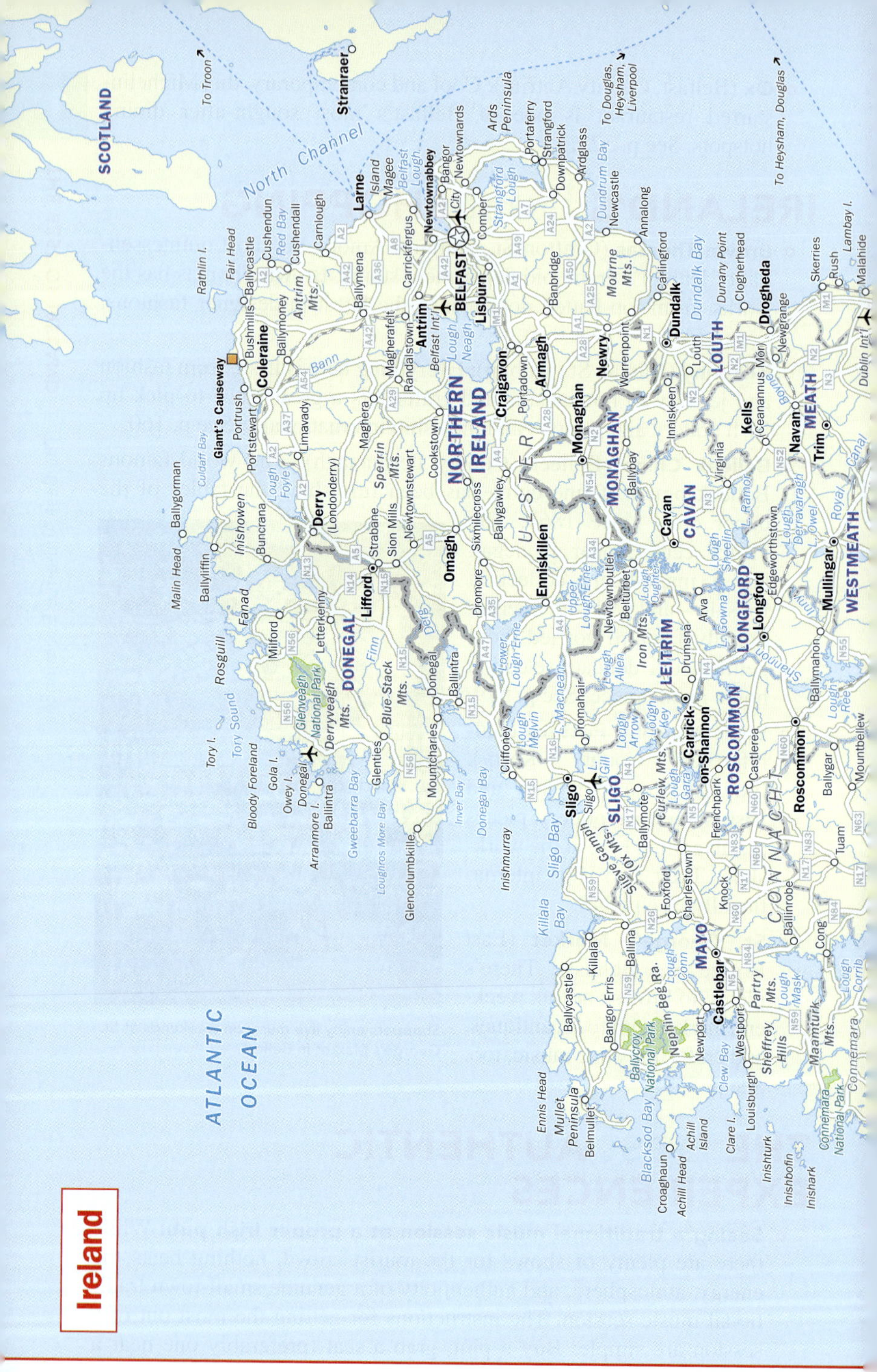

Ireland

IRISH SEA
CELTIC SEA
ATLANTIC OCEAN
St. George's Channel
WALES
To Liverpool
To Holyhead
To Fishguard
To Pembroke
To Swansea
To Roscoff
To Roscoff
0 30 miles
0 30 kms
DUBLIN
(Baile Átha Cliath)
Dún Laoghaire
Bray
Greystones
Wicklow
Wicklow Head
Avoca
Arklow
Shillelagh
Gorey
Courtown
Leixlip
Naas
KILDARE
DUBLIN
Wicklow Mts.
Wicklow Mts. National Park
WICKLOW
Rathvilly
Tullow
Carlow
CARLOW
Ferns
Enniscorthy
WEXFORD
Wexford Bay
Wexford
Wexford Harbour
Rosslare
Rosslare Harbour
Carnsore Point
Kilmore Quay
Saltee Islands
Wellington Bridge
Hook Peninsula
Hook Head
Blackstairs Mts.
Galway
GALWAY
Galway
Athenry
Ballinasloe
Tullamore
OFFALY
Bog of Allen
Droichead Nua (Newbridge)
Monasterevin
Mountmellick
Portarlington
Portlaoise
LEINSTER
LAOISE (LEIX)
Castledermot
Abbeyleix
Leighlinbridge
Nore
Barrow
Kilkenny
KILKENNY
Callan
Carrick-on-Suir
Waterford
Waterford
Waterford Hbr.
Dunmore East
WATERFORD
Comeragh Mts.
Clonmel
Dungarvan
Ring
Youghal
Knockadoon Head
Ballycotton
Castlemartyr
Tallow
Cappoquin
Knockmealdown Mts.
Cashel
Cahir
Tipperary
TIPPERARY
Limerick Junction
Thurles
Urlingford
Templemore
Roscrea
Moneygall
Birr
Cloghan
Shannon
Portumna
Borrisokane
Cloughjordan
Nenagh
Lough Derg
Scarriff
Ballina
Newport
Pallas Grean
Galtee Mts.
MUNSTER
Mitchelstown
Fermoy
Blackwater
Nagles Mts.
Carrigtchill
Cobh
Cork Harbour
Passage West
Cork
Cork Int'l
Blarney Castle
CORK
Kinsale
Kinsale Harbour
Old Head o' Kinsale
Courtmacsherry Bay
Clonakilty Bay
Galley Head
Rosscarbery
Bandon
Bandon
Skibbereen
Castletownshend
Baltimore
Cape Clear I.
Cape Clear
Toormore Bay
Crookhaven
Mizen Head
Dunmanus B.
Sheep's Head
Bantry
Bantry Bay
Glengarriff
Shehy Mts.
Macroom
Lee
Boggeragh Mts.
Millstreet
Banteer
Mallow
Buttevant
Charleville
Loughrea
Slieve Aughty Mts.
Rossaveal
Spiddal
Galway Bay
Carraroe
Lettermullen
North Sound
Kilronan
Inishmore
Inishmaan
Inisheer
Aran Islands
South Sound
Ballyvaughan
The Burren National Park
Doolin
Cliffs of Moher
Hag's Head
Ennistymon
Miltown Malbay
Spanish Pt.
CLARE
Ennis
Slieve Bernagh
Mutton I.
Newmarket-on-Fergus
Shannon
Sixmilebridge
Limerick
Donegal Pt.
Kilkee
Kilrush
Carrigaholt
Loop Head
Tarbert
Foynes
Patrickswell
Rathkeale
Adare
LIMERICK
Ballybunion
Listowel
Newcastle West
Kerry Head
Ballyheigue
Tralee Bay
Abbeydorney
Brandon Pt.
Castlegregory
Tralee
Castleisland
Kerry
Ballydesmond
Sybil Pt.
Dingle Peninsula
Dingle
Castlemaine
KERRY
Dunquin
Great Blasket I.
Dingle Bay
L. Leane
Killarney
Killarney National Park
Macgillycuddy's Reeks
Cahirsiveen
Valentia I.
Portmagee
Iveragh Pen.
L. Currane
Kenmare
Ballinskelligs
Ltl. Skellig
Skellig Michael
Kenmare R.
Beara Pen.
Castetownbere
Dursey I.
Bear I.
N59
N6
N18
N52
N62
N7
N78
N9
N81
N80
N11
N8
N10
N24
N76
N25
N21
N70
N72
N73
N20
N22
N71
M50

Enjoying a music session in a Galway pub.

smoldering peat fire), and wait for the action to begin. We've listed some of the best places in this book, including pubs such as the **Long Valley** in **Cork** (p. 267) or **Gus O'Connor's** and **McGann's** in little **Doolin, County Clare** (p. 362).

- **Getting lost down the back roads of County Kerry:** It's Ireland's most visited county by far, and if you stick to the beaten path, in summer it's thronged with tourists. Instead, veer off onto the winding back roads and allow yourself to get gloriously, hopelessly lost. There are always new discoveries to be made along its breathtaking byways. See p. 295.
- **Walking in the Burren** (County Clare): Ireland is full of memorable landscapes, but this is the most unique. For miles, this exposed coastal countryside has a haunting, alien feel, although it's strikingly beautiful, too. Try to be here as the sun goes down, when the craggy limestone plains turn an evening shade of red. See p. 359.
- **Taking a seaweed bath:** It may sound slimy, but bathing in seaweed is thought to have all sorts of therapeutic benefits for the skin and circulation—and it'll leave your skin silky soft. Start by opening the pores in a steam cabinet. We love the old-fashioned baths and

cabinets at **Kilcullen Seaweed Baths** in **Enniscrone, County Sligo** (p. 468).

- **Walking down the long stone passage at Newgrange** (County Meath): Sacred to the ancients, this passage tomb is more than 5,000 years old—that's older than the Egyptian pyramids or Stonehenge. Wander down the atmospheric central tunnel and try to visualize how many generations have passed since it was built—it's a mind-blowing exercise. See p. 181.
- **Browsing the English Market in Cork** (County Cork): Cork is a county made for foodies. In addition to Kinsale (p. 274), a coastal village that's become a hub for top restaurants, the eponymous main city is home to one of the country's finest (and oldest) food markets. A walk through here is a feast for the senses. See p. 256.
- **Hiking the path down to the Giant's Causeway** (County Antrim): Taking the half-mile walk down to this extraordinary natural wonder—37,000 columns of basalt sitting at the base of cliffs along the Antrim Coast—is like passing through a fantasy landscape. Geologists claim these rocks were formed millions of years ago by cooling volcanoes. But don't you prefer to believe they were really made by giants, as the ancients imagined? See p. 537.

2

IRELAND IN CONTEXT

As ever, it's a fascinating time to visit and see Ireland. A complex, small country with a tumultuous history, this is a land immensely rich with tradition, beauty, culture, and life. The past few decades have been a time of great change, first with the Celtic Tiger economy boom from 1995 to 2007, and then the property crash and economic slump that followed. In recent years the Republic of Ireland's economy has bounced back, and although the Covid-19 pandemic brought some temporary economic challenges, in 2022 Ireland's economy was Europe's fastest growing (growth moderated in 2023 and 2024). Meanwhile, Northern Ireland and the rest of the U.K. have been working through the aftereffects of Brexit, Britain's departure from the E.U.

IRELAND TODAY

The story of Ireland in the 21st century so far has been one of enormous change. The ups and downs of a turbulent economy took the country from dizzying boom at the turn of the new millennium to crushing bust after 2008, then most of the way back again.

But there are much more significant ways in which Ireland today is a very different place than it was a generation ago. In 2015, same-sex marriage was legalized, making Ireland the first country in the world to do so as the result of a referendum. Then, in 2018, after an even more extensive public debate, abortion was finally made legal too. The previous year, Leo Varadkar had become *Taoiseach* (prime minister, or head of the government), the first openly gay man to hold the post. For a country that had always been deeply conservative on social issues, these were all monumental sea changes—virtually inconceivable just a generation ago.

In recent years, Ireland had left behind one kind of identity and moved instead toward a more modern, liberal, European version of itself. While the Covid-19 pandemic (which saw tourism business closed for lengthy periods) and cost-of-living price increases (partly due to the Ukrainian conflict) have had impacts on life here in recent years, Ireland today is a vibrant, changing, growing destination and a *really* interesting place to visit.

FACING PAGE: A giant mechanical metal Pegasus, the mythical winged horse of Greek lore, at the 2024 Galway International Arts Festival.

THE MAKING OF IRELAND

The First Settlers

The date of the first permanent human habitation of the island has been long thought to be somewhere after the end of the last ice age, around the late 8000s B.C., although there is now evidence of earlier human presence going back some 34,000 years. Ireland's first colonizers, Mesolithic *Homo sapiens,* walked, waded, or floated across the narrow strait from what is now Britain in search of flint and, of course, food.

The next momentous prehistoric event was the arrival of Neolithic farmers and herders, sometime around 3500 B.C. Unlike Ireland's Mesolithic hunters, who barely left a trace, this second wave of colonizers began to transform the island at once. They came with stone axes that could fell a good-size elm in less than an hour. Ireland's hardwood forests receded to make room for tilled fields and pastureland. Villages sprang up, and more permanent homes, planked with split oak, appeared at this time.

Far more striking, though, was the appearance of massive megalithic monuments, including court cairns, *dolmens* (stone tables), round subterranean passage tombs, and wedge tombs. Thousands of these tombs are scattered around Ireland, and to this day only a small percentage of them have been excavated. These megalithic monuments speak volumes about the early Irish. To visit **Newgrange** ♥♥♥ (p. 181) and **Knowth** ♥♥♥

The prehistoric burial mound at Newgrange is estimated to be more than 5,000 years old.

(p. 181) in the Boyne Valley or **Carrowmore ♥♥♥** (p. 464) in County Sligo is to marvel at the mystical practices of the early Irish. Even today little is known about the meaning or purpose of these mysterious stone relics. Later Celtic inhabitants assumed that the tremendous stones and mounds were raised by giants, a race they called the people of the *sí*—a name that eventually became the *Tuatha Dé Danann,* and, finally, *fairies.* Over many generations, oral tradition downsized the mythical people into "little people," who were believed to have led a magical underground life in thousands of *raths* (earthwork structures) coursing the island like giant mole tunnels. All of these sites were believed to be protected by fairies, and tampering with them was thought to bring bad luck. So nobody ever touched them, and they have lasted to this day—ungraffitied, undamaged, unprotected by any visible fences or wires, but utterly safe.

The Celts

Of all the successive waves of outsiders who, over the years, shaped and swayed the timeline of Irish history, none made quite the impact of the Celts. They came in waves, originally from central Europe, beginning perhaps as early as the 6th century B.C. and continuing until the end of the first millennium. They fled the Roman invasion and clung to the edge of Europe—Ireland being, at the time, about as far as you could go to elude a Roman force. In time, they controlled the island and absorbed into their culture everyone they found there.

Despite their cultural potency, however, the Celts developed little in the way of centralized government, existing instead in a near-perpetual state of conflict with one another. The island was divided among as many as 150 tribes, grouped in alliances under five provincial kings. The provinces of **Munster, Leinster, Ulster,** and **Connaught** date from this period. The tribes fought fiercely among themselves over cattle (their "currency" and standard of wealth), land, and women. No one tribe ever ruled the entire island, though not for lack of trying. One of the most impressive monuments from the era of the warring Celts is the stone fortress of **Dún Aengus,** on the windswept hills of the Aran Islands (p. 395).

The Coming of Christianity

The Celtic chiefs neither warmly welcomed nor violently resisted the Christians who came ashore beginning in the 5th century. Although threatened, the pagan Celts settled for a bloodless rivalry with this new religion. In retrospect, this may have been a mistake.

Not the first, but eventually the most famous of these Christian newcomers was Maewyn Succat, a young Roman citizen torn from his Welsh homeland in a Celtic raid and brought to Ireland as a slave, where he was forced to work in a place called the Forest of Foclut (thought to be around modern County Antrim). He escaped on a ship to France, where he spent several years as a priest before returning to Ireland as a missionary. He

Deer graze at the pastoral monastic site of Glendalough.

began preaching at sacred Celtic festivals, a tactic that frequently led to confrontations with religious and political leaders, but eventually he became such a popular figure that after his death in 461, a dozen clan chiefs fought over the right to bury him. His lasting legacy was to establish in Ireland one of Europe's strongest Christian orthodoxies—an achievement for which he was later beatified as **St. Patrick.**

Ireland's conversion to Christianity was a somewhat negotiated process. The church at the time of St. Patrick was, like the man who brought it, Roman, yet for Ireland—an island still without a single proper town—Rome's system of dioceses and archdioceses simply didn't make sense. So the Irish adapted the church to their own situation, building isolated monasteries with extended monastic "families," each more or less autonomous.

For several centuries, Ireland flourished in this fashion, becoming a center of monastic learning. Monks and scholars were drawn here in droves, and were sent out in great numbers as well, to Britain and the Continent, as emissaries for the island's way of thinking and praying. Early monastic sites such as gorgeous **Glendalough ♥♥♥** in County Wicklow (p. 201), wind-swept **Clonmacnoise ♥♥♥** in County Offaly (p. 428), and isolated **Skellig Michael** off the Kerry coast (p. 326) give you an idea of how they lived, while striking examples of their scholarly work can be seen at **Trinity College ♥♥** (p. 104), which houses the Book of Kells, and the **Chester Beatty Library ♥♥♥** (p. 96) at Dublin Castle.

The Viking Invasions

The monastic city-states of early medieval Ireland might have continued to lead the world's intellectual development—but then the **Vikings** came along and ruined everything.

After centuries of relative peace, the first wave of Viking invaders arrived in Ireland in A.D. 795, making their base in the southeast, in what is now **Waterford City** (p. 215). Wealthy Irish monasteries were among their first targets. Unprepared and unprotected, the monasteries, which had amassed collections of gold, jewels, and art from followers around the world, were decimated. The round towers to which the nonviolent monks retreated for safety were neither high enough nor strong enough to protect them and their treasures from the onslaught.

Once word spread of the wealth to be found on this small island, the Scandinavian invaders just kept on coming. Experts in the arts of pillage and plunder, they had no knowledge of or interest in literature (in fact, most didn't know how to read), and they paid scant attention to the magnificent books they came across, passing them over for more obvious riches. This quirk of history allowed the monks to preserve their dying culture—and their immeasurably valuable work—for future generations.

monk-y **BUSINESS**

The Iliad and *The Odyssey* may have taken place on the turquoise depths of the Aegean, but it was on the dark waters of the Irish Sea that many classics of Roman and Greek literature survived the sack of Rome and the ensuing Dark Ages. But how did this happen? How did the Irish—in the words of bestselling author and historian Thomas Cahill—save civilization?

The year is A.D. 464. The mighty Roman Empire is on its knees, with the Eternal City under siege, its great libraries and universities about to be looted and burned. The world order is quite literally falling apart. Yet at the same time, in the far-flung backwater of Ireland, pagan Gaels are being converted to Christianity by an escaped Roman slave from Wales called Patricio—known today as St. Patrick.

As the Irish wholeheartedly embrace monastic life, centers of Christian learning pop up across the island, including the remote **Skellig Islands** (p. 326), where monks copy the Bible and other works. Masters of calligraphic arts, they produce beautiful illuminated texts such as the **Book of Kells** (p. 93). Gaeilge becomes the first vernacular language (slang, effectively) in Europe to have been written down. Some of Europe's finest minds flee the continental anarchy for Ireland, bringing books and learning with them. Knowledge-hungry monks duplicate great Latin and Greek works of literature.

After St. Patrick, Irish missionaries such as **Columcille** and **Columbanus** began to look abroad, where Europe had devolved into a fragmented patchwork of fiefdoms. Hardy Celtic monks set up new monasteries in France, Germany, Switzerland, and Italy, taking their skills with them. Beautifully decorated Irish manuscripts from this period have been found as far away as Russia, where the monks continued to advance the art of bookmaking.

After the Vikings left, Ireland enjoyed something of a renewal in the 11th and 12th centuries. Its towns grew, its regional kings continued to try (unsuccessfully) to unite the country under a single king, and its church came under increased pressure to conform to Vatican rules. All of these factors ripened Ireland for the next invasion.

A replica of a Viking longboat in Waterford City.

It was, tragically, an Irish king who opened the door to the next predator. **Diarmait Mac Murchada,** king of Leinster, whose ambition was to be king of all of Ireland, called on **Henry II,** the Norman king of England, to help him. Diarmait offered Henry a series of incentives: Not only did he bestow his eldest daughter on whoever led the army, he also offered overlordship of the Kingdom of Leinster. To put it bluntly, he made Henry an offer he couldn't refuse. So it was that an English expeditionary force, led by the Earl of Pembroke, Richard de Clare—better known as **Strongbow**—was sent to Diarmait's aid. After a successful invasion, victorious Strongbow remained in Ireland as governor, and thus gave the English their first foothold in Ireland. What Diarmait did not realize, of course, was that they would never leave.

The Norman Invasion

In successive expeditions from 1167 to 1169, the **Normans,** who had already conquered England, crossed the Irish Sea with crushing force. While Dublin Castle was for years the Norman seat of power, over the next century the Norman-English consolidated their power in other towns and cities.

Many of these settlers, however, grew attached to the island and began to integrate with the local culture; marriages between the native Irish and the invaders became commonplace. Inevitably, as time passed the Anglo-Normans became more Irish and less English in their loyalties.

Meanwhile, independent Gaelic lords in the north and west maintained their territories. By the late 1400s, English control of the island was effectively limited to **the Pale,** a walled and fortified cordon around what is now greater Dublin. (The phrase "beyond the pale" comes from this—meaning anything that is uncontrollable or unacceptable.)

English Power & the Flight of the Earls

The Tudor dynasty in England, which ruled from 1485 to 1603, changed all that, setting in motion the brutal reconquest of Ireland. In 1542, **Henry VIII** boldly proclaimed himself king of all Ireland—something even his warlike ancestors had stopped short of doing—and later that century his daughter, **Elizabeth I,** declared that all Gaelic lords in Ireland must surrender their lands to her, with the dubious promise that she would immediately grant them all back again.

A statue of the rebel chieftain "Red" Hugh O'Donnell in Donegal Town.

Unsurprisingly, the proposition was hardly welcomed in Ireland, and a rebel army was raised by two Irish chieftains, **Hugh O'Neill** and **"Red" Hugh O'Donnell.** They scored some significant victories early on, most notably over a force led by the Earl of Essex, whom Elizabeth personally sent to subdue them. Still, by 1603 O'Neill was left with few allies and no option but to surrender, which he did on March 23rd, the day before Elizabeth died. In 1607, after failing to win back much of their power, around 90 of O'Neill's allies fled to mainland Europe, possibly hoping for a Spanish invasion. This never happened. The **Flight of the Earls,** as it became known, marked a crucial turning point in Irish history—the point at which the old Gaelic aristocracy effectively came to an end.

The Coming of Cromwell

By the 1640s, Ireland was effectively an English plantation. Family estates had been seized and foreign (Scottish) labor brought in to work them. A systematic persecution of Catholics, stemming from Henry VIII's split from Rome, barred Catholics from practicing their faith. Resentment against thc English and their punitive laws led to fierce uprisings in Ulster and Leinster in 1641, and by early 1642 most of Ireland was again under Irish control. Unfortunately for the rebels, any hope of extending the victories was undermined by internal disunion. Sealing their fate was a decision to support the Royalist side in the civil war that had just broken out in England. After King Charles I of England was beheaded in 1648, **Oliver Cromwell,** the commander of the parliamentary forces, was installed as England's ruler, and it wasn't long before Cromwell's supporters took on his enemies in Ireland. A year later, the Royalists' stand collapsed in defeat at Rathmines, just south of Dublin.

Defeat for the Royalist cause did not, however, mean the end of war. Cromwell became paranoid that Ireland would be used to launch a French-backed insurgency; he also detested the country's Catholic beliefs. So as the hot, sticky summer of 1649 drew to a close, Cromwell set sail for Dublin with an army of 12,000 men and a battle plan so ruthless that it remains notorious to this day.

In the town of **Drogheda** (p. 183), more than 3,552 Irish soldiers were slaughtered in a single night. When a group of men sought sanctuary in the local church, Cromwell ordered the church burned down with them locked inside—an act so monstrous that some of his own men refused the order. On another day, in **Wexford,** more than 2,000 were murdered, many of them civilians. The trail of destruction rolled on, devastating counties **Galway** and **Waterford.** When asked where Irish citizens could go to be safe from him, Cromwell famously suggested they could go "to hell or Connaught"—the latter being the most far-flung, rocky, and unfarmable part of Ireland.

After a 7-month rampage that killed thousands and left churches, monasteries, and castles in ruins, Cromwell finally left Ireland in the care of his lieutenants and returned to England. Hundreds of years later, the memory of his infamous violence lingers painfully in Ireland. In certain parts of the country, people still spit at the mention of his name.

The Anti-Catholic Laws

Cromwell died in 1658, and 2 years later the English monarchy was restored. Still, anti-Catholic oppression continued in Ireland. Then in 1685 something remarkable happened: The new Stuart king, **James II,** refused to relinquish his Catholic faith after ascending to the throne. It looked for a while as if Catholic Ireland had found a royal ally at last. However, such hopes were dashed 3 years later, when James was ousted from power, and the Protestant **William of Orange** installed in his place.

James fled to France to raise support for a rebellion and then sailed to Ireland to launch his attack. He struck first at **Derry** (p. 563), laying siege for 15 weeks, before finally being defeated by William's forces at the **Battle of the Boyne.** The battle effectively ended James's cause, and with it, the hopes of Catholic Ireland for the best part of a century.

After James's defeat, English power was once more consolidated across Ireland. Protestant landowners were granted full political power, while laws were enacted to tamp down the Catholic population. Being a

Catholic in late-17th-century Ireland was not exactly illegal per se, but in practice life was all but impossible for those who refused to convert to Protestantism. Catholics could not purchase land, and existing landholdings were split up unless the families who owned them converted to Protestantism. Catholic schools were banned, as were priests and all forms of public Catholic worship. Catholics were barred from holding government office, practicing law, or joining the army. Those who refused to relinquish their faith were forced to pay a tax to the Anglican Church. And, because only landowners were allowed to vote, Catholics whose land had been taken away also lost the right to vote.

In Derry, cannons on the city walls held off Jacobite forces at the Siege of Derry in 1689.

The new British landlords settled in, planted crops, made laws, and sowed their own seeds. Inevitably, over time, the "Anglos" became the **Anglo-Irish.** Hyphenated or not, they were Irish, and their loyalties were increasingly unpredictable. After all, an immigrant is only an immigrant for a generation; whatever the birthright of the colonists, their children would be Irish-born and bred. And so an uncomfortable sort of stability set in for a generation or three, maintaining a very separate and unequal status quo: There were the haves, the wealthy Protestants, and the have-nots, the deprived and disenfranchised Catholics.

This unhappy peace held for some time. But by the end of the 18th century, the appetite for rebellion was whetted again—in the coffee shops and lecture halls of Europe's newest boomtown: **Dublin.**

The United Irishmen & the 1798 Rebellion

By the 1770s, Dublin was thriving as never before. As a center for culture and learning, it was rivaled only by Paris and London. Thanks to the work of such architects as James Gandon (who designed the **Custom House** ♥ [p. 110] and the **Four Courts** ♥ [p. 112]), its very streets were being remodeled in a grand, neoclassical style more akin to the great cities of southern Italy than of southern Ireland.

While the urban classes reveled in newfound wealth, stringent **Penal Laws** effectively cut off Catholic workers from their own countryside, driving them to pour into the city, looking for work. Alongside Dublin's buzzing intellectual scene, political dissent soon brewed. Even after a

The Four Courts in Dublin.

campaign by Irish politicians succeeded in getting many of the Penal Laws repealed in 1783, Dublin was a breeding ground for radicals and political activists. The results were explosive.

When war broke out between Britain and France in the 1790s, the **United Irishmen**—a nonviolent society formed to lobby for Catholic Irishmen to be admitted to the Irish Parliament—sent a secret delegation to persuade the French to intervene on Ireland's behalf against the British. Their emissary in this venture was a Dublin lawyer named **Wolfe Tone.** In 1796, Tone sailed with a French force bound for Ireland, determined to defeat forces loyal to the English crown. As luck would have it, though, they were turned back by storms.

In 1798, full-scale insurrection led by the United Irishmen spread across much of Ireland, particularly the southwestern counties of **Kilkenny** and **Wexford,** where a tiny republic was briefly declared in June in Wexford's Bull Ring square (p. 228). It was soon crushed by Loyalist forces, which then went on a murderous spree, killing tens of thousands of men, women, and children and burning towns to the ground. The nadir of the rebellion came when Wolfe Tone, having raised another French invasion force, sailed into Lough Swilly in Donegal and was promptly captured by the British. At his trial, Tone wore the uniform of a French soldier; he slit his own throat while in prison waiting to be hung.

The rebellion was over. In the space of 3 weeks, more than 30,000 Irish had been killed. As a final indignity in what became known as **The Year of the French,** the British tricked the Irish Parliament into dissolving itself, and Ireland reverted to strict British rule.

A Conflict of Conflicts

In 1828, a Catholic lawyer named **Daniel O'Connell**—who had earlier formed the Catholic Association to represent the interests of tenant farmers—was elected to the British Parliament as Member of Parliament for Dublin. (You can visit his home, in Caherdaniel, County Kerry; p. 328.) Public opinion was so solidly behind O'Connell that he was able to persuade the British prime minister that the only way to avoid civil war in Ireland was to force a **Catholic Emancipation Act** through Parliament. O'Connell remained an MP until 1841, when he was elected Lord Mayor of Dublin, a platform he used to push for repeal of the direct rule imposed from London after the 1798 rebellion.

O'Connell's enormous rallies—nicknamed "monster meetings"—were attended by hundreds of thousands and provoked the conservative

reading LIST

If you want to know about Ireland and the Irish, plenty of talented writers in and out of the country are willing to tell you.

Jonathan Bardon's *A History of Ireland in 250 Episodes* is a good general introduction to Irish history. The book is broken up into 250 short chapters—learned without being too dense, and a very useful primer.

To understand more about the Famine, try the British author **Cecil Woodham-Smith**'s *The Great Hunger.* Written in 1962, it's still viewed as the definitive dispassionate examination of this dark period in Irish history. *The Graves are Walking* by **John Kelly** also tells the harrowing story of the Famine between 1845-51, when Ireland lost a third of its population.

The author **Tim Pat Coogan,** son of an IRA volunteer, has written two excellent books, *The Irish Civil War* (2001) and *The Troubles: Ireland's Ordeal 1966–1996* (1997), both of which are essential reading for anyone wanting to understand the complexities of 21st-century Ireland. Coogan also wrote a controversial biography, *Eamon de Valera* (1995), criticizing the former Irish president's actions and legacy.

For a look at Ireland in recent history, try **John Ardagh**'s *Ireland and the Irish* (1995) or **F. S. Lyons**'s *Ireland Since the Famine* (1973). Or for something original (and slightly irreverent), check out *Ireland's Forgotten Past: A History of the Overlooked and Disremembered* (2020) by **Turtle Bunbury.**

In *Emigrants and Exiles: Ireland and the Irish Exodus to North America* (1988), Kerby A. Miller looks at the history of emigration of the Irish to America, while Aidan Doyle writes about the decline of the Irish language in *A History of the Irish Language: From the Norman Invasion to Independence* (2015).

American journalist **Patrick Radden Keefe** takes a deep dive into first-hand accounts of the Troubles in his 2019 bestseller *Say Nothing,* which was adapted into a TV series in 2024. Irish journalist **Fintan O'Toole** weaves recent Irish history into his own memoir of growing up in and around Dublin, *We Don't Know Ourselves* (2021).

Manchán Magan writes about myth and folklore in Irish history and its relationship to the land in *Listen To The Land Speak* (2022), and about the myths and monsters in Irish storytelling in *Wolf-Men and Water Hounds* (2023).

government to eventually arrest him on charges of seditious conspiracy. The charges were dropped, but the incident—coupled with growing impatience toward his nonviolent approach of protest and reform—led to the breakdown of his power base. "The Liberator," as he had been known, faded, his health failed, and he died on a trip to Rome.

The Great Famine

Even after anti-Catholic legislation began to recede, the vast majority of farmland available to Ireland's poor, mostly Catholic rural population was unfertile and hard to cultivate. One of the few crops that could be grown reliably was the potato, which therefore became the staple diet of the rural poor. So when, in 1845, a fungus destroyed much of the potato crop of Ireland, widespread devastation followed. (In County Kerry's Dingle Peninsula, the **Irish Famine Cottage**—see p. 344—stands as stark evidence of this desolation.)

To label the **Great Irish Famine** of the 1840s and '50s as merely a "tragedy" would be inadequate. It was, of course, tragic—but at the same time, the word implies a randomness to the whole sorry, sickening affair that fails to capture its true awfulness. The fact is that what started out as crop failure was turned into a disaster by the callous response of the British establishment.

The Irish Famine Cottage.

As the potato blight worsened, it became apparent to many landlords that their farm tenants would be unable to pay rent. Instead of helping to feed their now-starving tenants, these landlords shipped their grain overseas, determined to recoup what they were losing in rent. The British Parliament, meanwhile, was reluctant to send aid, putting the reports of a crisis down to, in the words of Prime Minister Robert Peel, "the Irish tendency to exaggerate."

People started to die by the thousands.

Eventually it became clear to the government that something had to be done. Emergency relief was sent to Ireland in the form of cheap, imported Indian cornmeal. However, this contained virtually no nutrients. Ultimately, it was malnutrition that spread such diseases as typhus and cholera, which claimed more victims than starvation itself.

To make matters worse, the cornmeal was not simply given to those in need of it. Fearful that handouts would encourage laziness among the "shiftless poor," the British government forced people to work for their food. Entirely pointless make-work projects were initiated, just to give the starving men something to do for their cornmeal; roads were built that led nowhere, and elaborate follies constructed that served no discernible purpose. Some of these still litter the countryside today, memorials to cruelty and ignorance.

One of the most difficult things to comprehend, more than a century and a half later, is the sheer futility of it all. For behind the statistics, the memorials, and the endless personal anguish lies perhaps the most painful truth of all: that the Famine was easily preventable. Enormous cargoes of imported corn sat in Irish ports for months, until the British government felt that releasing them to the people would not adversely affect market rates. Meanwhile, huge quantities of meat and grain were exported from Ireland. (Indeed, in 1847, cattle exports went up 33% from the previous year.)

Given the circumstances, it is easy to understand why so many chose to leave Ireland. More than a million emigrated over the next decade, about three-quarters of them to America, the rest to Britain or Europe. (For moving depictions of this emigration, visit Dublin's **EPIC The Irish Emigration Museum** [p. 114] and the ***Jeanie Johnston* Tall Ship** [p. 117], and County Wexford's **SS *Dunbrody* Famine Ship Experience** [p. 233].) The mass exodus drained the country. In 1841, Ireland's population was 8 million; by 1851 it was 6.5 million.

The Struggle for Home Rule

As the Famine waned and life returned to something like normality, the Irish independence movement gained new momentum. New fronts, both violent and nonviolent, opened up in the struggle for what was called **Home Rule.** Significantly, the Republicans now drew considerable support from overseas—particularly from America. There, groups such as the

Fenians fundraised and published newspapers in support of the Irish cause, while more audacious schemes—such as an 1866 "invasion" of Canada with fewer than 100 men—generated awareness, if little else.

Back home in Ireland, partial concessions were won in Parliament. By the 1880s, nationalists such as **Charles Stewart Parnell,** the MP for Meath, were able to unite various factions of Irish nationalists (including the Fenian Brotherhood in America) to fight for Home Rule. In a tumultuous decade of legislation, Parnell came close to winning Home Rule—until revelations about his long affair with Kitty O'Shea, the wife of a supporter, brought about his downfall as a politician.

By 1912, a bill to give Ireland Home Rule was passed through the British House of Commons but was defeated in the House of Lords. Many felt that the political process was all but unstoppable, that it was only a matter of time before the bill passed fully into law. Then World War I broke out in 1914, forcing the issue onto the back burner once again. Many in the Home Rule movement began to grow tired of pursuing their goal through legal political channels.

The Easter Rising

On Easter Monday 1916, a group of nationalists occupied the **General Post Office** ♥ (p. 112) in the heart of Dublin, from which they proclaimed the foundation of an Irish Republic. Inside were 1,500 fighters, led by schoolteacher and Gaelic League member **Patrick Pearse** and Socialist leader **James Connolly.**

The British government, panicking over an armed uprising on its doorstep while it fought a massive war in Europe, responded with overwhelming force. Soldiers were sent in, and a battle raged in the streets of Dublin for 6 days before the leaders of the rebellion were captured and imprisoned. (The walls of the post office and other buildings and statues up and down O'Connell St. still have bullet holes in them.) Pearse, Connolly, and 12 other leaders were imprisoned, secretly tried, and speedily executed.

Ultimately, though, the harsh British reaction was counterproductive. The ruthlessness with which the rebellion's ringleaders were pursued and dispatched acted as a lightning rod for many who were still on the fence about how best to gain Home Rule. It's a fact that has become somewhat lost in the ensuing hundred or so years: On that cold Monday morning when Patrick Pearse stood on the post office steps to read a treatise on Irish independence, a great many Irish didn't support the rebellion. Many believed that the best course of action was to lay low until the war had ended, when, they felt, concessions would finally be won. Others felt that the uprising was simply the wrong thing to do, as long as sons of Ireland were sacrificing their lives in the trenches of Europe.

The aftermath of 1916 all but guaranteed, for better or for worse, that Ireland's future would be decided by the gun.

Rebellion & the Anglo-Irish Compromise

A power vacuum was left at the heart of the nationalist movement after the Easter Rising, and it was filled by two men: **Michael Collins** (p. 282) and **Eamon de Valera.** On the surface, the two men had much in common: Collins was a Cork man who had returned from Britain in order to join the Irish Volunteers (later to become the **Irish Republican Army,** or IRA), while de Valera was an Irish-American math teacher who came back to Ireland to set up a new political party, **Sinn Féin.**

When de Valera's party won a landslide victory in the general election of 1918, its MPs took the provocative step of refusing to take their seats in London. Instead, they proclaimed the first **Dáil,** or independent parliament, in Dublin. De Valera went to rally support for the cause in America, while Collins stayed in Ireland to concentrate on his work as head of the Irish Volunteers. Tensions escalated into violence, and for the next 2 years, Irish nationalists fought a tit-for-tat military campaign against the British in Ireland. The low point of the struggle came in 1920, when Collins ordered 14 British operatives to be murdered in their beds. In response, British troops opened fire on the audience at a football game at **Croke Park** in Dublin (p. 113), randomly killing 12 innocent people.

A truce was eventually declared on July 9, 1921. Six months later, the Anglo-Irish treaty was signed in London, granting legislative independence

Dublin's General Post Office was the scene of fighting in the 1922 civil war.

to 26 Irish counties (known collectively as the **Irish Free State**). The compromise through which that freedom was won, though, was that six counties in the north would remain part of the United Kingdom. Sent to negotiate the treaty, Collins knew that that compromise—which he felt was the best deal he could get at the time—would not be accepted by the more strident members of his rebel group. He also knew they would blame him for agreeing to it in the first place. When he signed the treaty, he told the people present, "I am signing my own death warrant."

As he feared, nationalists were split between those who accepted the treaty as a platform on which to build, and those, led by the nationalist de Valera, who saw it as a betrayal. The latter group would accept nothing less than immediate and full independence at any cost. Even the withdrawal of British troops from Dublin for the first time in nearly 800 years did not quell their anger. The result was an inexorable slide into civil war. The flashpoint came in April 1922, when violence erupted around the streets of the capital, raging on for 8 days until de Valera's supporters were forced to surrender.

The government of the fledgling free state ordered that Republicans be shot on sight, leading to the deaths of 77 people. And Collins had been right about his own fate: Four months later, he was assassinated while on a visit to his childhood home.

A Republic at Last

The fallout from the civil war dominated Irish politics for the next decade. De Valera split from the Republicans to form another party, **Fianna Fáil** ("the Warriors of Ireland"), which won the election of 1932 and governed for the next 17 years. One of Eamon de Valera's more controversial decisions while in office was to keep Ireland neutral during World War II. His reasons included Ireland's relatively small size and economic weakness, as well as a protest against the British presence in Northern Ireland. Although that may have made sense to some extent, it left Ireland in the peculiar position of tacitly favoring one side in the war but refusing to help it. After the death of Adolf Hitler in April 1945, de Valera further alienated the Allies by sending his personal sympathies to the German ambassador. His stance didn't find much favor among the Irish population, either. During the war, as many as 300,000 Irish men still found ways to enlist in the British or U.S. armies. In the end, more than 50,000 Irish soldiers perished in a war their country had refused to join.

Ironically, de Valera was not to be the political leader to finally declare Ireland a republic. That distinction went to a coalition led by de Valera's opponent, **Douglas Hyde,** in 1948. Hyde's victory in the 1947 election was attributed to the fact that de Valera had become too obsessed with abstract Republican ideals to govern effectively.

Trouble on the Way

After World War II, 2 decades passed without violence in Ireland. Then, in the late 1960s, sectarian conflict erupted in the North. What started out as a civil rights movement, demanding greater equality for Catholics in Northern Ireland, soon escalated into a cycle of violence lasting 30 years.

It would be a terrible oversimplification to say that the **Troubles** were a clear-cut struggle between those who wanted complete Irish unification and those who wanted to remain part of the United Kingdom. That was, of course, the crux of the conflict. However, there were many other factors, such as organized crime and terrorism, together with centuries-old conflicts over religious, land, and social issues, all of which made the conflict even harder for outsiders to understand.

The worst of the Troubles came in the 1970s. In 1972, on a day forever remembered as "**Bloody Sunday**," British troops inexplicably opened fire on a peaceful demonstration in **Derry** (p. 563), killing 12 people—many of them shot while tending to the wounds of the first people injured. The IRA took advantage of public outrage over the shooting to begin their own civilian bombing campaign on the British mainland. The inexorable cycle of violence continued for 20 years. All the while, none of the myriad sides in the conflict would talk to each other. Finally, in the early 1990s, secret talks were opened between the British and the IRA, leading to an IRA ceasefire in 1994 (although the ceasefire held only shakily—an IRA bomb in Omagh 4 years later killed 29, the most to die on any single day of the Troubles).

Belfast street mural depicting IRA hunger striker Bobby Sands.

The peace process continued throughout the 1990s, helped significantly by the mediation efforts of U.S. President Bill Clinton, who became more involved in Irish affairs than any president before him. Eventually, on **Good Friday 1998,** a peace accord was finally signed in Belfast. The agreement committed all sides to a peaceful resolution of the conflict in Northern Ireland and reinstated self-government for the region in a power-sharing administration. However, it stopped short of resolving the territorial issue once and for all. In other words, Northern Ireland is still part of the U.K., and will be for the foreseeable future.

To some extent, the conflicts still rage more divisively than ever before. The difference is that, with notable exceptions, nowadays they are fought through the ballot box rather than the barrel of a gun. In 2005, the IRA fully decommissioned its weapons and officially dissolved itself as a paramilitary unit. Since then, there have been wobbles—including the occasional act of violence by splinter groups that don't want to accept peace—but these have been few and far between. Britain's Queen Elizabeth's 2011 visit to Ireland, and a 2016 decision by the (Protestant and staunchly pro-British) First Minister of Northern Ireland to attend centenary celebrations of the Easter Rising in Dublin, proved hugely meaningful.

Rebirth

While Northern Ireland struggled to find peace, the Republic of Ireland flourished. The 1990s brought unprecedented wealth and prosperity to the country, thanks in part to European Union subsidies, and partly to a thriving economy, nicknamed the **Celtic Tiger** for its new global strength. Ireland became a rich country, increasingly seen as one of the best places in the world to live and work.

However, that boom came crashing down after the banking crisis of 2008. The Irish government was forced to seek financial aid from the European Union, a package worth more than 50% of the whole economy, to save the country from bankruptcy. The op-ed pages of Irish newspapers expressed real feelings of betrayal and a sense of opportunity lost. Things have improved a lot since then, but the crash changed Ireland for good, as much in terms of its character as mere economics.

In the past decade, Ireland has addressed serious questions about its own identity. Certain things that once seemed indelible to Irish society are now evolving, and the country is becoming more socially liberal. The influence of the church is less keenly felt than it once was, particularly among the younger generation. One of the most powerful emblems of this change came in 2015, when a referendum to allow **same-sex marriage** passed by a landslide—making this the first country in the world to pass such a law through a popular vote. The **legalization of abortion,** once considered anathema here, became a reality in 2018.

IRELAND IN CULTURE

Literature

Ireland holds a place in literature disproportionate to its small size and modest population. Four writers from this tiny country have won the Nobel Prize in literature. Inspired by Ireland's unique beauty, the inequities of its political system, and its cruel legacy of poverty and struggle, the country's authors, poets, and playwrights wrote about the Irish for the Irish, and to raise awareness in the rest of the world. No matter where you live, you've probably been reading about Ireland all your life.

One of the country's best-known early writers, **Jonathan Swift** (p. 102) was born in Dublin in 1667 and educated at Trinity College. He left Ireland for England in 1688 to avoid the Glorious Revolution, and though he spent much of his adult life in London, he returned to Ireland when he was over 50 years old, at which point he began to write his most famous works. Greatly moved by the suffering of the poor in Ireland, he translated his anger into dark, vicious humor. His tract *A Modest Proposal* is widely credited with inventing modern satire. Swift's best-known works have political undertones—even *Gulliver's Travels* is a political allegory.

Best known for his novel *Dracula,* the novelist and theater promoter **Bram Stoker** was born in Clontarf, a coastal suburb of Dublin, in 1847. As a young man fresh out of Trinity College, he began reviewing theater productions for local newspapers, which is how he met the actor Henry Irving. He spent much of his time promoting and working for Irving, writing novels on the side for extra money. He lived most of his life in England, which largely inspired his work, although it is said that **St. Michan's Church** ♥♥ in Dublin (p. 107), with its ghostly crypt, and **St. Mary's Cathedral** ♥ in Killarney (p. 306) contributed to *Dracula*'s creepy feel.

A statue of Irish writer Oscar Wilde in Merrion Square, Dublin.

Born in Dublin in 1854, **Oscar Wilde** was a successful student at Trinity College, winning a scholarship to continue his studies in England at Oxford. After a flamboyant time there, he graduated with top honors and returned to Ireland, only to lose his girlfriend to Bram Stoker in 1878, after which he left Ireland forever. His writing—novels such as *The Picture of Dorian Gray,* plays including *The Importance of Being Earnest,* and books of poetry—were often overshadowed by his scandalous personal life. His works were largely inspired by British and French writers, and he spent the majority of his life abroad.

Similarly, **George Bernard Shaw,** who was born in Dublin in 1856 and attended school in the city, moved to England as a young man, and most of his work has a distinctly English feel. His plays are known both for their sharp wit and for their sense of outrage over unfairness in society and the absurdity of the British class system. He won both the Nobel Prize in literature (in 1925) and an Oscar (in 1939, for the screenplay of *Pygmalion*).

One of the leading figures of the Irish literary revival in the early 20th century, **William Butler Yeats** was born in Sandymount outside Dublin in 1865 and attended the Metropolitan School of Art in Dublin. His poetry and prose were heavily inspired by County Sligo, where he spent much of his time (and where he is buried, in **Drumcliffe** churchyard; p. 464). He won the Nobel Prize in 1923.

James Joyce was born in the Dublin suburb of Rathgar in 1882 and educated at Jesuit boarding schools, and later at Trinity College. He wrote vividly—and sometimes impenetrably—about Dublin, despite spending much of his life as an expat living nomadically in Europe. His controversial and hugely complex novels *Ulysses* and *Finnegans Wake* are his most celebrated (and least understood) works. They and his collection of short stories, *Dubliners,* touch deeply on the character of the people of Dublin. The **James Joyce Centre** ♥ (p. 116) is a mecca for Joyce fans.

The poet and playwright **Samuel Beckett** was born in 1906 in the Dublin suburb of Foxrock and educated at Trinity College. His work, however, was heavily influenced by German and French postmodernists, and he spent much of his life abroad, even serving with the Resistance in France during World War II. Best known for his complex absurdist play *Waiting for Godot,* he won the Nobel Prize in 1969.

A statue of novelist James Joyce, across from the General Post Office in Dublin.

The controversial writer, erstwhile terrorist, and bon vivant **Brendan Behan** was born in Dublin in 1923. Behan came by his revolutionary fervor honestly: His father fought in the Easter Rising, and his mother was a close friend of Michael Collins. When he was 14, Behan joined Fianna Éireann, the youth organization of the IRA, but was arrested on his first solo mission to blow up England's Liverpool Docks when he was 16 years old. His autobiographical book, *Borstal Boy,* describes this period in his life in exquisite detail. His play *The Quare Fellow* made him an international literary star, but he spent the rest of his life as a jolly, hopeless alcoholic, drinking his way through London, Dublin, and New York, better known for his quick wit and bons mots than for his plays.

Among modern Irish poets, the late **Seamus Heaney** may be the best known. Born in 1939 near a small town called Castledawson in Northern Ireland, as a child he won scholarships to boarding school in Derry and later to Queen's University in Belfast. His years studying classic ancient Greek and Latin literature and Anglo-Saxon writing heavily influenced his poetry, but all of his writing is steeped in the troubled region where he grew up. His works, including *The Cure at Troy* (based on the works of Sophocles), *The Haw Lantern, The Government of the Tongue,* and a modern translation of *Beowulf,* earned him the Nobel Prize in 1995.

Contemporary Irish novelists include the late award-winning writer **Edna O'Brien** (*The Country Girls, House of Splendid Isolation*); **Marian Keyes** (*Lucy Sullivan Is Getting Married, This Charming Man*); **Roddy Doyle** (*The Commitments, Paddy Clarke Ha Ha Ha*); and the late **Maeve Binchy** (*A Week in Winter, Circle of Friends*). The novels of **Anne Enright** (*The Gathering*) look at Ireland with sympathy and tremendous beauty. *The Spinning Heart,* by **Donal Ryan** (2012), gives an accurate and absorbing account of rural Ireland after the crash of 2008.

Anna Burns became Northern Ireland's first Booker Prize winner in 2018 with her riveting psychological novel *Milkman,* set amid the Troubles. Though born in the U.S., mystery writer **Tana French** has lived in Ireland most of her life, and her award-winning novels (*In the Woods, Faithful Place,* and others) were adapted into the TV series *Dublin Murders* in 2019. Younger writers on the rise include **Louise O'Neill** (*Only Ever Yours*), whose award-winning young-adult novels offer a bleak look at youth in Ireland; **Sally Rooney,** whose 2018 novel *Normal People* went on to become a hit TV series; and **Emer McLysaght** and **Sarah Breen** (*Oh My God, What a Complete Aisling*), whose hilarious novels find humor in all aspects of young Irish life. In 2023, Limerick-born novelist **Paul Lynch** won the Booker Prize for *Prophet Song,* a dystopian story set in Dublin. County Wicklow writer **Claire Keegan**'s beautiful short stories have been lauded worldwide. A movie adaptation of *Foster,* titled as *An Cailín Ciúin* (The Quiet Girl), was nominated for an Academy Award in 2023, while *Small Things Like These* was adapted into a movie in 2024.

Film & Television

Many controversial, complex, and difficult Irish subjects have been tackled by an international array of directors and actors. Here are some of the better-known ones—and a few obscure gems worth seeking out.

Man of Aran (directed by Robert Flaherty, 1934) is a "docufiction" about life on the Aran Islands. Long respected as a documentary, it's now known that much of it was staged by its American director. Still, it's an interesting view on what the islands looked like in the early 20th century.

Virtually unknown today, ***Maeve*** (directed by John Davis and Pat Murphy, 1982) is a fascinating piece of Irish independent film from the early 1980s, following an Irish expat in England who decides to return to strife-torn Northern Ireland.

The Commitments (directed by Alan Parker, 1991) may be the most famous Irish musical ever made. With its cast of young, largely inexperienced Irish actors playing musicians dedicated to American soul music, it's a delightful piece of filmmaking.

Michael Collins (directed by Neil Jordan, 1996) is a fine biopic about the Irish rebel, filmed largely on location and starring Irish actor Liam Neeson. ***Veronica Guerin*** (directed by Joel Schumacher, 2003) is a dark, fact-based film (with Australian actress Cate Blanchett doing an excellent Irish accent) about a troubled Irish investigative reporter on the trail of a drug boss. ***The Wind That Shakes the Barley*** (directed by Ken Loach, 2006), with a mostly Irish cast and English director, won the Palme d'Or at Cannes for its depiction of Ireland's early-20th-century fight for independence.

Intermission (directed by Jim Crowley, 2003) is a lively urban romance filmed on location in Dublin, featuring Irish actor Colin Farrell (talking in his real accent for a change). It's a great look at Dublin right in the middle of its economic boom. ***Once*** (directed by John Carney, 2007) is a touching, Oscar-nominated portrait of two struggling young musicians: an Irish singer (played by actor/musician Glen Hansard) and a Czech piano player trying to make it big in Dublin. The film was subsequently turned into a hit stage musical.

Silence (directed by Pat Collins, 2012) is a meditative, dreamlike art film about a sound recordist who travels deep into the Irish countryside in search of places completely free of manmade sound (spoiler alert: He has a hard time finding any).

Shadow Dancer (directed by James Marsh, 2012) is an exciting spy thriller set in early 1990s Belfast. A hit at the Sundance Film Festival, the film pulls off the rare trick of being about the Troubles without getting bogged down in politics. ***71*** (directed by Yann Demange, 2014) has been acclaimed as one of the best films about the Troubles in recent years. ***Good Vibrations*** (directed by Lisa Barros D'Sa and Glenn Layburn, 2013) tells the story of Terri Hooley, who in the 1970s opened a record store in the most bombed street in Belfast—the name reflected his

A Derry street mural celebrates the popular sitcom *Derry Girls*.

optimistic hope that music could bring warring communities together. (The store is still open on Winetavern St. in Belfast.)

Based on a popular TV sitcom, ***Mrs. Brown's Boys D'Movie*** (directed by Ben Kellett, 2014) is a broad slapstick comedy about a no-nonsense Dublin matriarch. The film became one of the most successful Irish films of the decade at the box office, despite being almost universally derided as terrible by critics (spoiler alert: They're right).

Calvary (directed by John Michael McDonagh, 2014) is a controversial drama about a small-town priest who receives a death threat from one of his parishioners, which leads him to discover dark truths about the community he lives in. Adapted from a novel by Colm Tóibín, ***Brooklyn*** (directed by John Crowley, 2015) is an incredibly touching drama about a young Irish woman (played by Saoirse Ronan) who emigrates to New York in the 1950s. ***Ordinary Love*** (directed by Lisa Barros D'Sa, 2019) is a searing romantic drama about a married couple facing a cancer diagnosis; many critics called it one of the best Irish films of the decade.

Irish actor Chris O'Dowd created and stars in ***Moone Boy*** (2012–15), a charming sitcom about his boyhood in small-town Roscommon. The hilarious coming-of-age sitcom ***Derry Girls*** (2018–22) follows a group of Londonderry teenagers who just happen to be growing up during the Troubles, while black comedy series ***Bad Sisters*** was an award-winner in 2022, with a second series debuting in late 2024.

Filmed on Achill Island and the Aran Islands, ***The Banshees of Inisherin*** (directed by Martin McDonagh, 2022) stars Colin Farrell, Brendan Gleeson, and Kelly Condon in a tragicomedy set in the remote west of Ireland in the 1920s, during the civil wars. It received nine Academy Award nominations and won three Golden Globes.

A movie adaptation of the short story ***Foster*** by Claire Keegan, titled as ***An Cailín Ciúin*** (The Quiet Girl) was nominated for an Academy Award in 2023. In 2024, the movie adaptation of her novella ***Small Things Like These*** was released, starting Irish actor Cillian Murphy.

Music

Music is inescapable in Ireland, and if you hear a band play in a bar and you like them, we strongly advise you to buy a CD from them.

In the days of Internet radio, the best way to discover new sounds is to tune in to Irish radio stations online. An excellent list of stations that stream live (including links) can be found at **radiofeeds.co.uk/irish.asp**. Good places to start are the stations run by **RTÉ,** the national broadcaster, particularly the music and entertainment-oriented **2FM** (rte.ie/2fm); **Today FM** (todayfm.com), a national station that's extremely popular with a young demographic; and **Q102** (q102.ie), a Dublin-based station that targets an over-35 audience with contemporary soft rock and ballads.

Some cool, quintessentially Irish names to check out, both in and out of the mainstream: **Damien Rice,** who has risen to huge chart success over the past decade; **Lisa Hannigan,** a singer-songwriter with a line in

Traditional music performance in an Irish pub.

THE IRISH language

Although English is the day-to-day language spoken by the majority of Irish people, Irish is the original Celtic language indigenous to these shores, and it is the national and first official language. You will see Irish (sometimes called Gaelic outside Ireland) on all road signs and official documents, and there are still places in Ireland where you will hear the Irish language being spoken. While only about 3% of Irish people speak Irish as their first language, it is still taught to all schoolchildren, and around 50% of the population can speak a little.

There are certain regions of Ireland, known as **Gaeltacht,** where Irish is predominantly spoken and official signage is in Irish rather than English. These areas are spread all over the country, but some of the biggest are in Donegal, Mayo, and Kerry. When you're driving around Gaeltacht districts, all the road signs will be in Irish—even emergency signs and place names. In this book we've included the Irish names as well as the English names for those places where you're likely to encounter this. (Donegal has a high proportion of native Irish speakers—more than a third of the residents of the Rosguill Peninsula, for example, speak Irish as their main language.)

You won't have any problem communicating with locals, however—nobody in Ireland speaks *only* Irish. While use of the language had been in decline, efforts to preserve and revive it have been successful and recent population surveys show the number of Irish speakers has increased year-on-year. It was made an official language of the E.U. in 2007, and the number of all-Irish schools is growing (around 1 in 12 schoolchildren is educated entirely through Irish). There are Irish TV and radio stations, several popular Irish language apps, and social media accounts that promote the language and help learners.

Here are some Irish words, to get you started:

Hello	*Dia duit*
Reply to hello	*Dia is Muire duit*
Goodbye	*Slán leat*
Excuse me	*Gabh mo leithscéal*
Please	*Le do thoil*
Thank you	*Go raibh maith agat*
My name is . . .	*. . . is ainm dom.*

infectiously romantic indie-pop; **Hozier,** a singer-songwriter from County Wicklow who has been making waves globally since 2014; **Burnt Out,** an angsty, artsy pair of indie-punk-influenced artists whose work is deeply rooted in Dublin's working-class culture; rapper **Jafaris,** part of an interesting new wave of Irish hip-hop artists; **Lyra,** a Cork native whose music draws comparisons to Enya and Kate Bush; **Soak,** an absurdly talented young Derry native who's been wowing the music world with her simple but enchantingly beautiful ballads; and **Eden,** an electronic music producer and songwriter who burst onto the international scene in 2016 and has been selling out venues across the world.

At the same time, traditional music is alive and well in Ireland, particularly in close association with Irish step dancing. The folk culture is primarily found outside of Dublin, although some pubs in the city do still showcase traditional music. Good places to catch live music are the coastal village of **Doolin,** in County Clare (p. 362); the lively pubs of

Cork City (p. 266); and the town of **Ballyshannon** in County Donegal (p. 480). Local pubs in small towns almost always can be counted on to host Irish music and sometimes dancing, too.

EATING & DRINKING IN IRELAND

Restaurants

Restaurants in Ireland are surprisingly expensive. The cost of eating out here is still well above the European average. On the plus side, Ireland's restaurants are varied and interesting—settings range from old-world hotel dining rooms, country mansions, and castles to sky-lit terraces, shopfront bistros, riverside cottages, thatched-roof pubs, and converted houses. There is huge appreciation for creative cooking, with an emphasis on seasonal and locally grown produce and meat.

Before you book a table, here are a few things you should know:

RESERVATIONS Except for self-service eateries, informal cafes, and some popular seafood spots, most restaurants encourage reservations, and most expensive restaurants require them. In the most popular places, Friday and Saturday nights are often booked up a week in advance, so have a few options in mind if you're booking at the last minute.

PRICES Meal prices at restaurants include national sales taxes (universally referred to as VAT, or Value Added Tax), at the rate of 13.5% in the Republic of Ireland and 20% in Northern Ireland. Some restaurants will include the tip as a service charge added automatically to the bill (usually listed at the bottom, just before the bill's total), especially for parties of six or more diners. Service charges generally range from 10% to 15%. When no service charge is added, tip around 12%, depending on the quality of the service. But do check your bill—some unscrupulous restaurants do not make it clear that you have already tipped, thus causing you to inadvertently tip twice.

TIPS FOR DINING bargains

- If you want to try a top-rated restaurant but can't afford dinner, see if they have an "**early bird**" early evening set menu or a **set-lunch menu.** You'll experience the same great cuisine at a much lower price.
- Try **pub food.** Pub menus usually include a mix of soups, sandwiches, burgers, steaks, and salads. In recent years, many pubs have converted or expanded into gastropubs and restaurants, serving excellent, unpretentious meals at (somewhat) reasonable prices. Check the menu before you sit down at a table (many places post them by their doors).
- Supermarkets and grocery stores in Ireland sell good **premade sandwiches** (much better than supermarket sandwiches in the U.S.) for a few euros, and some grocery stores have deli counters that will make up a fresh sandwich to order. These can make a good, cheap lunch or dinner.

DINING TIPS Don't be surprised if you are not ushered to your table as soon as you arrive at some upscale restaurants. This is not a delaying tactic—many of the better dining rooms carry on the old custom of seating you in a lounge while you sip an aperitif and perhaps peruse the menu. You are not under an obligation to have a cocktail, of course. It's perfectly fine to order a soft drink or just a glass of water.

Pubs

The pub is a mainstay of Irish social life—there are pubs in every city, town, and hamlet. Most people have a "local"—a favorite pub near home—where they go for a drink and conversation with neighbors, family, and friends. Pubs are more about socializing than drinking, and many people you see are just having a soft drink (a sparkling water, cola, or an orange or lemon soda). So even if you don't drink alcohol, feel free to go to the pub. It's a good way to meet the locals.

PUB HOURS Pubs in the Republic set their own hours, although closing times are bound by the type of alcohol license they have. Those with a regular license must shut by 11:30pm from Monday to Thursday, 12:30am on Friday and Saturday, and 11pm on Sunday. Those with late licenses can stay open until 2:30am Monday to Saturday and until 2am on Sunday. In Northern Ireland (which is governed by different laws), hours are slightly more restrictive, although this is currently the subject of debate. On Friday and Saturday nights, many pubs stay open until midnight or 1am, and a few even later than that, particularly in large towns and cities. It should also be noted that legal closing times can be hard to police in rural areas.

You'll notice that when "closing time" comes around, nobody clears out of the pub. "Closing time" is simply the time when the barmen must stop serving alcohol—often indicated by pub lights flickering briefly or a bartender shouting out "Last orders!" Anyone wanting to order one last drink does so then. You'll have about 20 to 30 minutes to finish before the pub closes. Eventually, bartenders shout something like "Time please!" or "All right folks," lights are turned up brightly, and patrons head to the exit.

TIPS ON ACCOMMODATIONS

Foreign visitors to Ireland should always have at least their first night's room booked, since you will be required to give an address at Immigration when you arrive at the airport. If you need help finding accommodations for subsequent nights once you're in Ireland, contact the local tourism office as soon as possible.

Booking in advance is your best strategy, especially in the summer and during peak times and festival events, when prices can rise and fall within the course of a week. Many hotels offer advance booking discounts several months ahead, and even if you book a month or two in advance, you can often get a better rate at a 4-star hotel than at a 2-star guesthouse—the most expensive hotels often offer in-advance discounts of up to 50%. So before you book that cheap hotel with no services, just have a peek at your dream hotel's prices and see if it's not as cheap, or maybe even cheaper. There is another option—if you are willing to take the risk. Hotels sometimes offer super last-minute discounts, but these are often limited to off-peak times, so prices very much depend on dates.

Accommodations in Ireland range widely in quality and cost. Often these variations are linked to location: A wonderful budget B&B in an isolated area of countryside may be cheap, while a mediocre guesthouse in Dublin or Cork may cost much more. Even in the same lodging, the size and quality of the rooms can vary, especially in older hotels and houses converted to B&Bs. Don't be discouraged by this, but do a little research so you know what you're booking.

Among your various options, **B&Bs** are often hard to beat. These smaller lodgings, usually in residential areas, can be charming and homey—we list several of the best in this book. Breakfast is included in the rate, and it's often hearty. Note that while most B&Bs are regulated and inspected by Failte Ireland under the National Quality Assurance Framework (look for the shamrock seal of approval), many perfectly fine establishments choose not to pay the annual fee that the stamp of approval requires—so don't assume that a place without the shamrock is subpar.

Hidden Ireland (hiddenireland.com; ✆ **098/66650**) is a collection of particularly elegant and unique B&Bs on the higher end of the price spectrum. Another interesting option if you're traveling in the countryside, especially if you're with children, is a stay in a **farmhouse B&B** on a family-run farm. Contact **B&B Ireland** (bandbireland.com) for information on farmhouse accommodation. For a selection of independent boutique hotels, manor houses, country hotels, and castles, contact **Original Irish Hotels** (originalirishhotels.com; ✆ **01/295-8900**); or for something more high-end, **Ireland's Blue Book** (irelands-blue-book.ie; ✆ **01/676-9914**) also has a great list of Irish country-house hotels, manors, and castles.

If you want to stay awhile and establish a base, consider renting a **self-catering** apartment, town house, or cottage. Self-catering is a huge business in Ireland. The minimum rental period is usually 1 week, although shorter periods are negotiable in the off-season. Families especially appreciate the convenience of having more room to spread out and a kitchen for preparing meals. **Rent an Irish Cottage** (rentacottage.ie; ✆ **061/411-109**) offers a selection of traditional cottages all over Ireland, fully modernized. The not-for-profit **Irish Landmark Trust** (irishlandmark.com; ✆ **01/670-4733**) offers historic properties, refurbished in period style, at prices lower than you might expect. On the more opulent end of the scale, **Elegant Ireland** (elegant.ie; ✆ **01/473-2505**) has anything from a chic seaside bungalow to a medieval castle with room for you and 20 of your BFFs.

Nowadays, Ireland's **hostels** are redesigning to attract travelers of all ages, including families. Many have private rooms and may cost a fraction of even a modest bed-and-breakfast. Contact **An Óige,** the Irish Youth Hostel Association (anoige.ie), or, in the North, **HINI** (Hostelling International Northern Ireland; hini.org.uk), for listings.

WHEN TO GO

A visit to Ireland in the summer is very different from a trip in the winter. Generally speaking, summer is when airfares, car-rental rates, and hotel prices are highest and crowds are most intense. But the days are long (6am sunrises and 10pm sunsets), the weather is warm, and every sightseeing attraction and B&B is open. In winter, you may get rock-bottom prices on airfare and hotels, but it will rain, the wind will blow, and many rural sights and a fair proportion of rural B&Bs and restaurants will be closed.

All things considered, we think the best time to visit is in spring and fall—the weather is a mix of seasons, prices are lower than in summer, and the crowds have yet to descend.

Weather

Rain is the one constant in Irish weather, although a bit of sunshine is usually just around the corner. The best of times and the worst of times are often only hours, or even minutes, apart. It can be chilly in Ireland at any time of year, so think *layers* when you pack.

Winters can be brutal, as the wind blows in off the Atlantic with numbing constancy, and strong gales are common. But deep snow is rare, and temperatures rarely drop much below freezing. In fact, Ireland is a fairly temperate place: January and February bring frosts but seldom snow, and July and August are very warm but rarely hot. The Irish consider any temperature over 68°F (20°C) to be "roasting" and below 34°F (1°C) bone-chilling.

Average Monthly Temperatures in Dublin

	JAN	FEB	MAR	APR	MAY	JUNE	JULY	AUG	SEPT	OCT	NOV	DEC
TEMP (°F)	36–46	37–48	37–49	38–52	42–57	46–62	51–66	50–65	48–62	44–56	39–49	38–47
TEMP (°C)	2–8	3–9	3–9	3–11	6–14	8–17	11–19	10–18	9–17	7–13	4–9	3–8

Holidays

The Republic observes the following national holidays, also known as bank holidays: New Year's Day (Jan 1); Imbolc or St. Brigid's Day (Feb 1); St. Patrick's Day (Mar 17); Easter Monday (variable), May Day (May

1); first Mondays in June and August (summer bank holidays); last Monday in October (autumn bank holiday); Christmas (Dec 25); and St. Stephen's Day (Dec 26). Good Friday (the Friday before Easter) is also observed. In Northern Ireland, the schedule of holidays is the same as in the Republic, with some exceptions: Summer bank holidays fall on the last Monday of May and August; it does not celebrate Imbolc; the Battle of the Boyne is celebrated on Orangeman's Day (July 12); and Boxing Day (Dec 26) follows Christmas.

In both Ireland and Northern Ireland, holidays that fall on weekends are celebrated the following Monday.

Ireland Calendar of Events

For the most up-to-date listings of events, check out **discoverireland.ie/whats-on** and **entertainment.ie**.

JANUARY

First Fortnight. Nationwide. This innovative festival challenges mental-health stigmas through art and culture. Events include plenty of comedy, music, and theater (firstfortnight.ie; ✆ **01/598-6263**). Early January.

Tradfest. Temple Bar, Dublin. Ireland's largest traditional music festival features exhibitions, film screenings, master classes—and, of course, lots of music performances. Most events take place in Temple Bar, but some are held farther afield (tradfest.com). Late January.

FEBRUARY

Dublin International Film Festival. Irish Film Centre, Temple Bar, and various cinemas in Dublin. Ten days of screenings of more than 100 films, from both Ireland and abroad, plus seminars and lectures on filmmaking (diff.ie; ✆ **01/662-4260**). Late February and early March.

MARCH

St. Patrick's Festival Dublin. This massive 4-day festival is open, free, and accessible to all. Street theater, carnival acts, sports, music, fireworks, and other festivities culminate in Ireland's grandest parade, with marching bands, drill teams, floats, and delegations from around the world (stpatricksday.ie; ✆ **01/604-0090**). On and around March 17.

St. Patrick's Day Parades. Held all over Ireland and Northern Ireland, celebrating Ireland's patron saint. March 17.

APRIL

Cúirt International Festival of Literature. Galway City. One of Ireland's most established literary festivals, Cúirt takes place over a week in Galway. The packed lineup includes panels, talks, spoken-word events, and theater (cuirt.ie; ✆ **091/569-777**). Mid- to late April.

International Pan Celtic Festival. For 5 days, the wider Celtic family (including Cornwall, Isle of Man, Scotland, Wales, and Brittany) unites for culture, song, dance, sports, and parades with marching bands and pipers. The festival moves to a different Celtic region every year—Ireland is a frequent host (panceltic.ie). April.

World Irish Dancing Championships. The premier international competition in Irish dancing features more than 4,000 contenders from as far away as New Zealand (clrg.ie). Location varies each year. April.

MAY

Belfast City Marathon. This 42km (26-mile) race of 17,000 international runners through the city starts at City Hall and finishes at the Maysfield Recreation Centre (belfastcitymarathon.com; ✆ **028/9060-5922**). Early May.

International Literature Festival Dublin. One of the biggest events in the Irish arts calendar, this 9-day festival draws high-profile authors from around the world. Events take place at venues across the city, including Dublin Castle (ilfdublin.com). Mid-May.

Dublin Dance Festival. Very much an international event, the DDF hosts dancers from around the globe as part of its innovative program, which has the self-proclaimed intention to "unlock new perspectives on our changing world" (dublindancefestival.ie; ✆ **01/679-8658**). Late May.

The Cat Laughs Comedy Festival. Various venues, Kilkenny Town. Past performers at this international festival of stand-up comedy include American comics Bill Murray, Zach Galifianakis, and Tig Notaro, and Ireland's Dara Ó Briain (thecatlaughs.com). Late May/early June.

JUNE

Carlow Arts Festival. This eclectic 10-day festival includes something for everyone, from visual arts, theater, and music to virtual reality and circus performances. Many events are family-friendly, and almost everything is completely free (carlowartsfestival.ie). Early June.

Taste of Dublin. Iveagh Gardens, Dublin. One of Ireland's biggest and most high-profile food festivals, where for 4 days visitors can sample dishes prepared by some of the country's top chefs and more than 100 artisan producers. (tasteofdublin.ie). Mid-June.

Bloomsday Festival. Various Dublin venues. This unique daylong fest celebrates Leopold Bloom, the central character of James Joyce's *Ulysses*, by replicating the sights, sounds, aromas, and tastes of Dublin on June 16, 1904, the day when *Ulysses* takes place. Ceremonies are held at the James Joyce Tower and Museum; guided walks visit Joycean sights (bloomsdayfestival.ie). June 11–16.

Cork Midsummer Arts Festival. Emmet Place, Cork City. The program includes musical performances and traditional Irish *céilí* bands, and always has a strong literary content. Bonfire nights are particularly popular (corkmidsummer.com). Mid-June.

Hinterland Festival. Kells, County Meath. Devoted to literature and the arts, Hinterland draws an increasingly high-profile guest list, including famous Irish writers (hinterland.ie; ✆ **083/096-9345**). Late June.

Irish Derby. The Curragh, County Kildare. Ireland's version of the Kentucky Derby or Royal Ascot is a fashionable gathering (***hint:*** jackets for men, posh hats for women) of racing fans from all over the world. It's one of the richest middle-distance horse races in Europe. Booking recommended (curragh.ie; ✆ **045/441-205**). Late June.

Dublin LGBTQ+ Pride Festival. An annual festival celebrating lesbian, gay, bisexual, transgender, and queer life in Dublin, it ends with a colorful Pride parade in the city. There are smaller Pride festivals in other locations around Ireland throughout the summer (dublinpride.ie). Last Saturday in June.

West Cork Chamber Music Festival. Bantry, County Cork. One of the biggest classical music festivals in Ireland, this presents a huge program of concerts, including work from the best up-and-coming new classical artists (westcorkmusic.ie; ✆ **027/52788**). Late June.

JULY

Galway International Arts Festival. Galway City. This 2-week fest features international theater, concerts, literary evenings, street shows, arts, parades, and music (giaf.ie). Mid-July.

Tread Softly. Sligo Town, County Sligo. The mythical landscape of Sligo is the inspiration for this 2-week festival celebrating the region's folklore and arts. Highlights include storytelling, guided walks, and art exhibitions (treadsoftly.ie). Late July or early August.

AUGUST

Fleadh Cheoil na hÉireann. Ireland's premier summer festival of traditional music, language, song, and dance since 1951 changes its host location every year. Competitions are held to select all-Ireland champions in categories of instruments and singing (fleadhcheoil.ie). Early to mid-August.

Kilkenny Arts Festival. Kilkenny Town. This weeklong event has classical and traditional music, plays, readings, films, poetry, and art exhibitions (kilkennyarts.ie). Early to mid-August.

Puck Fair. Killorglin, County Kerry. In one of Ireland's oldest festivals, the residents of this tiny Ring of Kerry town (p. 324) enthrone a goat as "king" over 3 days of merrymaking—open-air concerts, horse fairs, parades, and fireworks (puckfair.ie; ✆ **066/976-2366**). August 10–12.

Electric Picnic. Stradbally, County Laois. This midsize music festival, held on the grounds of Stradbally Hall, is known for its eclectic lineup. Recent acts have included Billie Eilish, Calvin Harris, and Kylie. Book early—tickets have been known to sell out within hours of going on sale the previous year (electricpicnic.ie). Mid-August.

Rose of Tralee International Festival. Tralee, County Kerry. A gala atmosphere prevails at this 5-day event (p. 336), with a full program of concerts, street entertainment, horse races, and a beauty-and-talent pageant leading up to the televised selection of the "Rose of Tralee" (roseoftralee.ie). Late August.

National Heritage Week. More than 400 events are held throughout the country, including walks, lectures, exhibitions, music recitals, and open-house days at historic buildings (heritageweek.ie; ✆ **056/777-0777**). Mid- to late August.

SEPTEMBER

Irish Antique & Fine Art Fair. The Royal Dublin Society, Ballsbridge, Dublin. Ireland's premier annual antiques fair, with hundreds of dealers from all over the island (iada.ie). Usually in September.

Dublin Fringe Festival. "Art is a power tool—start digging"—so proclaims the website of this super-cool fringe festival. Expect cutting-edge theater and other live performances over 2 weeks (fringe fest.com; ✆ **01/670-6106**). Mid-September.

Galway International Oyster and Seafood Festival. The highlights of this festival include the World Oyster Opening Championship, a grand opening parade, an art exhibition, a gala banquet, traditional music, and, of course, lots of oyster eating (galwayoysterfestival.com; ✆ **091/394-637**). Late September.

Dublin Theatre Festival. Showcases for new plays by every major Irish company, plus productions from abroad (dublin theatrefestival.ie; ✆ **01/677-8439**). Late September/mid-October.

OCTOBER

Baboró International Arts Festival for Children. Galway. A fun-filled, educational festival geared to kids 3 to 12 years of age, with theater, music, dance, museum exhibitions, and literary events (baboro.ie; ✆ **091/562-667**). Mid-October.

Guinness Cork Jazz Festival. Cork City. Ireland's second city stages a first-rate festival of jazz, with an international lineup of live acts playing in hotels, concert halls, and pubs (guinnesscorkjazz.com). Late October.

Bram Stoker Festival. Dublin. Bigger than you might expect, this 4-day celebration of the author of *Dracula* includes giant art installations, open-air film screenings, parades, and other Gothic fun (bramstokerfestival.com). Late October.

Fire dancer at the 2024 Púca Festival in County Meath.

Púca Festival. Trim and Athboy, County Meath. Halloween celebration with fire displays, storytelling, street parades, food and craft market, walking tours, comedy, and music performances (pucafestival.com). Late October.

Wexford Festival Opera. Wexford, County Wexford. Famous as much for its jubilant, informal atmosphere as its acclaimed productions of lesser-known 18th- and 19th-century operatic masterpieces, this festival also has classical music concerts and more (wexfordopera.com; ✆ **053/912-2144**). Late October/early November.

NOVEMBER

Cork International Film Festival. Cinemas throughout Cork. Now in its 70th year, Ireland's oldest film festival offers a plethora of international features, documentaries, short films, and special programs (corkfilmfest.org). Early to mid-November.

Mayo Dark Sky Festival. Newport, Mulranny, and Ballycroy, County Mayo. Talks, workshops, concerts, and guided night walks in Mayo Dark Sky Park at Wild Nephin National Park (mayodarkskyfestival.ie). November.

DECEMBER

Christmas Markets. You'll find Christmas fairs all over Ireland from late November through December. A handful of the best: **Killarney, Cork, Galway City, Belfast,** and Winterval in **Waterford** (winterval.ie). Expect quality local crafts, food, and general festive magic and sparkle. December.

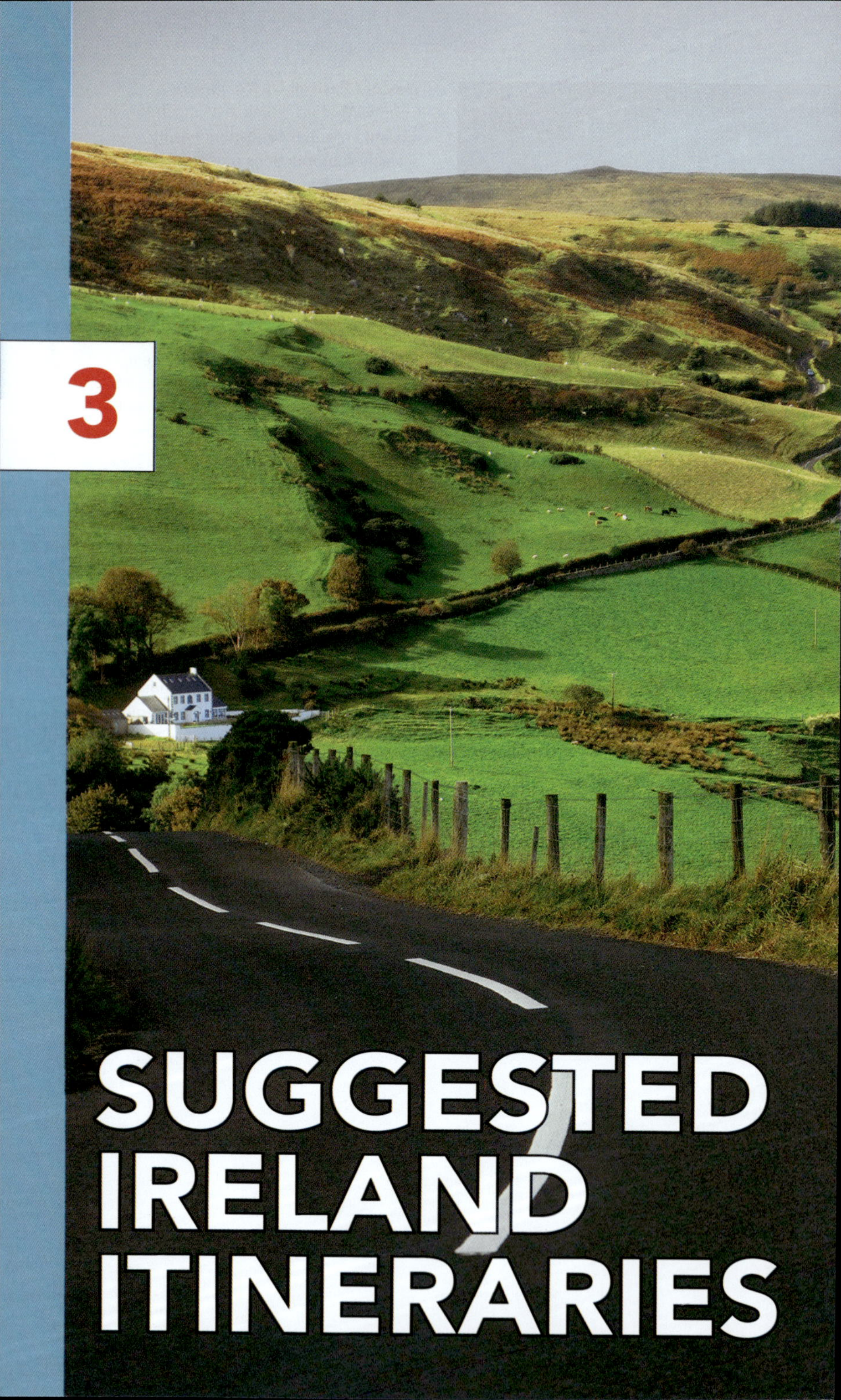
3
SUGGESTED
IRELAND
ITINERARIES

Ireland is a small island, so you can cover a lot of ground in a week and feel quite at home within two. But even with the best of intentions and all the energy in the world, you'll never see it all on a short visit. So rather than rushing to see everything or planning a big driving tour, choose your wish list early and pace yourself.

The suggested itineraries in this chapter will help you get the most out of this extraordinary and varied country—no matter how much time you have to see it. If you've only got a week to spend here, the southern regions probably have more to offer. They're generally easier to get around, and the major sights are closer together. If you're traveling with kids, Dublin and County Kerry have particularly rich troves of kid-friendly attractions. However, those in search of the road less traveled will be drawn northward, especially to places such as Mayo, Sligo, Donegal, and the beautiful Antrim Coast.

All of these tours (except one) assume that you have a week to see the country. Where there's potential for a longer trip, we've given some alternatives for an extended version. Pick and choose the parts that appeal to you, add in your own favorite shopping or scenic drives, and turn it all into a custom-made holiday for yourself.

Remember that while distances look small on the map, narrow roads can make for slow going. Our advice when planning your trip is to pick one or two areas or regions—the Southwest, West, or Northwest, for example—rather than trying to race around the whole (or half of the) island in a week.

THE REGIONS IN BRIEF

The island of Ireland is divided into two political units: the **Republic of Ireland,** which makes up the vast majority of the country, and **Northern Ireland,** which along with England, Scotland, and Wales is part of the United Kingdom. Of Ireland's 32 counties, all but six are in the Republic.

The island is also divided into four provinces: Ulster is north, Munster is south, Leinster is east, and Connacht is west. Each region is divided into counties:

In Ulster (to the north) Cavan, Donegal, and Monaghan in the Republic; Antrim, Armagh, Derry, Down, Fermanagh, and Tyrone in Northern Ireland.

FACING PAGE: **Scenic road in Connemara.**

In Munster (to the south) Clare, Cork, Kerry, Limerick, Tipperary, and Waterford.

In Leinster (to the east) Dublin, Carlow, Kildare, Kilkenny, Laois, Longford, Louth, Meath, Offaly, Westmeath, Wexford, and Wicklow.

In Connacht (to the west) Sligo, Mayo, Galway, Roscommon, and Leitrim.

DUBLIN & ENVIRONS With 40% of the Republic's population living within 97km (60 miles) of Dublin, the capital is the center of the profound changes that have transformed Ireland into a prosperous European country. Within an hour's drive of Dublin are Dalkey, Dún Laoghaire, Howth, Malahide, and many more engaging coastal towns, as well as the rural beauty of the Wicklow Mountains, horse country in Kildare, and the Neolithic ruins in County Meath.

THE SOUTHEAST The southeast offers sandy beaches, Wexford's lush countryside, Waterford City and its museums, Kilkenny's and Cahir's ancient castles, and the Irish National Heritage Park at Ferrycarrig.

CORK & ENVIRONS **Cork,** Ireland's second-largest city, is a buzzy university town and a congenial gateway to the south and west of the island. Within arm's reach are Blarney Castle (and its famous stone), the culinary

The colorful streets of Kinsale, County Cork.

and scenic delights of Kinsale, the historic emigration port of Cobh, and the dazzling landscape of West Cork.

THE SOUTHWEST The once-remote splendor of **County Kerry** has long ceased to be a secret, at least during the high season. The Ring of Kerry (less glamorously known as roads N70 and N71) encircling the Iveragh Peninsula is one of Ireland's most visited attractions. That's both a recommendation and a warning. While Killarney National Park provides a stunning haven from buses, the town of Killarney is filled with souvenir shops and tour groups. Marginally less visited highlights include the rugged Dingle Peninsula and two sets of islands with rich histories: the Skelligs and the Blaskets.

THE WEST The west of Ireland offers a first taste of Ireland's wild beauty and striking diversity, especially handy for those who fly into Shannon Airport. **County Clare**'s natural offerings—particularly the unique landscapes of the Burren—are unforgettable, and the county also has an array of impressive castles: Knappogue, Bunratty, and (just over the county line in Galway) Dunguaire.

GALWAY & ENVIRONS **Galway City** is busy, colorful, and funky—a youthful port and university town and the self-proclaimed arts capital of Ireland, with lots of theater, music, and dance. County Galway is the gateway to Connemara's moody, magical mountains and boglands. Offshore lie the atmospheric, mysterious Aran Islands.

THE MIDLANDS The lush center of Ireland, bisected by the lazy River Shannon, is a land of pastures, rivers, lakes, woods, and gentle mountain slopes. It's a retreat, in high season, from the throngs of tourists who crowd the coasts. The Midlands also hold remarkable sites—Birr Castle and its splendid gardens, for example, and Clonmacnoise, the evocative ruins of a famous Irish monastic center.

MAYO & SLIGO Farther up the coast to the north, past Galway, County Mayo offers the sweet town of Westport on Clew Bay and Achill Island (accessible by car), with its beaches and stunning cliff views. County Sligo inspired the poetry of W. B. Yeats, and offers a dense collection of stone circles, passage tombs, and cairns at such sites as Carrowmore, Knocknarea, and Carrowkeel, plus surfing beaches.

THE NORTHWEST In Ireland it's easy to become convinced that isolated austerity is beautiful. Nowhere is this more evident than in **County Donegal,** with its jagged, desolate coastline. (If you don't mind the cold, it offers some fine surfing.) Inland, Glenveagh National Park has as much wilderness as you could want.

NORTHERN IRELAND Across the border, Northern Ireland's six counties boast such attractions as the stunning **Causeway Coast,** the extraordinary basalt columns of the Giant's Causeway, and the Glens of Antrim.

IS NORTHERN IRELAND safe to visit?

In short, **yes.** Do not be put off visiting this wonderful part of Ireland because of its troubled past. It's been at peace for more than a quarter of a century. Belfast and Derry are *safer for visitors than almost any comparable American city,* and the Ulster countryside is idyllic and serene. So we really wouldn't worry.

That said, you do need to be aware of a few issues—particularly after Brexit. Be sensitive to the fact that there are still deep divisions here, and follow these basic rules:

- **Do not** discuss politics with anyone you don't know well.
- **Never** get involved in political or religious arguments relating to Northern Ireland.
- **Avoid** traditional Catholic or Protestant marches and parades, especially those by the Orange Order around July 12. They may look like local color, but they can get unpleasant quickly. People do get hurt.
- **Remain** informed. Follow the news to keep abreast of current events and any areas of tension.

The old city walls of **Derry,** the past glory of Carrickfergus Castle, and **Belfast**'s elaborate political murals and thriving food scene make a trip across the border worthwhile.

How to See Ireland

Let's get one thing straight: You don't *have* to rent a car to see Ireland. Millions of people don't. Ireland has a decent public transportation network, and you're spoiled for choice when it comes to tour bus excursions. And that's a fine way to do it. This is *your* trip, after all.

However, if your ideal Ireland involves wandering through the countryside, visiting small villages, climbing castle walls, hailing history from a ruined abbey, or finding yourself alone on a rocky beach—you cannot do those things independently without a car.

Short of hiring private guides, or taking some very expensive taxi rides, there just aren't many other options. Out of the main towns, public transportation exists, but it's slow and limiting. Most major sites in the countryside are doable on organized bus tours, but there's only so far that can take you. Fortunately, every major town has car-rental agencies, if you decide to explore by car.

Just remember to drive on the *left.*

The next step is deciding **where to start.** That decision can be made for you by where your flight arrives. If you're flying into **Shannon Airport** or **Cork Airport,** then it makes geographic sense to start out on the west coast. If you're flying into **Dublin,** you might as well explore that city first, then either head up to the North and the ruggedly beautiful Antrim Coast, or south down to the Wicklow Mountains, Kilkenny, Wexford, and Waterford.

Still, if you fly into Dublin but your heart is in Galway, no worries. You can traverse the width of the country in a couple of hours, thanks to motorways out of Dublin. Just bear in mind that rural roads are not well lit or well signposted, so driving at night should be avoided. Being lost in unfamiliar territory (where it can be many miles between villages) is no fun at all.

A WEEK FROM THE EAST TO SOUTHWEST

There's something terribly romantic about flying into Dublin. The compact, laidback city awaits a few miles down the road, packed with old-fashioned pubs, modern restaurants, and absorbing sights all laid out for walking. If you've never been here, a couple of days in Dublin make for a quick primer on Ireland. It's just enough time to do some shopping on **Grafton Street,** head up O'Connell Street to the **General Post Office,** or discover the Georgian beauty and museums around **St. Stephen's Green** and **Merrion Square.** You can give the surface of the city a good brush in a couple of days, and then head south to **Wicklow and Kilkenny,** and then on to **Waterford, Cork,** and **Kerry,** hitting many high points along the way.

Library Square at Trinity College in Dublin.

DAYS 1 & 2: Arrive in Dublin

If it happens that you're arriving from North America, you start with an advantage: Most flights arrive early in the morning, which effectively gives you an extra day's sightseeing. Check in to your hotel (or drop off your bags if check-in is not until the afternoon), order a cup of tea, take a minute to relax, get a map from your concierge, and then head out on foot.

Stay south of the River Liffey and head down Dame Street to **Dublin Castle** (p. 111), home of the magical **Chester Beatty Library** (p. 96) with its vast collection of gorgeous illuminated manuscripts. Later, take in **St. Patrick's Cathedral** (p. 103) and the vibrant green quadrangles and **Book of Kells** at **Trinity College** (p. 93) before heading over to Merrion Square, with its handsome granite architecture and two of the main sites of Ireland's **National Museum** (a third is on the west side of the city). The **Archaeology** museum has an extraordinary hoard of ancient gold, while the **Natural History** building contains a fascinating zoological collection from the past. It's a short stroll from here up to **St. Stephen's Green.** Rest your weary toes and soak up the floral view here. Then stroll down **Grafton Street** for some shopping before collapsing in your hotel.

On **DAY 2,** have a hearty breakfast in your hotel before striking out for the lively district of **Temple Bar.** Stroll north to the river, then take a right and walk along the noisy, vibrant waterfront to the landmark **Ha'penny Bridge.** Walk across and head east on **O'Connell Street,** where you pass its many statues to reach the bullet-ridden columns of the **General Post Office** (p. 112), site of the 1916 Easter Rising. After exploring the displays, head back to the river to Custom House Quay to wander amid the fascinating interactive exhibits in **EPIC The Irish Emigration Museum** (p. 114). If you have time, step aboard the *Jeanie Johnston* ship (p. 117) to learn more about the emigration story. Let someone else do the work in the evening, either on a walking tour—such as the **Irish Music Pub Crawl,** perhaps (p. 101)—or some good-natured scares aboard the **Dublin Ghost Bus** (p. 122). Those in search of less organized fun may prefer the simple, atmospheric pleasure of **An Evening of Food, Folklore & Fairies** (p. 175).

DAY 3: South to Wicklow & Kilkenny

It takes less than 2 hours to drive from the hustle and traffic of Dublin to the peace and quiet of the **Wicklow Mountains** (p. 205). Drive through the village of Enniskerry to the great estate of **Powerscourt** (p. 203) just past the village. After lunching in its Avoca Café, head on to **Glendalough** (p. 201) and feel your soul relax in the pastoral mountain and lake setting of this ancient monastic retreat. From

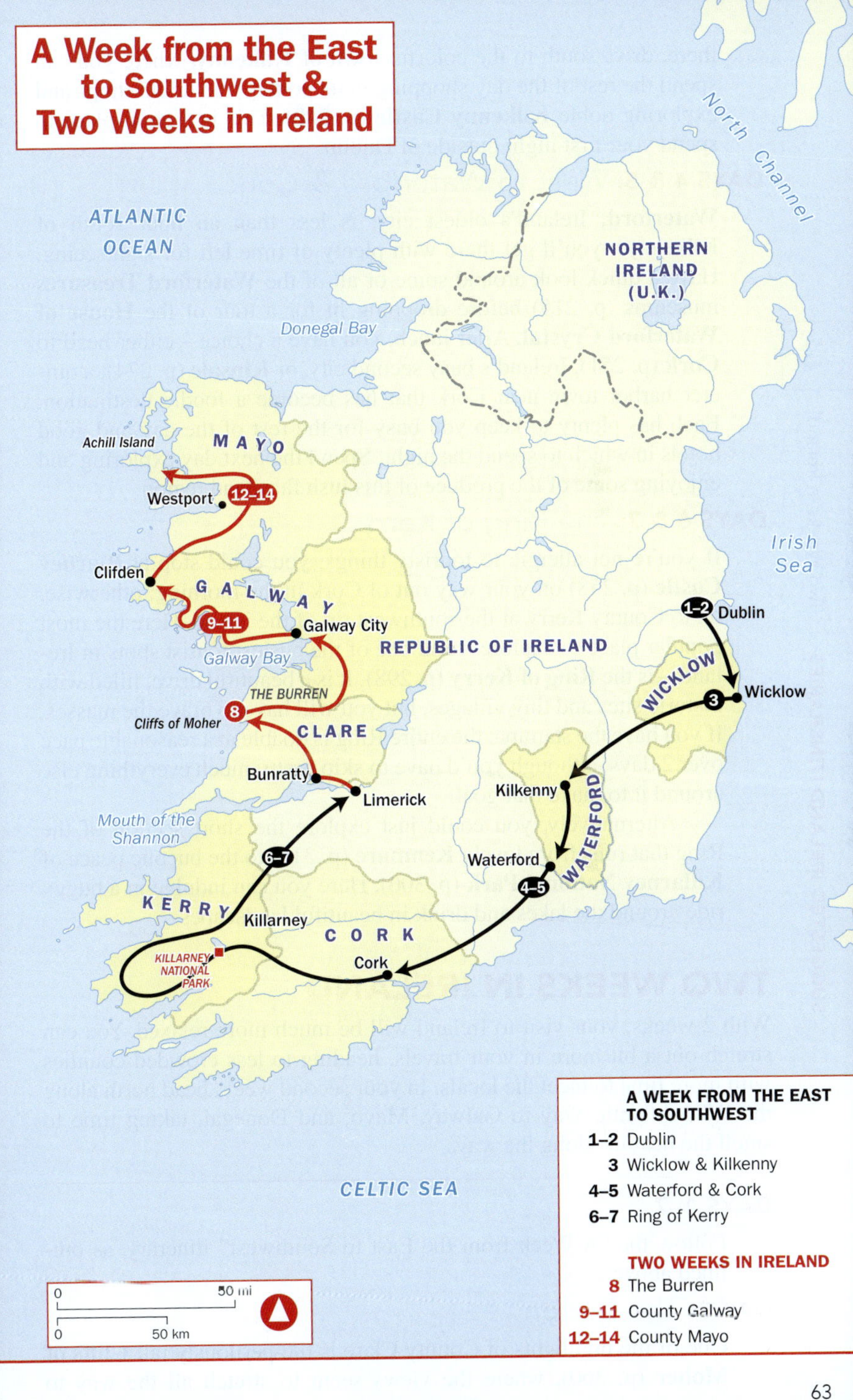
A Week from the East to Southwest & Two Weeks in Ireland
North Channel
ATLANTIC OCEAN
NORTHERN IRELAND (U.K.)
Donegal Bay
Achill Island
MAYO
Westport
12–14
Irish Sea
Clifden
GALWAY
9–11
Galway City
1–2
Dublin
REPUBLIC OF IRELAND
Galway Bay
WICKLOW
Wicklow
3
THE BURREN
8
Cliffs of Moher
CLARE
Bunratty
Limerick
Kilkenny
WATERFORD
Mouth of the Shannon
6–7
Waterford
4–5
KERRY
Killarney
CORK
KILLARNEY NATIONAL PARK
Cork
CELTIC SEA
0
50 mi
0
50 km
A WEEK FROM THE EAST TO SOUTHWEST
1–2 Dublin
3 Wicklow & Kilkenny
4–5 Waterford & Cork
6–7 Ring of Kerry
TWO WEEKS IN IRELAND
8 The Burren
9–11 County Galway
12–14 County Mayo

there, drive south to the colorful town of **Kilkenny,** where you can spend the rest of the day shopping in its pottery and crafts shops and exploring noble **Kilkenny Castle** (p. 240). This is a good place to spend your first night outside of Dublin.

DAYS 4 & 5: West to Waterford & Cork

Waterford, Ireland's oldest city, is less than an hour south of Kilkenny—you'll get there with plenty of time left for sightseeing. Have a quick look around some or all of the **Waterford Treasures** museums (p. 215) before dropping in for a tour of the **House of Waterford Crystal.** After lunch, you have a choice—either head to **Cork** (p. 251), Ireland's busy second city, or **Kinsale** (p. 274), a quieter harbor town near Cork that has become a foodie destination. Each has plenty to keep you busy for the rest of the day and good hotels in which to spend the night. Spend the next day exploring and enjoying some of the produce of this lush farmland region.

DAYS 6 & 7: The Ring of Kerry

If you're not allergic to touristy things, you could stop at **Blarney Castle** (p. 258) on your way out of Cork in the morning; otherwise, on to County Kerry at the southwest tip of the island. Here the most popular place to explore—and one of the busiest tourist spots in Ireland—is the **Ring of Kerry** (p. 298). It is a beautiful drive, filled with historic sites and tiny villages, but you will have to brave the masses. If you have the stamina, the entire Ring is doable at a reasonable pace over 2 days, although you'd have to skip pretty much everything else around it to make that goal.

Alternatively, you could just explore the short section of the Ring that runs from lovely **Kenmare** (p. 316) to the bucolic peace of **Killarney National Park** (p. 300). Here you can indulge in a buggy ride around the lakes and drink in beautiful landscapes.

TWO WEEKS IN IRELAND

With 2 weeks, your visit to Ireland will be much more relaxed. You can stretch out a bit more in your travels, heading to less crowded counties with more time to meet the locals. In your second week, head north along the Wild Atlantic Way to Galway, Mayo, and Donegal, taking time to smell the heather along the way.

DAYS 1–7

Follow the "A Week from the East to Southwest" itinerary, as outlined above.

DAY 8: The Burren

One of the highlights of County Clare is the perilously tall **Cliffs of Moher** (p. 360), where the views seem to stretch all the way to

America (although the price to park will make you shiver). Get there early before the crowds, and then spend the rest of the day exploring and marveling at the otherworldly limestone landscape of the **Burren** (p. 354) before a visit to **Bunratty Castle** (p. 359)—where medieval fortress meets historical theme park. The area is also home to another of the county's great medieval buildings, the exquisite ruins of **Corcomroe Abbey** (p. 358). Lovers of live music will want to spend the evening in the pubs of **Doolin** (p. 362), one of the very best places in Ireland for proper traditional music.

DAYS 9–11: County Galway

Start the day with a drive up to Galway City (it will take around an hour and a half from Doolin), your base for **DAY 9.** Spend a relaxing day walking the delightful streets of this artsy, vibrant town. Stay overnight in the city, and the next day, **DAY 10,** take a cruise out to the misty **Aran Islands** (p. 395) for a day trip or overnight stay. On **DAY 11,** go west to explore Connemara and its fabulous villages and beaches. **Connemara National Park** (p. 412) also has some great walks and hikes. Either return to your Galway City hotel each night or stay in a countryside B&B.

DAYS 12–14: County Mayo

On **DAY 12,** drive up from Galway through spectacular scenery, where the rocky shoreline plunges into the cobalt sea in glorious fashion. The south Mayo town of **Westport,** sitting at the edge of a picturesque river, is a delightful place to wander. With plenty of hotels, pubs, and restaurants, Westport makes a great base for a few days. Probably depending on whether or not you're traveling with youngsters, you could either spend a couple of hours at **Westport House and Adventure Park** (p. 448) or visit the **National Museum of Ireland: Country Life** (p. 447) near Castlebar. If it's a quiet retreat you're after, drive across the strangely empty flatlands to **Achill Island** (p. 448). The route along the coast and out across the bridge to the island is slow and winding, but the views are fantastic. If you do make it out to Achill, consider an overnight stay at the **Bervie** (p. 453), where the sea is right outside the door. History buffs can head north to the ancient archaeological site at **Céide Fields** (p. 450) along the coast.

DAY 14: Heading home

Depending on where you spent the night and at what time your flight leaves, you may be in for a long drive back to the airport, so start early. If you're flying from Ireland West, it's just a short drive to **Knock,** or if it's Shannon, take your time and perhaps a short detour to **Galway** for lunch. Expect the journey to Dublin airport to take at least 4 hours, but allow plenty of time in case of traffic backups around Dublin—they're virtually constant.

Kayaking at Westport House and Adventure Park in County Mayo.

THE BEST ADVENTURES IN IRELAND

With its miles of rugged Atlantic coastline and mountain ranges, lakes, rivers, and canals of all sizes, Ireland is a fantastic place for a few days of adventure. This might be a gentle walk, or cycle, or something more extreme like surfing or kitesurfing—and the good news is that there is always something to suit all levels no matter where you go. A national network of waymarked hiking trails (plus national-park and forest-park trails) provides plenty of walking and hiking options, or take to a mountain trail for something more challenging. Around the coast are surf schools and kayaking outfitters and opportunities to try kitesurfing or wing foiling. Inland, there are lakes, rivers, and canals to paddle on, plus greenways along old railway routes to walk or cycle. The best thing of all about this itinerary is that you don't have to give up seeing the bucket-list sights, archaeological attractions, and museums in an area. Have an adventure in the morning, recharge with a hearty lunch in a country pub, and then wind down in the afternoon with some leisurely browsing at a museum or heritage site.

DAYS 1 & 2: County Sligo

With the Dartry Mountains stretching north from the iconic flat-topped **Ben Bulben** mountain near Sligo Town, the Ox Mountains in the south of the county, and no end of long, golden beaches (plus loads of lakes and rivers), it's no surprise that County Sligo considers itself Ireland's adventure capital. Start the day with a dawn paddleboarding

tour on the Garavogue River with **Northwest Adventures** (p. 473) before a filling breakfast in **Sligo Town** and an afternoon exploring somewhere like **Carrowmore** (p. 464). You can also stretch your legs on an afternoon climb up **Knocknarea** (p. 466), an easy 30-minute stroll.

On **DAY 2**, drive to **Strandhill** for a 2-hour surfing lesson or rent a board for a couple of hours. Fall into **Shell's Café** afterwards for a post-surfing feed (p. 472). If the weather is stormy, head to the viewing point at **Mullaghmore** to watch some big-wave surfing action—the pro surfers fly in from around the world for the giant breaks in this corner of the county when the big storms hit.

SAVING MONEY ON trains & buses

The cost of rail travel can quickly mount up, but there are ways to save money. Whenever you can, *buy your tickets online in advance.* The sample fares listed in this itinerary are all prebooked; walk-up fares can be higher. The downside for booking that way is that you have to specify times of travel—but Irish Rail has a handy policy of letting you upgrade a prebooked ticket into something more flexible for just €10.

If you're going to be spending a lot of time on public transportation, you should also strongly consider buying a money-saving pass. **Eurail Pass** is good for travel on trains, and also offers discounts on Stena Line ferries and Irish Ferries routes between Ireland and England, Scotland, Wales, or France. You can select particular countries, or go for a Global Pass, which covers 28 European nations. If you choose to buy a pass for 3 days of unlimited travel in Ireland within 1 month, a pass starts at €143. The passes are valid throughout Ireland (including Northern Ireland). For details or for purchase, visit **eurail.com**. You can also buy Eurail Passes from **Railpass** (railpass.com; ✆ **877/375-7245** in the U.S.) and other travel agents.

While the pass can save you money, first check out route prices on **irishrail.ie**. It may work out cheaper just to book tickets for each journey. If you do buy a Eurail Pass, it's still advisable to make seat reservations to guarantee a space—this may cost a few extra euros each time in booking fees. Note that if you're already a resident of the European Union, you can travel with the Europeans-only equivalent of the Eurail Pass: the **Interrail Pass.** See **interrail.eu** for details.

Hikers can join a guided hike in **Ben Bulben** or one of the other surrounding hills with **Northwest Adventures** (p. 473), which also runs night hikes in Union Woods. Another nice way to see some of the County Sligo countryside is on horseback. Sign up for an hour or half-day of riding with the **Sligo Riding Centre** or **Island View Riding Stables** (p. 473).

DAYS 3–5: Galway & Connemara

Travel south to County Galway, where **Galway City** makes a great base for adventures in Connemara and beyond. You can spend your days out exploring the countryside and your nights soaking up the music, food, and pub culture of the city—or perhaps spend an evening or two in a country B&B to get the full nature experience.

One of the easiest hikes for adventures in Connemara is **Diamond Hill** in **Connemara National Park** (p. 412), one of the Twelve Bens. Allow around 3 or 4 hours for the full trail. Pick up a map of the trails from the visitor center, which also has a cafe for post-hike refreshments. From the summit, there are views down to **Kylemore Abbey** (p. 414) and out over the Atlantic. While you're on this side of Connemara, perhaps on **DAY 4** you can walk the Green Road along the stunning **Killary Fjord** (p. 421), a natural inlet that runs along the Mayo border. The walk takes 2 to 3 hours. You can also explore the fjord from the water on a boat tour or sign up for a land or sea adventure with either **Killary Adventures** or **Delphi Adventure Centre** (p. 422), both of which offer everything kayaking, windsurfing, and climbing and hiking.

On **DAY 5,** travel to south Connemara and spend time exploring the beaches around the village of **Roundstone**. Or take a ferry out to the **Aran Islands** (p. 395) from Rossaveel, for a day trip or overnight, where you can walk or cycle the quiet roads. A quieter island with lots of birds and beach walks is **Inishbofin** (p. 413)—the ferry sails daily from Cleggan. The Connemara pony is native to this region; a great way to get off the beaten path in the Galway countryside is on a day's pony trekking from **Diamond Equestrian Centre** or the **Point Pony Trekking and Horse Riding Centre,** Ballyconneely (p. 422). Head back to Galway City for some food and live music in the pubs for your last night in this region.

DAYS 6 & 7: County Clare & the Burren

Today we travel south to the **Burren** in County Clare, a fantastic place for adventure, with so much nature to see on its limestone-lined hills and beaches. Make sure to spend a day or two exploring **Burren National Park** to understand this unusual landscape and see some of its rare plants and wildflowers as well as heritage sites like **Poulnabrone** (p. 358) and **Corcomroe Abbey** (p. 358). Get a map of the park at the

The unusual landscape of Burren National Park.

Burren Centre (p. 357). If you have a couple of days, the 26-mile **Burren Way** (p. 359) is a great way to immerse yourself in the landscape and take some lesser-known trails (the trails can be rough, so wear solid hiking shoes).

On **DAY 7,** see the rock formations of the Burren underground at **Aillwee Burren Experience** (p. 354), a guided tour of some of the 3,280 feet of passages, with their bridged chasms and rocky waterfalls.

County Clare also has some of Ireland's best surfing beaches. Sign up for an afternoon surf lesson or rent a board for a sunset or sunrise surf in **Lahinch.** Lessons or rentals include wetsuits, and you can do private lessons or join in with a group. More experienced surfers can tackle the reef at Spanish Point, a little farther south. Stay overnight at **Armada House** (p. 364), overlooking the water, before leaving for your next destination.

THE BEST OF IRELAND FOR FAMILIES

Traveling with children is always a bit of an adventure, and you'll want all the help you can get. Luckily, Ireland—with its vast open countryside, farm hotels, and castles—is like a fairy-tale playground for kids. You may have trouble finding babysitters outside major towns, so just take the kids with you wherever you go—most restaurants, sights, and even pubs (during the day) welcome children. The best part of the country for those traveling with kids is arguably Cork and Kerry, where everything seems to be set up for families. Here's a sample itinerary for a kid-friendly trip.

DAYS 1 & 2: Dublin

The extensive greens of **Phoenix Park** (p. 121) are a great place for little ones to let off steam (it's the best place in the city for a picnic, too, if the weather's good). Within the park, **Dublin Zoo** (p. 123) is designed to appeal to the younger ones (you can take a train ride around the zoo, for instance). Inquisitive young minds will be inspired by the cabinets of curiosity and zoological treasures at the **National Museum of Ireland: Natural History** (p. 103). The guides at another museum, the **Little**

Biking in Phoenix Park.

Museum of Dublin (p. 117), do a great job putting into context the ordinary lives of Dubliners in the last hundred years for younger visitors. The interactive exhibits at **EPIC The Irish Emigration Museum** (p. 114) are a big kid magnet, and even younger kids (the braver ones anyway) are all but guaranteed to love a night aboard the **Dublin Ghost Bus** (p. 122).

DAY 3: County Cork

Okay, so it's not exactly untouched by the tourism fairy, but kids find plenty to love about **Blarney Castle** (p. 258), just outside Cork City. They can even kiss the famous stone, if they don't mind an attendant holding them upside-down. A few miles away, the **Fota Wildlife Park** (p. 272) is a well-designed zoo where docile animals (those that don't bite, kick, or stomp) roam among the visitors.

DAYS 4 & 5: County Kerry

Kerry is probably Ireland's most kid-friendly county, with enough to keep you busy for at least a couple of days. On the Dingle Peninsula, you might spot seals, dolphins, or basking sharks on a **Dolphin and Whale-Watching Tour** (p. 340). Don't overlook what **Killarney**

National Park (p. 300) has to offer little ones—what could be better than a ride around the mountains and lakes in an old-fashioned horse-drawn "jarvey"? On the Iveragh Peninsula, **Kenmare Bay Boat Tours** and seal-watching trips (p. 316) teach kids about conservation issues by putting them in touch with the underwater residents of Kenmare Bay. Meanwhile, an underground tour of the atmospheric **Crag Cave** (p. 335) is a surefire winner—as is a stop for high-energy playtime at the **Crazy Cave** (p. 335) adventure playground.

DAY 6: Bunratty Folk Park

You could spend most of a day at **Bunratty Castle & Folk Park** (p. 359), an attraction that combines one of Ireland's best medieval castles with a living-history museum. It's a brilliant re-creation of a 19th-century village, complete with costumed actors strolling down the street, chatting to passersby, and even working in the shops. Bunratty is also the setting for the lively **Medieval Banquet.** It's raucous but surprisingly good fun, as long as you don't mind that it's more touristy than authentic.

Medieval costumes at the Bunratty Castle & Folk Park.

DAY 7: Heading home

If you have time before the drive back to the airport, head into the otherworldly landscape of the **Burren** (p. 354), where young imaginations will be fired up by dolmens and other ancient sites. It's also where you'll find the **Burren Birds of Prey Centre** at Aillwee Cave (p. 356), a working aviary full of buzzards, falcons, eagles, and owls in flight.

BEYOND A WEEK . . .

If your trip extends beyond a week, your family will find plenty of standout attractions for kids farther north.

The **Atlantaquaria** (p. 408), just outside Galway City, is a state-of-the-art aquarium, while pony trekking across **Connemara National Park** (p. 412) is a unique way to see this beautiful, wind-swept landscape.

In Mayo, **Westport House and Adventure Park** (p. 448) has all the ingredients for high-activity fun; young girls in particular will enjoy learning about the region's real-life pirate hero, **Grace O'Malley** (p. 447).

If you're going as far as Belfast, the attractions around the Titanic Quarter hold plenty of youthful appeal. Try the hands-on science center, **W5** (p. 514), and the state-of-the-art **Titanic Belfast** museum (p. 510).

Finally, the **Causeway Coast Drive** (p. 534) has two key highlights that children adore: the perilous (but fun) **Carrick-a-Rede Rope Bridge** (p. 533) and the awe-inspiring alien shapes of the **Giant's Causeway** (p. 537).

EXPLORING ANCIENT IRELAND

Ireland treasures its ancestral past, with mysterious stone circles, cairns, and huge stone tables known as dolmens, standing perfectly preserved in pastures and on hillsides all over the island. Some of the oldest tombs predate the Egyptian pyramids by centuries, and in many cases, the meaning and purpose of several preserved sites remain intriguing riddles. To delve into this misty past, you'll need to be intrepid and cover a lot of ground in the car, but it'll be worth it—exploring these rocky symbols can be the most memorable part of any trip to Ireland.

DAY 1: Knowth & the Boyne Valley

After an early breakfast, head north from Dublin to the rich, rolling Boyne Valley (about an hour's drive north, just off the N2) to the **Brú na Bóinne Visitor Centre** (p. 181) and this extensive Neolithic burial ground. The huge necropolis holds numerous sites to visit, such as **Newgrange** (p. 182) and **Knowth** (p. 182). Book in advance to tour Newgrange—a tour here, early in the day before it gets crowded, is spectacular. You can also take a tour to the outside of Knowth. In the afternoon, head down the N3 to the **Hill of Tara** (p. 183), where mounds and passage graves date from the Bronze Age.

DAY 2: Céide Fields

It takes a couple of hours to drive from Dublin to this remote location in north County Mayo, but your efforts will be rewarded. This extraordinary ancient site (p. 450) holds the stony remains of an entire prehistoric farming village on top of a cliff, with a bonus of breathtaking views of the sea and surrounding countryside. Spend an hour exploring the 5,000-year-old site, and lunch in the excellent visitor center.

DAY 3: County Sligo

In the morning, drive east to County Sligo. On the N4, south of Sligo Town, visit the **Carrowkeel Passage Tomb Cemetery** (p. 463), which is perched on a hilltop with wide, sweeping views overlooking Lough Arrow. It's often very quiet early in the day—with luck you might have the 14 cairns and dolmens all to yourself. Then head on to

Sligo Town and follow signs to **Carrowmore Megalithic Cemetery** (p. 464). This extraordinary site has 60 stone circles, passage tombs, and dolmens scattered across acres of green pastures. They are believed to predate Newgrange by nearly a millennium. In the afternoon, if you're feeling energetic, climb to the nearby hilltop cairn of **Knocknarea** (p. 466)—thought to be the grave of folklore fairy Queen Maeve.

DAY 4: Inishmurray Island

After a relaxing morning, travel by boat to the island of **Inishmurray** (p. 465) off the coast of Sligo. Here you can spend the day wandering the impressively complete remains of an early monastic settlement founded in the 6th century. You can still make out its ancient chapels, beehive cells, and altars. If the weather is fine, pack a lunch and picnic on the sunny beach. Return to Sligo for the night.

DAY 5: The Burren

Today begins with another long drive, but you'll pass through some of the most beautiful parts of Galway and Mayo along the way. **The Burren,** in County Clare, is one of the richest areas of the country for ancient remains from the Neolithic period through medieval times. It has around 120 dolmens and wedge tombs—including the impressive **Poulnabrone Dolmen** (p. 358)—and as many as 500 ring forts. For more on this extraordinary region, see "The Burren" in chapter 9.

Visitors exploring the 6th-century ruins on Skellig Michael, home to early Christian monks and today a UNESCO World Heritage Site.

DAY 6: Skellig Michael

Right after breakfast, head south to County Kerry, where this starkly beautiful island sits 13km (8 miles) off the Iveragh Peninsula, a mute memorial to the hardy souls who once eked out a living amid its formidable cliffs (p. 326). Deeply observant early Christian monks punished their bodies by living here in miserable conditions, spending their days carving 600 steps into the hard stone, so they could climb up to their beehive huts and icy chapels. Today it is an unforgettable landscape, and the ruins of the monks' homes are profoundly moving. A trip out here by boat and an afternoon's exploration will take up much of the day. Once you return to the mainland, reward yourself with a relaxing evening in Kenmare.

DAY 7: Glendalough

Drive east today to County Wicklow, where the evocative ruins of the monastery at **Glendalough** (p. 201) are sprawled around two serene lakes nestled in a peaceful valley. Get a map from the visitor center before beginning your exploration of the round towers, chapels, and huts dotted around the wooded site. Don't miss the ancient church ruin known as **St. Kevin's Kitchen.** If the weather is warm, bring your lunch and picnic by the lake. You can easily spend a day here.

THE BEST OF THE NORTH & NORTHWEST

We start this tour in Belfast, a city that has undergone an immense transformation since the 1998 Good Friday Agreement, which finally established a detente in Northern Ireland. Tourism has steadily increased in this region over the last decade, thanks in part to **Titanic Belfast** (p. 510) and the many locations here used in the popular HBO series *Game of Thrones.* If the best sites of the Antrim Coast were in County Cork or Kerry, they'd be overrun with tourists; as it is, you can still visit a spectacular setting such as the Giant's Causeway and find yourself alone with nature. This tour then heads west to take in the best of counties Donegal and Sligo.

DAYS 1 & 2: Belfast

Northern Ireland's capital—and second-largest city on the island of Ireland—is a historic, vibrant town. Start with a visit to the **Ulster Museum** (p. 509) and experience some of the city's more recent past firsthand with a **Black Taxi Tour** (p. 506). The museums in the Titanic Quarter, such as the immense **Titanic Belfast** (p. 510), provide a more high-tech dose of history; alternatively, you could immerse yourself in the city's present by exploring its busy shopping districts. The **Belfast Botanic Gardens & Palm House** (p. 504) and **Queen's University** (p. 513) are also worth a look. Round off the day with a pint at one of Belfast's extraordinarily pretty pubs, like the **Crown Liquor Saloon** (p. 508), and a meal at one of the small but growing number of world-class restaurants.

DAY 3: County Antrim

One of the North's loveliest counties, Antrim is home to two gorgeous parks: **Castlewellan Forest Park** (p. 549), with formal gardens and gorgeous woodland walks, and the **Silent Valley Mountain Park** (p. 551), with beautiful walks and even more incredible views. Alternatively, the Causeway Coastal Route is one of Ireland's great coastal drives—and one of the least spoiled. Those who do this drive

will reap spectacular rewards. Start in **Carrickfergus,** with a brief stop to look around its medieval castle (p. 515), before heading north along the coast road. For the best views, take the **Torr Head Scenic Road** (p. 539), located just after the village of **Cushendun** (p. 536). It's an alternative signposted road running parallel to the main route, best for those with a good head for heights. From up here on a clear day, you can see all the way to the Mull of Kintyre in Scotland. The Causeway Coast's most remarkable attraction is the **Giant's Causeway** (p. 537), an uncanny natural rock formation comprised of thousands of tightly packed basalt columns. You could do the drive in about 2 hours, but you'll want to allow considerably longer than that to give yourself time to stop along the way. There are places along the coast to spend the night, or you could go straight on into **Derry** (p. 563), another hour farther from the Giant's Causeway.

DAY 4: Derry to Donegal

Straddling the border between Northern Ireland and the Republic, the vibrant city of Derry was for years synonymous with political strife. Though it's peaceful these days, it's still a divided place—the residents can't even agree on its name. Road signs from the Republic

Giant's Causeway on the Antrim Coast.

point to Derry; those in the North point to Londonderry. How can a place like that *not* be full of character and history? Walk the city walls, then check out the award-winning **Tower Museum** (p. 570) and the **Museum of Free Derry** (p. 568) before sampling some of the city's great restaurants.

DAYS 5 & 6: Donegal

You're really entering the wilds of Ireland now. Rise early and spend the morning driving up to **Malin Head** (p. 495), the northernmost tip of Ireland. It's a wild but breathtaking place. On the way back, visit **Doagh Famine Village** (p. 494) to learn about Ireland's history in an entertaining way. Then, either drive around Lough Swilly or take the car across on the ferry to the **Fanad Peninsula** and head for the wonderful **Rathmullan House** (p. 491), an elegant retreat on Lough Swilly waiting for you on your last night. Next day, visit **Glenveagh National Park** (p. 489) before driving across the county to the darling village of **Glencolumbkille** (p. 481). The excellent folk park here is well worth an hour of your time before you head on to the stone-cut town of **Ardara** at the foot of a steep hill—it's wall-to-wall arts-and-crafts shops and a pleasure to explore. Art lovers won't want to miss the revelatory gallery at **Glebe House** (p. 489).

DAY 7: County Sligo

Sligo Town (p. 460) has a few worthwhile attractions, but it's mostly useful as a lunch stop. The real reason to come this far lies in the surrounding countryside—the area has an astonishing concentration of ancient burial sites. Within a short drive from Sligo Town are two of the most incredible: **Carrowkeel Passage Tomb Cemetery** (p. 463),

Artisan weaving at Glencolumbkille Folk Village, a living-history park in a lush valley.

packed with 14 cairns, dolmens, and stone circles, and the impossibly ancient **Carrowmore Megalithic Cemetery** (p. 464). Here's something to ponder while clambering around the latter: The innocuously named tomb 52A is thought to be 7,400 years old, making it the earliest known piece of freestanding stone architecture in the world and a great finish to this trip.

Stone formation at Carrowmore Megalithic Cemetery.

4

DUBLIN

Dublin is an ancient city with a young soul. Grand old buildings line the banks of the River Liffey and the streets beyond; there are cathedrals, universities, pubs, and museums that are hundreds of years old. But the Irish capital is also one of Europe's most youthful cities, with a large population of university students and young workers. In fact, Dublin is the island's most cosmopolitan city by far—a vibrant, modern, European capital that wears that status on its sleeve. Busy bars and snazzy restaurants buzz alongside traditional pubs that have stood their ground for centuries. Chic boutiques and cafes fill medieval streets and historic buildings. Glass-and-steel offices holding the European headquarters of the world's biggest tech companies shine in the newly regenerated Docklands. This captivating city is yours to discover—and even if you think you know what to expect, you'll always be surprised by what you find.

ESSENTIALS

Arriving

BY PLANE **Aer Lingus** (aerlingus.com; ✆ **01/761-7834**), Ireland's national airline, operates regular, direct flights between Dublin Airport and numerous cities worldwide. From the United States, direct routes include Boston, Chicago, Los Angeles, New York (JFK and Newark), Philadelphia, Seattle, San Francisco, and Washington, D.C. (Not all of these routes operate in winter.) On the return journey, passengers bound for the U.S. may pre-clear customs and immigration at Dublin Airport (meaning you get to skip passport control on the American side). **American Airlines** (aa.com; ✆ **800/433-7300**), **Delta** (delta.com; ✆ **800/221-1212**), and **United** (united.com; ✆ **800/864-8331**) all fly direct to Dublin from at least one of those same cities. From Canada, direct flights are operated by **Air Canada** (aircanada.com; ✆ **1888/247-2262**). From Australia and New Zealand, **Quantas** (qantas.com; ✆ **13-13-13**) and **Air New Zealand** (airnewzealand.co.nz; ✆ **09/357-3000**) both fly to Dublin, with at least one change. Virtually all the major European airlines have direct flights to Dublin.

FACING PAGE: **Colorful mural outside Guinness Storehouse.**

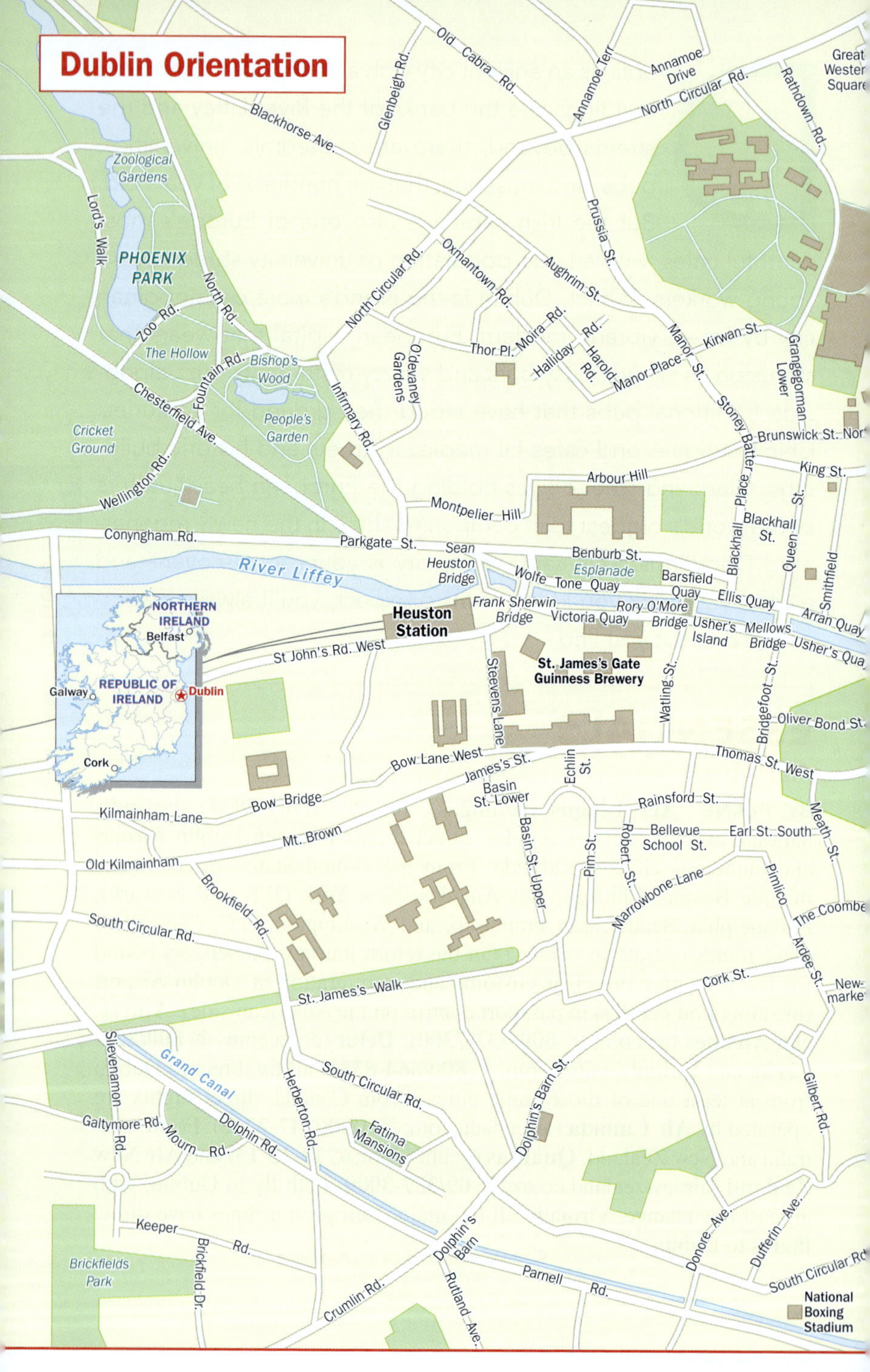
Dublin Orientation
Phoenix Park
Zoological Gardens
The Hollow
Bishop's Wood
People's Garden
Cricket Ground
River Liffey
Heuston Station
St. James's Gate Guinness Brewery
Grand Canal
Brickfields Park
National Boxing Stadium
Esplanade
Northern Ireland
Belfast
Republic of Ireland
Dublin
Galway
Cork
Old Cabra Rd.
Blackhorse Ave.
Glenbeigh Rd.
Annamoe Terr.
Annamoe Drive
North Circular Rd.
Rathdown Rd.
Great Western Square
Lord's Walk
North Rd.
Zoo Rd.
Fountain Rd.
Chesterfield Ave.
Wellington Rd.
Conyngham Rd.
Parkgate St.
Sean Heuston Bridge
Prussia St.
Aughrim St.
Oxmantown Rd.
Moira Rd.
Thor Pl.
Halliday Rd.
Harold Rd.
Manor Place
Manor St.
Kirwan St.
Grangegorman Lower
Stoney Batter
O'devaney Gardens
Infirmary Rd.
Arbour Hill
Montpelier Hill
Brunswick St. North
King St.
Blackhall Place
Blackhall St.
Queen St.
Smithfield
Benburb St.
Wolfe Tone Quay
Barsfield Quay
Ellis Quay
Arran Quay
Frank Sherwin Bridge
Victoria Quay
Rory O'More Bridge
Usher's Island
Mellows Bridge
Usher's Quay
St John's Rd. West
Steevens Lane
Watling St.
Bridgefoot St.
Oliver Bond St.
Thomas St. West
Bow Lane West
James's St.
Echlin St.
Basin St. Lower
Basin St. Upper
Bow Bridge
Kilmainham Lane
Mt. Brown
Old Kilmainham
Rainsford St.
Bellevue
School St.
Earl St. South
Meath St.
Robert St.
Pim St.
Marrowbone Lane
Pimlico
The Coombe
Ardee St.
Newmarket
Brookfield Rd.
South Circular Rd.
St. James's Walk
Cork St.
Slievenamon Rd.
Herberton Rd.
Dolphin's Barn St.
Gilbert Rd.
Galtymore Rd.
Mourn Rd.
Dolphin Rd.
Fatima Mansions
Keeper Rd.
Brickfield Dr.
Dolphin's Barn
Crumlin Rd.
Rutland Ave.
Parnell Rd.
Donore Ave.
Dufferin Ave.

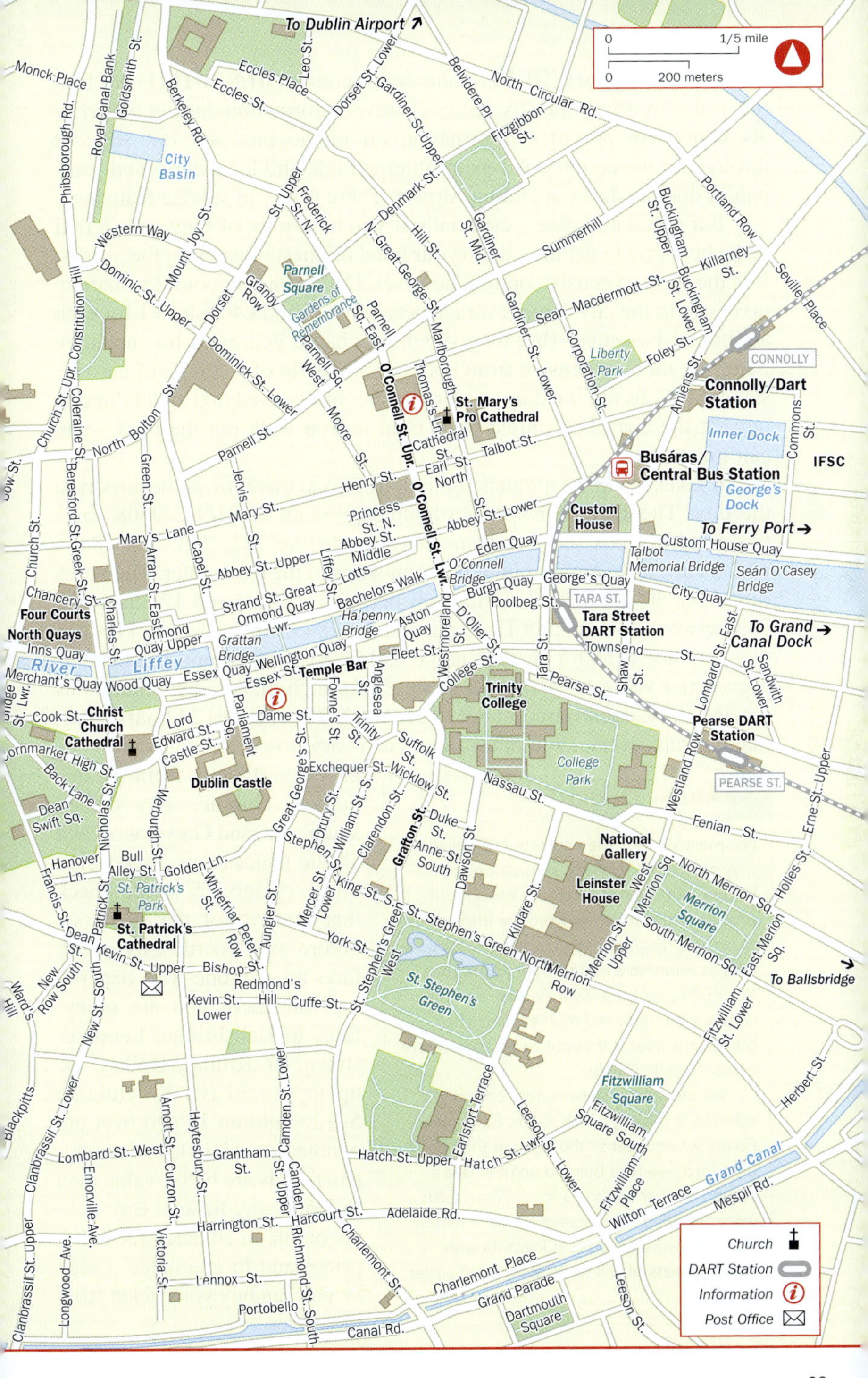

To Dublin Airport
0 1/5 mile
0 200 meters
Church
DART Station
Information
Post Office
City Basin
Parnell Square
Gardens of Remembrance
St. Mary's Pro Cathedral
Connolly/Dart Station
CONNOLLY
Liberty Park
Inner Dock
George's Dock
IFSC
Busáras/ Central Bus Station
Custom House
To Ferry Port
Custom House Quay
Talbot Memorial Bridge
Seán O'Casey Bridge
O'Connell Bridge
Ha'penny Bridge
Grattan Bridge
Four Courts
North Quays
River Liffey
Temple Bar
Tara Street DART Station
TARA ST.
To Grand Canal Dock
Trinity College
College Park
Pearse DART Station
PEARSE ST.
Christ Church Cathedral
Dublin Castle
National Gallery
Leinster House
Merrion Square
To Ballsbridge
St. Patrick's Park
St. Patrick's Cathedral
St. Stephen's Green
Fitzwilliam Square
Grand Canal
Dartmouth Square
O'Connell St. Upr.
O'Connell St. Lwr.
Grafton St.

Dublin Airport (DUB; dublinairport.com; ✆ **01/814-1111**) is 11km (6¾ miles) north of the city center. A travel information desk in the arrivals concourse provides information on public bus and rail services throughout the country. All major international and local car-rental companies operate desks at Dublin Airport. There is no rail service from here.

For speed and ease—especially if you have a lot of luggage—a **taxi** is the best way to get directly to your hotel or guesthouse from the airport. It is the most expensive option, however. Depending on your destination, taxi fares to the city center average between €25 and €40, plus €1 for each additional passenger (but they shouldn't charge you extra for luggage). Fares are more expensive from 8pm to 8am. A tip of a couple of euros is standard. Cabs are lined up at a first-come, first-served taxi stand directly outside the arrivals terminal (turn right as you walk out the door—you can't miss it).

It takes about 30 minutes (in light traffic) to travel from the airport to the city. The **Dublin Express** (dublinexpress.ie; ✆ **01/903-9508**) runs three express bus services from the airport—the 782, 783, and 784—which each have eight or nine different stops in the city center. The buses run every 30 minutes: the 782 from between 3:05am and 12:35am, the 783 between 1:45am and 12:15am, and the 784 from 5:30am to 11pm. A one-way fare is €8 for an adult and €3.50 for a child; a round-trip ticket is even better value at €10 for an adult, €5 for a child. Another shuttle bus service, **AirCoach** (aircoach.ie; ✆ **01/844-7118**) operates 24 hours a day, making runs every 15 minutes (hours can vary, so check in advance). Its buses go directly from the airport to Dublin's city center, south side, and Greystones. Not all the major stops are covered on every service, so do check that you've got the right one before you board. City-center fares are €12 one-way, depending on where you are going; fares to Ballsbridge, Leopardstown, or Killiney/Dalkey are up to €14.50 (€5–€7 children 5–12; children 13 and over are counted as adults), and round-trip tickets are better value than two one-way tickets. Buy tickets online in advance for better prices and to guarantee a seat, or you can buy your ticket from the driver.

Murky Origins

For most visitors, the very word "Dublin" may conjure up a heady, romantic mix of history, but the name actually has a more prosaic origin. It comes from the Irish words *dubh linn,* meaning "the black pool." Specifically, it refers to a natural inlet where the River Liffey met the River Poddle, and the waters were dark and murky. Long since buried, the inlet is thought to be somewhere around Dublin Castle.

An allusion to these watery origins still survives in the city's Irish name, *Baile Átha Cliath,* which means "the town of the hurdled ford"—a ford being a point where a stream or river crosses a road. When fords were "hurdled" in medieval times, it meant that they were covered at low tide with woven sheets of willow, making them easier to cross.

A cheaper but slower option is **Dublin Bus** (dublinbus.ie; ✆ **01/873-4222**), which has regular daily connections between the airport and the city center. These are normal commuter bus services, so luggage capacity is limited, and the bus may make up to 35 stops on the way to or from the airport, so the one-way trip takes around 50 minutes or more. Fares start at €2 adults, 90¢ children, which must be paid in coins (not notes), and change is not given; fares are cheaper with a prepaid **Leap Card** (p. 89). The city center is served by routes 16 and 41. The 16 bus runs from around 5:30am to 11:30pm; the 41 runs every half-hour through the day and night. Check routes and timetables before you arrive.

BY FERRY Passenger and car ferries from Britain arrive at the Dublin Ferryport, on the eastern end of the North Docks. Contact **Irish Ferries** (irishferries.ie; ✆ **0818/300-400**), **P&O Irish Sea** (poferries.com; ✆ **44/1304 44 88 88** for the U.K. call center), or **Stena Line** (stenaline.ie; ✆ **01/907-5555**) for bookings and information. Irish Ferries also sails to Dublin from Cherbourg in northern France. Buses and taxis serve both ports.

BY TRAIN Called *Iarnród Éireann* in Irish, **Irish Rail** (irishrail.ie; ✆ **01-836-6222**) operates daily train services to Dublin from all major cities and towns in Ireland including Cork, Galway, Limerick, Killarney, Sligo, Westport, Wexford, and Waterford, and from Belfast in Northern Ireland. Trains from the south, west, and southwest arrive at **Heuston Station,** St. John's Road; from the north and northwest at **Connolly Station,** Amiens Street; and from the southeast at **Pearse Station,** Westland Row. For the lowest fares, buy tickets in advance from the Irish Rail website.

BY BUS **Bus Éireann** (buseireann.ie; ✆ **01/836-6111**) operates daily express coach and local bus service from all major cities and towns in Ireland into Dublin's central bus station, **Busáras,** on Store Street. Buy tickets in advance online for the cheapest prices.

BY CAR If you are arriving by car from other parts of Ireland or on a car ferry from Britain, all main roads lead into the heart of Dublin and are well-signposted to the city center. The quickest way into Dublin from the airport is to take the Dublin Tunnel. The toll for cars is €3.50 (€12 during peak time, Mon–Fri 6–10am). You can pay using cash (euros or British pounds) or card. To bypass the city center, follow signs to the East Link toll bridge (€2.20) or the M50 toll highway (€3.50). The M50 circuits the city on three sides. From Wexford, Galway, or Belfast the drive takes around 2 hours; from Limerick 2½ hours; and from Cork 2½ to 3 hours. Your car-rental agency should inform you of all anticipated tolls.

Visitor Information

Visit Dublin (visitdublin.com; ✆ **1800/230-330**) operates two Discover Ireland tourist offices in Dublin city, at 3 Palace St. (Barnardo Square) and 14 Upper O'Connell St. Both are open Monday to Saturday 9am to 5pm.

For guides to what's on in Dublin, check out **Dublin Live** (dublinlive.ie/whats-on), **Dublin.ie** (dublin.ie/whats-on), **Lovin Dublin** (lovindublin.com/whats-on), **Totally Dublin** (totallydublin.ie), and **Visit Dublin** (visitdublin.com/whats-on).

City Layout

Dublin is divided by the curves of the River Liffey, which flows into the sea at the city's eastern edge. To the north and south, canals encircle the city center: The Royal Canal arcs across the north and the Grand Canal through the south. Traditionally, the area south of the river has been Dublin's buzzing, prosperous hub. It still holds many of the best hotels, restaurants, shops, and sights, but the Northside is on the upswing, with some new hotels giving it a trendy edge and competitive prices.

Dublin is compact and easily walked in an hour. In fact, a 45-minute walk from peaceful St. Stephen's Green, down bustling Grafton Street, and across the Liffey to the top of O'Connell Street offers a good overview of the city's prosperous present and storied past.

MAIN STREETS & SQUARES In the city center just south of the river, the main east-west artery is **Dame Street,** which merges with **College Green** at one end, and **Lord Edward Street** and on to **High Street** at the other.

Dame Street.

It connects Trinity College with Dublin Castle and Christ Church Cathedral. Just off Dame Street, you'll find the winding medieval lanes of the **Temple Bar** area, Dublin's party central, packed with noisy late-night bars and buzzing restaurants.

At its eastern end, where Dame Street becomes College Green, the sturdy gray stone walls of **Trinity College** make an excellent landmark to get your bearings. At the southwest corner of the campus is the bottom of **Grafton Street,** a lively pedestrianized thoroughfare lined with clothing boutiques, and side streets with restaurants and pubs. It leads, eventually, to the bucolic park of **St. Stephen's Green.** From there, head back down Kildare Street for museums, or along Merrion Row and down Merrion Street, passing Leinster House (seat of the Irish Parliament) to reach **Merrion Square,** another of Dublin's extraordinarily well-preserved Georgian squares.

To cross the River Liffey and get to the Northside, take the photogenic arch of the **Ha'penny Bridge** (p. 112); nearby **O'Connell Bridge,** which is wider than it is long; or the Ha'penny's sleekly modern neighbor, the **Millennium Bridge,** which is beautifully illuminated after dark. O'Connell Bridge leads directly onto broad **O'Connell Street,** the Northside's main thoroughfare, which runs north to **Parnell Square.** The street running along the Liffey's embankment is called the **North Quays** by everyone, though its name changes on virtually every block, reflecting the long-gone docks that once lined it.

Dublin Neighborhoods in Brief

TRINITY COLLEGE AREA On the south side of the River Liffey, Trinity College stands at virtually the dead center of the city. Its shady quadrangles and atmospheric stone buildings are surrounded by bookstores, shops, and noisy traffic.

TEMPLE BAR There are really two Temple Bars, depending on when you visit. During the day, Temple Bar is an artsy, cultured district full of trendy shops and modern art galleries. But such refinement gives way to an altogether more raucous atmosphere at night, when its myriad pubs, bars, and hip clubs draw partying crowds.

ST. STEPHEN'S GREEN/GRAFTON STREET AREA One of the main tourist areas of the city, this district is home to Dublin's finest hotels, restaurants, and shops. Filled with impressive Georgian architecture, today it is primarily a business and shopping zone.

KILDARE STREET & MERRION SQUARE Between Trinity College and St. Stephen's Green, this area is where you'll find the National Gallery, National Library, and two national museums. Leafy Merrion Square and its neighbor Fitzwilliam Square are surrounded by grand Georgian town

Pedestrians crossing the River Liffey via the cast-iron Ha'Penny Bridge, built in 1816.

houses, where some of Dublin's most famous citizens once lived; today they house offices for doctors, lawyers, and government agencies.

O'CONNELL STREET Lined with statues from bottom to top, O'Connell Street was the epicenter of the 1916 Easter Rising and the 1922 Civil War (bullet holes still pock the statue of its namesake, politician Daniel O'Connell). The surrounding area north of the Liffey was fashionable in the 19th century but lost much of its charm as it declined in the 20th century. The wide street has experienced some revitalization in recent years, with many great pubs, restaurants, and theaters within walking distance.

SMITHFIELD Urban renewal in the 21st century has transformed this formerly seedy market area into a lively district east of Phoenix Park, with such attractions as the Old Jameson Distillery.

THE LIBERTIES The Liberties district takes its name from the fact that it was once just outside the city walls and, therefore, exempt from Dublin's jurisdiction. Although it prospered in its early days, the Liberties fell on hard times in the 17th and 18th centuries and stayed that way for centuries. Today it is undergoing regeneration with the opening of new hotels and distilleries. For visitors, its main attraction is the Guinness brewery.

BALLSBRIDGE/EMBASSY ROW Immediately south of the Grand Canal, this upscale suburb is just barely within walking distance of the city center. Primarily a prestigious residential area, it is also home to hotels, restaurants, and embassies.

THE DOCKLANDS & THE IFSC The north and south quays of the River Liffey are home to the gleaming modern office and apartment blocks around the International Financial Services Centre (IFSC) on the north side, and Grand Canal Dock on the south side. The new builds include a number of hotels and restaurants. The area is also home to the 3Arena (north side) and Bord Gáis Energy Theatre (south side).

GETTING AROUND

If your stay in Dublin is short, geography is on your side. The vast majority of the capital's top sights are concentrated in the city center, which is small and very walkable. This leads to your first, most important (and quite frankly, easiest) decision: If you have a car, leave it behind at your hotel. Dublin's streets are choked with traffic, with baffling one-way streets and inadequate signage. If your feet get tired, there's a good tram and bus system, and taxis are everywhere.

By Bus

After walking, buses are the most convenient and practical way to get around the city center sights. **Dublin Bus** (dublinbus.ie; © **01/873-4222**) operates a fleet of double-deckers and single-deckers. Most originate on or near O'Connell Street, Abbey Street, and Eden Quay on the Northside, and at Aston Quay, College Street, and Fleet Street on the south side. Look for bus-stop markers resembling big yellow lollipops—they're

Leap Cards

If you're likely to use public transport a lot while in Dublin (which we highly recommend), do as the locals do: Get a **Leap Card,** a prepaid smart card for reduced-cost travel on all Dublin buses (including Nitelink), DART, Luas, and commuter trains. You can buy Leap Cards at some 400 shops in and around the city—look for the distinctive green logo depicting a somewhat over-excited frog in mid-leap. (In Dublin Airport, you can pick one up at the **Easons, Kiosk,** and **Spar** shops.) Ticket machines in some city center DART and railway stations also dispense Leap Cards. Or you can order them online at **leapcard.ie**. Unless you're here for more than a week, the best option is to ask for a Leap **Visitor Card,** which allows for unlimited travel on the network—including to and from the airport. It costs €8 for 24 hours, €16 for 3 days, and €32 for 7 days. It's valid at any time and the clock doesn't start until you first use it. There's also a **Freedom Ticket** from Dublin Bus, which combines a 3-day (72-hr.) travel pass that includes the airport 16 and 41 bus routes plus Luas and DART journeys, with a 48-hour hop-on, hop-off bus tour, all for €49. You buy the voucher online and redeem it at Dublin Bus Head Office or one of its specified retail locations in the city center.

every few blocks on main thoroughfares. To tell where a bus is going, look at the destination street and bus number displayed above its front window.

Bus service runs daily, starting at 6am (10am on Sun), with the last bus at about 11:30pm. On Friday and Saturday nights, **Nitelink** service runs from the city center to the suburbs from midnight to 4am. Buses operate every hour for most night runs. Bus schedules are posted on displays at bus stops, on **transportforireland.ie**, and on the Transport for Ireland **TFI Live** app, which contains bus stop maps. Both the website and app give live updates on the arrival time of the next bus at each stop. Bus arrival times are also on real-time digital displays at some bus stops.

You pay on board the bus, using an automatic fare machine located in front of the driver. You can pay with exact change (coins only) or with a smart card known as a **Leap Card** (p. 89). **No Dublin bus accepts notes or gives change.** A special **TFI 90-minute fare,** which covers not just bus journeys but DART trains and Luas trams (see below), costs €2 adults, €1 ages 19–23, and 65¢ for a child, if you are paying with a Leap Card.

By DART

An acronym for Dublin Area Rapid Transit, electric DART trains travel above ground, linking city center stations (including **Connolly Station, Tara Street,** and **Pearse**) with suburbs and seaside communities. Check a map to see if it serves your area. Service operates roughly every 10 to 20 minutes Monday to Saturday 6am to 11:30pm and Sunday 9:30am until 11pm. For more information, check the **Irish Rail** website (irishrail.ie; ✆ **0818/366-222**).

Modern Luas tram cars connect central Dublin sights with outlying neighborhoods.

By Tram

The sleek, modern (and wheelchair-accessible) light-rail tram system known as **Luas** (luas.ie; ✆ **1850/300-604**) runs from 5:30am to midnight Monday to Friday, 6:30am to midnight Saturday, and 7am until 11pm on Sunday. (The last trams to certain stations are earlier, so be sure to check the timetable.) There are two lines, Red and Green (see

learning the lingo: "BANK HOLIDAYS"

North Americans may be baffled by this phrase, which you'll see a lot on lists of opening times. It simply means a public holiday, often on a Monday. Banks, offices, and businesses are closed on bank holidays, while shops and attractions may run on reduced or Sunday hours.

Ireland has 10 regular bank holidays: New Year's Day (Jan 1); the first Monday in February; St. Patrick's Day (Mar 17); Easter Monday; the first Mondays in May, June, and August; the final Monday in October; Christmas Day (Dec 25); and St. Stephen's Day (Dec 26).

map inside the front cover of this guide). Ticket prices depend on the length of your journey and how many city zones it crosses. A single peak-travel journey within one zone costs €2, rising to €2.60 for two to eight zones. Ticket vending machines are located at every Luas stop. Purchase your ticket in advance using coins, paper money, or a credit card. Leap Cards are accepted on Luas.

On Foot

Marvelously compact, Dublin is ideal for walking. Just remember to look right and then left (and in the direction opposite your instincts if you're from North America) before crossing the street. Cross the road at the pedestrian crossings, which usually have pedestrian traffic lights.

By Taxi

Taxis are a cheap and handy way to get around Dublin, and you'll find them everywhere. You can either hail a cab on the street (if the light on top of the car is lit, it's available) or find one at the many taxi stands (called "ranks") throughout the city—located outside hotels, at bus and train stations, and on prime thoroughfares such as Upper O'Connell Street, College Green, and the north side of St. Stephen's Green. The taxi apps are **Free Now** and **Lynk.** If you use Uber, you will get a regular taxi, not a private car, thanks to the city's taxi regulations. You can also phone for a taxi (see "Fast Facts," p. 92).

By Car

We'll say it again: You do ***not*** want to drive around Dublin if you can possibly avoid it. However, if Dublin is your first stop on a wider tour of Ireland, you may want to rent a car to leave town and see the rest of the country. If that's the case, try **Hertz** (hertz.ie) at Dublin Airport (✆ **01/844-5466**) or 2 Haddington Rd. (✆ **01/668-7566**). **Europcar** (europcar.com) also has branches at Dublin Airport (✆ **01/812-2800**) and Spencer Dock off the North Quays (✆ **01/648-5900**).

[Fast FACTS] DUBLIN

ATMs/Banks Nearly all banks are open Monday to Friday 10am to 4pm. Convenient locations include the **Bank of Ireland,** at 2 College Green, 88 Camden St. Lower, and Trinity College; and the **Allied Irish Bank (AIB),** at 100 Grafton St. and 37 O'Connell St.

Currency Exchange Currency-exchange services, signposted as **Bureau de Change,** are in most Dublin banks and at many branches of the Irish post office system, known as **An Post.** A bureau de change operates daily during flight arrival and departure times at Dublin Airport. (It's handily situated in the baggage claim hall, just opposite carousels 6 to 10.) Some hotels and travel agencies offer currency exchange. ***Tip:*** The best rate of exchange is almost always when you use your bank card at an ATM.

Dentists For dental emergencies, have your hotel contact a dentist for you; otherwise, try **Smiles Dental Spa,** 28 O'Connell St. Lower (✆ **01/507-9201**), or **Molesworth Dental Clinic,** 2 Molesworth Place (✆ **01/661-5544**).

Doctors & Hospitals For emergencies, dial ✆ **999.** If you need a doctor, have your hotel contact one for you. Otherwise, you could try **Dame Street Medical Center,** 16 Dame St. (✆ **01/679-0754**), or the **Suffolk Street Surgery,** 107 Grafton St. (✆ **01/679-8181**).

Emergencies For police, fire, or other emergencies, dial ✆ **999.**

Luggage Storage If you arrive at your hotel too early to check in, or if checkout is in the morning and your flight isn't until the evening, many hotels will happily look after your baggage. Alternatively, there are luggage facilities at Terminal 1 Arrivals at Dublin Airport (see leftluggage.ie) or check out luggage storage services in the city like **Luggage Hero** (lugggehero.com), **Nannybag** (nannybag.com), or **Stasher** (stasher.com).

Mail The **General Post Office** on O'Connell Street (✆ **01/705-7600**) is open Monday through Saturday 8:30am to 6pm. **An Post** (anpost.com), the Irish postal service, has numerous smaller offices throughout the city.

Pharmacies Dublin does not have 24-hour pharmacies. **Hickeys Pharmacy** at 55 O'Connell St. (✆ **01/873-0427**) stays open until 8.30pm Monday to Saturday and to 8pm on Sunday. **Boots** at 12 Grafton St. (✆ **01/677-3000**) is open until 7:30pm Monday, Tuesday, Wednesday, and Friday, to 8pm on Thursday, and to 7pm on Saturday and Sunday. **City Pharmacy,** 14 Dame St. (✆ **01/670-4523**), is open until 9pm weekdays, 7pm on Saturday, and 6pm on Sunday. **Boots** branches at 20 Henry St. (✆ **01/873-0209**) and in the St. Stephen's Green Centre (✆ **01/478-4368**) are both open until 7pm Monday to Saturday and to 6pm on Sunday.

Taxis If you need to order a taxi, use the **Free-Now** or **Lynk** apps (you can also use Uber to hire a ride, but this will call a standard taxi), or try calling **VIP Taxis** (✆ **01/478-3333**), **Xpert Taxis** (xperttaxis.com; ✆ **01/667-0777**), or **Trinity Taxis** (✆ **01/708-2222**)

EXPLORING DUBLIN

Wandering Dublin—just walking along its streets, resorting to the map or your phone only if you get *really* lost—is one of the great pleasures of a visit here. The city center, where the vast majority of the sights are located, is small enough to traverse on foot. One minute you're walking along a quiet, leafy street and suddenly a beautiful row of Georgian houses or a

dublin PASSES

If you're planning a lot of sightseeing in Dublin, there are two Dublin passes on sale: an **All-Inclusive Pass,** which offers free admission over a set number of days to most major sights, hop-on, hop-off bus tours, and distillery tours; and an **Explorer Pass,** which gives admission to a set number of attractions over 60 days.

The All-Inclusive Pass is a bit pricey, given that so many of Dublin's sights are free. So, our advice is this: If you're going heavy on the sightseeing, buy the pass, but plan carefully how best to use it. For example, consider buying a pass good for 1 or 2 days, and then see all of the city's most expensive sights (the Guinness Storehouse, EPIC The Irish Emigration Museum, Big Bus Dublin tours, and so forth) on those days. On the other days of your trip, devote your time to the museums, parks, and galleries that charge no entrance fee. Or buy an Explorer Pass and cover the most expensive sites that you were going to visit. Do add up the admission costs of all your planned sights first, to make sure which pass is right for you and whether it works out as good value.

An All-Inclusive adult pass costs €79 for 1 day, €109 for 2 days, €134 for 3 days, €154 for 4 days, and €164 for 5 days. A child's pass for ages 5–15 is a little over half the adult price. An Explorer Pass, which is valid for 60 days, costs €79 adult/€39 child for three attractions, €99/€44 for four attractions, €109/€54 for five attractions, and €134/€64 for seven attractions. The passes are digital and can be purchased online at **gocity.com**. You then download an app to your phone and activate the pass when you visit the first attraction.

An alternative is the **DoDublin Days Out card** from Dublin Bus, which includes admission to six different attractions—The Little Museum of Dublin, MoLI (Museum of Literature Ireland), St. Patrick's Cathedral, EPIC The Irish Emigration Museum, Dublinia, and Christ Church Cathedral—and is valid for several months. The cost is €55 adults, €30 children, and €47 students and seniors. It's considerably cheaper than the combined admission costs of all six. You can buy the pass at **dodublin.ie**, and a voucher is sent by e-mail.

Georgian square like Merrion Square appears before you. Then, you find yourself facing the granite buildings of Trinity College, before stumbling upon some amazing old pub or tiny cafe you just have to stop at—and on and on. So, pack a sturdy pair of shoes, have your umbrella at the ready, and head out to discover how rewarding this wonderful old city can be.

Top Attractions

Book of Kells Experience ♥♥♥ LIBRARY One of Ireland's national treasures, this magnificent hand-drawn manuscript of the four gospels dates to the year 800, with elaborate calligraphy and colorful illumination drawn by Irish monks. It's an astonishing work of art, reverently displayed in Trinity College's Old Library. There's some effort involved in seeing it, however, with high prices and the likelihood of long queues. Up to now, a visit involved peering past other onlookers into the glass box

Áras an Uachtaráin (The Irish President's House) **1**
The Ark **30**
Book of Kells/Old Library **36**
Chester Beatty Library **37**
Christ Church Cathedral **29**
College Green **34**
Croke Park Stadium & GAA Museum **14**
The Custom House **23**
Dalkey Castle **50**
Dublinia **28**
Dublin Castle **32**
Dublin Liberties Distillery **41**
Dublin Zoo **2**
EPIC: The Irish Emigration Museum **24**
The Four Courts **20**
14 Henrietta Street **18**
Glasnevin Cemetery **12**
GPO Museum **22**
Guinness Storehouse **9**
Ha'Penny Bridge **26**
Hugh Lane Gallery **17**
Ireland's Eye Ferries **15**
Irish Film Institute **31**
Irish Museum of Modern Art **4**
Irish Rock 'n' Roll Experience and Wall of Fame **33**
James Joyce Centre **16**
Jameson Bow St. Distillery **11**
The Jeannie Johnston **25**
Kilmainham Gaol **5**
Leinster House **45**
The Little Museum of Dublin **42**
Marsh's Library **40**

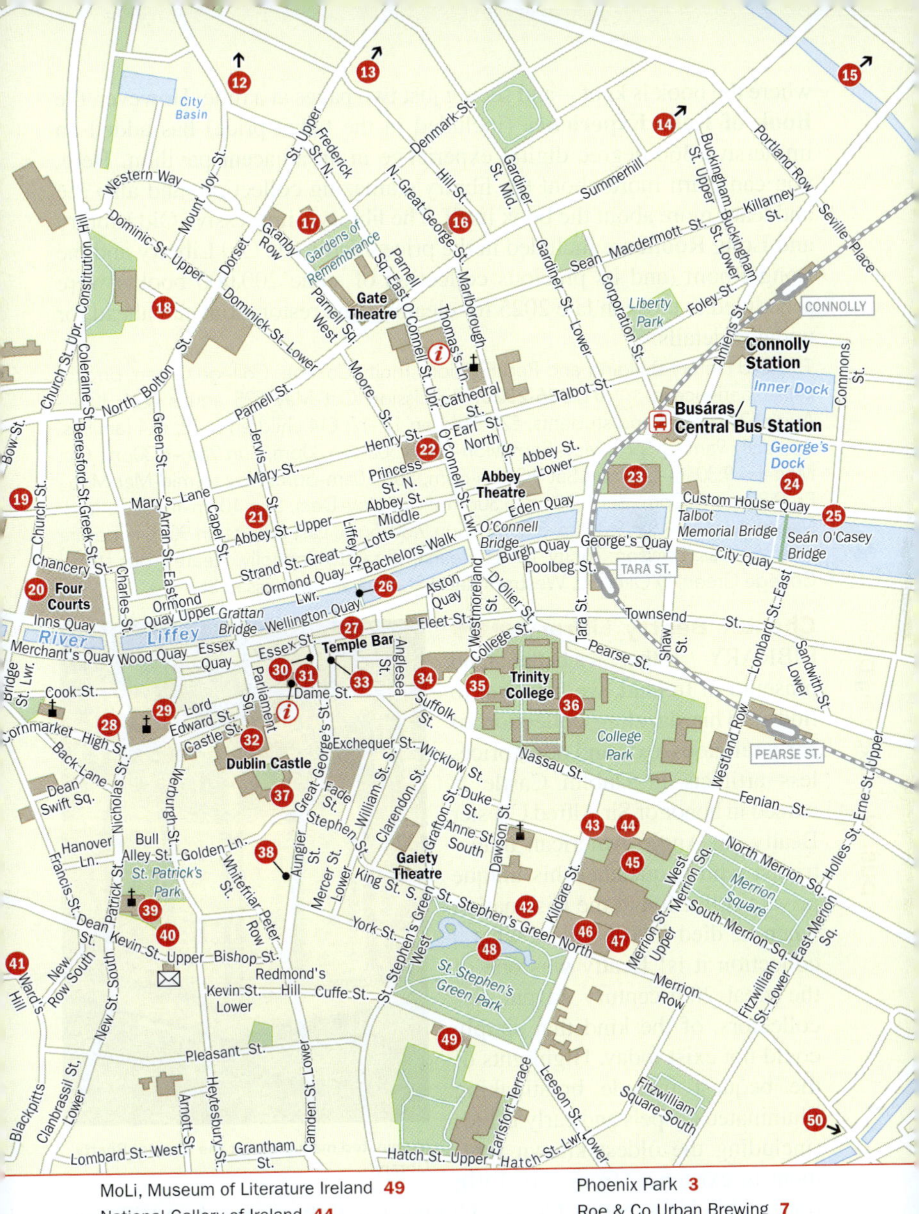

MoLi, Museum of Literature Ireland **49**
National Gallery of Ireland **44**
National Leprechaun Museum **21**
National Library of Ireland **43**
National Museum of Ireland: Archaeology **46**
National Museum of Ireland: Decorative Arts & History, Collins Barracks **10**
National Museum of Ireland: Natural History **47**
Newbridge House and Farm **13**
Pearse Lyons Whiskey Distillery **8**
Phoenix Park **3**
Roe & Co Urban Brewing **7**
St. Michan's Church **19**
St. Patrick's Cathedral **39**
St. Stephen's Green **48**
Teeling Whiskey Distillery **6**
Temple Bar Gallery **27**
Trinity College **35**
Urban Brewing **24**
Whitefriar St. Carmelite Church **38**

where the book is kept—and seeing just two pages at a time. However, the **Book of Kells Experience** (included in the ticket price) has added an immersive 360-degree digital experience in an adjacent pavilion. Here, you can learn more about the library's amazing collection, and also see and learn more about the book itself. The library's impressive Old Library and **Long Room** are included in the price. ***Note:*** The Old Library and the Long Room (and its precious collection of some 200,000 books) were scheduled to close in late 2025 for cleaning and restoration; call ahead for updated details.

The Old Library Building and Red Pavilion, Trinity College, College Green. bookofkellsexperience.ie. ✆ **01/896-2320.** Admission Oct–May €25 adults (€26 June–Aug); €21 seniors and students; €20 children 13–17; €14 children 6–12; €54 families. Apr daily 9am to 6pm. May–Sept Mon–Sat 8:30am–6:30pm, Sun 9am–6:30pm. Oct Mon–Fri 9:30am–5:30pm, Sat 9:30am-6pm, Sun 10am–5pm. Nov to mid-Mar Mon–Fri 9:30am–4:30pm, Sat 9:30am–5:30pm (5pm Nov–Dec), Sun 10am–4.30pm. Mid-Mar to Apr Mon–Sat 9:30am–5:30pm, Sun 9:30–5pm. Last admission 90 min. before closing. Luas: Dawson, Trinity. DART: Pearse, Tara St., Connolly. Nearest bus stops: College Green, D'Olier St., Westmoreland St., Pearse St., Nassau St.

Chester Beatty Library ♥♥♥

LIBRARY If there's a better small museum in Ireland, we have yet to find it. This dazzling collection of early religious texts and other priceless artifacts in Dublin Castle is named in honor of Sir Alfred Chester Beatty, an Anglo-American industrialist who bequeathed his unique private collection to the Irish nation when he died in 1968. And what a collection it is! Beatty was one of the great 20th-century adventurer-collectors, of the kind that simply could not exist today. Highlights of the bequest include breathtaking illuminated gospels and early Bibles (including the oldest known fragment in existence, from A.D. 150); impeccable 15th-century Qurans; Quranic scrolls from the 8th and 9th centuries; sacred Buddhist texts from Burma and Tibet; and Hebrew Pentateuchs and Torah scrolls. Though the core collection remains the same, exhibits are constantly changing, and you're unlikely to see the same manuscripts on every visit. Why queue and pay €25 to see two pages from the Book of Kells when you can lose yourself in this wonderful place for free?

Illuminated manuscript at the Chester Beatty Library.

On the grounds of Dublin Castle, Dame St. chesterbeatty.ie. ✆ **01/407-0750.** Free admission (suggested donation €10). Mon–Sat 9:45am–5:30pm (until 8pm Wed), Sun noon–5:30pm; closed Mon Nov–Feb. Luas: Trinity, St. Stephen's Green. DART: Tara St., Pearse. Nearest bus stops: Dame St., S. Great Georges St.

local hero: SIR ALFRED CHESTER BEATTY

Few people embody the term "citizen of the world" as much as Sir Alfred Chester Beatty. Born in New York in 1875, Beatty launched an American mining business that earned him the nickname "the King of Copper"—and a multimillion-dollar fortune to boot. This fabulous wealth gave him the means to pursue his passion for ancient manuscripts and works of art, and by the time he was an old man, his collection rivaled that of some of the world's greatest museums.

Beatty became a British citizen in the 1930s and was knighted by Queen Elizabeth II in 1954, after he made a generous bequest to the British Museum. However, he left the vast majority of his collection to Ireland—his ancestral home and a place dear to his heart. In return Beatty was made an honorary Irish citizen in 1957. He died 11 years later in Monaco but was brought back to Dublin for a state funeral.

Despite all this, Beatty is a surprisingly little-known figure in his adoptive home today. Some Dublin guides don't list the Chester Beatty Library among the city's top attractions, and some Dubliners have never heard of the collection, or the man himself.

Christ Church Cathedral ♥♥ CATHEDRAL This magnificent cathedral was designed to be seen from the river, so walk to it from the riverside in order to truly appreciate the size. It dates from 1038, when Sitric, Danish king of Dublin, built the first wooden Christ Church here. In 1171, the original foundation was extended into a cruciform layout and rebuilt in stone under the leadership of the Norman warrior Strongbow. The present structure dates mainly from 1871 to 1878, when a huge restoration took place—work that remains controversial to this day, as much of the building's old detail was destroyed in the process. Still, magnificent stonework and graceful pointed arches survive. (There's also a statue of Strongbow inside, and some believe his tomb is here as well, although historians are not convinced.) The best way to get a glimpse of what the original building must have been like is to visit the 12th-century crypt, which remains untouched. Tours are either 1-hour self-guided tours with audio guides or guided tours (check daily schedule on arrival).

Christchurch Place. christchurchcathedral.ie. ✆ **01/677-8099.** Admission €11.50 adults; €10 seniors and students; €4 children 11 and under; free for children 3 and under; €27 families. Book online for discounts. Free entry for prayer or services. Mon–Sat 9:30am–5pm; Sun 12:30–3pm. Last entry 45 min. before closing. Nearest bus stops: Lord Edward St., Patrick St., High St.

Hugh Lane Gallery ♥♥ ART MUSEUM This small art gallery, housed in the glorious classical Charlemont House, punches well above its weight. The strong collection of Impressionist works includes Degas's *Sur la Plage,* Manet's *La Musique aux Tuileries,* and Daumier's *In the Omnibus* (stolen from the gallery in 1992 but recovered in 2014). There are also sculptures by Rodin; a stunning collection of Arts and Crafts stained glass by Dublin-born artist Harry Clarke (don't miss his

GRAVE robbing

Three times in recent years, Dublin has found itself rocked by high-profile cases of theft and desecration at some of its most famous churches.

It all started on Saturday, March 3, 2012, when thieves staged an audacious raid on **Christ Church Cathedral** (p. 97). But they were not after money or priceless treasure: They had come instead for the preserved heart of St. Laurence O'Toole (1128–80), patron saint of Dublin.

The thieves hid in the cathedral overnight, then stole the relic, which was encased in a heart-shaped cage. Before leaving, they paused to light two candles on the altar. Nothing else was taken, leading the police to believe that the heart may have been stolen on the orders of a macabre collector.

All leads drew a blank, until 6 years later when—plot twist!—the heart was discovered, abandoned, in Phoenix Park. The relic was subsequently returned to its rightful place in the cathedral in 2018.

Rather more disturbing have been two incidents that have taken place at **St. Michan's Church** (p. 107). In 2019, a local man broke into the crypt, where he not only desecrated some of the mummified bodies laid to rest there, but also ripped the head off a centuries-old corpse and stole it as a memento. In this case, police were able to track down the thief, who was ultimately sent to jail. The head, meanwhile, was restored to the body with the help of a local undertaker. Then in June 2024 a man was arrested after starting a fire in the crypt. Water damage after the fire ruined five ancient mummies beyond repair. The man pled guilty in court but gave no reason for the criminal damage.

masterpiece, *The Eve of St. Agnes*); and numerous works by modern Irish artists. One room holds the maddeningly cluttered studio of the Irish painter Francis Bacon, moved here from London and reconstructed behind glass. Everything was moved—right down to the dust.

Parnell Sq. North 1. hughlane.ie. ✆ **01/222-5564.** Free admission. Tues–Wed 9:45am–6pm; Thurs 9:45am–8:30pm; Fri 9:45am–5pm; Sat 10am–5pm; Sun 11am–5pm. Luas: Parnell. DART: Connolly. Nearest bus stops: Parnell Sq., Dorset St. Upper, O'Connell St.

Kilmainham Gaol ♥♥ HISTORIC SITE Anyone interested in Ireland's struggle for independence from British rule should not miss visiting this former prison. Within these walls, political prisoners were incarcerated, tortured, and killed from 1796 until 1924. The leaders of the 1916 Easter Rising were executed here, along with many others. Future president Eamon de Valera was its final prisoner. To walk along these corridors through the grim exercise yard, or to venture into the walled compound, is a moving (at times even overwhelming) experience that will linger in your memory. An exhibition illuminates the brutal history of the Irish penal system; there's also a well-presented historical film. An art gallery on the top floor houses thought-provoking exhibitions. Only a limited

The central courtyard of Kilmainham Gaol, whose cells held many famous political prisoners over the years.

number of tickets are sold each day, and visits are by guided tour only—tours are 90 minutes, so allow 2 hours in total. The tours get completely booked up surprisingly far ahead, so do reserve your tickets online, especially if you're visiting in the summer.

Inchicore Rd., Kilmainham. kilmainhamgaolmuseum.ie. ✆ **01/453-5984.** Admission €8 adults; €6 seniors; €4 students and children 12–17; free for children 11 and under; €20 families. Museum daily 10:30am–5:15pm (July–Aug until 5:45pm). Last admission 1 hr. 15 min. before closing. Luas: Suir Rd. Nearest bus stops: Inchicore Rd., South Circular Rd., Inchicore Library.

National Gallery of Ireland ♥♥

ART MUSEUM The playwright George Bernard Shaw loved this place so much that he left it one-third of his royalties in perpetuity after he died. He saw it as paying a debt, so important was the gallery to his education. It is still a place to wander, wonder, and just be in thrall to so much beautiful art. Highlights of the permanent collection include paintings by Caravaggio, Gainsborough, Rubens, Goya, Rembrandt, Monet, and Picasso. The Irish national portrait collection is housed in one wing, while another area is devoted to

Monumental Wit

Few cities have such a love-hate relationship with their statues as Dublin. Locals have an acerbic rhyming nickname for each one, many of them unprintable. The very buxom statue of Molly Malone (heroine of the Irish folk song, who sold "cockles and mussels, alive alive, oh . . .") on Suffolk Street is variously known as "the Tart with the Cart," "the Trollop with the Scallop," or "the Flirt in the Skirt." In the same vein, the James Joyce statue on O'Connell Street is "the Prick with a Stick"; the statue of Anna Livia (a character in Joyce's *Finnegans Wake* who symbolized the Liffey), rising from an ornamental pond in Croppies Park, is "the Floozie in the Jacuzzi"; and, depending on whom you talk to, the Spire of Dublin on O'Connell Street is either "the Stiletto in the Ghetto," "the Skewer in the Sewer," "the Stiffy by the Liffey," or "the Nail in the Pale." The **Dublin Portal,** a two-way interactive webcam with New York City that opened in May 2024, was quickly nicknamed the "Zoom of Doom" and the "Eye in the Sty."

Gleaming metalwork on display in the National Museum of Ireland's outstanding archaeology museum.

the career of Jack B. Yeats (brother of W. B. Yeats), an Irish painter of some note. A €30-million renovation completed in 2017 reopened two wings and added a glass-covered courtyard. (Check out the gravity-defying, 7m/22-ft. freeform sculpture by Cork artist Joseph Walsh, which stands sentinel over the light-filled space.) Major exhibitions change regularly, and the subjects are often more imaginative than just the usual run of retrospectives and national landscapes. In keeping with the "art for all" ethos that so enamored Shaw, entry to the permanent collection and many of the temporary shows is free.

Merrion Sq. West. nationalgallery.ie. ✆ **01/661-5133.** Free admission. Mon 11am–5:30pm; Tues–Sat 9:15am–5:30pm (Thurs until 8:30pm); Sun 11am–5:30pm. Luas: Dawson. DART: Pearse. Nearest bus stops: Clare St., Merrion Sq., Nassau St.

National Museum of Ireland: Archaeology ♥♥♥ MUSEUM
The most impressive of the four sites that collectively make up the National Museum of Ireland, this excellent museum is devoted to the ancient history of Ireland and beyond, from the Stone Age up to the Early Modern period. Highlights include a stunning collection of Viking artifacts from archaeological digs in Dublin from the 1960s to the early 1980s—a haul so important that in one fell swoop the history of Viking settlement in Ireland was rewritten. There is also an enormous range of Bronze Age gold and metalwork, as well as iconic Christian treasures from the Dark Ages, including the Ardagh Chalice, the Moylough Belt Shrine, and the Tara Brooch. It's not just the relics of ancient Irish people that can be seen here—there are also four "bog bodies," human beings

DUBLIN walking tours

Small and compact, Dublin was made for walking. And you could hardly be in better or more learned hands than with the **Historical Walking Tours of Dublin** (historicaltours.ie; ✆ **087/688-9412**), whose guides are all history graduates from Trinity College, Dublin, and National University of Ireland. Established for more than 30 years, these engaging tours offer peerless historical insight. Tours leave from the Grattan statue opposite the front gate of Trinity College on College Green daily at 11am and 3pm May to September; daily at 11am April and October; and Friday to Sunday at 11am November to March. Tickets cost €19 adults, €17 students and seniors (accompanied kids 13 and under are free), and must be booked online in advance. An intriguing variety of private tours are also available—subjects include Medieval Dublin, Revolutionary Dublin, and Dublin's architecture. These should also be booked in advance, with a minimum of four people, and cost €250 to €300.

If you prefer a livelier pace, try the **Literary Pub Crawl** (dublinpubcrawl.com; ✆ **087/263-0270**). Walking in the footsteps of Joyce, Behan, Beckett, Shaw, and other Irish literary greats, this tour visits Dublin's most famous pubs and explores their deep literary connections. Actors provide humorous performances and commentary between stops. Tours start upstairs at the **Duke Pub,** 9 Duke St. (✆ **01/679-9553**), nightly at 7:30pm April to October; and Thursday to Sunday November to March. Tickets are €18 adults and €16 students. A limited number of tickets are sold on the night (cash only; doors open 7pm), but it's best to book online. The walking distance is around 1km (0.6 mile). No children are allowed for obvious reasons, but the tour organizers are keen to stress that the tour is safe and enjoyable for women traveling alone.

More sightseeing for the thirsty can be enjoyed on the **Traditional Irish Music Pub Crawl** (musicalpubcrawl.com; ✆ **01/475-3313**). Tours are led by two professional musicians, who describe the experience as a "moving concert," as you make your way from one famous musical pub to another in Temple Bar. Tours meet upstairs at the **Oliver St. John Gogarty** pub, Fleet and Anglesea streets (✆ **01/671-1822**). Tours run at 7pm from Sunday to Thursday, March to September. The cost is €22 and accompanied children 9 and over are allowed. On Friday and Saturday they run a musical dinner show starting at 6:30pm at **Flanagans Bar & Restaurant** on O'Connell Street; it includes Irish dancing and a three-course meal. The price is €59 adults, €45 children 13 and under, and €208 families. A show-only ticket is €29.

If you're looking for less booze and more history, the **1916 Rebellion Walking Tour** (1916rising.com; ✆ **086/858-3847**) takes you into the heat of the action at the General Post Office, explaining how the anger rose until the rebellion exploded on Easter Sunday in 1916. The 2-hour tour is well thought-out and run by local historians who authored a book on the events of that year. Tours are at 11:30am Monday to Saturday and 1pm Sunday, from March to October. Tickets cost €23 per adult and €14 per child aged 8 to 16. Children 7 and under are free. Booking is advisable. The tour starts at the **International Bar,** 23 Wicklow St.

whose remains were naturally preserved in bogs, sometime between 400 and 200 B.C., and the Faddan More Psalter, a book of psalms dating from around A.D. 800, which was found in a bog in 2006. Other notable artifacts include Ralaghan Man, a carved wooden Bronze Age statue from County

hard to love: **JONATHAN SWIFT**

The acerbic 18th-century wit Jonathan Swift, author of *Gulliver's Travels,* was born in Dublin, and except for a decade or so in England, lived in Ireland most of his life. After trying (and failing) to win a position at the English court, he became a Church of Ireland clergyman. Yet he continued to write and publish essays and poetry—in fact, he wrote his most controversial works while acting as dean of St. Patrick's Cathedral.

Many nations might have banned Swift for his scandalous writing. He certainly could not live in England—his works were considered too shocking. But the Irish always forgave him, and the church protected him, even after he published his most infamous essay, "A Modest Proposal," in 1729. In that essay, still read in English classes around the world, he advocated (ironically) that the Irish sell their children to be eaten as food in order to solve the problem of Irish poverty. He assured the reader that Irish babies would be delicious "whether stewed, roasted, baked or boiled . . ."

Satire was relatively unknown at the time, and many readers at first believed he was seriously recommending cannibalism. The essay caused public outrage and calls for him to be punished. But the church stood by him, as did the town, allowing him to continue to push the limits of 18th-century patience.

Swift believed passionately in humane treatment for the mentally ill, which in his time was unheard of. When he died, he bequeathed much of his estate to found St. Patrick's Hospital for the mentally ill. Typically, though, he couldn't just leave it at that. He wrote one last caustic verse about himself, and the country he loved:

"He left the little wealth he had
To build a house for fools and mad;
Showing in one satiric touch
No nation needed it so much."

Cavan; 2nd-century Roman figurines and homewares; and an extraordinary granite table made in Egypt circa 1870 B.C.

Kildare St. museum.ie. ✆ **01/677-7444.** Free admission. Tues–Sat 10am–5pm; Sun–Mon 1–5pm. Luas: Dawson. Nearest bus stops: Kildare St., Nassau St., St. Stephen's Green.

National Museum of Ireland: Decorative Arts & History, Collins Barracks ♥♥ MUSEUM This branch of the National Museum of Ireland tells the story of Irish (and world) history through fashion, jewelry, furniture, and other decorative arts, with the bulk of the collection spanning the 1760s to the 1960s. One gallery is devoted to the work of Eileen Gray (1878–1976), an Irish designer who became one of the most important figures of the Modernist movement; another showcases an extraordinary collection of Asian art bequeathed to the nation in the 1930s. Set in a converted 18th-century army building, the museum isn't entirely devoted to the arts: Eight galleries cover Irish military history from the 16th century to the present, including a fascinating section on the Easter Rising of 1916.

Collins Barracks, Benburb St. museum.ie. ✆ **01/677-7444.** Free admission. Tues–Sat 10am–5pm (July–Oct until 8pm Thurs); Sun–Mon 1–5pm. Luas: Museum. Rail: Heuston. Nearest bus stops: Sarsfield Quay, Parkgate St., Heuston Station.

National Museum of Ireland: Natural History ♥♥ MUSEUM The core collection at this museum has changed little since the museum was founded in the mid–19th century, and that's part of the attraction. Its display cases are filled with native Irish animals, from stuffed birds and mice to the skeletons of enormous sea creatures. While there are recent additions—including the Discovery Zone, in which visitors can open a series of drawers to discover unusual specimens within—it feels quaintly old-fashioned. Upstairs you'll find the most unique parts of the collection, such as the avian galleries and the "crystal jellies" collection: beautiful oversize glass models of microscopic sea creatures, made in the 19th century by the eccentric and brilliant Blaschka brothers of Dresden. There's no doubt this is a strange place—the locals call it "the dead zoo." Still, kids find it fascinating, and it is, in many ways, a trip into the past. ***Note:*** The museum closed in late 2024 for extensive refurbishment, so check online for reopening updates.

Merrion St. museum.ie. ✆ **01/677-7444.** Luas: St. Stephen's Green. DART: Pearse. Nearest bus stops: Merrion Sq., Clare St., St. Stephen's Green.

St. Patrick's Cathedral ♥♥ CATHEDRAL The largest—and most famous—church in Ireland, St. Patrick's is one of the most beloved places of worship in the world. The original church was built between 1220 and 1260 in honor of Ireland's patron saint, on a site where St. Patrick was said to have baptized converts; most of what you see now dates from the 14th century, along with some 19th-century renovations. The building is mainly Early English in style, with a square medieval tower that houses the largest ringing peal bells in Ireland; its spire, nearly 150 feet tall, soars above the city's low skyline. The main body of the church has a cavernous nave, glorious high ceiling, and historic displays. Tucked away at the back of the nave is a moving collection of war memorials, including a low-key tribute to the Irish dead of World War II. (Ireland was neutral in that war, but still around 300,000 men volunteered to fight with the Allies.) You can also see the tomb of the satirical 18th-century writer Jonathan Swift (see box on p. 102), once a dean at this cathedral. Free guided tours are offered at 10:30am and

St. Patrick's Cathedral is the largest church in Ireland.

A TOUR OF trinity college

A beautiful, grand, romantic place to wander around, the Trinity campus is open free of charge to the public year-round. No trip to Dublin is complete without spending a little while on the college grounds. Here are a few highlights (see map on p. 105):

Trinity's most striking and famous monument, the white **Campanile,** or bell tower, grabs your attention as soon as you enter through the main archway. Dating from the mid–19th century, it stands on the site of the college's original foundations, from 300 years earlier.

Built in the 18th century to a design by Thomas Burgh, the neoclassical **Old Library Building** is the only building on campus you have to pay to see. It's where you'll find the **Book of Kells Experience** (p. 93) and the library's magnificent **Long Room**—both of which are unmissable.

Home to the geography and geology departments, the **Museum Building** is one of Trinity's hidden gems. Built in the mid–19th century, it has Byzantine and Moorish influences. Walk through and look up to the glorious domed ceiling and the green marbled banisters.

Set between these two architectural masterpieces, the stark 1967 **Berkeley Library Building** sharply divides opinion with its austere modernism. Designer Paul Koralek's library honors Bishop George Berkeley, famed for his philosophical theory of "immaterialism" (things that can't be proven cannot exist), which went against the theories of both Isaac Newton and the Catholic Church. The gleaming sculpture outside the library is ***Sphere with Sphere*** by Arnaldo Pomodoro (1983).

Also facing the Old Library across Fellows Square, the 1970s **Arts Building** includes the **Douglas Hyde Gallery,** with a regularly changing program of modern art. Exhibitions switch out about every 3 months, and admission is always free.

Tucked away in the far northeastern corner of the campus, the **Science Gallery** is a combination art space, science museum, and debating forum, with exhibitions, workshops, public lectures, and even shows. It was closed for redevelopment at the time of print—check sciencegallery.com for updates.

One of the more benign remnants of English rule, the **College Park Cricket Pitch** is a small park where you'll often find a cricket match in progress on summer weekends. The sport is notoriously arcane for the uninitiated—but everyone can enjoy the picturesque sight of the players in their white uniforms.

2:30pm Monday to Saturday. There's also an irregular program of lunchtime classical-music recitals.

St. Patrick's Close. stpatrickscathedral.ie. ✆ **01/453-9472.** Admission €10 adults; €9 seniors and students; €4.50 children 6–12; free for children 5 and under; €28 families. Mon–Fri 9:30am–5:30pm; Sat 9am–5:30pm; Sun 9–11am and 1–3pm. Last admission 30 min. before closing. Guided tours Mon–Sat 10:30am and 2:30pm. Nearest bus stops: Patrick's Cathedral, Kevin St., Patrick St.

Trinity College ♥♥ UNIVERSITY The oldest extant university in Ireland, Trinity was founded in 1592 by Queen Elizabeth I to offer an education to the children of the upper classes and protect them from the "malign" Catholic influences elsewhere in Europe. Now it is one of the most respected universities on the continent. Among its alumni are Bram

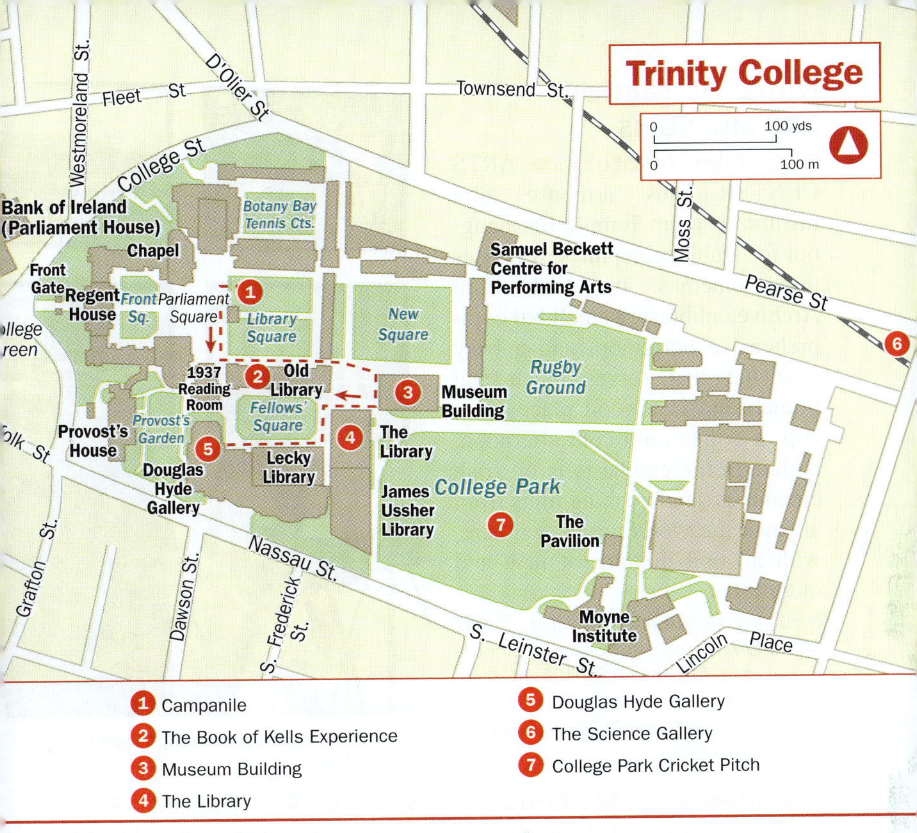

Stoker, Jonathan Swift, Oscar Wilde, and Samuel Beckett, as well as an array of rebels and revolutionaries. Step through the portico off College Green into the historic gray stone courtyard, and it wouldn't take much more than a lick of fog and a top hat or two to make you think you'd stepped back in time a century or more. The campus spreads across central Dublin just south of the River Liffey, with charming cobbled squares, lush gardens, and picturesque quadrangles. Most of the architecture dates from the 17th to the 19th century. You can wander the campus for free (see map above); alternatively, take either a guided **Trinity Trails** tour of all the main sights before you visit the Old Library and the Book of Kells Experience (p. 93). The 45-minute tour, guided by students, starts at the bell tower and gives an engaging view of the main attractions and points of interest, as well as some insider access around the 42-acre campus.

College Green. visittrinity.ie. ✆ **01/896-4499.** Guided campus tours €16 adults, free for children 11 and under, €50 families; with access to the Book of Kells Experience €33.50 adults, free for children 11 and under, €85 families. Tours run daily, June–Aug twice an hour 9am–5pm; Sept–May every hour 9am–3pm. Book online. Luas: Trinity, Dawson, Lower Abbey St. DART: Pearse, Tara St., Connolly. Nearest bus stops: College Green, D'Olier St., Westmoreland St., Pearse St., Nassau St.

More Attractions

ART MUSEUMS

Irish Film Institute ♥ ARTS CENTER This arthouse film institute is a hip Temple Bar hangout for Dublin cinephiles. It houses three cinemas, the Irish Film Archive, a library, a small but comprehensive bookshop, and a busy cafe bar that serves lunch and brunch and is a good place for a cup of coffee on a cold afternoon. Although the emphasis is on Irish cinema, groundbreaking films from all over the world are shown here, with a good mixture of new and older titles.

6 Eustace St., Temple Bar. ifi.ie. ✆ **01/679-3477.** Free admission. Cinema tickets €12–€15. Mon–Sun 11am–8pm. Luas: Trinity. DART: Pearse, Tara St. Nearest bus stops: Dame St., Parliament St., Wellington Quay.

The Irish Film Institute is a buzzing hangout for movie fans.

Irish Museum of Modern Art (IMMA) ♥♥ ART MUSEUM Set in the Royal Hospital Kilmainham, a beautiful 17th-century classical building with an impressive facade and courtyard, IMMA has a small but strong collection of modern art dating from the 1940s to the present day. Highlights include a striking series of mid-1970s photographs by Serbian conceptual artist Marina Abramovic; etchings and lithographs by Alice Maher, Louis le Brocquy, and Marcel Duchamp; and the Madden Arnholz Collection with around 2,000 old master prints, including works by Rembrandt. The beautifully restored grounds are also used as an exhibition space and worth a stroll, and there's also a courtyard cafe.

Royal Hospital Kilmainham, Military Rd., Kilmainham. imma.ie. ✆ **01/612-9900.** Free admission. Tues–Sat 10am–5:30pm (open 11:30am Wed), Sun and bank holidays noon–5:30pm. Last admission 45 min. before closing. Luas: Heuston. Nearest bus stops: Heuston Station, St. James's Hospital.

Temple Bar Gallery + Studios ♥♥ ART GALLERY/STUDIOS This big, rambling art gallery sums up all that is good about Temple Bar. Founded in 1983, it's one of the largest studio and gallery complexes of its kind in Europe, filled with innovative work by contemporary Irish artists—more than 30 of them, in a variety of disciplines, including sculpture, painting, printing, and photography. The level of creativity is dazzling, and it's run by helpful, friendly people. Only the gallery section is open to the public, but you can make an appointment in advance to view individual artists at work. The Studios host free talks and discussion panels, featuring the great and the good of the Irish arts scene. Check online for details.

5–9 Temple Bar. templebargallery.com. ✆ **01/671-0073.** Free admission. Tues–Fri 11am–6pm; Sat–Sun noon–4pm. Luas: Trinity. DART: Tara St. Nearest bus stops: Wellington Quay, Dame St.

CHURCHES & CATHEDRALS

St. Michan's Church ♥ CHURCH Built on the site of an earlier Danish chapel dating from 1095, this plain-looking 17th-century church is almost puritanical in its simplicity. The humble, whitewashed interior is pleasant, though not much to write home about in a city full of beautiful churches. Handel is said to have played his *Messiah* on the organ, which dates from 1724, but otherwise you'd be forgiven for wondering what the fuss is about. Well, unsuspecting visitor, prepare yourself for what lies beneath. There's something about the atmospheric conditions in the church's underground vaults that drastically slows decomposition, and the mummified remains of several people have lain here for centuries, in extraordinary states of preservation. A few still have their hair and fingernails. Among them are brothers Henry and John Sheares, who were executed as traitors in 1798 because of their connection to the rebellion. Another vault contains three mummies known as "the Crusader," "the Nun," and "the Thief." Their true identities were lost when the church records were destroyed during the Civil War of 1922. That crypt suffered vandalism in both 2019 and 2024 (p. 98) and at the time of print was still closed. Visiting the crypts is creepy and definitely not for the easily unnerved. It is said that Bram Stoker was inspired to write *Dracula* in part by having visited as a child. ***Note:*** The church is wheelchair-accessible, but the vaults are not.

Church St. cathedralgroupdublin.ie. ✆ **01/872-4154.** Admission €7 adults; €5 seniors, students and children; €18 families. Crypt: Feb–Oct Mon–Thurs 10am–12:30pm and 2–4:30pm; Nov–Jan 10am–2pm (winter hours may vary). Luas: Four Courts, Smithfield. Nearest bus stops: Church St., Arran Quay.

Whitefriar Street Carmelite Church ♥ CHURCH This 19th-century Byzantine-style church is unexpectedly (perhaps dubiously) one of the city's most romantic spots, as it holds the relics of St. Valentine. The pieces of bone are believed to be authentic; they were given to the church by Pope Gregory XVI in 1836. They're kept in a casket on an altar to the right of the main altar, but once a year (on St. Valentine's Day), they are carried out in procession for a special Mass. The church also holds an icon known as **Our Lady of Dublin,** a 15th-century woodcarving that, in 1824, was rescued from a nearby farm where it had been used as a pig trough.

56 Aungier St. whitefriarstreetchurch.ie. ✆ **01/475-8821.** Free admission. Daily 7:30am–5pm (except during Mass times Mon–Fri 8, 10, and 11:30am, 1:10 and 3pm; Sat 6pm; Sun 8 and 10:30am, 12:30 and 4pm). Luas: St. Stephen's Green. Nearest bus stops: Whitefriars St., Aungier St.

DISTILLERIES & BREWERIES

Dublin has had a long and interesting history of both brewing and distilling. It's said that whiskey was invented in Ireland, and Dublin was a whiskey powerhouse around the start of the 19th century, with no less than 37 distilleries supplying around 70% of the global market. The industry fell into decline from the 1920s, but has had a nationwide revival in recent years with the opening of new distilleries. In 2015, **Teeling Distillery** (p. 109) was the first distillery to open in the city in more than 100 years, offering a program of tours and tastings. This was followed by three more, all offering distillery tours: **Pearse Lyons Distillery** (pearselyonsdistillery.com; ✆ **01/691-6000;** tours from €22); **Dublin Liberties Distillery** (thedld.com; ✆ **086/107-6419;** tours from €17); and **Roe & Co** (roeandcowhiskey.com; ✆ **01/643-5999;** tours from €25). The birth of the craft brewing movement has seen breweries like **Urban Brewing** set up shop, with tours and tastings. (urbanbrewing.ie; ✆ **01/568-5989;** tours from €20). Meanwhile, the following three remain at the top of our list:

Guinness Storehouse ♥♥ MUSEUM Opened in 1759, the Guinness brewery at St. James's Gate is one of the world's most famous breweries, producing the distinctive dark stout known and loved the world over. The visitor experience at the Guinness Storehouse is self-guided and set out over seven floors, starting with an exhibit about the brewing

Enjoying a pint of Guinness at the Guinness Storehouse brewery.

process and ingredients, before delving into the brand's history and some of its famous advertising campaigns. There are two bars, plus the **Guinness Academy** (add €12) where you can learn how to pull a proper pint, and the **Stoutie** experience (add €8), which puts your selfie onto the head of a pint. Last but not least, stop in at the breathtaking **Gravity Bar,** where you can sample a glass of the famous brew in a glass-enclosed room 61m (200 ft.) above the ground, complete with 360-degree views of the city. There's also a gift shop, a **Connoisseur** tasting and storytelling experience (€95), and the full 3-hour **Guinness Brewery Tour** (€350). This is a large, lively space—plan around half a day here, and retreat somewhere quiet afterwards.

St. James's Gate. guinness-storehouse.com. ✆ **01/408-4800.** Admission €20 adults; €17 seniors and students over age 18; €10 children 5–17; free for children 4 and under; €51 families. Mon–Thurs 9:30am–5pm; Fri–Sat 9:30am–6pm; Sun 9:30am–5pm. Luas: St. James's Hospital. Nearest bus stop: James's St.

Jameson Bow St. Distillery ♥♥ MUSEUM Easy to spot from nearly a mile away by its chimney-shaped glass viewing tower, this distillery visitor center is a good place to come if you want to learn about one of Ireland's most famous whiskeys. There's no longer any actual distilling here (it's all been moved to Midleton Cork; see p. 272), but after learning how the whiskey is made, you get to sip a little of the old firewater yourself (or do a full tasting of four premium whiskeys for a few euros extra). Tours run throughout the day, about every 30 minutes, and last 45 minutes. Check opening times, as these can change.

Bow St., Smithfield Village. jamesonwhiskey.com. ✆ **01/807-2355.** 45-min. tour €26–€31 adults, €23–€28 seniors and students, €4 discount for off-peak tours, usually morning; €12 children 3–17 at all times, free for children 12 and under. Mon–Thurs 10am–6:30pm; Fri–Sat 10am–7pm; Sun 11.45am–6:30pm. Last tours 30 min. before close. Luas: Smithfield. Nearest bus stop: Smithfield.

Teeling Whiskey Distillery ♥♥♥ DISTILLERY TOUR If you want to soak up the inner machinations of a real working whiskey distillery, this is a great option. Your visit starts with an overview on the history of Irish whiskey and the highs and lows of the whiskey industry in Dublin over the years. Guides then take you through the whiskey-making process, with a walk through a live production area and past three whiskey stills, finishing with a whiskey tasting in a small barrel room. Tours last 45 minutes. Tickets are based on three different tasting options; all include Teeling small-batch whiskey or a soft drink (soda) or mocktail for under-18s (under-18s tickets can't be booked online). There's a cafe and gift shop on-site for all things whiskey.

13-17 Newmarket. teelingdistillery.com. ✆ **01/531-0888.** Tours €20–€35 adults, €10 children 10–18, free for children 9 and under. Tours every 20 min. Mon–Fri 11am–6pm; Sat 11am–7pm; Sun and bank holidays 11am–6pm. Gift shop Mon–Fri 10:30am–7:30pm, Sat 10:30am–8:30pm, Sun 12:30–7:30pm; cafe Mon–Fri 8am–4pm, Sat–Sun 10am–6pm. Nearest bus stops: Kevin St., Newmarket St.

HISTORIC ARCHITECTURE & BUILDINGS

Áras an Uachtaráin (The President's House) ♥♥ HISTORIC HOUSE Set in Phoenix Park, Áras an Uachtaráin was once the Viceregal Lodge, the summer retreat of the British viceroy, whose main digs were in Dublin Castle. From what were never humble beginnings, the original 1751 country house was expanded several times, gradually becoming the splendid neoclassical white mansion you see today, which now serves as the official residence of Ireland's president. Guided tours leave from the Phoenix Park Visitor Centre every Saturday. After an introductory historical film, a bus brings visitors to and from the house for a 1-hour tour of the state reception rooms (tours run a little longer in summer, when the gardens are included on the itinerary, weather permitting). Since the building is still the official home of the Irish president, a strictly limited number of tickets are given out, on a first-come, first-served basis. The house may occasionally be closed for state events, so check online or call ahead. ***Note:*** For security reasons, you need to bring photo ID; no backpacks, travel bags, strollers, cameras, or mobile phones are allowed on the tour.

Tours depart from Phoenix Park Visitor Centre. president.ie. ✆ **01/677-0095** (Phoenix Park Visitor Centre). Free admission. Sat 10 and 11:15am, 12:30, 1:45, and 3pm. Closed Dec 24–26. Nearest bus stops: Ashtown Gate, Castleknock Rd.

College Green ♥ ARCHITECTURAL SITE Across the street from Trinity College, this grand colonnaded building was originally Ireland's Parliament House. Its facade was allegedly the model for the Capitol building in Washington, D.C., with one key difference: It's completely devoid of windows. When Parliament House was built in the 1730s, it had windows, but they were bricked up in the early 1800s for security reasons. The Irish Parliament met here until 1801, when, by an extraordinary quirk of history, it was tricked into voting for its own abolition. (William Pitt the Younger, then Prime Minister of Britain, had promised sweeping reform of the anti-Catholic laws if Ireland agreed to a formal union with Britain. They did so, but then Pitt was deposed by King George III, the reforms never happened, and the Irish lost what little self-government they had.) Today the building is a branch of the **Bank of Ireland,** but you can see parts of the magnificent interior, featuring oak woodwork, 18th-century tapestries, and a sparkling crystal chandelier.

2 College Green. ✆ **01/661-5933.** Free admission. Mon–Fri 10am–4pm. Luas: Trinity. DART: Tara St. Nearest bus stops: College Green, Dame St., Nassau St., Westmoreland St., D'Olier St.

The Custom House ♥♥ ARCHITECTURAL SITE Completed in 1791, this beautifully proportioned Georgian building has a long, classical facade of graceful pavilions and arcades and a central dome topped by a statue of Commerce. The 14 keystones over the doors and windows are

Close-up of a Riverine Head at the Custom House.

known as the Riverine Heads, because they represent the Atlantic Ocean and the 13 principal rivers of Ireland. Although it burned to a shell in 1921, the building has been masterfully restored. The exterior is the main attraction here, but a visitor center opened in 2021 offers tours and exhibits telling the story of the controversy about the building's construction, how it was burned down during the Irish War of Independence, and how the landmark building was reconstructed. Visits are either self-guided or by guided tour (around 45 min.).

Custom House Quay. heritagireland.ie. ✆ **046/940-7146.** Self-guided tour €6 adults; €5 seniors; €3 children and students; free for children 11 and under; €15 families. Guided tours €8 adults; €6 seniors; €4 children and students; free for children 11 and under; €20 families. Four tours per day: 10:30am and 12:30, 2 :30, and 4pm. Visitor center daily 9:30am–5:30pm. Last admission 45 min. before close. Luas: Busáras. DART: Connolly, Tara St. Nearest bus stops: Custom House Quay, Eden Quay, Beresford Place.

Dublin Castle ♥ CASTLE The center of British power in Ireland for more than 700 years, this 13th-century castle was finally taken over by the new Irish government in 1922 following Ireland's independence. You can wander the grounds for free, but they're somewhat plain—the Gardaí (police) and government agencies use a significant section of the castle as office space. You'll need to take a guided or self-guided tour to see the impressive State Apartments, Viking Excavation, and the Gothic-style Chapel Royal, with its fine plaster decoration and carved-oak gallery. The castle's only extant tower is a 13th-century structure once used to imprison suspected traitors. A small museum dedicated to An Garda Síochána (the Irish police) is in the Treasury Building. In 1583 the castle's Upper Yard was the scene of Ireland's last trial by mortal combat; today it is dominated by an impressive Georgian structure called the Bedford Tower. The Irish crown jewels were kept in the tower until they were stolen in 1907 (they have never been recovered). If it's open, check out the Medieval Undercroft, an excavated site on the grounds where an early Viking fortress once stood. Self-guided visits are for timed slots and can be booked in advance online; tickets for guided tours are available from 10am to 4pm at the ticket desk. You can also download a free audio guide from the website. ***Note:*** This is a government building, so some areas may be closed for state events.

Dame St. dublincastle.ie. ✆ **01/645-8813.** Castle grounds free. State Apartments €8 adults; €6 seniors and students; €4 children 12–17; free for children 11 and under; €20 families. Daily 9:45am–5:45pm (last admission 5:15pm). Luas: Trinity. Nearest bus stops: Dame St., S. Great Georges St.

The Four Courts ♥ ARCHITECTURAL SITE Home to the Irish legal courts since 1796, this fine 18th-century building was designed by James Gandon (who also designed the Custom House; see above). It is distinguished by its graceful Corinthian columns, massive dome, and exterior statues of Justice, Mercy, Wisdom, and Moses. Badly damaged by the fighting during the Civil War of 1922, this building was later artfully restored, although some details, such as the statues of famous Irish lawyers that once adorned the niches of the Round Hall, were lost. No public tours are offered, but if you want to see the interior, slip in to watch a trial.

Inns Quay. courts.ie/four-courts. ✆ **01/888-6000.** Luas: Four Courts. Nearest bus stops: Inns Quay, Merchant's Quay, Ormond Quay.

General Post Office (GPO) ♥ HISTORIC SITE Don't be fooled by the nondescript name: With a facade of Ionic columns and Greco-Roman pilasters 60m long (197 ft.) and 17m high (56 ft.), the GPO is more than a post office—it is the symbol of Irish freedom. Built between 1815 and 1818, it was the main stronghold of the Irish Volunteers during the Easter Rising. On Easter Sunday, 1916, Patrick Pearse stood on its steps and read a proclamation declaring a free Irish Republic. It began, "In every generation the Irish people have asserted their right to national freedom and sovereignty." Then he and an army of supporters barricaded themselves inside. A siege ensued that ultimately involved much of the north of the city. Before it was over, the building was all but destroyed. It had barely been restored before civil war broke out in 1922, and it was heavily damaged again. It's still a working post office today, but you can learn all about the building's past at the excellent **GPO Museum** (p. 116) and even touch the bullet holes in the walls out front.

O'Connell St. visitdublin.com/general-post-office. ✆ **01/705-7000.** Free admission. Mon–Sat 8:30am–6pm, closed Sun and public holidays. Museum Mon–Sat 10am–5pm (last admission 4pm). Luas: Abbey St. Nearest bus stop: O'Connell St.

Ha'penny Bridge ♥ LOCAL LANDMARK Built in 1816, and one of the earliest cast-iron bridges in Europe, the graceful pedestrian-only Ha'penny Bridge (pronounced *Hay*-penny) is still the most attractive of Dublin's bridges. Officially named the Liffey Bridge, it's universally known by the toll once charged to cross it: half a penny. The turnstiles were removed in 1919 when passage was made free. The bridge is at its prettiest after sundown, when the old lamps atop its three filigreed arches are lit, and the underside at each end is illuminated in green.

Connects Wellington Quay and Lower Ormond Quay. bridgesofdublin.ie/bridges/hapenny-bridge/history. Luas: Jervis. Nearest bus stops: Bachelors Walk, Aston Quay.

Leinster House ♥ ARCHITECTURAL SITE The home of the Dáil (Irish House of Representatives) and Seanad (Irish Senate), this is the modern center of Irish government. Dating from 1745, it was originally known as Kildare House and was the seat of the Dukes of Leinster. Like the former Parliament House building at College Green (p. 110), it is said to have been a major influence on the architects of Washington, D.C.; the resemblance to Irish-born James Hoban's design for the White House, built 78 years later, is certainly clear enough. When the Dáil is not in session, guided tours are sometimes available; check online to see if they are running at all. ***Note:*** If you are booked for a tour, you need to bring photo ID (such as a driver's license or passport) to gain admission, and leave large or bulky bags at home. Because this is a government building, you should arrive a few minutes early to allow for security checks before your tour.

Kildare St. and Merrion Sq. oireachtas.ie. ✆ **01/618-3186** or 01/618-3781. Free admission. Entry by guided tour only, check online for details. Luas: St. Stephen's Green. DART: Pearse. Nearest bus stops: Kildare St., Nassau St., St. Stephen's Green.

MUSEUMS & LIBRARIES

14 Henrietta Street ♥♥♥ MUSEUM A tour of this town house on Henrietta Street takes you through 300 years of its history, from its construction as an elegant single-family home in the 1740s and its Georgian heyday as a social hub for the wealthy class through some of the city's social and economic decline and the home's later years as a tenement house—in 1911 it housed more than 100 people. The last residents left in the 1970s. The restoration of the house took more than 10 years, and 14 Henrietta opened as a museum in 2018. Some rooms are simply decorated (but not furnished) as they would have been in Georgian times, while others look as they would have in tenement times. A local guide brings the tour to life with personal stories and anecdotes. Tours start on the hour and take 75 minutes (note that the tours include stairs). Book in advance.

14 Henrietta St. 14henriettastreet.ie. ✆ **01/524-0383.** €10 adults; €8 seniors and students; €6 children 5–18; children 4 and under free. Wed–Sun 10am–4pm. Luas: Jervis St., Dominick St., or Broadstone. DART: Connolly. Nearest bus stops: Constitution Hill, Church St., Parnell Sq.

Croke Park Stadium & GAA Museum ♥♥ SPORTS MUSEUM Croke Park is the headquarters, and main sports ground, of the Gaelic Athletic Association (GAA), which oversees most of the traditional Irish sports—including hurling, camogie, and Gaelic football. The museum does a good job of setting out the history of Gaelic games and putting them into a wider historical context regarding the importance of sport to the Irish way of life. There are interactive exhibits, and you can take a tour of the stadium or hit the rooftop walkway on a thrilling skyline tour for views down into the stadium and right across the city (children must be age 12 and over to do the tour). The most excitement, of course, happens on match days—check the website if you want to hear the roar of the crowd for real.

Jones Rd. crokepark.ie. ✆ **01/819-2300.** Stadium tour and museum: €16 adults; €13 seniors and students; €11 children; €43–€45 families. Museum only: €9 adults; €7.50 seniors and students; €6.50 children; €21–€22 families. Skyline tour and museum: €22 adults; €20 seniors, students and children age 12 and over. Museum open Mon–Sat 9:30am–5pm, Sun and public holidays 10am–5pm. Stadium tours daily 11am–3pm (check online for times); skyline tour times vary, check website. On match days, check online to confirm hours. Luas: Connolly, Parnell, Marlborough. DART: Connolly. Rail: Drumcondra. Nearest bus stops: Ballybough Rd., Clonliffe Ave., Dorset St.

EPIC The Irish Emigration Museum ♥♥♥ MUSEUM This completely digital museum tells the fascinating stories of how and why millions of people emigrated from Irish shores in search of a better life—and the impact they made on other countries when they got there, in all fields from sports and music to science. Visits are self-guided and the exhibits have a fun interactive element, with plenty of high-tech storytelling. While not aimed specifically at children, the museum will keep younger visitors entertained as well as informed. You're given a "passport" with your ticket, which you can get stamped in each of the 20 galleries. There's also a genealogy center onsite. For help tracing your own Irish roots, you can book a consultation with a genealogist (€70–€172) either in person or online.

CHQ, Custom House Quay. epicchq.com. ✆ **01/906-0861.** Admission €19.50 adults; €17.50 seniors; €17 students; €13 ages 13–17; €10 ages 6–12; free for children 5 and under; €34–€49 families. Audio guide €2. Combined ticket with the *Jeanie Johnston* (p. 117) €30 adults; €26.50 seniors and students; €21.50 ages 13–17; €16 ages 6–12, children 5 and under free. Daily 10am–6:45pm (last admission 5pm). Luas: George's Dock. DART: Connolly, Tara St. Nearest bus stop: Custom House Quay.

Interactive displays at EPIC The Irish Emigration Museum.

Glasnevin Cemetery.

Glasnevin Cemetery & Visitor Center ♥♥ CEMETERY North of the city center, the Irish national cemetery was founded in 1832 and covers more than 50 hectares (124 acres). Most people buried here were ordinary citizens, but there are also many famous names on the headstones, ranging from revolutionary commander, Taoiseach (prime minister), and President Eamon de Valera to other political heroes and rebels including Michael Collins (p. 282), Daniel O'Connell, Countess Constance Markievicz (p. 465), and Charles Stewart Parnell. Literary figures also have their place here, such as writers Christy Brown (immortalized in the film *My Left Foot*) and Brendan Behan. The visitor center, **Experience Glasnevin,** has interactive exhibits devoted to the cemetery and its famous occupants. Guided tours allow you access to the beautiful O'Connell Crypt, resting place of "The Liberator" Daniel O'Connell (1775–1847); for an additional €5 you can climb to the top of the tower over O'Connell's monument. You can also take a self-guided tour (€8 adults, €6 seniors and students) with an audio guide and map. Printed maps showing who's buried where are sold in the visitor center. ***Tip:*** At 2:30pm every Friday to Sunday in summer, there is a reenactment of a famous speech that the 1916 revolutionary Pádraig Pearse made at the graveside of Fenian leader Jeremiah O'Donovan-Rossa (1831–1915).

Finglas Rd., Glasnevin. dctrust.ie/location/glasnevin.html. ✆ **01/882-6550.** Visitor center and tour €13 adults; €11 seniors, students, and children; €35 families. Visitor center daily 10am–5pm (including public holidays); tours Mon–Fri 2:30pm, Sat–Sun 11:30am and 2:30pm. Nearest bus stops: Glasnevin Cemetery, Botanic Gardens.

GPO Museum ♥♥ MUSEUM For years the General Post Office seemed to struggle with how best to preserve and present its historical credentials while also fulfilling the continuing needs of a working post office. Now, at last, it has the balance right with this informative little museum, which mainly focuses on the Easter Rebellion of 1916, during which the post office was a key player. Highlights include one of the few remaining original copies of the independence proclamation. Exhibits related to Irish history and the struggle for independence are told through thoughtfully presented interactive content. The cafe and gift shop are located in the building's beautiful courtyard. Informative guided tours of the museum cost an extra €2 over general admission; these run daily at 11am and 2:30pm (no morning tour on Sun).

O'Connell St. gpowitnesshistory.ie. ✆ **01/872-3101.** Admission €17 adults; €15 seniors and students; €8.50 children 5 and over. Mon–Sat 10am–5pm (last admission 4pm). Luas: O'Connell, Abbey St. DART: Tara St. Nearest bus stops: O'Connell St.

Irish Rock 'n' Roll Museum Experience and Wall of Fame ♥ MUSEUM Not so much a museum as a tour of a demo studio with a few exhibits thrown in, the Rock 'n' Roll Museum celebrates all things Irish rock. The tour culminates with the chance to form a "band" with your fellow visitors and lay down a track in the studio. Exhibits on display include vintage instruments and assorted memorabilia, such as a blank check signed by Bono for an autograph hunter. Outside, on Curved Street, is the **Irish Music Wall of Fame,** where giant photographic portraits of Ireland's top music stars, including Van Morrison, U2, and the Cranberries, adorn one side of the building.

Curved St., off Temple Bar. irishrocknrollmuseum.com. ✆ **089/449-0795.** Tours (must be prebooked) €22 adults; €19 seniors, students, and teenagers 13–18; €15 children 5–12; €65 families. Daily 10:30am–5pm. Luas: Trinity. DART: Tara St. Nearest bus stops: Dame St., College Green, Wellington Quay.

James Joyce Centre ♥ MUSEUM This idiosyncratic museum is set in a grand Georgian house that once belonged to the Earl of Kenmare. Joyce himself never lived here; he was, however, rather taken with a former owner of the house named Denis Maginni—an eccentric Irishman, who added an "i" to his name to give himself an air of Italian sophistication. (Maginni appears as a character in Joyce's masterpiece *Ulysses.*) Today the center functions as both a small museum and a cultural center devoted to Joyce and his work. Actual exhibits are a little thin on the ground, but the center holds interesting (at least for Joyce fans) lectures and special events, and also organizes a Joyce-themed walking tour of Dublin. Unsurprisingly, this place becomes an explosion of activity around Bloomsday (June 16), the date upon which the fictional events in *Ulysses* take place. Unlike the rest of Dublin, which makes do with a single day of celebrating its most famous 20th-century literary hero, the James Joyce Centre turns it into a week-long festival.

35 N. Great George's St. jamesjoyce.ie. ✆ **01/878-8547.** Admission €7 adults; €5 seniors and students; free for children 11 and under. Tues–Sat 10:30am–4:30pm (last admission 30 min. before closing). Luas: Parnell. DART: Connolly. Nearest bus stops: Parnell Sq., O'Connell St.

The *Jeanie Johnston* ♥♥♥ MUSEUM The beautiful tall ship tied up on the north quays in Dublin city is actually the *Jeanie Johnston,* a replica of a so-called "famine ship." It tells the story of the terrible humanitarian disaster and the two million people who fled Irish shores on ships like this for a better life in North America between 1845 and 1855. The 50-minute tour is an extremely moving experience. You stroll the breezy upper decks, then head below deck, where you can sense how grueling and cramped the voyages were—with passengers suffering from disease, seasickness, and starvation having to endure crowded conditions and bad weather. Remarkably, no lives were ever lost on the 16 Atlantic crossings of the original *Jeanie Johnston,* which later became a cargo ship before it sank in 1858. This replica was built in 2002, and it's a must-do if you want more insight into this tragic period in Irish history.

The *Jeanie Johnston* replica ship offers a glimpse into the desperate voyages of poor Irish people fleeing the Great Famine.

Custom House Quay. jeaniejohnston.ie. ✆ **01/473-0111.** €15 adults; €13 seniors and students; €12 ages 13–17; €10 ages 6–12; children 5 and under free; €34–€39 families. Combined ticket with EPIC (p. 114) €32 adults; €29 seniors and students; €23 ages 13–17; €17 ages 6–12; children 5 and under free. Tours daily every 30 min. 10am–4:30pm. Luas: George's Dock. DART: Tara St., Connolly. Nearest bus stop: Custom House Quay.

The Little Museum of Dublin ♥♥♥ MUSEUM Stuffed full of ephemera relating to the lives of ordinary Dubliners—art, toys, photographs, newspapers, prints, and other artifacts of the everyday—this delightful museum chronicles what it was like to live in the city throughout the 20th century. Thoughtfully laid out inside a Georgian town house, the vast majority of the items on display were donated by the people of Dublin, and the collection is growing all the time. Among the curios are genuine documents of social history, including items relating to the World War I, the struggle for independence, and the suffrage movement. Several objects have charming anecdotes connected—such as the music stand that, in June 1963, was hurriedly borrowed from the home of a local antiques dealer by visiting U.S. President John F. Kennedy, when he realized he had nowhere to put his papers during a speech. Entry is by guided tour (on the hour, every hour); tours are lively and informative, and guides are great with children. Book tickets online in advance during the high season. ***Note:*** **DoDublin** bus tour tickets (p. 122) include free entry to the museum.

15 St. Stephen's Green. littlemuseum.ie. ✆ **01/661-1000.** Admission €15 adults; €13 seniors and students; €35 families. Daily 9.45am–4:30pm. Last tour 4pm. Luas: Dawson, St. Stephen's Green. DART: Pearse. Nearest bus stops: St. Stephen's Green, Nassau St., Kildare St.

Marsh's Library ♥♥♥ LIBRARY Founded by the wonderfully named Narcissus Marsh, the Archbishop of Dublin, in 1701, this library is still much today as it was in the archbishop's time. Tall, long rows of books sit between paneled walls, and rolling ladders slant upward so readers can reach the high shelves. It is a magnificent example of a 17th-century scholar's library, its shelves filled with scholarly volumes, chiefly focused on theology, medicine, ancient history, and maps, along with Hebrew, Greek, Latin, and French literature. You can still see the wire cages where readers would be locked in with valuable tomes. It's still a working library, but readers are no longer imprisoned. The library has an excellent collection of books by and about Jonathan Swift (see box on p. 102), including volumes with his editing comments in the margins. Ironically, Swift himself said of Archbishop Marsh, "He is the first of human race, that with great advantages of learning, piety, and station ever escaped being a great man."

St. Patrick's Close. marshlibrary.ie. ✆ **01/454-3511.** Admission €7 adults; €4 seniors and students; ages 18 and under free. Tues–Fri 9:30am–5pm; Sat 10am–5pm. Luas: St. Stephen's Green. Nearest bus stops: Kevin St., Patrick's Cathedral.

MoLI (Museum of Literature Ireland) ♥♥♥ MUSEUM This museum dedicated to Ireland's rich literary tradition is in UCD Newman House, a historic Georgian town house on St. Stephen's Green where the original University College Dublin was founded (as the Catholic University of Ireland). A series of exhibits about Irish literature is spread across three floors, taking in everything from digital displays to a model of James Joyce's Dublin. There's also an interesting room with advice from writers, plus pen and paper if you feel inspired yourself. Look for rare items from the Joyce archive (he was a student in Newman House in 1902), including

Ireland's rich literary heritage is on display at MoLI (Museum of Literature Ireland).

the first copy of *Ulysses*. You can't see a page because it's closed up in a glass case, but copies are on display nearby. There are two guided tours a day. The shop is well worth a browse for books and literary-themed gifts, and the outdoor garden of the **Commons Café** is a gorgeous spot in nice weather.
UCD Newman House, 86 St. Stephen's Green. moli.ie. ✆ **01/716-5900.** €14.50 adults; €12 (or free Wed until noon) seniors, students and children; free for children 2 and under; €32 families. Add €3 for guided tour. Free 6–9pm on the first Fri of every month. Daily Mon 10:30am–5:30pm. Tours Mon–Sat 11am, 1 and 3pm; Sun 1pm. Last admission 4:30pm. Luas: St. Stephen's Green. DART: Pearse. Nearest bus stops: St. Stephen's Green, Leeson St.

National Leprechaun Museum ♥ MUSEUM/STORYTELLING Not quite what it seems from the outside, this is really more of an experience than a conventional museum. You go from room to room, each decorated in weird and imaginative and often wacky style, where storytellers spin tales from Celtic mythology. One room is done like an oversized living room, where adults can feel pixie-size while sitting on giant chairs and sofas. It's a bit strange—definitely a love-it-or-loathe-it experience (see p. 164 for how the leprechaun concept is viewed in Ireland). Although the emphasis is on fun and whimsy, the content is such that the experience isn't suitable for children under age 7. If you prefer your folklore darker, come in the evening for an adults-only version.
Jervis St. leprechaunmuseum.ie. ✆ **01/873-3899.** Day tours €18 adults, €16 seniors and students, €11 children 15 and under; night tours €20 adults (18 and over) only. Day tours every 30 min. 10:30am–5pm; night tours Thurs 7 and 8pm, Fri and Sat 7, 7:30, 8, and 8:30pm. Arrive at least 10 min. before tour. Luas: Jervis. DART: Tara St. Nearest bus stops: O'Connell St., Ormond Quay.

National Library of Ireland ♥ LIBRARY If you're coming to Ireland to research your roots, one of your first stops should be this library, where thousands of volumes and records yield ancestral information. Open at this location since 1890, it's also the principal library of Irish studies, particularly noted for its collection of first editions and the papers of Irish writers and political figures, such as W. B. Yeats, Daniel O'Connell, and Patrick Pearse. Parts of the collection are always on display to the general public (the Yeats exhibition is particularly good). The library also

HORSE-DRAWN carriage tours

Touristy it may be, but on a fine day you might hear horse-drawn carriages clattering around Dublin's streets, with tourists bundled up to keep warm while a driver comments on the sights as they clop past (or wait in traffic).

While horse-drawn carriages have been a long-standing tradition in Dublin, as with any place where these run, there are conversations about the welfare of the animals. Horses in Dublin must be licensed, which includes an annual inspection by a vet. If you have any concerns, before you hire a carriage, be sure to check whether your driver has a valid (current) horse license.

Drivers and their carriages usually congregate at the Grafton Street side of St. Stephen's Green. You can simply walk up to one and arrange your tour—anything from a short swing around the Green to a half-hour Georgian tour or an hour-long city tour. Rides are available on a first-come, first-served basis from April to October (weather permitting). The price should start at around €30 for a carriage ride around St. Stephen's Green, which covers four passengers.

Drivers also congregate outside the Guinness Storehouse. These may or may not be licensed. The official price is around €30 for a short trip to Temple Bar—however, there have been reports of unlicensed drivers trying to charge this per *person*, not per carriage, which would make the short trip extremely expensive. Before you set off, always make sure to clearly agree on the price *per person*, plus the start and end time and the exact drop-off location.

Alternatively, to book a tour in advance, try **Ned's Carriage Tours** (✆ **085/8135755** or Ned's Carriage Tours on Facebook), which does a 1-hour Georgian tour around Dublin for €120 for up to six passengers. Tours can also be customized to what you're interested in seeing.

has an unrivaled collection of maps of Ireland. For genealogy, a specialist **Family History Service** is open Monday to Friday from 9:30am until 5pm. It's free of charge. You can book an in-person consultation for guidance. You'll need to apply online for a reader's ticket for access to the Family History Room (nli.ie/family-history/family-history-service). The library has two other sites, both also with free admission. In Temple Bar, the **National Photographic Archive** (Meeting House Square; ✆ **01/603-0373;** daily 10am–4pm) always has some interesting photographic exhibitions; free tours of the photographic archive can be prebooked at ✆ **01/603-0346.** The **Seamus Heaney Listen Now Again** exhibition (Bank of Ireland Cultural and Heritage Centre, College Green; entrance via Westmoreland St.; daily 10am–4pm, last admission 3:30pm) features archive material and manuscripts from the poet's life and work.

2–3 Kildare St. nli.ie. ✆ **01/603-0200.** Free admission. Reading rooms: Mon–Fri 10:30am–12:30pm and 2–4pm (Tues also 5–7pm); Sat 9:30am–1pm (2 Sat per month, check dates online). Exhibitions: Tue–Wed 9:30am–7pm (last admission 6:30pm); Thurs–Mon 9:30am–5pm (last admission 4:30pm). Luas: Dawson. DART: Pearse. Nearest bus stops: Kildare St., Nassau St., St. Stephen's Green.

PARKS & GARDENS

Phoenix Park ♥♥ PARK The vast green expanses of Phoenix Park are Dublin's playground, and it's easy to see why. This well-designed, user-friendly park is crisscrossed by a network of roads and quiet pedestrian walkways that make its 704 hectares (1,739 acres) easily accessible. It's a working park—livestock graze peacefully on pasturelands, deer roam the forested areas, and horses romp on polo fields. The home of the Irish president (p. 110) is in the park, as is the **Dublin Zoo** (p. 123). The visitor center is partly located inside **Ashtown Castle,** a tower house built in the 1430s that was only discovered in 1978, when a later building that had completely enveloped it was demolished. Free parking is adjacent to the center. Next to the center, the **Phoenix Park Café** (✆ **01/255-4445**) serves healthy light lunches, scones, and cakes, while the quaint **Victorian Tea Rooms** (✆ **01/671-9376**) on Chesterfield Avenue serves great coffee and cakes. The park is 3km (2 miles) west of the city center on the north bank of the River Liffey.

Phoenix Park. phoenixpark.ie. ✆ **01/677-0095.** Free admission. Park open 24 hr.; visitor center 9:30am–6pm, last admission 45 min. before closing. Phoenix Park Café Mar–Sept Mon–Fri 9:30am–5pm, Sat–Sun 9:30am–5:30pm; Oct–Feb Mon–Fri 9:30am–4pm, Sat–Sun 9:30am–5pm. Victorian Tea Rooms daily 9:30am–5:30pm (closes 4:30pm Nov–Mar). Luas: Heuston. Nearest bus stops: Parkgate St., Castleknock Rd., Navan Rd.

St. Stephen's Green ♥♥ PARK This lovely city-center park is filled with public art, and there always seems to be something new and imaginative hidden amid its leafy walkways. Among them is a beautiful statue commemorating the Irish rebel Wolfe Tone (beside an affecting monument to the Great Famine) and a garden of scented plants for blind visitors. This is a great place for a summer picnic.

St. Stephen's Green. Luas: St. Stephen's Green. DART: Pearse. Nearest bus stop: St. Stephen's Green.

Especially for Kids

Sure, Dublin is rich in history and culture, but if you've got restless kids in tow, museums and historic buildings can get old fast. Luckily, the Irish capital also has a good complement of attractions that are tailor-made for families. Besides the attractions listed below, consider taking the **Dublin Ghost Bus** (see p. 122, if the kids are age 14 or over) or, if you've got jaded teenagers, the **Irish Rock 'n' Roll Museum Experience** (p. 116). A trip by DART to the heritage village of **Dalkey** (p. 124) or a seaside excursion to the fishing village of **Howth** for a boat trip (p. 125) can also be a welcome antidote to city touring. And don't overlook **Butlers Chocolate Experience** (p. 162), a treat for any kid with a sweet tooth.

The Ark: A Cultural Centre for Children ♥ ARTS CENTER This is a great option for children who are makers, thinkers, doers, listeners, and watchers. Age-specific programs are geared to small groups of kids from 2 to 12 years old. Mini courses (1–2 hr. long) are designed around themes in music, visual arts, and theater; there are also workshops in photography, instrument making, and the art of architecture. The custom-designed arts center has three modern floors that house a theater, a gallery, and a workshop for hands-on learning sessions. Tickets include one child and one adult; prices vary, expect to pay around €10 to €17.50 for events—some events and talks are free. Check the current schedule on the Ark's website.

11a Eustace St. ark.ie. ✆ **01/670-7788.** Ticket prices and event times vary; check online. Luas: Trinity. DART: Tara St. Nearest bus stops: Dame St., Wellington Quay.

DUBLIN bus tours

Convenient, comfortable, and—remember this when the heavens open in June—relatively immune to inclement weather, bus tours are a great way to pack a lot of sightseeing into a little time. And while Dublin has more than its fair share of standard tourist buses, some are more original.

Of the many "hop on, hop off" bus tours of the city, one of the best is the **DoDublin** tour (dodublin.ie; ✆ **01/703-3024**), thanks in part to the commentary of its witty driver-guides as you make your way among the sites. The 24-stop tour runs all around the city center, taking in sights such as **Trinity College** (p. 104), **Dublin Castle** (p. 111), and the **Guinness Storehouse** (p. 108). You can leave and rejoin the tour at any point, and as many times as you like within a 24- or 48-hour period, depending on which ticket you buy. The cost includes free entry into the **Little Museum of Dublin** (but you'll still need to book yourself on a tour; see p. 117) and the option of a free walking tour with a local guide. Buses run all day, every hour from 9am daily; the last tour starts its loop at 5pm. Many of the buses are multilingual. Tickets cost €32 adults, €30 seniors and students, and €12 children, and one child 15 and under travels free with every adult. Add €5 more for a 48-hour ticket. DoDublin also runs a 45-minute tour of the Docklands, a Ghostbus tour, and full-day excursions to attractions such as **Glendalough** (p. 201), **Powerscourt** (p. 203), and the **Cliffs of Moher** (p. 360). See website for details.

A spooky evening tour in a bus decked out in, um . . . spooky wallpaper, Dublin Bus's **Dublin Ghost Bus** (ghostbus.ie; ✆ **01/844-4265**) addresses Dublin's history of felons, fiends, and phantoms. You'll see haunted houses, learn of Dracula's Dublin origins, visit a graveyard, and even get a crash course in body snatching. It's all ghoulish fun, but not suitable for kids 13 and under. Tours leave at 7 and 9:30pm from Dublin Bus Headquarters at 59 O'Connell St. Upper. Tickets cost €35.

Likewise, the entertaining **Gravedigger Ghost Tour** (thegravedigger.ie; ✆ **01/907-3265**) takes you in pursuit of a few ghoulish and well-intentioned scares. Just when it all seems like too much for the faint-hearted, the bus stops at the Gravediggers Pub by Glasnevin Cemetery (p. 115) for a fortifying drink. Tickets cost €35, and tours depart from College Green every night at 7:45pm. Live actors and 4D technology help bring the whole spooky experience to life. Or should that be . . .

The Dublin Zoo's African Plains exhibit is home to giraffes, rhinos, and ostriches.

Dublin Zoo ♥♥ ZOO A perennial kid-pleaser, this modern, humane zoo in Phoenix Park provides a home for more than 235 species of wild animals and tropical birds. The animals live inside a series of realistically created habitats such as the African Plains, home to giraffes, rhinos, and ostriches; the Gorilla Rainforest, a 12,000-sq.-m (7½-sq.-mile) enclosure that houses five lowland gorillas; Asian Forest, home to Sumatran tigers and lions; the South American House, with an eclectic range of almost unbearably cute species, including tiny pygmy marmosets and two-toed sloths; and the Pacific Coast, where you can watch sea lions swim underwater and view a flamingo aviary that's big enough for the gracious birds to take flight. Playgrounds and gift shops are scattered throughout. Feeding times and scheduled keeper talks are posted on the zoo website (several times daily Mar–Sept; weekends only Oct–Feb). On-site is a restaurant, plenty of smaller cafes, and picnic areas for those who prefer to bring their own meals. There's a slight discount for booking online.

Phoenix Park. dublinzoo.ie. ✆ **01/474-8900.** Admission €20–€24 adults; €16–€19 seniors and students; €15–€18 children 3–15; free for ages 2 and under; €57–€67 families. Book online for discounts. Daily 9:30am–4pm. Last admission to zoo 1 hr. before closing; last admission to African Plains 30 min. before closing. Luas: Heuston (15-min. walk). Nearest bus stops: Infirmary Rd., Parkgate St.

Dublinia ♥ HERITAGE SITE Covering the history of Dublin from the Viking age through medieval times, this child-friendly history experience is presented as a series of interactive tableaux—complete with sound effects, smells, and audio "reconstructions" of *olde worlde* Dublin. Kids can try on clothes like the ones their ancestors may have worn, or even find themselves placed in the Dublin stocks. Check the website for details of special tours, with costumed guides, and other activities. Climb the 96 steps to the top of the viewing tower, which was once part of the (now vanished) medieval **Church of St. Michael the Archangel.**

St. Michael's Hill, Christ Church. dublinia.ie. ✆ **01/679-4611.** Admission €15 adults; €13.50 seniors and students; €7.50 children 3–12; €25–€37 families. Daily 10am–6pm (closes 5pm Oct–Feb). Last admission 1 hr. before closing. Luas: Four Courts. Nearest bus stops: High St., Patrick St., Dame St.

Outlying Attractions

Newbridge House and Farm ♥♥♥ MUSEUM AND FARM This gorgeous Georgian villa was built in 1747 as a country retreat and is still full of family-owned furniture and photos, making it one of Ireland's best-preserved historic interiors. A house tour is highly recommended (look out for the 1760s "Cobbe Cabinet of Curiosities") before a visit to the farm, which is home to horses, ponies, goats, pigs, ducks, rabbits, and lots more furry friends—some are traditional or rare breeds. It's 11 miles north of Dublin city, and also features a walled garden, cafe, and shop, with enough here to keep family members of all ages busy for a day or half-day out.

Hearse Rd., Newbridge Demesne, Donabate. newbridgehouseandfarm.com. ✆ **01/895-8262.** House tour and farm: €14 adults; €9.50 children; €10 seniors and students; €30–€42 families. Farm only: €10.50 adults; €8 children; €8.50 seniors and students; €25–€35 families. House, farm, and parkland tour: €18 adults; €14 seniors and students; €44 families. House tours daily 10 and 11am, and 2 and 3pm. Parkland tours 11am Sat and Sun.

Dalkey Castle & Heritage Centre ♥♥ HERITAGE SITE Housed in a 15th-century tower house, this center tells the history of venerable Dalkey town in a few sweet, if unsophisticated, displays. Don't leave without taking in the view from the battlements. Adjoining the center is a medieval graveyard and the **Church of St. Begnet** (Dalkey's patron saint), whose foundations date back to Ireland's early Christian period. Dalkey itself is worth a wander: A heritage town with plenty of historic buildings, it also has lots of charming pubs and restaurants. If you enjoy nature walks, climb **Killiney Hill** in Killiney Hill Park, just south of town, for great views of Killiney Bay, Bray Head, and the Wicklow Mountains. From Coliemore Harbour, a 10-minute walk from the train station, you can take a 5-minute ferry ride to clamber around rocky, abandoned **Dalkey Island,** with its ruined church and guard tower, wild goats, and adjacent seal colony.

Castle St., Dalkey (16km/10 miles SE of Dublin on R119). dalkeycastle.com. ✆ **01/285-8366.** Admission €16 adults; €15 seniors and students; €10.50 children 4–12. Apr–Oct Mon, Wed–Fri 10am–4:30pm (closes 4pm Nov–Mar); Sat–Sun 10:30am–4:30pm (closes 4pm Nov–Mar). Closed Tues. DART: Dalkey. Nearest bus stop: Dalkey.

Costumed interpreters on guard along the battlements of Dalkey Castle.

Ireland's Eye Ferries ♥♥ BOAT TRIP With cliffs, a harbor, and endless views over the Irish Sea, visitors flock to **Howth** village 10½ miles north of the city on sunny summer days to walk the cliff path and eat ice cream on the pier. Rather than joining the crowds on paths at the Summit or Baily Lighthouse, take this 1-hour boat trip around **Ireland's Eye,** a grassy isle just off Howth Harbour, to experience the area from the water. You will spot seals and, depending on the season, birds like gannets and puffins. If you are going to hike the cliffs, sign up for a Howth Safari Hiking Tour with sister company **Shane's Howth Adventures** (shaneshowthadventures.com) to see the less touristy trails and some secret spots on the peninsula.

West Pier, Howth. irelandseyeferries.com. ✆ **086/077-3021.** Boat trip €25 adults; €15 seniors, students and children; €60 families. Hourly 11am–4pm. Closed Jan to mid-Mar. DART: Howth. Nearest bus stop: Howth Harbour.

WHERE TO STAY IN DUBLIN

Lots of new hotels have opened up in Dublin in the past few years, many of them in areas such as the Docklands, the Liberties, and suburbs like Ranelagh. A number of the newcomers are bursting with personality, with uber-cool rooftop bars and retro design fittings. Dublin has many great classics too, ranging from Georgian town houses with character to grand dames where you can treat yourself to afternoon tea beside the fire. We've listed our favorites here.

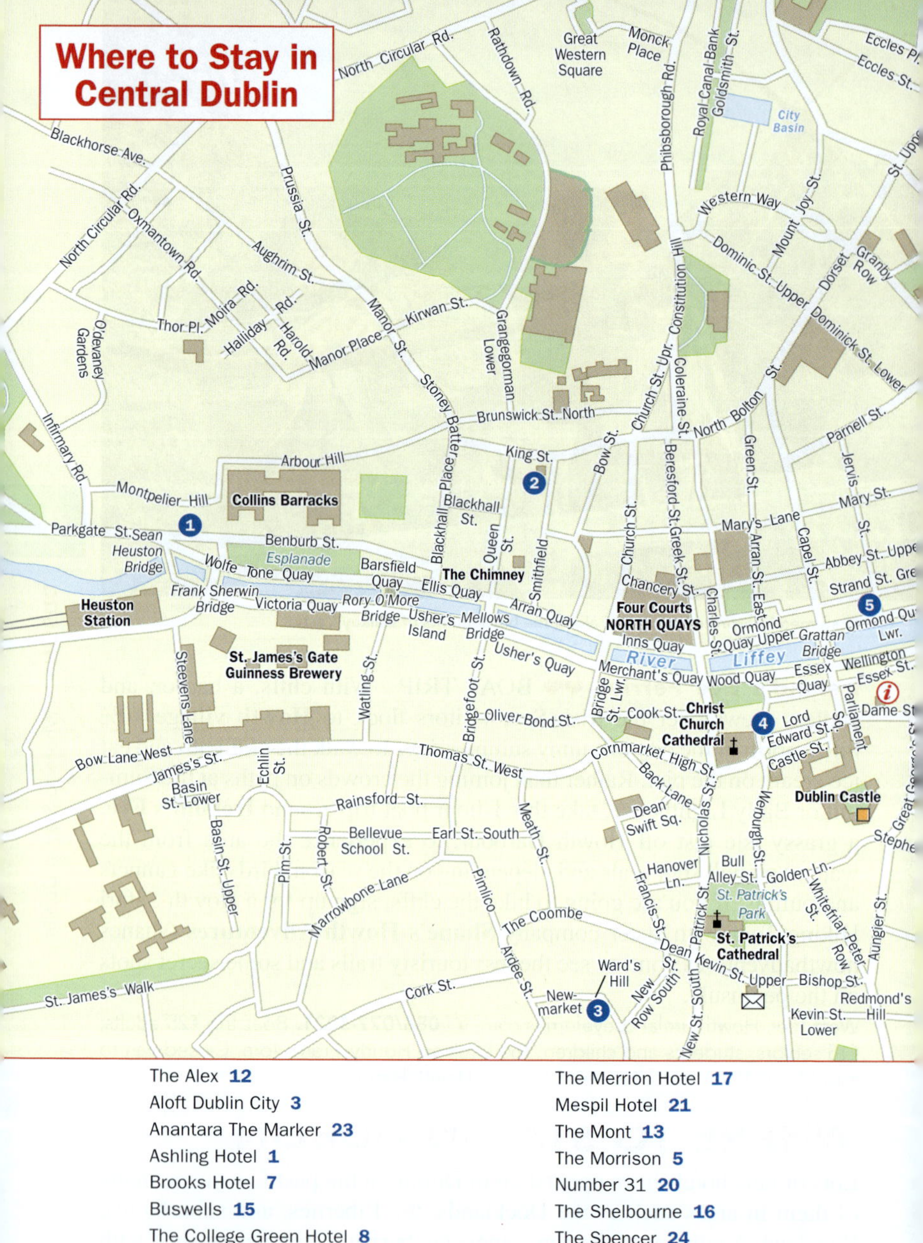

The Alex **12**
Aloft Dublin City **3**
Anantara The Marker **23**
Ashling Hotel **1**
Brooks Hotel **7**
Buswells **15**
The College Green Hotel **8**
Conrad Dublin **18**
The Grafton Hotel **6**
Grand Canal Hotel **22**
Harding Hotel **4**
Maldron Hotel Smithfield **2**
The Mayson **25**
The Merrion Hotel **17**
Mespil Hotel **21**
The Mont **13**
The Morrison **5**
Number 31 **20**
The Shelbourne **16**
The Spencer **24**
Trinity City Hotel **11**
Trinity Townhouse **14**
The Westbury **10**
The Wilder Townhouse **19**
Wren Urban Nest **9**

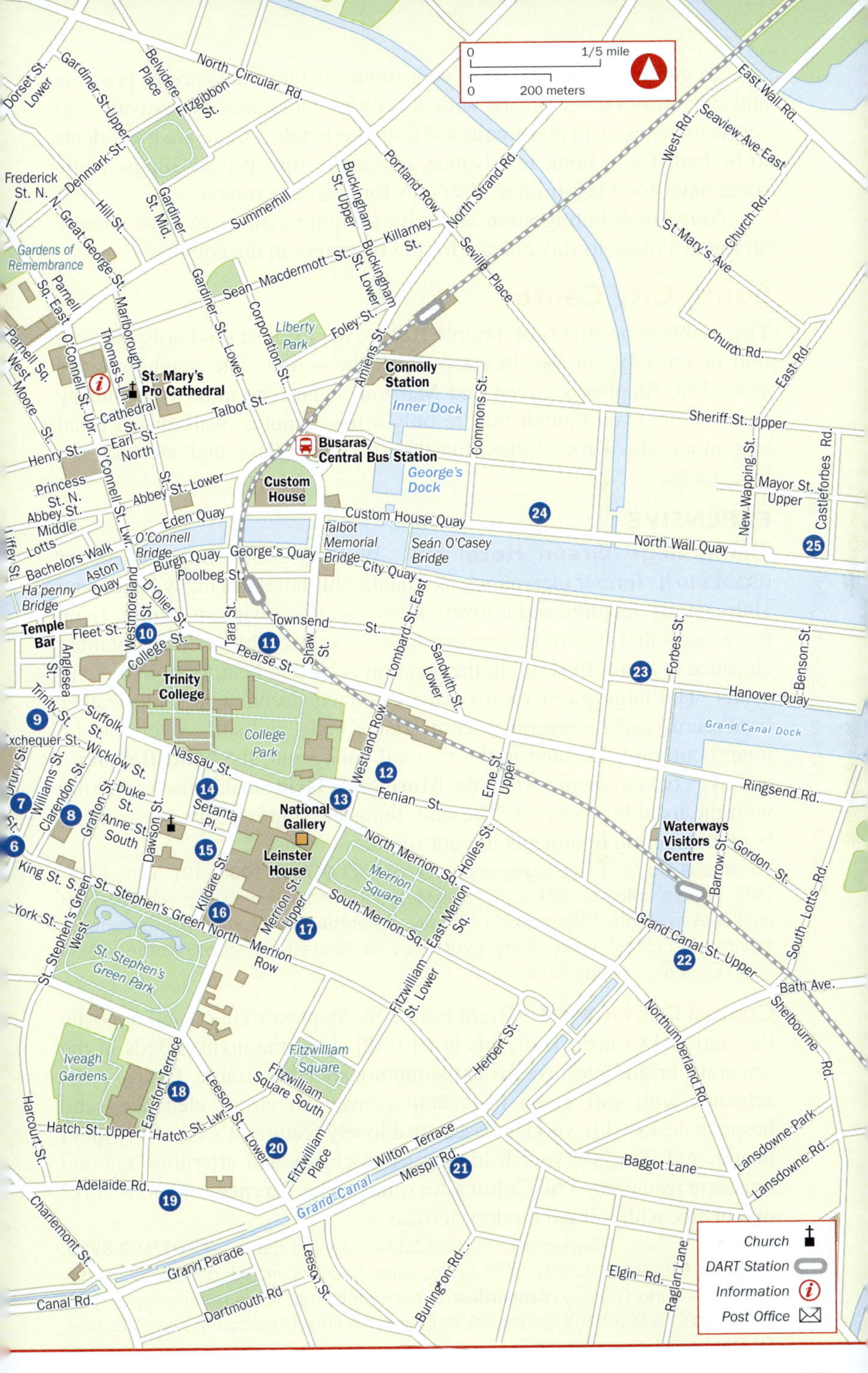
0
1/5 mile
0
200 meters
North Circular Rd.
Dorset St. Lower
Gardiner St. Upper
Belvidere Place
Fitzgibbon St.
Frederick St. N.
Denmark St.
Hill St.
Gardiner St. Mid.
Summerhill
Gardens of Remembrance
N. Great George St.
Parnell Sq. East
Parnell Sq. West
Moore St.
O'Connell St. Upr.
Thomas's Ln.
Marlborough St.
St. Mary's Pro Cathedral
Cathedral St.
Earl St. North
Henry St.
Princess St. N.
Abbey St. Middle
O'Connell St. Lwr.
Abbey St. Lower
Lotts
Liffey St.
Bachelors Walk
Ha'penny Bridge
Aston Quay
O'Connell Bridge
Eden Quay
Burgh Quay
Temple Bar
Fleet St.
Westmoreland St.
D'Olier St.
College St.
Anglesea St.
Trinity St.
Exchequer St.
Drury St.
Williams St.
Clarendon St.
Grafton St.
Suffolk St.
Wicklow St.
Duke St.
Anne St. South
Dawson St.
Nassau St.
Setanta Pl.
Trinity College
College Park
Kildare St.
King St. S.
St. Stephen's Green West
St. Stephen's Green North
York St.
St. Stephen's Green Park
Iveagh Gardens
Harcourt St.
Earlsfort Terrace
Hatch St. Upper
Hatch St. Lwr.
Leeson St. Lower
Adelaide Rd.
Charlemont St.
Canal Rd.
Grand Parade
Dartmouth Rd
Leeson St.
Gardiner St. Lower
Sean Macdermott St.
Corporation St.
Liberty Park
Talbot St.
Foley St.
Amiens St.
Buckingham St. Upper
Buckingham St. Lower
Portland Row
Killarney St.
North Strand Rd.
Seville Place
Connolly Station
Inner Dock
Commons St.
Busaras/ Central Bus Station
Custom House
George's Dock
Custom House Quay
Talbot Memorial Bridge
George's Quay
Poolbeg St.
Seán O'Casey Bridge
City Quay
North Wall Quay
Tara St.
Townsend St.
Pearse St.
Shaw St.
Lombard St. East
Sandwith St. Lower
Westland Row
Fenian St.
National Gallery
Leinster House
Merrion St. Upper
Merrion Row
North Merrion Sq.
Merrion Square
South Merrion Sq.
East Merrion Sq.
Holles St.
Erne St. Upper
Fitzwilliam St. Lower
Fitzwilliam Square
Fitzwilliam Square South
Fitzwilliam Place
Wilton Terrace
Mespil Rd.
Grand Canal
Herbert St.
Burlington Rd.
Baggot Lane
Elgin Rd.
Raglan Lane
Northumberland Rd.
Lansdowne Park
Lansdowne Rd.
Shelbourne Rd.
Bath Ave.
Grand Canal St. Upper
Waterways Visitors Centre
Barrow St.
Gordon St.
South Lotts Rd.
Ringsend Rd.
Grand Canal Dock
Hanover Quay
Benson St.
Forbes St.
New Wapping St.
Mayor St. Upper
Castleforbes Rd.
Sheriff St. Upper
East Rd.
Church Rd.
St Mary's Ave
West Rd.
Seaview Ave East
East Wall Rd.
Church
DART Station
Information
Post Office

To get the best price, book your rooms as far in advance as possible and avoid times that coincide with the city's major concerts, festivals, and sports matches. And don't write off four-star hotels—there are great deals to be had if you book in advance, especially for off-peak times, while some have good last-minute discounts for available rooms.

Note: Irish immigration authorities require visitors to have already arranged a place to stay at least for the first night in the country.

South City Center

The cobblestone streets of Temple Bar are the liveliest (and noisiest) section of the city, on the doorstep of all the action. The neighborhoods around St. Stephen's Green and Merrion Square are almost bucolic by comparison, even though they're only a few minutes' walk away. Head east along the River Liffey for the sparkling glass and steel of the Docklands.

EXPENSIVE

The College Green Hotel ♥♥ With its grand, imposing decor (thanks to its former incarnation as a bank), this hotel has many handsome 19th-century features and a lovely inner courtyard with an atrium. Even those parts that feel more modern have an impeccably well-maintained elegance to them. Best of all, the location is hard to beat, right in the city center. The large guest rooms have a refined decor, with wide leather headboards and outrageously comfortable beds, and some overlook the inner courtyard. Located in the original bank vault, the **Mint Bar** has a creative cocktail menu, while the **Morelands Grill** steakhouse is popular with the local business set. The only thing missing is a spa, but you can book pampering treatments in your room.

Westmoreland St. thecollegegreenhotel.com. ✆ **01/645-1000.** 191 units. €315–€675 double; €485–€3,500 suite. Breakfast included. Dinner, bed-and-breakfast packages available. Valet parking €35/day. **Amenities:** Restaurant; bar; gym; room service; Wi-Fi (free). Luas: Trinity. DART: Tara St. Nearest bus stops: Westmoreland St., D'Olier St., College Green.

Conrad Dublin ♥♥♥ Right beside St. Stephen's Green and opposite the National Concert Hall, this hotel is all about the luxury. Beds in the spacious, bright guest rooms are sumptuously comfortable. Earthy color schemes with soft green hues help convey an air of elegance—and bespoke desks with wooden bases are a lovely feature. It's blissfully quiet inside, and there's a stylish lounge for cocktails and afternoon tea and brasserie restaurant **The Coburg** for dinner. The **Terrace** is a more informal bistro, with a small outdoor terrace.

Earlsfort Terrace. hilton.com/en/hotels/dubhcci-conrad-dublin. ✆ **01/602-8900.** 192 units. €259–€462 double; €729–€2,885 suite. Breakfast included. Parking €30/day or valet parking €39/day. **Amenities:** 2 restaurants; bar; room service; gym; Wi-Fi (free). Luas: St. Stephen's Green. DART: Pearse. Nearest bus stops: Earlsfort Terrace, St. Stephen's Green, Leeson St.

The Merrion Hotel sets a tone of Georgian elegance.

The Merrion Hotel ♥♥♥ This luxurious five-star hotel is set in a row of Georgian town houses. The large, warm, and quiet rooms are all elegantly decorated in a traditional style, with king-size orthopedic beds. In the lobbies, fires crackle at the hearth, surrounded by button-backed chairs and velvet sofas. It's all lavish and peaceful. **Restaurant Patrick Guilbaud** has two Michelin stars and is one of the best restaurants in the city. There's also the pub-like **Cellar Bar,** the **No. 23** cocktail bar, and the **Garden Room,** another fine-dining alternative. The spa is a gloriously relaxing getaway, with a pool and thermal suite, but reserve your treatments in advance, as they do get booked up.

Upper Merrion St. merrionhotel.com. ✆ **01/603-0600.** 142 units. €350–€895 double; €895–€4,500 suite. Parking €20. **Amenities:** 3 restaurants; 2 bars; room service; spa; pool; gym; Wi-Fi (free). Luas: St. Stephen's Green. DART: Pearse. Nearest bus stops: Merrion Sq., Baggot St., Clare St.

The Shelbourne ♥♥ Dublin hotels simply don't come with a better historic pedigree than this. It was founded in 1824, making it 200 years old, and the Irish Constitution was written in this very building. A sense of history and elegance pervades the lobby rooms, with high ceilings, crystal chandeliers, and a grand staircase. Guest rooms have a contemporary elegance, with luxurious beds and large bathrooms. There's also a spa, pool, and gym. The hotel is a popular gathering spot for Dublin society—the **Horseshoe Bar** is a favorite of writers and politicians. Afternoon tea in the **Lord Mayor's Lounge** is a Dublin institution. The **Saddle Room** restaurant is the fine-dining option, and there is casual dining in the buzzing **No. 27 Bar and Lounge** or on the outdoor terrace.

27 St. Stephen's Green. theshelbourne.com. ✆ **01/663-4500.** 265 units. €345–€1,039 double; €1,152–€5,389 suite. Breakfast €18–€26. Dinner, bed-and-breakfast packages available. Valet parking €40/day. **Amenities:** 2 restaurants; 3 bars; gym; pool; spa; accessible rooms; Wi-Fi (free). Luas: St. Stephen's Green. DART: Pearse. Nearest bus stop: St. Stephen's Green.

The Westbury ♥♥♥ Basically conceived with well-heeled shopaholics in mind and popular with visiting celebrities, this top-end hotel just

The richly paneled 1824 bar welcomes guests at the Shelbourne.

steps from busy Grafton Street is a stylish retreat. The first-floor lobby is vast, with lots of comfy sofas for post-shopping cocktails or an excellent afternoon tea with bubbles. Bedrooms are sizable with large, comfortable beds and are decorated in warm tones, while some suites have their own rooftop terraces with city views. **Wilde** restaurant also has a beautiful terrace looking toward Grafton Street, the buzzing **Balfes** bistro is on the lower level, and the 1930s-style **Sidecar Bar** has its own martini trolley. Balfe St. doylecollection.com/hotels/the-westbury-hotel. ✆ **01/602-8900.** 205 units. €324–€710 double; €612–€4,800 suite. Breakfast included. Valet parking €40/day. **Amenities:** 2 restaurants; bar; room service; gym; Wi-Fi (free). Luas: Dawson. Nearest bus stops: St. Stephen's Green, Nassau St.

EXPENSIVE/MODERATE

The Grafton ♥♥ This modern hotel is probably more comfortable than it is flashy, but it's hard to beat the location, just steps from shopping and nightlife. Inside, rooms are modern and well-equipped, with muted tones and an Art Deco theme. Some rooms have small outside terraces, and a family room with two sets of bunks sleeps six. Food is available at **Bartley's Restaurant,** and the reception area has a bar and a small coffee dock. ***Our tip:*** Ask for a room overlooking Stephen Street—double glazing will keep you from hearing street noise, and you'll have super views across the rooftops and down to the passersby below.

Stephen St. thegrafton.ie. ✆ **01/255-2700.** 128 units. €159–€614 double. Breakfast €19.50–€22.50. Discount at nearby gym. Parking at nearby lot €16 for 24 hr. **Amenities:** Restaurant; bar; cafe; room service; Wi-Fi (free). Luas: St. Stephen's Green. Nearest bus stops: St. Stephen's Green, S. Great Georges St.

Trinity City Hotel ♥♥ This buzzing and stylish hotel is another with a hard-to-beat location. It's at the start of Pearse Street, just behind Trinity College and a short walk from Temple Bar. Choose from the range of room styles, with clean modern contemporary rooms in the main central building; stylish executive rooms in the old Victorian fire station building, with extra space and features like exposed brick walls; and old-style suites in the Georgian buildings, with small sitting rooms, antiques, and heritage features. The light-filled **Courtyard Restaurant** (which has outdoor dining in summer) is a good option for food, while the **Brunswick Bar and Lounge** also serves food and craft cocktails.

Pearse St. trinitycityhotel.com. ✆ **01/648-1000.** 262 units. €170–€511 double; €393–€736 suite. Lower rates do not include breakfast. Check online for offers. Limited valet parking €25. **Amenities:** Restaurant; bar; fitness center; Wi-Fi (free). Luas: Trinity. DART: Tara St. Nearest bus stops: Pearse St., Westmoreland St.

The Wilder Townhouse ♥♥ Just a short walk from St. Stephen's Green, this independent boutique hotel has many fans, drawn by its character and charm. Behind an impressive Victorian facade, guest rooms come in a variety of sizes, from tiny "Shoebox" doubles to spacious suites. All have tasteful decor in neutral tones and original features such as fireplaces, sash windows, and plaster cornices. Beds are comfortable with good mattresses; bathrooms are small but modern. Still, it's the thoughtful touches that bring people back. Books are left on bedside tables. Guests arriving after long flights are offered cups of tea or a complimentary drink from the bar. Staff are very helpful. A colorful breakfast buffet is served in the sunny garden room, and the bar hits the spot for a pre-dinner beverage. This is a find.

22 Adelaide Rd. thewilder.ie. ✆ **01/969-6958.** 42 units. €219–€488 double; €399–€628 suite. Breakfast included. Limited free parking (or on-street parking per hour). **Amenities:** Bar; Wi-Fi (free). Luas: Harcourt St. Nearest bus stops: Adelaide Rd., Earlsfort Terrace.

MODERATE

The Alex ♥♥ This stylish hotel near Trinity College has been gaining attention for its modern approach and spacious, well-designed rooms. Located on the site of an old train station, the hotel is designed within an inch of its life, with Art Deco touches mixed with elements that nod to its past as a station. Bedrooms are spacious and artfully designed with comfortable, king-size beds and soft throws made of Irish wool. Bathrooms

Guest rooms at the Brooks Hotel offer a tasteful refuge in the busy city center.

are sizable and up to date—some with freestanding tubs and separate showers. There's room to work in the bright lobby and good coffee on offer. The hotel restaurant is popular with locals for its light sandwiches and salads at lunch and tapas options for dinner.

41–47 Fenian St. thealexhotel.ie. ✆ **01/607-3700.** 103 units. €148–€540 double; €288–€600 suite. Lower rates do not include breakfast. Parking (in a nearby lot) €15/ day. **Amenities:** Restaurant; bar; room service; Wi-Fi (free). Luas: Dawson. DART: Pearse. Nearest bus stops: Merrion Sq., Nassau St., Westland Row.

Aloft Dublin City ♥♥ This outpost of the Marriott hotel chain's uber-modern Aloft brand is well located in the historic Liberties neighborhood, which has been undergoing a renaissance with a mix of old and new pubs and restaurants. It's around a 20-minute walk or 10-minute cab ride to a central point like Trinity College. The hotel has big windows, artfully simple rooms with good beds, and a low-key vibe. The vividly decorated bar is on the top floor, giving exceptional views all the way to the Wicklow Mountains on a sunny day. Even the reception desk is on the seventh floor, so this hotel is aptly named.

1 Mill St. marriott.co.uk/hotels/travel/dubal-aloft-dublin-city. ✆ **01/963-1800.** 202 units. €152–€467 double. **Amenities:** Restaurant; bar; Wi-Fi (free). Nearest bus stops: Kevin St., Clanbrassil St.

Brooks Hotel ♥♥♥ Brooks Hotel isn't much to look at from the outside, but on the inside, where it counts, it's attractive, warm, and welcoming. Only minutes from bustling Grafton Street, Brooks is an oasis of calm. Inside, the lounges have a muted color palette and traditional decor, with modern Irish art brightening the walls. The soundproofed rooms are compact but comfortable, with tasteful wallpaper and good desks. Beds have firm mattresses and soft linens, and a pillow menu lets you choose your firmness. Bathrooms are good size and modern. The joy is in the clever touches, including a small cinema where guests can watch movies (popcorn available on request). Plus, the hotel gives guests an Irish "book of the month." The **Bar and Brasserie** is a good option for a whiskey or light meal. Everything has been given great thought here.

59 Drury St. brookshotel.ie. ✆ **01/670-4000.** 98 units. €191–€476 double. **Amenities:** Restaurant; bar; Wi-Fi (free). Luas: Dawson. DART: Pearse. Nearest bus stops: Dawson St., St. Stephen's Green, S. Great Georges St.

Buswells ♥♥ An old-school air pervades this traditional hotel, a 5-minute walk from Grafton Street. The Georgian building's original features have been carefully maintained, from the intricate cornices of 19th-century plasterwork to the marble fireplaces, which warm the lobby on cold days. It can come as a surprise, therefore, to find that the guest rooms are modern and somewhat featureless. But even with its faults, this is a charming place on a peaceful street, with friendly staff and quiet rooms. Plus, you're in the very heart of the action. Guests with mobility problems should ask for a room on a lower floor; the old building has many staircases.

23–25 Molesworth St. buswells.ie. ✆ **01/614-6500.** 67 units. €114–€295 double. Lower rates do not include breakfast. Parking at nearby lot (€20/24 hr.). **Amenities:** Restaurant; bar; room service; Wi-Fi (free). Luas: Dawson. DART: Pearse. Nearest bus stops: Kildare St., St. Stephen's Green, Nassau St.

The Mont ♥♥♥ This stylish hotel has a super location for the museums, shopping, and nightlife of the south city (Trinity College and the National Gallery are just a few steps away). Rooms are design-led, with bright colors and block prints and an industrial vibe. The so-called "cosy doubles" are small, but beds are comfy and rooms come with all the mod cons. The biggest rooms are the spacious "dreamy suites," with large sash windows. The city views are great, but light sleepers should ask for an inside or courtyard room to avoid street noise. Downstairs, the **Sin Bin Bar** serves craft cocktails and snacks (there are plenty of restaurants on the doorstep) and has a sports theme with large projectors for key games. The gym is open 24/7. Check online for offers.

1-4 Merrion St. themonthotel.ie. ✆ **01/607-3800.** 96 units. €180–€450 double; €310–€580 suite. Lower rates do not include breakfast. Parking at nearby lot (€18/24 hr.). **Amenities:** Restaurant; bar; gym; Wi-Fi (free). Luas: Dawson. DART: Pearse. Nearest bus stops: Clare St., Merrion Sq.

Number 31 ♥ Tucked away on a quiet street near St. Stephen's Green, this B&B is made up of two houses—one Georgian town house and one modern mews—connected by an attractive courtyard. Rooms vary, but some have original features including high ceilings, sash windows, and decorative (not in use) fireplaces. All have modern bathrooms. Few rooms have air-conditioning, but each has a Dyson fan. Beds are mostly doubles, with orthopedic mattresses. Breakfast is epic here: fresh fruit compote, homemade cranberry-and-orange bread, and hot dishes made to order. ***Note:*** There are stairs but no elevator. This is an old house with character—but with that comes quirks like creaky floors and minimal soundproofing between floors, which may not suit light sleepers.

31 Leeson Close. number31.ie. ✆ **01/676-5011.** 22 units. €129–€484 double. Breakfast included. Parking (limited) €10 or on-street (€3.50/hr.). **Amenities:** Wi-Fi (free). Nearest bus stops: Leeson St. Upper, Wilton Trace.

Trinity Townhouse ♥♥ Originally built as town houses in the 1730s, this boutique hotel is set across three Georgian buildings on South Frederick Street. The location is fantastic, right in the heart of the fashionable south city area, steps from Grafton Street shops and Trinity College, not to mention pubs and restaurants. Some of the bedrooms retain a historic feel, with high ceilings and features like original fireplaces, while others are more modern. All have air-conditioning and up-to-date modern bathrooms. There's a small restaurant, too. These old houses are full of character but not well-soundproofed, plus there's no elevator, so you'll have to take the stairs to reach the upper floors.

29 S. Frederick St. trinitytownhousehotel.com. ✆ **01/617-0900.** 31 units. €165–€445 double. Parking at nearby lot (€22.50/24 hr. or €12.50 5–10am with discount ticket). **Amenities:** Restaurant; Wi-Fi (free). Luas: Dawson. DART: Pearse. Nearest bus stops: Nassau St., Dawson St.

INEXPENSIVE

Harding Hotel ♥ Just central enough not to require a long trek to the main tourist sites, but on a quieter street at the edge of the busy Temple Bar area, this is a reasonable option in the city center, and a bit of a find at these prices. The lobby's polished wood and floor-to-ceiling windows give off a pleasantly traditional vibe. Guest rooms are comfortable if plain; triple rooms typically cost just a little bit more than standard doubles, which makes them useful for families. It's not fancy, but it's pleasant and clean and has everything you need.

Copper Alley, Fishamble St. hardinghotel.ie. ✆ **01/679-6500.** 52 units. €119–€299 double. Breakfast not included in lower rates. No parking. **Amenities:** Restaurant; bar; accessible rooms; Wi-Fi (free). Nearest bus stops: Dame St., Essex Quay.

Mespil Hotel ♥ Just across the Grand Canal from all the sights, and a 10-minute walk from Merrion Square, this modern hotel has a lot to offer: sizable contemporary rooms with orthopedic beds, up-to-date bathrooms with walk-in rainfall showers, and pleasant canal views. Triple rooms often clock in at the same price as doubles—handy for families. The trendy **Lock Four** restaurant has a good menu that draws local office workers at lunch. The **Lounge Bar** is an attractive place for a tipple. One negative: The street can be noisy—light sleepers should ask for an upper-floor room. ***Tip:*** A **gourmet food market** is held nearby on Thursdays 11am until 2pm (irishvillagemarkets.com).

50–60 Mespil Rd. mespilhotel.com. ✆ **01/448-4600.** 255 units. €129–€249 double. Lower rates do not include breakfast. Parking free (limited) or on-street (€4/hr.). **Amenities:** Restaurant; bar; gym; room service; accessible rooms; Wi-Fi (free). Nearest bus stops: Burlington Rd., Baggot St.

Wren Urban Nest ♥♥ Tucked away on St. Andrew's Lane, just steps from Grafton Street and Temple Bar, this hotel makes no bones about its tiny rooms or "urban nests"—with a choice of "snug nest" (10 sq. m/108 sq. ft.) or "cosy nest" (12 sq. m/129 sq. ft.). Yet what the rooms lack in space, they make up for in clever design and details, such as storage cubbies, a fold-down desk, smart TV, minibar, power/rainfall shower, and good soundproofing. What's great is that the hotel is passionate about the environment and aims to be carbon neutral—it's not in your face about it, but you won't find single-use plastics here, energy is renewable, water comes in small cartons, and there's a machine in the corridor to fill your bottle. Even though you are surrounded by bars and restaurants, the food and cocktails at **ALT** bar and restaurant are superb; a large table is popular as a communal workspace.

St. Andrew's Lane. wrenhotel.ie. ✆ **01/223-4555.** 137 units. €109–€465 double. Breakfast not included in lower rates. Discount parking at nearby lot (€16/24 hr.). **Amenities:** Restaurant; bar; Wi-Fi (free). Luas: Dawson. DART: Tara St. Nearest bus stops: S. Great Georges St., Dame St., College Green.

The Docklands & IFSC

East of the city center, along the River Liffey, you'll find the sparkling glass-and-steel office blocks of the Docklands, which also has some worthy hotels and restaurants. The International Financial Services Centre (IFSC) is on the north side of the river, while the Docklands is on both sides.

EXPENSIVE

Anantara The Marker ♥♥♥ This sleek, ultra-modern hotel on Grand Canal Square overlooks the Grand Canal Quay waterfront in the south Docklands. It's a short walk from the city center, but the pedestrianized location means it's away from noise and traffic. Guest rooms are spacious and comfortable, with every luxury and high-end amenity. There's a relaxing spa, a 23m (75-ft.) pool, Jacuzzi, sauna, steam room, and a fully equipped gym. The excellent restaurant, **Forbes Street by Gareth Mullins** (p. 156), features creative menus with seasonal Irish ingredients. The **rooftop bar** is great in summer, with 360-degree views over the city and to the Dublin mountains. ***Tip:*** The hotel has courtesy bikes and a courtesy car for short local journeys and can arrange experiences like Docklands walking tours, sea swimming, and rooftop yoga.

Grand Canal Quay, Docklands. anantara.com/en/the-marker-dublin. ✆ **01/687-5100.** 187 units. €259–€532 double; €819–€2,213 suite. Breakfast included. Parking (€32/day) or valet parking (€40/day). **Amenities:** Restaurant; 2 bars; bikes; gym; pool; spa; courtesy car; Wi-Fi (free). DART: Grand Canal Dock. Nearest bus stops: Cardiff Lane, Pearse St.

The Spencer ♥♥ Set on the north bank of the River Liffey, this relatively recent addition to the IFSC skyline makes a great base for exploring. It's around a 15-minute walk along the river to O'Connell Street and 3 minutes' walk from the Luas. The bright rooms have a clean and simple design, with an emphasis on comfort over style; upgrade to a suite or junior suite for a private balcony overlooking the river. Downstairs, the lobby, bar, and restaurant are open plan, and the cuisine theme at **East Restaurant** is Asian fusion. One of the hotel's best features is a health club with a fully equipped gym and an 18m (59-ft.) swimming pool, great for recharging after sightseeing. The hotel is also ideally located for a visit to EPIC The Irish Emigration Museum (p. 114) and the *Jeanie Johnston* (p. 117).

Excise Walk, IFSC. thespencerhotel.com. ✆ **01/433-8800.** 209 units. €130–€399 double; €225–€637 suite. Lower rates do not include breakfast. Dinner, bed-and-breakfast packages available. Parking €25/24 hr. **Amenities:** Restaurant; bar; room service; gym; pool; Wi-Fi (free). Luas: Mayor Sq. DART: Connolly, Tara St. Nearest bus stop: North Wall Quay.

MODERATE

Grand Canal Hotel ♥ Right beside the Grand Canal, this large hotel is close to the Aviva Stadium and popular with sports fans. It's also a haven for business travelers and tourists looking for a pleasant, no-frills place to stay. Rooms are plain but large by Dublin standards. Downstairs, the **Waterbank Gastro Bar** serves good food and drinks (and gets packed on game days). The city center is a 20-minute journey away by DART. You could even walk if you wanted to work off one of the hearty hotel breakfasts—Trinity College is about 25 minutes on foot.

Grand Canal St. Upper. grandcanalhotel.ie. ✆ **01/646-1000.** 142 units. €139–€324 double. Breakfast not included in lower rates. Free parking. **Amenities:** Restaurant; bar; accessible rooms; Wi-Fi (free). DART: Grand Canal Dock. Nearest bus stops: Northumberland Rd., Mount St.

The Mayson ♥♥ This trendy hotel on the north city quays is divided between a modern new building and a restored redbrick warehouse and town house with lots of choice in room types. The old part has the restored pub **Bottle Boy,** plus **Elephant & Castle** restaurant, a handful of individually designed suites, and even a barber shop, while rooms in the new building are ultra-modern with floor-to-ceiling windows. The smallest rooms are tiny indeed (just 12 sq. m/129 sq. ft.), but all units have a speaker, fridge, and a great selection of snacks and drinks (for purchase) and bathrooms with rainfall showers. The terrace of **Ryleigh's** steakhouse on the sixth floor has views over the River Liffey. There is a small relaxation pool plus a large gym, a spin studio, and a climbing studio, and guests can join classes for €15. It's not a quiet hotel, but it's well-suited for guests craving buzz and action.

81/82 N. Wall Quay. themayson.ie. ✆ **01/245-7900.** 94 units. €159–€429 double; €399–€1,155 suite. **Amenities:** 2 restaurants; bar; gym; relaxation pool; Wi-Fi (free). Luas: The Point.

North of the Liffey & Smithfield

The area north of the Liffey has some good offerings in the way of hotels. It's also within walking distance of all the major sights and shops, and hotel rates tend to be lower on this side of the river. Head farther west of the city center to Smithfield if you'd rather not spend too much on lodging but still want to be within striking distance of attractions and nightlife,

EXPENSIVE

The Morrison ♥♥♥ Rooms at this chic city center hotel have cool, clean lines and a calming neutral color palette; some even have views of the River Liffey. The five-star is part of the Hilton Curio brand but has plenty of local personality—art is inspired by Dublin city, and song lyrics painted onto the walls here and there add an edge of Irish literary romance. There's good lighting and HDTV streaming TVs. The **Morrison Grill** is a lively spot overlooking the street and river, with a good selection of

Guest rooms at the Morrison have a chic, minimalist look.

seasonal dishes. It's next to funky cocktail lounge **Quay 14.** The afternoon tea here is dubbed "Fancy Pants Afternoon Tea"—how can you resist? The staff is excellent, and regulars swear that the amazing service never falters.

Lower Ormond Quay. morrisonhotel.ie. ✆ **01/887-2400.** 145 units. €170–€556 double. Lower rates do not include breakfast. Parking at nearby lot (€21.60/24 hr.). **Amenities:** Restaurant; bar; room service; gym; Wi-Fi (free). Luas: Four Courts. Nearest bus stops: Ormond Quay, Bachelors Walk, Wellington Quay.

MODERATE

Ashling Hotel ♥ Close to Heuston Station and Phoenix Park on the western end of the city, the Ashling is a modern six-story hotel. Basic double rooms have generic corporate-style decor, while deluxe rooms are more distinctive and spacious, with comfortable beds and large windows overlooking the city. The in-house restaurant is good, if nothing special. Central Dublin is a 10-minute tram ride or a 25-minute walk. ***Tip:*** Stroll through Croppies Acre Memorial Park, opposite the hotel, to see the bronze statue of Anna Livia, a character in James Joyce's *Finnegans Wake.* She appears to float in a pool of water—thus earning her the nickname "the Floozie in the Jacuzzi." For more on the acerbic wit of Dublin statues' nicknames, see p. 99.

Parkgate St. ashlinghotel.ie. ✆ **01/677-2324.** 226 units. €119–€288 double. Lower rates do not include breakfast. Dinner, bed-and-breakfast packages available. Parking €17.50/24 hr. **Amenities:** Restaurant; bar; Wi-Fi (free). Luas: Museum. Nearest bus stops: Parkgate St., Heuston Station.

Maldron Hotel Smithfield ♥ Part of a small Irish hotel chain, the Maldron Smithfield is a decent midprice option, a stone's throw from the Old Jameson Distillery. Guest rooms are modern and comfortable, and windows are soundproofed. Go for an upper-floor room with a balcony; the view across the low-slung skyline of Dublin's north side is lovely, particularly at sunset. The on-site restaurant and bar have fairly limited offerings, but several bars and restaurants are right outside, around Smithfield Square. Alternatively, the front desk can order you a pizza from a local delivery company (there's a menu in your room; pay in cash). While you're here, you should definitely visit the **Cobblestone** (p. 173), probably the best pub in Dublin for live traditional music, and less than 30 seconds from the hotel front door.

Smithfield Terrace. maldronhotelsmithfield.com. ✆ **01/485-0900.** 92 units. €133–€409 double. Breakfast included. Parking €18/24 hr. at adjoining lot. **Amenities:** Restaurant; bar; Wi-Fi (free). Luas: Smithfield. Nearest bus stops: Church St., Arran Quay, Stoneybatter.

Ballsbridge & the Southern Suburbs

South of the canal, this pricey Dublin residential neighborhood is coveted for its leafy streets and historic buildings. Half the foreign embassies in

Dublin are located out here. It's an upscale hotel quarter in part because of its trees, park, and usually peaceful streets (it can get busy on match or concert days at the Aviva or RDS). It's about a 10-minute cab or DART train ride, a 20-minute bus ride, or 30-minute walk from the center, but most hotels have parking, and it's handy for exploring south of Dublin and if you're driving to County Wicklow for the day. It's also on the Aircoach bus route from Dublin Airport.

EXPENSIVE

InterContinental Dublin ♥♥♥ Come here for the ultimate in five-star treatment and service and a retreat away from the buzz of the city center. It may look modern from the outside, but the InterContinental has been outfitted in a traditional style (plush carpets, elegant lamps, and chandeliers) more redolent of a historic hotel than its brick-and-glass exterior would suggest. Guest rooms are spacious, peaceful, and bright, some with views to Dublin Bay, and bathrooms are large with deep bathtubs. The hotel has a full-service spa, pool, a decent gym, and a host of thoughtful touches. For dining, **Seasons** restaurant is the more formal option; there's also the **Garden Terrace** and **Lobby Lounge,** a lovely place for afternoon tea (often with live piano), plus a well-stocked **Whiskey Bar.**

Simmonscourt Rd., Ballsbridge. intercontinentaldublin.ie. ✆ **01/665-4000.** 207 units. €334–€439 double; €634–€3,584 suite. Check website for special offers. Parking €20/night, valet parking €30. **Amenities:** Restaurant; bar; spa; pool; gym; Wi-Fi (free). DART: Sandymount. Nearest bus stops: RDS, Merrion Rd.

MODERATE

Aberdeen Lodge ♥♥ Drive up to this elegant Regency building in the springtime, and its front is so covered in ivy it looks like a vertical lawn. Inside, the decor is endearingly old-fashioned. Neat-as-a-pin public spaces are outfitted in heavy, antique-style furnishings and embroidered pillows scattered hither and thither. Guest rooms are comfortable and quiet, if a little plain, but bathrooms are modern. Some have views of the large garden, where guests can have tea—often in the company of the hotel's friendly cat or two golden retrievers. It's a short walk to Sandymount Village, Sandymount Beach, and the nearest DART station.

53–55 Park Ave., Ballsbridge. aberdeen-lodge.com. ✆ **01/283-8155.** 16 units. €214–€354 double. 3-night min. stay for some dates. Breakfast included. Free parking. **Amenities:** Restaurant; bar; use of nearby spa; Wi-Fi (free). DART: Sydney Parade. Nearest bus stops: St. John's Rd., Park Ave.

Ariel House ♥♥ This charming Ballsbridge guesthouse has won legions of fans over the years, and rightly so—it's a smoothly run, value-for-the-money operation on a quiet Victorian street. Ariel House is just a block from Aviva Stadium, one of Ireland's major sports grounds. Inside, the vibe is decidedly old-school. Simple guest rooms are tastefully decorated; the pleasant lounge has an honesty bar and piano (guests are free to tickle the ivories). Breakfasts offer good-size portions and plentiful options, and afternoon tea is served. The neighborhood is quiet enough to make you feel tucked away from the crowds (as long as it isn't match day or concert day at the Aviva, of course), with good links to central Dublin.

50–54 Lansdowne Rd., Ballsbridge. arielhouse.ie. ✆ **01/668-5512.** 37 units. €174–€344 double. Breakfast not included in lower rates. Free parking. **Amenities:** Honesty bar; room service; Wi-Fi (free). DART: Lansdowne Rd. Nearest bus stop: Merrion Rd.

The Devlin ♥♥ This on-trend small hotel is worth making the commute to Ranelagh. The quiet guest rooms are tiny but perfectly formed, with beds custom-made to fit the space, done up in crisp cotton sheets and firm mattresses. Everything is thought of—Smeg mini fridges hold drinks and nibbles, and shelves are stocked with power cables, USB adaptors, Dyson hair dryers, pod coffeemakers, even guitars in some cases. Bathrooms are tiny but modern, and the showers are good. Throughout, the decor is soothing, smoky grays and blues, with exposed brick and reclaimed oak touches. On the top floor, trendy **Layla's** restaurant offers drinks and French-influenced food with views of the rooftops. Get a pint and a burger in the **Americana Bar** on the ground floor, or grab coffee and a muffin from the **DIME** coffee hatch downstairs. The hotel even has its own 44-seater **Stella Cinema** with a good variety of listings. The Luas tram stops around the corner, sweeping you to the city center in 10 minutes.

117–119 Ranelagh. thedevlin.ie. ✆ **01/406-6550.** 40 units. €190–€400 double. On-street parking €2/hr.–€3.50/hr. (price varies per street). **Amenities:** Restaurant; bar; coffee shop; Wi-Fi (free). Luas: Ranelagh. Nearest bus stop: Ranelagh Rd.

WHERE TO EAT IN DUBLIN

If there's one thing we can say for certain, it's that there is no shortage of places to eat in Dublin. You can find any kind of cuisine, at just about any price. We've picked our favorites here and tried to include the best restaurants from all areas of the city. In addition to those listed below, we also love the smaller places that line the streets. **Bread 41** (41 Pearse St.; bread41.ie; no phone) is the place to come for the city's best organic sourdough and pastries—it's so popular, there's often a queue. If you're looking for breakfast in Temple Bar, **Stage Door Café** (11 Essex St. E.) is the place. Sit in the sunshine at an outdoor table and try the creamy scrambled eggs, savory omelets, and good coffee. Another great coffee shop near St. Stephen's Green is the super-trendy **Network Café** (39 Aungier St.; networkcafe.ie; no phone), which makes tasty takeouts like sourdough toast with kale, fried egg, Thai peanut sauce, and ginger; or a soda *farl* (thin pan-fried soda bread) with chorizo, hummus, fried egg, pepper, chili, and za'atar.

Temple Bar

MODERATE

The Bank on College Green ♥♥ PUB Built as a bank in 1895, at the height of Victorian opulence, this has to be one of the most handsome interiors in all of Dublin. Several remnants of the original were preserved when it was converted into a pub (including the old-style safes that you can still see downstairs). In the hour after local offices close, you'd be lucky to walk in and snag a table right away, but waiting for a table at least gives you an opportunity to admire the beautiful architecture. Tucked away behind the bar are bronze busts of the seven signatories of the 1916 Proclamation of Independence. A small and fairly traditional lunch menu of burgers, fish and chips, sandwiches, and salads gives way to a more extensive selection in the evening. Come on Sundays for brunch or to sample a traditional roast.

20–22 College Green. bankoncollegegreen.com. ✆ **01/677-0677.** Entrees €19–€39. Breakfast Mon–Sat 10:30am–noon, Sun 11am–noon; lunch daily noon–4pm; dinner 4–10pm. Luas: Trinity. DART: Tara St. Nearest bus stops: College Green, Dame St., Westmoreland St.

Where to Eat in Dublin

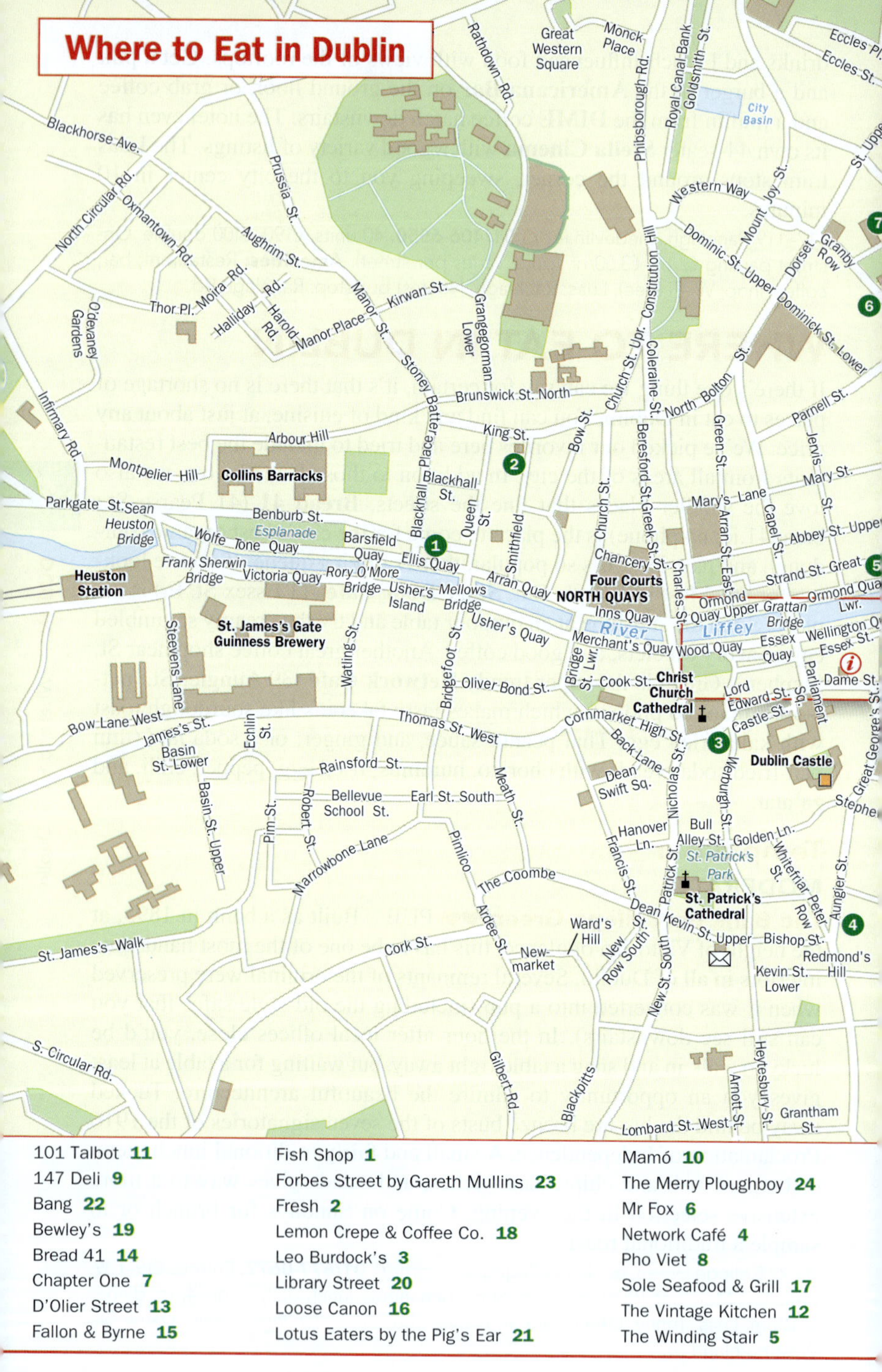

101 Talbot **11**
147 Deli **9**
Bang **22**
Bewley's **19**
Bread 41 **14**
Chapter One **7**
D'Olier Street **13**
Fallon & Byrne **15**
Fish Shop **1**
Forbes Street by Gareth Mullins **23**
Fresh **2**
Lemon Crepe & Coffee Co. **18**
Leo Burdock's **3**
Library Street **20**
Loose Canon **16**
Lotus Eaters by the Pig's Ear **21**
Mamó **10**
The Merry Ploughboy **24**
Mr Fox **6**
Network Café **4**
Pho Viet **8**
Sole Seafood & Grill **17**
The Vintage Kitchen **12**
The Winding Stair **5**

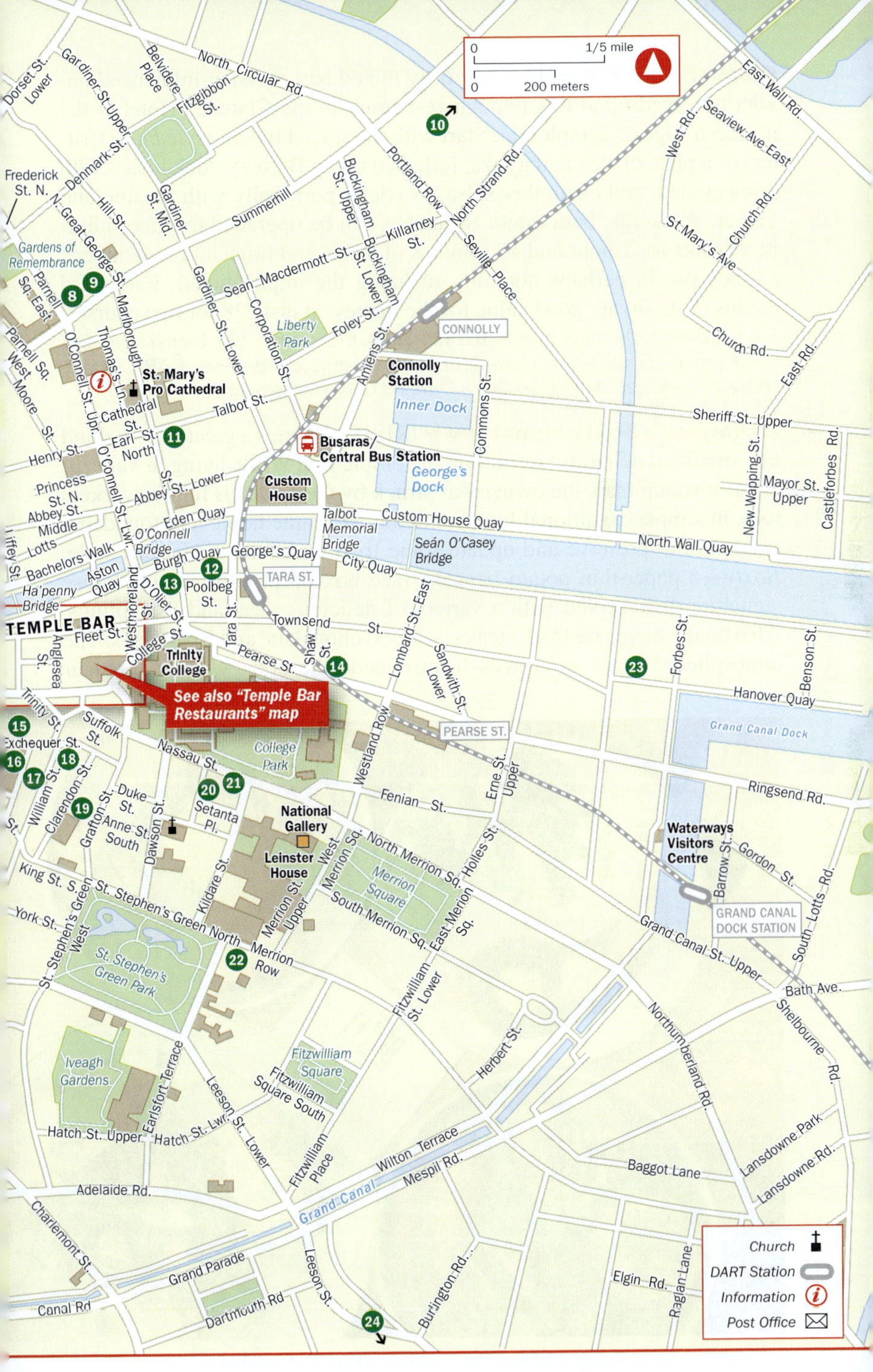

See also "Temple Bar Restaurants" map
Church
DART Station
Information
Post Office

Cleaver East ♥♥ ASIAN A tasty mixed bag of Asian-influenced flavors is served up at this popular restaurant in the Clarence Hotel at the northern edge of Temple Bar. Start with the spiced Indian-style *bhaji* (fritter) or a plate of steamed gyoza, followed up by Barbary duck breast with pomegranate and cucumber salsa, or sticky pork belly with sesame and ginger. Weekend "bottomless" brunches can be upgraded to offer unlimited drinks for 1 hour and 45 minutes (a "weekend brunch to remember," as they put it, perhaps not fully realizing the implications). Early-bird menus (5–6pm) are good value for the money, at just €28 for two courses. 6–8 E. Essex St. cleavereast.ie. ✆ **01/531-3500.** Entrees €23–€36. Dinner Wed–Sun 5–9:30pm. Brunch Sat–Sun 11am–4pm. Luas: Westmoreland, Jervis. DART: Tara St. Nearest bus stops: Wellington Quay, Ormond Quay, Parliament St.

Gallagher's Boxty House ♥♥♥ IRISH There's a great story behind this small but delightful restaurant in Temple Bar. While living in Venezuela as a young man, the owner was struck by the pride his fellow workers took in simple, traditional home cooking. He came home and founded a restaurant to preserve and update some Irish traditions in his own style. *Boxty*—a paper-thin potato pancake (see box on p. 146)—is the house signature dish, served with a variety of delicious meat and fish fillings. Also on the menu are thick steaks, seafood chowders, and Irish stews. The atmosphere buzzes as crowds form outside the door, waiting for their

In addition to boxty, Gallagher's Boxty House serves a range of Irish dishes.

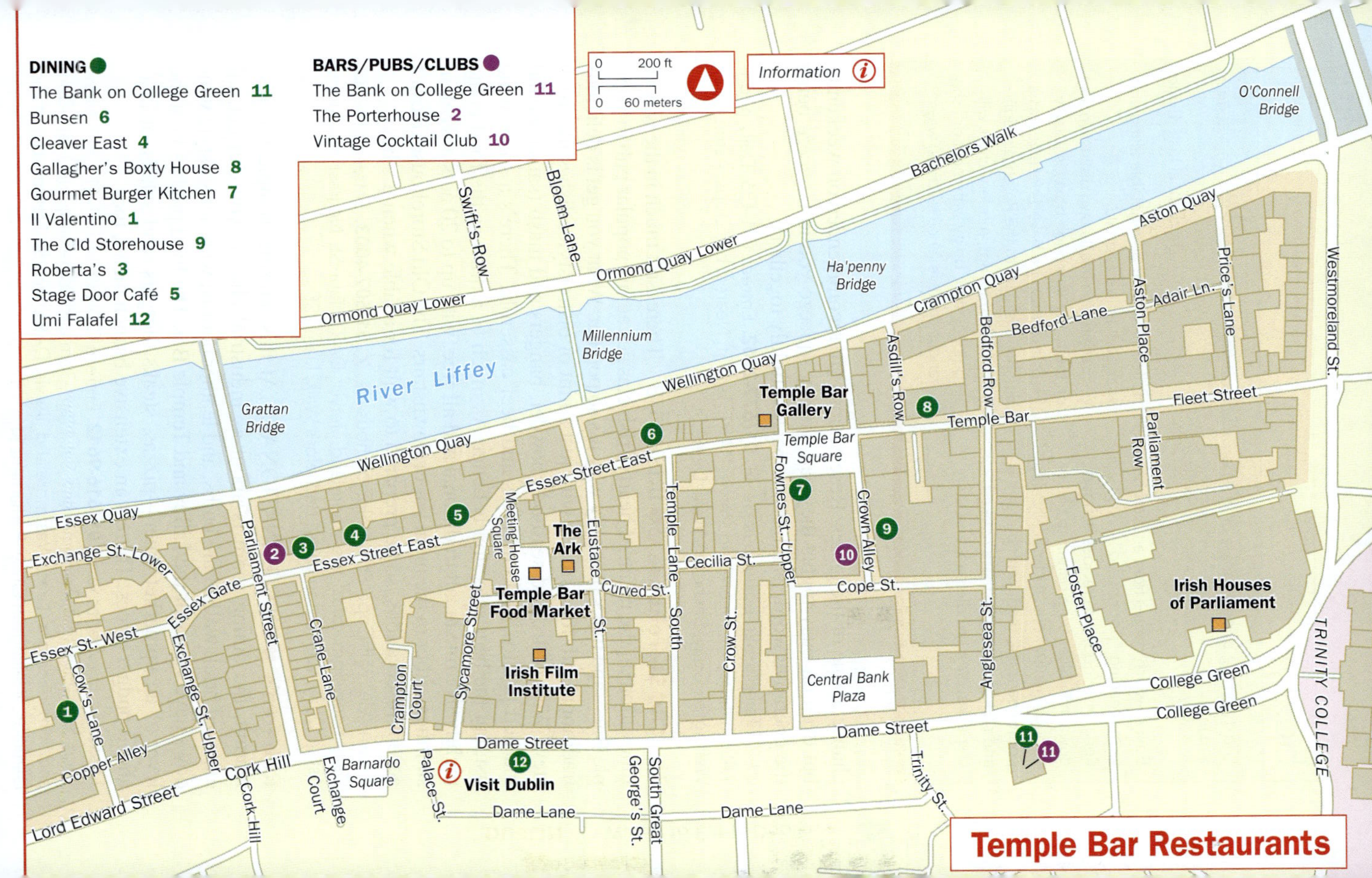

Temple Bar Restaurants
DINING
The Bank on College Green 11
Bunsen 6
Cleaver East 4
Gallagher's Boxty House 8
Gourmet Burger Kitchen 7
Il Valentino 1
The Old Storehouse 9
Roberta's 3
Stage Door Café 5
Umi Falafel 12
BARS/PUBS/CLUBS
The Bank on College Green 11
The Porterhouse 2
Vintage Cocktail Club 10
0 200 ft
0 60 meters
Information
River Liffey
O'Connell Bridge
Ha'penny Bridge
Millennium Bridge
Grattan Bridge
Bachelors Walk
Ormond Quay Lower
Swift's Row
Bloom Lane
Aston Quay
Crampton Quay
Wellington Quay
Essex Quay
Westmoreland St.
Price's Lane
Adair Ln.
Aston Place
Bedford Lane
Bedford Row
Asdill's Row
Fleet Street
Temple Bar
Parliament Row
Temple Bar Gallery
Temple Bar Square
Essex Street East
Fownes St. Upper
Crown Alley
Temple Lane South
Cecilia St.
Crow St.
Cope St.
Anglesea St.
Foster Place
Irish Houses of Parliament
Trinity College
College Green
Central Bank Plaza
Dame Street
Trinity St.
Dame Lane
South Great George's St.
Eustace St.
Curved St.
The Ark
Temple Bar Food Market
Irish Film Institute
Meeting House Square
Sycamore Street
Crampton Court
Palace St.
Visit Dublin
Barnardo Square
Exchange Court
Crane Lane
Parliament Street
Cork Hill
Exchange St. Lower
Exchange St. Upper
Essex Gate
Essex St. West
Cow's Lane
Copper Alley
Lord Edward Street

boxty

"Boxty on the griddle, boxty on the pan. If you can't bake boxty, sure you'll never get a man."

—Traditional Irish rhyme

Boxty—which comes from an old Irish term meaning "poor bread"—is a traditional Irish food, with recipes handed down in families from parent to child through generations. It's basically a thin potato pancake, made with buttermilk and sometimes eggs, that's cooked, crepelike, on a griddle pan, and then stuffed with meat or vegetable filling and wrapped up like a tortilla.

Each region has its own distinctive spin on the boxty. Although boxty is usually fried, it can also be baked or served as a dumpling (similar to the Polish pierogi). More often than not, modern chefs will accompany their boxty with meat or fish, in various creative (and delicious) ways.

chance at one of the tables. Reservations are recommended on weekends, but even on busy nights they can usually squeeze you in (*squeeze* being the operative word, as tables are packed tightly together).

20–21 Temple Bar. boxtyhouse.ie. ✆ **01/677-2762.** Entrees €24–€36. Daily noon–9:45pm. Luas: Westmoreland, Jervis. DART: Tara St. Nearest bus stops: Aston Quay, Wellington Quay, Bachelor's Walk, Dame St.

The Old Storehouse ♥♥ IRISH/PUB There isn't much in the way of innovation on the menu of hearty Irish classics at this popular pub in Temple Bar—and that's precisely why it's so popular. What you get is delicious traditional pub food mixed with just a hint of bistro style: dishes like Irish stew, West of Ireland seafood chowder, bangers and mash (sausages and mashed potato), and Guinness and beef casserole. There's a small wine list, but the beer selection is better. As much of a draw as the food is the nightly live music, all traditional and all free, with up to 20 acts a week in summer, either in the main bar or downstairs. The Old Storehouse doesn't accept reservations, so be prepared to wait for a table when it's busy.

Crown Alley, off Cope St. theoldstorehouse.ie. ✆ **01/607-4003.** Entrees €18–€36. Daily noon–9pm. Luas: Westmoreland, Jervis. DART: Tara St. Nearest bus stops: Aston Quay, Wellington Quay, Bachelor's Walk, Dame St.

Roberta's ♥♥ INTERNATIONAL At this buzzing Temple Bar restaurant, the dining room is about as industrial chic as you can get, all exposed brick walls, bare bulbs, and leather booths; warehouse-style windows have views of the Liffey and Temple Bar. The food pitches in at the level of an upmarket diner—pizzas, steaks, burgers, and salads, at just-above-budget prices. There's an extensive brunch menu, too.

1 Essex St. E. robertas.ie. ✆ **01/616-9612.** Entrees €22–€39; brunch €13–€19. Mon–Thurs 5pm–midnight; Fri 5pm–1am; Sat 11am–3pm and 5pm–1am; Sun 11am–3pm and 5pm–midnight. Luas: Westmoreland, Jervis. DART: Tara St. Nearest bus stops: Dame St., Wellington Quay, Parliament St.

INEXPENSIVE

Bunsen ♥♥ BURGERS This is one of the best places in Dublin for classic diner-style burgers. It's as stripped down as can be—choose from hamburger or cheeseburger, single or double, then pick a couple of toppings and what style of fries you want (hand-cut, shoestring, or sweet potato). And that's it. No veggie options are on the menu, though if you ask for a grilled cheese sandwich they'll happily fix you one. You can eat in the industrial-style dining room or get your slice of fast-food heaven to go. There are also branches at 36 Wexford St. (✆ **01/552-5408**), 3 S. Anne St. (✆ **01/652-1022**), 24 Baggot St. Upper (✆ **01/551-5833**), and 53 Dame St. (✆ **01/561-3853**).

22 Essex St. E. bunsen.ie. ✆ **01/559-9532.** Entrees €8.75–€11.75. Sun–Wed noon–9:30pm; Thurs–Sat noon–10:30pm. Luas: Westmoreland, Jervis. DART: Tara St. Nearest bus stops: Parliament St., Dame St., Wellington Quay.

Gourmet Burger Kitchen ♥ BURGERS There's something for everyone at this upscale minichain—get your burger classic and simple or opt for one of the more imaginative creations (such as the chicken, Camembert, and cranberry version, or the spicy Rocket Man, with habañero jam and paprika). Good veggie choices, too. Dessert options are a little limited, but the enormous shakes more than make up for that. Other Dublin branches are at 5 S. Anne St. (✆ **01/672-8559**) and 14 S. William St. (✆ **01/679-0537**).

Temple Bar Sq. gbk.ie. ✆ **01/670-8343.** Entrees €10.45–€16. Sun–Wed 11:50am–9:45pm; Thurs–Sat 11:45am–10:45pm. Luas: Westmoreland, Jervis. DART: Tara St. Nearest bus stops: Wellington Quay, Dame St., Parliament St.

Il Valentino ♥♥ CAFE This cheerful little cafe and artisan bakery in the heart of Temple Bar is perfect for a coffee and a diet-busting snack. Cakes and pastries are the specialty, and everything is made by hand on the premises. Try the almond croissant, raspberry or blueberry scones, or the pistachio eclair. It also serves breakfast and lunch, offering everything from breakfast brioches to tasty pizzas. There are two other branches, at 79 Mespil Rd., Ballsbridge (✆ **01/660-8114**), and 5 Gallery Quay, Grand Canal Dock (✆ **01/633-1100**).

Cow's Lane, Temple Bar. ilvalentino.ie. ✆ **01/633-4681.** Cakes and pastries €2–€7.15; sandwiches and pizza from €5.05. Daily 8am–6pm. Luas: Westmoreland, Jervis. DART: Tara St. Nearest bus stops: Parliament St., Dame St.

Umi Falafel ♥ MIDDLE EASTERN The mostly vegetarian menu at this cheap and cheerful place has something for everyone . . . as long as you like falafels. The spiced chickpea patties are freshly made and flash-fried, served up with plenty of creamy hummus and piled with cabbage, cucumber, radish, and other fresh vegetables. Salads are generously sized and inventive; the fattoush is our favorite—it features tomatoes, cucumber, parsley, dry mint, scallions, and lettuce, topped with toasted bread and pomegranate molasses. They also do a mean halloumi sandwich.

Takeout is available, or you can eat in the busy dining room. There are other branches in George's Street Arcade, Mary Street, Haddington Road, and Rathmines.

13 Dame St. umifalafel.ie. ✆ **01/670-6866.** Entrees €8.50–€14. Sun–Thurs noon–9pm; Fri–Sat noon–10pm. Luas: Trinity. DART: Tara St. Nearest bus stops: Dame St., College Green, Westmoreland St.

Trinity College Area

EXPENSIVE

D'Olier Street ♥♥♥ MODERN IRISH Chef James Moore worked around the world before opening D'Olier Street with two partners in December 2022. The restaurant sits in a bright, art-filled space in a landmark 19th-century building on the corner of D'Olier and Hawkins streets. The regularly changing 13-course menu takes local ingredients to the highest level of fine dining, with thoughtful artistic platings; it's divided into snack courses like quail Scotch egg with burger sauce and cornichon, fish courses like Kilmore Quay cod with basil and girolle, and meat courses like pork, gooseberry, cabbage, and gremolata, with desserts a divine sweet treat.

Chefs put the final touches on exquisitely plated dishes at D'Olier Street.

D'Olier Chambers, D'Olier St. dolierstreetrestaurant.com. ✆ **01/902-0720.** Tasting menu €128, 5-glass wine pairing add €88. Two dinner seatings 5–5:45pm and 8:15pm; lunch Fri noon–12:45pm. Luas: Westmoreland, Trinity. DART: Tara St. Nearest bus stops: D'Olier St., College St., Fleet St., Hawkins St.

Lotus Eaters by the Pig's Ear ♥♥ MODERN IRISH A deliciously inventive approach to traditional Irish tastes pervades at this super-cool restaurant overlooking Trinity College, which takes classic ingredients and adds an Asian influence. Oysters are offered with *nahm jim* and bonito sauce; grilled scallops come with satay and Thai basil; black cod gets a miso glaze. For extra flavor, you can add caviar, truffle, soy egg-yolk, duck liver, or bone marrow. There's also a three-course tasting menu (€60). Dishes are light and beautifully presented in an atmosphere of modern elegance. This is one of the city's most interesting restaurants.

4 Nassau St. lotuseaters.ie. ✆ **01/670-3865.** Entrees €18–€22. Tasting menu €60. Tues–Fri 5:30–9pm; Sat noon–2:30pm and 5:30–9pm. Luas: Dawson. DART: Pearse. Nearest bus stops: Nassau St., Kildare St., Merrion Sq.

The Vintage Kitchen ♥♥♥ IRISH Vintage artworks line the dining room of this stripped-down, funky little restaurant. (Everything's for sale, but there are no fixed prices, so just make an offer if you like something.) It's a small place with a limited number of tables, but you can see why people crowd in: The classic cooking is truly excellent, artfully presented in a contemporary style and generously proportioned. Start with the prawn risotto before sampling the 52° glazed filet of beef with beluga lentil, black onion-lime, *cavolo nero* (Tuscan kale), truffle-parmesan, and Cajun potato. There's a small wine and beer list. Make reservations for dinner.
7 Poolbeg St. thevintagekitchen.ie. ✆ **01/679-8705.** Lunch entrees €14–€24. 3-course dinner €65. Thurs–Sat noon–4pm; Mon–Sat 5:30–10pm. Luas: Trinity. DART: Tara St. Nearest bus stops: Hawkins St., Poolbeg St., D'Olier St., Westmoreland St., Pearse St.

Near Dublin Castle

MODERATE

Fallon & Byrne ♥♥ MODERN EUROPEAN A top-floor adjunct to the wonderful food and wine store **Fallon & Byrne Food Hall** (p. 163), this restaurant serves delicious seasonal Irish fare sourced from artisan producers. Nothing seems to have come very far: crab from the tiny port of Castletownbere, County Cork; lamb from Lough Erne; oysters from Carlingford. The menu manages a nice balance between ambitious dishes and more down-to-earth options. It also has vegetarian and vegan menus. And if you prefer to fend for yourself, an enormous selection of deli items is downstairs, available to go. There's also a small bistro menu available to enjoy over wine in the **Wine Cellar** (p. 170), in the basement.
11–17 Exchequer St. fallonandbyrne.com. ✆ **01/472-1010.** Entrees €26–€42. Mon–Thurs noon–9:30pm; Fri–Sat noon–10pm; Sun noon–8pm. Luas: Trinity. DART: Tara St. Nearest bus stops: S. Great Georges St., Dame St.

A seafood tower at Sole Seafood & Grill.

Sole Seafood & Grill ♥♥♥ SEAFOOD Connemara oysters, Dublin Bay prawns, West Cork mussels, Howth smoked salmon, shrimp, crab claws, clams, smoked mackerel: This cheerful seafood restaurant sources the best from the waters of Ireland and serves it all up in a lively space. There's a selection of oysters from different rocks along the coast, from Carlingford to Achill, plus three different types of caviar.

Presentation is immaculate—seafood towers are served either over crushed ice or steaming hot, and sole meunière is fileted at the table. There's also steak, chicken, and vegetarian options, and you can sit at the bar counter or at a standard table. An early-evening menu is €39 for two courses, €45 for three and is served from 5 to 6pm Monday to Friday and 1 to 5pm Saturday and Sunday.

18–19 S. William St. sole.ie. ✆ **01/544-2300.** Entrees €29–€60. Mon–Fri 5–10pm; Sat–Sun 1–10pm. Luas: St. Stephen's Green. DART: Pearse, Tara St. Nearest bus stops: S. Great Georges St., Dame St.

INEXPENSIVE

Leo Burdock's ♥♥ FISH & CHIPS Proof that not all good food experiences come with a hefty price tag, Leo Burdock's is probably the most famous fish and chip shop in Ireland. In fact, it's virtually *de rigueur* for passing celebrities to pop in; the photographic "wall of fame" includes Sandra Bullock, Russell Crowe, and Tom Cruise. But don't come expecting cutting-edge cuisine, because Leo Burdock's still trades on the same simple, winning formula it has used since 1913: battered fresh fish (cod, lemon sole, haddock, or ray) and thick chips (like very fat steak fries), all cooked the old-fashioned way, in beef drippings.

2 Werburgh St. leoburdock.com. ✆ **01/454-0306.** Fish and chips €15. Daily noon–11pm. Luas: Trinity. DART: Tara St. Nearest bus stops: Lord Edward St., High St., Patrick St.

Leo Burdock's fish-and-chips shop.

O'Connell Street/North of the Liffey

EXPENSIVE

Chapter One ♥♥♥ MODERN IRISH One of the city's most feted restaurants, with two Michelin stars, Chapter One delivers prix-fixe dining that uses innovative techniques and organic ingredients. Feast on gourmet dishes that fuse diverse parts, such as ravioli of Coolea cheese with pumpkin and black truffle, wild mallard with blackberry sauce, or game terrine with pickled cherry and brioche. Book the chef's table, located in the kitchen, if you want the full experience. The wine list is excellent, but you can also order a wine pairing or ask the advice of the excellent sommelier.

19 Parnell Sq. N. chapteronerestaurant.com. ✆ **01/873-2266.** 3-course lunch menu €85, 4-course dinner menu €160, 7-course tasting menu €190. Tues–Wed 6:30–9:30pm; Thurs–Sat noon–2pm and 6:30–9:30pm. Luas: Abbey St., O'Connell St. DART: Connolly. Nearest bus stops: Parnell Sq., Dorset St., O'Connell St.

Mr Fox ♥♥♥ IRISH/FRENCH Just across the square from Chapter One and likewise situated in the basement of a Georgian building, Mr Fox is another of the city's best restaurants. Here you'll find creative Irish cuisine with a French influence. Expect dishes like parmesan fondue with olive tapenade and cep butter; halibut with green curry, mussels, squash, and wild rice; and a potato tartlet with beef tartare and chipotle. The menu is short (officially five courses), but because some courses have three or four elements, you actually get 12 different dishes. The offerings are seasonal, and the menu changes every couple of months. The wine list is extensive, and a wine pairing (five wines, €70 per person) changes regularly to match the menu. There's also a vegetarian menu.

38 Parnell Sq. W. mrfox.ie. ✆ **01/874-7778.** 5-course set menu €93. Wed–Sat 5–9pm. Luas: O'Connell St. DART: Connolly. Nearest bus stops: Parnell Sq., Dorset St., O'Connell St.

The Winding Stair ♥♥ MODERN IRISH A sweet, old bookstore downstairs and a chic restaurant upstairs, the Winding Stair is just a stone's throw from the Ha'penny Bridge. The views of the Liffey are romantic, but it's the inventive modern Irish cooking that pulls in the crowds for lunch and dinner. After a starter of bleu cheese fritters with grilled pear, you could opt for a tranche of local Dunmore cod with crumbed mussels, or sea trout with trout caviar and pickled cucumber. Desserts are seductive here—you won't want to resist. The enormous wine list (we counted some 177 options on our last visit), helpfully arranged by character rather than region (for example, daring, robust, and bold reds; or fine, aged, and austere reds), features several decently priced options.

The chic and inventive Winding Stair, located above a vintage bookstore.

40 Lower Ormond Quay. winding-stair.com. ✆ **01/872-7320.** Entrees €27–€42. Mon–Tues 5–9:15pm; Wed–Sun noon–9;45pm. Luas: Jervis. DART: Tara St. Nearest bus stops: Ormond Quay, Bachelor's Walk, Wellington Quay.

MODERATE

101 Talbot ♥♥ IRISH/INTERNATIONAL This cheery and informal spot, a 3-minute walk from the General Post Office on O'Connell Street, is strong on delicious Irish cuisine with global influences and a healthy twist. The bright, airy dining room is lined with modern art. Specials may include roast cod with parmesan herb crust, or game pie with *champ* (mashed potato with scallion) and red wine sauce. The early-bird menu (two courses €29.95; 5–6:30pm) is a particularly good deal and popular with pre-theater diners attending the Abbey Theatre just around the corner.
101–102 Talbot St. 101talbot.ie. ✆ **01/874-5011.** Entrees €22–€31. Tues–Sat 5–11pm. Luas: Abbey St. DART: Connolly. Nearest bus stop: O'Connell St.

Pho Viet ♥♥ VIETNAMESE This bright and cheerful eatery is very popular with Dubliners, and it's easy to see why. It packs in the flavor in every single dish. From the crispy spring rolls to the big, steaming bowls of titular *pho* (a spicy meat and noodle soup), everything is memorable. Try the *pho dac biet* with beef (a mix of steak, brisket, and beef meatballs), and rice noodles plus sides of lemon, fresh chili, hoisin sauce and sriracha sauce for spice. Or stick to the traditional *pho ga*—chicken soup with rice noodles and fresh herbs. The atmosphere is lively, and the service quick and efficient. ***Tip:*** The lemon iced tea is the most refreshing option on the drinks list.
162 Parnell St. phokim.ie. ✆ **01/878-3165.** Entrees €15–€19. Sun–Thurs noon–10pm; Fri–Sat noon–11pm. Luas: Abbey St., Parnell St. DART: Connolly. Nearest bus stops: Parnell Sq., Dorset St.

INEXPENSIVE

147 Deli ♥♥ DELI Widely viewed as among the best sandwich makers in the city, the team at 147 pride themselves on piling it high and making it fresh. This small place just off O'Connell Street might not look like much from the outside, but sandwich magic is happening behind that counter. It has a few tables at the back where you can sit down with your pulled pork and slaw on sourdough bread or New York–style Reuben, among many others. There are also plentiful vegetarian options and outstanding coffee. Whatever way you go, you're likely to be happy. In the morning you can get poached eggs, fresh cinnamon buns, and breakfast sandwiches. If you're feeling rundown, try the mini-doughnuts—the sugar will save you.
147 Parnell St. Rotunda. 147deli.com. ✆ **01/872-8481.** Sandwiches €7–€14. Mon–Fri 9am–3pm; Sat 10am–3pm. Luas: Abbey St. DART: Connolly. Nearest bus stops: Parnell Sq., Dorset St.

Smithfield

MODERATE

Fish Shop ♥♥♥ IRISH This place is small, slightly out of the way, and has counter seating only, but it's worth a visit if you're in the

Smithfield area. The daily menu features the best locally caught fish, battered in beer and served with the finest wines (the amazing wine list alone is worth traveling for, with interesting categories like alpine wines, island wines, grower champagnes, and others). As well as fish such as hake, haddock, and lemon sole in batter, you might find oysters, cockles, and mussels on the menu, plus snacks like dressed crab on toast or squid with capers on toast.

76 Benburb St. fish-shop.ie. ✆ **01/5571-473.** Entrees €20–€35. Wed–Mon 12:30–2:30pm and 4–9:30pm. Luas: Smithfield, Museum. Nearest bus stops: Blackhall Place, Arran Quay.

INEXPENSIVE

Fresh ♥ INTERNATIONAL No, you haven't come to the wrong place—this *is* a supermarket. But step inside and you'll be met with a row of fresh cooking stations serving up delicious street food from around the world. The Mexican stand is popular, but for us the real standout is the incredible pan-Asian station, where a delicious pad Thai or crispy chili chicken can be whipped up in minutes, completely from scratch. Delicious, quality fast food doesn't come much fresher than this. Portion sizes are generous, and you can get a full meal, with nibbles on the side, for well under €20. There are a few tables, or you can get it all to go. It's a great option for lunch or an early, no-fuss dinner—but be aware that the food stations usually wind down by around 7pm. There are nine other branches around the city including the IFSC and Grand Canal Square.

Smithfield Sq. freshthegoodfoodmarket.ie. ✆ **01/5872-7587.** Hot food €5–€14. Mon–Fri 8am–10pm; Sat 9am–10pm; Sun 9am–9pm. Luas: Smithfield. Nearest bus stop: Arran Quay.

St. Stephen's Green/Grafton Street Area

EXPENSIVE

Bang ♥♥ MODERN IRISH The presence of so many Irish place names on the menu indicates how much this spot has embraced the Slow Food ethos. Many ingredients are regionally sourced from specialist Irish producers, with local flavors prevailing throughout. You may find Wicklow venison with charred parsnips and blackberries, chicken with black pudding and buckwheat, or a tasty filet of roasted halibut with cauliflower, fennel, and mussels. The wine list is expertly chosen, and there's a delightful seasonal cocktail menu—if it's on the menu when you're there, try the beehive julep, with spiced whiskey, Manuka honey, and black-walnut bitters.

11 Merrion Row. bangrestaurant.com. ✆ **01/400-4229.** Entrees €29–€43. Mon–Wed 5–9pm; Thurs–Fri 12:30–3pm and 5–9:30pm; Sat 1–3pm and 5–9:30pm. Luas: St. Stephen's Green. DART: Pearse. Nearest bus stops: St. Stephen's Green, Baggot St., Merrion Sq.

Library Street is known for its big flavors, as in this savory venison and endive dish, designed for sharing.

Library Street ♥♥♥ IRISH This is a small but buzzing space, with a big range of flavors. Chef patron Kevin Burke has designed the menu around four courses, but everything is meant to be shared. The menu changes with the seasons, but expect small snack plates like line-caught mackerel with tomato, or marinated peppers with salsa verde and kohlrabi, and larger mains like wild seabass with purple kale and bouillabaisse sauce, or salt-crusted venison with endive, pear, and beetroot. The service is great—the staff will talk through your choices to make sure they all work together, and there's a great wine list, too.
101 Setanta Place. librarystreet.ie. ✆ **01/617-0999.** Entrees €21–€38. Tues–Thurs 5–9pm; Fri–Sat 3–9pm. Luas: Dawson. DART: Pearse. Nearest bus stops: Nassau St., Dawson St., St. Stephen's Green.

MODERATE

Bewley's ♥♥ CAFE A Dublin landmark since 1927, Bewley's has a literary pedigree as well as a historic one: James Joyce was a regular (the cafe makes an appearance in his book *Dubliners*), and a host of subsequent literary greats made this their regular stop-off for a cup of tea and a bun or slice of cake. It's still hugely popular, and all the breads and cakes are made fresh each day on-site. ***Fun fact:*** The ornate faux-Egyptian facade (incongruously framing its never-really-used full name, "Bewley's

Oriental Café") is a relic of a European craze for all things ancient Egyptian, following the discovery of Tutankhamen's tomb just 5 years before the cafe opened.

78–79 Grafton St. bewleys.com. ✆ **01/672-7720.** Breakfast €10–€20; lunch entrees €13–€26. Mon–Fri 8:30am–5:30pm; Sat 8:30am–6pm; Sun 9am–6pm. Luas: Dawson. DART: Pearse. Nearest bus stops: Nassau St., Dame St.

INEXPENSIVE

Lemon Crepe & Coffee Co. ♥♥ CAFE This simple, straightforward eatery on South William Street serves fresh hot crepes, pancakes, eggs, and sandwiches, all made to order. Walk straight to the bar to order your Californian omelet, with guacamole and bacon, or the Power Crepe, filled with spinach, cheddar, and ham. The cafe serves both sweet crepes (with fillings like fruit, chocolate, and Nutella) and savory crepes (choose from cheese, meats, fish, or veggies), as well as a variety of sandwiches, waffles, and pancakes. If the weather's fine, sit out front and watch the world go by. It might not be the healthiest meal you have all day, but it will be delicious. The coffee is also excellent here, and the staff are friendly.

66 S. William St. lemonco.com. ✆ **01/672-9044.** Entrees €8.50–€12.50. Mon–Fri 8am–5pm; Sat 8:30am–6pm; Sun 9:30am–5pm. Luas: Dawson. DART: Pearse. Nearest bus stops: Dame St., College Green, St. Stephen's Green.

Loose Canon ♥♥♥ WINE BAR This tiny bodega-style wine bar does some of the city's best "toasties" (i.e., toasted or grilled cheese

Toastie to go from Loose Canon.

sandwiches), plus cheese and meat plates to accompany the wines. The list features some 10 to 12 wines by the glass and changes frequently, and the food menu is small, something like three different toasties plus a meat and cheese plate. But it's the flavor combos that get people talking: pairings like wild garlic and Cáis Dubh, Young Buck with sweet pepper, and Dunmore brie with plum chutney. Seating inside is extremely limited, but in fine weather sit outside for some people-watching or get your toastie to go and take it to St. Stephen's Green park.

29 Drury St. loosecanon.ie. ✆ **01/677-4215.** Entrees €9.75–€20. Mon–Tues 11am–10:30pm; Wed–Sat 11am–11:30pm; Sun 12:30–10:30pm. Luas: St Stephen's Green. DART: Pearse. Nearest bus stops: Dame St., College Green.

South Docklands

EXPENSIVE

Forbes Street by Gareth Mullins ♥♥♥ IRISH Forbes Street's chef Gareth Mullins brings together ingredients from the best Irish producers he can find, presenting them with creativity and craft. Two menu standouts are the incredible cuts of dry-aged beef from John Stone in County Longford and the fresh Flaggy Shore oysters from County Clare. You can choose dishes a la carte, small plates for sharing, or there's a pre-theater menu from 5 to 6.45pm Tuesday through Saturday (2 courses €39, 3 courses €45)—the Bord Gáis Energy Theatre is next door. The restaurant is based in the excellent **Anantara The Marker** hotel (p. 135), overlooking Grand Canal Dock.

Grand Canal Sq. forbesstreet.ie. ✆ **01/687-5104.** Entrees €23–€56. Tues–Sat 5–10pm. DART: Grand Canal Dock. Nearest bus stops: Pearse St., Cardiff Lane.

North of Dublin

EXPENSIVE

Mamó ♥♥♥ IRISH If you're taking a stroll in Howth, make sure to time it so that you can fall into this neighborhood bistro afterwards, whether it's for dinner, a quick bite at the counter, or a leisurely lunch on the terrace (weather permitting, of course). You might start with squash tart with pickled black trompette and Burgundy truffle, or cockles Portuguese, before tucking into the day's fish (fresh from the pier) with celeriac, razor clams, coco beans, and mussel mousse. An excellent *cotes de boeuf* for two sharing comes with crispy potatoes and bearnaise. Howth (p. 125) is a seaside village about 16km (10 miles) northeast of the city center. The restaurant is a 5-minute walk from the Howth DART station, while a cab here from the city should run you about €35–€45. Definitely worth the splurge.

Harbour House, Harbour Rd., Howth. mamorestaurant.ie. ✆ **01/839-7096.** Entrees €32–€45. Set weekday lunch menu 2 courses €37, 3 courses €42. Thurs–Sat 12:30–3pm and 6–9:15pm; Sun–Mon 1–7pm. DART: Howth. Nearest bus stops: Howth Village.

South of Dublin

MODERATE

The Merry Ploughboy ♥ IRISH/PUB An exuberant live show of traditional music and dancing accompanies dinner at this hugely popular pub in Rathfarnham, one of Dublin's farther-flung southern suburbs. Admittedly it's all very touristy, but you certainly get your money's worth—the show lasts 2 hours, and the menu, while limited, is actually pretty good. The show runs from 8 to 10pm, so if you want to have dinner as well, plan to arrive around 6:30 to 7pm. Expect plates of beef braised in Guinness and served with roasted root vegetables, or scampi cooked in tempura batter, served with chips (thick fries). Or you could skip the show and just go for the bar menu served in other sections of the pub. The only real drawback is the time it takes to get here (Rathfarnham is about 6km/3¾ miles from the city center), although a dedicated minibus will deliver you there and back to the city for a bargain round-trip price of €12. Edmondstown Rd., Rockbrook, Rathfarnham. mpbpub.com. ✆ **01/493-1495.** Dinner and show €62, child €42. Show only adult €32, child €28. Separate bar menu €17.95–€32.50. Pub open daily 12:30–9:30pm (until 8pm Sun); show daily 8pm. Special bus from central Dublin (€12/person return; must be prebooked). Pickups are at Nassau St. at 6:10pm and the Shelbourne Hotel at 6:15pm.

SHOPPING

There's no question: Dublin is a fantastic city for shopping. Independent shops and boutiques line up alongside their chain-store rivals, and you can often find excellent craftsmanship in the form of handwoven wool blankets and clothes, high-quality crafts and antiques, and chic fashions from the seemingly limitless line of Dublin designers.

The hub of mainstream shopping south of the Liffey is indisputably **Grafton Street,** which is also a popular site for buskers and street performers, where you're almost guaranteed an impromptu show, rain or shine. Grafton Street is crowned by the city's most fashionable department store, Brown Thomas (known as BT's; see p. 161), and the jeweler Weir & Sons (p. 164), but much better shopping is on the smaller streets radiating out from Grafton Street, such as **Duke Street, Dawson Street, Nassau Street,** and **Wicklow Street,** where you'll find shops that specialize in books, handicrafts, jewelry, gifts, and clothing. For clothes, look for tiny **Cow's Lane,** off Lord Edward Street in Temple Bar—it's popular with those in the know for its excellent boutiques selling the works of local designers. Also in Grafton's penumbra are **South William Street, Castle Market,** and **Drury Street,** all of which have smart boutiques and irresistible tiny shops. On South William Street, check out the **Powerscourt Townhouse Centre,** a small, elegant shopping center in a grand Georgian town house (p. 160). Not far away, the **George's Street Arcade** is a marvelous clutter of bohemian jewelry, used books, vintage clothes, and other things appealing to the alternative crowd (it even has a resident fortuneteller).

HOURS Generally, Dublin shops are open 10am until 6pm Monday to Saturday and until 8 or 9pm on Thursday. Most shops have Sunday hours, although these vary; some open at 10am, but most are open 11am to 6pm.

SHOPPING MALLS Dublin has several clusters of shops in multistory malls or ground-level arcades, ideal for indoor shopping on rainy days. On the south side, there's the gleaming wrought-iron-and-glass **St. Stephen's Green Centre,** at the top of Grafton Street (stephensgreen.com; ✆ **01/478-0888**), and the **Powerscourt Townhouse Centre,** 59 William St. S. (powerscourtcentre.com; ✆ **01/679-4144**). On the Northside, these include the **ILAC Centre,** off Henry Street (ilac.ie; ✆ **01/828-8900**), and the **Jervis Shopping Centre** (jervis.ie; ✆ **01/878-1323**), at 125 Abbey St. In the southern suburbs, about 8km (5 miles) south of the city center, the large **Dundrum Town Centre** on Sandyford Road (dundrum.ie; ✆ **01/229-1700**) has several major fashion outlets and high-street chains.

Art & Antiques

Caxton ♥♥ Antique prints from the 16th, 17th, and 18th centuries are a specialty of this wonderful art store. (In 2012, someone even identified a lost Renaissance masterpiece among the stock.) The prices can be astronomical, but even if you're not buying, for lovers of the antiquarian browsing here is like being a kid in a candy store. 63 Patrick St. ✆ **01/453-0060.** Nearest bus stop: Patrick St.

Christy Bird ♥ VARIETY IS OUR SPECIALTY proclaims a sign at this appealing antique store, which has been in business since the 1940s. And it certainly lives up to the promise, stocked with a happy jumble of knickknacks, collectibles, tat, and genuine antiques. The joy is that you never quite know what you're going to find. 32 S. Richmond St. christybird.com. ✆ **01/475-4049.** Luas: Charlemont, Harcourt St. Nearest bus stop: South Richmond St.

Jam Art Factory ♥♥♥ This is a treasure trove of works from Irish artists, with prints and art plus jewelry, ceramics, textiles, and other

The colorful shopfront of Jam Art Factory.

design items to take home or as gifts. A second branch of the shop is at 64–65 Patrick St. 14A Crown Alley. jamartfactory.com. ✆ **01/616-5671.** Luas: Trinity. DART: Tara St. Nearest bus stops: Dame St., Wellington Quay.

The Doorway Gallery ♥♥♥ Both new and established Irish artists display their work at this cheerful art gallery. There's always something wonderful to discover, and many prices are affordable, too. 24 S. Frederick St. thedoorwaygallery.com. ✆ **01/764-5895.** Nearest bus stops: Nassau St., St. Stephen's Green.

Green on Red ♥♥ Outstanding contemporary art can be found at this little gallery in the Docklands, about a mile northwest of the city center. It holds a dozen or so exhibitions per year. Park Lane, Spencer Dock. greenonredgallery.com. ✆ **087/245-4282.** Luas: Spencer Dock. Rail: Docklands. Nearest bus stops: Sheriff St., Oxford Terrace.

Books & Stationery

Eason ♥ There are outlets of this popular book chain all over Ireland, but this multi-story shop on O'Connell Street is one of the country's oldest, having been in business since 1819. Pretty much everything you could want is here, from history and local-interest titles to the latest bestsellers. Dublin alone has 11 other Eason branches, including ones at Nassau Street and Heuston Station. 40 Lower O'Connell St. easons.com. ✆ **01/858-3800.** Luas: Abbey St. Nearest bus stops: O'Connell St.

Hodges Figgis ♥♥♥ Another enormous *grande dame* Dublin bookshop, this one's even older than Eason—they've been dealing in the printed page here since 1768. Now owned by the Waterstones chain, Hodges Figgis is one of the go-to places in the city for books of all kinds. 56–58 Dawson St. waterstones.com/bookshops/hodges-figgis. ✆ **01/677-4754.** Luas: Dawson. DART: Pearse. Nearest bus stops: Dawson St., Nassau St., Kildare St., St. Stephen's Green.

Ulysses Rare Books ♥♥ When lovers of Irish literature and antiquarian books die, if they've been good they get to spend eternity in this shop. Formerly called Cathach Books, it's where to come for rare copies of Joyce, Yeats, Wilde, Behan, Stoker, and just about every luminary of the Irish canon you can think of. Prices range from the barely affordable (€375 for a rare 1927 *Dracula* on our last visit) to the stratospheric (€35,000 for a first-edition *Ulysses*), but it's simply heaven to browse. 10 Duke St. (off Grafton St.). rarebooks.ie. ✆ **01/671-8676.** Luas: Dawson. DART: Pearse. Nearest bus stops: Dawson St., Nassau St., Kildare St., St. Stephen's Green.

Crafts, Design & Housewares

Avoca ♥♥♥ An Irish institution, Avoca is a wonderland of vivid colors, soft blankets, light woolen sweaters, food, and gifts, all in a delightful shopping environment spread over three floors near Trinity College. Avoca fabrics are woven in the Vale of Avoca in the Wicklow Mountains (p. 205). The store also sells pottery, jewelry, and adorable little things you really don't need, but can't live without. Hands down, this is one of the best stores in Dublin. The top-floor **cafe** is a great place for lunch. 11–13 Suffolk St. avoca.ie. ✆ **01/677-4215.** Luas: Dawson. DART: Pearse. Nearest bus stops: Nassau St., Dame St., College Green.

The Design Tower ♥♥ A cutting-edge convocation of hot designers and craftspeople work at this former sugar refinery at the Grand Canal Quay on the eastern side of the city. Occupants include Seamus Gill, who makes extraordinary, almost organic-seeming silverware; conceptual artist and fashion designer Roisin Gartland; and jewelry designer Brenda Haugh, whose work includes interesting modern interpretations of Celtic motifs. Some designers here have walk-in shops, but most prefer appointments, so call ahead if you want to see someone specific. The Design Tower is near the Grand Canal Dock DART station, or about a 20-minute walk from Grafton Street. Grand Canal Quay. thedesigntower.com. ✆ **01/677-5655.** DART: Grand Canal Dock. Nearest bus stops: Grand Canal St., Pearse St.

Irish Design Shop ♥♥♥ Featuring all Irish designers and crafts, the Irish Design Shop has a thoughtful selection of everything from knits and homewares to Irish-made skincare products and art. Look for tweed throws, hand-knitted Aran hats, and cozy wool socks. 41 Drury St. irishdesignshop.com. ✆ **01/679-8871.** Luas: Dawson. DART: Pearse. Nearest bus stops: S. Great Georges St., Dame St., St. Stephen's Green.

Kilkenny ♥♥♥ The city's largest design and craft shop, Kilkenny has been here since 1976, and at this stage it is an Irish institution. You'll find a super selection of Irish designers with everything from pottery sets and ranges of crystal to clothing, jewelry, art, and all sorts of unique finds. You could easily lose a couple of hours in here, and it's a fantastic place for gifts or some Irish memento of your trip. For a post-shopping treat, a cafe on the first floor serves home-style Irish cooking and great desserts. 6 Nassau St. kilkennyshop.com. ✆ **01/677-7066.** Luas: Dawson. DART: Pearse. Nearest bus stops: Nassau St., Kildare St., Dawson St.

Powerscourt Townhouse Centre ♥♥ In a restored 1774 town house, this four-story complex consists of a central sky-lit courtyard and more than 60 boutiques, craft shops, art galleries, snack bars, wine bars, and restaurants. The wares include all kinds of crafts, antiques, paintings, prints, ceramics, leatherwork, jewelry, clothing, chocolates, and farmhouse cheeses. You can also book a behind-the-scenes tour to learn more about the house's history, where you'll poke around the old kitchen and cellars, the former Lord and Lady's bedrooms and dressing rooms, the music room, ballroom, and dining room. 59 S. William St. powerscourtcentre.ie. ✆ **01/679-4144.** Luas: St. Stephen's Green. DART: Pearse. Nearest bus stops: St. Stephen's Green, Dame St.

Department Stores

Arnotts ♥♥ Ireland's original department store, Arnotts first opened its illustrious doors in 1843. Its selection of womenswear, menswear, gifts, and beauty products is enormous. Arnotts stays open for late shopping until 9pm on Thursdays and 8pm on Fridays. Henry St. arnotts.ie. ✆ **01/805-0400.** Luas: Abbey St. DART: Connolly. Nearest bus stop: O'Connell St.

Brown Thomas ♥♥♥ The top-hatted doorman out front sets the tone for this great old Dublin institution filled with designer clothes and accessories. We've always found this a relaxed and friendly place, even if the credit card takes a bit of a beating. Stop by for most of the major fashion labels before getting your nails done, having a one-to-one at the cosmetics counters, or indulging at the bar and cafe or the elegant restaurant. 88–95 Grafton St. brownthomas.com. ✆ **01/605-6666.** Luas: Dawson, St. Stephen's Green. DART: Pearse. Nearest bus stops: Nassau St., Dawson St., St. Stephen's Green.

Fashion & Clothing

Costelloe & Costelloe ♥♥ This sweet clothing and accessories store sells a great range of handbags, pashminas, shrugs, and—delightfully—colorful fascinators and headpieces. Best of all, prices are quite reasonable. 14A Chatham St. costelloeandcostelloe.com. ✆ **01/671-4209.** Luas: Dawson, St. Stephen's Green. DART: Pearse. Nearest bus stops: St. Stephen's Green, S. Great Georges St.

Indigo & Cloth ♥♥ This trendy Temple Bar store started out selling men's clothing and now also sells lifestyle goods and some womenswear. For a break from browsing, the specialty cafe on the ground floor has some interesting brews. 9 East Essex St., Temple Bar. indigoandcloth.com. ✆ **01/670-6403.** Luas: Westmoreland. DART: Tara St., Pearse. Nearest bus stops: Dame St., College Green.

Kevin & Howlin ♥♥ There's nothing cutting-edge whatsoever about this place—and that's just why people like it. Dublin's go-to store for Donegal tweed, it's been selling handwoven jackets, coats, hats, and other traditional Irish countrywear since 1936. 31 Nassau St. kevinandhowlin.com. ✆ **01/633-4576.** Luas: Dawson, St. Stephen's Green. DART: Pearse. Nearest bus stop: Nassau St.

Louise Kennedy ♥♥♥ Undoubtedly one of the biggest names in contemporary Irish fashion—so respected that she was put on a postage stamp a few years ago—Louise Kennedy has dressed everyone from heads of state to Hollywood superstars. Her boutique in Merrion Square showcases the best of her current collection. Among the items she's famous for is the gorgeous "Kennedy bag," a limited-edition handbag that is a must-have among the Irish *glitterati*—yours for a mere €1,500. 56 Merrion Sq. louisekennedy.com. ✆ **01/662-0056.** DART: Pearse. Nearest bus stops: Merrion Square, Baggot St.

Om Diva ♥♥♥ Proof that not every designer emporium has to be the kind of place where they check your credit rating at the door, Om Diva is a delightful, cheery shop, with a great selection of designer women's fashion, handmade jewelry, vintage clothes, and accessories. One of Dublin's real finds. 27 Drury St. omdivaboutique.com. ✆ **01/679-1211.** Luas: Dawson, St. Stephen's Green. DART: Pearse. Nearest bus stops: Nassau St., S. Great Georges St.

Stable ♥♥ This small shop is filled with the best in contemporary Irish designs with luxurious wool and linen clothing, scarves, housewares, and accessories sourced from weavers, knitters, and other artisan producers around Ireland. 2 Westbury Mall, Balfe St. stable.ie. ✆ **01/675-3936.** Luas: Dawson, St. Stephen's Green. DART: Pearse. Nearest bus stops: Nassau St., S. Great George's St.

Quality Irish-designed wool and linen products at Stable.

Gourmet Food

Butlers Chocolate Café ♥♥ These chocolatiers now sell their delicious wares all over the world, but the business is still family-owned and -run. Their **Chocolate Cafés** are all over Dublin, including Grafton Street, Henry Street, and the airport, but the one on Wicklow Street is the flagship. In addition to an enormous selection of gourmet chocolates, it sells cakes, cookies, flapjacks—and a mean cup of joe. The hot chocolate is spectacular; try the white chocolate version for the purest hit of sweet choccy joy. True addicts can take a tour of the Butlers factory, just north of Dublin. 24 Wicklow St. butlerschocolates.com. ✆ **01/671-0591.** Luas: Dawson, St. Stephen's Green. DART: Pearse. Nearest bus stops: Nassau St., S. Great George's St.

Fallon & Byrne Food Hall ♥♥♥ This exceptional artisan food and wine store is like a high-end deli crossed with an old-fashioned grocer's—albeit a posh modern version. Produce is laid out in open crates, and shelves are stocked with epicurean treats of all kinds, including cheese, charcuterie, and a great selection of wine. There's also an outstanding restaurant on the top floor (p. 149) and a wine bar in the basement (p. 170). 11–17 Exchequer St. fallonandbyrne.com. ✆ **01/472-1010.** Luas: Dawson, St. Stephen's Green. DART: Pearse. Nearest bus stops: Nassau St., S. Great George's St., Dame St.

A trove of local Irish cheeses at Sheridans Cheesemongers.

Sheridans Cheesemongers ♥♥♥ Serious cheese lovers need look no further than this wonderful cheesemonger on South Anne Street. The shop stocks around 100 different varieties of cheese—French, English, Italian, you name it—but traditional Irish varieties are a particular specialty. They also sell other deli items, such as wine and cold meats, and do sandwiches to go. 11 S. Anne St. sheridanscheesemongers.com. ✆ **01/679-3143.** Luas: Dawson. DART: Pearse. Nearest bus stops: Nassau St., Dawson St., St. Stephen's Green.

Jewelry

DESIGNyard ♥♥♥ Some of Ireland's leading designers of contemporary jewelry have creations for sale here. Prices tend to be quite high—the cheapest items are around €100 and rise to thousands—but you'll be walking away with something beautiful and unique. They carry an especially beautiful range of engagement rings. By appointment only; advance bookings required. 25 S. Frederick St. designyard.ie. ✆ **085/198-0999.** Luas: Dawson. DART: Pearse. Nearest bus stops: Nassau St., St. Stephen's Green.

Gollum's Precious ♥ Come here for classic vintage and designer jewelry—especially French—with a particularly good collection of contemporary pearl earrings, bracelets, and necklaces. Ground floor, Powerscourt Townhouse Centre. gollumsprecious.ie ✆ **01/670-5400.** Luas: St. Stephen's Green. DART: Pearse. Nearest bus stops: S. Great Georges St., Dame St.

Rhinestones ♥ This small but delightful jewelry store specializes in costume jewelry, contemporary and vintage. The antique pieces go back to the early Victorian age, but the mid-20th-century collection has a particular air of glamour. 18 St. Andrews St. facebook.com/rhinestonesjewellers. ✆ **01/679-0759.** Luas: Trinity. DART: Pearse. Nearest bus stops: College Green, Nassau St.

Weir & Sons ♥♥ Established in 1869, this is the granddaddy of Dublin's fine-jewelry shops. It sells new and antique jewelry, as well as silver, china, and crystal; the ground floor of the main branch on Grafton Street also has a section devoted to 17th-, 18th-, and 19th-century antique silver from Ireland and Britain. A second branch can be found in Dundrum, about 7km (4⅓ miles) south of the city center. 96–99 Grafton St. and 1–3 Wicklow St. weirandsons.ie. ✆ **01/677-9678.** Luas: Dawson. DART: Pearse. Nearest bus stops: Nassau St., College Green.

STEP away FROM THE LEPRECHAUN: THREE ALTERNATIVE DUBLIN SOUVENIRS

Sure, you can stop by any of the multitude of souvenir stores in Dublin for a keychain shaped like a shamrock, something with sheep on it, or a T-shirt with an "amusing" slogan. But unless your friends really *do* want slippers shaped like a pint of Guinness, you'll score better points back home with one of these more authentic mementos.

- **A pennywhistle.** At Waltons (Blanchardstown Centre; waltons.ie; ✆ **01/960-3232**), which has been in the music business since the 1920s, you'll find instruments both traditional and modern, ranging from an authentic *bodhrán* (drum) starting around €40, to an "absolute beginners" Dublin tin whistle set, complete with DVD tutorial and songbook, for around €15. They also deliver.
- **Flapjacks.** If you ask for a flapjack in Ireland, you won't get a pancake, but a sweet biscuit (cookie to North Americans) made from rolled oats, butter, brown sugar, and honey, often with fruit, nuts, or yogurt added. These traditional treats can be bought in boxes at food stores, or grab one in a coffee shop for a couple of euros. They stay fresh for a few days and are sturdy enough to survive the trip home.
- **Hedgerow jam.** Known for its soft-as-silk handwoven wool items, Avoca (p. 159) offers more than just lovely clothing. You can also pick up a jar of their traditional Irish breakfast marmalade or the delightfully named hedgerow jam—each an Avoca specialty costing €6.65. (Meanwhile, buy yourself a luxurious Avoca blanket, dyed with traditional methods in vibrant shades of blue, green, or pink—a relative bargain, given their quality, starting at around €99.)

TEMPLE BAR street markets

On weekends, chic Temple Bar shopping isn't only indoors—it spills outside into three of Dublin's finest street markets.

The most glamorous of the three is the **Designer Mart,** a showcase for fashion designers and craftspeople from all over Ireland, which takes place in Temple Bar Square every Saturday from 10am until 4pm. The more low-key **Book Market** also takes up residence in Temple Bar Square on Saturdays, 10am to 5pm; there's always some piece of printed treasure or other to be unearthed among its secondhand book stalls.

A must for foodies, the **Food Market** makes its presence felt most of all, as tempting aromas waft around Meeting House Square on Saturdays, 9:30am until 3:30pm. Should the weather take a turn for the worse, a fancy retractable roof will keep you dry while you deliberate over which Irish farmhouse cheese to take away, before waiting in line for a freshly cooked snack.

For details on the Temple Bar street markets, check out **lovetemplebar.com**.

Specialist

Forbidden Planet ♥ Geeks, assemble! This treasure trove of comics, books, DVDs, and other assorted memorabilia celebrates everything cult. The range of comics and graphic novels is enormous. 5–6 Crampton Quay. forbiddenplanet.co.uk. ✆ **01/671-0688.** Luas: Jervis. DART: Tara St. Nearest bus stops: Aston Quay, O'Connell St.

The R.A.G.E. ♥♥ Imagine the kind of shop where 1980s teenagers hung out in John Hughes movies, and you've got this place about right. It stands for Record Art Game Emporium, and everything here is vintage—plenty of classic vinyl (all of which can be sampled first). You can even play some of the old video games on an original arcade machine. 8 Crow St., Temple Bar. therage.ie. ✆ **089/495-2347.** Luas: Trinity. DART: Tara St. Nearest bus stops: Aston Quay, Dame St.

SPORTS & OUTDOOR PURSUITS

BEACHES Plenty of fine beaches are accessible by city bus or DART, which follows the coast from Howth, north of the city, to Bray, south of the city in County Wicklow. Heading north up the coast, popular beaches include **Dollymount,** 5km (3 miles) away; **Sutton,** 11km (6¾ miles) away; **Howth,** 15km (9⅓ miles) away; and **Portmarnock** and **Malahide,** each 11km (6¾ miles) away. The southern commuter town of **Dún Laoghaire** (pronounced Dun *Lear*-y), 11km (6¾ miles) away, makes a particularly good day trip. Not only does it offer a small swimming beach (at Sandycove) and watersports (there are four yacht clubs), but it also has cafes and restaurants, two long piers, and a bucolic park with a buzzing Sunday market. For more details, see visitdublin.com.

The rocky beach at Howth Head.

GOLF Dublin is one of the world's great golfing capitals, with a quarter of Ireland's courses—including five of the top 10—within an hour's drive of the city. Visitors are welcome, but phone ahead and make a reservation. The following four courses—two parkland and two links—are among the best 18-hole courses in the Dublin area.

Elm Park Golf & Sports Club ♥, Nutley Lane, Donnybrook (elmpark.ie; ✆ **01/269-3438**), is a beautifully manicured par-69 course in the mostly residential south side of Dublin, only 6km (3¾ miles) from the city center. Greens fees are €120.

The respected links course at **Portmarnock Golf Club ♥**, in Portmarnock (portmarnockgolfclub.ie; ✆ **01/846-2968**), lies about 16km (10 miles) from the city center on Dublin's Northside, on a spit of land between the Irish Sea and a tidal inlet. Opened in 1894, this par-72 championship course has over the years hosted many leading tournaments, including the Dunlop Masters (1959, 1965), Canada Cup (1960), Alcan (1970), St. Andrews Trophy (1968), and many an Irish Open. You won't be surprised, then, to discover that fees are a bit pricey. It is open from April to October, and greens fees are €405 for 18 holes, €510 for 27 holes, and €595 for 36 holes, all including lunch.

Often compared to Scotland's St. Andrews, the century-old **Royal Dublin Golf Club ♥**, Bull Island, Dollymount (theroyaldublingolfclub.com; ✆ **01/833-6346**), is a par-73 championship seaside links on an island in Dublin Bay, 4.8km (3 miles) northeast of the city center. Like Portmarnock, it has been rated among the world's top courses and has played host to several Irish Opens. The home base of Ireland's legendary champion Christy O'Connor, Sr., the Royal Dublin is well known for its fine bunkers, close lies, and subtle trappings. Greens fees are €220 Monday through Thursday and €250 Friday and Saturday (€165–€190 Nov–Mar). Before 8:20am, greens fees are €195 Monday through Thursday and €180 Friday and Saturday.

the birds of **BULL ISLAND**

With a wealth of estuaries, salt marshes, sandflats, and islands, Dublin Bay provides a varied habitat for a number of bird species, making it surprisingly rewarding for bird-watching expeditions. Your all-around best bet lies just north of Dublin city harbor, in the suburb of Clontarf: a bird sanctuary called **Bull Island,** also known as the North Bull Island.

Bull Island isn't an island at all, but a 3km (2-mile) spit of marshland and sand connected to the mainland by a bridge. It was inadvertently created early in the 19th century by Captain William Bligh, of *Mutiny on the Bounty* fame. As head of the Port and Docks Board, Bligh ordered the construction of a harbor wall at the mouth of the River Liffey, in an effort to stop the entrance to Dublin Port from silting up. In fairly short order the shifting sands created this small landmass, a unique beachscape of dunes, salt marsh, and extensive intertidal flats that attracts thousands of seabirds.

Hundreds of species have been recorded on Bull Island, and some 40,000 birds regularly shelter and nest. In winter, they are joined by tens of thousands of migrants from the Arctic Circle, along with North American spoonbills, little egrets, and sandpipers. Together, they all make a deafening racket. A visitor center is open daily from 10am to 4:30pm; admission is free.

St. Margaret's Golf & Country Club ♥, in St. Margaret's, North County Dublin (stmargaretsgolf.com; ✆ **01/864-0400**), is a stunning par-72 parkland course 4.8km (3 miles) west of Dublin Airport. Greens fees are around €50 Monday to Wednesday and €70 Friday through Sunday.

HORSEBACK RIDING For trail riding through Phoenix Park, **Ashtown Riding Stables** (ashtownstables.com; ✆ **01/838-3807**) is ideal. It's in the village of Ashtown, adjoining the park and only 10 minutes by car or bus from the city center. You can also get there by train from Dublin Connolly station in less than 15 minutes; Ashtown station is directly opposite the stables. One hour starts at €65.

WATERSPORTS Lessons and equipment rental for watersports like paddleboarding, kitesurfing, and wingsurfing are available at **Pure Magic,** Clontarf, Howth and Dun Laoghaire (puremagic.ie; ✆ **01/805-4912**). The center is beside 17 hectares (42 acres) of enclosed fresh water. For guided kayaking tours on the River Liffey, try **City Kayaking** (citykayaking.com).

SPECTATOR SPORTS

GAELIC GAMES If your schedule permits, try to get to a **Gaelic football** or **hurling** match—the only indigenously Irish games and two of the fastest-moving sports around. Gaelic football is vaguely a cross between soccer and American football; you can move the ball with either your hands or feet. **Hurling** is a lightning-speed game in which 30 men use heavy sticks to fling a hard leather ball called a *sliotar*—think field hockey meets lacrosse. The women's version is called *camogie.* These amateur sports are played every weekend throughout the summer. Every county has a team, and the games culminate in September with the **All-Ireland Finals,** like an Irish version of the Super Bowl. For schedules and admission fees, check with the **Gaelic Athletic Association,** Croke Park, Jones Road (gaa.ie; ✆ **01/819-2300**), or to learn more about the sports, take a stadium tour or visit the **GAA Museum** at Croke Park (p. 113).

GREYHOUND RACING Races are held throughout the year at **Shelbourne Park Greyhound Stadium,** South Lotts Road. Contact **Greyhound Racing Ireland** (grireland.ie; ✆ **061/448-000**).

HORSE RACING The closest racecourse to the city center is the **Leopardstown Race Course,** off the Stillorgan road (N11), Foxrock (leopardstown.com; ✆ **01/289-0500**). This modern facility with all-weather, glass-enclosed spectator stands is 9.7km (6 miles) south of the city center. Racing meets—mainly steeplechases, but also a few flats—are scheduled throughout the year, two or three times a month.

RUGBY & SOCCER The **Aviva Stadium,** 62 Lansdowne Rd. (avivastadium.ie; ✆ **01/238-2300**), is, depending on your perspective, either a gleaming modern monument to Irish sports or one of Dublin's biggest eyesores. Either way, you really can't miss it. This is the official home of both the national rugby and football (soccer) teams.

DUBLIN AFTER DARK

Nightlife in Dublin is a mix of traditional old pubs, where the likes of Joyce and Behan once imbibed and where Irish music is often reeling away, and cool modern bars, where the hottest new international sounds fill the air, and the crowd knows more about Dior than the Dubliners. There's little in the way of crossover, although you'll find a couple of quieter bars and a few with an alternative angle.

WHAT'S ON Aside from the eternal "old" pubs, things change rapidly in the world of Dublin nightlife, so go online for the latest event listings. Dublin's tourism website **visitdublin.com/whats-on** offers a daily guide to art, theater, music, sports, and whatever other entertainment you're up for. You can search by type of experience or view complete events listings by date. Other sites like **Dublin.ie** at dublin.ie/whats-on or **entertainment.ie/events** also provide a comprehensive listing of the week's entertainment possibilities.

TICKETS As with any big city, ticket prices for shows vary considerably, from around €15 or €20 to over €100. Advance bookings for most large concerts, major plays, and so forth can be booked directly on the event or venue website, or through **Ticketmaster Ireland** (ticketmaster.ie; ✆ **1800/653-8000.**

Arenas & Concert Venues

3Arena ♥ This enormous indoor arena (previously known as the **O2**) is the biggest venue in Dublin, and the fifth-best attended in the world at this writing. It's the go-to place for major international acts, standup comedy, and other big-ticket entertainment events—all top-of-the-bill stuff. North Wall Quay. 3arena.ie. Book on ticketmaster.ie. Inquiries: ✆ **01/819-8888.** Luas: The Point. DART: Connolly. Nearest bus stops: E. Wall Rd.

National Concert Hall ♥♥ If classical music is more your thing, this is the place to be. The program also covers opera, world music, jazz, show tunes, and musicals. Something is on virtually every night; check the website for full listings. Earlsfort Terrace. nch.ie. ✆ **01/417-0077.** Luas: Harcourt. DART: Pearse. Nearest bus stops: Earlsfort Terrace, St. Stephen's Green.

Vicar Street ♥♥ Located west of Dublin Castle in the Liberties, this much-loved venue is definitely not Dublin's largest—its capacity is roughly 1⁄14th that of the 3Arena (see above)—but it attracts consistently big names in music and standup comedy. 58–59 Thomas St. vicarstreet.ie. ✆ **01/775-5800.** Nearest bus stop: Thomas St.

Sampling a pint at 37 Dawson Street.

Bars

Dublin bars generally open at noon and may stay open as late as 2:30am, depending on the day of the week.

37 Dawson Street ♥♥ This sumptuous cocktail bar is crammed with antiques and curios—everything from a stuffed bull's head on a polished wood wall to old anatomical drawings and ornate vases. Its cocktail list is as extensive and imaginative as the quirky surroundings would suggest, and at the back of the building is a proper, old-style whiskey bar. There's also a good restaurant. 37 Dawson St. 37dawsonstreet.ie. ✆ **01/902-2908.** Luas: Dawson. DART: Pearse. Nearest bus stops: Dawson St., St. Stephen's Green, Nassau St.

Café en Seine ♥♥ At this elegant, 1920s-style cafe/bar, the interior is all terribly Gatsby, with hanging lamps, glass ceilings, faux-baroque furniture, and polished brass statuettes. The cocktail list is straight-up fun, the whiskey menu a page long, and the atmosphere appropriately decadent. They also serve a bistro menu until 9pm, and on Sundays there's a popular jazz brunch from noon to 5pm. 40 Dawson St. cafeenseine.ie. ✆ **01/677-4567** for bookings. Luas: St. Stephen's Green. Nearest bus stops: Dawson St., Nassau St.

Dakota ♥♥ Small but perfectly curated, this stylish bar on South William Street has a hip clientele and an outstanding selection of bottled beers and cocktails. The crowd is young and the atmosphere raucously sophisticated. 9 S. William St. dakotabar.ie. ✆ **01/672-7696.** Luas: St. Stephens's Green. DART: Tara St. Nearest bus stops: Dame St., College Green.

The Vintage Cocktail Club ♥♥♥ There's a definite speakeasy vibe to this Temple Bar cocktail lounge, starting with the super-discreet black door marked only with the initials VCC. Brilliantly—perhaps uniquely?—the cocktail menu is divided into eras, starting with those invented in the 1400s (who knew?) and going up to the 1940s, before leaping forward to the VCC's own decadent creations. It really feels as if you've joined a club, discovering this place—but sorry, kiddo, you have to be over 23. 15 Crown Alley. vintagecocktailclub.com. ✆ **01/675-3547.** Luas: St. Stephen's Green. Nearest bus stops: Wellington Quay, Dame St.

Wine Cellar ♥♥ In the basement at the wonderful Fallon & Byrne (p. 149) sits this equally wonderful wine bar. The concept is simple: Pick a bottle from the multitude on display in the candlelit cellar (with or without the advice of the waitstaff), pay €1 corkage Sunday to Tuesday, or €10 corkage Wednesday through Saturday, and enjoy. Of course, you can also order off the wine list, and there's a menu of bistro-style food. 11–17 Exchequer St. fallonandbyrne.com. ✆ **01/472-1010.** Luas: Dawson. DART: Pearse. Nearest bus stops: Dawson St., Nassau St., Dame St.

The Wool Shed ♥ Looking for somewhere to watch a big game? This is the place. Enormous TV screens flank the bar, showing whatever's hot in the sporting world—football (the European kind), rugby, U.S. sports (including football, the American kind), and whatever else is on the schedule. They also serve crowd-pleasing bar food. Parnell St. woolshedbaa.com. ✆ **01/872-4325.** Luas: Jervis. Nearest bus stops: Parnell Sq., O'Connell St.

Comedy Clubs

The International Bar & Comedy Cellar ♥♥ Hosted by the International Bar, the Comedy Cellar is one of the country's top comedy clubs, showcasing the best young pretenders in the world of Irish standup every

Wednesday night. Keep an eye on the website and the club's Facebook page to see who's on when you're in town. Tickets cost €12 to €15. The International, 23 Wicklow St. intercomedydublin.com/the-comedy-cellar. ✆ **01/677-9250.** Wed 9:30pm (doors open 9pm). Luas: Trinity. DART: Pearse, Tara St. Nearest bus stops: College Green, Dame St., Nassau St.

Laughter Lines ♥♥ What is it about Dublin on a Wednesday that everybody needs cheering up? Another midweek pub takeover, this one happens at the Duke on Duke Street, the last Wednesday night of every month at 8:30pm (show starts 9pm). The talented company improvises sketches according to whatever the audience suggests. It's chaotic and great fun. Tickets are €10 including a free pint of beer. The Duke, Duke St. facebook.com/LaughterLinesDublin. ✆ **083/097-9624.** Wed 8:30pm. €5. Luas: Dawson. DART: Pearse. Nearest bus stops: Dawson St., Nassau St., St. Stephen's Green.

Nightclubs

Admission to nightclubs varies, from free if you arrive early-ish to around €20 for the very fanciest places. Prices are usually higher on Friday and Saturday nights. Check club websites before going so you won't be surprised. Along with the clubs listed below, check out weekend events at the **Gaiety Theatre** (p. 175).

Panti Bar ♥♥ One of Dublin's most famous gay bars and clubs, this place is hugely popular and riotously good fun. Saturday night is cabaret night, often hosted by drag queen Panti Bliss herself, and on Sundays there's a "gay ole' tea dance" from 3pm. Panti's tireless campaigning for LGBTQ+ rights has recently made her quite a public figure; to watch her here, in her natural habitat, in full fabulous flow, is a thing to behold. 7–8 Capel St. pantibar.com. ✆ **01/874-0710.** Luas: Jervis, Four Courts. Nearest bus stops: Ormond Quay, O'Connell St.

Whelans ♥♥ With a pub at the front and live music stages to the rear, this is one of the city's best-loved music venues, and the fun keeps going after 11pm with club nights at Whelan's Upstairs. Monday to Thursday, you'll find silent discos with two different DJs; indie clubs take over on Fridays and Saturdays, showcasing local acts from different genres. You can buy tickets at the door; club admission is free if you attended a gig in the main live-music venue earlier in the night. 25 Wexford St. whelanslive.com. ✆ **01/478-0766.** Silent disco €5; Indie club €10. Luas: Harcourt, St. Stephen's Green. Nearest bus stops: Camden St., Kevin St.

Pubs

How could you go to Dublin and not stop by a pub or two? More than mere drinking dens, pubs are the secular temples of Ireland, a cultural

Dublin's oldest pub, the Brazen Head.

export that has conquered the world. The Irish didn't invent the pub, exactly, but many would say they perfected it. In *Ulysses,* James Joyce referred to the puzzle of trying to cross Dublin without passing a pub; his characters quickly abandoned the quest as impossible and stopped to have a few pints instead. You may want to look upon that as a challenge.

Pub hours generally begin as early as 10:30 or 11am (12:30pm on Sun) and last orders are at 11:30pm Monday to Thursday, 12:30am on Friday and Saturday, and 11pm on Sunday, after which you'll need to head to a nightclub if you crave more action.

The Bank on College Green ♥♥ This handsome place was built as a bank in 1892, at the height of Victorian opulence. While it's also an appealing place to eat (p. 141), you can enjoy its stunning interior just as well by simply grabbing a pint or a wee dram. 20 College Green. bankoncollegegreen.com. ✆ **01/677-0677.** Luas: Trinity. DART: Pearse. Nearest bus stops: College Green, Dame St., Westmoreland St.

The Brazen Head ♥♥♥ This is a serious contender for the coveted title of "oldest pub in Ireland," having served the locals continually since at least 1661 (although an alehouse was reputedly on the same spot for hundreds of years before that—they claim 1198 as the foundation date, and who's to argue?). It was once a hangout for Irish revolutionaries, and Joyce mentioned the place in *Ulysses,* although today it's more famous for lively traditional music sessions. Every night features a different act; worthies who've played here include Van Morrison, Tom Jones, and Garth Brooks. 20 Lower Bridge St. brazenhead.com. ✆ **01/679-5186.** Luas: Smithfield. Nearest bus stops: Merchant's Quay, High St.

The Cobblestone ♥♥♥ We recently asked a Dublin taxi driver to recommend the best place for live music in Temple Bar. Answer: "Now why would you bother, when the Cobblestone is so close?" This is an authentic musician's place, as much a traditional music venue as a pub, such is the standard of the music. Free sessions are in the front bar nightly, with ticketed acts in the **Backroom,** a dedicated performance space. The pub is on the Northside, 5 minutes' walk from the Old Jameson Distillery (p. 109). 77 N. King St., Smithfield. cobblestonepub.ie. ✆ **01/872-1799.** Luas: Smithfield. Nearest bus stop: Church St.

Davy Byrnes ♥♥ "He entered Davy Byrnes," wrote Joyce of Leopold Bloom, the hero of *Ulysses.* "Moral pub. He doesn't chat. Stands a drink now and then. But in a leap year once in four. Cashed a cheque for me once." Given its impeccable literary connections, it's no surprise that many writers make this pub a pilgrimage spot when they're in town. Joyce himself was a regular, although the food has improved since his day—the menu of pub classics and sandwiches is actually pretty good, and reasonably priced. *Ulysses* fans will be delighted to hear that you can still order a gorgonzola sandwich, Bloom's snack of choice. 21 Duke St., off Grafton St. davybyrnes.com. ✆ **01/677-5217.** Luas: Dawson. DART: Pearse. Nearest bus stops: Dawson St., Nassau St.

Doheny and Nesbitt ♥♥♥ From the outside, this pub brings to mind a Victorian medicine cabinet, all polished wood with a rich blue-and-gold sign. Its proximity to the political heart of the capital makes it a perennial hangout for politicos, lawyers, economists, and those who write about them—which can make for some spectacularly good eavesdropping. (Its name inspired a catchphrase, "the Doheny and Nesbitt School of Economics," to describe the movers and shakers who used to shoot the breeze here during Ireland's boom years of the 1990s and 2000s.) To admire its cozy interior, a midweek daytime visit is best—this place gets packed in the evenings (especially summer weekends), even more so when a big sports match is on. 5 Baggot St. Lower. dohenyandnesbitts.ie. ✆ **01/676-2945.** Luas: St. Stephen's Green. DART: Pearse. Nearest bus stops: St. Stephen's Green, Baggot St., Merrion Sq.

Grogan's Castle Lounge ♥♥♥ There's a friendly, chatty vibe at this satisfyingly old-fashioned place, considered one of Dublin's "quintessential" pubs. You'll find little modern about the dimly lit, atmospheric interior, save for the incongruous art collection on the walls (if you like a piece, ask—most of it is for sale). Grogan's reputation rests mostly on its eclectic clientele, ranging from grizzled old folks who've been coming here for years to hipsterish artsy types in search of a low-fi hangout. 15 S. William St. groganspub.ie. ✆ **01/677-9320.** Luas: Trinity, Dawson. DART: Pearse, Tara St. Nearest bus stops: S. Great Georges St., St. Stephen's Green, Dame St.

Kehoe's ♥♥ This lovely old pub is virtually sepia-toned, with its burnt-orange walls and acres of polished walnut. That's an appropriate analogy for the atmosphere, too—easygoing and frequently packed in the evenings. Kehoe's is best enjoyed in daylight hours, when you can observe the local characters and soak up the old-school Irish pub atmosphere. A particularly appealing feature is the original "snugs"—tiny private rooms, almost like booths. 9 S. Anne St. kehoesdublin.ie. ✆ **01/677-8312.** Luas: Dawson. DART: Pearse. Nearest bus stops: Dawson St., Nassau St.

The Long Hall ♥♥♥ The gorgeous, polished walnut-and-brass interior of this Victorian pub is liable to elicit purrs of delight from thirsty patrons as soon as they walk in the door. Undoubtedly one of Dublin's most, well . . . *Irish* of pubs, the Long Hall is named for the bar that runs the entire length of the interior. Regulars have to fight for space alongside the tourist crowd, but it's worth squeezing in for a look at the interior. Not that staying here for a few pints is anything like a chore. 51 S. Great George's St. visitdublin.com/the-long-hall. ✆ **01/475-1590.** Luas: Trinity. DART: Tara St. Nearest bus stops: S. Great Georges St., Dame St.

Neary's ♥ A favorite hangout of Dublin's theatergoers—and actors, stage crews, and just about everyone else from the Gaiety Theatre (p. 175) behind it—it's full of Victorian features, such as the wonderful globe lanterns out front, held aloft by a brass arm emerging from the brickwork. The upstairs bar is a quiet retreat during the day. 1 Chatham St. nearys.ie. ✆ **01/677-8596.** Luas: St. Stephen's Green. DART: Pearse. Nearest bus stops: St. Stephen's Green.

Victorian lanterns outside of Neary's, a favorite pub of theatergoers.

SPINNING AN IRISH yarn OR TWO

The concept of the wonderful **An Evening of Food, Folklore & Fairies ♥♥♥** is timeless, yet brilliant in its simplicity. No high-tech smoke and mirrors, just compelling tales from Irish folklore, passionately told by masters of the storytelling craft. To be clear, this is storytelling for all ages, not just children, and it's a brilliant revival of an ancient art. The whole thing takes place in an atmospherically lit room in **The Stag's Head pub** in Dame Court. The storytellers spin their absorbing yarns, with tales of the Irish landscape, superstitions, and culture. The show finishes early in the evening so it can be done pre-dinner, and if you haven't had your fill of Irish tradition by the end of it all, you can go and listen to live music in a bar somewhere like O'Donoghue's on Merrion Row or the **Cobblestone** (p. 173).

The storytelling evenings are held every Tuesday and Thursday 5 to 6.30pm. Tickets are €23 adults and €15 children 6–14 (minimum age 6). Contact irishfolktours.com (✆ **086/826-5312**).

The Porterhouse ♥♥ This lovely pub in Temple Bar was the first in Dublin to sell only microbrewery beers. Most are produced by the Porterhouse's own minichain, and the range is constantly updated, so you never know what you'll get from one visit to the next. A relaxed, jovial vibe and hearty pub lunches make it a perfect pit stop on a long day's sightseeing. There's also live music every night. 16–18 Parliament St. porterhousebrewco.ie. ✆ **01/679-8847.** Luas: Trinity. DART: Tara St. Nearest bus stops: Dame St., Parliament St.

Theater

Abbey Theatre ♥♥ Since 1903, the Abbey has been the national theater of Ireland, and it remains one of the country's most respected and prestigious theaters. The original theater, destroyed by fire in 1951, was replaced in 1966 by the current functional, if uninspired, 492-seat house. In addition to its main stage, there's a 127-seat basement studio, the **Peacock,** presenting newer, more experimental work. 26 Lower Abbey St. abbeytheatre.ie. ✆ **01/878-7222.** Ticket prices generally €15–€49. Event times vary; check online. Luas: Abbey St., O'Connell St. DART: Tara St., Connolly. Nearest bus stop: O'Connell St.

Gaiety Theatre ♥ The elegant little Gaiety, opened in 1871, hosts a varied array of performances, everything from opera to classical Irish plays and Broadway-style musicals. (The Gaiety's annual pantomime, or Christmas show, is a big event on the city's theatrical calendar.) Don't forget to check out the ornate decor while you're there. The Gaiety Theatre, S. King St. gaietytheatre.ie. ✆ **01/646-8600.** Ticket prices generally €20–€50. Event times vary; check online. Luas: St. Stephen's Green. DART: Pearse. Nearest bus stop: St. Stephen's Green.

The Gate Theatre ♥♥ Just north of O'Connell Street off Parnell Square, this 370-seat theater was founded in 1928 by Irish actors Hilton Edwards and Micheál Mac Liammóir to provide a venue for a broad range of plays; its program today still includes a blend of modern works and the classics. Although less known by visitors, the Gate is easily as distinguished as the Abbey. Cavendish Row, Parnell Sq. gatetheatre.ie. ✆ **01/874-4045.** Ticket prices generally €20–€40. Event times vary; check online. Luas: O'Connell St. Nearest bus stops: Parnell Sq., O'Connell St.

DAY TRIPS FROM DUBLIN

5

Driving in or out of Dublin, through suburbs and then out along big, bland, modern highways, it would be easy to assume the region immediately surrounding the capital is a little . . . dull? But don't be fooled. The Dublin hinterland is like the safety curtain at a Broadway show—it might not look like much, but just wait until you see what's on the other side. Within an hour's drive north, south, or west of Dublin, you will find some of Ireland's most iconic ancient ruins, historic homes, and castles, set in miles of beautiful countryside. And while it's possible to see any of them on a quick day trip from the capital, the area has plenty of fine hotels and restaurants should you want to spend more time here. And who could blame you?

North of Dublin lie the remnants of Ireland's most ancient civilizations at **Newgrange** and **Knowth,** while the green hills of the **Boyne Valley** hold the long-lost home of early Irish kings. To the west, **Kildare** is Ireland's horse country, dotted with handsome historic homes and some topnotch hotels and restaurants. South of Dublin, the beautiful, brooding **Wicklow Mountains** rise from the countryside, dotted with early Christian ruins, gardens, forests, and peaceful river valleys.

ESSENTIALS

Arriving

BY CAR Most attractions listed in this chapter are easily accessible by car in about an hour from Dublin, in reasonable traffic. There's the catch: Roads around the city are good, but traffic can be a problem, particularly during rush hour, when everything slows to a crawl. You can get excellent maps from one of the **Dublin Tourist Information Centres** (visitdublin.com; ✆ **1800/230-330**).

BY BUS **Bus Éireann** (buseireann.ie; ✆ **01/836-6111**) operates services from the central bus station (Busáras) out to each of the regions listed in this chapter, although there aren't always practical links to the more remote sites. If you're looking to visit attractions by bus, the best bet is probably to take a tour—see the box on p. 180.

PREVIOUS PAGE: A view of the gardens from a Powerscourt Estate terrace.

Counties Louth & Meath

Brú na Bóinne, Newgrange & Knowth **6**

Drogheda **7**

Hill of Tara **10**

Loughcrew **2**

Monasterboice **4**

Newgrange Farm **8**

Old Mellifont Abbey **5**

Proleek Dolmen **1**

St. Colmcille's House **3**

Trim Castle **9**

County Kildare

Castletown House **11**

The Curragh Racetrack **14**

Irish National Stud and Japanese Gardens **13**

Kildare Heritage Centre **12**

Moone High Cross **18**

St. Brigid's Cathedral **15**

Counties Wicklow & Carlow

Avondale House and Beyond the Trees **24**

Brownshill Dolmen **19**

Glendalough **21**

Glenmacnass Waterfall **22**

Huntington Castle and Gardens **26**

Mount Usher Gardens **23**

The Powerscourt Estate **17**

Russborough House **16**

St. Mullin's Monastery **27**

Vale of Avoca **25**

Wicklow Mountains National Park **20**

bus trips FROM DUBLIN

Although you'll need a car to fully explore the regions around Dublin, virtually all of the big attractions can be visited on guided bus tours. Most leave from central Dublin, quite early in the day, and deposit you back around 5 or 6pm. Book tours directly with the operator. Here are a few of the most popular ones:

Newgrange Tours by Mary Gibbons (newgrangetours.com; ✆ **086/355-1355**) are among the most respected of the guided tours that visit the ancient burial site. Mary is an excellent guide, and her tours have an allocated entry slot at Newgrange, meaning you don't have to wait. Tours run daily from several pickup points in Dublin, between 9 and 10am (returning about 5:30pm). This includes a break for lunch (meal not included in the price). The tour costs €75.

Glendalough Bus (glendaloughbus.com; ✆ **01/281-8119**) runs day trips from the north side of St. Stephen's Green to Glendalough every day at 11:30am. Return tickets cost €23 adults and €14 children; you buy them from the driver. You can also catch the bus from Bray at 12:10pm; the return fare from there is €16 (€9 children).

The **Wild Wicklow Tour** (wildwicklow.ie; ✆ **01/280-1899**) takes in Dún Laoghaire Harbour and Killiney Hill, before heading to Glendalough and the Sally Gap. They even take you to a pub for lunch (not included in the price). The tours—which are perhaps skewed toward more youthful travelers—leave from several points in Dublin, "early but not too early" (8:35–9:25am), and return at around 5:30 or 6pm. Tickets cost €55 adults and €40 children (plus online booking fee).

Paddy Wagon Tours (paddywagontours.com; ✆ **01/823-0822**) runs a number of rather touristy trips from Dublin to places all over Ireland, from near (**Kilkenny** and **Glendalough**) to about the farthest you can get from Dublin and still be in Ireland (the **Dingle Peninsula, Cliffs of Moher,** and **Giant's Causeway**). Tickets start at €33 and rise to around €99. The longest day tours take about 12 hours, door to door. Paddy Wagon also runs 2- and 3-day tours that include accommodations; see the website for details.

BY TRAIN **Irish Rail** (irishrail.ie; ✆ **1850/366-222**) trains leave Dublin's Heuston station for Kildare at least once an hour. The journey takes between 25 and 45 minutes. Several direct trains depart daily from Dublin's Connolly station to Wicklow; the journey takes an hour.

NORTH OF DUBLIN: COUNTIES MEATH & LOUTH

North of Dublin's conurbation, the River Boyne rolls through the rich, fertile countryside of counties Meath and Louth. The Boyne is more than a river—it's an essential part of Irish lore, linking Ireland's ancient past (the prehistoric passage tombs of Newgrange, the storied Hill of Tara) with more modern history (the infamous 1690 Battle of the Boyne, when the Protestant King William III defeated the exiled Catholic King James II for the crown of England). Today the Boyne Valley is a much more peaceful place, but it offers visitors a wealth of historic treasures tucked away among miles of farmland and smooth, rolling hills.

Visitor Information

The **Dundalk Tourist Office** on Market Square, Dundalk, Co. Louth (visit louth.ie; ✆ **042/935-2111**), is open Monday to Friday 9am until 5pm. The **Drogheda Tourist Office** (West St., Drogheda, Co. Louth; drogheda.ie; ✆ **041/987-2843**) is open Monday to Saturday 9am until 5pm (closed Sat Oct–Mar). The **Brú na Bóinne Visitor Centre**, the center for Newgrange and Knowth (see below), is at Newgrange, Donore, Co. Meath (heritage ireland.ie; ✆ **041/988-0300**), and keeps the same hours as those ancient sites.

Exploring North of Dublin

On the surface, County Meath looks like placid farm country—small rolling hills covered in emerald-green grass. But don't be fooled: Its most breathtaking historical sights lie underground. Meath's fertile soil and rich river land have attracted settlers for more than 8,000 years, and much of what they left behind has yet to be found. Archaeologists believe that they have uncovered only a fraction of the archaeological wealth of this region; new discoveries are made constantly.

Brú na Bóinne, Newgrange, and Knowth ♥♥♥ ANCIENT SITE

Brú na Bóinne, which translates to "palace of the Boyne" in Irish, is a

The massive prehistoric burial mound of Newgrange is an engineering marvel and an archaeological mystery.

World Heritage Site and a national park, home to some of Ireland's best-known prehistoric monuments: Newgrange, Knowth, and Dowth. **Newgrange,** the most well-known, is one of the archaeological wonders of Europe. Built as a burial mound more than 5,000 years ago—long before the Egyptian pyramids or Stonehenge—it sits atop a hill near the Boyne, massive and mysterious. Newgrange is so old that when it was built there were still woolly mammoths living in parts of Europe. The mound is 11m (36 ft.) tall and approximately 78m (256 ft.) in diameter. It consists of 200,000 tons of stone, a 6-ton capstone, and other stones weighing up to 16 tons each, many of which were hauled from as far away as County Wicklow and the Mountains of Mourne. Each stone fits perfectly in the overall pattern, and the result is a watertight structure, an amazing feat of engineering. The question remains, though: Why? Even as archaeologists found more elaborate carvings in the stones, they deduced no clues as to whether it was built for gods, kings, or long-forgotten rituals. Inside, a passage 18m (59 ft.) long leads to a central burial chamber that sits in pitch darkness all year, except for 5 days in December. During the winter solstice (Dec 19–23), a shaft of sunlight travels down the arrow-straight passageway for 17 minutes, where it hits the back wall of the burial chamber. You can register for a lottery to be in the tomb for this extraordinary event, although competition is fierce—and these days it's livestreamed on the Internet as well.

The extraordinary prehistoric burial site at **Knowth** was only discovered in 1968, and much of it is yet to be excavated. It is mainly composed of two massively long underground burial chambers, the longer of which stretches for 40m (131 ft.). In the mound, scientists found the largest collection of passage tomb art uncovered thus far in Europe, as well as a number of underground chambers and 300 carved slabs. Surrounding the mound, 17 satellite graves are laid out in a mysterious, complex pattern. And still, no one has a definitive answer to the biggest riddle of all: What was it all for? Even now, many of Knowth's secrets have not been uncovered—excavation work is constant here, and there is no access for visitors to the inner chamber or passage.

Tip: These sites have no direct access; you have to visit as part of a tour from the Brú na Bóinne Visitor Centre near Donore, where you park and take a shuttle bus the rest of the way. You should book weeks in advance, as soon as you know the day you'll be coming—space is limited and it's one of Ireland's most popular historic sites. There are three tours—the **Brú na Bóinne tour and Newgrange chamber** allows you inside the passage at Newgrange, where you can walk down past the elaborately carved stones and into the chamber, which has three sections, each with a basin stone that once held cremated human remains. The tour also visits the exterior of Knowth. The **Newgrange tour** includes access to the chamber as well. The **Knowth tour** visits the exterior of Knowth only with no access to Knowth's inside chamber. All of the tours include the self-guided exhibition at the Visitor Centre—you can also just visit the exhibition only.

Brú na Bóinne Visitor Centre, on N51, 2km (1¼ miles) west of Donore. heritage ireland.ie. ✆ **041/988-0300.** Brú na Bóinne tour and Newgrange chamber: €18 adults; €16 seniors; €12 students and children 12 and over; free for children 11 and under; €48 families. Newgrange tour and exhibition, or tour of Knowth exterior and exhibition: €10 adults; €8 seniors; €5 students and children 12 and over; €25 families. Visitor Centre only: €5 adults; €4 seniors; €3 students and children 12 and over; €13 families. Visitor Centre open daily May–Aug 9am–5:45pm; Sept 9am–5:15pm; Oct–Jan 9am–4:15pm; Feb–Apr 9:30am–4:45pm. Last admission 45 min. before closing. Knowth is closed Oct–Mar. Book all visits online before visiting.

Drogheda ♥ TOWN A modest industrial commuter town of 40,000 people, 56km (35 miles) north of Dublin, Drogheda (pronounced *Draada* in the local accent) has two historic churches—both, confusingly, with the same name. The bigger of the two, **St. Peter's Roman Catholic Church,** in the town center, is remarkably impressive, with its French Gothic rose window and imposing 68m (222-ft.) spire. But its main claim to fame is grislier: St. Peter's contains the shrine of St. Oliver Plunkett (1625–81), the Archbishop of Armagh, who was beheaded in London for his part in an alleged plot to assassinate King Charles II—becoming the last Catholic martyr to die in England. His severed head can still be seen, shriveled and wizened inside a glass case, as the centerpiece to his shrine. The other St. Peter's, **St. Peter's Church of Ireland,** a simple gray stone church at the northern end of the town, has its own notorious backstory, dating to 1649, during Oliver Cromwell's bloody conquest of Ireland. On September 11, after an 8-day siege, around 2,000 Irish soldiers loyal to the deposed monarch, Charles I, were massacred. Fleeing the carnage, 140 took refuge in St. Peter's steeple. Refusing to heed their surrender, Cromwell ordered them burned alive using wood from the pews—an act so heinous that some of his own men refused, risking a charge of mutiny. St. Peter's has been rebuilt twice since the terrible event. (Check out the spooky carved skeletons on one tomb in the nave.) The small **Drogheda Museum** is located in the 17th-century **Millmount Fort,** overlooking the town, where the walls were finally breached at the end of the siege. The guided tours are a little long, so stick with the self-guided version.

St. Peter's R.C. Church: West St.; saintpetersdrogheda.ie; ✆ **041/983-8537;** daily 10am–5pm. **St. Peter's Church of Ireland:** Peter and William sts.; drogheda.armagh.anglican.org; no phone; daily 10am–3pm. **Millmount Fort:** Off John St.; discoverboynevalley.ie; ✆ **041/983-3097;** admission €8 adults, €4 seniors, students, and children, €20 families; daily 9:30am–5:30pm, last admission to tower 1 hr. before closing.

Hill of Tara ♥♥ ANCIENT SITE Legends and folklore place this hill at the center of early Irish history. Ancient tombs have been discovered that date back to the Stone Age; pagans believed that the goddess Queen Maeve reigned from here. By the 3rd century, a ceremonial residence had been built here for the most powerful men in Ireland—the high kings, who ruled as much by myth as by military strength. Every 3 years they would hold a weeklong *feis* (a kind of government session/wild party twofer), at which more than 1,000 princes, poets, athletes, priests, druids, musicians, and jesters celebrated. Laws were passed, disputes settled, and matters of defense decided. After the last *feis* was held in A.D. 560, Tara went into a decline as the power shifted. Today, little is left of the hill's great heritage, save for grassy mounds and some ancient pillar stones. All that survives of the Iron Age forts are depressions in the soil. That said, it's still a great spot with views that extend for miles. You can learn the hill's history at a visitor center in the old church beside the entrance. Guided tours are available for those who want to know what lies beneath the smooth, green surface.

Signposted on N3, about 12km (7.4 miles) S of Navan. hilloftara.org. ✆ **046/902-5903** (visitor center); 041/988-0300 (off-season). Free admission to Hill of Tara. Admission to visitor center €5 adults; €4 seniors; €3 students and children; €13 families. Hill open year-round. Visitor center: Mid-May to mid-Sept daily 10am–6pm. Last admission 1 hr. before closing.

Loughcrew Cairns and Gardens ♥♥ ANCIENT SITE Loughcrew is a two-for-one deal: beautiful 19th-century pleasure gardens dotted with lakes, perfect for picnicking, and, just a short distance away, one of the biggest megalithic burial grounds in Ireland. The 30 passage tombs of Loughcrew are known locally as *Slieve na Calliaghe,* which translates as "The Hill of the Witch." With such an atmospheric name you'd expect something good to look at, and sure enough, the three hills topped like crowns with symmetrical tombs can be seen from miles away. The site is aligned with both the equinox and the pagan day of Samhain (Halloween), so that twice a year the dawn sun lights a heavily carved stone within one cairn. Crowds gather each year to see the phenomenon. Access to the cairns is free—the climb is steep, so wear appropriate footwear. There are guides on-site daily from May to September. From N3, take R195 through Oldcastle toward Mullingar; 2.4km (1½ miles) out of Oldcastle, look for the signposted left turn and follow signs.

Outside Oldcastle. heritageireland.ie. ✆ **049/854-1240.** Cairns: Free admission. Guided tours of cairns daily 10am–5pm mid-May to mid-Sept. Gardens (loughcrew.com; ✆ **049/854-1356**): €8 adults; €6 seniors; €4 children; €22 families. May–Oct daily 10am–5pm. Garden tours €20 per person or €60 per group (book in advance). Closed Jan–Mar.

Monasterboice ♥♥ RELIGIOUS SITE This atmospheric monastic site holds a peaceful cemetery, one of the tallest round towers in Ireland, ancient church ruins, and two excellent high crosses, all surrounded by trees and green fields. The site is said to have been founded in the 4th century by a follower of St. Patrick named St. Buithe. The name "Buithe" was corrupted to Boyne over time, and thus the whole region is named after him. A small monastic community thrived here for centuries, until it

HIGH CROSSES: icons OF IRELAND

You see them all over Ireland, often in the most picturesque rural surroundings, standing alone like sentries: high Celtic crosses with stories carved into every inch of space. Haunting and ancient as they seem to us today, when they were created, these carved stones served a practical purpose: They were books, of sorts, in the days when books were rare and precious. Think of the carvings, which illustrate biblical stories, as cartoons explaining the Bible to an illiterate population. Originally, the crosses were probably brightly painted, but the paint has long been lost to the wind and rain.

Muiredeach's High Cross at Monasterboice (p. 184) has carvings telling, from the bottom up, the stories of Adam and Eve, Cain and Abel, David and Goliath, and Moses, as well as the wise men bringing gifts to the baby Jesus. At the center of the old cross, the carving is thought to be of Revelation, while at the top St. Paul stands alone in the desert. The western side of the cross tells the stories of the New Testament, with, from the top down, a figure praying, the Crucifixion, St. Peter, Doubting Thomas, and, below that, Jesus's arrest. On the base of the cross is an inscription of the sort found often carved on stones in ancient Irish monasteries. It reads in Irish, "A PRAYER FOR MUIREDACH FOR WHOM THE CROSS WAS MADE." Muiredach was the abbot at Monasterboice until 922, so the cross was probably made as a memorial after his death. Another excellent example of a carved high cross is the **Moone High Cross** ♥, which is not too far away (p. 194).

Really intrigued by high crosses? Then head southwest to the **Ahenny High Crosses** in County Tipperary (p. 379).

was seized and occupied by Vikings in the 10th century. The Vikings were, in turn, defeated by Donal, the high king of Tara, who is said to have single-handedly killed 300 of them. Today only a little is left, but the **Muiredeach's High Cross** is worth the trip all on its own. Dating from 922, the near-perfect cross is carved with elaborate scenes from the Old and New Testaments (see box, above). Two other high crosses are more faded, and one was smashed by Cromwell's forces. The site is now accessible to wheelchair users.

Off the main Dublin road (N1), 9.7km (6 miles) NW of Drogheda, near Collon. Free admission. Daily dawn–dusk.

Newgrange Farm ♥♥ FARM After all that history, the kids will thank you for bringing them to this busy farm, where farmer Willie Redhouse and his family offer a 1½-hour tour. You can feed the ducks, groom a calf, and bottle-feed the lambs and kid goats. Children can hold a newborn chick, pet a pony, play with the pigs, and look at pheasants and rare birds in the aviaries. Tractor rides cost an extra €3. The high point of the week occurs every Sunday afternoon (and on Irish national holidays), when the sheep take to the track with teddy bear jockeys for the weekly derby. (Call to check race times.) Demonstrations show farm skills such as threshing and horseshoeing, and sheepdogs show off their herding skills. The farm has kids' play areas, a coffee shop, and plenty of picnic space. The price is a little steep, but family discounts kick in at just one adult and one child.

Off N51, 3.2km (2 miles) E of Slane (signposted off N51 and directly W of Newgrange monument). newgrangefarm.com. ✆ **041/982-4119.** Admission €10.50 per person; family rates for 2–10 people €21–€94. Mid-Mar to Aug daily 10am–6pm. Last admission 5pm.

Old Mellifont Abbey ♥♥ RELIGIOUS SITE/RUINS Founded in the 12th century, this was Ireland's first Cistercian monastery, and it grew to be the most important. Much of it is gone now, but enough is left to give you an idea of what Mellifont was like in its day, when it was the center of Cistercian faith in Ireland, with more than 400 monks living and working within its walls. You can see the outline of the cross-shaped nave, as well as the remains of the cloister, refectory, and the warming room (the only part of the monastery with heating—after all, monks were supposed to live lives of suffering). Mellifont was closed in the 16th century during Henry VIII's dissolution of the monasteries, and a manor house was built on the site for an English landlord, using the abbey stones. A century later, that house would be the last place where Hugh O'Neill, the final Irish chief, stayed before surrendering to the English and then fleeing to Europe (see "English Power & the Flight of the Earls," p. 29). At the informative visitor center next door, you can find out more about the monastery and its long, complex history.

The ruins of Old Mellifont Abbey in County Louth, the first Cistercian monastery in Ireland.

Tullyallen, signposted off R168, 9.7km (6 miles) W of Drogheda. heritageireland.ie. ✆ **041/982-6459** or 041/988-0300 (out of season). Free admission to grounds. Visitor center admission €5 adults; €4 seniors; €3 students and children; €13 families. Visitor center and guided tours late May to mid-Sept daily 10am–5pm; last admission 45 min. before closing.

Proleek Dolmen ♥ ANCIENT SITE This huge dolmen is said to resemble a giant's finger when viewed from a distance. That is subjective, to say the least. But fingerlike or not, it's an impressive sight. The massive 35-ton capstone looks alarmingly precarious, balanced on top of three smaller stones like a crude, misshapen tripod. The top of the capstone is invariably covered with pebbles, thanks to a local legend that says if you can throw a stone and it stays there, your wish will come true. You can reach the dolmen down a paved footpath from the parking lot of the **Ballymascanlon House Hotel** (ballymascanlon.com; ✆ **042/935-8200**) near Dundalk; the dolmen is a 5-minute walk away. To find the hotel from Dublin, take exit 18 for Dundalk North off the M1, then take the N52 off the first roundabout, and the road to Ballymascanlon from the second. The hotel is about 3km (1¾ miles) down this road.

On the grounds of Ballymascanlon House Hotel, Dundalk. No phone. Free admission.

St. Colmcille's House ♥ RELIGIOUS SITE Sitting incongruously near more modern houses in Kells, like a memory of Ireland's distant past, this narrow gray stone house is all that's left of a long-lost monastic settlement that once stood where the town now sprawls. Most of the nearly windowless building dates to the 10th century, although some sections predate that by another hundred years. Some experts believe it was once a scriptorium, where monks wrote and illuminated books—and quite possibly where the Book of Kells (p. 93) was produced. The first-floor room still contains traces of an ancient fireplace and entryway; a narrow staircase ascends to a dark vault just under the roof.

About 180m (590 ft.) NW of St. Columba's Church, Church Lane, Kells. No phone. Free admission. Open on request—contact Kells Courthouse Tourism and Cultural Hub, ✆ **046/924-7508** more than 24 hr. in advance to arrange.

Trim Castle ♥♥ CASTLE A skeletal reminder of the clout once wielded by Anglo-Normans in Ireland, this ruined edifice is an inspiring sight. The Norman lord Hugh de Lacy occupied the site in 1172 and built the enclosed cruciform keep. In the 13th century, his son Walter enlarged the keep, circled it with a many-towered curtain wall, and added a great hall as an upgraded venue for courts, parliaments, and feasts. After the 17th century, though, it was abandoned and lay in ruins for hundreds of years. Few paid much attention to it, until Mel Gibson chose to use it as a setting for the 1995 film *Braveheart.* The Irish Heritage Service restored it as a "preserved ruin." Entry to the main part of the castle is by guided tour only, but arrive early if you're visiting in summer—space is limited and the tour can't be

A Gruesome Find at Trim Castle

In 1971, when excavation work was underway at Trim Castle, workers made a macabre discovery: While digging to the south of the central keep, they uncovered the remains of 10 headless men. Historians believe that the bodies date from the 15th century. During a time of high crime in 1465, King Edward IV ordered that all robbers be beheaded, and their heads displayed on spikes to intimidate those who might be considering a career in crime. Presumably, these men had all suffered that fate.

in advance, so it often sells out. ***Note:*** The hour-long tour is unsuitable for small or unruly children and for anyone unable to maneuver steep climbs or afraid of formidable heights.

Castle St., Trim. heritageireland.ie. ✆ **046/943-8619.** Admission €5 adults; €4 seniors; €3 students and children; €13 families. Mid-Mar to Sept daily 10am–5pm; Nov to early Feb weekends 9am–4pm; mid-Feb to mid-Mar and Oct daily 9:30–4:30pm; last admission 1 hr. before closing.

Where to Stay North of Dublin

Bellinter House ♥♥ On the banks of the River Boyne outside Navan, this imposing gray stone Palladian country house was designed by the same man who built **Russborough House** (p. 204) and **Powerscourt** (p. 203). The hotel has been restored to resemble a 19th-century country getaway, with an atmosphere of relaxed elegance. Its drawing room is a lovely space, where you can take afternoon tea or just relax in front of the fire with a good book. Most guest rooms are less glamorous than the public areas; the more expensive rooms are, inevitably, the most beautiful. But all have large, modern bathrooms and comfortable beds. The restaurant is highly rated for its French-influenced Irish cuisine and locally sourced meat and produce. Breakfasts are huge—even the tea selection is enormous. A small spa holds a sauna, steam room, and outdoor hot tub, and guests are free to explore the sprawling grounds and fish on the river. Get directions from the hotel before setting out—on a tiny farm road, this place can be hard to find.

Bellinter, Navan, Co. Meath. bellinterhouse.com. ✆ **046/903-0900.** 42 units. €129–€369 double. Breakfast included. Free parking. **Amenities:** Restaurant; bar; spa; Wi-Fi (free).

The Cottages ♥♥ You can't get closer to the sea than these historic thatched cottages on the beach in County Meath, just outside the village of Bettystown, where the sound of the waves will lull you to sleep. Each cottage is perfectly restored and equipped with exposed beams, comfortable beds, warm bed covers, full kitchens, and living rooms with just enough space. Bathrooms have freestanding showers and deep bathtubs. All cottages have TVs and Wi-Fi, but long walks on the beach and strolls into the picturesque village will undoubtedly keep you busy. Book early; with just six cottages, it's understandably popular.

Coast Rd., Bettystown, Co. Meath. cottages-ireland.com. ✆ **041/982-8104.** 6 units. €190–€570 per cottage per night. 3-night min. stay. Free parking. **Amenities:** Wi-Fi (free).

Ghan House ♥♥ Overlooking Carlingford Lough, Ghan House is a sweet, old-fashioned hotel. The good-size guest rooms are traditionally furnished, with antiques and sofas. Most are in the main 17th-century building, though there is also a modern extension, and many have views of the lake or mountains. "Superior" rooms have half-tester beds and deep

The Cottages sit on a beach overlooking the Irish Sea.

Victorian bathtubs. The award-winning restaurant serves up excellent modern Irish cuisine, and the owners hold cooking and wine-tasting classes on-site. Check the website for special offers.

2 Ghan Rd., Carlingford, Co. Louth. ghanhouse.com. ✆ **042/937-3682.** 12 units. €220–€390 double. Breakfast included. Free parking. **Amenities:** Restaurant; bar; Wi-Fi (free).

Headfort Arms Hotel ♥♥ Originally built in 1780 as a town house for the Marquis of Headfort while he waited for his country estate to be built, the Headfort Arms has been a family-run hotel for years. It still has a certain old-world charm (mixed in with mod cons like high-speed broadband and an in-house spa). You can opt to stay in one of the heritage rooms in the main house, which have high ceilings, fireplaces, and freestanding baths, or in the more modern wing. There are good dining options too, with gastropub fare at the **Kelltic Bar,** breakfast, carvery lunches, and evening grills at **Café Therese,** or fine dining at the **Vanilla Pod** (p. 191).

Headfort Place, Kells, Co. Meath. headfortarms.ie. ✆ **046/924-0063.** 45 units. €109–€448 double. Breakfast included. Free parking. **Amenities:** Restaurant; cafe; bar/gastropub; spa; room service; Wi-Fi (free).

The Station House ♥♥♥ This charming hotel in the Boyne Valley was originally built as a railway station in 1862. The hotel has lush gardens and is set on 12 acres, surrounded by forests and fields. Inside, the room decor has a "country luxury" vibe, and many rooms still have original Victorian features such as sash windows. The Station Master Suite has a floral decor and a freestanding bath, while the tiny two-level Signal Suite, set in the old signal box, is an adorable nook. Unwind after exploring with home cooking in the **Signal Restaurant** or casual bites in the **Platform Bar**. It's a romantic spot, so don't be surprised if a wedding is booked in too.

Kilmessan, Co. Meath. stationhousehotel.ie. ✆ **046/902-5239.** 19 units. €180–€410 double. Breakfast included. Check online for offers. Free parking. **Amenities:** Restaurant; bar; Wi-Fi (free).

Trim Castle Hotel ♥♥ This modern hotel is a stone's throw from the castle (you really could hit it with a rock quite easily, not that we're encouraging you). The hotel lounges and restaurants are bright and cheerful. Guest rooms are not huge but are well-appointed, with modern bathrooms. Some rooms have direct views of the evocative castle ruins. The bistro-style **Jules Restaurant** offers reasonably priced classic Irish fare (three-course Sun lunch €32), and a lovely rooftop patio is a fine place to take a coffee and soak up the view. You can get great gastropub options like burgers and steaks in the **Bailey Brasserie,** while the **BoAnn Café** serves brunch, light bites, and sweet treats. Check the website for deeply discounted deals, particularly in spring.

Castle St., Trim, Co. Meath. trimcastlehotel.com. ✆ **046/948-3000.** 68 units. €145–€275 double. Breakfast included. Free parking. **Amenities:** Restaurant/bar; cafe; room service; Wi-Fi (free).

Where to Eat North of Dublin

This isn't one of Ireland's foodie regions, but that doesn't mean there aren't good options. This is a great area for simple, homey Irish food. In addition to the places listed below, plenty of places offer lighter bites. In Carlingford, **Ruby Ellen's Tea Rooms** (Newry St.; facebook.com/rubyellenstearooms) is legendary for its decadent homemade cakes, fluffy scones, and pots of piping-hot tea. In Drogheda, the tiny town-center **Ariosa Café** (Saint Laurence St.; ariosacoffee.com) offers the best cup of joe north of Dublin, roasting its own beans to make sure each cup is perfect. Also in Drogheda, take a healthy break at the **Bare Food Company** (15 West St.; thebarefoodcompany.ie; ✆ **041/983-5529**), with great vegan options, from its creamy bircher muesli to fresh, green salads and veg-packed sandwiches. In a converted barn outside Dundalk on the M1 motorway, the rustic and beautiful **Strandfield House** (strandfield.com; ✆ **042/937-1856**), a hybrid cafe/florist/bakery, uses local ingredients in all its recipes, offering obscure local cheeses, fabulous tarts and quiches, fresh pizzas, bread, pastries, and, well, big bouquets of roses. Expect a short wait—it's insanely popular.

The Bay Tree ♥♥♥ IRISH This restaurant isn't much to look at from the outside, but inside it's a cozy, romantic space. The cooking is top-notch, allowing the freshest, local ingredients—some of which come from the restaurant's own gardens—plenty of space to shine without overloading the palate. Start with a fig and Roquefort tart garnished with 25-year-old balsamic, then try the duck confit with mulled-spice red cabbage, or salmon filet with glazed Brussels sprouts. Follow it up with a rich sticky toffee pudding with hot toffee sauce, or a super-fresh baked Alaska, straight from the oven. The Bay Tree has an attached guesthouse with pleasant, modern bedrooms, costing from €120 to €150 per night.
Newry St., Carlingford, Co. Louth. baytree.ie. ✆ **042/938-3848.** Entrees €22–€38. Thurs 5–8:30pm; Fri–Sat 5–9pm; Sun 1–7:30pm.

Burke's Restaurant ♥ INTERNATIONAL The Burke family have run this friendly, unpretentious little diner for more than 25 years, making it a local institution. The enormous, overflowing full Irish breakfasts are a staple (and pretty reasonable at €11.50, given that they provide enough carbs to power you for a week). The lunch menu focuses on comfort food: fried chicken, burgers, and fresh local fish. Drop by in the afternoon for tea and sample the delicious house-recipe pancakes. The restaurant is just around the corner from St. Peter's Church on West Street.
6 Peter St., Drogheda, Co. Louth. ✆ **041/984-3498.** Entrees €12–€18. Mon–Sat 9am–3pm.

The Glyde Inn ♥♥ IRISH Overlooking scenic Dundalk Bay, this waterfront pub and restaurant in Annagassan is famed for its clever way with local seafood. Dishes are simple and classic. The seafood chowder is creamy and rich, served with warm, homemade bread. Regulars come for the lobster—caught that morning—but there are plenty of other options. From fish and chips to the catch of the day (if razor clams are on the menu, definitely try them), this is hearty fare in a relaxed setting.
Main St., Annagassan, Co. Louth. theglydeinn.ie. ✆ **042/937-2350.** Entrees €18–€34. Wed–Sun noon–8pm.

Vanilla Pod ♥♥ MODERN EUROPEAN Imaginative Irish cooking with international influences is the focus of this great little restaurant in Kells. The menu is seasonal and showcases regional flavors in dishes like herb-crumbed scallops with gin and lemon thyme; honey- and plum-glazed duck breast; or rack of local lamb with pea and lettuce gratin. It's located at the Headfort Arms Hotel (p. 189) in Kells.
Headfort Arms Hotel, John St., Kells, Co. Meath. headfortarms.ie. ✆ **046/924-0084.** Entrees €19–€27. Thurs–Sat 5–10pm; Sun 12:30–9:30pm. Closed Mon–Wed.

WEST OF DUBLIN: COUNTY KILDARE

The flatlands of Kildare are rich in more ways than one. The fertile soil produces miles of lush pastures perfect for raising horses, and the population is one of the most affluent in the country, with plenty of cash for buying horses. Driving through the smooth rolling hills, home to sleek thoroughbreds, you might notice a similarity to the green grass of Kentucky—in fact, the county is twinned with Lexington, Kentucky. This is the home of the Curragh, the racetrack where the Irish Derby is held, and smaller tracks at Naas and Punchestown.

Once the stronghold of the Fitzgerald Clan, Kildare is named after the Irish *cill dara,* or "Church of the Oak," a reference to St. Brigid's monastery, which once sat in the county, surrounded by oak trees. Brigid (see box on p. 195) was a bit ahead of her time as an early exponent for women's equality—she founded her co-ed monastery in the 5th century.

Visitor Information

The **Kildare Town Tourist Office and Heritage Centre** is in the refurbished 19th century Market House in Market Square, Kildare Town (kildareheritage.com; ✆ **045/530672**). It's open Monday to Saturday from 9:30am to 1pm and 2 until 5pm. As well as tourist information, it has a gift shop and the **Legends of Kildare** virtual reality experience. This tells the story of some of the area's well-known characters including St. Brigid, and the history of the town itself. Shows take 30 minutes and run Tuesday to Saturday every half-hour between 10am and 4:30pm, and cost €9.50 adults, €7.50 seniors and students, €6.50 children, and €30 to €41 families. The minimum age is 10. The **Kildare Town Historic Guided Walking Tour** starts at the Heritage Centre on Saturdays at 11:30am from June to August. The hour-long tours are led by a local historian and visit St. Brigid's Cathedral (p. 194) and other key sites; they cost €5 per person.

Exploring West of Dublin

Castletown House ♥♥ HISTORIC HOUSE The fine, symmetrical architecture of this spectacular Palladian-style mansion has been imitated many times across Ireland over the centuries. Made of clean, white stone, with elegant rows of tall windows, Castletown was built between 1722 and 1729, designed by Italian architect Alessandro Galilei for William Connolly, who was at the time speaker of the Irish House of Commons. Today, it's beautifully maintained, and the fully restored interior is worth the price of admission. Entry is by guided tour only, though you're free to wander around the surrounding parkland at your leisure. Two interesting follies on the estate were built as make-work for the starving population during the Famine: One is a graceful obelisk, the other an extraordinarily playful barn, created as a higgledy-piggledy inverted funnel, around which winds a fanciful stone staircase. It is aptly named the Wonderful Barn.

Signposted from R403, off main Dublin-Galway Rd. (N4), Celbridge. castletown.ie. ✆ **01/628-8252.** House: €10 adults; €8 seniors; €5 students and children; €25 families. Grounds: Free admission. House: Mar to early Nov daily 10am–5pm (last admission 1 hr. before closing) by guided tour only; call ahead or check tour times online. Grounds: 7am–7:30pm year-round.

The Curragh ♥ RACECOURSE The country's best-known racetrack, the Curragh has hosted races for hundreds of years. The first recorded race took place here in 1727, but historians believe races were held at this site long before then. Today it's a modern flat track—there's nothing left of whatever may have stood here centuries ago. But its place in history is assured, and it is home to the **Irish Derby,** the premier horse race of Ireland, held every year on the last Saturday of June. Races take place at least one Saturday a month from March to October; check the Curragh website for full details on all races and tickets, including premium packages. Derby day tickets are inevitably more expensive than for other races; expect to pay upwards of €30 or €50 with transport to and from Dublin (prebooking is essential). On non-race days, the Curragh runs 90-minute "behind the scenes" tours, where you can visit locations like weighing rooms and parade rings.

The nearest train station is Kildare Town (a free shuttle runs from there to the track on race days); trains run direct from Waterford, Cork, Limerick, Galway, and Dublin's Heuston station, with fares starting at around €15. **Dublin Coach** (dublincoach.ie; ✆ **01/465-9972**) runs a "Race Bus" from Westmoreland Street in central Dublin on race days; fares start at around €12.

Dublin-Limerick Rd. (N7), The Curragh. curragh.ie. ✆ **045/441205.** Standard race days €15–€20 adults; discount for seniors and those 25 and under; free for children 17 and under (with adult). Hours vary; 1st race usually 1:30pm (or 5pm for evening races), but check newspapers or website. Behind the scenes tours €25–€55.

Irish National Stud and Japanese Gardens ♥♥♥ MUSEUM/FARM/GARDENS Many of Ireland's fastest horses have been bred on the grounds of this famous stud farm. Horse lovers and racing fans will be in heaven walking around the expansive grounds and watching the well-groomed horses being trained; guided tours run regularly. One of the highlights here, especially if you are in a small group, is the **Irish Racehorse Experience**—a fun, interactive exhibit where you get to own, name, train, and equip your "racehorse" before becoming the jockey and riding the racehorse simulator in a real-time race, to see how your choices worked out. After all the excitement, take a walk in the tranquil **Japanese Gardens,** which date from 1906 and have pagodas, ponds, and bridges over trickling streams. The beautifully designed visitor center has a

A mare and foal at the Irish National Stud, home of many of Ireland's finest thoroughbred racehorses.

restaurant and shop. A garden dedicated to St. Fiachra—the patron saint of gardeners—lies in a beautiful natural setting of woods and wetlands.

Off the Dublin-Limerick Rd. (N7), Tully. irishnationalstud.ie. ✆ **045/521617.** Admission including Irish Racehorse Experience €22 adults; €17 seniors and students; €14 children; free for children 3 and under; €55 families. Book online for discounts to these prices. Racehorse experience for ages 8 and up only. Daily 9am–5pm; last admission 1 hr. before closing. Closed Jan to early Feb.

Moone High Cross ♥ RELIGIOUS SITE Amid the picturesque ruins of Moone Abbey, this magnificent high cross (see box on p. 185) is nearly 1,200 years old. The abbey, established by St. Columba in the 6th century, lies in evocative ruins around it. The cross features finely crafted Celtic designs as well as biblical scenes: the temptation of Adam and Eve, the sacrifice of Isaac, and Daniel in the lions' den. Among the carvings are several surprises, such as a carving of a Near Eastern fish that reproduces when the male feeds the female her own eggs, which eventually hatch from her mouth.

Signposted off N9 on southern edge of Moone. kildareheritage.com/moone-high-cross. No phone. Free admission. Daily dawn–dusk.

St. Brigid's Cathedral ♥ CHURCH Built on the site of St. Brigid's monastery, which was founded in the 5th century, this beautiful 13th-century church dominates central Kildare. Its exquisite stained-glass windows portray Ireland's three great saints: Patrick, Colmcille, and Brigid. The round tower on the grounds is the second tallest in the country

(33m/108 ft.); it dates to the 10th century, although its original pointed roof was later replaced by a Norman turret. If the groundskeeper is in, you can climb the stairs to the top for €6. Near the tower, a strange-looking stone with a hole at its top is known as the "wishing stone"—according to lore, if you put your arm through the hole and touch your shoulder when you make a wish, then your wish will come true. The cathedral is closed to visitors from October to April, but you can usually visit the grounds year-round, free, by inquiring at the Heritage Centre on Market Square (p. 192). Market Sq., Kildare Town. stbrigidscathedral.com. ✆ **045/521229.** Cathedral €4; round tower €6. Cathedral: May–Sept Mon–Sat 10am–1pm and 2–5pm; Sun 2–5pm; last admission 15 min. before closing. Grounds: daily dawn–dusk.

Where to Stay West of Dublin

Barberstown Castle ♥♥ Although parts of this hotel were built as recently as the early 2000s, enough genuine old castle is still on view as you approach for it to look and feel satisfyingly, well, *castle*-like. The oldest section dates from the 13th century, and the castle has had 37 owners since then—including rock star Eric Clapton, who held regular music sessions when he lived here in the 1980s. Even the modern guest rooms manage to feel pleasantly antique; some have four-poster beds. Family rooms are available, too. The formal **Barton Rooms** restaurant serves classic

local hero: ST. BRIGID

Modern-day feminists have embraced this 5th-century Irish saint, and for good reason. Brigid was a headstrong girl who fought against the oppressive, patriarchal rules of her time. When her father picked a husband for her, she refused to marry him. Legend holds that when her father insisted that the wedding should go forward, she pulled out her own eye to prove she was strong enough to resist his plans. He backed down, and the mutilated girl joined a convent. When she took her vows, however, the bishop accidentally ordained her as a bishop rather than a nun. It is said that as soon as that happened, she was miraculously made beautiful again.

As she grew older, Brigid remained a rebel. She founded a monastery in Kildare but insisted that it be open to both nuns and monks—something unheard of at that time. Word of the monastery, and of its unusual abbess, soon spread throughout Europe, and she became a powerful figure in European Christianity. Her followers marked their homes with a plain cross woven from river reeds. In some Irish homes, you'll still find crosses made in precisely that way.

One of Brigid's strangest rules for her monastery was that a fire should always be kept burning, day and night, tended by 20 virgins. Long after she died, the fire at St. Brigid's burned constantly, tended as she said it should be. This continued as late as 1220, when the bishop of Dublin insisted that the tradition, which he viewed as pagan, be stopped. But there is still a fire pit at **St. Brigid's Cathedral ♥** (p. 194), and a fire is lit in it every February 1, on St. Brigid's feast day. Since 2023, St. Brigid's Day has been an official annual public holiday in Ireland.

(and quite pricey) Irish bistro fare, while there's more casual dining at the **Garden Bar.**

On R403, Straffan, Co. Kildare. barberstowncastle.ie. ✆ **01/628-8157.** 55 units. €165–€295 double; €255–€1,530 suite. Breakfast included. Free parking. **Amenities:** Restaurant; bar; room service; Wi-Fi (free).

Cliff at Lyons ♥♥♥ This peaceful country retreat is set along the Grand Canal and is a collection of historic village houses now containing a boutique hotel and a superb spa with an outdoor thermal area. Rooms are all different and in stone buildings along tree-lined pathways; some have four-poster beds and freestanding bathtubs. The Lily Pond rooms all face the main water feature. There are also small cottages to rent. The **Mill** restaurant serves country classics (much of the produce is grown on-site) and is named after an old mill, on the grounds. There are bicycles if you wish to cycle along the canal (the **Pantry** cafe does great takeout for picnics), plus a cute home store. Check the website for special stay-and-dine or spa offers.

Lyons Rd., Celbridge, Co. Kildare. cliffatlyons.ie. ✆ **01/630-3500.** 38 units. €229–€639 double. Breakfast included. Free parking. **Amenities:** 2 restaurants; bar; bikes; spa; Wi-Fi (free).

Martinstown House ♥♥ An elegant country house getaway near the famous Curragh racecourse (p. 193), Martinstown dates mostly from the 1830s. Bedrooms are decorated with more than a few nods to its early Victorian origins, with heritage color schemes and antique-style furniture. Excellent four-course dinners (€65) are served around a single, long, candlelit table, which gives the appealing sense of an upper-class house party

The Victorian-era Martinstown House, a country retreat near the Curragh racecourse.

from a bygone age. Expect seasonal fare such as roast duck with spiced red cabbage, or grilled sole with lemon and caper butter. The downside is that you have to reserve 24 hours in advance, and a minimum of 12 guests are required at dinner. So, unless you're traveling in a large group, it might be worth determining if any of your fellow guests want to eat here on the same night as you. ***Note:*** Although the Curragh is just 8km (5 miles) away, a frustrating road layout means that driving between the Martinstown and the racecourse takes up to a half-hour each way. ***Note:*** This place can get booked up *really* far in advance.

Off L6078 (follow signs for Martinstown), Ballysax, The Curragh, Co. Kildare. martinstownhouse.com. ✆ **045/441269.** 6 units. €175–€295 double. Breakfast included. Free parking. **Amenities:** Restaurant; Wi-Fi (free).

Where to Eat West of Dublin

County Kildare is beloved by Dubliners for its horses and outlet shopping (the outlet mall **Kildare Village** [kildarevillage.com] has more than 120 designer stores), but the restaurants aren't too shabby, either. In addition to the options below, try **Agape** on Market Square in Kildare Town (facebook.com/agapegourmetfoodbar) for gourmet sandwiches or lunches and light dinners; or the **Green Barn** at the Burtown House and Gardens in Athy (burtownhouse.ie). Inside an actual converted barn, this light-filled restaurant grows much of its food in the beautiful gardens here, which are also open to the public. Try the leek and kale pie or the warm goat cheese and honey fritter, and then wander the grounds.

The Brown Bear ♥♥ EUROPEAN In the pretty village of Two Mile House outside Naas, this multi-award-winning restaurant located on the owner's family farm offers local produce and innovative cooking in a relaxed environment. Expect starters like scallops with pumpkin and black pudding, or foie gras with apple and walnut. Main dishes could include duck breast with red cabbage and pickled carrots, or cod with white beans and prawns. The chefs use a light touch and let the fresh produce sing.

Two Mile House, Naas. thebrownbear.ie. ✆ **045/883561.** Entrees €19–€36. Wed–Sat 5:30–9pm; Sun 1–3pm and 4:30–7pm.

Cunningham's ♥ THAI/PUB FOOD Inside and out, Cunningham's is a fairly traditional, run-of-the-mill Irish pub—which makes it all the more unlikely that it also serves some of the best Thai food in the area. Delicious authentic-style meals are prepared by the Thai chef, Chock, and served in the bar nightly. You could go for a spicy red, green, or panang curry, made with coconut and chilis; or a classic pad Thai served with crispy wontons. The menu also has traditional pub options, such as burgers and steaks and Sunday roast, but it's the Thai food that packs in the crowds. Some nights include live music.

Main St., Kildare Town. cunninghamskildare.com. ✆ **045/521780.** Entrees €21–€34. Bar: Mon–Sat 5–9pm; Sun 1–7pm. Restaurant: Wed–Thurs 5–9pm; Fri–Sat 5–9:30pm; Sun 1–7pm.

Hartes ♥♥ GASTRO PUB A multiple winner for "Best Restaurant in Co. Kildare," Hartes looks like a traditional pub from the outside. But expect no Irish stew here. The owners are dedicated to locally grown produce and sustainable farming practices, and the chefs can tell you where every piece of meat or seafood came from in dishes like the local goat cheese and fig tart, or the chicken wings with dry chili rub and mint yogurt. For mains, try the chicken and chorizo cassoulet, or the halloumi fritters with chickpea tagine—but save room for dessert. The chocolate fondant with 70% dark chocolate is a personal favorite of ours.
Market Sq., Kildare Town. harteskildare.ie. ✆ **045/533557.** Entrees €19–€39. Tues 4:30–9pm; Wed–Thurs 12:30–4pm and 5–9pm; Fri–Sat 12:30–4pm and 5–9:30pm; Sun 12:30–8pm.

Neighbourhood ♥♥♥ MODERN IRISH In what was a former pub on the main street in Naas, chef Gareth Naughton and his team have created a culinary hotspot, taking the highest-quality local ingredients and adding a twist. Salt-aged duck breast comes with carrot, duck sausage, prune ketchup, and duck sauce; roasted cod is accompanied by miso cauliflower, boudin noir, mussels, and seaweed. The all-day dinner menu is short, with around six entrees, and there are two sharing specials, which

local hero: SILKEN THOMAS

Nobleman and rebel rolled into one, Silken Thomas was an unlikely revolutionary. More properly known as Thomas FitzGerald, the 10th Earl of Kildare, he was born in 1513 to illustrious parents—his father was governor of Ireland—and spent much of his childhood at the court of King Henry VIII in England.

Thomas returned to Ireland as a young man, to follow in his father's footsteps and rule on behalf of the king. However, when word reached him that his father had fallen out with Henry and been executed, Thomas raised a rebellion. It began with a blistering attack on Dublin Castle. That failed, but the English were rattled. Thomas and his men retreated to the relative safety of County Kildare, expecting a counterattack at any moment. And indeed it came . . . but by stealth. While Thomas was temporarily absent from his garrison, a guard was bribed to let in a small group of English soldiers, who massacred everybody inside.

Thomas and his remaining men fought valiantly for a while longer. The struggle was futile, however, and Thomas eventually agreed to surrender in return for a promise that he and his closest compatriots would be spared. But King Henry wasn't one for keeping his word. Thomas and his men were sentenced to death by hanging, drawing, and quartering.

On a bleak February morning in 1537, Thomas and the others were hanged by the neck, but cut down before they died. Then they were cut open, their bowels and genitals removed and then burned in front of their eyes. They were finally killed by beheading, after which their corpses were cut into quarters and placed on spikes. Such was the wrath of kings.

Despite this chilling end, Thomas remains a folk hero. But why the unusual nickname? The sobriquet "Silken Thomas" comes from the fact that Thomas always dressed in the height of fashion. And when his army of 200 men rode into battle, they wore ribbons of silk streaming from their helmets.

change each day. As well as the a la carte menu, there's a good-value early-bird menu available up to 6pm Wednesday through Saturday, with two courses for €30 or three courses for €35.

1 N Main St., Naas, Co. Kildare. neighbourhoodnaas.com. ✆ **045/954-466.** Entrees €28–€45. Wed–Fri 5–9:15pm; Sat 11am–2:30pm and 5–9:15pm; Sun noon–3:30pm and 5–8pm. Fixed-price menu Wed–Sat to 6pm.

Silken Thomas ♥ INTERNATIONAL Named for a real-life knight and dashing rebel (see box on p. 198), this atmospheric pub offers simple, tasty, unfussy meals in a jovial atmosphere. The menu is something of a global tour, with Mexican fajitas, Chinese stir-fries, and Indian curries happily served alongside burgers, salads, and fish and chips and other familiar Irish fare. There's also a carvery (buffet-style station serving roast meat and vegetables) from noon daily and a substantial breakfast menu.

16 Market Sq., Kildare Town. silkenthomas.com. ✆ **045/522232.** Entrees €19–€25. Mon–Sat 9am–8:30pm; Sun 9am–8pm.

Sports & Outdoor Pursuits in Kildare

GOLF The flat plains here create excellent parkland layouts, including the Arnold Palmer–designed, par-72 **K Club** in Straffan (kclub.ie; ✆ **01/601-7200**). The club has two courses, with greens fees ranging from €90 to €125 (South course) and €130 to €225 (North course).

WALKING The way-marked **Grand Canal Way,** a long-distance walking path that cuts through part of Kildare, passes through such scenic towns as Sallins, Robertstown, and Edenderry, where you can find a room and stock up on provisions. For more information, go to **irishtrails.ie/Trail/Grand-Canal-Way/18**, or contact the Kildare tourist office (p. 192).

SOUTH OF DUBLIN: COUNTIES WICKLOW & CARLOW

Wicklow's northernmost border is just a dozen or so miles south of Dublin, making it one of the easiest day trips from the city. The centerpiece of the region is the beautiful **Wicklow Mountains.** The highest peak is just 1,102m (3,035 ft.) high, but the hills are traversed by the well-marked **Wicklow Way** walking path, which wanders for miles past mountain tarns and secluded glens. Tucked into the mountains are the isolated monastery and lakes of **Glendalough** and picturesque villages such as **Roundwood, Laragh,** and **Aughrim.** Along the coast, the busy town of **Bray** is 12.6km (7¾ miles) south of Dún Laoghaire. Farther south is the coastal town of **Greystones** and, just inland, the charming villages of **Enniskerry** and **Avoca.** A handful of historic stately homes and gardens dot the countryside.

Just over the border of County Wicklow lies **County Carlow,** one of Ireland's smallest counties, bordered to the east by the Blackstairs Mountains and to the west by the fertile limestone land of the Barrow Valley and the Killeshin Hills. Its most prominent feature is the 5,000-year-old granite formation known as **Brownshill Dolmen.**

A WALK FROM bray

At the southern end of the DART line from Dublin, the town of **Bray** is within reach for an afternoon excursion from the city. The seafront boardwalk was popular in Victorian times and still has a handful of amusement arcades and pubs. Bray's greatest pleasure is probably the stunning coastal view of Killiney Bay, Dalkey Island, and Bray from the rocky promontory of **Bray Head.** Follow the beachside promenade south through Bray; at the outskirts of town, the promenade turns left and up, beginning the ascent of Bray Head. Shortly after the ascent begins, a trail branches to the left—this is the cliffside Bray to Greystones walk, which continues another 5km (3 miles) along the coast to Greystones. From the center of Greystones, a DART train (check times on irishrail.ie) will take you back to Bray. It's an easy walk, about 2 hours each way, but don't attempt it in bad weather or strong winds, when the cliffside path becomes treacherous. Check before visiting, as it is sometimes closed because of landslides.

Visitor Information

The **Wicklow Tourist Information Office,** Fitzwilliam Square, Wicklow Town (visitwicklow.ie; ✆ **040/469117**), is open year-round Monday to Friday 9am until 5pm (closed Sat–Sun). The **Carlow Tourist Office,** Library Building, College Street, Carlow Town (carlowtourism.com; ✆ **059/913-0411**), is open year-round Monday to Friday 10am until 5pm, plus February to October on Saturday 10am to 1pm and 1:30 to 4:30pm, June through August Sunday and bank holidays from 2 to 4:30pm.

Exploring South of Dublin

Avondale House and Beyond the Trees ♥♥ HISTORIC HOUSE/ NATURE SITE Avondale House was built in 1777, and from 1904 to 1915 the estate became the "birthplace of Irish forestry" when the Irish state experimented with tree species, planting different varieties to see which would best suit Irish forestry. The Treetop Walk is an elevated 1.4km (0.85-mile) walkway that sweeps past the tops of trees like oaks, spruces, and giant redwoods. There's lots of information and interactive elements along the way—including a viewing tower and an optional giant slide at the end—suitable for all ages. The walks along the forest park trails are just as nice. You can also take one of the house tours of **Avondale House** (1½ hr.) or grab a bite to eat at the **Seed Café.** Next door to the cafe is a children's play area.

Rathdrum, Co. Wicklow. beyondthetreesavondale.com. ✆ **0404/46111.** Treetop walk or house tour €16 adults; €14 seniors and students; €13 children 4–17; free for children 3 and under; €30–€42 families. Half-hour house tour €11 adults and children 12–17; free children 11 and under. Combination ticket for Treetop Walk and house tour €29 adults; €25 seniors and students; €23 children 4–17; free for children 3 and under; €54–€76 families. Treetop Walk Mar–Aug 9am–7pm; Sept 9:30am–7pm; Oct to mid-Nov 9:30am–5pm, mid-Nov to Jan noon–4pm; Feb 10am–5pm. Avondale House daily, tour times vary. Parking €5 per car.

Brownshill Dolmen ♥ ANCIENT SITE Resembling an elephant about to topple slowly to one side, this megalithic stone table has crouched in this green field in County Carlow for millennia. No one knows its purpose, though archaeologists suspect the dolmen was built as a portal tomb to mark the burial place of a long-dead king. The gigantic stack of stones is estimated to be 5,000 years old, and for many centuries, people believed it had been built by giants. Today, archaeologists say the vast capstone—believed to weigh a colossal 100 tons—was likely rolled into place up an earthen ramp that was then destroyed. Faced with the sheer massiveness of these stones, you may prefer to stick with the tale about the giants.
Off Rathvilly Rd., Carlow Town. carlowtourism.com/attraction/brownshill-dolmen-2. No phone. Free admission. Daily dawn–dusk. Access via parking lot and enclosed pedestrian pathway.

Glendalough ♥♥♥ RELIGIOUS/NATURE SITE Tucked away amid deep forests and surrounded by rolling hills, this evocative, misty glen is a truly magical place. Glendalough means "valley of the two lakes," and you can easily walk around both lakes, or climb the hills to take in the beauty of this extraordinary site from above (you can get maps at the visitor center at the entrance). The area is part of Wicklow Mountains National Park (p. 205). Each of the many walking trails traversing the area takes in scenic vistas and wildlife, as well as some hidden ruins. The oldest ruins are **Teampall na Skellig,** across the lake at the foot of towering cliffs (unfortunately, there's no boat service and they cannot be visited), and the cave known as **Kevin's Bed,** believed to be where a monk known as St. Kevin lived when he first arrived at Glendalough. More accessible are the ruins of the monastic village he founded—accessed from the main road or along the path from the upper lake to the lower lake. Here, there's a nearly perfect round tower, 31m (102 ft.) high and 16m (52 ft.) around the base, as well as hundreds of timeworn Celtic crosses and several chapels. One of these is St. Kevin's Chapel, often called **St. Kevin's Kitchen,** a fine specimen of an early Irish barrel-vaulted oratory with a miniature round belfry rising from a stone roof. First established by St. Kevin in the 6th century, Glendalough was originally devoted to Christian worship and scholarly learning. Sacked first by the Vikings and later by the English, it was eventually abandoned by the monks who sought refuge here. Those beautiful round towers were actually hideouts with retractable ladders that the monks would pull up after them when the raiders arrived. Most of the buildings were destroyed in repeated attacks, but enough survive to ensure the ruins are a striking and atmospheric spectacle in this peaceful valley.
Signposted from R756, 2km (1⅓ miles) W of Laragh, Co. Wicklow. heritageireland.ie. ✆ **040/445-352.** Free admission to national park, lakes, and Glendalough monastic village. Visitor center admission €5 adults; €4 seniors; €3 students and children; €13 families. Daily 9:30am–6pm (closes at 5pm mid-Oct to mid-Mar); last admission 45 min. before closing. Car parking in Upper Lake car park €5 per car (fee includes one free admission to visitor center).

Glenmacnass Waterfall ♥ NATURE SITE A wide strip of silver running down a rugged hill, the Glenmacnass Waterfall is more pretty than spectacular. It doesn't plummet so much as slip through the rugged countryside and down Mt. Mullagheleevaun. From the parking lot near the top of the hill there's a well-signposted path to the falls, but take care on the rocks, which can be slippery.

Laragh, Co. Wicklow. Follow Military Rd. through the Sally Gap and Laragh to the top of Glenmacnass Valley, and then watch for signs to the waterfall. Free admission.

Huntington Castle and Gardens ♥♥ CASTLE This place has all the makings of a spectacular haunting. It's built on the site of a 14th-century abbey, which was itself built on top of a Druid temple (a modern shrine to the Egyptian goddess Isis lies in the basement, in what used to be the kitchens and dungeons). The rambling, 17th-century crenelated manor house is overgrown with vines that turn blood-red in the fall. It should come as no surprise then that the castle claims to be the most haunted building in Ireland. The owners say it is plagued by ghosts of Druids who cause mists in the fields and showers of blood. Other than that, it's very nice. The interior can only be seen by guided tour, which includes areas that were closed until recently, such as the old kitchens and drawing room. The gardens are beautiful—many of the plants date back to the 18th century—and the unusual 17th-century water features have been restored to working condition. Don't miss the walking path guarded on either side by ancient yew trees. An adventure playground keeps little ones busy. If you're not afraid of ghosts, the castle offers historic guest rooms in the old part of the castle; rooms start at around €260.

Clonegal (off N80, 6.5km/4 miles from Bunclody), Co. Carlow. huntingtoncastle.com. ✆ **053/937-7160.** Guided tours: €13.50 adults; €12.50 seniors and students; €6 children 11 and under. May–Sept daily tours hourly 1–4pm; Oct–Dec and Feb–April Sat–Sun tours hourly 1–3pm. Gardens and playground only: €6.95 adults; €3 children 4–12. May–Sept daily 11am–5pm; Oct–Dec and Feb–April Sat–Sun only (same hours). Last admission 1 hr. before closing.

Armor and hunting trophies line a hallway in rambling Huntington Castle.

Mount Usher Gardens ♥♥ GARDENS Spreading out on 8 hectares (20 acres) at the edge of the River Vartry, this peaceful and romantic site was once an ancient lake. Since 1868 it's been a riverside garden, designed in a distinctively informal style, with fiery rhododendrons, fragrant

The sweeping gardens and grounds of Powerscourt Estate.

eucalyptus trees, giant Tibetan lilies, and snowy camellias competing for your attention. Attuned to their natural setting, these gardens have an almost untended feel—a sort of floral woodland. The spacious **Avoca Garden Café** overlooks the river and gardens.

Off the N11, Ashford, Co. Wicklow. mountushergardens.ie. ✆ **040/449672.** Admission €10 adults; €8 seniors and students; €5 children 4–16; free children 3 and under. Daily 10am–5:30pm (closes 5pm Nov–Mar). Last admission 1 hr. before closing.

Powerscourt Estate ♥♥♥ GARDENS/HISTORIC HOUSE The gardens of this magnificent estate are truly gorgeous, with classical statuary, a shady grotto made of petrified moss, a peaceful Japanese garden, and a massive, over-the-top fountain from which statues of winged horses rise. Landscaper Daniel Robertson designed the gardens between 1745 and 1767, and they take full advantage of splendid views of the Sugar Loaf mountain and surrounding countryside. Legend has it that thanks to crippling gout, Robertson oversaw the work while being carted around in a wheelbarrow, sipping port as he went. When the bottle was dry, work was done for the day. The whole thing is impressive enough that back in 2014, *National Geographic* magazine named Powerscourt's the third-greatest gardens in the world. At the estate's garden center, you can learn everything there is to know about the plants that thrive here, and even pick up seeds to take home (although beware of Customs rules for such things). Sadly, the 20th century was not kind to the Palladian house itself, when it was abandoned and then gutted by fire. It has since been partially restored, and a few rooms are open to the public, but only on Sundays and Mondays in May through September. The estate also has a playground and gift shops. If you feel energetic, follow the well-marked path over 7km (4 miles) to the picturesque **Powerscourt Waterfall**—the highest in Ireland at 121m (397 ft.); you can also drive here, following signs from the estate. The waterfall is at its most powerful in the days after a heavy rainfall. Powerscourt is only about 20km (12½ miles) south of Dublin and can be reached by city bus 44 or 185 to Enniskerry village, approximately a 25-minute walk from the estate.

On R760, Enniskerry, Co. Wicklow. powerscourt.com. ✆ **01/204-6000.** Gardens: €13.50 adults (€10 Nov–Feb); €11.50 seniors (€9); €10 students (€8.50); €5 children 5 and over; €32 families (€25). Waterfall: €7.50 adults; €6.50 seniors; €6 students; €3.50 children 15 and under; free children 2 and under; €19 families. Gardens: Mar–Oct daily 9:30am–5:30pm (or at dusk if earlier); Nov and Feb 9:30am–5pm; Dec–Jan 9:30am–4:30pm. Last admission ½ hr. before closing. Garden Pavilion: daily 9:30am–5:30pm. Powerscourt Waterfall: May–Aug 9:30am–7pm (last admission 6pm); Mar–Apr and Sept–Oct 10:30am–5:30pm (last admission 5pm); Nov–Feb 10:30am–4pm (last admission 3:30pm).

Russborough House ♥♥ HISTORIC HOUSE Sprawling low across the green landscape, this somber gray stone villa was built between 1741 and 1751. The designer was Richard Cassels, the same man who designed the much more fanciful Powerscourt House (see above). Today, however, Russborough is known not for its architecture but for housing a small but mighty art gallery. In the 1950s, the house was bought by Sir Alfred Beit, a member of the De Beers diamond family, specifically to hold his massive trove of personal art, and it displays one of the most exquisite small rural art collections you're likely to find anywhere. Although many of the most valuable paintings have been moved to other museums after a series of robberies, you can still view works by Vermeer, Gainsborough, and Rubens. The house can be explored only by guided tour, and there is certainly a lot to see: ornate plaster ceilings by the Lafranchini brothers, huge marble mantelpieces, and fine displays of silver, porcelain, and furniture. Kids will be amused by a fiendish maze and a "fairy trail" on the grounds that tells the story of Russborough's resident fairy. The grounds also hold traditional craft workshops where you can see artisans in action, including a blacksmith and a candlemaker. The estate's other attraction is the **National Bird of Prey Centre** (nationalbirdofpreycentre.ie; ✆ **045/857-755**), home to hawks, owls, falcons, and eagles from different parts of the globe. Check the website for details on how to book a private "hawk walk" through the grounds with a trainer and one of the resident big birds. The center is open daily July through September, Wednesdays to Sundays April to June, and weekends only October through March.

Signposted from N81, 3.2km (2 miles) S of Blessington, Co. Wicklow. russborough.ie. ✆ **045/865-239.** House tour: €14.50 adults; €12 seniors and students; €6.50 children 6–15; free children 5 and under. Maze and fairy trail: €3; €12 families. Outdoor family ticket: maze, parklands, and fairy trail €30. National Bird of Prey Centre: €9 adults; €7 seniors; €6 students and children 6–15; €25 families. House tour Mon–Fri noon–3pm; Sat–Sun 10am–4pm. Parklands daily 9am–6pm. Cafe and shop daily 9:30am–5pm. National Bird of Prey Centre tours Sat–Sun 1:30, 2:30, and 3:30pm; Wed–Fri 2:30 and 3:30pm. All-day parking €4.

St. Mullin's Monastery ♥ RELIGIOUS SITE This monastery has an idyllic setting in a sleepy hamlet beside the River Barrow, surrounded by low hills. These are the ruins of a monastery founded by St. Moling (Mullin) in roughly A.D. 614. In the Middle Ages the monastery ruins were a popular destination, especially at the height of the Black Death in 1348. By tradition, pilgrims would cross the river barefoot, circle the burial spot of St. Mullin nine times, and drink from the healing waters of the saint's well. These waters are still the subject of an annual pilgrimage on or near July 25. A number of rebels from the 1798 Rising are buried here.

On the Barrow Dr., 12km (7½ miles) N of New Ross, St. Mullins, Co. Carlow. Free admission. Daily dawn–dusk.

Vale of Avoca ♥♥ NATURE SITE Basically a peaceful green river valley, the Vale of Avoca is the "Meeting of the Waters" where the Avonmore and Avonbeg rivers join to form the Avoca River. Pleasant as it is, we'd probably never have heard of it were it not for the 19th-century poet Thomas Moore, who wrote, "There is not in the wide world a valley so sweet/As the vale in whose bosom the bright waters meet . . . ." Just 3km (2 miles) away, the charming riverside village of **Avoca** makes a good stop. Here you can tour the traditional mills where **Avoca Handweavers** (avoca.com) still make their coveted blankets, sweaters, and other beautiful homewares, more than 300 years after they spun their first looms. Watch the weavers at work on a tour of the woolen mill, which also has a gift shop (of course) and cafe. The mill is signposted on the R754 road heading north out of the village, and tours run daily from March to October.

Rte. 755, Avoca, Co. Wicklow. avoca.com/en/stores-and-cafes/avoca-village. Tours €8 adults; €6.50 seniors and students; €5 children 5–16; free for children 4 and under. Tours daily 9am–6pm summer; 10am–4pm winter.

Wicklow Mountains National Park ♥♥♥ NATURE SITE Stretching into the mountains around Glendalough, this hilly national park is popular with hikers walking the Wicklow Way, a trail that cuts across the park (p. 209). In the high season, you'll find an information station at the Upper Lake at Glendalough where you can get maps and route guides. Behind the center is a sweet little "sensory garden" (free admission) containing a variety of plants chosen for their scent, texture, and even the sounds of the wildlife they attract. The closest parking is at Upper Lake, where you'll pay a few euros per car. ***Note:*** The Irish National Parks & Wildlife Service warns that ticks carrying Lyme disease are known to live in the hills. Although the risk of contracting the disease is small, you should dress in long sleeves, wear a hat, avoid hiking in shorts, and check for ticks afterward. Don't panic too readily if you find one, though; ticks need to be attached for at least 24 hours for infection to take place, and fewer than 100 cases are reported annually in the whole of Ireland.

Heathlands mantle the panoramic Wicklow Mountains.

In the park service's reassuring words, "Remember, be aware, but don't worry."

Glendalough, Co. Wicklow. wicklowmountainsnationalpark.ie. ✆ **0404/45425.** Free admission to national park. Glendalough Visitor Centre: €5 adults; €4 seniors; €3 students and children; €13 families. Park open 24 hr. Visitor center daily 9:30am–6pm (to 5pm Mar–Oct). Last admission to center 45 min. before closing. Car parking in Upper Lake car park €5 per car (fee includes one free admission to visitor center).

Where to Stay South of Dublin

BrookLodge & Macreddin Village ♥♥♥ A winning combination of top-end hotel, spa, and holiday village, BrookLodge is a luxurious hideaway. Guest rooms are understated and contemporary in design, while suites—which come with a stylish mezzanine level—offer plenty of extra room for not much greater cost. The hotel is surrounded by an entire village of activities, from golf, hiking, and horseback riding to an artisan baker, deli, and crafts store. The peaceful spa, **Wells,** is worth trying out—treatments start at €60. The main restaurant, the excellent **Strawberry Tree ♥♥♥** (p. 210), was the first in Ireland to gain full organic certification.

Macreddin Village (btw. Aughrim and Aghavannagh), Co. Wicklow. brooklodge.com. ✆ **040/236444.** 86 units. €134–€380 double; €234–€570 suite. Breakfast included. Free parking. **Amenities:** 2 restaurants; 2 pubs; golf course; gym; pool; room service; spa; Wi-Fi (free).

The Lord Bagenal ♥♥ This cheerful, modern hotel on the banks of the River Barrow loses points for character, but the air-conditioned bedrooms are spacious and comfortable. Ask for a room with a view of the river. This is a good choice for families; in addition to family rooms that cost very little more than doubles, the staff here will help organize activities, such as kayaking or fishing on the Barrow. The in-house restaurant serves rich, French-influenced cuisine in a formal setting, while the bar, with its cozy open fires and relaxed atmosphere, offers a simple, crowd-pleasing menu (steaks, burgers, local fish, and the like).

Main St., Leighlinbridge, Co. Carlow. lordbagenal.com. ✆ **059/977-4000.** 39 units. €125–€315 double. Breakfast included. **Amenities:** Restaurant; bar; room service; Wi-Fi (free).

Powerscourt Hotel ♥♥♥ The grand, sweeping Palladian-style frontage of this gorgeous hotel, part of the Marriott chain, is almost as impressive as its historic namesake, Powerscourt House (p. 203). Guest rooms are large and elegantly furnished. The lounges are gorgeous, with soaring ceilings, beautiful furniture, and exquisite views. The spa is positively sci-fi in its sleek design—the pool is lit by illuminated Swarovski crystals—and the list of treatments includes everything from hot stone treatments to a "shillelagh massage" in which you are, we kid you not, rubbed down with a lucky stick. The hotel has three eateries of varying levels of formality: The **Sika Restaurant** serves outstanding modern Irish menus (€85 for three courses); the marginally less formal **Sugar Loaf Lounge** offers a lavish afternoon tea (€60 per person); and the casual **Sally Gap Bar & Brasserie** is the place for great steaks and seafood. ***Be aware:*** This is a lovely hotel, but it's not intimate—200 rooms can make it feel crowded, and service can slip. The child-friendly policy, while great for families, is not conducive to pure relaxation. People come here for the style and the luxury—but not peace.

Powerscourt Estate, near Enniskerry, Co. Wicklow. powerscourthotel.com. ✆ **01/274-8888.** 200 units. €242–€466 double; €404–€916 suite. Breakfast included. Free parking. **Amenities:** 2 restaurants; bar; gym; pool; pub; room service; spa; Wi-Fi (free).

Wicklow Way Lodge ♥♥ This B&B looks unassuming from the outside, but step inside and you'll find a simple haven of tranquility and charm. Guest rooms are tastefully furnished, with lots of polished wood and toasty underfloor heating. Enormous windows take advantage of the glorious view—a fantasia of rolling hills and verdant green in spring, while in the fall, the mist rolls in across a blanket of autumnal hues. Breathe in the air and feel your soul relax—this is the Ireland you came for, isn't it? There's one family room, though note that very young kids aren't allowed because of the house's split-level layout. Hosts Marilyn and Seamus are a joy, genuinely kind and helpful and full of tips for the best walking paths. Glendalough (p. 201) is just 6km (4 miles) from here. There's homemade bread at breakfast, with fresh local eggs—and try the porridge, too! Plan ahead, though—the lodge can get booked up almost a year in advance.

Oldbridge, Roundwood, Co. Wicklow. wicklowwaylodge.com. ✆ **01/281-8489.** 5 units. €170–€220 double. Breakfast included. Free parking. **Amenities:** Wi-Fi (free in lounge only).

Where to Eat South of Dublin

Wicklow is close enough to Dublin for residents to commute, so it has a gentrified restaurant scene. In addition to the options listed below, there are many small, independent places to stop for lunch or light food. In the charming village of Delgany, **Firehouse Bakery** (Old Delgany Inn; thefirehouse.ie) will ruin your diet with its freshly baked pastries, tarts, and cakes. It's the perfect place to grab breakfast or lunch on the go. In Enniskerry, **Poppies** (The Square; facebook.com/poppiesireland) is a terrific quick stop for light lunches eaten in and picnic fodder to take out. Freshly made sandwiches, quiches, and cakes are the specialty.

Chakra by Jaipur ♥♥♥ INDIAN If you need a break from Irish food, this outstanding Indian restaurant is one of the best in the area. It's not the most idyllic location, in a concrete-and-glass shopping mall down a rather nondescript street in Greystones, but that's really the only disappointing thing about it. The food is excellent: Indian cuisine, with all its spice, infused with the flavors of Ireland. You might start with a plate of Barbary duck breast tikka with passionfruit and orange, before moving on to a traditional butter chicken made with local honey. It's a must-visit for lovers of Indian food.

1st floor, Meridian Point, Church Rd., Greystones. chakra.ie. ✆ **01/201-7228.** Entrees €26–€28. Tues–Thurs 5–10pm; Fri–Sat 5–10:30pm; Sun 2–9pm.

Harbour Kitchen ♥♥♥ SEAFOOD Not surprisingly for a restaurant at Greystones Harbour, the Harbour Kitchen specializes in fish, served

Discover Michelin-starred Indian food in County Wicklow, at Chakra by Jaipur.

WALK THIS WAY: hiking IN COUNTY WICKLOW

Loved by hikers and ramblers for its peace, isolation, and sheer beauty, the **Wicklow Way** is a 132km (82-mile) signposted walking path that follows forest trails, sheep paths, and country roads from the suburbs south of Dublin up into the Wicklow Mountains and down through country farmland to Clonegal in County Carlow.

It takes about 5 to 7 days to walk its entirety, with overnight stops at B&Bs and hostels along the route. You can also organize baggage transfers and guides. Most people, however, choose to walk sections as day trips. (***Tip:*** The southern section, through Tinahely, Shillelagh, and Clonegal, is much gentler and less hilly.) You can pick up information and maps at the Wicklow Mountains National Park Visitor Centre at Glendalough, or get more information on the Wicklow Way, including maps and suppliers, at **visitwicklow.ie**.

St. Kevin's Way, an ancient pilgrims' route more than 1,000 years old, has recently been restored. The path runs for 30km (19 miles) through scenic countryside from Hollywood to Glendalough. As it winds among roads, forest paths, and open mountainside, the route visits many of the historical sites associated with St. Kevin.

Leaflets containing maps and route descriptions for other walks can be found at tourist offices. Folks who prefer less-strenuous walking may enjoy the paths around the lakes at **Glendalough.**

with a creative flair (there are steak, chicken, and vegetarian options, too). This is a lovely, bright space over the Beach House Pub with exposed brick walls and high, wood-beamed ceilings adding atmosphere and sea views to complete the ambience. Many ingredients are locally sourced, and wild treats like seaweed and nettles make an appearance. Some menu highlights include crab with dressed celery and wasabi buttermilk; scallops with potato puree, smoked lardons, and garden peas; and wild halibut with house gnocchi, confit leeks, and ash beurre blanc.

Beach Rd., Greystones. harbourkitchen.ie. ✆ **01/517-0197.** Entrees €20–€42. Wed–Sat 5–9:30pm; Sun 1–8pm.

Hunter's Hotel ♥♥♥ IRISH Run by the same family for more than 200 years, this gorgeous old coaching inn with gardens is known for its good, traditional-style food. Afternoon tea and dinner are served daily, and there are weekend lunches. Expect dishes like roast lamb, roast beef, and roast duck with all the trimmings, followed by apple crumble. It's a great stop if you're passing through the area, but if you fancy staying on longer, there are 2 acres of gardens plus a river walk for a post-meal stroll, and the hotel has 16 bedrooms.

Newrath Bridge, Rathnew. hunters.ie. ✆ **0404/40106.** Sat lunch 2 courses €38, 3 courses €47; Sun lunch 3 courses €48. Dinner 2 courses €40, 3 courses €50 (Sat €48–€60). Afternoon tea Mon–Fri 1–5:30pm, Sat 4–5.30pm, Sun 4:30–5.30pm; lunch Sat 1–4pm, Sun 2 sittings at 12:30 and 2:45pm; dinner daily 7:30–8:30pm.

The Pigeon House ♥♥♥ MODERN IRISH This award-winning restaurant in Delgany village is renowned for its innovative but unpretentious approach. In an old, converted inn, the dining room has an airy feel. It's open for breakfast, brunch, and lunch, and all meals are delicious. Breakfast has everything from pancakes to a full grill; lunch options vary from light salads to sturdy meals like beef pie with thyme puff pastry, harissa, and honey carrots. Sweet potato falafel is served with roasted red pepper hummus, mint and mango yogurt, feta, dukkah, and grilled flatbread. Everything is understated and absurdly fresh. There's a good cocktail list, too.

Delgany. pigeonhouse.ie. ✆ **01/287-7103.** Entrees €16–€20. Daily 9am–3pm.

The Strawberry Tree ♥♥♥ MODERN IRISH The main restaurant of the excellent **BrookLodge** complex (p. 206) is rightly regarded as one of the best places to dine in the region. The beautiful, blue-tinged dining room makes a wonderful setting for any gathering. This was the first restaurant in Ireland to receive full organic certification, and that ethos guides the outstanding modern Irish menu, which takes localism seriously. Depending on the season, you might dine on wild Kilmore Quay sole with Jerusalem artichoke and fermented whey, or beef filet with seasonal vegetables and bone gravy. If you're feeling gregarious, book a place at the "big table"—a communal table that seats up to 40, at which you're served a set menu in the style of a feast.

At BrookLodge, Macreddin Village (btw. Aughrim and Aghavannagh). brooklodge.com. ✆ **040/236444.** Fixed-price menu €78. Wed–Sun 6:30–9:30pm (also Mon–Tues in July–Aug).

Sports & Outdoor Pursuits in Wicklow

CYCLING **Cycling Safaris** (cyclingsafaris.com; ✆ **01/260-0749**) offers a weeklong tour of Dublin and Wicklow starting at €1,045 per person, including bed, breakfast, and luggage transfers.

HORSEBACK RIDING The hillside paths of Wicklow are perfect for horseback riding. More than a dozen stables and equestrian centers in the area offer horses for hire and riding lessons. Rates average around €70 to €90 per hour. **Brennanstown Riding School,** Hollybrook, Kilmacanogue, Co. Wicklow (brennanstownrs.ie; ✆ **01/286-3778**), offers beginner's treks up picturesque Little Sugar Loaf Mountain.

WATERSPORTS & ADVENTURE SPORTS Deep in the Wicklow Mountains, the Blessington Lakes are a 2,000-hectare (4,940-acre) playground of tranquil, clean, speedboat-free water. At the Hidden Valley Holiday Park in Rathdrum, **Wicklow Adventures** (hiddenvalley.ie; ✆ **086/727-2872**) offers high-octane outdoor activities, including laser tag. A standard daily ticket costs €24 per child, €16.50 per adult, and €7.50 per senior; it's free for children 3 and under.

6

THE SOUTHEAST

It doesn't take long to feel like you're deep into the Irish countryside as you travel to the counties south of Dublin. For a start, the accent changes—subtly but unmistakably, a mellifluous dialect creeps in, with a musical lilt all its own. The three main counties of the Southeast—**Waterford, Wexford,** and **Kilkenny**—are close enough together that you could use any as a base for exploring the region by car. (It's a little trickier by public transport, unless you stick to the main towns.) Waterford's tourism slogan "Where Ireland Begins" definitely has a grain of truth to it. Waterford City, the eponymous capital, is Ireland's oldest, founded by Viking invaders in A.D. 914. Wexford and Kilkenny are both rich in medieval heritage, including Kilkenny Castle, one of Ireland's most impressive medieval buildings.

ESSENTIALS

Arriving

BY BUS **Bus Éireann** (buseireann.ie; © **01/836-6111**) operates direct service several times a day from Dublin's central bus station (**Busáras**) into Kilkenny, Wexford, and Waterford. The trip to Kilkenny takes upwards of 2 hours; to Wexford and Waterford, closer to 3.

BY TRAIN **Irish Rail** (irishrail.ie; © **1850/366-222**) operates several trains daily between Dublin and Kilkenny, Wexford, and Waterford. The journey to Kilkenny takes about 90 minutes; to Waterford, a little over 2 hours; and to Wexford, 2½ hours.

BY FERRY Ferries from Britain sail to Rosslare Harbour, 19km (12 miles) south of Wexford Town. Contact **Irish Ferries** (irishferries.ie; © **0818/300-400**) or **Stena Line** (stenaline.com; © **01/907-5555**) for bookings and information.

BY CAR The drive from Dublin to Kilkenny, Waterford, or Wexford is nearly all via motorway. From Dublin to Wexford, take N/M11 south. For Kilkenny, take the M7 southwest out of Dublin, then split off onto M9. If you're heading to Waterford, stay on M9 for another 50km (31 miles) after the turnoff for Kilkenny. The drive to Kilkenny is about 1½ hours, and to Waterford or Wexford about 2 hours, but considerably longer if you're caught in Dublin's terrible rush-hour traffic. For car-rental information in Dublin, see p. 91.

PREVIOUS PAGE: Biking the Waterford Greenway.

Kilkenny, Wexford & Waterford
0 10 miles
0 10 kms
CLARE
Ballina
Killaloe
Nenagh
OFFALY
Roscrea
Abbeyleix
LAOISE (LEIX)
Castledermot
Baltinglass
WICKLOW
Rathdowney
Ballinakill
Durrow
Graigue
Carlow
Rathvilly
Hacketstown
Aughrim
Tullow
Tinahely
Arklow
Templemore
Ballyragget
Templetuohy
Johnstown
Leighlinbridge
Shillelagh
Castleconnell
Newport
Milestone
Urlingford
Freshford
Dunmore Cave
Ballon
Slaney
CARLOW
Clonegal
Gorey
Nore
Whitehall
Limerick
Thurles
Kilkenny
Bagenalstown
Bunclody
Courtown
Littleton
KILKENNY
Barrow
Borris
Mt. Leinster
TIPPERARY
Camolin
IRISH SEA
Pallas Grean
LIMERICK
Bennettsbridge
Ballingarry
Ballymurphy
Ferns
Dundrum
Kells
Callan
Graiguenamanagh
Blackstairs Mts.
Lough Gur
Limerick Junction
Cashel
Oola
Stoneyford
Thomastown
Enniscorthy
Kilmuckridge
Hospital
Drummin
Knocktopher
Inistioge
Bruff
Tipperary
Fethard
Suir
WEXFORD
Ninemilehouse
Bansha
Newinn
Clonroche
Ballyhale
Oilgate
Wexford Bay
Galtee Mts.
Cahir
New Ross
Adamstown
Kilmallock
Rathkeevin
Carrick-on-Suir
Lukeswell
Curracloe
Galtymore
Kilfinane
Clonmel
Wexford
Wexford Harbour
Ardfinnan
Knockanaffrin
Mooncoin
Wellington Bridge
Johnstown Castle
Comeragh Mts.
Portlaw
Cheekpoint
Rosslare
Mitchelstown
Clogheen
Killinick
Rosslare Harbour
Kilcommon
Waterford
Duncannon
Doneralle
Knockmealdown Mts.
Kilmacthomas
St. George's Channel
Lady Island Lake
Glanworth
WATERFORD
Dunmore East
Kilmore Quay
Cappoquin
Tramore
Carnsore Point
Castletownroche
Fermoy
Lismore
Lemybrien
Hook Peninsula
Blackwater
Bunmahon
Annestown
Waterford Harbour
Hook Head
Saltee Islands
To Fishguard
Ballymacmague
Tallow
Dungarvan
To Pembroke
NORTHERN IRELAND
CORK
Ring
Belfast
Kilmona
Clashmore
Grange
Watergrasshill
Youghal
REPUBLIC OF IRELAND
Galway
Dublin
Blarney
Carrigtohill
Ardmore
Castlemartyr
CELTIC SEA
Cork
Midleton
Ballymacoda
Map Area
Passage West
Cobh
Cork
To Roscoff
Cork Int'l
Cloyne
Ballycotton

Getting Around

Getting from Dublin to the centers of Kilkenny, Wexford, or Waterford by public transport is easy. It's also relatively simple to travel between the three cities. However, as with most rural areas in Ireland, getting *around* the countryside by public transport once you're there is extremely difficult. Unless you're sticking to the big towns, your best option is to rent a car.

BY BUS Direct buses connect Waterford and Wexford every couple of hours; most journeys take an hour. A few buses per day run between Kilkenny and Waterford; the journey takes 1 to 2 hours, depending on whether you have to change buses (which you almost always do). No convenient bus routes connect Kilkenny and Wexford; you'll have to change in Waterford.

BY TRAIN A half-dozen or so trains daily travel between Kilkenny and Waterford; the journey takes 35 minutes. Getting from Kilkenny or Waterford to Wexford by train involves multiple changes and can take all day; avoid this route if at all possible.

BY CAR If you take public transport to the Southeast and then want to drive around the countryside, you can easily pick up a rental car in one of the main towns. In Kilkenny, **Enterprise Rent-a-Car** has a branch at the Kilkenny Car Complex, Dublin Road (enterprise.ie; ✆ **056/775-3318**). **Hertz** has a branch in Wexford Town, on Ferrybank (✆ **053/915-2500**), or

ghost language: **YOLA**

The extinct Yola language of County Wexford was a dialect of medieval English that survived in Ireland from the 12th century to the mid-1800s. The very name "Yola" is, in fact, Yola for "old."

Much of what we know of Yola is thanks to the work of a man named Jacob Poole, who compiled glossaries from native speakers between 1800 and 1827. Somewhat more celebrated, however, is the happy accident of history that occurred when the Earl of Mulgrave, Lord Lieutenant (governor) of Ireland, visited Wexford in 1836. To his surprise, Mulgrave was greeted by a local dignitary who gave his welcome speech entirely in Yola. A full transcript survives, and its evocative closing lines are enough to show how strange, yet slightly familiar, Yola must have sounded:

"Wi Irishmen ower generale houpes be ee-boud, az Irishmen, an az dwelleràs na cosh an loyale o' Baronie Forthe, w'oul daie an ercha daie, our meines an oure gurles, praie var long an happie zins, shorne o'lournagh an ee-vilt wi benisons, an yersel and oure gude zovereine, till ee zin o'oure daies be var aye be ee-go to'glade . . . ."

With Irishmen our common hopes are inseparably bound up, as Irishmen, and as inhabitants, faithful and loyal, of the Barony Forth, we will daily and every day, our wives and our children, implore long and happy days, free from melancholy and full of blessings, for yourself and our good sovereign, until the sun of our lives be gone down the dark valley . . . .

you can try **Budget** at Rosslare Ferryport (budget.ie; ✆ **053/913-3318**). In Waterford, **Enterprise** has a branch on Cork Road (enterprise.ie; ✆ **051/304-804**).

BY FERRY Driving between Waterford and Wexford involves a circuitous route via New Ross—or you can cut the distance in half by taking the handy car ferry from the poetically named **Passage East,** about 12km (7½ miles) east of Waterford (passageferry.ie; ✆ **051/382-480**). Regular crossings run Monday to Saturday 7am until 8pm, Sunday and public holidays 9:30am to 8pm; in summer (June–Aug) ferries run until 9pm. Tickets per car are €10 one-way, €14 round-trip. Discounts are available for multiple crossings.

COUNTY WATERFORD

County Waterford is set along Ireland's southeast coastline, with plenty of rolling countryside as well as bays and beaches dotted along the way. Waterford City itself is a small but vibrant city set slightly inland on the River Suir, near the head of Waterford Harbour. It is the oldest city in the country, first settled by Viking invaders in the 9th century, and many of the city's best heritage sites can be found in the historic Viking Triangle.

Visitor Information

The **Waterford Tourist Information Centre** is located in the Medieval Museum on Cathedral Square, Waterford (visitwaterford.com; ✆ **1800/230-330**). It's open Monday to Friday 9am until 5pm, Saturday 10am to 5pm, and Sunday and bank holidays 11am to 5pm.

Exploring Waterford City

Bishop's Palace ♥♥ MUSEUM One of six separate museums that are known collectively as **Waterford Treasures,** the Bishop's Palace focuses on life in the city from 1700 until the mid–20th century. Costumed guides show you around the collection, which includes impressive displays of 18th-century furniture, art, and fashion. The Georgian drawing room is dominated by Willem Van der Hagen's fascinating 1736 landscape painting of Waterford City—the oldest landscape of an Irish city in existence—depicting long-vanished Waterford landmarks such as the medieval Christ Church Cathedral, demolished in 1773. Appropriately, given its close proximity to the famous factory (p. 218), the museum also holds the earliest surviving pieces of Waterford Crystal, including a decanter dating from 1789. The 3D *Masterpieces in Glass* experience uses virtual reality to explore the storied history of glassmaking in Waterford.

The Mall. waterfordtreasures.com/bishops-palace. ✆ **051/849-650.** Admission €10; free for children 12 and under with paying guest. Included in the €18 Freedom of Waterford ticket; see p. 216. Mon–Fri 9:15am–5pm; Sat 10am–5pm; Sun and public holidays 11am–5pm (June–Aug opens 10am Mon–Fri and 9:30am on Sat). Last admission 4:20pm.

viking triangle tours & the FREEDOM OF WATERFORD

For those who like their history entertaining and fast, the **Epic Tour of the Viking Triangle** walking tour offered by the Waterford tourism office takes in 1,100 years of local history in 45 minutes. Enthusiastic guides lead you to several points of interest within the so-called "Viking Triangle" of central Waterford, starting at the **Bishop's Palace** (p. 215) and moving swiftly through **Reginald's Tower** (p. 220), Greyfriars Church, the **Chorister's Hall** (p. 220), and **Christ Church Cathedral** (see below). You don't get to linger inside any of these places (some you won't see further than the lobby), so think of it as a whistle-stop history primer rather than anything in depth. Depending on the guide, the tour's raucous style can be heavy on audience participation, which may not be to everybody's taste, but kids get a kick out of the wacky vibe. Tours operate daily year-round at noon, 2, and 4pm; meet outside the Bishop's Palace on the Mall. On its own, the tour costs €10 adults, free for children 12 and under, but it's also included in the €18 **Freedom of Waterford** ticket, which bundles together admission to the tour plus the **Medieval Museum** (p. 220), **Bishop's Palace, Irish Museum of Time** (p. 219), and **Irish Silver Museum** (p. 219). For details, see waterfordtreasures.com and select the "Freedom of Waterford" ticket option.

Christ Church Cathedral ♥♥ CATHEDRAL Waterford's most important church building is a beautiful example of late-18th-century architecture. Corinthian columns top grand marble plinths, rising up to meet the stucco, with its delicate filigreed detail. The current building, designed by John Roberts, was finished in 1773, replacing one built by the Vikings in the 11th century. (One solitary pillar remains from the original building.) This was where Strongbow, the first English lord to invade Ireland, married an Irish princess—thus gaining a permanent foothold into Irish nobility. Christ Church's Catholic counterpart, the Holy Trinity Cathedral (also designed by John Roberts), is on Barronstrand Street (p. 218).

Cathedral Sq. christchurchwaterford.com. ✆ **051/858958.** Free admission. Apr–Oct Mon–Sat 10am–5pm (closes 4pm some Mon, Thurs, and Fri); Nov–Mar Mon–Sat noon–2pm.

Garter Lane Arts Centre ♥♥ ARTS CENTER One of Ireland's largest arts centers, the Garter Lane occupies two buildings on O'Connell Street. Number 5 holds exhibition rooms and artists' studios, and no. 22a, a former Friends meetinghouse, is home of the Garter Lane Theatre, along with an art gallery and courtyard. The gallery showcases works by contemporary and local artists, and hosts a varied program of music, dance, and films.

O'Connell St. garterlane.ie. ✆ **051/855038.** Many events and exhibits free; ticketed events around €15–€30. General opening: Tues–Sat 11am–5:30pm; individual performance and event times vary.

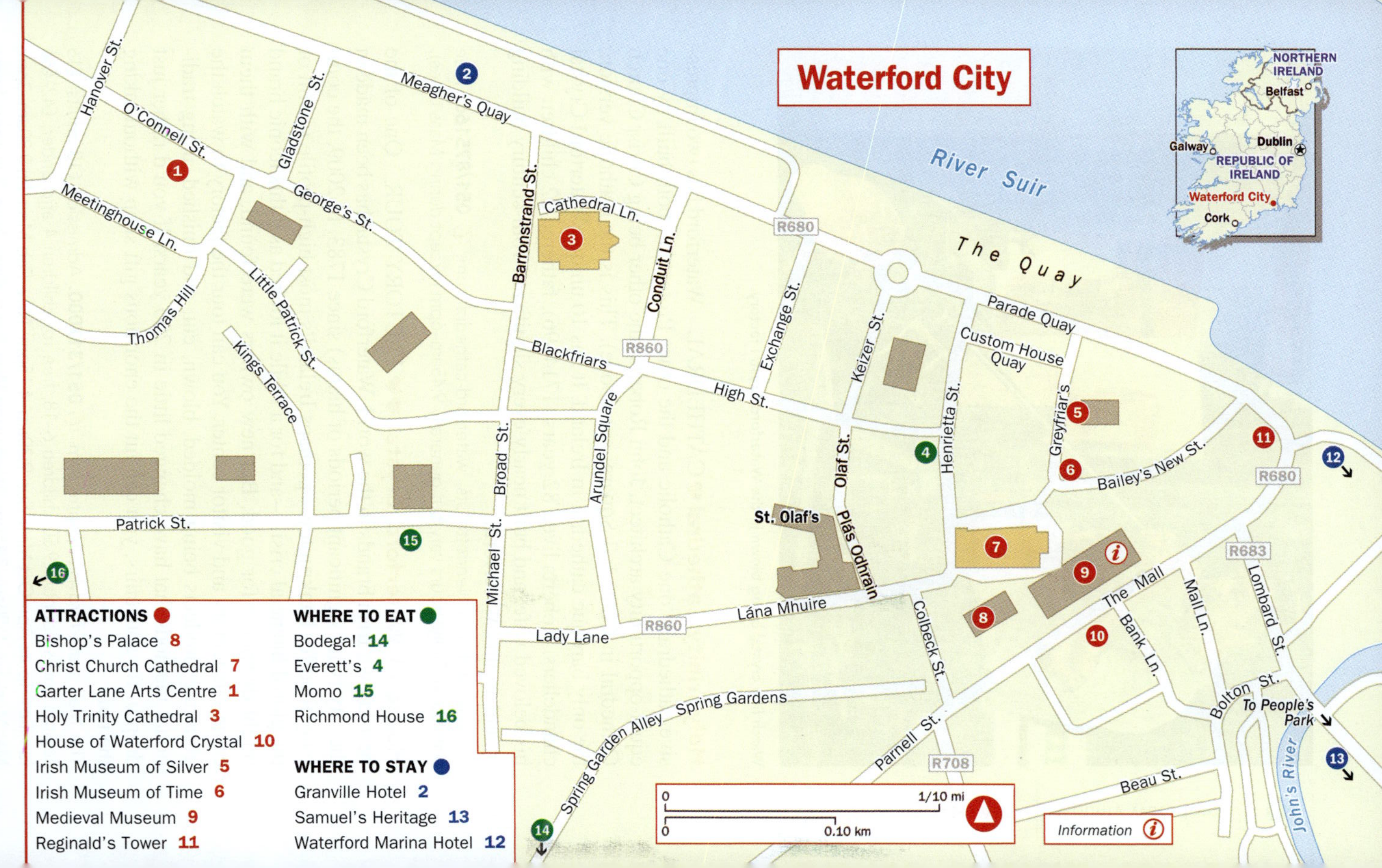
Waterford City
River Suir
The Quay
NORTHERN IRELAND
Belfast
Dublin
Galway
REPUBLIC OF IRELAND
Waterford City
Cork
Hanover St.
O'Connell St.
Meetinghouse Ln.
Gladstone St.
Meagher's Quay
George's St.
Barronstrand St.
Cathedral Ln.
Conduit Ln.
Thomas Hill
Little Patrick St.
Kings Terrace
Blackfriars
R860
R680
Exchange St.
Keizer St.
Parade Quay
Custom House Quay
High St.
Henrietta St.
Greyfriar's
Bailey's New St.
Olaf St.
St. Olaf's
Plás Odhrain
Arundel Square
Broad St.
Michael St.
Patrick St.
Lady Lane
Lána Mhuire
Colbeck St.
The Mall
Bank Ln.
Mall Ln.
Lombard St.
R683
Bolton St.
To People's Park
John's River
Beau St.
Parnell St.
R708
Spring Gardens
Spring Garden Alley
0
1/10 mi
0.10 km
Information
ATTRACTIONS
Bishop's Palace 8
Christ Church Cathedral 7
Garter Lane Arts Centre 1
Holy Trinity Cathedral 3
House of Waterford Crystal 10
Irish Museum of Silver 5
Irish Museum of Time 6
Medieval Museum 9
Reginald's Tower 11
WHERE TO EAT
Bodega! 14
Everett's 4
Momo 15
Richmond House 16
WHERE TO STAY
Granville Hotel 2
Samuel's Heritage 13
Waterford Marina Hotel 12

Watch fine crystal being blown in the Waterford Crystal factory.

Holy Trinity Cathedral ♥ CATHEDRAL Waterford has two impressive cathedrals, one Catholic and the other Protestant, both built by one equal-opportunity architect, John Roberts (the other being Christ Church Cathedral in Cathedral Square; see above). This is the Catholic version, the only baroque cathedral in Ireland. It has 10 unique Waterford Crystal chandeliers. Roberts lived 82 years (1714–96), fathered 22 children with his beloved wife, and built nearly every significant 18th-century building in and around Waterford.

Barronstrand and Henrietta sts. waterford-cathedral.com. ✆ **051/875166.** Free admission. Daily; hours vary but generally 9:45am–6pm (except during Mass times).

House of Waterford Crystal ♥♥ FACTORY TOUR One of the best-known Irish brands in the world, Waterford Crystal has been made in the city (with significant periods of hiatus) since 1783. In 2009, the company filed for bankruptcy—perhaps Ireland's most high-profile victim of the global financial crisis—and for a while it looked as if this iconic brand might disappear for good. But new owners were found, and with them came this factory and visitor center. You can tour the factory to watch the glittering products being molded, blown, cut, and finished, using traditional methods that have changed little in 200 years. If you'd rather just drop in for souvenirs, you can hit the enormous gift shop without taking the tour.

The Mall. waterfordvisitorcentre.com. ✆ **051/317000.** Admission €18 adults; €16 seniors and students; €9.50 children 6–18; free for children 4 and under; €42–€66 families. Tours Apr–Oct Mon–Sun 9:30am–4:15pm; Nov–Feb Mon–Fri 9:30am–3pm; Mar Mon–Sun 9:30am–3:15pm. Store open Mon–Sat 9:30am–5pm; Sun noon–5pm.

The Irish Museum of Time is set inside a refurbished 1880s-era neo-Gothic church.

Irish Museum of Time ♥♥♥ MUSEUM This delightful horological museum, located in a restored Gothic-style church, tells the story and science of time. There are rows of grandfather clocks, decorative wall clocks, and displays of pocket watches over two levels, and the collection includes early European timepieces—including a London-made clock from William Clement, whose invention led to the accuracy (and the "tick-tock") in clocks. Don't miss the very cleverly designed restroom at the rear. Just down the street on Cathedral Square, you can also visit another of the city's Waterford Treasures museums, the **Irish Silver Museum** (waterfordtreasures.com/museum/the-museum-of-silver; admission €5, free for children 11 and under), which has a collection of silver treasures dating from Viking times to the Victorian era.

An exhibition case of silver treasures at the Irish Silver Museum.

Greyfriars St. waterfordtreasures.com/the-museum-of-time. ✆ **051/849501.** Admission €5 adults; free for children 11 and under. Mon–Sat 10am–5pm; Sun and bank holidays 11am–5pm; open until 6pm June–Aug. Admission for both museums is also included in the €18 Freedom of Waterford ticket, p. 216.

Medieval Museum ♥♥ MUSEUM As the name promises, the fascinating Medieval Museum has many artifacts from the city's medieval period, including richly embroidered cloth-of-gold vestments, intricate metal badges worn by pilgrims to the Holy Land, and the lavishly illustrated Charter Roll of Waterford dating from 1373. In common with other Waterford Treasures such as the Bishop's Palace (p. 215) and Reginald's Tower (see below), costumed guides are on hand in corny but enjoyable fashion, to add medieval flavor. The building itself is as much a treasure as the items on display: Though a modern design, it incorporates two medieval structures that were inaccessible for years, the 15th-century **Wine Vault** and the impressive 13th-century **Chorister's Hall,** with its vaulted stone ceiling.

Cathedral Sq. waterfordtreasures.com/medieval-museum. ✆ **051/849501.** Admission €10; free for children 11 and under with paying guest. Also included in the €18 Freedom of Waterford ticket, p. 216. Mon–Fri 9:15am–5pm; Sat 10am–5pm; Sun and bank holidays 11am–5pm; June–Aug open until 6pm. Last admission 40 min. before closing.

The Great Charter Roll of Waterford, called "medieval Ireland's version of the Book of Kells," is on display in the city's Medieval Museum.

Reginald's Tower ♥♥ MUSEUM Built around the year 1000, this Viking-era stone tower is Ireland's oldest building still in day-to-day use. Today it houses a museum devoted to that period in Waterford's history. While much of it is interpretive in nature, a number of items are on display, too: fragments of Viking pottery, coins, and jewelry, including the stunning Waterford Kite Brooch—an ornamental clasp dating from the late 11th century, intricately patterned with fine threads of gold and silver. Be careful when climbing the old stone staircase—in order to confound attackers, these "stumble steps" were designed to be deliberately uneven, hence easy to trip over (also oriented in such a way to make wielding a sword impossible if you're right-handed—so better leave yours behind).

The Quay. waterfordtreasures.com/reginalds-tower. ✆ **051/304-220.** Admission €5 adults; €4 seniors; €3 students and children; €13 families. Daily 9:30am–5:30pm; closes 5pm early Dec to early Mar. Last admission 45 min. before closing.

Waterford City Walking Tours ♥♥ TOURS Local guide Jack Burtchaell is well versed in the history, folklore, and witty anecdotes of his home city. From mid-March to October he conducts this engaging hour-long tour of the old city twice daily, leaving from the reception area of the Granville Hotel on the Quay at noon and 2pm. You don't have to book in advance—just show up a little before departure time.

The Quay. jackswalkingtours.com. ✆ **051/873-711.** Tour €10. Mid-Mar to Oct daily noon and 2pm.

Farther Afield in County Waterford

Ardmore High Cross ♥ RELIGIOUS SITE Ardmore (Irish for "the great height") is a very ancient Christian site—St. Declan, its founder, is said to have been a bishop in Munster as early as the mid–4th century, well before St. Patrick came to Ireland. Tradition has it that the small stone oratory in a cemetery high above Ardmore marks his burial site. St. Declan's Oratory is one of several stone structures composing the ancient monastic settlement. The most striking is the perfectly intact 30m-high (98-ft.) round tower. On-site are also ruins of a medieval cathedral and, nearby, St. Declan's well and church. A lovely 4km (2.5-mile) cliff walk takes around an hour. Ardmore is near the border with County Cork, about 70km (43 miles) southwest of Waterford City.

On R673, Ardmore. No phone. Free admission. Daily dawn–dusk. From the main N25 road, turn onto R673 and follow signs to Ardmore.

A WALK TO mahon falls

The point where the narrow Mahon River reaches the top of the Comeragh Mountains makes for a beautiful, rugged view, as it tumbles hundreds of feet down the rocky slopes in a spray of silvery white. The walk to the falls is popular with hikers, both for the sheer stony loveliness of it (you can see all the way from the falls to the sea) and because it's a fairly short distance—about a 15-minute walk in each direction. The 80m (262½-ft.) waterfalls are on the R676 between Carrick-on-Suir and Dungarvan. At the tiny village of Mahon Bridge, 26km (16 miles) south of Carrick-on-Suir, turn west on the road marked for Mahon Falls, then follow signs for the falls and the Comeragh Drive. In about 5km (3 miles), you reach a parking lot along the Mahon River (in fact, just a tiny stream). The trail begins across the road. Follow the stream along the floor of the valley to the base of the falls. From here you can see the fields of Waterford spread out below you, and the sea a glittering mirror beyond. Walking time is about 30 minutes round-trip.

Hiker takes in Mahon Falls in the Comeragh Mountains.

Lismore Castle Gardens and Arts ♥♥ GARDENS/GALLERY High above the River Blackwater, this turreted medieval fortress dates from 1185, when Prince John of England (later the infamous King John who signed the Magna Carta) established a castle on this site. The grounds, surrounded by thick defensive walls dating from 1626, are spread across nearly 7 acres. They're peaceful and quite lovely to stroll, dotted with sculptures and offering views of the massive castle (which, sadly, is not open to the public). Also on the grounds is **Lismore Castle Arts** (lismorecastlearts.ie; ✆ **058/54061**), a gallery devoted to contemporary visual arts, with a good program of exhibitions and big-name featured artists such as Ai Weiwei and Dorothy Cross. Entry is included in the price for the gardens. The gallery has a second space at **St. Carthage Hall,** located on Chapel Street in Lismore (✆ **058/54061**), open Saturday and Sunday from noon to 5pm, during exhibition periods only (call or go online to check the schedule). Admission is free.

Lismore, Co. Waterford (6.5km/4 miles W of Cappoquin via N72). lismorecastlegardens.com. ✆ **058/54061.** Gardens and gallery: €9 adults; €7.50 seniors and students; €6.50 children; €25 families. Mid-Mar to Oct daily 10:30am–5:30pm; last admission 1 hr. before closing.

Where to Stay in County Waterford

Cliff House Hotel ♥♥♥ This award-winning luxury boutique hotel on County Waterford's coast will wow you from the start with extraordinary sweeping sea views. Inside, things get even better, because this place is known for its superb service, innovative food, and elegant rooms. Standard rooms are not huge, but they are well appointed, with king beds and bathrooms with rainforest showers and free-standing bathtubs. Many have private balconies with breathtaking views. If you need more privacy and money is no object, you can rent a cottage or beach house on the grounds. The Michelin-starred **House Restaurant** melds fresh local seafood and produce with cutting-edge techniques. There's also a more casual **Bar Restaurant** for relaxed dining and afternoon tea. Finally, the peaceful spa and pool will work away any tension you have left.

Middle Rd., Ardmore. cliffhousehotel.ie. ✆ **024/87800.** 39 units. €259–€830 double. Free parking. **Amenities:** Restaurant; bar; room service; pool; spa; Wi-Fi (free).

Granville Hotel ♥♥ With its elegant, sienna-colored frontage, this welcoming hotel in Waterford City was built in the late 1700s and has been in business continuously since 1865. The interior retains something of a manor house feel, with rich color schemes, deep red carpeting, and antique furniture. Guest rooms are comfortable and reasonably spacious—not all have air-conditioning, however, so make sure to request this when you book if it's important to you. Some rooms overlook Waterford Quay, with its field of gently bobbing yacht masts. The hotel bar is

Spacious guest rooms at the Granville Hotel overlook Waterford Quay.

popular with locals, and the **Bianconi Restaurant** offers excellent Irish and European cooking. Staff could hardly be friendlier or more helpful.
Meagher's Quay, Waterford. granvillehotel.ie. ✆ **051/305555.** 100 units. €111–€180 double. Breakfast not included in lower rates. Dinner, bed-and-breakfast packages available. Parking at Clock Tower lot (opposite the hotel) free for guests (limited spaces). **Amenities:** Restaurant; bar; room service; Wi-Fi (free).

Samuel's Heritage ♥♥ This charming B&B on the outskirts of Waterford (just a little too far to be considered walking distance from the center) overlooks open fields on one side and the River Suir on the other. Sally, Des, and family have converted their home into a modern, well-equipped lodging, with surprisingly good amenities for a countryside B&B, such as a mini-gym and infrared sauna. The bright and cheery guest rooms have ample space and a few extras, such as flatscreen TVs and free Wi-Fi. Family rooms sleep up to four. The delicious breakfast options include smoked salmon with eggs from their own hens.
Halfway House, Dunmore Rd., Waterford. samuelsheritage.com. ✆ **051/875094.** 6 units. €130–€150 double. Breakfast included. Free parking. **Amenities:** Gym; sauna; Wi-Fi (free).

Waterford Marina Hotel ♥ This modern, well-run hotel overlooking the River Suir isn't particularly characterful, but it's in a great location, a short walk from the center of Waterford. Rooms are clean and have everything you need, including comfortable beds. Family rooms are an exceptionally good value and sleep up to four, usually for just €30 or €40 more than the standard double rates. Some bedrooms have lovely views over the water. Special offers are often listed on the website, including packages that cover dinner in the excellent restaurant. ***Tip:*** Ask for an upper-floor room—the views are better, and you're a bit above the ruckus when there's street noise at night.

Canada St., Waterford. waterfordmarinahotel.com. ✆ **051/856-600.** 81 units. €129–€229 double. Breakfast not included in lower rates. Free parking. **Amenities:** Restaurant; bar; room service; accessible rooms; Wi-Fi (free).

Where to Eat in County Waterford

Waterford's restaurant scene is pretty impressive for such a small city. Luxury restaurants abound (many of the best listed here), but a good number of small eateries are perfect for light meals. In Kilmacthomas, **Coach House Coffee** (the Workhouse; coachhousecoffee.ie; ✆ **051/295-654**) offers fantastic coffee, sandwiches, and light lunches in the historic environment of a converted workhouse and is a great stop on the Waterford Greenway (p. 227). In Tramore, the **Seagull Bakery** specializes in sourdough bread and the freshest baked goods to take with you (4 Broad St.; seagullbakery.ie; no phone).

Bodega! is a lively place for modern Irish food in Waterford City.

Bodega! ♥♥ MODERN IRISH/EUROPEAN A restaurant with an exclamation point in the name isn't really the sort of place you'd expect to sit up straight, and Bodega! certainly does its best to cultivate a funky vibe. Order a cocktail from the extensive list while you peruse the menu, then go all out with some local beer-battered fish and chips, or roast corn-fed chicken with roasted garlic and Madeira sauce. Sink yourself into a food coma with a luscious dessert of warm chocolate fondant.
54 John St., Waterford. bodegawaterford.com. ✆ **051/844177.** Entrees €20–€36. Wed–Thurs 4:30–9pm; Fri–Sat 4:30–10pm; Sun 1–7:45pm.

Everett's ♥♥♥ MODERN IRISH/EUROPEAN Food critics have been singing the praises of this Waterford restaurant since it opened in 2018 and immediately began stacking up the awards. An eponymous venture by respected chef Peter Everett, it's tucked inside a humble 15th-century building in the medieval quarter. The food is a modern take on Irish cuisine, with the ingredients so fresh and local, expect to see the farmer's name on the menu. Try dishes like seared Wexford scallops with squash and nduja or Andarl Farm pork ravioli with Granny Smith apple and celeriac, followed by roast Comeragh Mountain lamb with coco beans and lamb jus or featherblade of local beef with confit turnip and horseradish. The dessert plate of Irish cheeses is lush, or you can dive into desserts like chocolate soufflé with homemade raspberry ice cream. Book early online.
22 High St., Waterford. everetts.ie. ✆ **051/325174.** Fixed-price menu €41–€52; lunch €37–€39. Dinner Tues–Sat and bank holiday Sun 5:30–9:30pm; lunch Fri–Sat 12:30–2pm.

Momo ♥♥ IRISH Often hailed as one of the best restaurants in Ireland, Momo is a sure bet for interesting, innovative cooking without pretensions. Although the menu always features a few interesting vegetarian options (and plenty of gluten-free as well), the emphasis is on meaty dishes like slow-cooked beef rib, or pork filet wrapped in serrano ham. Appetizers might include prawns, mussels, and Gubbeen chorizo pil pil, or Toonsbridge buffalo mozzarella with salad. The lunch menu is similar, but also includes sandwiches (from €12) including a toastie with ham, scamorza cheese, and red onion jam. The light-filled dining room is artfully designed, the perfect place to linger over a glass of wine.
47 Patrick St., Waterford. momorestaurant.ie. ✆ **051/581509.** Entrees €20–€29. Tues–Sat noon–3pm and 5–9pm; Sun 1–8pm.

Richmond House ♥♥♥ MODERN IRISH The grounds of this 18th-century mansion hide away a bountiful produce patch, where the chef gets most of the fruit and vegetables for the restaurant's kitchen. This is something of a dining destination for people in this part of Ireland, and it's easy to see why—the food is a hugely successful combination of Irish and Continental flavors. Menus change daily, according to what's fresh and in season, but you're likely to find locally sourced lamb, beef, and seafood served with sides like *champ* (mashed potato and spring onion) or something freshly picked from the garden. The wine list includes a better-than-average selection of wines by the glass. Richmond House also has a few guest rooms (around €140–€190 per night).

Signposted from N72, Cappoquin. richmondcountryhouse.ie. ✆ **058/54278.** Fixed-price menu €60. Daily 6–9pm. Closed Dec 22–Jan 10.

The Tannery ♥♥ IRISH This restaurant and cookery school in a converted 19th-century leather factory has been racking up awards for innovative cuisine since 1997. Its fresh approach to fine dining—all food, no pretension—has earned it loyal fans around the world. The menu changes constantly, but expect starters like crab crème brûlée with pickled cucumber or grilled trout with pickled fennel and orange butter sauce. Mains might include roast cod with cauliflower, sweetheart cabbage, and a mussel and herb velouté; or guineafowl breast served with roast parsnips, buttered sprouts, and a port and redcurrant sauce. If you don't order the chocolate and coffee mousse with hazelnut caramel for dessert, we want to know why. Chef Paul Flynn also offers master classes in cooking (from €195 per day). You can stay nearby in one of the elegant rooms in a restaurant-owned town house (from €210 per night).

10 Quai St., Dungarvan, Co. Waterford. tannery.ie. ✆ **058/45420.** Fixed-price menu €70. Early bird (5:30–6:30pm) €45. Wed–Sat 5:30–9pm; Sun 12:30–3:30pm.

Sports & Outdoor Pursuits in Waterford

CYCLING From Waterford City, you can ride 13km (8 miles) to Passage East and take the ferry (p. 215; fare with bicycle €3 one-way, €4 round-trip) to Wexford and the beautiful Hook Peninsula (p. 232). Or continue on from Passage East to Dunmore East, a picturesque seaside village with a small beach hemmed in by cliffs. For a scenic cycling route along an old railway line, try the **Waterford Greenway** (p. 227).

FISHING **Knockaderry Reservoir** is an enormous 28-hectare (70-acre) fishery 12km (7½ miles) southwest of Waterford City, great for catching rainbow trout. You can purchase day permits (€25) from the Centra supermarket on the main R680 road in Kilmeaden; boat hire from €15 (waterfordflyfishing.ie). The **Fort William Fishery,** Glencairn, Lismore (fortwilliamireland.com/fishing; ✆ **087/829-2077**), is renowned for its wild salmon; permits cost between €70 and €100 per day, depending on the month. They also rent cottages, sleeping up to eight, for €1,000 to €1,200 per week; see the website for details.

GOLF County Waterford has rich pickings for golf fans. Clubs and resorts include three 18-hole championship courses. **Waterford Castle Hotel & Golf Resort,** The Island, Ballinakill, Waterford (waterfordcastleresort.com/golf; ✆ **051/878203**), is a par-72 parkland course on a small island; greens fees are around €30 to €55. **Faithlegg Golf Club,** Faithlegg House, Waterford (faithlegggolfclub.com; ✆ **051/380587**), a

cycling THE GREENWAY

Off-road greenways—special walking or cycling trails along former railway lines—have become popular in Ireland in recent years, and more are in development. The 46km (28-mile) **Waterford Greenway,** on the old railway line between Waterford City and Dungarvan, takes in rolling countryside, bridges, viaducts, and the quarter-mile-long Ballyvoyle tunnel, which dates from 1878. You will also pass old railway stations, medieval ruins, and Norman castles and see the Viking settlement at Woodstown, with plenty of scenic and seaside views along the way.

You can choose from various bike hire companies, and some will also shuttle your luggage and/or bring you back to your starting point. Rates start at around €25 per day or €45 for an e-bike. Check out **Waterford Greenway Bike Hire** (waterfordgreenwaybikehire.com; ✆ **051/295-955**) or **Waterford Greenway** (waterfordgreenway.com; ✆ **085/232-4111**).

Beyond the Southeast, other scenic greenways include the **Great Western Greenway** in Mayo (p. 456) and the **Limerick Greenway** (p. 377).

par-72 parkland course beside the River Suir, charges greens fees of €30 to €80. **Dungarvan Golf Club,** Knocknagranagh, Dungarvan (dungarvan golfclub.com; ✆ **058/43310**), a par-72 parkland course, has greens fees of €35 to €40.

SAILING, PADDLEBOARDING & SEA KAYAKING From May to September, the **Dunmore East Adventure Centre,** Dunmore East (dunmore adventure.com; ✆ **051/383783**), offers 2-hour sailing taster sessions for €65 as well as a variety of sailing lessons. A 1-hour kayaking or stand-up paddleboarding session is €30. Summer programs for children are also available.

COUNTY WEXFORD

The countryside in this area feels so peaceful and bucolic, Dublin might as well be hundreds of miles away. Wexford is known for its long stretches of pristine beaches and for the evocative historic monuments in Wexford Town and on the Hook Peninsula. The modern English name of Wexford evolved from *Waesfjord,* which is what the Vikings called it when they invaded in the 9th century. The Normans captured the town at the end of the 12th century; you can still see remnants of their fort at the Irish National Heritage Park.

Visitor Information

The **Wexford Tourist Information Centre** is at Wexford Arts Centre, Cornmarket, Ferrybank South, Wexford (visitwexford.ie; ✆ **1800/230-330**). It's open June through mid-September Monday to Saturday 9am until 5:30pm.

Exploring Wexford Town

The Bull Ring ♥ SQUARE/STATUE In the 17th century, this town square was a venue for bull baiting, a sport introduced by the butcher's guild. (Tradition maintained that after a match, the hide of the ill-fated bull was presented to the mayor and the meat was used to feed the poor.) But it played a greater part in history in 1798, when the first declaration of an Irish republic was made here. A memorial statue honors the Irish pikemen who fought for the cause. Today, activity at the ring is much tamer: An excellent outdoor market is held every Friday and Saturday from 9am to 5pm.

Off N. Main St.

Cornmarket ♥ SQUARE Until a century ago, this central marketplace buzzed with the activity of cobblers, publicans, and more than 20 other businesses. Today it's just a wide street dominated by the Wexford Arts Centre, a structure dating from 1775.

Off Upper George's St.

Irish National Heritage Park ♥♥ HERITAGE SITE On the banks of the River Slaney, just outside of Wexford Town, this 14-hectare (35-acre) living-history park is great fun. It provides an ideal introduction for visitors of all ages to life in ancient Ireland, from the Stone Age to the Norman invasion. Each reconstructed glimpse into Irish history is well crafted and has its own natural setting and wildlife. There are regular 30-minute tours on prehistoric Ireland, early Christian Ireland, and the age of invasion. There's also a nature trail and interpretive center, complete with gift shop and cafe. Kids can easily be kept amused for half a day here.

Ferrycarrig (about 4.8km/3 miles W of Wexford, signposted from N11). irishheritage.ie. ✆ **053/912-0733.** Admission €14 adults; €12 seniors and students; €9 children; free for children 4 and under; €32–€38 families. July–Aug daily 9:30am–6:30pm (last admission 5pm); Mar–Jun and Sept–Oct daily 9:30am–5:30pm (last admission 4pm); Nov–Feb daily 9:30am–5pm (last admission 3pm). Tour times vary (check website).

John Barry Monument ♥ STATUE This bronze statue, a gift from the American people in 1956, faces out to the sea as a tribute to the titular Mr. Barry, a Wexford native who became the father of the American Navy. Born at Ballysampson, Tacumshane, 16km (10 miles) southeast of Wexford Town, Barry immigrated to the colonies while in his teens and became one of the U.S. Navy's first commissioned officers. In 1797, George Washington appointed him head of the U.S. Navy.

Crescent Quay.

National Opera House ♥♥ CONCERT HALL This modern opera house, with its large but rather garish copper-plated tower, is a somewhat awkward addition to the Wexford skyline. The biggest event in its calendar is the prestigious **Wexford Festival Opera (wexfordopera.com)**,

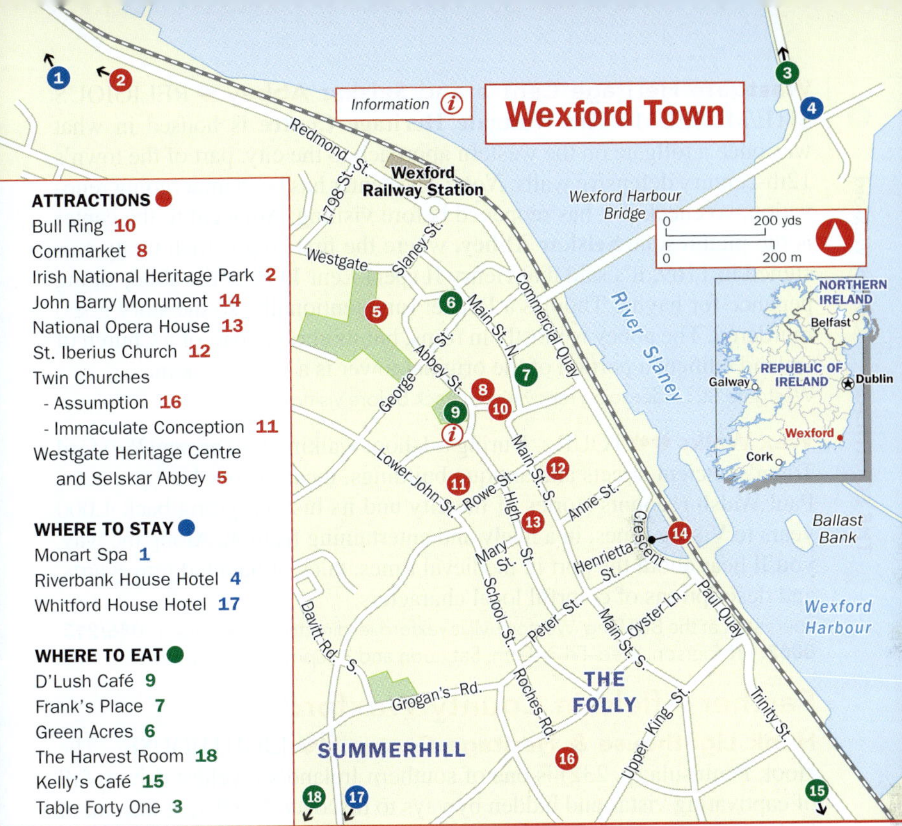

held for 2 weeks each October/November, attracting aficionados from all over Ireland and beyond. Opera lovers will be in heaven—but book early if there's something you really want to see. Tickets start at around €35, rising to €164 for the best seats.

High St. nationaloperahouse.ie. ✆ **053/912-2144.** Ticket prices vary; generally €20–€60. Event times vary; call ahead.

St. Iberius Church ♥♥ CHURCH Erected in 1660, St. Iberius was built on hallowed ground—the land has been used for houses of worship since Norse times. The church has a lovely Georgian facade and an interior known for its superb acoustics. Concerts are sometimes held here; see local listings for details.

N. Main St. No phone. Free admission. Tues–Thurs 10am–4pm; Sun 11am–12:30pm.

The Twin Churches: Church of the Assumption and Church of the Immaculate Conception ♥♥ CHURCHES Dominating Wexford's skyline, a pair of 69m (226-ft.) spires top these twin Gothic Revival structures (1851–58), designed by architect Robert Pierce, a pupil of Augustus Pugin (designer of the Houses of Parliament in London).

Bride and Rowe sts. ✆ **053/912-2055.** Free admission; donations welcome. Daily 8am–6pm.

Westgate Heritage Centre and Selskar Abbey ♥ RELIGIOUS SITE/MUSEUM The **Westgate Heritage Centre** is housed in what was once a tollgate on the western approach to the city, part of the town's 12th-century defensive walls. ***Note:*** The center has been undergoing renovation, so check if it has reopened before visiting. Adjacent to the center is the picturesque **Selskar Abbey,** where the first Anglo-Irish treaty was signed in 1169; it's said that Henry II spent Lent 1172 at the abbey doing penance for having Thomas à Becket (unintentionally, so the story goes) murdered. The abbey is mostly in ruins, but its choir is part of a Church of Ireland edifice; a portion of the original tower is a vesting room.
Westgate St. Undergoing renovation; check before visiting.

Wex Walks ♥♥ TOUR During a 1-hour walking tour around Wexford Town's ancient streets and antique buildings, local history buff and actor Paul Walsh recounts stories of the city and its history, going back 1,000 years to Viking times, in a lively and entertaining fashion. Along the way, you'll hear about the port in medieval times, tales of haunted graveyards, and descriptions of colorful local characters.
Tours start at the Bull Ring, Wexford. visitwexford.ie/directory/wexwalks. ✆ **086/213-8062.** €15/person. Wed–Fri 3:30pm; Sat noon and 2:30pm; Sun 2:30pm.

Farther Afield in County Wexford

Hook Lighthouse & Heritage Centre ♥♥ LIGHTHOUSE The Hook Peninsula (p. 232) is one of southern Ireland's loveliest drives, full of captivating vistas and hidden byways to discover. Nestled at the end of it all is this picturesque old lighthouse, the oldest part of which dates from

Hook Lighthouse is the world's oldest lighthouse still in continuous use.

the 13th century, making it the world's oldest lighthouse still in continuous use. Guided tours do an excellent job of telling the history of the lighthouse and of the surrounding peninsula, which has been occupied since at least the 5th century A.D. There is an active program of special events, too, from art courses to ghost tours. ***Tip:*** The drive from Waterford is drastically shorter if you take the Passage East car ferry (p. 215). Hook Head is 30km (18⅔ miles) southeast of Waterford, 47km (29 miles) southwest of Wexford.

Hook Head. hookheritage.ie. ✆ **051/397-055.** Admission €12 adults; €10 seniors and students; €6 children 5–17; free for children 4 and under; €16–€34 families. Visitor center: daily 9:30am–5pm (until 6pm July–Aug). Lighthouse tours run every half-hour.

A TRIP THROUGH HISTORY: EXPLORING THE ring of hook

A wild and rugged place of rocky headlands and secluded beaches, the **Hook Peninsula** juts out between Bannow Bay and Waterford Harbour in southwest County Wexford. In medieval times, these inlets were significant landing spots for travelers from Britain to Ireland, as archaeological remains attest. Today, the peninsula is a popular driving or cycling route (see map on p. 231), as well as a magnet for hikers on the Wexford Coastal Pathway (p. 239) and for birders watching the spring and fall passerine migration.

Start your exploration at the town of **Wellington Bridge,** 22km (14 miles) southwest of Wexford Town via R733. Just west of Wellington Bridge on R733 is a roadside stop on the left by a cemetery; from here you can look across Bannow Bay to the ruins of **Clonmines,** a Norman village established in the 13th century. It's a fine example of a walled medieval settlement, with remains of two churches, three tower houses, and an Augustinian priory. You can drive to the ruins—just follow R733 another mile west to a left turn posted for the Wicklow Coastal Pathway and continue straight on this road where the pathway turns right. The ruins are on private land, so ask permission at the farmhouse at the end of the road.

Continuing west on R733, turn left on R734 at the sign for the Ring of Hook, and turn right at the sign for **Tintern Abbey** ♥ (p. 234). Founded by Welsh monks in the 13th century, its beautiful grounds contain a restored stone bridge that spans a narrow sea inlet.

As R734 continues south, you come to **Baginbun Head,** where the Norman presence in Ireland was first established with a victory over the Irish at the Battle of Baginbun. Today it's a peaceful scene, with a fine beach nestling against the cliffs, but from the beach you can still see the outline of the Norman earthwork fortifications on the head.

The **tip of the peninsula, Hook Head,** with its line of low cliffs eroded in places for blowholes, has been famous for shipwrecks since Norman times. Its historic **lighthouse** (p. 230) has been on this site since the early 13th century.

The Ring of Hook road returns along the western side of the peninsula, passing the beaches at **Booley Bay** and **Dollar Bay.** On a promontory overlooking the town of **Duncannon** is a **fort** built in 1588 to protect Waterford Harbour from the Spanish Armada. Just north of Duncannon, along the coast at the village of **Ballyhack,** a ferry runs to County Waterford (p. 215), and there's a Knights Hospitallers castle on a hill.

A visit to the Hook Peninsula wouldn't be complete without a stop at **Dunbrody Abbey,** in a field beside the road about 6.5km (4 miles) north of Duncannon. The abbey, founded in 1170, is a magnificent ruin and one of the largest Cistercian abbeys in Ireland. Despite its grand size, it bears remarkably little ornamentation. Tours are sometimes available; inquire at the visitor center across the road.

Irish Agricultural Museum and Famine Exhibition ♥♥ MUSEUM Absorbing and at times deeply affecting, this excellent museum on the grounds of Johnstown Castle illuminates how important agriculture has been to the history of this region. Exhibits are devoted to, among other things, traditional crafts, dairy farming, country furniture, and historic machinery. Of course, no farming museum in Ireland would be complete without mention of its greatest catastrophe: the Great Famine, which killed about a million people in the mid–19th century (and was responsible for the emigration of a million more). You can also stroll the grounds as part of the ticket. Booking is not required for the museum or grounds, but you need to prebook if you wish to add a castle tour.

Johnstown Castle Estate, Bridgetown Rd., off Wexford-Rosslare Rd. (N25). johnstowncastle.ie/irish-agricultural-museum. ✆ **053/918-4671.** Gardens and museum: €10.50 adults; €8 seniors and students; €4.50 children 5–16; children 4 and under free; €26 families. Castle tours (extra): €5.50 adults; €4 seniors and students; €2.50 children 5–16; €12 families. Gardens and museum daily 9am–5:30pm (closes 4:30pm Nov–Mar); last entry 1 hr. before closing. Castle tours May–Sept 11 and 11:30am, noon, 1:30, 2, and 3pm; Oct–Apr 11am, noon, 1 and 2pm.

SS *Dunbrody* Famine Ship Experience ♥♥♥ MUSEUM This huge, life-size reconstruction of a 19th-century tall ship is exactly the kind of vessel on which a million or more people emigrated from Ireland to escape the Great Famine. An interpretive history center, the SS *Dunbrody* offers an engaging way to learn about that history—particularly for youngsters, who will find it less stuffy than a conventional museum. Actors in period dress lead the tours, describing in great detail what life on

Costumed interpreters at the SS *Dunbrody* Famine Ship Experience bring to life the emigrant experience of the Famine years.

local hero: JFK, GREAT-GRANDSON OF NEW ROSS

U.S. President John F. Kennedy was born in America, but Patrick Kennedy (1823–58), his great-grandfather, was a son of Ireland, raised in the small riverside town of New Ross in County Wexford. That connection to the Kennedy family history draws thousands of visitors a year.

The house near New Ross where he lived until 1848 has been converted into a museum dedicated to the Kennedy family's Irish history. The **Kennedy Homestead** (kennedyhomestead.ie; ✆ **051/388264**) in the tiny village of Dunganstown, 8km (5 miles) south of New Ross, is a humble, one-story traditional stone building. John F. Kennedy himself visited the homestead in June 1963, meeting his cousins during what he reportedly called "the happiest 4 days of my life." The story of that visit is one of the exhibits at the modern visitor center on the grounds, where you can also see rare memorabilia (some acquired through the Kennedy Library archival collection in Boston) and learn what the family's life was like in the dangerous world of 19th-century Ireland, as well as the circumstances that led to Patrick Kennedy's decision to emigrate. It's open daily 9:30am to 5:30pm (last admission 5pm); entry costs €10 adults, €9 seniors, €7 children and students, and €25 to €35 families.

Another nearby JFK site of interest is the **John F. Kennedy Arboretum** (heritageireland.ie; ✆ **051/388171**), a beautiful lakeside garden and wildlife haven dedicated to the late president. It's signposted from R733, about 12km (7½ miles) south of New Ross. Guided tours are held daily at noon and 3pm. Opening times are May to August daily 10am until 8pm; April and September daily 10am until 6:30pm; and October to March daily 10am to 5pm. Last admission is 1 hour before closing. Entry costs €5 adults, €4 seniors, €3 students and children, and €13 families.

board was like for the passengers. It's a moving experience. The SS *Dunbrody* is in New Ross, 36km (22⅓ miles) west of Wexford.

The Quay, New Ross. dunbrody.com. ✆ **051/425239.** Admission €14 adults; €13 seniors; €9 students and children; €32–€48 families. Daily 9am–6pm (closes 5pm Oct–Mar); last tour 1 hr. before closing.

Tintern Abbey ♥ HISTORIC SITE In a lovely rural setting overlooking Bannow Bay, Tintern Abbey was founded in the 12th century by William Marshall, the Earl of Pembroke, as thanks to God after he nearly died at sea. The parts that remain—nave, chancel, tower, chapel, and cloister—date from the early 13th century, though they have been much altered since. The grounds are extraordinarily beautiful and include a stone bridge spanning a narrow sea inlet. A visitor center has exhibitions on the history of the abbey, as well as a small cafe. Don't miss a stroll in the restored Colclough Walled Garden on the grounds.

Note: This is not the Tintern Abbey that William Wordsworth wrote about in his famous poem of the same name; however, the monks who named this abbey were Cistercians from the other Tintern, located in Wales—they simply gave this one the same name.

Signposted 19km (12 miles) S of New Ross off R733, in Saltmills. heritageireland.ie/places-to-visit/tintern-abbey. Admission €5 adults; €4 seniors; €3 students and children; €13 families. Daily June–Aug 10am–5.30pm; mid-Mar to May and Sept to early Nov 10am–5pm. Last admission 45 min. before closing. Closed early Nov to mid-Mar.

Where to Stay in County Wexford

In Wexford, choice within the town is limited; you'll do much better opting for a place in the countryside, where there's a satisfying mixture of bucolic farmhouses and luxurious getaways.

Monart Spa ♥♥ A luxurious, restorative, grown-up retreat, Monart is one of Ireland's top destination spas. It's a sumptuous, impeccably designed place, nestled beside a lake. Guest rooms are surrounded by woodland, and most have little balconies or patios overlooking the grounds. The spa has a thermal suite equipped with a pool, salt grotto, indoor and outdoor saunas, and an aroma steam room. To maintain the air of serenity, children are not allowed. Rooms have no coffee machines, kettles, or Wi-Fi; there is a cafe, however, or you can order tea or coffee via room service and use Wi-Fi in the reception building.

On L6124, The Still (about 5.2km/3⅓ miles W of Enniscorthy). monart.ie. ✆ **053/923-8999.** 68 units. €378–€480 double; €620–€750 suite. Breakfast included. 2-night min. some summer weekends. Dinner, bed-and-breakfast, and spa packages available. Free parking. **Amenities:** 2 restaurants; bar; afternoon tea; cafe; pool; room service; spa; Wi-Fi (free) in main building.

Riverbank House Hotel ♥♥ This cozy midsize hotel just outside the town center in Wexford has lovely views of the River Slaney. Rooms overlooking the river have suitably huge picture windows. Beds are comfortable and very large; some are four-posters. Family rooms come with one double and one single bed. The bar and restaurant are pleasant spaces, filled with natural light. The casual pub-style food is good, too—offering unfussy, international dishes of the something-for-everyone variety—and in good weather, you can dine on the terrace overlooking the river. The genuinely cheerful staff helps it all run smoothly.

The Bridge, Wexford. riverbankhousehotel.com. ✆ **053/912-3611.** 23 units. €88–€248 double. Breakfast not included in lower rates. Free parking. **Amenities:** Restaurant; bar; room service; Wi-Fi (free).

Whitford House Hotel ♥♥ Located a few miles outside the Wexford town center, the Whitford House Hotel makes a relaxing getaway for the whole family. Rooms are moderate in size and pleasant in decor, with neutral color schemes and a mix of modern and traditional furnishings. The lounges and bar are popular and often busy—the hotel has a friendly, social vibe. It offers plenty of amusements for small children, including a playground and a kiddie pool. For the grown-ups, an adults-only pool area has a Jacuzzi, steam room, and sauna. The **Seasons Restaurant** produces solid fare—nothing too innovative but reliably good, the kind of place where local families go for meals on special occasions. The **Forthside Bar & Bistro** is perfect for more casual fare around a wood-burning stove. New Line Rd., Wexford. whitfordhotelwexford.ie. ✆ **053/914-3444.** 36 units. €105–€245 double. Breakfast not included in lower rates. Spa packages available. Free parking. **Amenities:** Restaurant; bistro/bar; pool; gym; spa; Wi-Fi (free).

Woodbrook House B&B ♥♥ This grand Georgian mansion is reached down a long, private road, tucked away at the foot of the Blackstairs Mountains near Enniscorthy. Owners Giles and Alexandra FitzHerbert bought the house in ramshackle condition and have coaxed it back to regal beauty. Soaring ceilings, curving staircases, long hallways, original wood and stone floors, light tumbling through towering windows, breathtaking mountain views—expect all of that and comfortable beds. The decor is eclectic, with lots of antiques; everything looks loved and lived in. The owners are excellent cooks and use produce from the garden and local farms, so we recommend booking **dinner** (€50) during your stay. Make some time to wander the gorgeous grounds and breathe that fresh air. Woodbrook, Killanne, Enniscorthy. woodbrookhouse.ie. ✆ **053/925-5114.** 3 units. Open Easter–Sept. €170–€180 double. Breakfast included. Free parking. **Amenities:** Wi-Fi (free).

Where to Eat in County Wexford

Wexford isn't as famous for its cuisine as Cork or Waterford, but there's a growing foodie movement. Along with the restaurants listed below, plenty of places offer lighter cuisine. **D'Lush Café** (Cornmarket, Wexford;

Creative small plates and tapas accompany a great wine list at Frank's Place in Wexford Town.

facebook.com/dlushcafewexford) in the Wexford Arts Centre claims to have the best coffee in Wexford, and we believe them. It also uses fresh, seasonal ingredients in sandwiches, tarts, soups, and breakfasts. At the edge of Wexford Town, **Kelly's Café** (Drinagh Retail Park; kellyscafe.ie; ✆ **053/916-8800**), an outpost of the popular Kelly's Resort Hotel and Spa, is a handy option for homemade breakfast and lunch, with a gourmet twist—we love the scrambled eggs on sourdough toast and the poached eggs with avocado, but the homemade pastries are even better. The mood is casual, the food is great, the coffee is strong. When you don't know what you want, try popping into **Green Acres** (Selskar St., Wexford; greenacres.ie; no phone), an upscale food hall with a delicatessen, restaurant, art gallery, and wine cellar, all featuring carefully selected food to eat in or take out. It's the perfect place to put together a picnic.

Frank's Place ♥♥ MODERN IRISH This wine bar, deli, market, and cafe is set in a former bakery that goes back five generations in the owner Frank's family. The atmosphere is both buzzing and relaxed. At lunch, small plates include bruschetta of Wexford strawberry and goat cheese, or mixed seafood chowder. The dinner menu is tapas style, with plates like red mullet with chorizo and basil, or risotto of smoked hake with parmesan and *rocket* (arugula). A great wine list includes a number of fine and rare vintages.

54 N. Main St., Wexford. franksplace1860.ie. ✆ **053/918-9109.** Lunch entrees €6–€20; dinner tapas €10–€14. Mon–Thurs 9am–6pm; Fri–Sat 9am–8:45pm; Sun 10am–5:30pm.

The Harvest Room Restaurant at Dunbrody House ♥♥♥ IRISH Chef Kevin Dundon's cooking has made him one of Ireland's best-known chefs (he's a regular on TV). At the Harvest Room, fish is from the coast off the nearby Hook Peninsula, dairy, meat, and poultry are sourced from local farms, and most of the fruit, veggies, and herbs are grown in the country house's gardens. Both the menu and wine list change with the seasons—expect dishes like mountain lamb in spring, local crab in summer, parfaits with fruit compotes in fall, and slow-cooked venison in winter. Kevin also runs a cookery school with lots of 1-day courses. Once you get here, you won't want to leave, so thankfully **Dunbrody House** is also a plush country-house hotel with elegant bedrooms

The elegant Harvest Room Restaurant in the Wexford countryside.

(from €300 per night). Look out for special dinner and foodie packages and events.

Arthurstown. dunbrodyhouse.com/harvest-room-restaurant.html. ✆ **051/389600.** 3-course set menu €75. Wed–Sun 6–9:30pm. Closed Jan.

Table Forty One ♥♥ IRISH Local chef Andrew Duncan worked in top restaurants and hotels around the world before returning to his home town of Gorey to open this restaurant. The focus is on local ingredients from the countryside of the Southeast, served in a way that keeps the fine-dining experience relaxed and informal. The short menu (around four options for each course) changes weekly and might feature a dish like wild mushroom risotto, rump of Wexford lamb with garden peas and baby turnips, or Andrew's signature filet steak served with mushroom and smoked bacon jam.

41 Main St., Gorey. tablefortyone.ie. ✆ **053/942-1366.** Fixed-price menu 2 courses €36; 3 courses €44. Wed–Sat 5–9pm; also Sun of bank holiday weekends 5–9pm.

Sports & Outdoor Pursuits in Wexford

BEACHES County Wexford's beaches at **Courtown, Curracloe, Duncannon,** and **Rosslare** are good for walking, jogging, and swimming.

BIRD & WILDLIFE WATCHING Besides the **Wexford Wildfowl Reserve ♥♥** (wexfordwildfowlreserve.ie) in North Slob, about 6.4 km (4 miles) northeast of Wexford Town, bird-watchers head for **Hook Head** (p. 232), a good spot in spring and autumn for seeing the passerine migration. In addition to swallows, swifts, and warblers, look for the less common cuckoos, turtle doves, redstarts, and blackcaps.

In May, June, and July, **Great Saltee Island** is excellent for watching seabirds, when the island's southern cliffs become mobbed with nesting birds and their young. Plentiful species include puffins, which nest in underground burrows, as well as graceful guillemots, cormorants, kittiwakes, gannets, and Manx shearwaters. The island is privately owned, but visitors are welcome as long as they do not disturb the bird habitat and the island's natural beauty. A daily ferry to the islands from Kilmore Quay runs between April and September (salteeferry.com; ✆ **087/252-9736;** €30 adults, €15 children 11 and under; book online). ***Note:*** You may need to walk on slippery stones or seaweed or in shallow water when you land. Landings don't take place in rough weather. **Kilmore Quay Angling** (kilmoreangling.com; ✆ **087/213-5308**) offers an "eco-cruise" around the Saltee Islands, to see seals and birds (without landing); expect to pay €25 adults, €15 children.

KAYAKING **The Irish Experience** (theirishexperience.com; ✆ **087/097-6749**) runs sea kayaking trips exploring coves and sea caves on the Hook Peninsula from April to October (weather permitting), while telling fascinating stories of the area's history. Sunset trips in summer are particularly magical. Trips cost from €35 to €80 for adults, prices for children and teens vary per trip, and some trips have minimum age limits; book online.

walk this way: THE WEXFORD COASTAL PATHWAY

Along the entire coastline you'll see brown signs with a picture of a hiker on them, marking the **Wexford Coastal Pathway,** which meanders along the coast via pristine beaches and country lanes—and, unfortunately, some stretches of busy roads. At the north end, however, there's a peaceful beach walk from **Clogga Head** (County Wicklow) to **Tara Hill,** 14km (8 miles) south, ending with panoramic views from atop Tara Hill. South of Wexford Town, another good section runs from **Rosslare Harbour** around Carnsore Point to **Kilmore Quay.**

Yet another fine coastal walk is near Wexford Town in the **Raven Nature Reserve,** an area of forested dunes and uncrowded beaches. To get there, take R741 north out of Wexford, turn right on R742 to Curracloe village, and at Curracloe turn right to drive just over a mile to the beach parking lot. The nature reserve is to your right. By car it's a half-mile south, but you can also walk there along the beach. It's 5km (3 miles) to Raven Point, where at low tide you can see the remains of a shipwreck, half-buried in the sand.

COUNTY KILKENNY

Kilkenny City stands on the site of an old monastery from which it takes its name. A priory was founded here in the 6th century by St. Canice; in Irish, *Cill Chainnigh* means "Canice's Church." In medieval times, it was a prosperous walled city. Much of its medieval architecture has been skillfully preserved, including long sections of the medieval wall, and the Medieval Mile, a trail of historic sites, runs from Kilkenny Castle to St. Canice's Cathedral. Farther afield, the gentle countryside is full of captivating old ruins, from the majestic **Kells Priory** to the haunting remains of **Jerpoint Abbey.**

Visitor Information

The **Kilkenny Tourist Office** is at 79A High St., Kilkenny (visitkilkenny.ie; ✆ **1800/230-330**). It's open Monday to Saturday from 9am until 5pm. It sometimes closes for lunch on quieter days, and hours can vary in winter.

Exploring Kilkenny City

Black Abbey ♥♥ CHURCH This Dominican church, founded in 1225, is named Black Abbey after the Black Friars, another name for the Dominicans, who wore various black capes over their white habits. The abbey's blackest days came in 1650, when Oliver Cromwell used it as a court from which to dispense summary justice, before destroying it completely; by the time he left, all that remained were the walls. The abbey was rebuilt and opened in 1816 as a church; a new nave was completed in 1866, and the entire building was fully restored in 1979. Among the elements remaining from the original abbey are an alabaster sculpture of the

Art gallery in Kilkenny Castle.

Holy Trinity that dates from 1400, and a pre-Reformation statue of St. Dominic carved in Irish oak, which is believed to be the oldest such piece in the world. The huge Rosary Window, which represents in stained glass the 15 mysteries of the rosary, is nearly 45 square meters (484 sq. ft.); it was created in 1892 by Mayer of Munich.

Abbey St. (off Parliament St.). ✆ **056/772-1279.** Free admission; donations welcome. Daily May–Sept 8am–8pm; Oct–Apr 8am–6:30pm. No visits during worship (Mass times Mon–Sat 10:30am and 1:05pm; also closed for Sat vigil 6:10pm and Sun 9am, noon, and 6pm).

Kilkenny Castle ♥♥♥ CASTLE Standing majestically beside the River Nore on the south side of Kilkenny City, this stunning medieval castle was built in the 12th century and remodeled in Victorian times. From its sturdy corner towers to its battlements, Kilkenny Castle retains the imposing lines of an authentic fortress. The exquisitely restored interior includes a library, drawing room, and bedrooms, all decorated in 1830s style. The former servants' quarters are now an art gallery. The 20-hectare (49-acre) grounds include a riverside walk, extensive gardens, and a well-equipped children's playground. This is a very busy site, so arrive early (or toward the end of the day) to avoid waiting. Visits can be self-guided or by guided tour (book online in advance).

The Parade. kilkennycastle.ie. ✆ **056/770-4100.** Admission self-guided tour €8 adults; €6 seniors; €4 students and children 12–17; children 11 and under free; €20 families. Guided tour tickets €4 extra. Daily Apr–Sept 9:15am–5:30pm; Oct–Mar 9:30am–5pm. Last admission 30 min. before closing. Closed Dec 24–27 and 31.

Kilkenny Walking Tours ♥♥ TOURS Local historian Pat Tynan leads you through the streets and lanes of medieval Kilkenny on this lively

ATTRACTIONS

Black Abbey 2

Kilkenny Castle 7

St. Canice's Cathedral 1

WHERE TO STAY

Butler House 10

Lawcus Farm Guesthouse 11

Pembroke Kiklenny 9

WHERE TO EAT

Campagne 6

Foodworks 3

Gourmet Store 4

Kyteler's Inn 5

Ristorante Rinuccini 8

walking tour. Tall-sounding (but 100% true) tales are really Pat's strong point; he's a mine of trivia, much of it rather sensational (his own website sells the tour with promises of "black death, whippings, burnings, crime, jails, theft and prostitutes"—now how's *that* for a pitch?). Tours depart daily from the tourist office on High Street and last about 70 minutes.
c/o Kilkenny Tourist Office, 79A High St. kilkennywalkingtours.ie. ✆ **087/265-1745.** Tickets €30. Mid-Mar to Oct Mon–Sat 11am and 2pm; Sun and all tours Nov–Feb must be prebooked; call for availability.

St. Canice's Cathedral ♥♥ CATHEDRAL The church that gave Kilkenny its name stands at the northern end of the city at the end of the Medieval Mile. Built in the 12th century, it was restored after the English invasion led by Oliver Cromwell in the mid–17th century. It is noteworthy for its rich interior timber and stone carvings, its colorful glasswork, and the structure itself. On the grounds, amid the tombstones in the churchyard, looms a massive round tower, believed to be a relic of the ancient church (although its original conical top has been replaced by a slightly domed roof). If you want to climb to the top of the tower, it will cost you a few more euros and burn more calories than you can count. ***Note:*** The cathedral has no parking, so use the lot on Dean Street or park in the city center.

Interior of St. Canice's Cathedral.

The Close, Coach Rd. stcanicescathedral.ie. ✆ **056/776-4971.** Cathedral: €7.50 adults, €6.50 seniors and students, €5 children 6–18, €19 families. Round Tower: €7 adults, €6.50 seniors and students, €4.50 children 6–18, €17 families. Combined ticket: €12 adults, €10 seniors and students, €8 children 6–18, €30 families. Cathedral: May–Sept Mon–Sat 9am–6pm, Sun 1–6pm; Oct–Apr Mon–Sat 10am–5pm, closed Sun. Round Tower (weather permitting): June–Aug Mon–Fri 9am–6pm, Sun 2–6pm. Last climb 30 min. before closing. ***Note:*** You must be over 140cm (4½ ft.) to climb the tower.

Farther Afield in County Kilkenny

Duiske Abbey ♥ CHURCH A fine example of an early Cistercian abbey, Duiske Abbey was founded in 1204. Although it was officially suppressed in 1536, monks continued to occupy the site for many years. In 1774, the tower of the abbey church collapsed. In 1813, the roof was replaced, and religious services returned to the church, but the abbey didn't approach its former glory until the 1970s, when a group of locals mounted a reconstruction effort. Now, with its fine lancet windows and a large effigy of a Norman knight, the abbey is the pride of Graiguenamanagh. The adjacent visitor center has an exhibit of Christian art and artifacts.

Upper Main St., Graiguenamanagh. villageofthemonks.com/duiskeabbey. ✆ **059/972-4238.** Free admission; donations welcome. Daily 8am–6pm.

Dunmore Cave ♥♥ UNDERGROUND CAVERNS This gloomy series of chambers, formed over millions of years, contains some fine calcite formations. The caves have been known to humans for at least a millennium; they are first recorded in written records from the 9th and 10th centuries. These records, known as the *Triads of Ireland,* indicate that a bloody Viking massacre took place here in the year A.D. 928. No conclusive proof has ever been found, but evidence unearthed by archaeologists in more recent years confirms that Vikings used the caves. Exhibits at the visitor center tell the story. Access to the cave is by guided tour only. Dunmore is about 11km (7 miles) from Kilkenny City.

Off Castlecomer Rd. (N78), Ballyfoyle. heritageireland.ie. ✆ **056/776-7726.** Admission €5 adults; €4 seniors; €3 students and children; €13 families. June–Aug daily 9:30am–6pm (last tour 5pm); Mar–May and Sept–Oct daily 9:30am–5pm (last tour 4pm); Nov–Feb Wed–Sun 9:30am–5pm (last tour 3pm). Tours may end early in winter depending on sunset.

Jerpoint Abbey ♥♥♥ CHURCH About 18km (11 miles) southeast of Kilkenny, this atmospheric Cistercian monastery dates from the 12th

Exquisite medieval stone carvings at Jerpoint Abbey.

century. Highlights of the ethereal ruins, which are preserved in a peaceful country setting, include a sculptured cloister arcade, Romanesque architecture in the north nave, and unique stone carvings on the medieval tombs (some of which have traces of original paint on them). The staff is quite friendly and knowledgeable about the local area. Ask for details of where to find the mysterious, ghostly ruins of the **Church of the Long Man,** about 16km (10 miles) away. If you're lucky, they'll be able to direct you—it's very hard to find otherwise and a local secret you may find yourself sworn to keep. ***Tip:*** If you're here in spring or autumn, plan your visit toward the end of the day. Wandering around these ancient places as the walls are blushed in peach and gold from the setting sun is an unforgettable experience.

On N8, 2.5km (1½ miles) SW of Thomastown. heritageireland.ie. ✆ **056/772-4623.** Admission €5 adults; €4 seniors, students, and children; €13 families. Daily 9am–5:30pm (closes 5pm Mar, 4:30pm Oct, 4pm Nov); closed Dec to mid-Mar (except for prebooked tours). Last admission 45 min. before closing.

Jerpoint Glass Studio ♥♥ CRAFT STUDIO Here you can witness the creation of Jerpoint glass, which you've probably been admiring in shops all across Ireland. The lines of the glasses, goblets, and pitchers are simple and fluid, highlighted by swirls of color. Watch the glass being blown and then blow your budget next door at the shop.

Stoneyford. jerpointglass.com. ✆ **056/772-4350.** Shop and gallery: Mon–Sat 10am–5pm; Sun and bank holidays noon–5pm. Glassblowing demonstrations: Mon–Thurs 10am–4pm; Fri 10am–1pm. No demonstrations on public holidays.

Kells Priory ♥♥ RELIGIOUS RUINS With its encompassing fortification walls and towers, Kells is a glorious ruined monastery enfolded into the sloping south bank of the King's River. In 1193, Baron Geoffrey FitzRobert founded the priory and established a Norman-style town beside it. The current ruins date from the 13th to 15th centuries. The priory's wall has been carefully restored, and it connects seven towers, the remains of an abbey, and foundations of chapels and houses. You can tell by the thick walls that this monastery was well fortified, and those walls were built for a reason—it was frequently attacked. In the 13th century, it was the subject of two major battles and burned to the ground. (Despite the similar name, this is not the same monastery where the famous Book of Kells [p. 93] was stored for years.) The priory is less than half a mile from the village of Kells, so if you have time to spare, cross the footbridge behind it, which takes you on a beautiful path across the river and to a riverside walk leading to a picturesque old mill.

Kells. heritageireland.ie. ✆ **056/772-4623.** Free admission. Guided tours June–Sept Wed–Sun 9:30am–5pm (last tour 4pm). Take N76 S from Kilkenny, follow signs for R699/Callan and stay on R699 until you see signs for Kells.

Where to Stay in County Kilkenny

Butler House ♥♥ The former Dower House of Kilkenny Castle, this elegant 18th-century house is full of charm, with a mix of modern fittings and original features like ornate ceilings, marble fireplaces, and picture windows. Some rooms have garden views or castle views, and some ground-floor rooms have garden access. The location could not be better, right in the center of town—one entrance leads to a walled garden connected to the castle yard, while another entrance opens onto Patrick Street. Ask the friendly staff where to go in town, but allow time to soak up the gardens too, especially in fine weather.

16 Patrick St. butler.ie. ✆ **056/772-2828.** 17 units. €150–€360 double. Breakfast included. Free parking. **Amenities:** Restaurant; bar; afternoon tea; Wi-Fi (free).

Lawcus Farm Guesthouse ♥♥♥ Perfect peace and tranquility await you at this gorgeous farmyard B&B, deep in the Kilkenny countryside. Make no mistake: This is the real deal ("Helping us on the farm at feeding time is greatly appreciated," says the website), but hosts Mark and Ann-Marie go out of their way to welcome guests. The early-19th-century farmhouse has been beautifully renovated. Guest rooms are decent size, with plenty of natural light. It's a pastoral setting to die for—you're right next to a river, where you can go wild-water swimming or try your hand at fishing for trout. Home-cooked breakfasts are delicious, but you'll have to fend for yourself at dinner. (Your hosts can recommend nearby places.) The guesthouse has family rooms, and a self-contained lodge for couples, the Tree House, set on a rocky outcrop down by the river, costs €280 for 2 nights, including breakfast in the main house. The only snag in this rural idyll? Lawcus Farm doesn't accept credit cards (they are "working on it"), but you can send payment by PayPal (without having an account).

Stoneyford (from the R713, pass Stoneyford sign and turn to right of small bridge; follow signs to B&B). lawcusfarmguesthouse.com. ✆ **086/603-1667.** 6 units. €140–€250 double. Breakfast included. 2-night min. stay; discounts for stays of 3 or more nights. Children 4 and under free (1/party). Free parking. **Amenities:** Wi-Fi (free).

Mount Juliet Estate ♥♥♥ Tucked away on a 500-acre estate in the lush Kilkenny countryside, Mount Juliet offers a choice of two rural hideaways: the historic Manor House, which dates from 1757, or Hunter's Yard, a gorgeous conversion of the former stables. At both, rooms are spacious and decorated with elegant restraint—large beds are swathed in fine linens, bathrooms are bang up to date, and all have peaceful, bucolic views. You're walking distance from charming Thomastown, with its pretty churches and sweet cafes. The Manor House is the more well-known, formal, and expensive of the two, renowned for its service and Michelin-starred restaurant, **Lady Helen ♥♥♥**. But we like Hunter's Yard's low-key vibe. **The Hound** restaurant **♥♥** is bright and relaxed,

High tea at Mount Juliet Estate.

with a chilled-out gastropub approach that features fresh, local ingredients without pretension. It's also significantly cheaper across the board. Whichever property you choose, though, it's very unlikely you'll be disappointed.

Mount Juliet Estate, Thomastown. mountjuliet.ie. ✆ **056/777-3000.** 32 units (Manor House); 93 units (Hunter's Yard). €270–€524 Manor House double; €225–€554 Hunter's Yard double. Breakfast included. Free parking. **Amenities:** Restaurant; bar; spa; pool; room service; Wi-Fi (free).

Pembroke Kilkenny ♥♥ Just 200m (656 ft.) from Kilkenny Castle (from the upper floors you can see the castle's turrets poking up over rooftops), this is a cosmopolitan hotel in the center of Kilkenny City. Bedrooms are bright and comfortable, with plenty of space. The in-house **Statham's** restaurant serves excellent seasonal Irish cooking featuring local food producers. The sophisticated bar is a lively spot for a cocktail or glass of wine and also has a more casual bar-food menu. The **Mint Medispa** offers treatments including Bio-Penta infusion facials and massages (from €80 for 40 min., with facials from €120).

11 Patrick St., Kilkenny. pembrokekilkenny.com. ✆ **056/778-3500.** 74 units. €129–€329 double. 2-night min. stay on some dates. Dinner and spa packages available. Breakfast included. Free parking. **Amenities:** Restaurant; bar; spa; room service; Wi-Fi (free).

Where to Eat in County Kilkenny

Kilkenny has a small but growing restaurant scene, and among the options are excellent coffee shops and cafes. One of the best is the **Gourmet Store** (56 High St.; facebook.com/gourmetstorekk), a sunny cafe/deli in Kilkenny Town. It's the perfect stop for breakfast or lunch on the go, offering freshly made bagels, sandwiches, salads, and soups, as well as all the ingredients for a picnic. Another spot to try in Kilkenny Town is **Foodworks** (7 Parliament St.; foodworkskk.ie; no phone), an airy, modern eatery that's winning awards for its fresh approach to light cuisine. Think tasty breakfasts, glorious salads, towering sandwiches, and cakes you'll dream of for days. There's also a great wine list—you're on vacation, you know. For richer fare, besides the places below, try **Lady Helen** at Mount Juliet (see above), a Michelin-starred restaurant tucked away in the countryside, or **Statham's** at the Pembroke Kilkenny (see above), now run by the former executive chef at Mount Juliet.

Campagne ♥♥♥ BISTRO The chef at this outstanding French-Irish restaurant, about a 10-minute walk from Kilkenny Castle, once ran the kitchen at Dublin's superlative **Chapter One ♥♥♥** (p. 150). The sleek and atmospherically lit dining room has colorful modern art on the walls. The three-course fixed-price menus are short but subtly inventive, showcasing dishes like monkfish with chicken and girolle lasagne, braised fennel and roast chicken butter sauce, or filet of beef with crushed celeriac and spinach. For dessert, try the figs roasted in muscatel, or walnut and olive oil cake with gingerbread ice cream. The extensive wine list is well chosen, with particularly strong French options. Locals make this one-Michelin-star restaurant their top choice for special occasions—but if you find the prices too high, come for the early-bird menu (Wed–Thurs 5:30–6:45pm, Fri–Sat 5–5:30pm), priced at €48 for three courses.

5 The Arches, Gas house Lane. campagne.ie. ✆ **056/777-2858.** 3-course fixed-price menu €80. Dinner Wed–Thurs 5:30–9pm, Fri–Sat 5–9:30pm; lunch Sun 12:30–2:30pm. Open 6–8pm Sun on some bank holiday weekends.

Kyteler's Inn ♥♥ PUB In business for over 6 centuries, this vintage inn serves decent pub food—sandwiches, Irish stew, burgers, fish and chips—but it's the atmosphere you really come for. With all the exposed flagstones and cozy nooks, it's hard to think of a more satisfyingly Irish-looking pub. The place is named after noted hellraiser Alice Kyteler, who died in 1324. She poisoned at least three of her husbands, ran the inn as a den of debauchery, and was sentenced to be burned as a witch. But she escaped, and nobody saw or heard from her again. Unless, that is, you believe some of the more colorful tales about this place after dark. . . .

Kieran St. kytelersinn.com. ✆ **056/772-1064.** Lunch entrees €7–€17.50; dinner entrees €17–€28. Mon–Thurs 10:30am–11:30pm; Fri–Sat 10:30am–12:30am; Sun 12:30–11pm (food served until about 10pm).

Ristorante Rinuccini ♥♥♥ ITALIAN This extremely popular restaurant opposite Kilkenny Castle packs in diners for delicious Italian food with an Irish accent. The basement-level dining room gets very busy, but the food more than makes up for it. The homemade pasta is as good as you'd expect, and on the specials board, local produce really comes into its own: catch of the day fresh from Kilmore Quay; Silver Hill duck baked with sweet *aurum* (an Italian liqueur); and spinach and ricotta ravioli in a gorgonzola sauce. Desserts are equally good—try the classic tiramisu filled with zabaglione. Make reservations, especially if you're coming on a weekend.

1 The Parade. rinuccini.com. ✆ **056/776-1575.** Lunch 2 courses €32, 3 courses €40; dinner entrees €24–€40. Reservations recommended. Mon–Sat 12:30–2:30pm and 5–9:30pm; Sun 12:30–8pm.

Sports & Outdoor Pursuits in Kilkenny

GOLF **Mount Juliet Golf and Country Club** in Thomastown (mountjuliet.ie; ✆ **056/777-3000**) is an excellent course 16km (10 miles) south of Kilkenny City. The 18-hole, par-72 championship course, designed by Jack Nicklaus, charges greens fees of €65 to €110. Even closer to the city is the 18-hole championship course at the **Kilkenny Golf Club** in Glendine (kilkennygolfclub.com; ✆ **056/776-5400**), an inland par-71 layout with greens fees of €40 to €50.

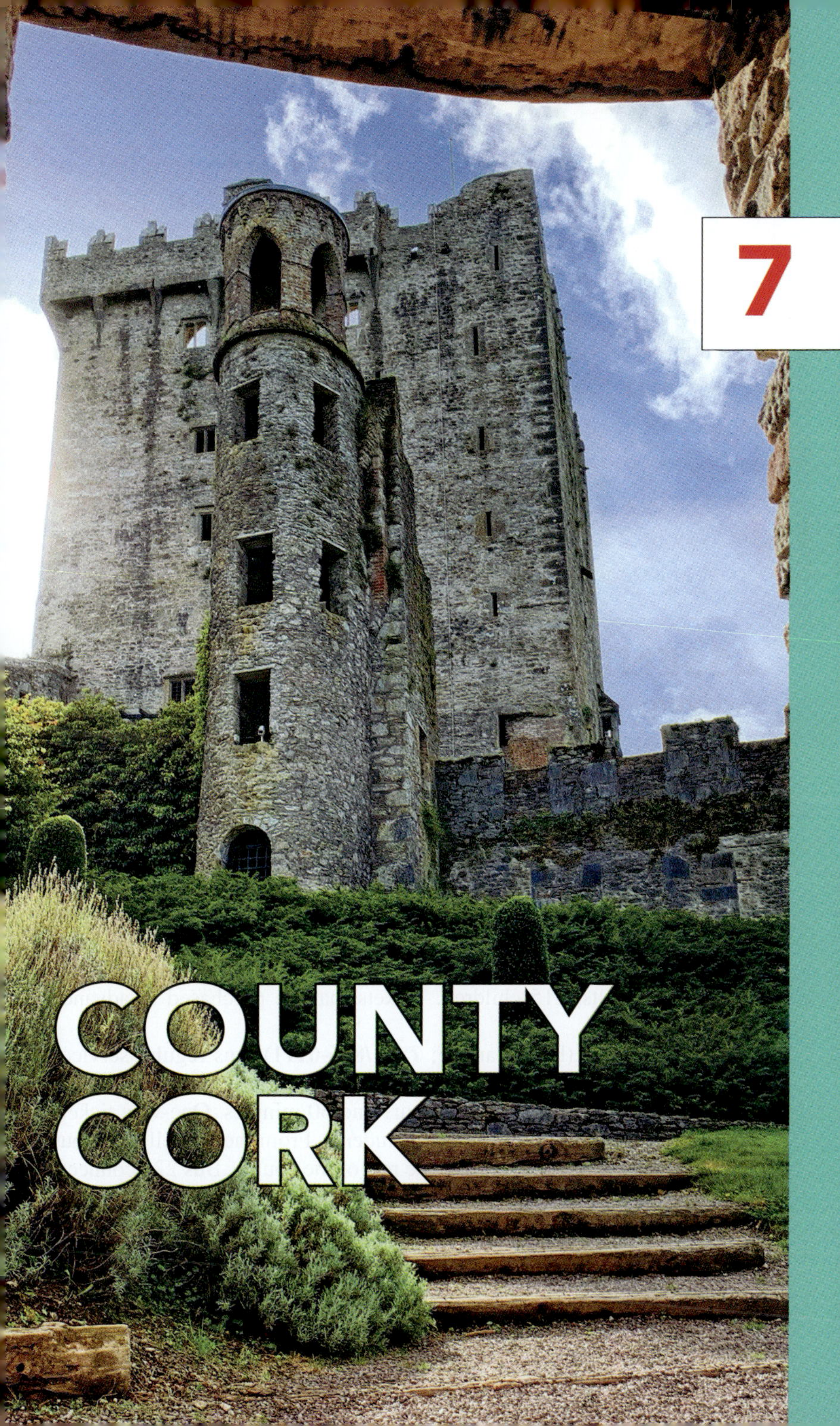

7

COUNTY CORK

With its lively capital city, quiet country villages, rocky hills, picturesque beaches, and long, peaceful miles of lush green farmland, it's easy to see why Cork is one of Ireland's most popular destinations. St. Fin Barre is credited with the name—in the 6th century, he built a monastery on a swampy estuary of the River Lee, giving it the Irish name *Corcaigh* (marsh). Stop in **Cork City** for wonderful restaurants and good hotels. Keep going to see the pretty harbor town of **Kinsale,** famous for its gourmet food scene; the storied seaport of **Cobh** in East Cork; or the barren beauty of **Cape Clear Island** in craggy West Cork. Cork is also the start (or end) point of the **Wild Atlantic Way** (p. 275), which runs 2,500km (1,550 miles) along the west coast of Ireland.

ESSENTIALS

Arriving

BY BUS **AirCoach** (aircoach.ie; ✆ **01/844-7118**) runs a regular direct service from Dublin to Cork City. You can catch the bus either at Dublin Airport or Aston Quay in Dublin city center; from there, the journey to Lower Glanmire Road in Cork City takes 3 hours, traffic permitting. Buses start at 6:25am from Terminal 2, 5 minutes later from Terminal 1, and then on the hour every hour from Aston Quay all day until midnight, the last bus leaving Terminal 2 at 11:25pm. One-way tickets to Cork are €22 adults, €11 children; round-trip tickets are €31.50 adults, €15 children. Tickets from Cork to Dublin are €20 adults, €10 children; round-trip tickets €30 adults, €15 children. Tickets may be purchased in advance online.

Bus Éireann (buseireann.ie; ✆ **01/836-6111**) runs regular services from all parts of the Republic to the Cork bus station (Parnell Place). The trip from Dublin takes around 3 hours and 30 minutes. One-way tickets are €14 adults, €9 children, and €12 students. From the Parnell Place bus station, Bus Éireann buses run to the rest of the county. Bus 226 connects Cork with Kinsale. Buses also arrive on Pier Road.

PREVIOUS PAGE: **Blarney Castle.**

BY TRAIN **Iarnród Éireann/Irish Rail** (irishrail.ie; ✆ **1850/366-222**) travels to Cork City from Dublin and other parts of Ireland. Trains arrive at Kent Station, Lower Glanmire Road, in eastern Cork City (✆ **021/455-7277**). Kinsale does not have a train station.

BY FERRY There are no longer any direct ferry routes into Cork from Britain. However, **Brittany Ferries** (brittany-ferries.com; ✆ **021/427-7801**) sail twice a week between Roscoff, in France, and Cork's Ringaskiddy Ferryport.

BY CAR Cork is easily reachable on the M8 from Dublin, N25 from Waterford, and N22 from Killarney. To rent a car in Dublin, see p. 91; to rent a car at Shannon Airport, see p. 354. To hire a car in Cork, try **Enterprise Rent-A-Car,** Kinsale Road (✆ **021/497-5133**), or **Dollar Car Rental** at Cork Airport (✆ **021/496-5849**).

BY PLANE **Cork Airport (ORK),** Kinsale Road (corkairport.com; ✆ **021/431-3131**), is served by several airlines, including **Aer Lingus, British Airways, Air France,** and **Ryanair.** Cork is the Republic of Ireland's second busiest airport (and the fourth in Ireland overall, after Dublin and the two airports in Belfast). It has direct flights to and from several European countries, including the U.K. and France.

Visitor Information

Cork Tourist Information Centre (discoverireland.ie; ✆ **1800/230-330**) is at 125 St. Patrick St., Cork. It's open Monday to Saturday from 9am to 5pm (also open Sun June–Sept). **Kinsale Tourist Information Office** at Emmet Place, Kinsale (kinsale.ie; ✆ **021/477-3481**), is open Monday to Saturday from 9am to 5pm (open Sun June–Sept). **Cobh Tourist Office,** in Market House, Casement Square, Cobh (✆ **021/481-3301**), is open Monday to Friday from 9am until 4:45pm. There are year-round tourist offices in Bandon, Fermoy, Mallow, Midleton, and Youghal, and seasonal tourist offices in Baltimore, Bantry, Clonakilty, Glengarriff, Macroom, Schull, and Skibbereen.

CORK CITY

While Cork City has a population of only 225,000 residents, it's a busy, attractive, cultured place with the feel of a much larger city. The presence of University College Cork keeps the population young, the creative class dynamic, the pubs interesting, and the number of affordable restaurants plentiful. It has its flaws—traffic gets congested, and some areas can feel gritty and crowded. But lose yourself in the narrow lanes of the old Huguenot Quarter or wander MacCurtain Street at night and you'll understand the unique spirit of this real Irish city, which is not a tourist trap. Cork City is compact and best seen on foot—park the car and strike out.

City Layout

Cork City center is set on an island, so don't be confused if you come across not one River Lee but two. These two channels divide the city into three sections:

FLAT OF THE CITY The downtown core is bounded by two channels of the River Lee. Its main shopping thoroughfare is bustling **St. Patrick Street,** which curves up to **St. Patrick's Bridge. Oliver Plunkett Street** is also full of shops and cafes. Nearby, **South Mall** is a wide, tree-lined street with attractive Georgian architecture and a row of offices; linking them at their western end is **Grand Parade,** a spacious thoroughfare that blends 18th-century bow-fronted houses with the remains of the old city walls. It holds businesses and shops as well as **Bishop Lucey Park.** The pedestrianized lanes around French Church Street and Carey's Lane, the old **Huguenot Quarter,** are lined with cafes, restaurants, and small shops.

NORTH BANK St. Patrick's Bridge leads over the river's north channel to the hilly north side of the city, where St. Patrick Street becomes **St.**

CORK: THE rebel CITY

Travel in County Cork today, and all that appears in front of you are rolling green hills and bucolic farmscapes. But this county was once at the heart of the battle for Ireland's soul.

For centuries, the county had a reputation for defiance and revolt. Once the seat of power in South Munster, it changed hands many times as the English and Irish battled for control. Devastated by the Great Famine, Cork became a center of the 19th-century Fenian movement, when the label "Rebel Cork" was first widely used. It certainly lived up to the name during Ireland's early-20th-century battle for independence. It was a battle of wills, and Cork refused to surrender.

The British troops occupying Cork at the time—a paramilitary force nicknamed the "Black and Tans" for the color of their uniforms—were among the most repressive in the country. The struggle came to a head in 1920 when Thomas MacCurtain, mayor of Cork City, was killed by the Black and Tans. His successor, Terence MacSwiney, was arrested, and later died in a London prison after a hunger strike lasting 75 days.

On December 11 of that year, after an attack by the IRA, the British forces set fire to Cork City center, apparently as payback. The library, City Hall, and almost all the buildings on St. Patrick Street were burned to the ground. More than 300 buildings were destroyed in the ensuing conflagration—virtually the entire city was smoldering rubble. As the fires blazed, two men suspected to be members of the IRA were shot as they slept, also allegedly by the occupying military troops.

The atrocity's bitter legacy ensured that fighting would rage on in Cork, even as peace talks took hold elsewhere in Ireland. Cork resisted peace agreements to the end, even a treaty negotiated by Cork native son Michael Collins (p. 282). And it ensured that Cork natives would embrace their identity as Rebel Cork forevermore.

Cork City
ATTRACTIONS
Blarney Castle 8
Cork Butter Museum 9
Cork City Gaol 1
Cork Public Museum 2
Crawford Art Gallery 11
English Market 13
Mutton Lane Mural 12
St. Anne's Church and Shandon Tower 10
St. Fin Barre's Cathedral 7
University College Cork and Glucksman Gallery 3
Information
WHERE TO EAT
Cafe Paradiso 6
Cask 19
Ecofish 21
5Points Café 24
The Glass Curtain 23
Goldie 17
Greene's 22
Market Lane 16
Orso 15
Paladar 18
WHERE TO STAY
The Address 25
The Dean 26
Hayfield Manor 4
Imperial Hotel 14
The Metropole 20
The Montenotte 25
The River Lee 5
0 1/8 mile
0 1/8 km
St. Anne's
Firkin Crane Centre
Opera House
Bus Station
City Hall
St. Francis's
UCC East Campus
Granary Theatre
Beamish & Crawford Brewery
Cork City Tours
Elizabeth Fort
St. Fin Barre's Cathedral
Cork Public Museum
University College Cork Main Campus
GREENMOUNT
THE LOUGH
River Lee
North Channel
South Channel
Mardyke Gardens
Fitzgerald Park
Bishop Lucey Park
N20
N22

Patrick's Hill. And is it ever a hill! It's got an incline so steep it'll remind you of San Francisco. East of St. Patrick's Hill, lively **MacCurtain Street** runs past the train station and out to the M8 motorway. West of St. Patrick's Hill is Shandon, one of the city's oldest neighborhoods, with the tall spire of **St. Anne's Church** its chief landmark.

SOUTH BANK Across the river's south channel, the largely residential South Bank is where you'll find **St. Fin Barre's Cathedral,** the site of St. Fin Barre's 6th-century monastery, and, farther west, the campus of **University College Cork.**

Exploring Cork City

Cork Butter Museum ♥♥ MUSEUM With a name like this, it's no surprise that this fun little place has turned up on several "world's quirkiest museums" lists, but it's more than just a celebration of tasty Irish dairy produce. From 1770 until the 1920s, Cork was the world's largest exporter of butter, peaking at half a million casks annually by the turn of the 20th century. The museum chronicles that industrial past, using butter as a springboard to explore wider stories about Irish farming, society, and industry, from the Middle Ages onward. It's surprisingly enlightening.

O'Connell Sq., Shandon. corkbutter.museum. ✆ **021/430-0600.** Admission €5 adults; €4 seniors and students; €2 youth 17 and under; children 11 and under free. June–Sept Mon–Sat 10am–4pm, Sun and bank holidays 11am–4pm; Oct–Nov Wed–Sat 10am–4pm; Sun and bank holidays 11am–4pm.

Cork City Gaol ♥♥ HERITAGE SITE Like something out of a Victorian novel, this early-19th-century jail is an austere and highly atmospheric building. It opened in 1824 as a women's prison. Famous inmates included the extraordinary Countess Constance Markievicz (see box on p. 465). The first woman elected to the British parliament, she was sentenced to death for her part in the 1916 Easter Rising (her sentence was commuted because of her sex, to which she reportedly responded, "I do wish you had the decency to shoot me"). Earlier in its history, the jail was the last place in Ireland many convicts were held before being shipped off to Australia. This colorful past is well-presented, with the aid of costumed mannequins in key positions. Somewhat incongruously, in 1927, after the building ceased to be used as a prison, it became the site of Ireland's first radio station. A small museum tells this story, complete with a restored studio from the period.

Convent Ave., Sunday's Well. corkcitygaol.com. ✆ **021/430-5022.** Admission €11 adults; €9 seniors and students; €7 children; €34 families. Additional €2 for audio guide or guided tour. Daily 10am–5pm (closes at 4pm Nov–Feb). Guided tours at 2pm (hourly tours July–Aug).

Cork Public Museum ♥♥ MUSEUM This simple, rather endearing civic museum is a good place to get an overview of the city's history. Displays include a few objects from Cork's ancient past, including an Iron Age helmet and some of the oldest tools ever discovered in Ireland. But it's

strongest when it comes to the traditional crafts made in the city during the 19th and 20th centuries, including silverware and intricate lace from the Victorian period. There are also very good collections relating to the lives of local revolutionaries, including Michael Collins (p. 282). The museum is located on the west side of Cork, in the middle of Fitzgerald Park—near the Western Road, about a 10-minute walk from the city center.
Fitzgerald Park. corkcity.ie/en/cork-public-museum. ✆ **021/427-0679.** Free admission. Tues–Fri 10am–4pm; Sat 11am–4pm. Closed Mon, Sun, and bank holidays.

Crawford Art Gallery ♥♥♥ ART MUSEUM One of the top art galleries in Ireland, the Crawford has impressive collections of sculpture and paintings. The Irish School is particularly well-represented with works from John Butts (1728–65), including his fine 1755 panorama of Cork City, and Dublin-born Harry Clarke (1889–1931), one of the most celebrated illustrators of the early 20th century, who also produced some incredible early Art Deco–influenced stained glass. The gallery has a strong collection of works by female Irish artists from the mid–19th century onward; check out the extraordinary abstract work of Mainie Jellett (1897–1944) and the Cubist painter Norah McGuinness (1901–80). The gallery also has a program of temporary exhibitions.
Emmet Place. crawfordartgallery.ie. ✆ **021/480-5042.** Free admission. Mon–Sat 10am–5pm (Thurs until 8pm); Sun and bank holidays 11am–4pm. Last entry 15 min. before closing. Free tours Thurs 6:30pm, Sun and bank holidays 2pm.

Sculptures in the Crawford Art Gallery in Cork.

English Market ♥♥ MARKET HALL The name of this bustling food market harks back to the days of English rule—it was first granted a charter in 1610 during the reign of King James I. The current market building dates from 1788, although it was redesigned after being gutted by fire in the 1980s. Inside is a cornucopia of fresh produce, including super-traditional Cork delicacies—some of them tempting, others less palatable to outsiders. (Mmm, tripe! Pig's trotters? Anyone?) Happily, there are lots of tasty treats too, like local cheeses, handmade cakes, and a specialist chocolate shop, with plenty of takeaway snacks.

Grand Parade; enter from St. Patrick St., Grand Parade, Oliver Plunkett St., or Princes St. englishmarket.ie. ✆ **021/ 492-4258.** Free admission. Mon–Sat 8am–6pm.

The handsome English Market offers plenty of gourmet browsing.

Mutton Lane Mural ♥ PUBLIC ART This riotously colorful mural along the walls of Mutton Lane, down one side of the Mutton Lane Inn, is intended to represent the essence of Cork. It depicts musicians performing the traditional "Pana Shuffle," and all of the characters featured are real local people. It is a vivid evocation of peace and community spirit, beloved locally—so much so, claim the owners of the pub, that it has never been vandalized by graffiti (impossible to prove, of course). The mural was painted by local artist Anthony Ruby in 2004. Its historical provenance can be dated by the following message, which is hidden within the colorful scene: "DEDICATED TO EVERYONE EXCEPT GEORGE BUSH." The lane leads into the English Market.

Mutton Lane, off St. Patrick St.

St. Anne's Church and Shandon Tower ♥♥ CHURCH Cork's most recognizable landmark, also known as Shandon Church, is famous for its giant pepper-pot steeple and eight melodious bells. Pretty much wherever you stand in the downtown area, you can see the stone tower crowned with a gilt ball and distinctive fish weathervane. The clock, added in 1847, made it the first four-faced clock tower in the world (beating London's Big Ben by just a few years). Until fairly recently, due to a quirk of clockworks, it was known as "the four-faced liar" because each side showed a different time—except on the hour when they all somehow managed to synchronize. Disappointingly, perhaps, that charming oddity has now been repaired. Climb the 1722 belfry tower for a chance to ring the famous Shandon Bells. (Be warned, though: It's 132 steps up to the belfry, and the gap narrows to a claustrophobic half-meter—that's just over 1½ ft.—near the entrance to the belfry.) If you continue on the somewhat precarious climb past the bells, you'll be rewarded with spectacular views over the surrounding countryside.

Church St., Shandon. shandonbells.ie. ✆ **021/450-5906.** Free admission. Clock tower €6 adults; €5 seniors and students; €3 children; €15 families. June–Sept Mon–Sat 10am–4:30pm, Sun 11:30am–4:30pm (closes 4pm Mar–May and Oct, 3pm Nov–Feb). Last entry to tower 30 min. before closing.

St. Fin Barre's Cathedral ♥♥ CATHEDRAL With its three soaring spires dominating the Cork skyline, this Church of Ireland cathedral sits on the very spot St. Fin Barre chose in A.D. 600 for his church and school (according to legend). A much smaller medieval tower was demolished to make way for the current building, which dates from the early 1860s—there's nothing left of the original aside from a few pieces of decorative stonework inside. In this building, the architect, William Burges (1827–81), embraced the French Gothic style popular at the time. The interior is highly ornamented with some stunning mosaic work. The bells were inherited from a 1735 church that also previously stood on this site. The cathedral hosts occasional exhibitions; check the website for listings of what's on.

Bishop St. corkcathedral.com. ✆ **021/496-3387.** Admission €8 adults; €7 seniors and students; free for children 15 and under. Mon–Sat 9am–5pm; Sun Apr–Oct 12:30–2pm and 4:30–5pm. Closed Sun (except for services) Nov–Mar.

University College Cork and Glucksman Gallery ♥♥ UNIVERSITY Part of Ireland's national university, with about 21,000

A quiet corner on the campus of University College Cork.

students, this center of learning is housed in a pretty quadrangle of Gothic Revival–style buildings. Colorful gardens and wooded grounds grace the campus. An audio tour of the campus takes in the **Crawford Observatory,** the Harry Clarke stained-glass windows in **Honan Chapel,** the landscaped **President's Garden,** and the **Stone Corridor,** a collection of stones inscribed with the ancient Irish *ogham* written language. Hour-long guided tours, given by students, leave from the visitor center at 3:30pm every Wednesday or 3pm on Saturday. Also on the campus, the innovative **Lewis Glucksman Gallery** has an excellent program of exhibitions. Expect to see cutting-edge photography, painting, sculpture, and a few items from the university's ever-expanding permanent collection. A good cafe and shop are also on-site.

Visitor center: North Wing, Main Quad, Western Rd. ucc.ie/en/discover/visit. ✆ **021/490-1876.** Free admission. Mon–Sat 9am–5pm; Sun 11am–5pm. Glucksman Gallery: glucksman.org. ✆ **021/490-1844.** Free admission (€5 suggested donation). Tues–Sun 11am–5pm.

Outside Cork City

Blarney Castle ♥♥ CASTLE Though the runaway favorite for the hotly contested title of "cheesiest tourist attraction in Ireland," Blarney Castle is nonetheless an imposing structure beloved by many. Constructed in the late 15th century, it was once much bigger; the massive square

Blarney House.

tower is all that remains of the vast medieval building. But, be honest, that's not why you've heard of this place, right? Its most famous attraction, and probably the most disappointing magical rock you'll ever kiss in your life, is the eponymous "Blarney Stone." Whoever first decided that this particular slab had mystical powers certainly didn't have the convenience of visitors in mind; after trudging up a series of narrow, poorly lit staircases, you'll find it wedged underneath the battlements, far enough to make it uncomfortable to reach, but not so far that countless tourists cannot lie down, stick their heads outside, and kiss it in hopes of achieving lifelong loquaciousness. There's no extra charge for kissing the Blarney Stone, though it's customary to tip the attendant who holds your legs (you might want to do it *before* you're slung over the edge). Thanks to Covid, a special cleaning spray is used on the stone after each person. Have we sold you on the experience yet? Snark aside, there is definitely more to see here. Take time to explore the atmospheric dungeons beneath the castle, and if you need a break from the tour-bus groups, the gardens are not only very pretty, but much less crowded. On the grounds is the later **Blarney House,** built in 1874 in the then-fashionable Scottish Baronial style with imposing gray stone and filigreed turrets that make it resemble a mini-Hogwarts. It's still a private residence, but you can tour the interior (June–Aug only, Mon–Sat 10am–2pm). Blarney Castle is 8km (5 miles) outside the city on R617. You can easily get here by taxi or bus—the number 215 stops about twice an hour (once per hr. on Sun). Ask the driver to let you off at the stop nearest the castle. ***Tip:*** Save a few euros on the admission price by booking online.

The Gift of Gab (or Is It Just Blarney?)

Can being held upside down and backwards from the top of a tall castle to kiss a rock really bring you the ability to talk up a storm? Well, Blarney Castle's association with the gift of gab does go back a long way. The popular version has it that Queen Elizabeth I (1533–1603) invented the notion in a fit of exasperation at then–Lord Blarney's tendency to prattle on at great length without ever agreeing to anything she wanted. The custom of actually kissing the stone, though, is less than a century old. Nobody knows quite when, how, or why it started, but around here they've got a thousand possible tales, some involving witches and others the crusaders. But don't believe them—it's all a bunch of . . .

Blarney. blarneycastle.ie. ✆ **021/438-5252.** Admission €22 adults; €17 seniors and students; €10 children 6–16; free for children 5 and under; €55 families. Jan–Mar and Nov–Dec 9am–5pm; Apr and Oct 9am–5:30pm; May–Sept 9am–6pm. Last admission 1 hr. before closing; times can change due to bad weather/poor light.

ORGANIZED TOURS

Cork City Tours ♥♥ Riding on open-top buses, you can hop on and off to explore the sights of Ireland's second city. The buses run all day in a loop from March through October (as frequently as every half-hour

July–Aug). Tour highlights include the Cork City Gaol, St. Anne's Church (Shandon Bells), and University College Cork. While the tour begins at the tourist office (42 Grand Parade), you can buy a ticket on the bus at several stops; check out the route on the Cork City Tours website.
corkcitytours.com. ✆ **021/430-9090.** Tickets €22 adults; €18 seniors and students; €9 children 6–15; free for children 5 and under; €50 families. Number of tours according to seasonal demand. June–Aug daily tours 9:30am–4:30pm every 30 min.; May and Sept daily tours 9:30am–4:15pm every 45 min.; Mar–Apr and Oct daily tours 9:30am–3:30pm every 90 min. Times refer to start of tours at Grand Parade, which depart from St. Patrick St. 5 min. later; complete circuit takes about 75 min.

Where to Stay in Cork City

Cork City has a good selection of hotels for all budgets and tastes, with many new openings plus refurbishments of old favorites in recent years, from no-frills to stylish design statements. Choose the city center if you plan to walk around, or somewhere on the outskirts with parking if you plan to do a bit of sightseeing in the county by car. Book ahead for the best room rates and try to avoid busy festival times.

EXPENSIVE

Hayfield Manor ♥♥♥ Everything about this elegant manor house is plush, from the sofas, decor, and grand piano in the lobby to comfy rooms where old-fashioned glamour meets all five-star luxuries. Located just

A grand fireplace in the imposing lobby of Hayfield Manor.

outside town and right beside U.C.C. (University College Cork), Hayfield has two restaurants: **Orchids,** for afternoon tea and dinner, and the more informal **Perrotts** in the conservatory, for lunch and dinner. The indoor pool, outdoor hot tub, and courtyard garden provide a welcome retreat after a day in the city—check out the courtyard's glass-walled bar **Bloom** for brunch or cocktails. In the evening, cozy up with a book after dinner in the library or drawing room. Nice touches include a local brand of cosmetics in the **Beautique Spa** and a golf putter in every room.

Perrott Ave., College Rd. (beside U.C.C.). hayfieldmanor.ie. ✆ **021/484-5900.** 88 units. €257–€575 double; €660–€1,500 suite. Dinner and other packages available. Free parking. **Amenities:** 2 restaurants; bar; valet parking; gym; room service; spa; swimming pool; outdoor hot tub; Wi-Fi (free).

The Montenotte ♥♥ Those who like to stay perched above the action, rather than right in the thick of it, will doubly appreciate one of the chief selling points of the stylish Montenotte: fantastic views across Cork City and the River Lee, with landscaped gardens and terraces to admire it all from. The hotel, once a house owned by a merchant prince, has been renovated from top to bottom in recent years, and is now a sophisticated place to stay. The hotel's **Bellevue Spa** offers treatments in an elegant setting, and the health club has a 20m (65-ft.) pool, sauna, Jacuzzi, and gym. There's even an in-house cinema. The cool, modern color schemes in the good-size guest rooms are offset with traditional patterns. The **Panorama Bistro** offers topnotch bistro cooking—with a superb view from the dining room, of course, and the **Glasshouse** cocktail bar has equally impressive vistas. For a secluded sanctuary within the hotel grounds, book a standalone Woodland or River suite. Each sleeps two, with a freestanding bath and woodland or river views from a private terrace.

Middle Glanmire Rd. themontenottehotel.com. ✆ **021/453-0050.** 107 units. €192–€340 double; €550–€680 Woodland or River suite. Breakfast not included in lower rates. Dinner, bed-and-breakfast packages available. Free parking. **Amenities:** Restaurant; bar; cinema; gym; swimming pool; room service; spa; Wi-Fi (free).

The River Lee ♥♥ A 5-minute walk from the city center, this shiny, modern hotel overlooks the River Lee (as you may have guessed). Guest rooms are quietly chic, with an understated modern style and huge windows that make the most of city or river views. Executive rooms have access to a private lounge with panoramic views of the city. The **River Club** terrace is the place to be in good weather; there's also a restaurant and a stylish cocktail bar with rare whiskeys from the Midleton Distillery in East Cork. The health club includes an indoor 20m (65-ft.) swimming pool, with complimentary Pilates and spin classes for guests.

Western Rd. doylecollection.com/hotels/the-river-lee-hotel. ✆ **021/425-2700.** 182 units. €212–€325 double. Breakfast not included in lower rates. Dinner, bed-and-breakfast packages available. Underground parking €12. **Amenities:** Restaurant; bar; gym; room service; swimming pool; Wi-Fi (free).

MODERATE

The Address ♥♥ The impressive redbrick exterior of this hilltop 1870s mansion on the northeast outskirts of Cork gives way to a snazzy lobby with black-and-white checkered floors. The guest rooms continue the stylish theme, based around traditional-style furniture. Pay the extra for an upper-floor room with a city view or balcony. **North** restaurant is a bright bar and restaurant filled with floor-to-ceiling bookcases; a comfy outdoor terrace comes with heaters; and the fitness center has a sauna. Be aware that the hotel can get booked up by wedding parties in the summer.

Military Hill. theaddresscork.com. ✆ **021/453-9000.** 70 units. €123–€226 double. Breakfast not included in lower rates. Free parking. **Amenities:** Bar/restaurant; gym; room service; Wi-Fi (free).

The Dean ♥♥ While its Horgan's Quay setting beside the Kent train station is not in the center of town (it's about a 15-min. walk), you might feel as if you're in the heart of the action simply while checking in. The emphasis here is on "fun," and the lobby buzzes with a cocktail and spritz bar and pumping tunes. Rooms are compact (from 20 sq. m/215 sq. ft.) but feature retro-style gadgets and generously sized showers. Rooftop restaurant **Sophie's** has an outdoor terrace with views over the developing docklands area. There's a well-equipped Power Gym and studios (fitness classes cost extra), plus a small relaxation pool and steam room, on the ground-floor level. Check online for packages.

Horgan's Quay. thedean.ie/cork. ✆ **021/234-1200.** 114 units. €141–€270 double; €338–€570 suite. Parking at Kent Station €9.50/24 hr. **Amenities:** Restaurant; bar; gym; hydrotherapy pool; room service; steam room; Wi-Fi (free).

Imperial Hotel ♥♥ This city-center hotel is surprisingly affordable for the amenities it offers, with elegantly restored public areas that are redolent of a much more expensive kind of hotel altogether. The guest rooms are perhaps a little plain by comparison, and the most basic rooms are small, but upgrading just a little gets you ample space and a bit more style. Hotel restaurant **Sketch** specializes in local meats and seafood, while **Lafayette's** cafe has delicious pastries and scones and **No.76** bar serves light bar food. Unwind in the **Escape Spa,** which offers a long list of indulgent, revitalizing treatments, starting at about €110 for a 50-minute facial or a back, neck, and shoulder massage. One hour in the vitality suite, with a Jacuzzi, steam room, and sauna costs €20 for hotel guests and €30 for non-residents.

76 South Mall. imperialhotelcork.com. ✆ **021/427-4040.** 125 units. €175–€336 double. Lower rates do not include breakfast. Dinner, bed-and-breakfast, and spa packages available. Parking at nearby lot (€15). **Amenities:** Restaurant; bar; cafe; room service; spa; Wi-Fi (free).

INEXPENSIVE

The Metropole ♥♥ Handily located on MacCurtain Street in the historic Victorian Quarter and dating from 1897 itself, the Met is an elegant redbrick building with Hogwarts-like roof peaks and turrets. Despite its age, the hotel's 112 small-ish rooms are up to sparkling modern standards, with marble bathrooms, comfortable beds, and fast Wi-Fi. The smallest rooms are tiny indeed—branded "cozy" by the hotel, these 9-sq.-m (97-sq.-ft.) singles come with a twin bed and just enough room for you and a suitcase. The standard double isn't huge, but it's pleasantly decorated, and the executive room has a king-size bed and seating area. Downstairs is a pretty, statue-surrounded swimming pool, with sauna and Jacuzzi. The ground-floor bar is popular with locals as well as guests. Breakfast earns raves from regulars, but there are plenty of other restaurants nearby if you crave variety.

MacCurtain St. themetropolehotel.ie. ✆ **021/464-3700.** 112 units. €153–€274 double. Nearby parking €10. **Amenities:** Restaurant; bar; gym; pool; room service; Wi-Fi (free).

Where to Eat in Cork City

Cork City is smattered with trendy eateries. The latest development is the happening outdoor dining scene, with tables along pedestrianized streets (such as Princes St.) off Oliver Plunkett Street. Cafes around the city range from old-fashioned spots serving traditional fry-ups to hipster joints with high-energy brunches and in-house roasteries. Whether casual or high-end, Cork's restaurants take advantage of the county's abundant supplies of fresh farm produce, cheese, and seafood.

As well as the dining highlights below, there are some casual favorites. On MacCurtain Street in the Victorian Quarter, hit **5Points Café** (59 MacCurtain St; 5points.ie; no phone) in the morning for breakfast *baps* (bread rolls) and bagels with the full works: sausage, bacon, black pudding, and relish. For cocktails and sharing plates in the evening, take a stroll to **Cask** (48 MacCurtain St.; caskcork.com; ✆ **021/450-0011**) or **Paladar** (6 Bridge St.; paladar.ie; ✆ **021/229-0045**). **Ecofish** (45a MacCurtain St.; ecofishcork.com; ✆ **085/200-5450**) does excellent takeout fish and chips, scampi, and chargrilled prawns.

Brewing Up Loyalty

There is a definite sense of civic loyalty when it comes to drinking stout in this town. Yes, Ireland is known for its love of Guinness, but in Cork you're more likely to find locals drinking the two locally brewed stouts: Murphy's or Beamish. In fact, walk into any pub and order a "home and away" and you'll be presented with a pint of Murphy's (or Beamish) and one of Guinness.

Cafe Paradiso ♥♥♥ VEGETARIAN An inventive, classy vegetarian restaurant on the Western Road strip, Cafe Paradiso does such magnificent things without meat that even passionate carnivores will find plenty to love. Try tasty starters like cheddar croqueta with roast pepper and fermented chili and then move on to the cauliflower and cashew korma. There's also a vegan menu. Desserts are heavenly; if it's on the menu, try the chocolate tart with brown butter ice cream and hazelnut. ***Note:*** The restaurant does not allow infants or small children.

16 Lancaster Quay. paradiso.restaurant. ✆ **021/427-7939.** 6-course menu €68. Tues–Sat 5–9:30pm.

The Glass Curtain ♥♥♥ MODERN IRISH This elegant dining space has roots as a culinary institution: It was once one of the city's bakeries. Today, it champions the organic, sustainable offerings of the food producers, brewers, and distillers of County Cork (and beyond), adding a creative twist of flavor to seasonal produce with offerings like monkfish with spiced langoustine coulis and spring onion, or saddle of lamb with carrot, coffee, and sunflower seeds. Some dishes, such as the whole John Dory with girolle mushrooms or the 1.1kg porterhouse steak, are designed to be shared between two. Go for the full five-course tasting menu (€85) to really sample the range of flavors on offer. Add a wine pairing for €45.

Unit A, Thompson House, MacCurtain St. theglasscurtain.ie. ✆ **021/451-8659.** Entrees €24–€40. 5-course tasting menu €85. Tues–Thurs 5:30–9pm; Fri–Sat 5–9pm.

Goldie ♥♥♥ IRISH/SEAFOOD The food here is all about wild Irish seafood with a "whole catch" approach (they use everything the boat brings), so the menu changes daily. Sea vegetables are foraged by the chefs, vegetables come straight out of a community garden, and there's a zero-waste policy. The setting is informal; go for counter seating for views of the open kitchen or the plant-filled upstairs section. Prepare for delicious snacks like Achill Island sea salt and vinegar *parnisse* with crème fraîche tartar, or mains like oak-smoked jerk mackerel with rhubarb and apple salsa, or steamed Roaringwater Bay mussels with creamed leek and dashi broth—made with foraged seaweed. Ales (brewed with no additives) from Elbow Lane brewery across the road are crafted to suit the food.

128 Oliver Plunkett St. goldie.ie. ✆ **021/239-8720.** Entrees €20–€29. Wed–Sat 5–10pm.

Greene's ♥♥ IRISH This contemporary dining room on MacCurtain Street, with dark wood floors, stone walls, and tall plants, has a calm and relaxed feel. The menu offers around six choices for each course, with starters like beetroot and goat's cheese or scallops with coriander and lime. For main courses, the focus is on locally sourced fish, beef, or lamb and seasonal vegetables. The specialty (and a good talking point) is steak on the stone, a prime cut served sizzling to the table so you can cook it to your liking. An unexpected touch (and good backdrop for photos) is the backlit waterfall in the courtyard.

48 MacCurtain St. greenesrestaurant.com. ✆ **021/455-2279.** Entrees €21–€35. Tues–Fri 4–9:30pm; Sat and bank holiday Sun 3–10pm.

Market Lane ♥♥ IRISH This friendly, informal downtown restaurant serves Irish-inflected bistro food. It's a let-down-your-hair kind of place, with the menu consisting mostly of traditional, unpretentious cooking,

Ice cream and raspberry parfait at Market Lane.

done very well. Think sophisticated comfort food: slow-cooked bacon with parsnip and scallion mash, or pan-roasted monkfish with Morteau sausage and spring greens. There are vegetarian and vegan options and lighter choices at lunch. But don't miss dessert! Try the delicious orange and vanilla bread and butter pudding. Gourmet sandwiches are served at lunch.

5–6 Oliver Plunkett St. marketlane.ie. ✆ **021/427-4710.** Entrees €17–€30. Daily noon–9:30pm (until 10pm Thurs, 10:30pm Fri–Sat).

Orso ♥♥♥ IRISH/MEDITERRANEAN This place is like a ray of warm Mediterranean sunshine in downtown Cork City. Traditional flavors of southern Europe and North Africa meet Irish influences, and the result is nothing short of delightful. It's open from late morning, so you can pop in for a late breakfast or brunch of Syrian *manoushi* bread with poached egg and caramelized onion, or smoked salmon and scrambled eggs. The lunch menu is long and varied, but it's really at dinnertime when the excellent cooking comes into its own. Plates might include mussels with Bombay aloo cream, coriander, and lime, or *rogan josh* (curried meat) cannelloni with spinach and feta. Nearly everything on the wine list is available by the glass, and the small cocktail menu is intriguing—try the delicious basil smash.

8 Pembroke St. orso.ie. ✆ **021/243-8000.** Dinner entrees €22–€27. Mon–Sat 11am–3:30pm and 4–10pm; closed Sun and bank holidays.

Cork City Shopping

St. Patrick Street is the main shopping thoroughfare, though many stores are scattered throughout the city on side streets and in lanes. In general, shops are open Monday to Saturday from 9:30am until 6pm, unless indicated otherwise. Many shops remain open until 9pm on Thursday and Friday, and some are open on Sunday noon to 5pm. **Winthrop Arcade,** off Winthrop Street, is the best of a handful of covered shopping arcades in the city. The main full-size shopping mall is **Merchant's Quay Shopping Centre,** Merchant's Quay and St. Patrick Street (mqsc.ie; ✆ **021/427-5466**). Cork's best department store is **Brown Thomas,** 18–21 St. Patrick

St. (brownthomas.ie; ✆ **021/480-5555**), its three floors filled with the same kind of upscale items found in the main branch in Dublin (p. 161).

ARTS & CRAFTS

Cork Craft & Design ♥♥ This spacious, airy shop on the city's outskirts features work from dozens of craftspeople living in County Cork. The constantly evolving offerings vary from modern to traditional, and include pottery, woodwork, fabric, paintings, and sculpture. Open Monday to Saturday until 5pm. 27a St. Patrick's Woollen Mill, Douglas. corkcraftanddesign.com. ✆ **021/436-8365.**

BOOKS

Eason ♥ The large and nicely designed Cork branch of this major Irish bookstore chain has titles on just about everything under the sun, from bestsellers to travel guides (you know, just in case you lose this one). 113–115 St. Patrick St. easons.com. ✆ **021/427-0477.**

Vibes and Scribes ♥ This cheery secondhand bookstore stocks titles in a huge array of genres, as well as gifts and crafty knickknacks. A second branch, also selling stationery and art and craft supplies, is at 3 Bridge St. (✆ **021/450-5370**). 21 Lavitt's Quay. vibesandscribes.ie. ✆ **021/427-9535.**

FASHION & CLOTHING

Blarney Woollen Mills ♥♥ On the grounds of **Blarney Castle ♥♥** (p. 258), this is the flagship outlet of an Irish chain that specializes in traditional Irish gear: Aran sweaters, cashmere and other knitwear, tweeds, country clothing, capes, and accessories. It also stocks a large range of Irish crafts, such as Waterford Crystal and Celtic-style jewelry. Open daily until 6pm. On the grounds of Blarney Castle, Blarney. blarney.com. ✆ **021/451-6111.**

Monreal ♥♥ Designer handbags, belts, and other accessories are for sale at this boutique in the Winthrop Arcade. The gorgeous stock of shoes includes some rather cool lace-up Wellington boots—a handy way of staying stylish, whatever the Irish weather throws at you. Winthrop Arcade, off Winthrop St. monreal.ie. ✆ **021/480-6746.**

Cork City After Dark

PUBS

An Spailpín Fánac ♥♥ One of Cork's oldest pubs (it opened in 1779), this is a wonderful spot to hang out with a pint and while away an hour or two. It's also one of the best pubs in the city for live music (p. 267). 28–29 S. Main St. facebook.com/anspailpinfanac. ✆ **021/427-7949.**

The Idle Hour ♥♥ This is the sort of place you go if you want some good lively *craic* (fun), loud music, and a young crowd. It's an extremely popular pub, especially during sports matches, shown here on huge TVs. Albert Quay. theidlehour.ie. ✆ **021/496-5704.**

a tuneful pint: CORK'S MOST MUSICAL PUBS

Cork has a deserved reputation as home to some of Ireland's best pubs for live, traditional music. It's virtually a rite of passage to catch a session while enjoying a pint or two (and it's stout in these parts, by the way—Murphy's or Beamish, not Guinness—if you really want to fit in).

Just follow your ears to find the best places, but to get started, here are a few of the most respected spots. **An Bodhrán** (the name refers to a type of drum made from goatskin), 42 Oliver Plunkett St. (facebook.com/AnBodhranCork; ✆ **021/427-4544**), has live sessions nightly, as does the cozy **An Spailpín Fánac** (which means "the wandering labourer"), 27 S. Main St. (✆ **021/427-7949**). The succinctly named **Sin é** (literally, "That's It"), 8 Coburg St. (✆ **021/450-2266**), has been one of Cork's top live-music pubs for decades. It has sessions most nights at 7pm, but those on Tuesday, Friday, and Sunday are particularly good. There's traditional Irish music every Thursday night at the atmospheric **Long Valley Bar,** 10 Winthrop St. (thelongvalleybar.com; ✆ **021/427-2144**)—but if you've had your fill of the tin whistle by this point, come on Monday nights at 9:30pm to catch the lively program of spoken-word events; see obheal.ie for more details.

John Henchy & Sons ♥♥ Full of appealing Victorian features, this fantastic pub looks as if it has hardly changed since it first opened in 1884. It's got a private area ("snug") that was originally built to allow ladies to visit the pub without fear of impropriety. St. Luke's Cross. facebook.com/HenchysBar. ✆ **021/450-7833.**

The Long Valley ♥♥ A cheerful, gregarious air pervades at this long-standing favorite of the Cork pub scene. The crowd is a mix of stalwart locals and hip young things. It also has a good program of live music and spoken word. 10 Winthrop St. thelongvalleybar.ie. ✆ **021/427-2144.**

THE PERFORMING ARTS

Cork Opera House ♥♥ Near the river on Emmet Place, the Cork Opera House is the region's preeminent venue when it comes to opera and other live concerts (classical, trad, folk, rock, country), plus dance, standup, and more. Emmet Place. corkoperahouse.ie. ✆ **021/427-0022.** Tickets around €25–€50.

The Firkin Crane Cultural Centre ♥♥ Named after two Danish words for measurements of butter, the Firkin Crane is set in a quirky Victorian-era rotunda on the North Bank, just downhill from St. Anne's Church/Shandon Bells. It's one of Ireland's major centers for contemporary dance, hosting touring companies in addition to showcasing new talent. Many performances are free. The only downside is that performances

The Guinness Cork Jazz Festival

Held every year since 1978, this is Ireland's biggest and most prestigious jazz festival. Big names such as Ella Fitzgerald, Oscar Peterson, and Stephane Grappelli have played here over the years, with more than 1,000 performers from all over the world taking part annually. It's held at various citywide venues in late October. Visit **guinnesscorkjazz.com** for details. Tickets go on sale in early September; prices vary, and some events are free.

are infrequent—usually just a handful per month—and the most headline-grabbing tend to be during the Guinness Cork Jazz Festival (see above). John Redmond St., Shandon. firkincrane.ie. ✆ **021/450-7487.** Ticket prices and performance times vary by event.

Sports & Outdoor Pursuits in Cork City

GAELIC GAMES Hurling and Gaelic football are both played on summer Sunday afternoons at Cork's **Páirc Uí Chaoimh Stadium,** Marina Walk (✆ **021/201-9200**). The stadium recently underwent a €100-million redevelopment. Check the local newspapers for match listings or visit the **Gaelic Athletics Association** website at gaa.ie.

STAND-UP PADDLEBOARDING See the city from the water on a 2-hour stand-up paddleboarding tour with **Cork City SUP** (corkcitysup.ie; ✆ **086/259-7688**) on the River Lee from St. Mary's Priory Church on Popes Quay. After a short lesson (beginners welcome), you'll paddle past famous landmarks and under the city bridges while hopefully remaining balanced on the board. All equipment is provided (but there are no changing facilities on-site). The cost is €55 per person.

URBAN KAYAKING A lovely way to see the city from the water is on a relaxed 2½-hour under-the-bridges kayaking tour with **Atlantic Sea Kayaking** (atlanticseakayaking.com; ✆ **028/21058**), where you'll glide past historical sites and hear stories of the Rebel City's history. You can also do a sunset tour. The cost is €70 per person (over 12s only; Thurs–Sat June–Sept). Atlantic Sea Kayaking also offers guided kayaking trips in West Cork (p. 293).

EAST CORK

Along the coast just east of Cork City are a number of attractions worth venturing away from the city for, most within an easy hour's drive. While families will probably make a beeline for **Fota Wildlife Park** on the shore of Lough Mahon, foodies will love **Ballymaloe House** and its famous cooking school, while whiskey buffs can visit **Jameson Distillery** in Midleton. A vital piece of Ireland's history is told at the harbor town of **Cobh,** which under its former name of Queenstown was once Ireland's chief port of emigration and the last port of call for the *Titanic*. If you have more

County Cork
Ballymaloe Cookery School 16
Bantry House 7
Cape Clear Island (Oileán Chléire) 3
Charles Fort 10
Cobh 14
Cummingeera 4
Desmond Castle 11
Drombeg Stone Circle 8
Dursey Island 1
Fota House & Gardens 13
Fota Wildlife Park 13
Gougane Barra 6
Ilnacullin (Garinish Island) 5
Kinsale Pottery and Arts Centre 12
Michael Collins Centre 9
Midleton Distillery Experience 15
Mizen Head 2
LIMERICK
KERRY
CORK
TIPPERARY
WATERFORD
Ballyheigue
Abbeydorney
Ardfert
Tralee
Castleisland
Mt. Eagle
Farranfore
Castlemaine
Killorglin
Killarney
The Paps
Dingle Bay
Caragh Lough
Lough Leane
L. Guitane
Killarney National Park
Macgillycuddy's Reeks
Valentia I.
Cahirsiveen
Portmagee
Ballinskelligs
Waterville
Sneem
Kenmare
Little Skellig
Skellig Michael
Caherdaniel
Kenmare River
Beara Peninsula
Knockboy
Shehy Mts.
Caha Mts.
Glengarriff
Ballylickey
Adrigole
Whiddy I.
Bantry
Bantry Bay
Ahillies
Cahermore
Dursey I.
Bear I.
Sheep's Head Peninsula
Sheep's Hd.
Durrus
Ahakista
Ballydehob
Dunmanus Bay
Schull
Crookhaven
Mizen Head
Toormore Bay
Roaringwater Bay
Cape Clear
Cape Clear I.
Sherkin I.
Baltimore
Skibbereen
Castletownshend
Unionhall
Glandore
Leap
Rosscarbery
Clonakilty
Clonakilty Bay
Drimoleague
Dunmanway
Timoleague
Courtmacsherry
Courtmacsherry Bay
Old Head of Kinsale
Kinsale
Kinsale Harbour
Bandon
Enniskean
Shanlaragh
Ballingeary
Macroom
Lee
Coachford
Ballymakeery
Poulgorm Bridge
Millstreet
Boggeragh Mts.
Cloonbannin
Ballydesmond
Kanturk
Banteer
Newmarket
Dromcolliher
Charleville
Buttevant
Doneralle
Castletownroche
Mallow
Kilmona
Blarney
Blarney Castle
Cork
Cork Int'l
Halfway
Carrigaline
Ringaskiddy
Crosshaven
Cork Harbour
Cobh
Passage West
Carrigtohill
Midleton
Cloyne
Ballycotton
Knockadoon Head
Castlemartyr
Youghal
Clashmore
Watergrasshill
Nagles Mts.
Blackwater
Fermoy
Glanworth
Mitchelstown
Galty Mts.
Kilfinane
Ballyporeen
Clogheen
Kilcommon
Knockmealdown Mts.
Cappoquin
Lismore
N20
N21
N70
N72
N71
N22
N73
N8
ATLANTIC OCEAN
CELTIC SEA
To Swansea
To Roscoff
NORTHERN IRELAND
Belfast
REPUBLIC OF IRELAND
Dublin
Galway
Map Area
Cork
0 10 miles
0 10 kms

point of departure: A DAY IN COBH

If you're a foreigner with an Irish surname, this bustling seaside town could be more important to you than you realize. Cobh (pronounced *cove,* meaning "haven") used to be called Queenstown, and it was once Ireland's chief port of emigration. For thousands of Irish emigrants, particularly during the Famine years and in the early 20th century, Cobh was the last bit of Ireland they ever saw. It was also the last port of call for the RMS *Titanic* before it sank in April 1912. That story is expertly told at **Cobh: The Queenstown Story** (Deepwater Quay; cobhheritage.com; ✆ **021/481-3591**). Part of the Cobh Heritage Centre, the exhibition is open daily from 9:30am to 6pm (closes 5pm mid-Oct to mid-Apr). Last admission is 1 hour before closing. Tickets cost €15 adults, €12 seniors and students, €9.50 youth 13–18, €8 children 12 and under, and €37 families.

A short walk from the Cobh Heritage Center, the ***Lusitania*** **Memorial** (Casement Sq.) commemorates the British luxury liner sunk just off the Cork coast by a German U-boat on May 7, 1915, killing 1,198 passengers. Queenstown was the base for the heroic Irish rescue efforts that saved 764 lives. Across Casement Square from the memorial, the **Titanic Experience** (titanicexperiencecobh.ie; ✆ **021/481-4412**) is more of a themed attraction than a museum—it's just a few re-created rooms from the ship and a series of exhibits about the ill-fated voyage, emptying into a very busy gift shop. From April to September it's open Monday to Friday 9am until 6.30pm, and Saturday and Sunday 9am to 7pm, with tours every 15 minutes (Oct–Mar 10am–5:30pm, tours every 30 min.); last admission 1 hour before closing. Entry costs €12 adults, €10.50 seniors and students, €8 children, and €24 to €41 families.

It's worth the effort to climb the hill to the handsome neo-Gothic **St. Colman's Cathedral** (cobhcathedralparish.ie; ✆ **021/481-3222**). Started in 1868, the cathedral was the country's most expensive religious building of its time. The largest of its 47 bells weighs 3½ tons, and the organ has nearly 2,500 pipes. The interior is vast and ornate, including a beautiful nave and precipitously high chancel arch. It is also a popular venue for concerts and recitals.

If you want to discover more about Cobh's role in the *Titanic* story, an hour-long **Titanic Trail** walking tour visits several related sites, putting it all into the context of the town's maritime history. In truth, this is a general historical tour of the town with just a couple of *Titanic* connections, but it's informative, nonetheless. The tour departs from the Commodore Hotel, 4 Westbourne Place, at 11am and 2pm daily mid-March to October (the rest of the year, there's one daily tour at 11am if there are prebookings). It costs €19.50 adults and €10 children 11 and under (plus a booking fee). Call ✆ **087/276-7218** or book tickets at **titanic.ie**.

Harbor view of historic Cobh.

time to spend, stay on an extra day or two and visit **Ballycotton** village for cliff walks and to tour its island lighthouse, or the beach town of **Youghal** (pronounced *yawl*) near the Waterford border.

Arriving

If you're driving from Cork City, take the main Waterford road (N25) east. Exit at R624 for Fota and Cobh; exit at Midleton for Ballycotton and Shanagarry; Youghal has its own signposted exit. **Irish Rail** (irishrail.ie; ✆ **021/455-7277**) operates a daily train service between Cork City and Cobh via Fota Island. The journey takes about half an hour. It also operates regular services to Midleton. **Bus Éireann** (buseireann.ie; ✆ **021/450-8188**) also provides a daily service from Cork City to Cobh and other points in East Cork.

Exploring East Cork

Ballymaloe Cookery School ♥♥ SCHOOL Professional and amateur cooks flock here from all over the world to sit near the whisk of Darina Allen. It was Darina's mother-in-law, Myrtle, who elevated Irish "country house" cooking to gourmet status at **Ballymaloe House ♥♥♥** (p. 273). This led to the founding of this famous cooking school, which offers courses ranging in length from a half-day to 12 weeks. The extensive **gardens** and organic farm are open to visitors all year (guided tours can be booked). The **Ballymaloe Farm Shop,** open Monday through Saturday from 9:30am to 5:30pm, sells fresh produce (including Ballymaloe's delicious brand of relish) plus takeaway teas, coffees, and lip-smackingly good sweet treats.

Shanagarry. ballymaloecookeryschool.ie. ✆ **021/464-6785.** Half-day courses €120–€235. Open year-round; schedule varies. Gardens and farm: admission €8.50 adults; €7 seniors and students; €6.50 youth 8–16; free for children 7 and under; €25 families. Garden tours from €7.50 per person (book in advance). Mon–Sat 9:30am–5:30pm.

Fota House & Gardens ♥♥ HISTORIC HOUSE This is one of two popular attractions on Fota Island, a small island in Cork Harbour that is fully accessible by road. Built in the 1820s, Fota House is considered to be one of the finest examples of a Regency mansion in Ireland, and there are twice-daily guided tours of the elegant, classically influenced interior. Don't miss the working Victorian kitchen garden. Meanwhile, **Fota Arboretum** is a must-see for horticulturalists. The 27-acre grounds include walled gardens with a number of exotic plants that defy the odds and thrive in the island's unusually mild microclimate. For overnight stays and golf, check out nearby **Fota Island Resort** (fotaisland.ie; ✆ **021/488-3700**), with three championship golf courses and a spa.

Fota Island, Carrigtwohill. fotahouse.com. ✆ **021/481-5543.** House tours: €12 adults; €10 seniors and students; €6 children; €28 families. July–Aug daily noon, 2, and 3pm; Mar–June and Sept daily noon and 2pm; Oct Sat–Sun noon and 2pm. Gift shop and cafe: Mar–Sept daily 10:30am–5pm; Oct Sat–Sun 10:30am–5pm. Arboretum and gardens free; walled garden open Apr–Sept Mon–Thurs 8:30am–4:45pm, Fri 8:30am–3:45pm, Sat–Sun 11am–5pm. Parking fee €3.

Fota Wildlife Park ♥♥ ZOO Many of the animals in this thoughtfully designed park—including kangaroos, macaws, and lemurs—have the run of 16 hectares (40 acres) of grassland, free to roam without any apparent barriers and mingling with human visitors and one another. The more dangerous animals, such as cheetahs and gibbons, are behind conventional fencing. Besides visiting the menagerie of exotic creatures, kids can ride on a tour train, and visitors of all ages learn about the conservation and breeding program. The park also has picnic areas and a gift shop. The **Savannah Café** (one of two in the park) is in view of the meerkat exhibit, so you may find yourself being watched by curious eyes while you eat your lunch.

Fota Island, Carrigtwohill. fotawildlife.ie. ✆ **021/481-2678.** Admission €21 adults; €16 seniors and students; €14 children 15 and under; children 3 and under free; €61–€77 families. Book online for discounts. Daily 9:30am–6pm. Last entry 1½ hr. before closing.

Midleton Distillery Experience ♥♥ DISTILLERY Whiskey distilling has been undergoing a revival in Ireland in recent years, with new distilleries opening around the country, many offering tours and tastings. The Jameson Distillery in Midleton, however, is one of the originals—in fact, this is where all Jameson is now made. While it's been a working distillery since 1975, the visitor experience has recently undergone a multi-million-euro upgrade. A 1½-hour guided tour takes you around the plant to see how Jameson whiskey and other brands are produced and hear stories of people who have worked there. You can add a 20-minute whiskey tasting to sample the goods. A 2-hour Behind The Scenes tour includes

Jameson Whiskey's main distillery in Midleton welcomes visitors with guided tours and tastings.

tastings (€75), and a 2-hour 45-minute Distiller's Apprentice tour (€150) includes a sampling of whiskey straight from the cask.

Midleton. jamesonwhiskey.com. ✆ **021/461-3594.** Tours €26–€31 adults; €23 students and seniors; for tastings add €30. Daily 10am–6pm.

Where to Stay & Eat in East Cork

Ballymaloe House Hotel ♥♥ Most famous for its well-known cookery school—where you can take full- and half-day courses (p. 271)—Ballymaloe also has an inviting country hotel just 3 miles from the school. Comfortable guest rooms are furnished in traditional country-house decor, with floral-print wallpaper, antique-style furniture, and original art on the walls. For a bit more privacy, you can choose from one- and two-bedroom self-catering cottages or a faux castle tower (complete with balcony on the battlements). The kitchen is the real draw here—the restaurant produces fantastic gourmet dinners nightly, lavish five-course affairs with seasonal menus (€100/person); there's also Sunday lunch (€65) or a four-course Sunday dinner (€85). The (largely French) wine list is extensive, with an iPad version that includes video information pages.

Shanagarry. ballymaloe.ie. ✆ **021/465-2531.** 33 units. €275–€400 double. Breakfast included. Dinner, bed-and-breakfast packages available. Closed Jan to mid-Feb. **Amenities:** Restaurant; room service; Wi-Fi (free).

Bayview Hotel ♥♥ If ever a view qualified as a "wow factor," this would be it: miles of coastline dotted with islands and headlands, and fishing boats bobbing gently in the harbor. Guest rooms are basic but pleasant, with modern furnishings. Each room has a sea view. The **Capricho** restaurant serves good modern Irish cuisine, using plenty of local produce, including fish direct from the pier; prices are high (two courses €48, three courses €70). Hotel guests have free use of the spa and health club at sister property the **Garryvoe Hotel** (garryvoehotel.com; ✆ **021/464-6718**), a 10-minute drive away.

Ballycotton. thebayviewhotel.com. ✆ **021/464-6746.** 35 units. €230–€325 double. Breakfast included. Dinner, bed-and-breakfast packages available. Oct–Dec Fri–Sun only; closed Jan and Feb. **Amenities:** Restaurant; bar; use of nearby health club; room service; Wi-Fi (free).

Ferrit & Lee ♥♥ IRISH This lovely dining space in an old stone building just yards from the Midleton Distillery (p. 272) is worth a stop for lunch or dinner. The two chefs are local to the area, and all the produce is sourced from East Cork suppliers—look out for chowder made with seafood fresh off the pier in Ballycotton, or roasted red pepper risotto with Ardsallagh goat's feta, asparagus, and toasted hazelnuts. The signature dish is slow-cooked featherblade of beef marinated in Jameson whiskey and served with carrot and parsnip puree, tenderstem broccoli, seasonal potatoes, and a thyme jus. The lunch menu has some lighter dishes such as soup and filled baguettes, and there's outdoor seating both at the front and back.

Distillery Walk, Midleton. ferritandlee.ie. ✆ **021/463-5235.** Entrees lunch €13.50–€24.50, dinner €24–€36. Tues–Sat noon–9pm. Closed Sun–Mon.

Terre ♥♥♥ FRENCH/ASIAN Winning rave reviews, a Michelin star within its first year of opening, and a second star just a year later, Terre has been one of the most exciting additions to the Cork culinary map in recent years, and it's worth a special trip to the period rooms of the manor house at Castlemartyr Resort, a half-hour's drive east of Cork City. Here chef Vincent Crepel, who has worked in some of the world's best restaurants, offers a modern take on classical French cooking, adding plenty of Asian flavors. On the 10-course tasting menu, which is served over 3½ hours, lobster might be accompanied by artichokes *barigoule,* samphire and makrut consommé, or Wagyu beef with barley koji. It's expensive (add the wine pairing and you won't see much change from €500), but when the chef says he aims to bring joy to your soul, who's worrying about budgets?
Castlemartyr Resort, off the N25, Castlemartyr. terre.ie. ✆ **021/421-9053.** Dinner €200; wine pairings €100–€230; tea pairing €70. Wed–Sat 6:30–8:30pm and some Sun lunches.

Chef Vincent Crepel adds Asian flavors to classical French cuisine at Terre.

KINSALE

A half-hour's drive south of Cork City (take N27 to the R600, aka Kinsale Rd., or N71 to the R607), **Kinsale** is a charming fishing village sitting on a picturesque harbor, surrounded by green hills. Considered the gateway to West Cork, Kinsale is also the start of the **Wild Atlantic Way** (p. 275). This artsy town of 5,000 residents enchants with its narrow winding streets, well-kept 18th-century houses, imaginatively painted shopfronts, window boxes overflowing with flowers, and a harbor full of sailboats. Picturesque as it is, however, Kinsale has a more eventful history than you might think. In 1601, it was the scene of a major sea battle between Protestant England and Catholic Spain—one in which Irish rebels played a covert part. You can learn all about this fascinating conflict on one of local man Barry Moloney's absorbing **Kinsale Historic Strolls** (p. 276).

Exploring Kinsale

Charles Fort ♥♥ HISTORIC SITE Southeast of Kinsale, at the head of the harbor, this coastal landmark dating from the late 17th century was

The Wild Atlantic Way

The Wild Atlantic Way is a 2,500km (1,550-mile) coastal driving route stretching the entire length of the west coast of Ireland. The trail, which runs from Kinsale in County Cork all the way to Malin Head in County Donegal (p. 495), can be a handy navigator to some of the main sights and viewpoints. The route is well signposted with brown road signs bearing a thick white squiggle in a blue box (like two Ws linked together forming a wave), with "N" indicating the northbound route and "S" indicating the route going south. A number of "discovery points" along the way, marked by brown metal posts with the WAW wave on them, provide information about the area. More information, including a full list of the points of interest covered, can be found at **wildatlanticway.com**.

named after Charles II, who was king of England and Ireland at the time it was built. A classic star-shaped fort, it was constructed after the Battle of Kinsale (1601) to replace medieval Ringcurran Castle, which had been reduced to rubble by the English army. The building was strengthened throughout the 18th and 19th centuries, and the fort remained in use as a military garrison right up until the British left in 1921. It suffered extensive damage during the civil war and has only recently been restored. Across the river, the smaller **James Fort** dates to the reign of King James I (1603–25) and was later captured in 1690 by the forces of (Protestant)

Charles Fort guarded Kinsale's harbor for centuries.

King William I during his war with the deposed (Catholic) James II—part of the same conflict that is still commemorated by Protestant "Orange marches" in Northern Ireland.

Summercove. heritageireland.ie. ✆ **021/477-2263.** Admission €5 adults; €4 seniors; €3 students and children; €13 families. Daily 10am–6pm (closes 5pm Nov to mid-Mar). Last admission 1 hr. before closing.

Desmond Castle ♥ MUSEUM This small, squat stone fortress doesn't really look like a castle, in part because it sits incongruously halfway up a residential street. Built around 1500 as the Customs house for Kinsale Harbour, in the late 17th century it was turned into a prison—at which time its history took several dark detours, including a fire that gutted the building in 1747, roasting alive the 54 French soldiers imprisoned within. Later, during the Great Famine, it was used as a workhouse. Inside is a small museum. ***Note:*** The castle and museum have been closed since 2018 for conservation work, so check the website before visiting.

Cork St. heritageireland.ie. ✆ **021/477-4855.** Admission €5 adults; €4 seniors; €3 students and children; €13 families. Mid-Apr to early Oct daily 10am–6pm (closed rest of year). Last admission 45 min. before closing.

Kinsale Historic Stroll ♥♥♥ TOURS One of the most pleasant ways to spend an hour in these parts is to take local resident Barry Moloney's excellent walking tour—or "historic stroll," as he prefers to call it—of Kinsale town. Barry and his fellow guides lead visitors around the main sights, and their local knowledge is second to none. Highlights include the 12th-century St. Multose Church; a walk past Desmond Castle (see above); and the harbor, where the 17th-century Battle of Kinsale is recounted with an enthusiasm only found in people who really love their subject. Barry asserts that the battle was perhaps the most significant turning point in Irish history. The tour starts outside the tourist office at 11:15am every day. From May to September, there's also an earlier tour at 9:15am (except Sun). You pay at the end or, in their words, "drop out for free if you're not delighted." That probably doesn't happen very often.

Departs from Kinsale Tourist Office, Pier Rd. historicstrollkinsale.com. ✆ **087/250-0731.** Tours €8 adults; €1 children. May–Sept Mon–Sat 9:15 and 11:15am, Sun 11:15am; Oct and Mar daily 11:15am. Nov–Feb private tours only.

The colorful streets of Kinsale.

THE scilly WALK

Effectively a miniscule suburb across the harbor from Kinsale, the village of Scilly—pronounced "silly"—clings to a strong sense of its own identity. Its unusual name is thought to hark back to fishermen from the Scilly Isles (off the coast of Cornwall, England) who settled here during the 17th century.

To explore the area, follow the signposted pedestrian path that runs along the sea from Scilly to Charles Fort. (You can pick up maps of the full route at the Kinsale tourist office.) Take the righthand road around the village, skirting along the coast, and join the marked pedestrian trail by the waterside. Along here are lovely views across the harbor to Kinsale and the stout remains of **James Fort** (p. 275).

You'll pass another tiny hamlet on the outskirts of Kinsale, **Summer Cove,** which is as sweet a place as its halcyon name suggests. Black-and-white toy-town houses, with splashes of green and red, face the harbor as gulls circle overhead and the waves froth and bubble along the harbor walls.

A short walk uphill from Summer Cove lies **Charles Fort** (p. 274), built to defend the port from foreign invaders. Local lore has it that until the 19th century, access to this stretch of water was controlled by a massive chain floating on timber kegs between the two shores that could be drawn tight at a moment's notice.

The Scilly Walk ends here, but if you continue south along the sea, you'll find another path that follows the headland to the tip of **Frower Point,** which affords great views across the harbor to the Old Head of Kinsale. The total distance from Kinsale to Frower Point is 8km (5 miles) each way, and every part of it is rewarding.

Kinsale Pottery and Arts Centre ♥♥ ART STUDIO This excellent ceramics workshop outside of Kinsale sells beautiful, original items of pottery from delicate tea sets and tableware to ornamental masks. The shop is full of surprises, and prices aren't too steep. A two-floor gallery always has some interesting pieces on display. If you're looking for an alternative way to spend a day or more, the workshop also runs pottery courses where you can learn the basics of the craft and go home with your own creations. Prices start at around €75 for a half-day adult course (plus the cost of shipping what you make after it's fired, finished, and glazed, if you're unable to pick it up in person a week later). All materials are included in the price.

Ballinacurra. kinsaleceramics.com. ✆ **085/880-8395.** Free admission. Daily 10am–5pm.

Where to Stay in Kinsale

Actons Hotel ♥♥ Built in the mid–19th century, this pleasant, well-run property overlooking Kinsale Harbour has been a hotel since the 1940s, and a renovation has added a few modern touches. Guest rooms aren't huge, but they're nicely designed, with very large beds and lovely harbor views. In a town where it's easy to find accommodations with character but lacking modern conveniences, you'll welcome the few extras such as an elevator (rare around here) and a swimming pool. The hotel's two restaurants are good, but you've also got Kinsale and all its wonderful restaurants on your doorstep.

Pier Rd. actonshotelkinsale.com. ✆ **021/477-9900.** 77 units. €185–€315 double; €280–€625 suite. Breakfast included. Dinner, bed-and-breakfast packages available. Free parking. **Amenities:** 2 restaurants; bar; room service; gym; pool; Wi-Fi (free).

Blue Haven Hotel ♥♥ There's something wonderfully old-school about this chic town house hotel in the middle of Kinsale. Rooms are traditionally decorated with antique-style furniture and heritage-print wallpaper. The only snag is street noise, so ask for an upper-floor room if you're a light sleeper. Appropriately enough for a hotel in such a foodie town, the hotel has good dining options—a bar and bistro, a garden terrace, and fine dining at **Rare,** with five- and seven-course menus or small plates menus featuring seafood and produce from local farms.

3–4 Pearse St. bluehavenkinsale.com. ✆ **021/477-2209.** 16 units. €149–€358 double. Breakfast included. Dinner packages available. **Amenities:** 2 restaurants; bar; room service; Wi-Fi (free).

Desmond House ♥♥ This lovely, historic B&B is one of the best places to stay in Kinsale. Desmond House was built in the mid–18th century, making it one of the oldest and best-preserved Georgian buildings in town. Grainne and Paddy Barnett Byrne bought the building several years ago and have only made it better. Guest rooms are generously sized with big, comfortable beds, and spacious bathrooms. Many of the ingredients for the delicious breakfasts come straight from the **English Market ♥♥** in Cork (p. 256), and the building is sustainably run with solar panels, full recycling, and an eco-friendly approach.

42 Cork St. desmondhousekinsale.com. ✆ **021/477-3575.** 4 units. €230 double. Breakfast included. 2-night minimum stay. **Amenities:** Wi-Fi (free).

Pier House ♥♥ There's something wonderfully bright and cheerful about this sweet place. Hosts Pat and Ann have done a beautiful job converting the 19th-century town house into a B&B, with a maritime feel and subtle splashes of modern art. A few of the rooms have little balconies, and guests are welcome to bring wine back with them if they want to spend a leisurely hour admiring the views of the harbor or garden (ask for a room with a view). You'll have to fend for yourself for meals (including breakfast), but this is hardly a chore in foodie-friendly Kinsale.

Pier Rd. pierhousekinsale.com. ✆ **021/477-4169.** 10 units. €170–€190 double. Closed Dec and Jan. **Amenities:** Wi-Fi (free).

Where to Eat in Kinsale

Kinsale is famous as a foodie hub, and for good reason—there's an excellent restaurant on every corner. But if you're looking for lighter fare, the town has plenty of outstanding options. These include **Flying Poet** (44 Main St.; flyingpoet.ie; ✆ **085/263-5431**), a small aviation-themed cafe serving light-as-air scones and tea, or fresh sandwiches and coffee. It also sells books to take with you on the road. Serving breakfast and lunch, **Leona's** on **9 Market Street** offers creamy, steaming-hot porridge or perfectly cooked eggs in the morning, while lunch could be fish cakes or local Wagyu beef burger. The coffee and desserts here are addictive. The **Lemon Leaf Café Bar and Townhouse** (70 Main St.; lemonleaf.ie; ✆ **021/470-9792**) has a great menu and space for families with young children—on sunny days, kids are drawn to the courtyard, while parents will welcome the lunchtime seafood chowder or Mediterranean salad piled high with falafel and a litany of fresh veggies.

Kinsale Food Tours (kinsalefoodtours.com; ✆ **085/107-6113**) will take you on a 2½-hour culinary odyssey around the town on foot, with lots of stories and tastings, from €80 per person.

Bastion ♥♥♥ IRISH This funky, creative restaurant is a big hit with local diners, and it got international attention when it snagged a Michelin star in 2019. An eight-course tasting menu brings updated Irish flavors to the fore, from the tender filet served with smoked potato cream and onion crumble to the melt-in-your-mouth confit duck. The exquisitely presented desserts are a treat—try the poached pear with mascarpone, perhaps washed down with a sweet glass of orange muscat. Dinner is served at 7:15pm, and there's a shorter four-course tasting menu at 5:15pm. ***Note:*** Children 12 and under are not permitted, and there is just one menu for all, so food allergies/intolerances are not accommodated. Reservations open 30 days in advance.

Corner of Main and Market sts. bastionkinsale.com. ✆ **021/470-9696.** Tasting menu €150 at 7:15pm; 4-course tasting menu €80 at 5:15pm. Optional wine pairing €55. Thurs–Sun 5–9pm.

The Black Pig ♥♥♥ BISTRO/TAPAS This charming cafe-bar has won hearts as much for its warm atmosphere as for the excellent food and wine. Gently flickering candlelight and bookcases filled with well-thumbed tomes set the laidback tone. The menu has constantly changing local specialties: smoked duck breast with orange and fennel; oak-smoked salmon with horseradish cream; or perhaps a delicious plate of Oysterhaven oysters. The wine list is outstanding, with over 170 vintages on offer. This is a popular spot, especially on weekends, so booking is advisable.

66 Lower O'Connell St. theblackpigwinebar.com. ✆ **021/477-4101.** Entrees €17–€38. Wed–Sun 5:30–11:30pm.

Kinsale Foodie Fests

Food lovers from all over Ireland—and even farther afield—descend on Kinsale each February for **Kinsale Restaurant Week,** when the town's restaurants show off their offerings with a special two-course menu. In October, the **Kinsale Mad Hatters** festival takes over town for a fun day, with walking tours led by costumed guides (you can follow characters like Alice or the March Hare) to participating restaurants. Learn more and book tickets at kinsalerestaurants.com.

Meat dishes served at Finns' Farmcut come directly from the Finn family farm in north Cork.

Finns' Farmcut ♥♥♥ MODERN IRISH The menu here is ambitious without being overly complicated, with a focus on the seasons and plenty of space to let the ingredients breathe. Grass-fed beef and lamb come direct from the Finns' family farm in Mitchelstown in north County Cork, all prepared in a charcoal oven affectionally known as Bertha. As you'd expect from Kinsale, the seafood comes straight from the harbor, so you never know exactly what will end up on the menu that night.

6 Main St. finnsfarmcut.com. ✆ **021/470-9636.** Entrees €22–€42. Tues–Fri 5:30–9pm; Sat 5–9pm.

Fishy Fishy ♥♥♥ SEAFOOD Widely respected, hugely popular, and yet brilliantly simple, Fishy Fishy is one of the best restaurants in Kinsale. The skillfully prepared fresh seafood comes from a small number of trusted local suppliers. Exactly what's cooking depends on the day's catch, but you can expect to find platters of chilled seafood or the signature Fishy Fishy pie of salmon and white fish in a creamy sauce. Look out for the truffle fries. The **Blue Room** wine bar serves small plates (opening hours vary; usually open at weekends).

Crowleys Quay. fishyfishy.ie. ✆ **021/470-0415.** Entrees €19–€28. Wed–Sun noon–9pm. Closed Jan.

Man Friday ♥♥♥ MODERN IRISH/SEAFOOD The dining room at Man Friday overlooks the bay in Scilly, a perfect setting for the reliably excellent food served here. We can't resist the seafood—citrus-and-gin-cured salmon rolls with fennel and orange salad, scallop and sea bass ceviche, or local oysters—although the beef and lamb options are excellent, too. For dessert, try the flourless chocolate torte with crème fraîche. Ask to sit in the conservatory for the most heavenly views.
Scilly. manfridaykinsale.ie. ✆ **021/477-2260.** Entrees €24–€42. Tues–Sat 5–9:30pm. Open Sun of bank holiday weekends.

Max's ♥♥♥ MODERN IRISH Husband-and-wife team Anne Marie and Olivier have run this excellent seafood restaurant since the '90s and have a seemingly effortless way of making diners feel welcome. The menu changes seasonally, but the main flavors are all local and ingredients are sometimes foraged by chef Olivier. Fish dishes depend on the local catch; favorites like hake, sea bass, and monkfish are always given a creative twist. There's usually a lamb dish on the menu and wild game in winter.
48 Main St. maxs.ie. ✆ **021/477-2443.** 2-course dinner €46. Mon–Wed and Fri–Sat 6–10pm. Closed periodically Nov–Mar, so reserve ahead.

The Spaniard ♥♥ BISTRO The portrait on the sign of this atmospheric old inn shows Don Juan de Aguila, the Spanish commander who led a force of 4,000 men against the English at the Battle of Kinsale in 1601. The English won, but Don Juan became a hero in local folklore. The inn dates from around 50 years after the battle, and it's a popular place for

Dating from the 17th century, the Spaniard serves up homey pub food.

local hero: **MICHAEL COLLINS**

Among the heroes of Ireland's struggle for independence, Michael Collins seems to be Cork's favorite native son. Affectionately referred to as "the Big Fella," Collins was the commander-in-chief of the army of the Irish Free State, which finally won the Republic's independence from Britain in 1921.

Collins was born in 1890, and, along with seven brothers and sisters, he was raised on a farm in Sam's Cross, just outside the little town of **Clonakilty.** He emigrated to England at 15, like many other young Irish men seeking work in London. In his 20s he joined an Irish revolutionary group, the Irish Republican Brotherhood (I.R.B.), and first came to fame in 1916 as one of the planners and leaders of the Easter Rising (p. 36). Although it aroused passions among the population, the Rising was in fact a military disaster, and Collins—young but clever—railed against its amateurism. He was furious about the seizure of prominent buildings—such as Dublin's General Post Office (p. 112)—that were impossible to defend, impossible to escape from, and difficult to get supplies into.

After the battle, Collins was arrested and sent to an internment camp in Britain, along with hundreds of other rebels. There his stature within the I.R.B. grew, and by the time he was released, he had become one of the leaders of the Republican movement. In 1918, he was elected a member of the British Parliament, but like many other Irish members, he refused to go to London, instead announcing that he would sit only in an Irish parliament in Dublin. Most of the rebel Irish MPs (including Eamon de Valera) were arrested by British troops for their actions, but Collins avoided arrest, and he later helped de Valera escape from prison. Over the subsequent years, de Valera and Collins worked together to create an Irish state.

After lengthy political wrangling and much bloodshed (Collins orchestrated

good, homey pub food like fish pie or fish and chips, with roasts on Sunday. An eclectic program of live music runs nightly.

Junction of Scilly and Lower Rd. thespaniard.ie. ✆ **021/477-2436.** Entrees €15–€30. Mon–Thurs 10:30am–11:30pm; Fri–Sat 10:30am–12:30am; Sun 12:30–11:30pm. (Food served until about 9pm daily.)

The Supper Club ♥♥ MODERN IRISH Good food, a nice vibe, and bespoke craft cocktails—this restaurant seems to have hit on the right formula for a relaxed but tasty supper in the center of this foodie town. The menu ranges from "lite bites" like Oysterhaven oysters, mussels, and smoked Cooleeney brie to a full supper menu including dishes like 18-hour beef short-rib, pan roast filet of hake, and the supper club burger, (which also comes as a vegan option), accompanied by sides like twice-cooked fries with truffle mayo. Delicious house cocktails include the gin-based "Scilly Walk" and the vodka-based "Thyme Folks Please!"—the latter a play on words for pub closing time in Ireland.

2 Main St. thesupperclub.ie. ✆ **021/470-9233.** Entrees €19–€36. Tues–Sat 5:30–9:30pm.

an assassination that essentially wiped out the British secret service in Ireland), Collins was sent by de Valera in 1921 to negotiate a treaty with the British government. In the meeting, British Prime Minister David Lloyd George agreed to allow Ireland to become a free republic, as long as that republic did not include the largely Protestant counties of Ulster, which would stay part of the United Kingdom. Knowing he could not get more at the time and determined to end the violence, Collins reluctantly agreed to sign the treaty, hoping to renegotiate later. After signing the document Collins said, "I have just signed my death warrant."

As he'd expected, the plan tore the new Republic apart, dividing the group now known as the IRA into two factions: those who wanted to continue fighting for all of Ireland, and those who favored the treaty. Fighting soon broke out in Dublin, and the civil war was underway.

The battles stretched on for 10 months. In August 1922, Collins, weary of the war, was on a peace mission in his home county. Stopping at a pub near his mother's birthplace, he and his escort were on the road near Béal na Bláth when Collins was shot and killed. Precisely who killed him—his own men or the opposition—was never known. On his rapid rise to the top, he'd made too many enemies. He was 31 years old.

The **Michael Collins Centre** (michaelcollinscentre.com; ✆ **086/811-3317**), located on the farm where he grew up, is a good place to learn more about the man. In addition to an hour-long tour, featuring a film and a visit to the actual ambush site, the center runs in-depth guided trips around the local area. (These last 3½ hr. and are probably for Collins devotees only.) The center is signposted off N71, 5.6km (3½ miles) west of Clonakilty. It's open mid-June to mid-September, Monday through Saturday from 11am until 4pm. Admission costs €8 adults; €5 students; €4 children; and €25 for a family.

Sports & Outdoor Pursuits in Kinsale

FISHING Kinsale is one of the southern Irish coast's sea-angling centers. The area has numerous shipwrecks for wreck fishing (not the least of them the *Lusitania,* near the Old Head of Kinsale). Try **Kinsale Angling** (1 Rampart Lane, The Ramparts; kinsale-angling.com; ✆ **021/242-9000**) for charter boats. They also run diving and whale- and dolphin-watching trips. Fishing half-days start from around €55; call for more information.

GOLF Embraced by the sea on three sides, the nothing-short-of-spectacular **Old Head Golf Links** (oldhead.com; ✆ **021/477-8444**) is Tiger Woods's favorite Irish course and was once named one of *Golf Magazine*'s "Top 100 Courses in the World." Course managers work hard to ensure that crucial wildlife habitats are not disturbed. But golfing here costs big money: Greens fees in high season (May to mid-Oct) are a whopping €450 for one 18-hole round (closed Nov to mid-Apr). You can also stay overnight in the recently added suites, which have views across the golf course to the Atlantic, or indulge at the thermal spa.

SAILING There's excellent sailing out from Kinsale Head. **Sovereign Sailing** (sovereignsailing.com; ✆ **021/477-4145**) offers a full range of yacht-sailing options for all ages and levels of experience. Between March and November, full- or half-day sails from Kinsale leave every day. Rates vary widely based on the kind of sailing you try, but a half-day trip on a 27-foot day yacht costs €235 for up to four people, and a 40-foot yacht is €395 for up to eight people.

WATERSPORTS The **Oysterhaven Activity Centre** (oysterhaven.com; ✆ **021/477-0738**), 8km (5 miles) from Kinsale, rents out kayaks, SUPs (stand-up paddleboards), windsurfing gear, and sailing dinghies. Prices start from €20 per hour for windsurfing equipment, €12–€18 per hour for kayaks, €30 for dinghies, and €15 for SUPs. Sailing, SUP, kayaking, and windsurfing lessons are also available (€30–€120). Things get pretty busy in summer, so try to book ahead as much as possible.

WEST CORK

You might say that West Cork is like County Kerry without the crowds. Like Kerry, it's got a photo-friendly craggy topography and jagged Atlantic coastline; and just as in Kerry, it's impossible to make good time on West Cork's narrow, sinuous roads as they twist along rivers, through valleys, around mountains, and through lovely small towns. Those willing to slow down and go with the flow are amply rewarded. In places, the route hugging the coast narrows to just one lane and delivers heart-stopping views.

Some of the most beautiful coastal scenery (and severe weather) is on West Cork's islands. **Cape Clear Island,** home to a bird-watching observatory, is also a well-known Gaeltacht: Schoolchildren and adults alike come here to work on their Irish language skills each summer. **Dursey Island,** off the tip of the Beara Peninsula, is accessible by cable car. The sheltered **Garinish Island** in Glengarriff is the site of Ilnacullin, an elaborate Italianate garden.

Arriving

The N71 is the main road into West Cork from north and south, looping around its coast; the east-west N22, on its way from Cork City to Killarney, also passes through some of West Cork. **Bus Éireann** (buseireann.ie; ✆ **021/450-8188**) provides daily bus service to and from the principal towns in West Cork. Find bus schedules online.

Exploring West Cork

Bantry House ♥♥ HISTORIC HOUSE Built around 1750 for the earls of Bantry, this Georgian house is filled with exquisite furniture and objets d'art from all over Europe, including Aubusson and Gobelin tapestries said to have been made for Marie Antoinette. The gardens, with original statuary, are beautifully kept—climb the steps behind the building for a breathtaking panoramic view of the house, gardens, and Bantry Bay. Inside, stop by the exhibition on the ill-fated Spanish Armada, which, led by the Irish rebel Wolfe Tone, attempted to invade the country near Bantry House in 1769. Fully guided tours (included in the ticket price) take place daily at 2pm; otherwise, you're free to wander by yourself. And if you really love it here, you can spend the night (doubles €230–€250).

Bantry. bantryhouse.com. ✆ **027/50047.** Admission €14 adults; €11.50 seniors and students; €5 youth 5–16; children 4 and under free; €33 families. June–Aug daily 10am–5pm; mid-Apr to May and Sept–Oct Wed–Sun and public holiday Mon 10am–5pm. Last entry 30 min. before closing. Closed Nov to mid-Apr.

Cape Clear Island *(Oileán Chléire)* ♥♥ HERITAGE/NATURE SITE The southernmost inhabited point in Ireland, 13km (8 miles) off the mainland, Cape Clear Island has a permanent population of just a hundred residents. It is a bleak place with a rock-bound coastline and no trees to break the rush of sea wind, but it's also starkly beautiful. In early summer, wildflowers brighten the landscape, and in October, passerine migrants, some on their way from North America and Siberia, fill the air. Seabirds are abundant during the nesting season, especially from July to September. A bird observatory is at the **North Harbour,** with a warden in residence from March to November. You can stay at the observatory overnight, on a self-catering basis (birdwatchireland.ie; €40 per night). There are no hotels on the island, so any other accommodation is based around house rentals, small B&Bs, or yurt glamping at **Chléire Haven** (chleire-haven.com; ✆ **086/197-1956**).

You can get to the island by ferry with **Cape Clear Ferries** (capeclearferries.com; ✆ **028/39159;** return tickets €20 adults, €12 students, €9 children, €49–€50 families) and explore it all at your own pace; alternatively, take the **Fastnet Rock Lighthouse Tour** with the same ferry company (fastnettour.com; €44 adults, €30 seniors and students, €12 children,

Walk to Abandoned Cummeengeera

Stark and eerie, **Cummeengeera** ♥ is an abandoned village in a wild, remote valley near Lauragh, on the Kerry side of the Beara Peninsula. The walk to the village gives you a taste of the rough beauty of this mountainous area and a sense of the extent to which people in pre-Famine Ireland would go to find a patch of arable land. To get to the start of the walk, take R571 from Castletown up along the coast toward the town of Lauragh. Just west of Lauragh, turn onto the road for Glanmore Lake, signposted on the right. After approximately 1km (⅔ mile), turn right at a road posted for "stone circle." Continue 2km (1¼ miles) to the point at which the road becomes dirt, and park on the roadside. From here, there is no trail—just walk up the valley to its terminus, about 2km (1¼ miles) away, where the ruins of a village hug the cliff's base. Where the valley is blocked by a headland, take the route around to the left, which is less steep. Return the way you came. The whole walk—4km (2½ miles)—is of moderate difficulty.

€95 families), which runs a couple of times a week from June to August, weather permitting (call for current sailing times). It starts at Baltimore or Schull on the mainland and stops at Cape Clear Island for 2 to 3 hours, enough time to stroll around and also take in the island's heritage center, before a boat ride out to sea that circles **Fastnet Rock.** Home to nothing but a magnificent lighthouse, Fastnet was traditionally known as "Teardrop Island," not for its shape but because it was the last piece of Ireland emigrants saw on their way to America.

Cape Clear Island. capeclearisland.ie.

Drombeg Stone Circle ♥♥ ANCIENT SITE This ring of 13 standing stones is the finest example of a megalithic stone circle in County Cork. The circle dates from 153 B.C., and little is known about its ritual purpose. However, the remains of two huts and a cooking area just to the west of the circle give some clue; it's thought that heated stones were placed in a water trough (which can be seen adjacent to the huts) and the hot water was used for cooking. This section has been dated to sometime between A.D. 368 and 608.

Signposted off R597 btw. Rosscarbery and Glandore, just east of Drombeg village. No phone. Free admission (open site).

Dursey Island ♥♥ HERITAGE/NATURE SITE This is a real adventure: a barren promontory extending into the sea at the tip of the Beara Peninsula. The island offers no amenities for tourists, but the adventurous will be rewarded with beautiful seaside walks, a 200-year-old signal tower, and a memorable passage from the mainland via cable car. To get there, take R572 past Cahermore to its terminus. As you sway wildly in the wooden cable car, you'll wonder whether or not to be reassured that someone saw fit to place some holy water and the text of Psalm 91 inside. ("If you say, 'the Lord is my refuge,' and you make the most high your dwelling, no harm will overtake you.") At this point you might be wondering whether a ferry would have been a wiser option. It wouldn't: Apparently the channel between the island and mainland is just too treacherous to permit regular crossing by boat. Cable cars run all year, 7 days a week. Crossings can't be prebooked—it's always first come, first served—and you can only pay with cash. The island has no shops, pubs, restaurants, or lodging of any kind. Bring food, water, and warm clothing. The crossing is very popular in summer, and numbers are sometimes restricted on the island on particularly busy days. **Dursey Boat Trips** (durseyboattrips.com; ✆ **083/898-9999**) runs a 1½-hour trip around the island and nearby Bull Rock from Garinish Pier (tickets €60 adults, €30 ages 6–12) but does not actually land on the island.

Dursey Island, about 21km (14 miles) W of Castletownbere (follow R572). durseyisland.ie. ✆ **027/73851.** Cable-car round-trip €10 adults; €5 children 4–16; free for children 3 and under; cash only. Mar–Oct daily 9:30am–7:30pm; Nov–Feb 9:30am–4:30pm. Cable car stops for lunch 1–1:30pm.

Visitors travel from the mainland to Dursey Island via a 10-minute crossing over Dursey Sound aboard Ireland's only cable car.

Gougane Barra ♥♥ HERITAGE/NATURE SITE One of County Cork's most beautiful spots, Gougane Barra (which means "St. Fin Barre's Cleft") is the name of both a tiny old settlement and a forest park a little northeast of the Pass of Keimaneigh, 24km (15 miles) northeast of Bantry, well signposted off R584. If you're coming from the east, it's about 30km (18½ miles) southwest of Macroom. Its loveliest feature is a dark, romantic lake, which is the source of the River Lee. This is where St. Fin Barre founded a monastery in the 6th century, supposedly on the small island connected by a causeway to the mainland. Nothing remains of that community; the island's elfin chapel and eight small circular cells date from the early 1700s, along with a modern chapel. Still, the setting is idyllic, with rhododendrons spilling into the still water as swans glide by. Signposted walks and drives lead through the wooded hills.
7km (4½ miles) W of Ballingeary (signposted off R584). gouganebarra.com. Park admission €5 per car (in coins).

Ilnacullin (Garinish Island) ♥♥ GARDEN Officially known as Ilnacullin, but usually referred to as Garnish (or "Garinish"), this little island is a beautiful and tranquil place. It used to be little more than a barren outcrop, its only distinguishing feature a Martello tower left over from the Napoleonic Wars of the early 19th century. Then, in 1919, the English landscaper Harold Peto was commissioned to create an elaborate Italianate garden, with classical pavilions and myriad unusual plants and flowers. The island's uncommonly mild microclimate allows a number of subtropical plant species to thrive here; George Bernard Shaw is said to have written *St. Joan* under its shady palm trees. The island can be reached for €10 per person round-trip (€5 children 6–15) on a ferry operated out of Glengarriff by **Harbour Queen Ferries** (harbourqueenferry.com; ✆ **027/63116**). Boats run back and forth about every 20 to 30 minutes. ***Note:*** The Harbour Queen doesn't take credit cards. The nearest ATMs are in Bantry.

Glengarriff. garinishisland.ie. ✆ **027/63040.** Admission (gardens) €5 adults; €4 seniors; €3 students and children; €13 families. July–Aug daily 9:30am–5:30pm; Apr–June and Sept 10am–5:30pm; Oct 10am–4:30pm. Last landing 1 hr. before closing. No landings Nov–Mar.

Mizen Head ♥♥ VIEWS At Mizen Head, the very extreme southwest tip of Ireland, the land falls precipitously into the Atlantic breakers in a procession of spectacular 210m (689-ft.) sea cliffs. You can cross a suspension bridge to an old signal station, now a visitor center, and stand on a rock promontory at the southernmost point of the mainland. The sea view is spectacular—bad weather may close the bridge, but it's worth a trip here regardless of the weather. On wild days, tremendous Atlantic waves assault the cliffs, while on clear days, you might see dolphins leaping from the surf and seals basking on the rocks. A huge renovation in the early 2010s added new bridges, viewing platforms, and a simulated ship's bridge. On the way out to Mizen Head, you'll pass Barleycove Beach, a gorgeous stretch of sand and rock. There's also a cafe and gift shop.

From Ballydehob, take R592 and then R591 to Goleen and follow signs to Mizen Head. mizenhead.ie. ✆ **028/35000.** Admission €7.50 adults; €6 seniors and students; €4.50 children 5–14; free for ages 4 and under; €25 families. June–Aug daily 10am–6pm; Sept–Oct daily 10:30am–5pm; Nov–Mar Sat–Sun 11am–4pm. Mar–May 10:30am–5pm. Opening times may vary and are weather-dependent.

Admiring the spectacular sea cliffs at the southernmost tip of Ireland, Mizen Head.

Where to Stay in West Cork

Eccles Hotel & Spa ♥♥ This charming hotel has a gorgeous setting overlooking Bantry Bay. The building has been open to guests since 1745, though it has undergone many renovations and additions since then, welcoming famous guests along the way. **Garnish Restaurant**'s Chef Eddie Attwell is passionate about local food; he forages and grows his own produce, and guests are welcome to join him on morning walks. The

Seawater therapy treatments top the spa menu at the luxurious Inchydoney Lodge & Spa.

Harbour Bar serves casual eats, and the spa is divine—one treatment room has a bathtub overlooking the bay. This is a great base for exploring the area—the hotel has bicycles for guests and can arrange everything from golf to kayaking. The so-called "cosy" rooms are on the small side but priced accordingly, so check when booking. Ask for a bay rather than a forest room if you want sea views.

Glengarriff Harbour. eccleshotel.com. ✆ **027/63093.** 57 units. €200–€280 double. Breakfast included. Free parking. **Amenities:** Restaurant; bar; spa; room service; Wi-Fi (free). Closed Jan to mid-Feb.

Dunmore House ♥♥ This delightful hotel overlooking the sea in Clonakilty dates back to 1934 but has modernized with the times along the way—and is now run by the fourth generation of the same family. It's all about the ocean here, with sea views from the gardens, outdoor terrace, and some bedrooms. Make time to explore the walkways of the cliff garden, which has lovely seating areas overlooking the water. Food is top-notch: Many of the vegetables and salads served in **Adrift Restaurant** are grown in the hotel's own garden. You can also eat in the more casual bar area (get there early to nab a spot beside the open fire).

Clonakilty. dunmorehousehotel.ie. ✆ **023/883-3352.** 30 units. €205–€320 double. Breakfast included. Check website for offers. Free parking. **Amenities:** Restaurant; bar; garden; Wi-Fi (free). Closed Jan–Feb.

Inchydoney Lodge & Spa ♥♥♥ So close to the beach you could almost dive into the Atlantic from your balcony, this famously luxurious spa hotel is dreamy. The spa specializes in thalassotherapy treatments, using seawater; the full list of what's offered may relax you just by reading it. Guest rooms are sophisticated and modern, with huge windows that open out onto amazing views of the sea. The **Gulfstream Restaurant** serves French- and Mediterranean-influenced cooking, with fresh seafood a particular specialty. The hotel also has a pub and bistro if you're after something simpler. Unlike some high-end spas, Inchydoney is a great option for families, with its dedicated children's lounge; the hotel can also arrange family-friendly activities such as kayaking, whale-watching, surfing, and cycling.

Clonakilty. inchydoneyisland.com. ✆ **023/883-3143.** 67 units. €220–€360 double. Breakfast included. Dinner, bed-and-breakfast packages available. Free parking. **Amenities:** 2 restaurants; bar; pool; room service; spa; Wi-Fi (free).

Where to Eat in West Cork

With its microclimate and clear waters, West Cork has a wealth of food artisans producing everything from cheese, preserves, and smoked fish to whiskey and mead made in the area. Weekly farmers markets are a great source for local foods and often a hive of social activity. Look for meet-the-maker experiences while you're there. You can take master classes in smoking wild fish or go on coastal foraging tours at the **Woodcock Smokery** (woodcocksmokery.com; ✆ **028/36-232**) in Gortbrack, just west of Castletownshend; drop into **Clonakilty Black Pudding** visitor center to learn more about the Irish breakfast staple (clonakiltyblackpudding.ie; ✆ **023/883-4835**); or visit **Clonakilty Distillery** (clonakiltydistillery.ie; ✆ **023/887-8020**) to learn about whiskey distilling or blend your own gin.

West Cork has lots of food trucks (many in converted horseboxes) as well. On the Beara Peninsula, look for the **Beara Barista** caravan (facebook.com/BearaBarista) on Ballydongan Beach in Allihies for hot dogs made with Gubbeen Smokehouse sausages. Near Courtmacsherry, **Bean & Berry** at Garretstown beach is known for its açai smoothie bowls; and the food truck park at **Quills** in Glengarriff offers treats like woodfired pizza from **Pizza Base** or steak burgers and sausage baps from **Fire and Feast.**

Blairscove ♥♥ IRISH This has to be one of the most picturesque dining rooms in Ireland. A former barn, it may have originated as an 18th-century watchtower. The menu isn't cutting-edge, but that's kind of the point. Instead, what you get (after a charmingly retro buffet of appetizers) are traditional Irish flavors elegantly updated, such as rack of lamb with an herb crumb, or monkfish with mussels, celeriac, leek, and saffron cream. Desserts are rich and delicious. If you want to make even more of a night of it, Blairscove offers B&B lodging for €200 to €370 a night for two people sharing.

Barley Cove Rd., Durrus. blairscove.ie. ✆ **027/61127.** 3-course menu €85. Mid-Mar to Nov Tues–Sat 6–9:30pm.

Dede at the Customs House ♥♥♥ TURKISH/IRISH A tiny seaside village like Baltimore is not where you'd expect to find Turkish fusion cooking, but the talented chef Ahmet Dede has earned two Michelin stars with his inventive creations and exquisite presentation. The tasting menu changes weekly and features local produce. Sample courses might be langoustine with wasabi, crème fraîche, raki, and asparagus, or aged beef with carrot, grapefruit, pepper, tarhana sauce, and *firik*. There are different menus for carnivores, pescatarians, and vegetarians. Baltimore. customshousebaltimore.com. ✆ **028/48248.** Lunch tasting menu €100; dinner €180. Reservations essential. Thurs–Fri 5:30–8:30pm; Sat 12:30–2pm and 5:30–8:30pm; Sun 12:30–2:30pm.

Chef Ahmet Dede features local Cork produce in his stellar Turkish fusion cooking at Dede at the Customs House.

The Heron's Cove ♥♥ SEAFOOD It's all about the bounty of the sea at this laid-back restaurant about 15km (9 miles) from **Mizen Head** (p. 288). All the seafood is caught on the West Cork coastline; expect Bantry Bay organic salmon, tempura monkfish, or perhaps some lemon sole filet prepared in a creamy white-wine sauce. You can sit outside on a terrace overlooking the harbor if the weather's good. It also offers B&B lodging in pleasant guest rooms with harbor views for €120 to €130 per night. Harbour Rd., Goleen. heronscove.com. ✆ **028/35225.** Entrees €20–€30. June–Aug Tues–Sun 7–9:45pm; Apr–May and Sept–Oct Fri–Sat 7–9:45pm. Opening times and dates may vary.

Mary Ann's ♥♥ SEAFOOD/PUB FOOD The handsome exterior of this friendly pub in Castletownshend, near Skibbereen—in fact, the *only* pub in the village—makes a super photo op, with red-orange paint and neat black windows looking satisfyingly pub-like. Fortunately, the food is just as good. This being the West Cork coast, seafood is often what stands out: fresh, local crab salad, lobster, local scallops, prawns, fish pie with plenty of, guess what, local ingredients—but there are meatier choices as well, such as the rump of lamb with potato gratin and red wine jus. Fish and chips (fried haddock) are also great. You can eat in a little courtyard terrace if you're blessed with sunshine. Castletownshend. facebook.com/maryannspubandrestaurant. ✆ **028/36146.** Entrees €18–€37. Daily noon–9pm.

walk this way: THE SHEEP'S HEAD LOOP

A jagged strip of land reaching out into the Atlantic on the western side of County Cork, the Sheep's Head Peninsula is well worth a visit. It's a place of wild, rocky scenery, ice-blue lakes, and spectacular coastal views. It is also an isolated place; you'll likely find yourself alone for large stretches of time, with the expansive sea views all to yourself. Which, in bustling modern Ireland, is enough to make it worth the trip.

To see it the easy way, drive the **Sheep's Head Loop,** which begins just outside Bantry along the tiny road to Kilcrohane. It takes you through the coastal village of **Ahakista,** where you can stop to explore a Bronze Age stone circle, and on to tiny **Durrus,** home to the rocky ruins of the Cool na Long Castle. The main draw here, though, is the natural beauty. The north side of the peninsula is all sheer cliffs and stark, rocky scenery, unmarred by modern development (the sunsets on this side are unbelievable), while the more lush southside road runs right along the wondrous Dunmanus Bay.

To explore the peninsula in more depth, however, you could walk the **Sheep's Head Way,** voted "Best Walk in Ireland" by *Country Walking* magazine a few years ago. The windy coastal walk is certainly ambitious, making an 89km (55-mile) loop around the peninsula. Most walkers choose to explore only the tip, from the point where the road ends down to the stumpy 1960s-era lighthouse, which keeps oil tankers from running aground. If you try the longer walk, be aware that the route is rough in places, particularly on the north side. The south side of the peninsula is greener and the path well-traveled.

The *Guide to the Sheep's Head Way* by Stephen Bosch (2003), available in local shops and tourist offices, combines history, poetry, and topography in a fantastic introduction to the region. The lavishly illustrated guide *Walking the Sheep's Head Way* by Amanda Clarke (2014) helpfully breaks the walk into all its various stages.

Restaurant Chestnut ♥♥♥ FRENCH/IRISH This tiny (18 seats at six tables) former pub earned sudden fame when it received a Michelin star in 2019. It's an unassuming place, with ceilings so low that tall customers have to stoop to get inside. But size isn't everything, and here it's all about the food. The opener is homemade smoked butter with warm sourdough bread just out of the oven. The seven-course set menu is ever-evolving but features dishes such as paper-thin slices of celeriac wrapped around local Young Buck cheese; fresh local mussels with seaweed and tapioca; and crisp scallops with parsley and yeast. This is experimental cooking, playful and unpredictable—tiny, complex dishes designed to challenge your expectations. A four-course tasting menu gives a good overview of the food. ***Note:*** Vegetarians and anyone with dietary restrictions should notify the restaurant when they book. Upstairs is a casual dining space, for small plates and snacks.

Staball Hill, Ballydehob. restaurantchestnutwestcork.ie. ✆ **028/25766.** 7-course set menu €149, 4-course set menu €70. Reservations essential (released 2 months in advance). No children 11 and under. Wed–Thurs 6–9pm; Fri–Sat 5–9pm. Closed mid-Dec to Mar.

Sports & Outdoor Pursuits in West Cork

BEACHES **Barleycove Beach** is a vast expanse of pristine sand with a fine view out toward the Mizen Head cliffs; despite the trailer park and holiday homes on the far side of the dunes, large parts of the beach never seem to get crowded. Take R591 to Goleen and follow signs for Mizen Head. **Inchydoney Beach,** on Clonakilty Bay, is famous for both its gorgeous beach and the luxe **Inchydoney Lodge & Spa** (p. 289).

CYCLING The **Mizen Head, Sheep's Head,** and **Beara peninsulas** offer fine roads for cycling, with great scenery and few cars. The loop around Mizen Head, starting in Skibbereen, is a good 2- to 3-day trip; a loop around the Beara Peninsula from Bantry, Glengarriff, or Kenmare takes at least 3 days at a casual pace. In Bantry, you can rent bicycles and e-bikes from **O'Donovan Cycles,** Market St., Bantry (odonovancycles.ie; ✆ **086/128-0307**); expect to pay around €20 per day (€120 per week), or €50 per day (€280 per week) for an e-bike.

DIVING The **Baltimore Diving Centre** in Baltimore (baltimorediving.com; ✆ **086/241-2855**) provides equipment and boats to certified divers to explore the many shipwrecks, reefs, and caves off Cork's western coast. Cost is from €90 per dive including equipment. Various 3-hour to 14-day certified PADI courses are available for all levels of experience.

FISHING The West Cork coast is known for its many shipwrecks, making this one of the best places in Ireland for wreck fishing. **Courtmacsherry Sea Angling Centre,** Woodpoint House, Courtmacsherry (courtmacsherryangling.ie; ✆ **086/825-0905** or 023/884-6427), offers angling aboard an Aquastar fishing boat that can reach the wreck of the *Lusitania* in about 40 minutes. A day's fishing costs around €80 per person. Rod hire is €10 per day. They also run dolphin- and whale-watching excursions for €50 per person. Self-drive boat hire starts at €85 for a half-day. **Bantry Bay Charters** (bantrybaycharters.ie; ✆ **083/089-6828**) offers everything from 3-hour mackerel fishing trips to full-day sea angling trips, whale-watching, and diving. Trips start from €60 for a 3-hour marine wildlife tour to around €600 per boat for a half-day of sea angling (min. eight people).

KAYAKING With hundreds of islands, inviting inlets, and sea caves, the West Cork coast is a sea kayaker's paradise. About 6km (4 miles) east of Baltimore, **Lough Hyne,** one of the largest saltwater lakes in Europe, offers warm, still waters for beginners, a tidal rapid for the intrepid, and access to a nearby headland riddled with caves. **Atlantic Sea Kayaking** (atlanticseakayaking.com; ✆ **028/21058**) specializes in guided trips on Lough Hyne as well as along the coastal bays and inlets from Castlehaven Bay near Skibbereen. They also run night kayaking trips in both locations, starting at dusk.

WALKING A spectacular coastal walk begins along the banks of **Lough Hyne,** cupped in a lush valley of exceptional beauty. To get there, follow signs for Lough Hyne along R595 between Skibbereen and Baltimore; a parking lot is at the northwest corner of the lake. The wide trail proceeds gradually upward from the parking lot through the woods on the west slope of the valley; once you reach the hilltop, you'll see a sweeping view of the coast from Mizen Head to Galley Head. Walking time to the top and back is about 1½ hours.

WHALE-WATCHING The Atlantic waters off the southwest coast are some of the best for spotting dolphins, porpoise, and basking sharks, plus—if the season is right—fin, humpback, and minke whales, who all come here to feed. On a whale-watching boat trip you can also see lots of bird life and seals and admire the bays, cliffs, and caves from the water. Try **Atlantic Whale and Wildlife Tours** for a 3- to 4-hour trip from Courtmacsherry (atlanticwhaleandwildlifetours.com; ✆ **087/774-4401**) or **Cork Whale Watch,** which runs from Reen Pier near Union Hall in Cork City (corkwhalewatch.com; ✆ **086/327-3226**). Trips with **Baltimore Sea Safari** range from 20 minutes to 2 hours and take in a seal colony (baltimoreseasafari.ie; ✆ **028/207-53**).

COUNTY KERRY

8

Rolling green fields, lakes and mountains, picture-postcard towns, and craggy ocean vistas . . . there's a reason why so many visitors to Ireland put County Kerry at the top of their itineraries. Charming, colorful towns like Kenmare and Dingle make perfect stops on any Irish tour. Kerry's peaceful green valleys are just what everyone hopes for when they come to Ireland. And therein lies the rub! With massive popularity comes massive crowds. The height of summer is incredibly busy here—if it's peace you want, ideally, you should hit these hills in the late spring or fall, when it's much quieter (but still just as beautiful). There's an antidote for even the busiest times, however: Should you find that the tour-bus traffic on the **Ring of Kerry** is getting to you, simply turn off onto a small country lane, and within seconds you'll find yourself virtually alone in the peaceful Irish countryside.

ESSENTIALS

Arriving

BY BUS **Bus Éireann** (buseireann.ie; ✆ **064/663-0011**) operates regularly scheduled service into Killarney and Dingle from all parts of Ireland. **Local Link Kerry** routes connect Kerry towns and villages (locallinkkerry.ie; ✆ **066/714-7002**).

BY TRAIN Trains from Dublin, Cork, and Galway arrive daily at **Killarney Railway Station** (irishrail.ie; ✆ **064/663-1067**), Railway Road, off East Avenue Road, and **Tralee Casement Station** (irishrail.ie; ✆ **066/712-3522**). Kenmare and Dingle do not have train stations.

BY CAR Getting to Killarney from Cork is easy—just head northeast out of Cork City on N22; the distance is about 85km (53 miles). To get to Killarney from Dublin, take M7 southwest to Limerick, then N21 (which also leads to Tralee, gateway to the Dingle Peninsula), and N22 to Killarney. The total journey is about 310km (193 miles). Kenmare and Killarney are connected by the main N71 Ring of Kerry Road; they're only 33km (20½ miles) apart, but allow plenty of time because of the winding nature of the road (and, in summer, tour-bus traffic). To hire a car in Killarney, try **Budget** at the International Hotel on Kenmare Place (budget.ie; ✆ **064/663-4341**) or for Tralee, try **Enterprise** on John Joe Sheehy Road

PREVIOUS PAGE: The Gap of Dunloe.

(enterprise.ie; © **066/711-9304**). For details on car rentals in Dublin, see p. 91; for Shannon Airport car rentals, see p. 354.

BY PLANE **Ryanair** (ryanair.com; © **01/255-5212**) has two flights per day from Dublin into the miniscule **Kerry County Airport** in Farranfore (kerryairport.ie; © **066/976-4644**), about 16km (10 miles) north of Killarney. Ryanair also operates a handful of flights every week from London's Luton and Stanstead airports, Manchester, Frankfurt in Germany, Faro in Portugal, and Alicante in Spain. **Chalair Aviation** (en.chalair.fr; © **0033/892-700-499**) operates flights between Kerry and Brittany, Normandy, and the Pyrenees in France. Fewer flights are scheduled in winter.

Visitor Information

The **Killarney Tourist Information Centre** is at Beech Road, Killarney (killarney.ie; ✆ **1800/230-330**). The **Kenmare Tourist Office** is at the Kenmare Heritage Centre, Market Square, Kenmare (kenmare.ie; ✆ **064/664-1233**). The **Tralee Tourist Office** is at the Ashe Memorial Hall on Denny Street, Tralee (✆ **066/712-1288**). The **Dingle Tourist Office** is on the Quay, Dingle (✆ **066/915-1188**), or contact **Dingle Peninsula Tourism** (dingle-peninsula.ie; ✆ **066/915-2448**). All stay open year-round.

Organized Tours

If you're not confident in hiring a car and driving yourself around County Kerry's tourist-clogged roads, plenty of companies will take you to see the major sights on organized bus tours. Most depart from **Killarney,** the most popular base for exploring the Ring of Kerry. Prices vary enormously according to itinerary, but expect to pay somewhere in the region of €25 to €50 per person. Two recommended operators are **Wild Kerry Day Tours,** 100 New St. (wildkerrydaytours.com; ✆ **064/663-1052**), and **Dero's Tours,** 22 Main St. (derostours.com; ✆ **064/663-1251**). Both run full-day tours of the Ring of Kerry, tours to Dingle and the Slea Head Peninsula, and a variety of tours around Killarney National Park.

THE RING OF KERRY

This green and beautiful stretch of countryside is one of the world's most photographed places, and for good reason: Gorgeous panoramas of mountains, valleys, rolling hills, and seaside await around every curve. It's no surprise, then, that the 178km (110-mile) two-lane road encircling the **Iveragh Peninsula** is such a massive draw for visitors—it's by far the most popular scenic drive in Ireland. The **Ring of Kerry** is both the actual name of the road—or, if you want to be pedantic, a section of the N70, N71, and N72 highways—and the collective name given to the many attractions in the area. Nearly all of County Kerry's most popular sights are either on or within a short distance of the Ring, including the stunning **Killarney National Park.**

What you won't find, at least in the summertime, is much in the way of peace. Bicyclists avoid the route because so many tour buses thunder down it from early morning until late in the day. Of course, if you yearn for peace and quiet, you can simply skedaddle off the busy highway and onto the many narrower country roads. There's so much beauty here, it doesn't really matter how you see it. Often the greatest pleasures can be found along a scenic side road or a quiet byway just begging to be explored.

Tip: You can drive either way along the Ring of Kerry, but a counter-clockwise route gives you the best views. Very large vehicles are always meant to travel this way to avoid accidents and nasty traffic jams around the Ring's perilously narrow bends.

The area's main hub is the small but busy town of **Killarney,** conveniently sited on the edge of spectacular **Killarney National Park,** which includes the breathtaking **Killarney Lakes** and the scenic **Gap of Dunloe.** Most people traveling the route start and finish at Killarney, but smaller, quieter **Kenmare** makes for a good alternative base.

Killarney & Killarney National Park

Killarney's ample stock of restaurants, pubs, and hotels keeps it buzzing with visitors throughout the year. Given this, tourism is a bit more in-your-face here than anywhere else in Kerry—in the summer its narrow streets are prone to tour-bus traffic jams. That aside, Killarney has much to offer, and plenty of beauty to go with the bustle.

The main attraction is the valley in which Killarney nestles—a verdant landscape of mist-wreathed lakes and rugged hills so spectacular that "even an ad man would be ashamed to eulogize it," as author and playwright Brendan Behan once said. It's easy to escape the crowded streets to explore the quiet rural splendor of the 65-sq.-km (25-sq.-mile) **Killarney National Park:** Start at the main visitor center at **Killarney House and Gardens** (p. 300) to pick up maps and information before you decide which part of the park to explore. The **Killarney Tour** guided hop-on, hop-off bus (killarneytour.com; ✆ **087/250-8122**) runs around every hour to Ross Castle, Torc Waterfall, Muckross House, and Muckross Abbey. Single tickets are €6 to €7; day tickets cost €15 adults, €13.50 students, €12.50 youth 12 to 18, and €10 kids 11 and under.

A hiking group climbs Mangerton Mountain, just above the lake known as Devil's Punchbowl, in Killarney National Park.

killarney NATIONAL PARK

A huge, rambling wilderness with breathtaking scenery, **Killarney National Park** ♥♥♥ is an essential stop along the Ring of Kerry. Within the park's borders are lakes, mountains, and two estates—**Muckross** (p. 302) and **Knockreer** (p. 306). The main visitor center for the park, located in **Killarney House and Gardens** (killarneynationalpark.ie; ✆ **01/539-3620**), is just a 5-minute walk from Main Street in the town center. Stop by here to pick up maps and take in an exhibition before you get started. The visitor center is open daily 9:15am to 1pm and 2 to 5pm in summer, 9am until 5:30pm in winter.

Cars are banned from most of the trails that traverse the park, so you'll have to explore it on foot—or else hire a **"jarvey,"** or "jaunting car," an old-fashioned horse-and-buggy. Jarveys can be booked from **Killarney Jaunting Cars,** Muckross Close (killarneyjauntingcars.com; ✆ **064/663-3358**). Drivers also often congregate in one of the small parking lots on the main N72 Ring of Kerry Road, between the edge of Killarney Town and the entrance to Muckross House, and at Kate Kearney's Cottage at the Gap of Dunloe.

Three lakes dot the park. The largest, the **Lower Lake,** is sometimes called **Lough Leane** or Lough Lein, translated as "the lake of learning." It's more than 6km (3¾ miles) long and holds 30 small islands that seem to rise from the mist. The most celebrated of Killarney's islands, the lovely **Innisfallen** ♥♥ (p. 302), is on the Lower Lake. Nearby are the **Middle Lake** or **Muckross Lake,** and the smallest of the three, the **Upper Lake.**

Several marked trails are available for exploring the beauty of Killarney Park:

Blue Pool Nature Trail: Starting behind the Muckross Park Hotel, this trail winds for a relaxing 2.3km (1.5 miles) through coniferous woodland beside a small lake. The trail is named for the lake's unusually deep blue-green color, a result of copper deposits in the soil.

Cloghereen Nature Trail: Incorporated into a small section of the Blue Pool trail, this walk is fully accessible to blind visitors. A guide rope leads you along the route, lined by plants identifiable by scent and touch. An audio guide is available from the Muckross House visitor center for a small deposit.

Mossy Woods Nature Trail: One of the park's gentler trails, this route starts from Middle Lake (Muckross Lake) and runs just under 2km (1.2 miles). The moss-covered trees and rocks it passes are a major habitat for bird life. You'll also see several strawberry trees (*Arbutus*), something of a botanical mystery—they're common in these parts but found almost nowhere else in Northern Europe. The route offers incredible mountain views.

Old Boat House Nature Trail: This short lakeside walk begins at the 19th-century boathouse below Muckross Gardens and goes .8km (.5 mile) around a small peninsula by Middle Lake.

Arthur Young's Walk: Starting on the road to Dinis Island, this longer (4.8km/3 miles) hike traverses natural yew woods, then follows a 200-year-old road on the Muckross Peninsula.

TOWN LAYOUT

Killarney may be the most important town in the region, but this is Ireland, so this "metropolis" is much smaller than you'd expect, with a full-time population of only about 14,500. Of course, this number swells considerably at the height of tourist season—and it feels like it. The town

is laid out around one central thoroughfare, **Main Street,** which becomes **High Street** at the northern end. The principal cross streets are **New Street** and **Plunkett Street** (which becomes **College St.**). The Deenagh River edges the western side of town; **East Avenue Road** edges the eastern side. The busiest section of town is at the southern tip of Main Street, where it curves to meet East Avenue Road, then curves again to head south to the Muckross road and the entrance to Killarney National Park.

The best and fastest way to get around town is on foot (those with mobility problems can call a taxi—nowhere is all that far from anywhere else in this town, so fares are low).

A signposted **Tourist Trail,** which visits all the highlights, takes less than 2 hours to complete. Download a map from **killarney.ie**.

TOP ATTRACTIONS IN KILLARNEY & KILLARNEY NATIONAL PARK

Gap of Dunloe ♥♥♥ VIEWS A narrow pass between the Purple Mountains and the dark, rocky hills known as MacGillycuddy's Reeks, the winding Gap of Dunloe rises through mountains and wetlands just west of Killarney National Park. The route through the gap (called Gap of Dunloe Rd., naturally) passes craggy hills, meandering streams, and deep gullies, and it ends in the park at the Upper Lake. Some of the roads can be difficult around here, so many people choose to explore by bicycle (p. 315) or by "jarvey" (p. 300). While cars are not strictly banned from this road (it's not technically part of Killarney National Park), it's not advisable to drive all the way through the Gap. Drive into the scenic countryside—perhaps as far as **Kate Kearney's Cottage** (p. 312)—park your car, and then proceed on foot or by bike or rent a jarvey car from one of the drivers here.

Signposted from N72 (Ring of Kerry Rd.), Killarney.

Innisfallen ♥♥ HERITAGE/NATURE SITE Shrouded in forest, this small island appears to float peacefully on the Lower Lake in Killarney National Park. Behind the trees is what's left of a 7th-century monastery that flourished for 1,000 years. It's thought that Brian Boru, the great Irish chieftain, and St. Brendan the Navigator received their education here. From 950 to 1320, the "Annals of Innisfallen," a chronicle of early Irish history, was written at the monastery. You can reach Innisfallen by taking an open boat tour from Reen Pier near Ross Castle. The total trip is around 1 to 1½ hours (the crossing to the island takes 10–15 min.).

Lower Lake, opposite Ross Castle, Ross Rd. (signposted from N71, Ring of Kerry Rd.), Killarney. visitinnisfallen.com. ✆ **064/663-0200.** €15 adults; €12 children 11 and under. Daily Mar to early Nov, departing hourly 10am–3pm.

Muckross House & Gardens ♥♥ HISTORIC HOUSE Built in 1843, this elegant, neo-Gothic Victorian house at one of the entrances to Killarney National Park offers an enlightening glimpse at how both masters and servants of the house once lived—the grand, *Downton Abbey*–like formal dining room contrasts starkly with the Victorian kitchens and

A farmhand milks cows the old-fashioned way at Muckross Traditional Farms.

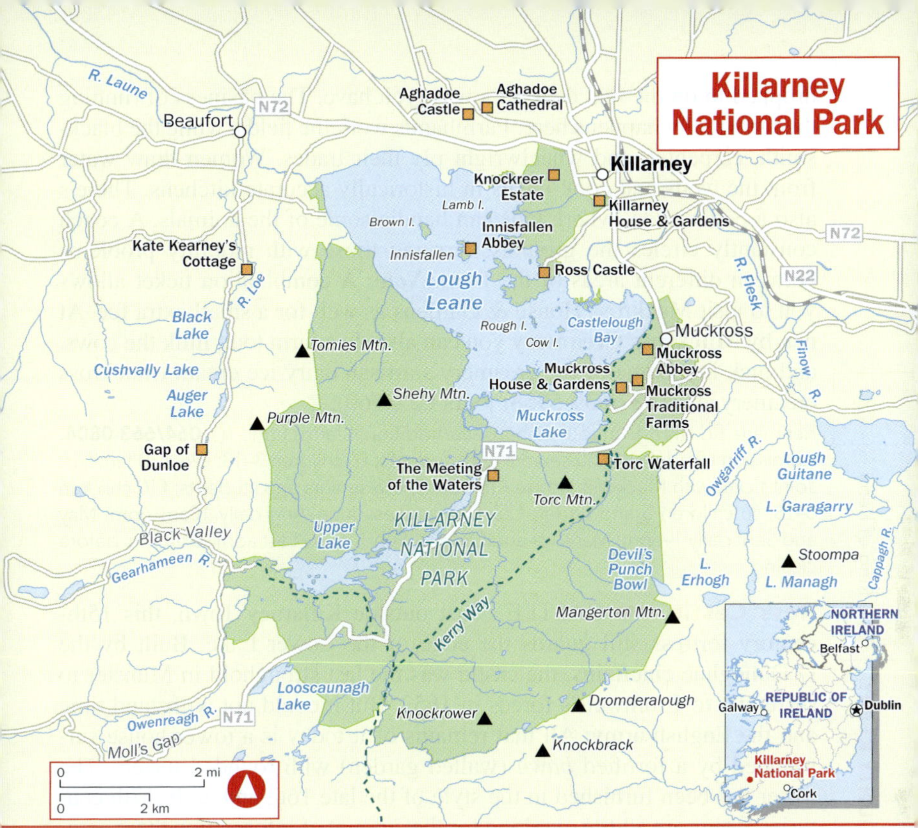

servants' quarters below stairs. The landscaped gardens are beautiful and a riot of color in high summer. The pleasant cafe, overlooking some manicured flowerbeds, is a lovely spot to linger over a cup of tea. A traditional weavers' and craft shop is also on the grounds, along with the evocative ruin of the 15th-century **Muckross Abbey,** founded about 1448 and burned by Cromwell's troops in 1652. The abbey's central feature is a vaulted cloister around a courtyard that contains a huge yew tree, thought to be as old as the abbey itself. William Makepeace Thackeray once called it "the prettiest little bijou of a ruined abbey ever seen."

On N71 (Ring of Kerry Rd.), 6km (3¾ miles) S of Killarney. muckross-house.ie. ✆ **064/663-0804.** Admission €9 adults; €7.50 seniors and students; €6 children 6–18; free for children 5 and under; €26–€30 families. Joint ticket with Muckross Traditional Farms: €16 adults; €13 seniors and students; €10 children 6–18; €6 children 5 and under; €33–€37 families. House: daily 9:15am–7pm (closes 6pm Apr–June and Sept–Oct, 5:30pm Nov–Mar). Last admission 90 min. before closing.

Muckross Traditional Farms ♥♥ HERITAGE SITE Not far from the Muckross House estate, these farms demonstrate traditional life as it was in previous centuries in County Kerry. It's cleverly done—the farmhouses and barns are so authentically detailed that you feel as if you've dropped in on the real deal. In a way, you have. The business of running the farm really happens here: Farmhands work the fields, while the blacksmith, carpenter, and wheelwright ply their trades. Women draw water from the wells and cook meals in historically accurate kitchens. There's also a petting zoo, where kids can handle some of the animals. A coach constantly circles the grounds, ferrying those with mobility problems between different areas of the farm. ***Note:*** A combination ticket allows you to visit Muckross House & Gardens as well for a small extra fee. At nearby **Muckross Creamery** you can also do a farm tour, milk the cows, and tuck into some of the creamery's artisan dairy ice cream (muckross creamery.ie; ✆ **087/639-5958;** tours €25–€60).

Kenmare Rd. (N71). muckross-house.ie/traditional-farms.html. ✆ **064/663-0804.** Admission €9 adults; €7.50 seniors and students; €6 children 3–18; €26–€30 families. Joint ticket with Muckross House €16 adults; €13 seniors and students; €10 children 6–18; €6 children 5 and under; €33–€37 families. June–Aug daily 10am–6pm; May and Sept daily 1–6pm; Mar–Apr and Oct Sat–Sun 1–6pm. Last admission 1 hr. before closing.

Ross Castle ♥♥ CASTLE Just outside Killarney Town, this 15th-century fortress still guards the edge of the Lower Lake. Built by the O'Donoghue chieftains, the castle was the last stronghold in Munster to surrender to Cromwell's forces in 1652. But it could not withstand time and the English army: All that remains of it today is a tower house surrounded by a fortified *bawn* (walled garden) with rounded turrets. The tower has been furnished in the style of the late 16th and early 17th centuries. Tours are a little overlong for the amount of information there actually is to impart, but it's worth it to see inside the castle. Luckily, you can wander the grounds at leisure. In good weather, the best way to reach the castle is via a lakeside walk (it's 3km/2 miles from Killarney). From the castle, you can also take boat tours of the lake (p. 305).

Ross Rd., signposted from N71 (Ring of Kerry Rd.). heritageireland.ie. ✆ **064/663-5851.** Admission €5 adults; €4 seniors; €3 students and children; €13 families. Mar to early Nov daily 9:30am–5:45pm. Last admission 45 min. before closing.

What's in a Name: MacGillycuddy's Reeks

This marvelously named mountain range just west of Killarney is quite a sight to behold. Formed of red sandstone, the mountains were gradually shaved down by glaciers until the peaks reached the gentle shape they hold today. The name, however, sounds anything but dignified. It may help to know that the mountains were named after an ancient and noble clan that once predominated in this area, the Mac Gilla Machudas, and the word "reek" is an old Irish term for a peaked hill.

Torc Waterfall ♥♥ NATURE SITE A walk through sylvan woods, populated with red deer, brings you to this popular beauty spot. The 18m

Torc Waterfall.

(60-ft.) falls are impressive, and well worth the 5-minute walk from the dedicated parking lot on the Ring of Kerry Road. More strenuous but even more rewarding is the climb up the 100 or so steps next to the falls, which take you up to **Friar's Glen**—so-called because it was a hideout for priests during Cromwell's invasion—with its sweeping views across the Killarney Lakes. The river that feeds the falls rises on a mountainside a few miles away; the source is evocatively known as the Devil's Punchbowl.

Off N71, about 1.5km (¾ mile) S of Muckross House (in the direction of Kenmare), Killarney.

OTHER ATTRACTIONS IN THE KILLARNEY AREA

Aghadoe Cathedral ♥ RUINS/RELIGIOUS SITE These evocative ruins look more like a crumbling parish church than a cathedral, but that's exactly what stood here until the hamlet of Aghadoe was sacked by the forces of Oliver Cromwell in 1652. Ivy grows along a roofless nave, and decaying stone walls give way to a hillside graveyard. The tiny round tower, a few yards away, is the sole remnant of a monastery dating from 1027. Adjacent to the ruins is a viewpoint with breathtaking views over the Lower Lake, 1.6km (1 mile) away. Squint and you can also see Ross Castle on the far shore. There's a small (free) parking lot next to Aghadoe Heights Hotel (p. 306), just across the street. It's worth booking afternoon tea at the hotel—the dining room has extraordinary views of the lake and serves tasty scones and cakes.

About 5km (3 miles) NW of Killarney off N22/L2019; Ard Na Be Rd., Aghadoe. Follow signs for Aghadoe Heights. Free admission. Daily dawn–dusk.

Killarney Water Bus ♥♥ BOAT TOURS From the harbor at **Ross Castle ♥♥** (see above), the ***MV Pride of the Lakes*** takes you on an hour-long waterborne cruise. The covered boat ride is a little on the touristy side, but the views of the park from the lake are gorgeous. You can also take a tour that combines a lake cruise with a "jaunting car" ride around the park. ***Tip:*** Ross Castle is included on the hop-on, hop-off bus tour from Killarney town center (p. 298), so you could make the boat tour your first activity. The bus takes less than 10 minutes to the castle. The return journey to town is longer, so add in plenty of sightseeing stops on the way.

The Pier, Ross Castle, Ross Rd., off N71 (Ring of Kerry Rd.), Killarney. killarneylaketours.ie. ✆ **064/663 2638.** €15 adults; €12 seniors; €8 children 3–12; €40 family. June–Sept daily 11am, 12:30, 2:30, and 4pm; Apr–May and Oct 12:30 and 2:30pm. Times may change according to weather.

Knockreer Estate ♥ GARDENS The grand old house that once stood here burned down in the early 20th century; what you see today is a modern building of the same name on the same site, which serves as the park's education center. Still, the estate's lovely old gardens remain, with 200-year-old trees setting off sweet wildflowers and azaleas to fragrant effect. A signposted walk takes you past beautiful views of the Lower Lake and the valley; a pathway leads down to the River Deenagh. Main access to Knockreer is through Deenagh Lodge Gate, opposite St. Mary's Cathedral in Killarney Town.
Main entrance on Cathedral Place, off New St., Killarney. Free admission.

The Meeting of the Waters ♥ NATURE SITE One of the most tranquil spots in Killarney National Park (and not to be confused with the more famous place with the same name in County Wicklow; see p. 205), this is where the Upper, Middle, and Lower lakes converge. You can hike from Muckross House (about 5km/3 miles), or park at the unmarked lot about 1.6km (1 mile) south of the **Torc Waterfall** (p. 304) parking area on the main Ring of Kerry Road. From here, the walk down a signposted path takes about 15 minutes, although "unofficial" side paths also lead you to the shore at different points. The views from these side paths are just as lovely (and often free of people), but take care—the ground is uneven in places. Good, sturdy walking shoes are recommended.
Off N71, about 2.4km (1½ miles) S of Muckross House, Killarney.

St. Mary's Cathedral ♥ CATHEDRAL If you think this limestone cathedral looks more Castle Dracula than local church, it may be because New Street was once the home of Bram Stoker, who spent summers in Killarney while he was a student at Trinity College Dublin. Officially known as the Catholic Church of St. Mary of the Assumption, it's designed in the Gothic Revival style and laid out in the shape of a cross. Construction began in 1842, was interrupted by the Famine, and concluded in 1855 (although the towering spire wasn't added until 1912).
Cathedral Place, off New St. ✆ **064/663-1014.** Free admission. Daily 9am–6pm.

WHERE TO STAY IN KILLARNEY

Expensive

Aghadoe Heights ♥♥ Luxurious, welcoming, and with one of the best views in Ireland, this is among the country's top spa hotels. Perched on a hill to the north of Killarney Town, the modernist building boasts floor-to-ceiling windows that take in the full, glorious panorama of Lough Leane in Killarney National Park. (In winter, an atmospheric fluke can mean that you're literally above the clouds here, an effect that's nothing short of fairy-tale.) The **Lake Room** serves French-influenced seasonal Irish cuisine with an emphasis on fresh seafood in an elegant atmosphere. Alternatively, you can graze on lighter fare in the adjacent lounge and

Views of Lough Leane from the Lake Room at the Aghadoe Heights hotel.

piano bar and take in the views over drinks on the terrace. When you're not out sightseeing, take a relaxing break in the opulent spa and thermal suite. Take time to explore the ethereal ruins of **Aghadoe Cathedral,** directly across the street (p. 305).

About 5km (3 miles) NW of Killarney, signposted off N22; Ard Na Be Rd., Aghadoe. aghadoeheights.com. ✆ **064/663-1766.** 74 units. €269–€539 double; €619–€950 suite. Breakfast included. Spa and dinner, bed-and-breakfast packages available. Free parking. **Amenities:** 2 restaurants; bar; pool; room service; spa; gym; tennis court; Wi-Fi (free).

Cahernane House ♥♥ A neo-Gothic mansion on the outskirts of Killarney National Park, Cahernane is a luxurious retreat. The decor is authentically grandiose: Public areas have the feel of a traditional gentlemen's club, filled with antique furniture, stag heads on the wall, and the scent of a peat fire hanging heavy in the air. Guest rooms are more modern, though no less elegant, and some bathrooms have deep clawfoot tubs. Many of the rooms have private patios. Of the two house restaurants, the excellent, formal **Herbert's Restaurant** has beautiful views of two mountain ranges, and the more relaxed **Cellar Bar** serves lighter meals among the beautifully lit arches of an old wine cellar.

Muckross Rd. cahernane.com. ✆ **064/663-1895.** 48 units. €233–€359 double; €323–€429 suite. Breakfast included. Dinner, bed-and-breakfast packages available. Free parking. **Amenities:** Restaurant; bar; room service; Wi-Fi (free). Closed Jan–Feb.

The Europe ♥♥♥ Tucked away at the edge of the Lakes of Killarney, with splendid views from every floor, the Europe is widely seen as one of the best hotels in Ireland. The modern white building looks plain from the outside, but inside it is exceptional. Guest rooms are spacious, most overlooking the glorious Lakes of Killarney. Beds are enormously comfortable, and rooms are quiet. The hotel has two dining options: the gastropub-like **Brasserie** and the elegant **Panorama** for fine dining, with its jaw-dropping views of Lough Leane and the MacGillycuddy's Reeks and its highly-rated Irish cuisine with European influences. The Europe has numerous lounges where you can sip tea, read a book, or savor a whiskey. Downstairs, soak in the indoor/outdoor pool at the award-winning

Set right on Killarney's Lower Lake, the Europe is a sleekly modern hotel with a full roster of luxury amenities.

spa while taking in more lake and mountain views, or walk right down to the lake's edge. This is one of our favorites.

Fossa Rd. theeurope.com. ✆ **064/667-1300.** 180 units. €355–€595 double; €720–€3,000 suite. 2-night minimum stay weekends and in high season. Free parking. **Amenities:** 2 restaurants; bar; room service; spa; gym; Wi-Fi (free).

Killarney Park ♥♥ Conveniently located in the center of town, the lemon-yellow five-story building has appealing arched attic windows. Rooms are not huge, but they're comfortable and up to date. Premium rooms are larger and have king beds and separate seating areas. Afternoon tea is popular with visitors and locals alike. The **Peregrine** restaurant serves the best seasonal Kerry produce in an elegant but relaxed atmosphere with comfortable banquettes and cozy horseshoe-shaped booths; the **Garden Bar** has a more informal menu that includes sandwiches and steaks. The spa is an oasis, with an indoor pool and outdoor hot tubs overlooking the gardens. Indulge in a treatment if you can.

East Ave. killarneyparkhotel.ie. ✆ **064/663-5555.** 67 units. €349–€720 double; €850–€1,735 suite. Breakfast not included in lower rates. Free parking. **Amenities:** Restaurant; bar; room service; pool; spa; Wi-Fi (free).

Moderate

Earls Court House ♥♥ Just outside the center of Killarney, on a quiet street with views of the mountains, Earls Court House is a pleasingly old-fashioned kind of B&B. Guest rooms are simple but pleasant, featuring polished wood furniture and buttermilk-colored walls. A few have four-poster beds and Jacuzzi baths, and family rooms sleep up to four. You can have afternoon tea in one of two guest lounges, where fires are lit in winter and games and books are available.

Woodlawn Rd. killarney-earlscourt.ie. ✆ **064/663-4009.** 24 units. €150–€212 double. Breakfast included. 2-night min. summer weekends. Free parking. **Amenities:** Library; self-service laundry; Wi-Fi (free). Closed Jan–Feb.

Killarney Plaza ♥♥ This large, modern hotel couldn't have a better location if you like to be in the thick of the action—it's right in the middle of Killarney town center. The accommodations are functional, contemporary, and comfortable rather than luxurious—think U.S. chain hotel and you're close enough. (Indeed, this place is big with tour groups, from the U.S. and elsewhere.) The buffet breakfast offers a vast selection, and there are two in-house restaurants: the **Tan Yard** restaurant and **Café du Parc** bar—although being this centrally located in Killarney, you're hardly short of choice at your doorstep. The good in-house spa, gym, and 15m (50-ft.) pool lets you recharge after a day of sightseeing.

Town Centre, Killarney. killarneyplaza.com. ✆ **064/662-1111.** 198 units. €195–€250 double; €295–€320 suite. Breakfast included. Free parking. **Amenities:** 2 restaurants; 2 bars; pool; gym; spa; Wi-Fi (free).

Killeen House Hotel ♥♥ This charming country-house-style hotel has a peaceful setting in Aghadoe, around 10 minutes' drive from Killarney Town. A former rectory built in 1838, the building has a homey, welcoming atmosphere inside. The hotel is surrounded by gardens, perfect for a relaxing stroll or refreshments, while in cooler weather, there are seats beside the fire in the cozy lounge. One of the best things about staying here is the wonderful **Rozzers** restaurant (p. 313), offering both fine dining (check online for dinner-and-B&B packages) and a bar-food menu. The filling breakfast will keep you going all day.

Aghadoe. killeenhousehotel.com. ✆ **064/663-1711.** 23 units. €150–€215 double. Breakfast included. Free parking. **Amenities:** Wi-Fi (free). Weekends only Nov–Dec. Closed Jan–Feb.

The Ross ♥♥ This charming small hotel in the middle of Killarney (sister hotel to the Killarney Park Hotel, across the road) packs lots of personality into four walls. Within easy walking distance to most of the town's sights and shops, it's beautifully designed, especially the fabulous gastropub **The Lane,** with an all-day food menu and a great list of cocktails, and the snazzy **Polly's Lounge,** which prides itself on its cocktails. Beds are comfortable, and rooms are big enough to easily accommodate families with kids; many have views of the town. Room decor is simple but pleasant.

East Ave. theross.ie. ✆ **064/663-1855.** 29 units. €170–€270 double. Breakfast included. **Amenities:** Restaurant; bar; Wi-Fi (free).

spa life, **IRISH-STYLE**

It's fair to say Ireland is blessed with more than a few top-rated spas—and some of the top spas cluster around Kenmare and Killarney. The best ones use the beautiful natural settings to spectacular effect and borrow their treatments from the Irish countryside. Everything from Irish spring water to peat mud and local river stones are used to coax forth beauty from tired, work-dulled skin and hair. None of these spas are cheap, but they're a wonderful way to treat yourself on the road.

Treatments at the spa at the **Aghadoe Heights Hotel & Spa** (p. 306) outside Killarney are designed to awaken the senses—the grounding ritual is a pressure massage designed to soothe mental anxiety as well as ease tension. Spa and hotel guests can spend time in the exquisite thermal suite, which has an array of steam rooms, saunas, tropical showers, cooling rooms, and hot tubs. Treatments range from about €130 to €230.

The **Easanna Spa** at the **Sheen Falls Lodge,** off N71, Kenmare (sheenfallslodge.ie; ✆ **064/664-1600**), features a pool shaped like a flower, each petal forming a kind of relaxation space. You can have a hot stone massage or facial and then float off in total relaxation. Room rates here start at around €300. Treatments range from about €90 to €235.

The spa at the **Killarney Park Hotel** (p. 308) is a modern, peaceful oasis in the center of Killarney, with a soothing pool and such exotic treatments as the thousand flower detox wrap, in which you are soaked in green tea balm and wrapped up cozily while it gets to work, or the lime and ginger salt scrub, designed to revitalize tired skin. Treatments range from about €75 to €225.

Anú Spa at the **Brehon Hotel** (thebrehon.com; ✆ **064/663-07000**), named after a Celtic earth goddess, has revitalizing treatments that take inspiration from around the world, including Indian head massages, Ayurvedic scrubs, and even an anti-aging facial using 23-carat gold minerals. Continue restoring your body or soul afterwards in the vitality suite, which has a sauna, steam room, ice fountain, and swimming pool. Rooms start at €140. Treatments range from €80 to €230.

At the **Sámas spa** in the elegant **Park Hotel Kenmare,** Shelbourne Street, Kenmare (parkkenmare.com; ✆ **064/664-1200**), you can soak in the warm spa pool while gazing out over the mountains. Spend an hour relaxing in the thermal suite (rock sauna, ice fountain, tropical mist shower), before your treatment. ***Note:*** The thermal suite is strictly for spa guests only. Rooms start at about €325; treatments cost €145 to €265, according to the time booked (1 hr., 90 min., or 2 hr.).

The artfully lit **ESPA spa** in the **Europe** hotel (p. 307) offers exquisite views of the lake and the hills from the indoor/outdoor pool. There's a full thermal suite to steam your cares away, and the massages and facials here earn raves from regulars. Treatments range from €135 to €390.

Treatments at the **Spa at the Muckross Park Hotel**, Muckross, Killarney (muckrosspark.com; ✆ **064/662-3400**), include an energy-shot massage to clear both body and mind, plus a range of facials. The vitality suite is perfect for a post-treatment recharge, with a vitality pool, hot tubs, sauna, steam room, ice fountain, tropical shower, and thermal loungers. Treatments cost from €70 to €170.

Aghadoe Spa in the Aghadoe Heights Hotel.

Inexpensive

Larkinley Lodge ♥♥ A great option just a few blocks from the center of Killarney, Larkinley Lodge is a modern guesthouse in a beautifully converted town house. Toni and Danny Sheehan are gregarious hosts with an eye for detail. Guest rooms are small but just the right mix of traditional and modern, with minimal clutter and muted color schemes. Triple rooms only cost a little more than doubles. ***Note:*** They don't serve breakfast but do have tea and coffee facilities. The location is about a 10-minute walk into central Killarney, not far from great pubs and restaurants yet in a quiet neighborhood where you can escape the evening street noise.

Lewis Rd. larkinley.ie. ✆ **087/238-9537.** 6 units. Doubles from €120. Free parking. **Amenities:** Wi-Fi (free).

WHERE TO EAT IN KILLARNEY

A bustling tourist town, Killarney offers lots of food options. In addition to the restaurants listed below, there are ample places to stop for a quick coffee, a light meal, or a freshly made sandwich. If you're buying a takeout coffee, take note that the cafes no longer use single-use cups. You can either bring your own reusable cup or pay a refundable deposit of €2. For sweet treats, order some hand-crafted chocolates with coffee at **Lir Café** (6 Kenmare Place; lircafe.com; ✆ **064/663-3859**). For a summer treat,

Murphy's Ice Cream (37 Main St.; murphysicecream.ie; ✆ **087/052-3145**) is one of the best things Ireland has to offer on a sunny day.

Bricín ♥♥ IRISH Located above a craft store on Killarney's main street, this is a long-standing favorite on the local dining scene. *Bricín* means "little trout" in Irish, and seafood is one of the strong points of the traditional Irish menu. Locally reared meat is also often on the menu, served with interesting sauces, such as supreme of chicken with thyme jus and cinnamon. The house specialty, however, is what this place is renowned for: *boxty,* a savory pancake stuffed with several different types of filling (see box on p. 146). The dining room is an old-fashioned kind of place, complete with stained-glass windows and an open fireplace. ***Tip:*** Bricín serves a great-value early-bird menu (two courses €27, three courses €30) from 6 until 6:45pm.

26 High St. bricin.ie ✆ **064/663-4902.** Entrees €21–€37; fixed-price menu €43. Tues–Sat 6–9:30pm. Closed early Jan to early Mar.

Harrow ♥♥♥ IRISH Seasonal local produce gets a creative flourish in this contemporary dining space, where chef John O'Leary's menu nods to classic French cuisine. The menu focuses on local seafood and dry-aged cuts of Irish beef, with dishes like pan-fried Atlantic monkfish with smokey paprika and Catalan mussel stew, or dry-aged beef with portobello pesto, black garlic, and celeriac. Make sure to leave room for desserts like chocolate fondant with cocoa nib tuille and stout ice cream.

27 High St. harrowkillarney.com ✆ **064/663-0766.** Entrees €25–€42; 3-course set menu €49.50. Wed–Sun 5–9:30pm.

Kate Kearney's Cottage ♥ INTERNATIONAL Unofficially considered the gateway to the Gap of Dunloe, this cheerful pub is hugely popular. It's more than a little touristy, but the stick-to-your-ribs pub food is pretty tasty. The menu offers everything from toasted sandwiches to pizzas, plus a daily roast, all best washed down with a restorative pint. Semi-regular "Irish Nights" offer a package of dinner and a show of traditional music; call or check the website for upcoming dates. The pub is named after a feisty local woman who carved out a reputation as a maker of illegal *poitín* (moonshine) that she called Mountain Dew.

Gap of Dunloe, Beaufort, signposted from N72 (Ring of Kerry Rd.). katekearneyscottage.com. ✆ **064/664-4146.** Entrees €12–€21. Daily noon–11pm (food until 8pm).

Quinlan's Seafood Bar ♥♥ SEAFOOD With a family business of fish shops, it's no surprise that the catches here are right off the boat, "from tide to table," as they say. The fare is simple and straightforward. Fish and chips, with a light batter and a giant portion of chunky fries, come hot from the fryer. Have it with mushy peas, and you're deep into a true Irish dinner. If you fancy more sophisticated dishes, the menu obliges, with scallops in butter, boiled Irish lobster, lemon sole in a buttery sauce, and prawns so fresh they all but swim off the plate. Also run by the

Table for four at Rozzers, where local Irish ingredients get a haute cuisine twist.

Quinlan brothers is the slightly more upscale **The Mad Monk** (21/22 Plunkett St.), serving delicious Portmagee crab claws, Dingle Bay squid, and Atlantic prawns as well as fish and chips and wine.

77 High St. seafoodbar.ie/killarney. ✆ **064/662-0666.** Entrees €17–€22. Mon–Thurs and Sun 12:30–8:30pm; Fri–Sat 12:30–9pm.

Rozzers ♥♥♥ MODERN IRISH This is a popular spot for fine dining, with a simple menu combining the best local Irish ingredients with classic French influences—Kerry beef might be served with a celeriac gratin wild mushroom fricassee, sweet carrot puree, and a port wine sauce. There's often roast rack of Ring of Kerry lamb as well as oysters, salmon, and monkfish, or chateaubriand with Irish beef for a treat. Decor is old-style—the building is an Edwardian rectory from 1838—but the country-house hotel setting is charming, and you can also stay over if you like (p. 309); check for dinner and B&B packages. Book your table well in advance.

At the Killeen House Hotel, Aghadoe. killeenhousehotel.com/en/rozzers-killarney-restaurant. ✆ **064/663-1711.** 3-course fixed-priced menu €65. Mid-March to Oct Mon–Sat 6–9pm; Nov–Dec Sat–Sun 6–9pm. Closed Jan–Feb.

Stonechat ♥♥ IRISH All the food at this relaxed, friendly little place on Fleming's Lane is locally sourced, with good fish and meat favorites like seafood chowder and an 8-ounce chargrilled filet steak. Look out for dishes like wild hake, baked and served with spinach and vegetables, or slow-cooked Kerry lamb shank with mustard mash and tomato and red wine sauce. There's a good choice of vegetarian and vegan dishes on the menu too, and most of the dishes are gluten-free.

8 Fleming's Lane, Killarney. thestonechat.com. ✆ **087/683-5421**. Entrees €18–€37. Tues–Sat 3–10pm. Closed Jan–Feb.

KILLARNEY SHOPPING

Shopping hours in Killarney are usually Monday to Saturday 9am to 6pm, but from May through September many stores are open every day until 9 or 10pm. Killarney has more souvenir and craft shops than you can shake a *shillelagh* at; a few of the best are listed below.

Aran Sweater Market ♥♥ Rows of soft wool sweaters, skirts, hats, and scarves in colors ranging from traditional cream to bright blues, reds, and ochre await in this town center store. All are Irish made, most from pure wool. 19 College Square. aransweatermarket.com. ✆ **064/662-3102.**

Bricín ♥♥ This little craft store sells traditional ceramics, jewelry, and clothes. Many of the wares on sale here were made locally. Upstairs is one of the town's best restaurants (p. 312). 26 High St. bricin.ie. ✆ **064/663-4902.**

The Dungeon Bookshop ♥♥ One of Killarney's most popular independent bookstores, the Dungeon stocks a good range of secondhand books. 99 College St. facebook.com/TheDungeonBookshop. ✆ **064/663-6536.**

Killarney Art Gallery ♥♥ This gallery showcases work from respected Irish artists as well as new and local talent. 32 Main St. killarneyartgallery.com. ✆ **087/276-7999.**

Mr. McGuire's Olde Sweet Shop ♥♥ This charming traditional candy store is a delight for kids of all ages. Candy is measured out from tall jars into little bags, or you can pick out some very giftable packages straight from the shelf. College Square. ✆ **064/667-1764.**

Muckross Craft Shop ♥♥ Part of the Walled Garden, a small shopping complex on the grounds of **Muckross House ♥♥** (p. 302), this place has a good stock of Irish crafts, pottery, clothing, cards, and quality gifts—and many items are made locally. Muckross House, Muckross Rd. muckross-house.ie. ✆ **064/667-0147.**

KILLARNEY AFTER DARK

The mainstay of nightlife in Killarney is the lively pub scene. The town has more than its fair share of good places to enjoy a pint and some live traditional music. All of these places can get pretty packed on a busy summer's night—so come early to stand a chance of getting a seat.

Charlie Foley's ♥♥ Every trip to Killarney should include at least one pint at Charlie Foley's. The old pub dates from 1896 and is a local institution, one of the places in town where you might actually meet Irish people instead of tourists. Take a seat in the snug or at the bar and wait for the local gossip to flow. New St. charliefoleys.ie. ✆ **064/663-4311.**

Killarney Grand ♥♥ This hugely popular pub is one of the best places in the region to hear traditional Irish music—and for free. Nightly live sessions start at 9pm; there's also a nightclub and a piano bar. The atmosphere gets pretty raucous, and the crowds can really pack in here (definitely standing-room-only), but the music is always good. Some of the biggest names in Irish music have played here over the years; you never know when you might catch the next big thing. A "neat" dress code is enforced at the door—meaning you don't have to wear your best duds, but don't walk in looking too scruffy, either. Main St. killarneygrand.com. ✆ **064/663-1159.**

The Laurels ♥ Another very popular pub for live music, here the traditional music sessions (and sometimes Irish dancing) take place several times a week, usually starting at around 9pm. The pub also serves good food, including stone-baked pizzas. Main St. thelaurelspub.com. ✆ **064/663-1149.**

O'Connors ♥♥ At this traditional pub, the program of live music is extensive, with bands playing every night—both scheduled and, occasionally, spontaneous. It doesn't stop there, either; you might catch a play, some standup comedy, or even a spoken-word event. 7 High St. facebook.com/oconnorskillarney. ✆ **086/034-6949.**

Tatler Jack ♥ For Gaelic sports fans, this is the place to go. Football and hurling matches are shown on big-screen TVs, and traditional music is played on many nights in summer. Expect to find a raucous atmosphere. 23–29 Plunkett St. tatlerjack.ie. ✆ **064/663-2361.**

OUTDOOR PURSUITS IN THE RING OF KERRY

CYCLING **Killarney National Park,** with its lakeside and forest pathways, trails, and roads, is a paradise for bikers. Bike rental charges start from €20 per day (€45 for an e-bike) and from €125 per week at **Killarney Rent-a-Bike** (killarneyrentabike.com; ✆ **064/663-1282**), with locations on Beech Road, College Street, and Muckross Road. **WildNHappy** (wildnhappytravel.com/tour/killarney-cycling-tour; ✆ **086/389-0171**) runs half-day cycling tours, costing from €45 and starting from the Tourist Information Centre on Beech Road.

FISHING Fishing for salmon and brown trout in Killarney's unpolluted lakes and rivers is a popular pastime. Brown trout fishing is free on the

The Best Drive in Ireland?

It takes about 45 minutes to drive between Killarney and Kenmare, but it's one of the most picturesque routes in the country. It's easy enough to find—just follow signs for N71 through Killarney National Park, taking care not to get onto the quicker but infinitely less romantic back roads instead (your GPS or map app may try and take you this way by default). If you're setting out from Kenmare, the drive begins along gentle foothills; from Killarney, it's sun-dappled, sylvan woods. Either way, before long you hit wide, sweeping vistas of lakes and mountains, guaranteed to catch your breath and steal your heart. Fortunately, there are plenty of places to pull over and gawp at the scenery, including **Ladies View**—so-called because it was, apparently, a favorite of the ladies-in-waiting to Queen Victoria during her Ireland visit in 1861. The viewpoint has a handy **cafe** (ladiesview.com) with a solid menu (homemade soups, Guinness stew, fresh pastries), a craft shop, bar, and a rooftop alfresco terrace for panoramic views. All the best viewpoints have small, free parking areas, so don't be tempted to pull over illegally on the narrow road—and don't forget to leave time to take all those dreamy pictures.

lakes, but a permit is necessary for the rivers Flesk and Laune. Salmon fishing anywhere requires a special license. Permits, licenses, tackle, bait, rod rental, and other fishing gear can be obtained from **O'Neill's,** 6 Plunkett St. (facebook.com/oneillsofkillarney; ✆ **064/663-1970**). The shop (which was started in 1947) also arranges *ghillies* (fishing guides) for around €150 to €200 per day on the Killarney Lakes.

GOLF Overlooking the Atlantic Ocean, on the southwestern part of the Ring of Kerry, the par-72 **Waterville Golf Links,** Waterville (watervillegolflinks.ie; ✆ **066/947-4102**), is considered one of the best courses in Ireland. The 6,200-yard course also has the distinction of containing a "Mass Hole," a relic of the days when Catholic Mass had to be celebrated in secrecy. Greens fees are €300 to €325 April to October, €120 November to March. Visitors are always welcome at the championship courses of the **Killarney Golf & Fishing Club,** Killorglin Road (N72), Fossa (killarneygolfclub.ie; ✆ **064/663-1034**), 5km (3 miles) west of the town center. Widely praised as one of the most scenic golf settings in the world, it has two 18-hole courses—Killeen and Mahony's Point—with gorgeous lake and mountain layouts. There is also a 9-hole course, **Lackabane.** Greens fees are €85 to €175, depending on the course and the time of day.

HORSEBACK RIDING Many trails in the Killarney area are suitable for horseback riding. Scenic rides cost from €60 per hour at **Killarney Riding Stables,** N72, Ballydowney (killarneyridingstables.com; ✆ **064/663-1686**). Lessons and weeklong trail rides can also be arranged.

STARGAZING While the **Kerry International Dark Sky Reserve** is a designated dark-sky area on the Iveragh Peninsula (Ring of Kerry), most places in County Kerry—away from urban areas—are good for viewing the night sky on a cloudless night, thanks to the county's low light pollution. For a guide to what you are seeing, sign up for a 90-minute stargazing tour (€50) in Caherdaniel (kerrydarkskytourism.com; ✆ **087/600-7820**).

Kenmare

Kenmare is a sweet little town with flower boxes at every window, lots of restaurants, and plenty of places to stay. Originally called Neidin (pronounced Nay-*deen,* meaning "little nest" in Irish), Kenmare is indeed a little nest of verdant foliage and colorful buildings nestled between the River Roughty and Kenmare Bay. And while it certainly gets more than its fair share of visitors in the summer, Kenmare isn't as frenetic as Killarney. If you crave a quieter life, this can make it a more pleasant place to stay—especially if you have the freedom of a car.

EXPLORING KENMARE

Kenmare Bay Boat Tours ♥♥ BOAT TOUR This fun 90-minute cruise with live commentary by Pat the skipper makes for an engaging introduction to Kenmare Bay and its wildlife—specifically the dolphins, sea otters, and gray seals you might see frolicking nearby, plus the foxes

Shops and restaurants line Kenmare's lively main street, Henry Street, with the scenic Kerry countryside just a few minutes' drive away.

and goats sometimes spotted along the shoreline. There's a covered seating area, but it's more fun to view the seals from the open part of the deck (make sure to dress warmly). Boats depart from the pier next to the Kenmare suspension bridge; they also offer a 70-minute sunset tour. Sailing times vary, depending on the tides, and reservations are recommended.
The Pier. kenmarebayboattours.com. ✆ **087/711-0240.** €30 adults; €15 children aged 5–17; €80 families. Daily May–Aug; Sept Tues–Wed and Fri–Sun; Feb–Apr and Oct Sat–Sun. Call or check website for departure times.

Kenmare Druid Circle ♥ PREHISTORIC SITE On a small hill near the market square, this large Bronze Age druid stone circle is magnificently intact, featuring 15 standing stones arranged around a central boulder that still bears signs (circular holes, a shallow dent at the center) of having been used in ceremonies. To find it, walk down to the market square and follow signage on the left side of the road. There's no visitor center and no admission fee; it's just sitting in a small paddock.
Off the Square. kenmarestonecircle.com.

Kenmare Farmer's Market ♥♥ MARKET If you're visiting midweek, be sure to check out this small but lively open-air market held every Wednesday in Kenmare's main square. The emphasis is on food from small artisan producers from across the region. Traders may come here from quite far afield to sell their wares, although the bulk of what's for sale is locally sourced. It's a fun market to browse your way through.
The Square. facebook.com/kenmaremarket18. No phone. Wed 9am–5pm. Some stalls may close in bad weather.

Tom Crean Brewery ♥♥ BREWERY TOUR The famous Irish Antarctic explorer Tom Crean was from Annascaul on the Dingle Peninsula in County Kerry, and his granddaughter Aileen, a trained chef, set up this brewery, restaurant, and guesthouse. On the 1-hour tour you'll learn all about how the beer is brewed and the family history of exploration before sampling some of the brew. The brewery's shop sells some of the beers plus gifts and posters.

Main St. tomcreanbrewerykenmare.ie. ✆ **087/161-2929.** €20 adults; €8 children 17 and under; €48 families. Tours Mar–Dec Fri–Mon 3pm; book online.

WHERE TO STAY IN KENMARE

Expensive

Park Hotel Kenmare ♥♥♥ This circa-1897 hotel is an elegant option. Large, traditionally decorated rooms with open fireplaces, grand oil paintings, and imposing staircases fill the ground floor. All around are spectacular views of the lake and green hills. This is a formal place—the staff is polite but not snobbish and will help arrange anything you need. Bedrooms are quiet and spacious; some have four-poster beds. There's a 12-seater cinema where you can watch a movie of your choice from the hotel library. The restaurant has lavish modern European a la carte menus or a seven-course tasting menu for €130. But the extraordinary **Sámas spa** (p. 310) might prove so distracting that you forget to do anything else at all.

Kenmare High St. parkkenmare.com. ✆ **064/664-1200.** 46 units. €325–€635 double. Breakfast included. Free parking. **Amenities:** Restaurant; bar; cinema; golf course; pool; room service; spa; Wi-Fi (free).

On verdant grounds overlooking Kenmare Bay, Park Hotel Kenmare offers spacious, well-appointed guest rooms.

Sheen Falls Lodge ♥♥♥ This elegant hideaway on the River Sheen outside Kenmare was built in the 17th century as a nobleman's hunting lodge, but now it is a hotel more famous for its massages than its venison. Expect spacious rooms with luxurious decor (all have views of the grounds or the dappled river). **The Falls** restaurant offers exceptional Irish-influenced European cuisine in formal surroundings. The extensive grounds offer opportunities for horseback riding, shooting, fishing, golf, and tennis. You can have high tea in the sun lounge or champagne in the cocktail bar, but it's the spa that most people rave about. Try one of the exclusive treatments, then soak in the heated pool. Bliss.

Knockduragh. sheenfallslodge.ie. ✆ **064/664-1600.** 66 units. €250–€770 double; €370–€2,090 suite. Free parking. **Amenities:** Restaurant; bar; cinema; golf course; pool; tennis; horseback riding; room service; spa; Wi-Fi (free).

Moderate

Brook Lane Hotel ♥♥ Just a mile outside of Kenmare, this hotel doesn't look like much from the outside but offers a lot on the inside. Attractively designed rooms made cozy by underfloor heating, plus big, comfortable beds topped with soft linens, are just the answer after a long day of exploring. The in-house **Casey's** bar and restaurant is run by the outstanding team behind sister restaurant **No. 35** (p. 321), so no need to go out for dinner. Handy, quiet, and affordable.

Sneem Rd. brooklanehotel.com. ✆ **064/664-2077.** 22 units. €135–€355 double. **Amenities:** Restaurant; bar; Wi-Fi (free).

Lagom Restaurant & Townhouse ♥♥♥ The rooms at this stylish townhouse in the center of Kenmare (above the restaurant) are all about simple Scandinavian-style luxury, with wood floors and a color palette that takes inspiration from the local surroundings (the name "lagom" comes from the Swedish concept of balance). Make sure to book dinner at **Lagom Restaurant** (✆ **064/664-8423**) on the ground floor, which has a separate entrance—the menu focuses on the best local produce with seasonal flavors. The breakfast menu offers a great choice of dishes, too. ***Tip:*** The town house has two upper floors, each with a set of stairs, so ask for the lower floor if you have heavy baggage.

36 Henry St. lagomkenmare.com. ✆ **087/977-2310.** 10 units. €155–€170 double. Accommodation for ages 16 and over only. Breakfast included. Paid on-street parking, or free parking nearby. **Amenities:** Restaurant; Wi-Fi (free). Weekends only in Jan.

Inexpensive

The Happy Pig ♥♥ At this cozy guesthouse around 15 minutes' walk from Kenmare Town, each room has either a garden or mountain view. The house is full of art and antique-style furnishings, and there's a sitting room with a library to relax in and a patio for good weather. Bikers will love this place—there's storage for bicycles and motorbikes and a heated drying room for hiking/biking gear. Tasty breakfasts here include options like organic eggs with smoked salmon, and home-baked scones.

Sneem Rd. thehappypig.ie. ✆ **083/059-4747.** 6 units. €125–€170 double. Breakfast included. Free parking. **Amenities:** Wi-Fi (free). Closed Jan to mid-Mar.

Rockcrest House ♥♥ You get a homey welcome from hosts Marian and David at this typical Irish B&B, just a 5-minute walk from the town center—enough to be close to restaurants and shops but also to enjoy a rural feel in a quiet country setting. Rooms are spacious if basic, and there are two single rooms available for solo travelers. The full Irish breakfasts will set you up for the whole day, including a vegetarian version.

Gortmullen. visit-kenmare.com/rockcresthouse. ✆ **064/664-1248.** 5 units. €115–€125 double. Breakfast included. Free parking. **Amenities:** Wi-Fi (free).

WHERE TO EAT IN KENMARE

Kenmare is a lovely place to linger over a cup of tea or a light lunch, and there are plenty of places to do just that. If you're looking for a hot breakfast or a chilled-out lunch, **Rookery Lane** (Bridge St.; rookerylane.ie; ✆ **064/664-8392**) is a good spot for poached eggs and fluffy pancakes, with colorful burrito bowls. (It also has four guest rooms; €170–€180 double.) Another terrific breakfast and lunch option, **Poffs** (New Rd.; facebook.com/poffsfood; ✆ **064/664-0645**) serves sandwiches piled high with fixings. We love the scrambled eggs with flaked smoked mackerel. For tasty takeout woodfired pizzas, try **Boxed** (The Square; facebook.com/boxedwoodfiredpizza.ie; ✆ **064/668-6020**). You can also eat your way around town with **Kenmare Foodie Tours** (kenmarefoodies.com), where local food enthusiast Karen Coakley introduces you to the town's food producers with tasty samples. Tours last 2½ to 3 hours, cost €85, and run every Wednesday in summer at around 11am.

The Boathouse Bistro, at Dromquinna Manor.

The Boathouse Bistro ♥♥ BISTRO/SEAFOOD This casual seafood bistro at Dromquinna Manor has an outside seating area overlooking Kenmare Bay, making it perfect for a warm summer night or as a good lunch stop on a sunny day. The menu serves dishes like pan-seared salmon or the house-special fish cakes with mango salsa. Or you could just have a burger and

sea-salted french fries while you take in the wonderful view. The bistro closes for much of the winter.
On N70, 5km (3 miles) W of Kenmare. dromquinnamanor.com. ✆ **064/664-2889.** Entrees €22–€42. May Wed–Sun 12:30–9pm; June–Aug Thurs–Tues 12:30–9pm.

The Lime Tree ♥♥ MODERN IRISH This internationally praised restaurant in a charming historic building offers an elegant twist on Irish comfort food. The menu is smart and varied without being overly complicated, with plenty of locally sourced ingredients—black pudding from Sneem, salmon from Kenmare, County Kerry lamb. You might start with a duck croquette with pickled plums, or prawn cocktail with cognac-infused sauce, then go on to a baked filet of salmon with lemon crumb crust, or sirloin of beef with onions, shallot, and garlic butter. Try the crepes for dessert, served with pralines, ice cream, and a rich butterscotch sauce.
3A Shelbourne St. limetreerestaurant.com. ✆ **064/664-1225.** Set menu 2 courses €50, 3 courses €57. Wed–Mon 6–9:30pm.

Maison Gourmet ♥♥ BAKERY A little touch of *la vie Parisienne* on the very un-French streets of Kenmare, this artisan bakery serves freshly made sandwiches, omelets, pancakes, filled croissants—and excellent organic coffee. The patisserie is so tempting it's hard even to walk past it without dreaming of a delicious slice of cake or tart. Eat in or take out.
26 Henry St. maisongourmetkenmare.com. ✆ **064/664-1857.** Pastries €2.20–€5, brunch €9.50–€14. Daily 8am–5pm.

Mulcahys ♥♥ IRISH This place is popular with locals and visitors alike for relaxed dining in a casual atmosphere and contemporary setting. As well as filling mains, it has a good choice of small plates and sharing options—though you might not want to share your tasty lobster and crab croquettes or beef cheek with potato. The restaurant can be loud when it's full, so bear that in mind when choosing a time to eat. If it's on the menu, try a glass of Killahora Apple Ice Wine made in nearby County Cork.
Main St. mulcahyskenmare.ie. ✆ **064/664-2383.** Entrees €21–€33. Tues–Sat 5–9pm.

No. 35 ♥♥ IRISH/INTERNATIONAL "Local produce" is a term you see a lot in the best restaurants, but this place really takes it a step further—all the meat it serves was reared on its own farm. The menu is short and simple; you might start with some cured salmon with rye, cucumber, and dill, followed by catch of the day with orange, fennel, and smoked almonds or featherblade beef with cabbage and Jerusalem artichoke. The dining room is small, and this place can get packed, so reserve ahead.
35 Main St. no35kenmare.com. ✆ **064/664-1559.** Entrees €21–€25. Fri–Tues 5–9pm.

The Strawberry Field ♥♥♥ PANCAKES This 200-year-old "pancake cottage" is a true delight, set in a traditional farmhouse cottage with a homely interior complete with a wood-burning stove. Pancakes come in sweet or savory versions, with fillings like bacon and cheddar cheese, or beetroot hummus and salad. The bright yellow building is also home to an

art and crafts shop, with pieces by local artists, so as well as leaving full, you might own a new cast-iron teapot, painting, or piece of jewelry after your visit.
Blackwater, Moll's Gap, Sneem Road. strawberryfield-ireland.com. ✆ **064/668-2977.** Pancakes €4.75–€10.50. Wed–Sun 10am–5:15pm.

KENMARE SHOPPING

The Ring of Kerry has many good craft and souvenir shops, but those in and around Kenmare offer some of the best choices in terms of quality. Kenmare shops are open year-round, usually Monday to Saturday from 9am to 6pm. From May to September, many shops remain open until 9 or 10pm, and some open on Sunday from noon to 5 or 6pm.

Avoca at Moll's Gap ♥♥ Creative, colorful, and with what must be one of the world's best-appointed parking lots, this branch of Avoca is on a mountain pass just off the main Ring of Kerry Road, 10km (6 miles) north of Kenmare. Though quite small, it sells a good selection of the crafts, knitwear, and upscale knickknacks for which the Wicklow-based company is famous. The cafe upstairs is also a great pit stop for a light lunch or cup of tea. Moll's Gap (on R568, signposted from main N71 Ring of Kerry Rd.). avoca.ie. ✆ **066/916-5000.**

Lorge Chocolatier ♥♥♥ Benoit Lorge makes exquisite artisanal chocolates in every form, from bars and boxes to truffles, hot chocolate, chocolate spreads, and nougat. They're wonderful creations, elegantly presented—the gift boxes are little works of art in themselves. Too bad their precious, tasty cargo must be eaten. All of it. Right now. 18 Henry St. and N71, Bonane. lorge.ie. ✆ **064/667-9994.**

Quills Woollen Market ♥♥ Housed in a delightfully multicolored row of shops in the center of Kenmare, this long-standing business specializes in traditional Irish knitwear—particularly heavy-knit Aran sweaters, coats, and cardigans. It also sells Irish tweeds, shawls, linens, and various decor pieces like plush sheepskin rugs. It's a great place to stock up on authentic souvenirs. Other branches of Quills are in Killarney, Glengarriff, Ballingeary, and Sneem. Main St. irishgiftsandsweaters.com. ✆ **064/664-1078.**

Quills Woollen Market.

SPORTS & OUTDOOR PURSUITS IN KENMARE

ADVENTURE SPORTS **Eclipse Ireland,** Blackwater Bridge, Kenmare (eclipseireland.com; ✆ **064/668-2965**), offers a host of high-thrills activities and outdoor fun, including kayaking, archery, raft building, fishing, and trekking. See the website for the full list.

CYCLING You could conceivably cycle directly from Kenmare to Killarney National Park (about 13.2km/8½ miles), although the main Ring of Kerry Road is narrow, with sharp bends, and can get clogged with tour-bus traffic in summer. Ask for alternative cycling routes when you rent bikes, either from **Finnegan's Corner** at 37 Henry St., Kenmare (finneganscorner.com; ✆ **064/664-1083**), or **Eclipse Ireland,** Blackwater Bridge, Kenmare (eclipseireland.com; ✆ **064/668-2965**). Rates are around €25 per day or €50 for an e-bike.

KAYAKING & SUP On a guided kayaking or SUP (stand-up paddle-boarding) tour of Kenmare Bay with **Emerald Outdoors** (emerald outdoors.ie; ✆ **083/031-7011**), you might spot some seals. On the 2½-hour night kayaking tour, look for bioluminescent plankton lighting up the water beneath you as you paddle under the silhouette of the Caha mountains. Tours cost from €65.

Driving the Ring of Kerry Road

Whether you're setting out from Kenmare or Killarney, it's best to follow the Ring of Kerry tourist route in a counterclockwise direction. This means that you'll begin by heading west out of Killarney on the N72 road. (The road number will change to N70 for most of the loop as it circumnavigates the Iveragh Peninsula; it becomes N71 when you swing back through Kenmare.) About 22km (16½ miles) northwest from Killarney is the next major stop: **Killorglin,** a smallish town that lights up in mid-August when it hosts a traditional horse, sheep, and cattle fair called **Puck Fair** (see box on p. 324). For the rest of the year, Killorglin is a pretty, quiet town, well worth a wander, with the River Laune running straight through the town center.

SOS: GPS

You can drive either way along the Ring of Kerry, but we recommend a **counterclockwise** route for the most spectacular views. Drivers of very large vehicles also stick to this direction in order to avoid bottlenecks on the perilously narrow bends. This all worked fine for years—until modern technology intervened with the spread of GPS technology and mapping apps. Now some drivers unfamiliar with the route are being sent by their devices in a clockwise direction, thus causing all sorts of chaos, including some of the worst traffic jams ever seen on the Ring. These problems are rare, but expect high traffic in the summer.

As you continue on what is now the N70, glimpses of Dingle Bay will soon appear on your right. **Carrantuohill,** Ireland's tallest mountain at 1,041m (3,414 ft.), is to your left, and bleak vistas of open bog land

Killorglin: The Puck Stops Here

Sleepy little **Killorglin** wakes up every year on August 10, when the annual **Puck Fair** (puckfair.ie) incites a 3-day explosion of merrymaking and pageantry. Ireland's oldest festival and one of the last remaining traditional fairs, it's technically an agricultural show; the apex of the event involves capturing a mountain goat (the name Puck Fair comes from the Irish words *Aonach an Phoic*, fair of the he-goat), which is then declared "King Puck" and paraded around town on a throne, wearing a crown. It's bonkers, but quite a lot of fun. Nobody knows how it began, but one story dates to Cromwell's invasion of Ireland in the mid-17th century. English soldiers, foraging for food in the hills above the town, tried to capture a herd of goats. One goat escaped to Killorglin and alerted the villagers to mount a defense. Others say the fair is pre-Christian, connected with the pagan feast of Lughnasa on August 1. As you cross the old stone bridge over the River Laune, look out for the whimsical statue of the goat on the eastern side—and know that it stands in honor of this town's love for the goat.

constantly come into view. Along this coast, the Ring winds around cliffs and the edges of mountains, often with nothing but the sea below—another reason you will probably average only 50kmph (31 mph), at best. As you travel along, you'll notice the remnants of many stone cottages dotting the fields along the way. Most date from the mid-19th-century Great Famine, when millions of people starved to death or were forced to emigrate. This area was particularly hard hit, with the Iveragh Peninsula alone losing three-quarters of its population.

Glenbeigh is next on the Ring, a sweet little seafront town with a sandy beach and streets lined with palm trees.

Continue along the sea's edge to **Cahersiveen,** soon after which you can branch off the N70 onto R565 to visit the lovely seaside town of **Portmagee,** which is connected by a bridge to leafy **Valentia Island,** where you can visit the lighthouse (p. 329). In the 18th century, the Valentia harbor was notorious as a refuge for smugglers and privateers; it's said that John Paul Jones, the Scottish-born American naval officer in the War of Independence, also anchored here quite often. From Valentia you can take a boat trip to arguably the most magical site of the Ring of Kerry: the island of **Skellig Michael** ♥♥♥ (see box on p. 326), where medieval monks built a monastery in exquisite isolation. Visitor numbers are limited and the island is very popular, so boat trips must be booked well in advance. If you can't get a boat slot, however, Valentia Island's **Skellig Experience** (p. 329) gives you a good taste of the island's enduring fascination.

Head next for **Waterville,** an idyllic beach resort located between Lough Currane and Ballinskelligs Bay. For years it was a favorite retreat of Charlie Chaplin; there's even a statue of him near the beach. Here's another rewarding detour: Follow the sea road north of Waterville (R567) to the Irish-speaking village of **Ballinskelligs** ♥♥ (p. 327), with its

The Ring of Kerry
1 Kenmare
2 Killarney
3 Killorglin
4 Glenbeigh
5 Valentia Island
6 Skellig Michael
7 Waterville
8 Ballinskelligs
9 Derrynane
10 Staigue Fort
11 Sneem
Ballyduff
Slieve Mish Mts.
Sybil Pt.
Dingle Peninsula
Castlemaine
Annascaul
Castlemaine Harbour
N70
Ventry
Dingle
(An Daingean)
Killorglin
Great Blasket I.
Inch Pt.
N72
Slea Head
Rosbehy Pt.
Caragh Lough
Glenbeigh
Beaufort
Killarney
Dingle Bay
Inishabro
Inishvickillane
Ring of Kerry
Gap of Dunloe
Lough Leane
Beenkeragh
L. Acoose
Kells
Caher
Carrantuohill
Killarney National Park
Canglass Pt.
N70
Coomashaharn L.
MacGillycuddy's Reeks
Cahergall Fort
Ladies' View
Ballycarbery Castle
Moll's Gap
Valentia Lighthouse
Cahersiveen
Iveragh Peninsula
ATLANTIC OCEAN
Knightstown
Valentia I.
KERRY
R568
N71
Kilgarvan
Inny
Skellig Experience
Mastergeehy
Derriana L.
Kenmare
Bray Head
Portmagee
N70
N70
Ring of Kerry
Cloonaghlin L.
NORTHERN IRELAND
An Gleann
N71
Belfast
L. Currane
Sneem
Waterville
Ballinskelligs
St. Finan's Bay
Ballybrack
Staigue Fort
Tuosist
Galway
Dublin
REPUBLIC OF IRELAND
Ballinskelligs Bay
Castlecove
Little Skellig
Bolus Head
Derrynane
Beara Peninsula
Skellig Michael
Derrynane House Nat'l Historic Park
Caherdaniel
Kenmare River
Map Area
Cork
Deenish I.
Lamb's Head
Caha Mts.
Scariff I.
0 5 miles
0 5 kms
Coulagh Bay
CORK
Adrigole
Bantry

a great, mysterious wonder: A TRIP TO THE SKELLIG ISLANDS

"Whoever has not stood in the graveyard on the summit of that cliff, among the beehive dwellings and beehive oratory, does not know Ireland through and through . . . ."

—George Bernard Shaw

The craggy, inhospitable Skellig Islands rise precipitously from the sea. Here gray skies meet stormy horizons about 14km (8 miles) off the coast of the Iveragh Peninsula. From the mainland, **Skellig Michael** and **Little Skellig** appear impossibly sharp-angled and daunting even today—just imagine how perilous the mere act of getting there would have been in the 6th and 7th centuries. Back then, a group of monks built a community on the steepest, most wind-battered peaks. Over time, they carved 600 steps into the cliffs and built monastic buildings hundreds of feet above the ocean. The complex is now a UNESCO World Heritage Site.

There is something tragic and beautiful about the remains of the ancient oratories and beehive cells there. Historians know very little about these monks and how they lived, although they obviously sought intense isolation. Records relating to the Skelligs indicate that even here, all but completely hidden, the monastery was discovered by Vikings, who attacked it as they did all the Irish monastic settlements. Monks were kidnapped and killed in attacks in the 8th century, but the settlement always recovered. To this day, nobody knows why the monks finally abandoned the rock in the 12th century.

Landing is only possible on **Skellig Michael** ♥♥♥, the largest of the islands, where the ruins of the monks' church can be reached by way of rambling stone staircases up the sides of cliffs at the edge of the cobalt sea. Due to its protected status, there's an annual quota for the number of visitors allowed. This was rarely a problem in the past—until a little film franchise called *Star Wars* came along. *The Force Awakens* and *The Last Jedi* were filmed here in 2014 and 2016 respectively (it's

medieval monastery slowly rotting away. The scenic **Skellig Ring** coastal drive leads from here; a sandy Blue Flag beach is just past the post office by Ballinskelligs Bay, and at the end of the beach are the remnants of a 16th-century castle.

Continuing on the N70, the next point of interest is **Derrynane** ♥♥ (p. 328), at **Caherdaniel.** Derrynane is the former seat of the O'Connell clan and erstwhile home to Daniel O'Connell, "the Liberator" who freed Irish Catholics from the last of the English Penal Laws in the 19th century. From there, watch for signs to the prehistoric ruins of **Staigue Fort** ♥♥ (p. 329), about 3km (2 miles) off the main road in a farmer's field.

Sneem, the next village on the circuit, is a colorful little hamlet where houses are painted in vibrant shades, creating a beautiful tableau. The colors—blue, pink, yellow, and orange—burst out on a rainy day, like a little touch of the Mediterranean. There's not much to do in Sneem, but the spectacularly rugged island where Luke Skywalker exiles himself in *The Force Awakens* and *The Last Jedi*—and where Rey finds him), and since then, demand to visit Skellig Michael skyrocketed. So, if you want to have the unique experience of making landfall on Skellig Michael in the summer, it takes a bit of planning. Boat tours to the island are run by individual local companies rather than a central ferry operator. Most, though not all, tours leave from the Portmagee harbor; be sure to check when you book. There are about a dozen of them, most contactable only via their cellphones or their websites, or at their stalls on the beach near Portmagee. Bookings need to be made as far in advance as possible. *Do not assume that you can get a place on the day.* Our advice is to book as soon as you know your travel dates, and be prepared for cancellations in inclement weather.

The Skellig Michael Cruises Company (skelligmichaelcruises.com; ✆ **087/617-8114**) is one of a few boat services currently offering online booking, and it has a good word-of-mouth reputation. Another recommended option with online booking is **Casey's Skellig Islands Tours,** which also offers an ecotour of the puffins and other rare birds that inhabit the islands (skellig islands.com). The Cork and Kerry tourist information centers can also assist, as can your hotel.

The **Skellig Experience** visitor center on Valentia Island (p. 329) offers two boat trips around the Skelligs: a sea cruise ***around*** the Skelligs, which **does not make landfall** (the cost, including admission to the center, is €50 adults, €45 seniors and students, €35 children, and €165 families); or the **Skellig Michael Landing tour** (€125 per person), which allows you to view the monastic ruins up close.

Here's a last little fun fact for *Star Wars* fans: The porgs from *The Last Jedi* were a late addition because it proved impossible to keep all the puffins who live on Skellig Michael out of the shots. Instead of trying to digitally remove the hundreds of inquisitive birds, it was decided to paint over them—and thus, the fluffy little porgs were born.

it's worth a stop just to see it. From here, you're no distance at all from Kenmare, and you've made your way around the Ring.

TOP ATTRACTIONS ON THE RING OF KERRY DRIVE

Ballinskelligs & the Skellig Ring ♥♥ RUINS/RELIGIOUS SITE
West of Waterville, across a small bay, the coastal village of Ballinskelligs contains the absurdly picturesque ruins of **St. Michael Ballinskelligs,** a medieval priory overlooking the sea. A beautiful sandy beach also features the remnants of a 16th-century castle. Ballinskelligs is a starting point for the so-called **Skellig Ring,** a stunning coastal drive that takes in some of the best viewpoints of the mysterious Skellig Islands (see box, above). It also passes through some of the most dramatic scenery in the county, and with the merest fraction of the traffic that can clog the Ring of Kerry. ***Be warned, however:*** Its very remoteness means that this route can be tough going, and the roads are very mountainous in places. This is also

The beach at Ballinskelligs.

the edge of Gaeltacht territory, where Irish is the primary language on road signs. To find the Ring, head south through Ballinskelligs. About .5km (⅓ mile) after the pink An Post building, you'll come to a crossroads. The Skellig Ring (*Morchuaird na Sceilge* in Irish) is signposted to the right. The signs continue throughout the route.

Visitor Information Point: Cafe Cois Trá, Ballinskelligs Beach, Ballinskelligs. ✆ **066/947-4888.** Cafe open daily 9am–6pm (hours may be reduced in winter).

Derrynane House National Historic Park ♥♥ HISTORIC HOUSE Irish political leader and Parliament member Daniel O'Connell (1775–1847) became known as "the Great Liberator" for his successful campaign to repeal the laws that barred Catholics from holding office. He became particularly famous in his lifetime for his so-called "monster meetings," vast public rallies held across the country (one, on the Hill of Tara, was reckoned to have been attended by nearly a million supporters). His house at Caherdaniel contains a museum devoted to his life. Not everything will be of interest to those unfamiliar with his story, but a few items—such as the gilded carriage from which he greeted crowds after a spell as a political prisoner—are worth seeing, as is the setting.

Signposted from N70 (Ring of Kerry Rd.), approx. 3.5km (2 miles) from Caherdaniel. derrynanehouse.ie. ✆ **066/947-5113.** Admission €5 adults; €4 seniors; €3 students and children; €13 families. Mid-Mar to Sept daily 10am–4:45pm; Oct daily 10am–4pm; mid-Nov to early Dec Sat–Sun 10am–3pm. Last admission 45 min. before closing. Tearoom open Mar–Nov.

The Skellig Experience ♥♥ VISITOR CENTER On Valentia Island (reached via a road bridge from Portmagee), this innovative visitor center is devoted to the Skellig Islands and their history. It tells you all about the extraordinary history of Skellig Michael's ancient monastic edifices and the natural history of these seabird-rich islands. The center also offers various boat trips out to see the islands (p. 326).

Valentia Island. skelligexperience.com. ✆ **066/947-6306.** Admission €6 adults; €5 seniors and students; €3.50 children; €17 families. Apr–Sept daily 10am–6pm; Oct daily 10am–5pm; Mar and Nov 5 days a week (days vary each week) 10am–5pm. Last entry 45 min. before closing. Closed Dec–Feb.

Staigue Fort ♥♥ ANCIENT SITE This well-preserved, surprisingly large prehistoric fort is built of rough stones without mortar of any kind. The walls are 4m (13 ft.) thick at the base. Historians are not certain what purpose it served—it may have been a hilltop fortress or a kind of prehistoric community center—but experts think it dates from around 1000 B.C. It's an open site with no visitor center. Look for signs and hike up the path through the field. It's quite something to see.

Off N70 just outside Castlecove, on a small farm road (follow signs 4 km/2½ miles to site). Daily 9am–7pm.

Valentia Lighthouse ♥♥ HERITAGE SITE There's something fascinating about the lonely life of a lighthouse keeper. The last keeper lived here with his family until the lighthouse was automated in 1947, and you can learn more about the conditions and the isolation they must have faced during a visit here. As well as the stunning location overlooking the sea on Valentia Island, the lighthouse has lots of history—it was built on the site of Fleetwood Fort, which dates way back to 1653. The lighthouse opened in 1841. On a 45-minute guided tour you can explore the fort, visit the lightkeeper's house, and climb the 21 steps of the lighthouse tower. The former kitchen is now home to tearooms.

Cromwell Point, Valentia Island. valentialighthouse.ie. ✆ **066/947-6985.** Admission €8.50 adults; €7.50 seniors and students; €5 children 11 and under; €21.10 families. Mar–Oct 10:30am–5:30pm. Last entry 5pm.

At Valentia Lighthouse, re-created rooms evoke the isolated life of keepers and their families.

WHERE TO STAY ALONG THE RING OF KERRY

Although the Ring of Kerry is easily driven as a day excursion from Killarney or Kenmare, don't overlook the option of staying overnight in the countryside or in one of the small towns along the Ring—and it just may save you a few euros, too.

Ard na Sidhe Country House ♥♥♥ *Ard na Sidhe* means "Hill of the Fairies" in Irish, and this beautiful Arts and Crafts house does look quite magical as it appears in the folds of the green Irish hills near Killorglin. With only 18 bedrooms and tucked away on gorgeous grounds, it's the perfect place to hide away from the world. Rooms are done in muted shades with firm king-size beds, modern bathrooms, and peaceful views. The lounges are like elegant living rooms, with sofas clustered around wood-burning fireplaces. The in-house restaurant is simply fabulous, with European-influenced Irish cuisine, using locally sourced, seasonal produce in a relaxed but delightful setting. This place is well worth the drive. Caragh Lake, Killorglin. ardnasidhe.com. ✆ **066/976-9105.** 18 units. €275–€290 double. Breakfast included. Free parking. **Amenities:** Restaurant; croquet; Wi-Fi (free). Closed mid-Oct to mid Apr.

Kells Bay House & Gardens ♥♥ Anyone who loves gardens, birdsong, and the sea will fall in love with this place. It's on the Ring of Kerry overlooking Dingle Bay, making it a great stop if you are driving the Ring. The 17 hectares (42 acres) of gardens are famed for exotic plants and

Guest room in the Ard na Sidhe Country House.

ferns; owner Billy Alexander, a renowned horticulturist, won a gold medal at England's prestigious Chelsea Flower Show in 2021. Rooms are cozy, and most in the main house have garden views; others have mountain or bay views, and some have all three. Private suites to the side of the house are adjacent to a primeval forest and walled garden. What's nice about an overnight stay here is that you can roam the gardens freely when day visitors have left, and you have direct access to a beach.

Kells, Cahersiveen. kellsbay.ie. ✆ **066/947-7975.** 9 units. €110–€290 double. 2-night minimum stay in peak season. Rates include garden entry. Free parking. **Amenities:** Restaurant; bar; Wi-Fi (free). Closed Jan.

The Moorings ♥♥ A bright, cheery building overlooking the seafront in Portmagee, the Moorings has guest rooms as well as a popular bar and restaurant. Rooms are decently sized, and decor is fresh and modern; some rooms have sea views, and there are larger rooms for families. You won't need to go far for dinner, with local produce and fresh seafood in the **Moorings Restaurant** or **Bridge Bar** (the daily specials often feature the catch of the day), and the bar has regular traditional music sessions. They can also arrange Skellig boat trips (p. 326) from the nearby pier. This is a lively spot.

Portmagee. moorings.ie. ✆ **066/947-7108.** 17 units. €120–€180 double. Breakfast included. Free parking. **Amenities:** Restaurant; bar; Wi-Fi (free).

Parknasilla Resort ♥♥ Set on a 500-acre estate right on the lake shore overlooking Kenmare Bay, Parknasilla has some of the loveliest views along the Ring of Kerry. The classically decorated rooms have either mountain or sea views, and cottages and villas dot the tree-lined grounds. You'll have plenty to do here, with walking trails, a walled garden, tennis courts, and a 12-hole golf course, plus extra activities like kayaking or guided seashore walks. There's a heated indoor pool, but you can also have a refreshing dip in the Atlantic waters and then relax in one of the outdoor hot tubs or heated outdoor infinity pool afterwards.

Sneem. parknasillaresort.com. ✆ **064/667-5600.** 85 units. €290–€420 double; €450–€550 suite. Breakfast included. Free parking. **Amenities:** Restaurant; bar; tennis; golf; swimming pool; gym; Wi-Fi (free). Closed Jan to mid–Mar.

Quinlan & Cooke ♥♥ More of a restaurant-with-rooms than a small hotel, this is a stylish and unique place to stay. Bedrooms are open-plan contemporary spaces with a minimalist vibe: polished wood floors, huge skylights, and clawfoot tubs, plus a few high-tech extras such as Bose stereos. The guest lounge looks as if it's tumbled from the pages of a decor magazine, with deep velvet sofas and a cozy wood-burning stove. The superb restaurant **QC's** specializes in fresh local seafood (such as Valentia scallop Mornay) and steaks cooked to perfection, accompanied by sides like scallion mashed potatoes. A continental breakfast is served in the room (there's no cooked breakfast option).

3 Main St., Cahersiveen. qc.ie. ✆ **066/947-2244.** 11 units. €150–€250 double. Breakfast included. Free parking. **Amenities:** Restaurant; gym; Wi-Fi (free).

walk this way: THE KERRY WAY

Serious hikers test their chops on the **Kerry Way,** a long-distance trail that traverses extraordinary scenery while roughly following the Ring of Kerry. Ireland's longest marked hiking trail, the 202km (126-mile) route includes several "green roads" (old, unused roads built as Famine relief projects and now converted into walking paths).

The first stage, from Killarney National Park to Glenbeigh, travels inland over rolling hills and past pastoral scenes. The second stage circles the Iveragh Peninsula and takes in spectacular ocean views, passing through picturesque towns including Cahersiveen, Waterville, colorful Sneem, and lovely Kenmare. The final inland walk brings you via the old Kenmare Road back to Killarney.

The walk is steep in places—the highest point is 385m (1,200 ft.) in a section known as Windy Gap. There are long stretches of wilderness between civilization—walkers attempting the entire path, or even substantial portions of it, need to prepare carefully. But some short stretches can be easily accessed and make for gentle afternoon walks, suitable for amateurs.

Maps outlining the route, and the best short walks, are available from the Killarney and Kenmare tourist offices. For details, see **kerryway.com**.

WHERE TO EAT ON THE RING OF KERRY DRIVE

Some of the best foodie options are found in the area hotels—**Ard na Sidhe Country House** in Killorglin (p. 330) has one of the finest restaurants on the Ring of Kerry, and Quinlan & Cooke's **QC's** in Cahersiveen (qc.ie; see above) is a stellar gastropub, with gorgeous seafood sourced by the owner's own fishing fleet. **The Moorings** (p. 331) in Portmagee also features local seafood fresh from the harbor.

Caherdaniel

The Blind Piper ♥♥ IRISH This friendly, lively pub is one of the top places to eat in Caherdaniel. The menu is straightforward comfort food—toasted sandwiches, hake with mushy peas and fries, or roast of the day with mashed potato, vegetables, and gravy. Live traditional music sessions liven up the place on Tuesday and Thursday nights in July and August from 9:30pm. ***Note:*** The Blind Piper is a bit hard to find. Turn off N70 road in Caherdaniel next to the big red building in the center of the village. The pub is bright yellow.

Off main Ring of Kerry Rd. (N70), Caherdaniel. blindpiperpub.ie. ✆ **066/947-5126.** Entrees €14–€30. Daily 12:30–7:45pm.

Killorglin

Bianconi ♥♥ GASTROPUB In a rambling Victorian pub, this restaurant has a surprisingly modern menu. Light meals are served up to 5:30pm, with toasted sandwiches on bloomer bread, huge, fresh salads, and seafood chowder. The dinner menu starts at 6pm, and the dishes are true gastropub fare. Start with the Dingle goat's cheese cheesecake, or the oak smoked salmon and baby prawn roulade. Mains might include an Irish prime beef steak with a choice of sauces and sides, the seafood platter, or tempura fish and chips. Upstairs, the stylish guest rooms (€105–€160) are a great option if you need a place to base yourself.

Lower Bridge St., Killorglin. bianconi.ie. ✆ **066/976-1146.** Lunch €5–€25, dinner entrees €21–€37. Daily 10:15am–5:30pm and 6–9pm.

Jack's Coastguard Restaurant ♥♥ SEAFOOD/MODERN IRISH This cheery restaurant lists "Water's Edge" as its address. That's not so much a street name as a description; it's right on the harbor in Cromane, a tiny village near Killorglin. The dining room is a bright, modern space boasting beautiful views of the bay, while a pianist plays away in the corner. As you can imagine, the specialties are mostly seafood, but the menu always finds room for some meatier options, too. For dessert, try the delicious apple and blackberry crumble.

Water's Edge, Cromane Lower, Killorglin. jackscromane.com. ✆ **085/746-9233.** Entrees €25–€38. Bar daily 4–11pm; restaurant Thurs–Sun 5–9pm. Sun lunch 1–3pm. Winter hours vary. Closed Jan. Reservations encouraged.

Kingdom 1795 ♥♥ MODERN IRISH This gorgeous restaurant takes its casual style from its former life as a pub—1795 is the date of the first lease—and it has been given a stylish contemporary update by its owners, host Suzi and chef Damien, with informal seating and marble-topped tables. The food is exquisite: creative dishes largely based on seasonal ingredients from local suppliers. You might see Wagyu beef blade and brisket served with cabbage, stout mustard, and house butter, as well as seafood and duck, or a kohlrabi pie with truffle ketchup, ramsons, and Coolattin cheese.

Main St., Killorglin. kingdom1795.com. ✆ **066/979-6527.** Set menu: 2 courses €50, 3 courses €60. Wed–Sun 6:30–9pm.

Portmagee

The Fisherman's Bar ♥♥ IRISH This traditional Irish pub near the pier at Portmagee has some of the freshest seafood on the menu, with everything from crab claws to squid, prawns, lobster, and smoked salmon. Order the platter for a true feast. Meat options include juicy steaks and burgers. Add a fresh pint of stout and you're all set—and a bonus is the outside seating in good weather.

2 Harbour View, Portmagee. fishermansbarportmagee.com. ✆ **066/947-7103.** Entrees €16–€32. Daily noon–4:30pm and 6–8:30pm (closes 8pm Oct–May).

Sneem

Bridge Café & Bistro ♥♥ CAFE This cafe and bistro right beside the river in Sneem is a great place to stop for breakfast or lunch while touring the Ring of Kerry. The food here is unpretentious and fabulously fresh. Choose the full Irish breakfast, a stack of pancakes, or zested avocado mash on toast in the morning, or tasty fish, chips, and mushy peas for lunch. There's outdoor seating, and dogs are catered to with a special menu of "pup cakes" and "pooch bowls." The gourmet hot chocolates and coffees are excellent, and it even serves cocktails.

Bridge St., Sneem. ✆ **064/667-5858.** Entrees €6–€24. Thurs–Tues 9am–5pm. Closed Wed.

The Village Kitchen ♥♥ IRISH This busy village cafe has a country kitchen vibe and a simple menu of staples like soup, fish and chips, burgers, toasted sandwiches, and scones, all of which it does very well. The Village Toastie comes with a side salad and chips, and the Wicklow Farmhouse brie toastie will keep you going for the day. All this might explain why the cafe gets busy—expect to see everyone from passing tourists to the local parish priest. It has some tables outside for fine weather.

3 Bridge St., Sneem. facebook.com/villagekitchensneem. ✆ **064/664-5281.** Entrees €11–€18. Tues–Sun 9:30am–4pm. Closed Mon.

Wharton's Traditional Fish & Chips ♥♥ FISH & CHIPS Not actually a restaurant at all, but a food truck on the roadside at Templenoe, between Sneem and Kenmare (it's around 6km/3½ miles from Kenmare), this is an outstanding "chipper," with a traditional menu of (usually) cod and hake—although asking if you'd prefer your fish battered or fried in breadcrumbs is a nice twist. It's nothing fancy, but that's half the point—this is real Irish fast food.

Greenane, Templenoe. facebook.com/whartonstraditionalfishandchips. ✆ **083/348-7505.** Entrees around €14.50 (half portions from €10). Tues–Sun 4–8pm (days can vary depending on the week).

TRALEE

With a population of 24,000, the Kerry capital is nearly twice the size of Killarney. It's a lively workaday place, rather than a tourist center, but the advantage of basing yourself here is that you are surrounded by locals rather than tourists. Tralee Town is near both the Ring of Kerry and the Dingle Peninsula, but it's also a gateway to the lesser-explored North Kerry, popular for its beaches and golf courses. It's also home to **Siamsa Tíre,** the National Folk Theatre of Ireland (siamsatire.com; ✆ **066/712-3055**), which has a program of festivals and performances celebrating Ireland's cultural heritage.

Exploring In & Around Tralee

Blennerville Windmill ♥♥ LANDMARK Reaching 20m (66 ft.) into the sky, this snow-white windmill must surely be the most photographed object in Tralee. Perched at the edge of the river, the windmill has blades that still turn, which makes it rare in this part of the world. Built in 1800, it flourished until 1850, when it was largely abandoned. After decades of neglect, it was restored and is now fully operational. You can

The restored Blennerville Windmill.

climb to the top and see some of its complex inner workings in detail. The visitor complex is also home to the Kerry Model Railway and an exhibition on emigration (Blennerville was a major point of departure). The windmill is about a mile outside central Tralee on N86.

Windmill St., Blennerville. blennervillewindmill.ie. ✆ **066/712-1064.** Admission €8 adults; €6 seniors and students; €4 children; free for children 4 and under; €22 families. June–Aug daily 9:30am–5:30pm; Apr–May and Sept–Oct Tues–Sat 9:30am–5pm. Closed Nov–Mar.

Crag Cave ♥♥ UNDERGROUND CAVERNS Although they are believed to be more than a million years old, these limestone caves were not discovered until 1983. Visitors take 70 steps down 3,753m (12,310 ft.) into the well-lit cave passage, for a self-guided audio tour (make sure your phone is charged in advance) to see the massive stalactites and fascinating caverns. It's touristy but interesting nonetheless. Be prepared to climb back up the steps, and dress warmly as the cave temperature is 10°C (50°F). A children's play area (endearingly called **Crazy Cave**) is an extra €9 per child (€7 ages 1–2, €5 ages 7–11 months, free for accompanying adults). The **Garden Cafe** is a useful stop for a quick bite.

College Rd., Castleisland (turn left off N21 onto Main St., then left onto College Rd.). cragcave.com. ✆ **066/714-1244.** Admission €15 adults; €12 seniors and students; €6 children; free children 3 and under; €35–€40 families. Apr–Nov daily 10am–6pm; Dec Thurs–Sun 10am–6pm; Jan–Mar Fri–Sun 10am–6pm. Tours every half-hour May–Aug, no set times rest of year.

Kerry County Museum ♥ MUSEUM Spanning several thousand years of history up to the present day, this museum's galleries cover Kerry's ancient past; the coming of the Normans and the medieval period; the Famine years; and the struggle for independence. The fun part is the Medieval Experience, where you can wander around a re-created medieval town, with requisite sound effects, dressed-up mannequins, and the like (children can dress in costume). The museum is in the town's Ashe Memorial Hall, the same building as the Tralee tourist information center, beside Tralee Town Park.

Ashe Memorial Hall, Denny St. kerrymuseum.ie. ✆ **066/712-7777.** Admission €5 adults, free for accompanying children; €10 families. June–Aug daily 9:30am–5:30pm; Sept–May Tues–Sat 9:30am–5pm. Last admission 4pm.

The Seanchaí: Kerry Writers' Museum ♥♥ MUSEUM In the heritage town of Listowel, this imaginative museum's innovative displays

COULD YOU BE THE rose OF TRALEE?

A 19th-century song about a local girl named Mary O'Connor is at the root of this unique festival, which sets out each year to find and crown the famous **Rose of Tralee.** William Mulchinock's tear-jerker tune about the girl he was stopped by fate from marrying so caught the public's imagination that more than 100 years later, it is still performed in Irish pubs worldwide. Thus, in 1959 the idea was born for a contest to crown the loveliest lass in Tralee.

The competition has evolved from a beauty pageant to an international event that celebrates all that's good about Irish culture and heritage. While many Irish people view it as slightly cheesy, it does connect the global Irish community around the world—the winner takes on an ambassadorial role to represent Ireland and the festival with a year-long international tour that includes charity work.

Every August, the town fills with the 32 young women vying for the title, many flying in from around the world. The contest rules are fairly generous in terms of who is Irish, not to mention Traleean—the rules require contestants to be of Irish birth or ancestry, so past winners have been from places as far-flung as the U.S. and Australia. Each "rose" is accompanied by a designated male escort for the festival (escort in the old-fashioned sense—they provide support and companionship for the Roses and that's it), and to reward the best escort, there is even a "Rose Escort of the Year" award.

The festival lasts 5 days, during which time the entire town becomes somewhat obsessed with it—restaurants, pubs, and theaters all get involved in hosting events related to the Rose of Tralee.

If you want to join in the fun, or if you know a girl with an Irish last name who would make a good Rose, contact the **Rose of Tralee Festival Office** (roseoftralee.ie; ✆ **066/712-1322**).

often feel more like art installations devoted to the life and work of various Kerry writers from the past and present. Life-size statues sit hunched over books and even propping up a bar, with the text of their best-known works covering them from head to toe. Self-guided audio tours take 1½ hours. Listowel is 26km (16 miles) northeast of Tralee on N69. Drop in to **Listowel Castle** next door to see the remains of the 15th-century fortress. 24 The Square, Listowel. kerrywritersmuseum.com. ✆ **068/22212.** Admission €10 adults; €8 seniors and students; €5 children 11–17; €20 families. Mon–Fri 10am–5pm; also open Sat 10am–5pm July–Aug; last admission 4pm. Listowel Castle: The Square, Listowel. heritageireland.ie. ✆ **086/3857209**. Admission and tours free. May–Sept daily 10am–6pm. Last admission 5:15pm.

Where to Stay & Eat in Tralee

Ballygarry Estate Hotel ♥♥ Also on the outer edge of Tralee, this is a pleasant country inn. The original manor house has been extended over the years, but the inside still has an old-world feel. Elegant guest rooms maintain the country-mansion air, and superior rooms are spacious, with king-size beds. The in-house **Nádúr Spa** is a relaxing hideaway, while the outdoor hot tubs and thermal garden overlooking fields and distant mountains are a calming oasis. There are also complimentary bicycles for guests, a gym, foraging walks, a children's fairy trail, and woodland walks. The **Brasserie** restaurant serves excellent modern Irish food, and there's also **Owen Mac's** pub and more formal **Restaurant 58.** Check the website for special offers.

Signposted off N21, Leebrook, approx. 3.3km (2 miles) W of Tralee. ballygarry.com. ✆ **066/712-3322.** 64 units. €139–€264 double; €259–€509 suite. Breakfast included. Free parking. **Amenities:** Restaurant; bar; spa; Wi-Fi (free).

Ballyseede Castle ♥♥♥ If you were to imagine a romantic Irish castle—with turrets, drawing rooms filled with antiques, portraits and marble fireplaces, plus luxurious bedrooms, Ballyseede Castle would probably fit the bill. It even has two Irish wolfhounds, plus 30 acres of gardens and woodland for strolls. It's all done with homey charm rather than over-the-top luxury, and the best thing about it is that to stay or eat here will not break the budget—the "cosy rooms" offering particular value. For dining, there's a choice of **O'Connell Restaurant** or the **Stone Room,** plus a more informal menu and afternoon tea served in the bright **Orangery** or on the outside terrace. Needless to say, it's a popular wedding venue. It's just outside Tralee, so the location is handy for exploring the Dingle Peninsula and North County Kerry.

Signposted off N21, approx. 5km (3.1 miles) W of Tralee. ballyseedecastle.com. ✆ **066/712-5799.** 45 units. €207–€322 double; €335–€529 suite. Breakfast included. Free parking. **Amenities:** 2 restaurants; bar; Wi-Fi (free).

Kate Brown's ♥♥ IRISH This is a charming country-style pub and restaurant in the village of Ardfert, around 9km (5½ miles) northwest from Tralee Town. The outdoor seating fills up quickly on a fine day. The good selection of seafood dishes ranges from beer-battered fish and chips to baked Dingle crab au gratin. Steaks from a local farm come in 10-ounce Hereford sirloins, rib-eyes, and filets. The menu also has vegetarian dishes and salads, plus daily specials. Leave room for dessert or the selection of Irish cheese.

Farranwilliam, Ardfert. katebrowns.ie. ✆ **066/713-4055.** Entrees €11–€38. Mon–Sat 10:30am–11:30pm; Sun noon–11:30pm.

The Oyster Tavern ♥♥ IRISH Once a country pub, this popular restaurant in the village of Spa, around 11km (7 miles) west from Tralee Town, has been serving the freshest seafood since the 1970s, including oysters from the natural beds on the nearby shore, which can be ordered by the half-dozen. The restaurant menu features everything from seafood chowder or steamed mussels to poached monkfish and seafood tagliatelle (meat dishes, too). The shorter bar menu has a selection of light bites or mains, and there are regular live music sessions in the bar.

The Spa, Knockanush West. theoystertavern.ie. ✆ **066/713-6102.** Entrees €16–€30. Mon–Wed 5–9pm; Thurs–Sat 5–9:30pm; Sun 12:30–8pm.

Sports & Outdoor Pursuits in Tralee

GOLF The Arnold Palmer–designed **Tralee Golf Club,** Fenit/Churchill Road, West Barrow, Ardfert (traleegolfclub.com; ✆ **066/713-6379**), overlooking the Atlantic 13km (8 miles) northwest of town, is one of the most spectacularly situated courses in Ireland. Greens fees are a pricey €375 in high season (mid-Apr to mid-Oct), and €200 for the first two weeks in April.

Former U.S. President Bill Clinton's favorite Irish course, **Ballybunion Golf Club,** Ballybunion (ballybuniongolfclub.ie; ✆ **068/27146**), is about 40km (25 miles) north of Tralee in the northwest corner of County Kerry. This facility has two challenging 18-hole seaside links, both on cliffs overlooking the Shannon River estuary and the Atlantic. Tom Watson has rated Ballybunion's Old Course one of the finest in the world, while the Cashen Course was designed by Robert Trent Jones, Sr. Greens fees are €125 for the Cashen Course and €350 for the Old Course (or play both for €450).

CYCLING The **Tralee to Fenit Greenway** is a 13.6km (8.45-mile) walking and cycling route along the old railway from Tralee town through rolling countryside to the seaside village of Fenit, with mountain and sea views along the way. At **Tralee Bike Rental** (traleebikerental.ie) on Edward Street (behind Tralee Train Station), bike hire starts from €25 per day.

THE DINGLE PENINSULA

North of the Ring of Kerry, the Dingle Peninsula offers its own scenic drives, lively pubs, and ancient heritage sites, without all the tourist congestion. In summer, Dingle Town can get busy with travelers, but otherwise this is a sleepy little place, filled with color and wonderful to explore. The peninsula is also in the Gaeltacht or Irish-speaking area so road signs and place names will be in Irish.

West of Dingle Town, a stunning coastal drive known as the **Slea Head Drive** is lined with archaeological sites and has views over the Blasket Islands. (It's also a memorable route for cycling.) Some of Ireland's finest beaches line both sides of the peninsula (p. 349), and the views are spectacular. Walkers can tackle the challenges of the **Dingle Way** (p. 348).

Exploring the Dingle Peninsula

DINGLE TOWN

A charming, brightly colored little town at the foot of steep hills, **Dingle** (which is called ***Daingean Uí Chúis*** in Irish—the town is in the Gaeltacht or Irish-speaking area) is worth a visit for a stroll around its pubs, cafes, and Irish craft shops. It also has plenty of hotels and restaurants so it's a good base for exploring the region and it's one of the starting points for

The Dingle Peninsula
Ballyferriter 6
The Blasket Centre (Ionad an Bhlascaoid Mhóir) 5
Dingle Oceanworld Aquarium 1
Dunbeg Fort 4
Eask Tower 2
Gallarus Oratory 7
Irish Famine Cottage 3
Sciuird Archaeological Adventures 1
ATLANTIC OCEAN
The Seven Hogs (Magharee Is.)
Tralee Bay
Brandon Pt.
Maharees Peninsula
Brandon Bay
Brandon
L. Gill
Castlegregory (Caislean an Ghriare)
Dingle Way
Beenmore
Brandon Mtn.
Cloghane
Fermoyle
Stradbally
Camp
Stradbally Mtn.
NORTHERN IRELAND
Belfast
Dublin
Galway
REPUBLIC OF IRELAND
Map Area
Cork
Ballynabuck
Feohanagh
L. Cruite
Brandon Pk.
L. Slat
Dingle Peninsula
The Three Sisters
Smerwick Hbr.
Murreagh
Slea Head Drive
Conor Pass
Slievanea
L. Anscaul
Sybil Pt.
Ballyferriter
An Cnapan Mor
Cnoc Mhaoilionain
N86
Clogher
R559
Pilgrim's Route
Dingle (An Daingean)
Lispole
Annascaul
Inch
R559
Ventry
N86
Lugnagappul
R561
Inishtooskert
Dunquin
Kinard
Ventry Hbr.
Blasket Islands
R559
Reenbeg Pt.
Parkmore Pt.
Bull's Hd.
Minard Hd.
Kilmurray Bay
Cromane
Inch Pt.
Slea Head
Tearaght
Great Blasket Island
Dingle Bay
Inishnabro
Inishvickillane
0 2 miles
0 2 kms

boats and ferries to Dingle Bay and the Blasket Islands. The town is lively in summer: Its busiest time is in August, when the **Dingle Races** draw crowds to watch the horses run every other weekend. (The racetrack is just outside town on N86.) In the last week of August, the **Dingle Regatta** fills the harbor with traditional Irish *currach* boats in a vivid display of color and history.

Boat Tours of Dingle Bay ♥♥ BOAT TOUR Dingle Bay's most famous former resident, Fungie the dolphin, put the area on the map from 1983 to 2000, when he drew dolphin-loving crowds to see his interactions with swimmers, kayakers, and tour boats. His legacy lives on, and there's still a chance to see dolphins on a boat trip in Dingle Bay. One of the best is the 4-hour Dolphin & Whale Watching Tour with **Blasket Island Eco Marine Tours** from Ventry Pier, 7km (4⅓ miles) from Dingle, where an on-board wildlife guide will point out marine habitats around the coastline and the Blasket Islands (p. 342), with the chance to spot puffins and seals too. The full-day tour includes 3 hours on Great Blasket Island (p. 342); they also offer a 3-hour **Morning Sea Safari.** From Dingle Town, the 3-hour Blasket Island Adventure Tour with **Dingle Dolphin Tours** takes in Dingle Bay and the islands, where you might spot seals, dolphins, whales, and basking sharks depending on the season and weather. A 1-hour Dingle Bay cliff tour (€15 adults; €10 children) explores tunnels, cliffs, sea caves, and the Dingle Lighthouse.

Blasket Island Eco Marine Tours, Ventry Pier: marinetours.ie. ✆ **086/335-3805**. Ecotour €79/person; full-day tour €89/person; morning sea safari €59 adults or €29.50 children 11 and under. Apr–Oct daily 1pm (ecotour) or 10am (full-day tour). **Dingle Dolphin Tours,** The Pier, Dingle: dingledolphin.com. ✆ **066/915-2626.** €60 adults; €40 children (tour recommended for ages 10 and over). July–Aug daily 2pm; Apr–June and Sept to mid-Oct Wed and Sat 2pm. All tours weather permitting.

Dingle Oceanworld Aquarium ♥♥ AQUARIUM Though it's quite small, given the ticket price, this is a nicely designed aquarium, home to lots of sea critters in creatively designed tanks. You can walk through an aquarium tunnel with fish swimming above and around you, visit a butterfly oasis, and interact at the touch tank, where kids can pet starfish and rays. The aquarium also has some super-cute Antarctic Gentoo penguins. This compact, hands-on, interactive place makes a good reward for your kids for being patient while you took pictures of a pile of rocks back up the road. For feeding times and talks, see online timetable.

Dingle Harbour. dingle-oceanworld.ie. ✆ **066/915-2111.** Admission €20 adults; €15.50 seniors and students; €14 children 3–16; €63–€72 families. Daily 10am–6pm. Last admission 1 hr. before closing.

Eask Tower ♥ LANDMARK Built in 1847 as a Famine relief project, this 12m-tall (39-ft.) tower is built of solid stone nearly 5m (16 ft.) thick with a wooden arrow pointing to the mouth of the harbor. It is certainly interesting to look at, but the main reason for making the 1.6km (1-mile) climb to the summit of Carhoo Hill is to see the incredible views of Dingle Harbour, and, on the far side of the bay, the Iveragh Peninsula.

Carhoo Hill. From Dingle, follow Slea Head Rd. 3.2km (2 miles), turn left at road signposted for Colâiste Ide, and continue another 3.2km (2 miles).

Sciúird Archaeological Adventures ♥♥ TOUR For serious history buffs, these tours are a great opportunity to get deeper insight into how prehistoric settlers and early Christians left their mark on the Dingle Peninsula. Led by archaeologist Micheál O Coileain, the tours last 3 hours and involve a short bus journey and some easy walking. Four or five monuments, from the Stone Age to medieval times, are on the route. Tours start from the top of the pier, although pickups from your hotel are possible if you're staying locally. Tour groups are limited to 12 people and reservations are required, at least a day or so in advance if possible.

Dingle Town. ancientdingle.com. ✆ **087/419-8617.** Tour €50 per person. Apr–Sept daily 10am; rest of year by appointment.

THE SLEA HEAD DRIVE

Looping around the western tip of the Dingle Peninsula, the magnificent **Slea Head Drive ♥♥♥** offers rugged coastal vistas, unspoiled islands, and mossy archaeological sites—some of the Wild Atlantic Way at its best. At any tourist information center, you can get a Dingle Peninsula map with the various ruined abbeys, old forts, and main sightseeing points

Spectacular coastal vistas lie at every turn along the Slea Head Drive.

listed on it. Sights below are listed in the order you'll pass them when you drive the loop clockwise (the road is narrow, and you need to drive it clockwise to avoid bottlenecks where only one vehicle can pass). This way, you also get the wow factor of sweeping coastal views as soon as you leave Dingle. ***Note:*** This is in the Gaeltacht (Irish-speaking) area, so by law, all signs—even road-hazard signs—are in Irish.

Leaving Dingle by car, head southwest along R559 through the town of Ventry, following the **Slea Head Drive** road markers. **Slea Head (*Ceann Sléibhe*),** at the southwestern edge of the peninsula, has pristine beaches, great walks, and extensive archaeological remains such as **Dunbeg Fort (*Dún Beag*)** ♥ (p. 343). After rounding the Head, go north to the village of **Dunquin *(Dún Chaoin),*** stunningly situated between Slea Head and Clogher Head, where you can catch ferries to the abandoned **Blasket Islands (*Na Blascaodaí*)** (see below). Just past Dunquin is the **Great Blasket Centre *(Ionad an Bhlascaoid)*** (p. 343), which has a cliff-top viewing point.

Back on the Slea Head Drive, the scenery opens up to take in some stark moorland on your right, in contrast to the ever-spectacular coastal views on the left. There are plenty of spots to safely pull over for pictures on this stretch. If the sun is out, this section is jaw-dropping. The weather is also dramatic; incoming squalls can hit you suddenly, like an icy, wet wall. Pause to browse the excellent pottery at **Louis Mulcahy** ♥♥ (p. 348), which looks out toward **Clogher Strand,** a pretty, coastal inlet (at the 2 o'clock position if you're standing outside the pottery).

A few miles north and east along the coast, the sleepy village of **Ballyferriter (*Baile an Fheirtearaigh*)** ♥ has an Iron Age fort and **Músaem Chorca Dhuibhne** (westkerrymuseum.com; June–Sept daily 10am–5pm), with exhibits on the area's natural and cultural heritage plus a small bookshop and cafe. Continue along R559 and you'll soon see signs for the **Gallarus Oratory** (p. 343), a beautifully preserved early Christian church. From here, continue on the loop back to Dingle, 8km (5 miles) farther along R559, and you've completed the Slea Head Drive.

The Blasket Islands ♥♥ HERITAGE/NATURE SITE Overshadowed by the more famous Skelligs (p. 326), the Blaskets are another group of mysterious, abandoned islands off the Kerry coast, but with more recent stories to tell. For hundreds of years these were home to an isolated community with a rich tradition of storytelling and folklore—all in Irish, of course—that was well documented in the late 1800s. In 1953, however, the islands were considered too dangerous for habitation, and the Irish government ordered a mandatory evacuation. The only island you can actually visit is the largest, **Great Blasket,** where the cottage ruins remain—an eerie ghost town in an outstandingly beautiful setting. There are free daily 1-hour tours of the abandoned village in summer (btw. 11:30am–2:30pm). A stunning 13km (8-mile) walking route stretches to the west end of the island, passing sea cliffs and beaches of ivory sand.

Great Blasket Village.

Worth a visit beforehand (or if you don't get out to the island itself) is the **Great Blasket Centre *(Ionad an Bhlascaoid)*,** on the mainland in Dunquin, which tells the story of the islands through thoughtful exhibits; there's also a cliff-top viewing point and cafe. You can reach Great Blasket Island by 20-minute ferry (weather permitting) from Dunquin Pier in April through September, from 10:30am to 1:30pm, returning from 2 to 5pm (blasketferry.ie, ✆ **087-4488-330**). Return tickets are €40 adults and €25 children 15 and under. Six-hour trips aboard the ***Peig Sayers*** (greatblasketisland.net/boat-trips; ✆ **086/313-5098**), a rigid inflatable vessel, include a 3½- to 4-hour stop on Great Blasket; it leaves from Dingle Marina at 11am daily from April through October. The cost is €85 per person. Full-day trips with **Blasket Island Eco Marine Tours** (p. 340) from Ventry also include a landing on Great Blasket.

Great Blasket Centre (*Ionad an Bhlascaoid*), Dunquin (*Dún Chaoin*). blasket.ie. ✆ **066/915-6444.** Admission €5 adults; €4 seniors; €3 students and youth; children 7 and under free; €13 families. Late Mar to mid-Nov daily 10am–6pm. Last admission 45 min. before closing.

Dunbeg Fort *(Dún Beag)* ♥ RUINS Sitting atop a sheer cliff just east of Slea Head, outside the village of Ventry, this 5th-century fort's stony walls rise from the cliff edge as if they were always part of it. The round Iron Age structure's stone walls are still mostly sturdy, although part of the fort fell into the sea during storms in 2014 and 2017. Walk around the fort to see where other fortifications and "beehive" huts were built inside the walls thousands of years ago. There's also a mysterious underground passage. A short video at the visitor center gives more information about the fort's history, and there's also a cafe.

Fahan, Slea Head Dr. dunbeagfort.com. ✆ **086/173-7724.** Admission €3.50 adults; €2.50 students and seniors; €1.50 children. Apr–Oct daily 10am–4pm.

Gallarus Oratory ♥ RELIGIOUS SITE Built sometime between the 7th and 9th centuries, this tiny, beehive-shaped chapel is one of the best-preserved pieces of early Christian architecture in Ireland. Its walls and roof are made entirely of dry stones without mortar—yet the interior stays remarkably dry (not quite dry enough, sadly, to avoid damage during the heavy floods that hit Ireland in 2014, though the repairs are seamless). If the visitor center is closed, you can just walk around back and straight up

KERRY SEAS: IRELAND'S NEWEST national park

Ireland's newest and largest national park is based around the coastal waters off County Kerry and was created to protect the area's marine diversity and coastal landscape. *Páirc Náisiúnta na Mara, Ciarraí*—Kerry Seas National Park—is also Ireland's first marine park, and it became a reality when the lands around 455m-high (1,496-ft.) Conor Pass (the scenic mountain road that crosses the Dingle Peninsula; see p. 345) were brought into public ownership in 2024. The 70,000-acre park is quite spread out (don't expect one entrance gate or visitor center) and includes various sites including islands off the County Kerry coast such as the Skelligs (p. 326); an underwater limestone reef called the Kerry Head Shoal; the sand dunes at Inch Beach; the waters around the Blasket Islands (p. 342); and some of 952m (3,123-ft.) Mount Brandon, on the Dingle Peninsula. Plans for future educational and visitor facilities in the park were being developed at press time.

the little path to the next field, where the oratory is located. You can't get any closer than this by car, but the uphill walk only takes a minute or two from the parking lot. Nearby is the single surviving tower of 15th-century **Gallarus Castle.** Tours are self-guided, but you can watch the 10-minute film inside the visitor center for information about the site.

Gallarus. gallarusoratory.ie. ✆ **066/915-5333.** Free admission to site. Visitor center €5 adults; €4 seniors and students; €12 family. Apr–Oct daily 9am–7pm or on request during off-season. Signposted down small farm road off R559, 7km (4⅓ miles) NW of Dingle, 4.8km (3 miles) W of Ballyferriter.

Irish Famine Cottage ♥ HERITAGE SITE This cottage isn't a replica; it's a real dwelling, maintained as it would have been at the time it was abandoned during the Great Famine years of the mid–19th century. The humble stone building, scattered with pieces of furniture, is a stark and haunting sight, perched on a windswept cliff overlooking the coast. You can't go inside, but looking in through the windows gives a powerful enough impression of what life was really like for the rural poor. Kids get a little bowl of feed to give to the animals in the field. ***Note:*** The cottage is a short walk uphill from the parking lot, so it may not be suitable for those with mobility problems. They also run **sheepdog demonstrations,** where visitors can see a farmer herding sheep with his dogs, and a **Petting Farm** with ponies, donkeys, and lambs.

Signposted from R559, Slea Head Dr., Fahan, Ventry. dinglesheepdogs.com/cottage. ✆ **087/762-2617.** Famine cottage €3. Cottage, sheepdog show, and petting farm €10. Apr–Oct Mon–Sat 9am–6pm.

OTHER SCENIC DRIVES

If you're heading back toward Killarney and the Ring of Kerry from here, there are two routes—the main N86 (known locally as the "Low Road"), which is pretty enough, or the smaller but more memorable "High Road," which goes over the mountains via the **Conor Pass.** The road is narrow and lacks passing places at a few points you really wish it didn't, but the views are nothing short of incredible—and to preserve its beauty, the area is now part of the **Kerry Seas National Park** (p. 344). The best viewpoint is a small parking area next to a waterfall, just after you begin descending through the pass. To go this way, take R559 (Spa Rd.) east out of Dingle; on the outskirts of town, when you hit a fork in the road, follow signs for Conor Pass and Tralee, to the right.

The High Road eventually meets up with the main N86, just after the nothing-much village of **Camp**—where there's another scenic alternative for the adventurous. Instead of going the way your GPS or maps app will probably steer you around trafficky Tralee, veer off down the tiny, unnamed road signposted for **Aughils,** on the right as you pass through Camp. This lovely route takes you first by a stretch of modern but idyllic houses (you'll probably dream briefly about moving here), before crossing beautiful moorland, then through another picturesque mountain pass. It then joins up with the R561 coast road, just 10 minutes or so from Castlemaine on the Ring of Kerry. But beware—although this way can definitely be a shortcut, especially in rush hours, we mean it when say the road is tiny! The last time we took this route the receptionist at our hotel raised an eyebrow and exclaimed "in a *rental car?*" (We do not recommend either this or the Conor Pass in heavy rain or icy weather.) But remember, fortune favors the brave. Especially those with good tires.

Where to Stay on the Dingle Peninsula

Benner's Hotel ♥♥ An easy walk from everything in Dingle Town, this 300-year-old inn is a local institution, with plenty of traditional charm. Done in a neutral decor, rooms have a modern look. Some have antique furnishings such as four-poster beds, and most come with town views. The bar downstairs is a great place to have a pint after a day of sightseeing. Or you can retreat with a drink to the library room if you prefer some quiet.

Main St. dinglebenners.com. ✆ **066/915-1638.** 52 units. €139–€364 double. Breakfast included. Free parking. **Amenities:** Bar; Wi-Fi (free).

Castlewood House ♥♥♥ Overlooking the glassy expanse of Dingle Bay, this lovely, whitewashed house is filled with art and antiques. Its location is exceptional, and views of the shimmering water, framed by distant mountains, are breathtaking. Guest rooms are chic and comfortable, with designer furniture and bathrooms with Jacuzzi tubs. Breakfasts are outstanding—including porridge with a dash of whiskey, homemade breads, oranges in caramel, kippers with scrambled eggs, and omelets with smoked salmon. Despite the rural feel, Dingle Marina is only a 10-minute walk away, but you might just want to curl up beside the fire in the drawing room with a book from the library.

The Wood. castlewooddingle.com. ✆ **066/915-2788.** 12 units. €130–€235 double; €180–€280 suite. Breakfast included. Free parking. **Amenities:** Wi-Fi (free). Closed Dec to mid-Feb.

Ceann Sibéal Hotel ♥♥ Being based in the village of Ballyferriter, west of Dingle on the Slea Head Drive, is ideal for those who prefer a more rural experience to the hubbub of Dingle Town itself—and the mountain views at the Ceann Sibéal are calming after a busy day of sightseeing. Rooms in this family-run hotel are basic but comfortable, and a restaurant/bar offers a menu with local ingredients. A bonus: Ballyferriter village's three traditional pubs are just steps away.

Ballyferriter. ceannsibealhotel.com. ✆ **066/915-6433.** 26 units. €120–€220 double. Breakfast included. Free parking. **Amenities:** Restaurant; bar; Wi-Fi (free).

Dingle Skellig Hotel ♥♥ With sweeping views of Dingle Bay, this modern hotel at the edge of Dingle Town is a great option for those looking for a little relaxation or a place with space for kids (there's a kids' club during school holidays). Rooms are spacious and comfortable, divided into classic styles or deluxe with air-conditioning and firm king-size beds. Everything's done in neutral tones, and some rooms come with balconies with fabulous views. Breakfast is served buffet style, and the **Coastguard** restaurant enjoys bay views. The hotel has a pool, a eucalyptus steam room, and a gym, and the **Peninsula Spa** offers relaxation with sea views and an outdoor hot tub for hotel guests. The self-service laundry is ideal if you're midway through a road trip.

Farran Dingle Bay. dingleskellig.com. ✆ **066/915-0200.** 152 units. €180–€330 double; €240–€650 suite. Breakfast included. Free parking. **Amenities:** 2 restaurants; bar; lounge; pool; spa; gym; laundry. Wi-Fi (free). Closed Jan–Feb.

Where to Eat on the Dingle Peninsula

Bean in Dingle ♥♥ CAFE A little slice of metropolitan cool right in the middle of Dingle, Bean serves one of the finest cups of joe we've had in Ireland. Bean hand-roasts its own specialty coffee, and you can buy it in bags to bring home—try the house blend "An Fear Marbh," named after the Blasket island Inis Tuaisceart, which looks like a sleeping giant. Have your coffee to go or sit at the long, communal wooden table and linger over a black pudding sausage roll or a slice of tasty cake—baked by the owner's mother and grandmother.

Green St. beanindingle.com. ✆ **087/299-2831.** Items €3–€6. Mon–Sat 8:30am–5pm; Sun 10am–4pm.

Doyle's Seafood Restaurant ♥♥ SEAFOOD Doyle's is simply one of the best places in the region for seafood; a lot of what you find on the menu depends on the catch of the day. The restaurant offers a smattering of mains, but the focus here is a menu of small sharing plates featuring delicacies like crispy crab cakes, chorizo and tomato mussels, steamed lobster, and chargrilled tuna. Vegetarians are well served with a menu of starters and entrees, and dishes like duck spring rolls and pan-slow-braised beef satisfy the carnivores. The wine list is extensive.

4 John St. doylesrestaurantdingle.ie. ✆ **066/915-2674.** Small plates €8–€25; entrees €22–€36. Mon–Sat 5–9pm.

Fenton's ♥♥♥ IRISH The Fenton family have been in farming and fishing for generations, and practically everything served here is local—the rib-eye is Dexter Beef grass-fed on the cliff-top family farm, seafood (like wild hake or black sole) is from local fishermen, and even the herbs are grown in the family's walled garden. Patricia Fenton herself oversees everything here—don't miss her delicious soda bread scones—and it's all set in a colorful, airy space on Green Street, once the home of Patricia's grandfather's mackerel yard.
Green St. fentonsrestaurantdingle.com. ✆ **066/915-2172.** Entrees €25–€37. Tues–Sat 5:30–9:30pm.

Out of the Blue ♥♥ SEAFOOD The name of this much-loved restaurant could refer to the sea it sits next to or the bright blue building it occupies. Either way, there's nothing here but seafood, but it's some of the freshest in the country, and the day's catch is listed on blackboards outside. The place is casual, but the cooking isn't. The seafood chowder is creamy and rich, chargrilled tuna is served with lentil salad, and the smoked salmon is house-cured. It has only a few tables, so booking is essential, but you can do it online.
Waterside. outoftheblue.ie. ✆ **066/915-0811.** Entrees €22–€33. Daily 4–9pm.

Reel Dingle Fish ♥♥ FISH & CHIPS Dingle is not short of an authentic "chipper" or two, and this is one of the best in town. Everything's

Bean in Dingle is the place to go for a cup of coffee and a slice of tasty cake.

cooked the traditional way—fish in batter, with piping-hot chips, and no messing around—but the menu has a greater-than-average choice of fresh fish to choose from, including hake, monkfish, pollock, and locally smoked haddock, in addition to the usual cod and plaice. It also sells homemade burgers crafted from local beef.

Bridge St. facebook.com/ReelDingleFish. ✆ **066/915-1713.** Fish and chips €9.90–€13.50. Tues–Sun 1–10pm.

Dingle Peninsula Shopping

An Gailearai Beag ♥♥♥ A showcase for the West Kerry Craft Guild, "the small gallery" is a treasure trove of crafts and art, handmade by local artists (who take it in turns to staff the shop). Shelves are dotted with everything from soaps made with Irish seaweed and hand-stitched ornaments of Irish cottages and puffins to colorful prints and greeting cards of local Dingle scenes. Also check out **Piglet,** a shop and gallery next door, for more. 18 Main St. angailearaibeag.com. ✆ **066/915-2976.**

Brian de Staic Jewellery Workshop ♥♥ A respected jewelry designer who has built up quite a following since he first appeared on the scene more than 30 years ago, Brian specializes in modern interpretations of ancient Celtic motifs; you'll find everything from pendants and brooches to earrings, bracelets, and crosses. Some of his work is based on instantly recognizable designs; others are more subtle and abstract. Green St. briandestaic.com. ✆ **066/915-1298.**

Louis Mulcahy Workshop ♥♥ Louis Mulcahy's pottery is all beautifully made, from vases and ornaments to kitchenware and tea sets. Everything can be shipped worldwide. The workshop on the Slea Head

walk this way: THE DINGLE WAY

The **Dingle Way** begins in Tralee and circles the peninsula, covering 153km (95 miles) of gorgeous mountain and coastal landscape. The most rugged section is along Brandon Head, on the peninsula's north coast, where the trail passes between Mount Brandon and the ocean. Farther west, the section between Dunquin and Ballyferriter (24km/15 miles) follows an especially lovely stretch of Atlantic coast. For more information, pick up maps from local tourist offices.

Ireland Walk Hike Bike (irelandwalkhikebike.com; ✆ **066/718-6181**) has a selection of self-guided walks and hikes on the Dingle Way, ranging between 3 and 10 days. Prices include maps/apps, accommodation, and luggage transfers. It also runs fully guided hiking trips on both the Dingle Peninsula and the Kerry Way (p. 332).

A Dingle Way itinerary is also offered by **Hidden Ireland Tours,** Dingle (hiddenirelandtours.com; ✆ **251/751-3087** in the U.S., or 087/235-5293), which does guided hiking tours around the Kerry Way and Killarney National Park (p. 300).

Drive sprawls over a two-story building with gorgeous views down to the coast; it's open daily year-round until 6pm (or 5:30pm in winter months). On R559, 16.5km (10⅓ miles) NW of Dingle. Clogher, Ballyferriter. louismulcahy.com. ✆ **066/915-6229.**

Original Kerry ♥♥ Everything here is designed and made in Kerry—including gorgeous ceramics, knitwear, glass art, and wood in colors and designs evoking local landscapes and seascapes. Look for hand-stitched belts and leather journals featuring Celtic patterns by Uisce Leather; ceramics by Sinéad Lough; knitwear by Fiadh Durham; and jewelry by Brian de Staic (see above). originalkerry.shop. ✆ **083/852-0705.**

Sports & Outdoor Pursuits in the Dingle Peninsula

SPECTATOR SPORTS

HORSE RACING The **Dingle Races** are a major event in the Irish horse-racing calendar, with 20 or so events taking place over a long weekend in mid-August. The incredibly picturesque Ballingtaggart Racecourse is just outside Dingle, on the road to Tralee. For more information, visit dingleraces.ie.

ROWING Held over a couple of days in mid-August, the **Dingle Regatta** (facebook.com/dingleregatta2016) is where you'll see *currach* or *naomhóg* racing in traditional wooden boats covered with canvas (in the old days they used animal skins) and tar. See the regatta's Facebook page for dates—search for "Dingle Regatta." Also check **dingle-peninsula.ie** for information on annual rowing regattas in Ballydavid (June), Ventry (July), and Brandon (Aug).

OUTDOOR PURSUITS

BEACHES The Dingle Peninsula is home to several spectacular beaches. The most famous is **Inch Strand**—a 5km-long (3-mile) creamy stretch of sand dunes in the town of Inch (*Inse*). It makes for a beautiful stop on the coast road into Dingle, with a beach cafe (open summer only) and a colony of semi-wild ginger cats that live among the slopes of its parking lot, ever hopeful for scraps. On Kilmurray Bay, **Minard Beach,** in the shadow of Minard Castle, giant sandstone boulders form a beach unlike anything you've ever seen. It's definitely *not* safe for swimming, but ideal for a stroll or a picnic.

The calmest beaches for swimming in this area are east of Castlegregory, on the more protected west side of Tralee Bay. The beach at **Maherabeg** has a coveted European Blue Flag (meaning it is exceptionally unpolluted and environmentally safe), and the beaches of **Brandon Bay** are particularly scenic—great for walking and swimming. These beaches are all popular surfing spots when the wild Atlantic is doing its thing.

CYCLING Traditional and electric bikes can be rented at **Dingle Bikes** (dinglebikes.com; ✆ **086/084-8378**); they will deliver to your hotel or B&B. Regular bikes are €25 and e-bikes €50 for the day (9am–7pm), and you are provided with maps, a helmet, and lock. Or try **Paddy's Bike Shop,** Dykegate Lane (paddysbikeshop.com; ✆ **066/915-2311**), where regular bikes are €25 per day, e-bikes €45. Both hire shops can suggest a number of day trips or overnight touring options.

DIVING & WATERSPORTS On the north coast of the Dingle Peninsula, Castlegregory on protected Tralee Bay is the region's go-to place for watersports. **Waterworld,** Harbour House, Scraggane Pier, Castlegregory (waterworld.ie; ✆ **066/713-9292**), is a diving center that offers packages including diving and room and board at good rates. Classes for beginners are available. The house is a short boat ride from most of the diving sites. You can take surfing, windsurfing, or wing-foiling lessons at **Jamie Knox Watersports,** Brandon Bay, Castlegregory (jamieknox.com; ✆ **066/713-9411**), run by former professional windsurfer Jamie Knox. They have three bases between Castlegregory and Fahamore. Surfing lessons start at €40, windsurfing from €45, and winging from €120, including all equipment. **Brandon Adventures** (brandonadventures.com) runs "surf and turf" adventure packages with surfing, stand-up paddleboarding, hiking, and coastal walks (depending on the weather) plus 2 nights' accommodation in a gorgeous country lodge, from €275 per person.

9

THE BURREN & BEYOND

COUNTIES CLARE, LIMERICK & TIPPERARY

North of County Kerry, the west coast of Ireland has long drawn visitors entranced by its stunning landscapes. From the verdant farmland along the Shannon River, head north to the towering Cliffs of Moher, drive winding roads to the extraordinary alien landscape of the Burren National Park, or travel inland and wander through the ancient, ruined fortress known as the Rock of Cashel. However far you go, whether along the Wild Atlantic Way coast or past lush farmland, there's always something wonderful to catch your eye.

Bordering Kerry to the north, but entirely separated by the broad Shannon Estuary, **County Clare** is a rugged and beguiling county. Its principal draw is the region known as the Burren, a stark and desolate rocky landscape filled with mysterious, ancient stone dolmens—it's quite unlike anywhere else in the country. As if that wasn't enough to impress, Clare also has the famous coastal Cliffs of Moher, a place of high drama and majestic beauty. The contrast with its neighbor, **County Limerick,** could hardly be more pronounced: Limerick is distinguished by the swirls and eddies of the Shannon River and its verdant countryside. To the east, **County Tipperary** is filled with pleasant, emerald-green farmland. In truth, Tipperary doesn't contain much that's worth going out of the way for, with one major exception: the Rock of Cashel, one of Ireland's most spectacular medieval ruins. It's worth a trip across the country all on its own.

ESSENTIALS

Arriving

BY PLANE Several of the big airlines operate regular scheduled flights into **Shannon Airport,** off the Limerick–Ennis road (N18), County Clare (shannonairport.com; ✆ **061/712000**), 24km (15 miles) west of Limerick City. If you need a taxi, you can catch one at the airport or prebook with **Shannon Airport Taxis** (shannonairportcab.com; ✆ **061/471-538**). Alternatively, **Bus Éireann** (buseireann.ie; ✆ **1850/836-611**) provides regular bus service from Shannon Airport to **Colbert Station** in Limerick.

BY BUS **Bus Éireann** (buseireann.ie; ✆ **1850/836-611**) provides regular bus service from all parts of Ireland to most towns listed in this chapter, although service isn't frequent in the most rural areas, and many of the sights located outside of towns and villages are not served by public transportation.

PREVIOUS PAGE: Cows grazing by the medieval ruins of the Rock of Cashel.

Counties Clare, Limerick & Tipperary
0 10 miles
0 10 kms
ATLANTIC OCEAN
Galway Bay
Aran Islands
Inishmore
Inishmaan
Inisheer
Kilronan
South Sound
Cliffs of Moher
Hag's Head
Spanish Pt.
Mutton I.
Donegal Pt.
Scattery I.
Galway
Barna
Furbogh
Spiddal
Oranmore
Clarinbridge
Athenry
Craughwell
Loughrea
Kinvara
Ballyvaughan
Murroogh
Slieve Elva
The Burren National Park
Lisdoonvarna
Doolin
Ennistymon
Lahinch
Liscannor
Corofin
Inagh
Miltown Malbay
Quilty
Knockalough
Kilkee
Kilrush
Carrigaholt
Tarbert
Ballybunion
Listowel
Ballyheigue
Tralee
Castleisland
Farranfore
Mt. Eagle
Abbeyfeale
Newcastle West
Dromcolliher
Ardagh
Foynes
Rathkeale
Askeaton
Ballingarry
Charleville
Newmarket
Kanturk
Buttevant
Doneralle
Mitchelstown
Kilfinane
Kilmallock
Bruff
Hospital
Lough Gur
Croom
Adare
Patrickswell
Pallaskenry
Limerick
Cratloe
Bunratty
Sixmilebridge
Shannon
Newmarket-on-Fergus
Clarecastle
Ennis
Tulla
Slieve Bernagh
Killaloe
Ballina
Scarriff
Mountshannon
Lough Graney
Maghera
Gort
Slieve Aughty Mts.
Cashlaundrumlahan
Woodford
Killimor
Portumna
Lough Derg
Borrisokane
Nenagh
Puckhaun
Cloughjordan
Ballingarry
Moneygall
Roscrea
Birr
Banagher
Cloghan
Ferbane
Craughwell
Shannon
Clonaslee
Slieve Bloom Mts.
Arderin
Mountrath
Portlaoise
Portarlington
Clonygowan
Monasterevin
Emo
Ballyroan
Abbeyleix
Ballinakill
Durrow
Rathdowney
Johnstown
Freshford
Ballyragget
Urlingford
Templetuohy
Templemore
Slievekimalta
Castleconnell
Newport
Milestone
Thurles
Littleton
Ballingarry
Cashel
Dundrum
Pallas Grean
Golden Vale
Oola
Limerick Junction
Tipperary
Emly
Galtee Mts.
Galtymore
Bansha
Newinn
Cahir
Ardfinnan
Clogheen
Kilcommon
Knockmealdown Mts.
Ballyporeen
Fethard
Rathkeevin
Clonmel
Comeragh Mts.
Knockanaffrin
Carrick-on-Suir
Mooncoin
Suir
Callan
Kells
Knocktopher
Ninemilehouse
Ballyhale
Inistioge
Bennettsbridge
Kilkenny
Nore
Waterford
Tramore
Lemybrien
CLARE
GALWAY
OFFALY
LAOISE (LEIX)
KILKENNY
TIPPERARY
LIMERICK
CORK
KERRY
WATERFORD
N6
N18
N52
N62
N7
N8
N78
N9
N10
N76
N24
N25
N20
N21
N73
NORTHERN IRELAND
REPUBLIC OF IRELAND
Belfast
Dublin
Galway
Cork
Map Area

BY TRAIN **Irish Rail** (irishrail.ie) operates direct trains from Dublin, Cork, and Killarney, with connections from other parts of Ireland, to Limerick's **Colbert Station,** Parnell Street; to **Clonmel** and **Thurles** in County Tipperary; and to **Ennis** in County Clare.

BY CAR Although several of the major sights in this region can be reached on public transportation, you really need a car for the more remote places. Shannon Airport has desks for international car-rental chains **Avis** (avis.ie; ✆ **061/715600**), **Budget** (budget.ie; ✆ **061/471361**), **Hertz** (hertz.ie; ✆ **061/471369**), **Enterprise** (enterprise.ie; ✆ **061/704914**), and **Europcar** (europcar.ie; ✆ **061/206040**).

COUNTY CLARE

At first glance Clare seems a pleasantly pastoral place, with its miles of pasture and softly rolling fields. But head to the coast and a dramatic landscape awaits, with plunging cliffs and crashing waves. Turn north from there and you'll find visual drama of a different kind, courtesy of the stark, rocky landscapes of the Burren.

Visitor Information

The **Burren Centre** in Kilfenora (theburrencentre.ie; ✆ **065/708-8030**) is the place to go for information on the Burren region. In addition, visitor information points are on Arthur's Row in **Ennis** (✆ **065/682-8366**) and at the **Cliffs of Moher** (✆ **065/708-6141**).

Exploring the Burren

The **Burren National Park** ♥♥♥ (p. 357) is far and away the county's greatest attraction. You could spend several days exploring its profound wilderness, although a day is plenty to hit the high points. One of the best ways to explore the Burren is to take the R480. In a series of corkscrew turns, the road curves from **Corofin** through gorgeous scenery north to **Ballyvaughan,** a delightful little village overlooking the blue waters of Galway Bay. **Lisdoonvarna,** on the park's western edge, is a small and charmingly old-fashioned town that has long been known for its natural mineral springs. Each summer, it draws thousands of people to bathe in its sulfuric streams, iron creeks, and iodine lakes (see box on p. 363).

Aillwee Burren Experience ♥♥ CAVES The story of how the deep Aillwee cave system came to be discovered starts with a curious dog. In 1944, a local farmer followed his dog into a small crevice in the hillside. The man was astonished to find that it opened into a huge cavern with 1,000m (3,280 ft.) of passages running straight into the heart of a mountain. The publicity-shy farmer kept it to himself for decades before eventually spreading the word. Professional cave explorers later uncovered its magnificent bridged chasms, deep caverns, frozen waterfall, and hollows created by hibernating brown bears (which have been extinct in Ireland

County Clare
Aillwee Burren Experience 4
Bunratty Castle & Folk Park 10
Burren Centre 6
Caherconnell Stone Fort 5
Cliffs of Moher 1
Corcomroe Abbey 3
Craggaunowen 9
Doolin 2
Ennis Friary 8
Poulnabrone Dolmen 7
Scattery Island 11
Galway
Oranmore
Rossaveal
Carraroe
Lettermullen
Inverin
Spiddal
Furbogh
Barna
Clarinbridge
Craughwell
Loughrea
Killimor
Galway Bay
North Sound
South Sound
Black Head
Murroogh
Kinvara
N18
Inishmore
Kilronan
Inishmaan
Inisheer
Aran Islands
Slieve Elva
Ballyvaughan
Slieve Aughty Mts.
GALWAY
Gort
Woodford
Lough Derg
Lough Graney
Maghera
Doolin
Lisdoonvarna
Burren Way
The Burren National Park
Kilfenora
Ennistymon
Corofin
Cliffs of Moher
Liscannor
Hag's Head
Lahinch
ATLANTIC OCEAN
Inagh
CLARE
Mountshannon
Scarriff
Slieve Bernagh
Tulla
Spanish Pt.
Miltown Malbay
Ennis
Mutton I.
Quilty
Clarecastle
Quin
Killaloe
Ballina
N7
Newmarket-on-Fergus
N67
N68
Sixmilebridge
TIPPERARY
Donegal Pt.
Knockalough
Shannon
Bunratty
Castleconnell
Newport
Cratloe
Kilkee
Limerick
Pallaskenry
Kilrush
Golden Vale
Killimer
Foynes
Carrigaholt
Scattery I.
Askeaton
LIMERICK
Patrickswell
N24
Tarbert
Adare
Loop Head
KERRY
Rathkeale
N21
0 10 miles
0 10 kms
NORTHERN IRELAND
Belfast
REPUBLIC OF IRELAND
Galway
Dublin
Map Area
Cork

Wildflower spotting in the Burren.

for 10,000 years). Guided cave tours are excellent here, usually led by geology students from area universities. Enjoy the spookiness when they turn out the lights for a minute so you can experience the depth of the darkness inside. Tours last approximately 30 minutes and are conducted continuously. Tickets include entry to the **Burren Birds of Prey Centre,** a working aviary designed to mimic the natural habitat of the buzzards, falcons, eagles, and owls that live there. For €110 per person, you can take a private, 45-minute "Hawk Walk," where a handler shows you the birds up close and teaches you how to handle a hawk for yourself. It culminates in a guided forest walk, where you learn how to release the bird and call it back. (The handlers need at least a day's notice, ideally more, to arrange a Hawk Walk—you can't book on the day. Tickets include admission to the cave and the Birds of Prey Centre.) A couple of on-site craft shops sell Aillwee's own brand of cheese, among other things.

Off R480, near Ballyvaughan. aillweecave.ie. ✆ **065/707-7036.** Admission to caves and Birds of Prey Centre: €27 adults; €25 students and seniors; €17 children 5–16; €61–€91 families; free for children 4 and under. Daily 10am–5pm (late Nov to Christmas closed Sat–Sun). Visits are timed: morning visits 10am–1:30pm, afternoon visits 1:30–5pm.

Caherconnell Stone Fort ♥ ANCIENT SITE Built sometime around the year A.D. 950, this rugged early medieval ring fort was used on and off as a defensive structure until the 1600s. It's one of the best-preserved ruins of its kind in Ireland; the dry stone walls are around 3m (approximately 9 ft.) tall in places, and equally as thick. Evidence of a much earlier structure, possibly dating to the Neolithic period, has been found nearby (though there's very little to see). The site is rich in artifacts, thanks to the high-caliber metalwork that was produced here in the Middle Ages, and you'll often see archaeology students at work here. A visitor center has a cafe and an exhibition focusing on the Burren's forts, dolmens, and other ancient monuments. More entertainingly, you can also see sheepdog "trials" (demonstrations, that is—they haven't done anything wrong) at the fort from March to October. Check website for the weekly calendar of sheepdog trials.

On R480, 1km (¾ mile) N of the Poulnabrone Dolmen (see below), near Carran. caherconnell.com. ✆ **065/708-9999.** Admission to fort: €8.50 adults; €6 children; free for children 4 and under; €23–€35 families. Sheepdog demos: €10 adults; €7 children; free for children 4 and under; €27–€41 families. Joint ticket fort and demos: €17 adults; €12 children; free for children 4 and under; €46–€70 families. May–Sept 10am–5pm (July–Aug until 5:30pm); Mar–Apr and Oct 10:30am–4:30pm. Last tour 45 min. before closing.

THE burren NATIONAL PARK

The otherworldly landscape of the **Burren National Park** spreads across 1,653 hectares (4,083 acres) carved by nature from bare carboniferous limestone, both desolate and beautiful. Sheets of rock jut and undulate in a kind of moonscape as far as you can see. Amid the rocks, delicate wildflowers somehow find enough dirt to thrive; ferns curl gently around boulders, moss softens hard edges, orchids flower exotically, and violets brighten the landscape. With the flowers come butterflies that thrive on the rare flora. Even the Burren's animals are unusual: The pine marten (small weasels), stoat (ermine), and badger, all rare in the rest of Ireland, are common here.

The Burren began to develop 300 million years ago when layers of shells and sediment were deposited under a tropical sea. Many millions of years later, those layers were exposed by erosion and poor prehistoric farming methods. Since then, it's all been battered by the Irish rain and winds, producing the haunting landscape you see today. Humans first began to leave their mark here about 7,000 years ago. The park is particularly rich in archaeological remains from the Neolithic through the medieval periods—dolmens and wedge tombs (approximately 120 of them), ring forts (500 of those), round towers, ancient churches, high crosses, monasteries, and holy wells.

Though there's no official entrance, the park is centered at Mullaghmore Mountain—and like all national parks in Ireland, it's completely free to enter (burrennationalpark.ie; ✆ **065/682-7693**).

The **Burren Centre** (theburrencentre.ie; ✆ **065/708-8030**), on R476 to Kilfenora, provides an informative overview with films, landscape models, and interpretive displays. Admission to the center is €8 adults, €7 seniors and students, €4 children ages 6–15, and €25 families (free for children 5 and under). It's open daily June to August 9am until 5pm, mid-March to May and September to October 10am until 4pm (the center is closed Nov to mid-Mar). A craft shop and tearoom are also on-site. The center is next to the ruins of **Kilfenora Cathedral,** which has some interesting wall carvings—look for the heads above what's left of the doors and windows.

Corcomroe Abbey ♥♥ RELIGIOUS SITE/RUINS Set jewel-like in a languid green valley bounded by rolling hills, the jagged ruins of this Cistercian abbey are breathtaking. Donal Mór O'Brien founded the abbey in 1194, and his grandson, a former king of Thomond, is entombed in the structure's northern wall. Some interesting medieval and Romanesque carvings are set in the stone, including one of a bishop with a crosier. Corcomroe is a lonely spot, except for Easter morning, when people come from miles around to celebrate Mass. On your visit, look for a mound, surrounded by trees, beside the road on the way out—it's the remains of an ancient ring fort.

Signposted from L1014, near Oughtmama. archaeology.ie/monument-of-the-month/archive/corcomroe-abbey-co-clare. No phone. Free admission (open site).

Poulnabrone Dolmen ♥ ANCIENT SITE This portal tomb is an exquisitely preserved prehistoric site, made all the more arresting by the alien Burren landscape in which it sits. Its dolmen (stone table) is huge and surrounded by a natural pavement of rocks. The tomb has been dated back 5,000 years. When it was excavated in the 1980s, the remains of 16 people were found. And yet, it's still a mystery how the gigantic boulders were moved and lifted—the capstone alone weighs 4½ tonnes (5 tons). In summer, you shouldn't have much trouble finding this site; just look for all the tour buses—at times they literally block the road.

On R480, 1km (¾ mile) S of Caherconnell Stone Fort (see above), near Carran. burrengeopark.ie/discover-explore/geosites-discovery-points/poulnabrone. No phone. Free admission (open site).

The ruined nave of Corcomroe Abbey.

walk this way: THE BURREN WAY

With its unique terrain and meandering walking paths, the Burren lends itself beautifully to walking. The **Burren Way** is a 42km (26-mile) signposted route stretching from Ballyvaughan to Liscannor, incorporating old "green roads"—unpaved former highways that crisscross the Burren landscape in inaccessible areas. (Most were created during the Great Famine as work projects for starving locals.) An information sheet outlining the route is available from any tourist office. You can also download trail maps of marked Burren walks at the **Burren National Park**'s website (**burrennationalpark.ie**)—free guided walks are offered in the summer.

Or explore the landscape with local experts. Author **Tony Kirby** (heartofburrenwalks.com; ✆ **087/292-5487**) leads fascinating 2½-hour walks in the Burren, featuring everything from the limestone pavements to the monuments and wild plants. Dates vary and are posted in advance online. The cost is €25 adults and free for kids 16 and under. Marie McGauran of **Burren Experience** (mullaghmore-burren.com; ✆ **086/821-9441**) will also take you on a 2-hour nature walk to some remote and beautiful areas in the park that you can only reach on foot. Walks cost €35 for adults, free for accompanying children 11 and under.

Exploring the Clare Coast

One of Ireland's most photographed places, the **Cliffs of Moher** draw thousands of visitors to Clare's remote reaches every day of the year, rain or shine. Rising to vertiginous heights above the Atlantic Ocean, the cliffs are undeniably impressive. The site is well worth a visit, but be aware that in the high season, the crowds can rather spoil the effect. Farther along the Clare Coast, **Lahinch** is an old-fashioned Victorian seaside resort, with a wide beach and long promenade curving along the horseshoe bay. The beach is great for surfing, and golfers love the outstanding links course (p. 369). The Clare Coast is in fact dotted with seaside resorts with varying degrees of crowds and beauty, such as **Kilrush, Kilkee, Miltown Malbay,** and **Ennistymon.** You'll also stumble across places with quirky names, like Puffing Hole, Intrinsic Bay, Chimney Hill, Elephant's Teeth, Mutton Island, and Lover's Leap.

Traditional Irish music is always on heavy rotation in Clare. The secluded fishing village of **Doolin,** near Lahinch, is the unofficial capital of Irish traditional music. The village is also a departure point for boat trips to the beautiful and isolated **Aran Islands** (p. 395).

Bunratty Castle & Folk Park ♥♥ HERITAGE SITE Built in 1425 and restored in the 1950s, Bunratty is an impressive early-15th-century castle, and home to two major tourist attractions: a "living-history" re-creation of a 19th-century village, and a riotous nighttime medieval banquet. You can tour the interior of the castle, which is surprisingly complete, including a fine collection of medieval furniture and art. The restored walled garden is a beautiful place to wander around. However, the folk park is probably the bigger draw here. Actors in period costume wander around as you walk through the authentic-looking village center, complete with everything from a post office and schoolroom to a doctor's office. You can go inside each and chat with the "occupants." Meanwhile, professional craftspeople work their trades, using traditional methods. There's even a Victorian-style pub. It's all great fun, and a brilliant way to imbue kids with a sense of history. In the evenings, the **medieval banquet** takes over the castle's Great Hall. After a full sit-down meal, actors and musicians in medieval garb put on a lively show of music, dancing, and folk stories. Note that this is the full "tourist" experience, and some people might find the "Irishness" a little over the top. It can sell out months in advance, so either book in advance or just enjoy the Folk Park and castle by day and look for a more authentic music experience in a County Clare pub at night.

Costumed interpreters go about their daily business in the re-created 19th-century village at Bunratty Castle.

Signposted from N18 (Shannon-Limerick Rd.), Bunratty. bunrattycastle.ie. ✆ **061/711-222.** Castle and folk park €17 adults; €12 seniors, students and children 4–18; free for children 3 and under; €40–€63 families. Daily 9:30am–5:30pm; last admission 4pm. Medieval banquet €60 adults; €40 children 4–10; daily 5:30 and 8:30pm.

Cliffs of Moher ♥♥ NATURAL SITE The cries of nesting seabirds are faintly audible over the roar of the Atlantic crashing against the base of these breathtaking cliffs. Undulating for 8km (5 miles) along the coast, the cliffs tower as high as 214m (702 ft.) over the sea. In bad weather, access is (understandably) limited—the wind can be dangerous here. When the weather is fine, a guardrail offers you a small sense of security as you peek over the edge. (Some visitors always insist on climbing over it for a better view of the sheer drop or a selfie—needless to say, this is against the rules and extremely dangerous.) On a clear day, you can see the Aran Islands in Galway Bay as misty shapes in the distance. Look the other way, however, and you'll see a constant throng of tour groups, coaches, and cars. The enormous visitor center houses gift shops, a high-tech "Cliffs of Moher Experience," and various other exhibits that feel designed to wring every last cent out of this natural wonder. Furthermore, the visitor center has the only parking, which you can't use without buying visitor center entry tickets—effectively turning it into a steep *per person* parking charge (the road is too narrow to park elsewhere). Needless to say, the cliffs are overwhelmingly popular, and in summer it can be crowded during the day. But if you visit during off-peak times and book tickets online, prices are much cheaper. (In July–Aug, the cliffs stay open until 9pm; arriving late in the day is a good way to see the view without a crowd.) Head up the path beside the visitor center to the 19th-century **O'Brien's Tower** for the best view of the cliffs—it's a knockout spot for photos, and admission is included in the ticket price. To see the cliffs for free, walk along the Coastal Walk north from either **Doolin** or **Liscannor.** The entire walk is 20km (12.4 miles) and takes around 4½ hours. There's also a 5.6km (3.5-mile) trail running south to Hags Head, which takes around 2 hours. ***Note:*** These trails can be uneven and exposed and should be avoided in windy or foggy weather. Always stay on the official trail—the cliff edge is unstable, and there have been a number of injuries and even fatalities.

Near Liscannor. cliffsofmoher.ie. ✆ **065/708-6141.** Visitor center admission (includes parking) €7 adults, seniors, and students; free for accompanied children 12 and under; €14 families. Daily May–Aug 8am–9pm; Mar–Apr and Sept–Oct 8am–7pm; Nov–Feb 9am–5pm. Tower and cliffs may be inaccessible in bad weather.

O'Brien's Tower at the Cliffs of Moher.

Craggaunowen ♥♥ HERITAGE SITE Following the successful castle-plus-open-air-museum template of **Bunratty Castle** (p. 359), Craggaunowen focuses on what life would have been like for its Bronze Age inhabitants. A reconstructed "crannog" shows how Celts lived, worked, and defended themselves from the Iron Age right through to the middle of the first millennium. (Records indicate, in fact, that scattered communities lived like this as late as the 1600s.) Other reconstructions include a 4th-century ring fort and underground passages known as *souterrains,* thought to have been used for cool storage. (Incidentally, some archaeologists believe there are real souterrains at **Caherconnell Stone Fort**—see p. 356—that have yet to be excavated.) Costumed historian-guides

Historic settlement at Craggaunowen.

provide demonstrations of techniques the inhabitants would have used to cook, build, weave, and so on. Also on display is the Brendan Boat, a replica of the kind of vessel Vikings are believed to have sailed to America; it was built in 1976 by explorer Tim Severin, who used it to do just that—a 4,500-mile journey that took him and his crew just over a year. The 16th-century **Craggaunowen Castle** is also on the grounds (included in the price).

Kilmurray, near Quin. craggaunowen.ie. ✆ **061/711-222.** Admission €9.90 adults; €7.75 seniors; €8 ages 4–18; free for children 3 and under; €28–€43 families. Daily 10am–5pm. Last admission 1 hr. before closing. Closed mid-Sept to Easter.

Doolin ♥♥ VILLAGE Doolin's old pubs and restaurants ring with the sound of fiddle and accordion all year long, earning this secluded fishing village a reputation as the unofficial capital of Irish traditional music. Most famous among them is **Gus O'Connor's Pub** (Fisher St.; gusoconnorsdoolin.com; ✆ **065/707-4168**), set among a row of thatched fisherman's cottages, about a 10-minute walk from the seafront. Great though the craic is here, the pub's fame inevitably draws crowds, and it can get packed to the rafters on a busy night. If you're looking for something a little less touristy, head up the road to **McGann's** (Main St.; mcgannspubdoolin.com; ✆ **065/707-4133**); it's not so unrelentingly jammed as Gus O'Connor's. In fact, on many nights, there are no locals in Gus's at all—they're all here, downing pints of Guinness and listening to the fiddles. Feel free to join them. Doolin is on R479, about 7.8km (4¾ miles) west of Lisdoonvarna.

Tourist Information Centre: Next to the Hotel Doolin, Fitz's Cross, Doolin. doolin.ie. No phone.

Ennis Friary ♥ RELIGIOUS SITE/RUINS When you walk around what's left of Ennis Friary, it can be hard to get a sense of its original scale. Records show, however, that in 1375 it was the home and workplace for no less than 350 friars and 600 students. Founded in 1241, this Franciscan abbey was a famous seat of learning in medieval times, making Ennis a focal point of Western Europe for many years. It was finally forced to close in 1692, and thereafter fell into ruin, but the partly restored site contains beautifully sculpted medieval tombs, decorative fragments, and carvings, including the famous McMahon tomb, with its striking representations of the Passion. The nave and chancel are the oldest parts of the friary; other structures, such as the 15th-century tower, transept, and sacristy, are also rich in architectural detail.

Abbey St., Ennis. heritageireland.ie. ✆ **065/682-9100.** Admission €5 adults; €4 seniors; €3 children and students; €13 families. Mid-Mar to Sept daily 10am–6pm; Oct daily 10am–5pm. Last admission 45 min. before closing. Closed Nov to mid-Mar.

Scattery Island ♥♥ ISLAND/RUINS Atmospheric monastic ruins dating from the 6th century perch upon this unspoiled island in the Shannon Estuary near Kilrush, on Clare's south coast. A high, round tower and several churches are all that remain of an extensive settlement founded by St. Senan. Ferries depart multiple times a day and take around 30 minutes to cross to the island. Island visits are usually 2 or 2½ hours—tickets include a 1-hour guided monastic village walking tour and free time for a

LOVED UP IN lisdoonvarna

If you've been looking for love in all the wrong places, clearly you've never been to Lisdoonvarna. This County Clare town lives for *l'amour.*

There's a Matchmaker Pub on the main street (inside the Imperial Hotel) and local resident Willie Daly is a professional matchmaker. Every September, the town hosts the month-long **Lisdoonvarna Matchmaking Festival** (matchmakerireland.com). Thousands of lovelorn singletons come in search of The One, and locals cheer them on. Up and down each street, every atmospheric corner is used for mixers and minglers. Residents stir the pot by hosting romantic breakfasts, dinners, games, and dances. There's music in every pub, and crowds on the narrow village streets.

So good are their intentions and so charming is their belief in true love—in the idea that there really is somebody out there for everybody, and that they might find each other in a far-flung corner of western Ireland—that you, too, may believe.

walk, picnic, or swim. A longer Great Island Experience gives visitors 4 to 5 hours on the island (selected dates only). The island has no shops or food facilities, so bring a packed lunch.

Kilrush Marina, Kilrush. scatteryislandtours.com. ✆ **085/250-5512.** Round-trip ferry and tour tickets €32 adults; €20 ages 13–17; €15 children 3–12; €25 seniors and students; €85–€95 family. June–Aug up to 4 tours per day 9am–4pm; May and Sept Sat–Sun 2 tours per day 8am–4pm. Tour times vary according to tide times; call in advance or book online.

Where to Stay in County Clare

County Clare contains the most unique and special places to stay in the region. That said, it's perhaps a little surprising that there aren't more of them. Fortunately, there are some real gems among their number.

Armada House ♥♥ Dating back to around 1810, this elegant house has been thoughtfully restored, with classical style mixed with antiques and colorful art. Some rooms have four-poster beds, and most have sea views. Breakfast is designed to make the most of produce from local County Clare producers. Soak up the sea views from the lounge or beside the fire, or order a hamper to take with you while out exploring. Guests benefit from the amenities of sister property, the **Armada Hotel,** across the road, which has a restaurant, bistro, and pub, plus guest activities like

Antiques and art blend with modern comfort at Armada House.

yoga, guide runs, and knitting sessions. Spanish Point is about a 30-minute drive down the coast from the Cliffs of Moher.

Spanish Point. armadahotel.com/armada-house. ✆ **065/707-9000.** 13 units. €210–€290 double; €325–€400 suite. Breakfast included. Free parking. **Amenities:** Bar; Wi-Fi (free). Closed Sun–Thurs Nov–Jan.

Dromoland Castle ♥♥♥ If you've always wanted to stay in a real Irish castle, Dromoland might just fit the bill, with its huge gray stone walls, battlements, and Gothic features, right down to suits of armor in the hallways. It's a five-star hotel so it's pricey—but if you can splash out for a night of luxury, it's worth it. A castle has stood here since 1014 and was rebuilt over the years. The current buildings date to the 1700s and 1800s but have been fully modernized. Dinner at the **Earl of Thomond** dining room is worth dressing up for (gentlemen will need a jacket), with a nine-course tasting menu (€145) or a la carte options. You can also have afternoon tea in the **Gallery** or arrange a picnic basket and explore the 450-acre grounds for the day—it has an 18-hole golf course, lake fishing, tennis, falconry, and a spa, plus a pool and gym in the golf club (just a short walk or golf-buggy ride from the main castle), home to the **Fig Tree Restaurant,** a less formal option for dinner.

Newmarket-on-Fergus. dromoland.ie. ✆ **061/368-144.** 97 units. €399–€1,157 double; €1,363–€3,780 suite. Check website for discounts. Breakfast included. Free parking. **Amenities:** 2 restaurants; bar; concierge; gym; golf course; pool; room service; Wi-Fi (free).

Fergus View ♥♥ There are breathtaking views to be had at this sweet B&B near Corofin, one of the gateways to the Burren. You could sit for ages marveling at the long vista of rolling fields and rambling hills, joined by the wonderful owner, Mary, as she brings you a fortifying tray of tea to sip by the open fire. Mary and Declan are also experts on the Burren and all this area has to offer visitors and will happily share their encyclopedic knowledge. Guest rooms are small and simple, but beds are comfortable.

On R476 in Kilnaboy, 3.2km (2 miles) N of Corofin. fergusview.com. ✆ **065/683-7606.** 3 units. €120 double. Breakfast included. Free parking. **Amenities:** Wi-Fi (free). Closed Nov–Easter.

Gregans Castle Hotel ♥♥ An elegant 18th-century house in an extraordinary setting, Gregans is not in fact at all castle-like, but don't let that bother you. The unique location, deep in the Burren, makes this one of the most peaceful hotels in Ireland. It's been delighting guests for decades, including J. R. R. Tolkien, who was apparently so inspired by the otherworldly views that he drew on them to describe Mordor in *The Lord of the Rings*. Guest rooms are design-magazine chic, with modern furnishings and bay windows. There are no televisions, to better enable guests to get maximum peace from their stay. If you can't stretch to the cost of a night here, consider booking a table in the restaurant, **Gregans**

Castle ♥♥♥ (p. 367), for modern Irish cooking, or opt for a light lunch in the **Corkscrew Bar** or afternoon tea at weekends.

Ballyvaughan. gregans.ie. ✆ **065/707-7005.** 22 units. €325–€505 double; €475–€730 suite. Breakfast included. Check website for dinner, bed-and-breakfast deals. Free parking. **Amenities:** Restaurant; bar; Wi-Fi (free). Closed Dec to mid-Feb.

Sheedy's ♥♥ Less than an hour from Shannon Airport and 10 minutes from the Cliffs of Moher, Sheedy's location, lying at the edge of the charming country town of Lisdoonvarna, could hardly be better. The owners pride themselves on offering rural charm with all the comforts of any urban home and fireplaces to sit by with hot tea on a cold day. Spacious guest rooms are all done in low-key classic country-house style, with armoires (called wardrobes here) and armchairs. It's not fussy; instead, it's pleasantly home-like. The award-winning in-house restaurant prides itself on using local meat and seafood in its French-influenced cooking. Try this place and you'll undoubtedly become a regular.

Main St., Lisdoonvarna. sheedys.com. ✆ **065/707-4026.** 11 units. €230–€250 double. Breakfast included. Check website for offers. Free parking. **Amenities:** Restaurant; bar; Wi-Fi (free). Closed Oct–Apr.

Where to Eat in County Clare

Historically County Clare doesn't have the foodie reputation of somewhere like Cork, but that has been changing. In addition to the restaurants listed below, there are many stellar places to get light meals. The **Wooden Spoon** in Killaloe (Bridge St.) is popular with locals for its cakes, sandwiches, quiches, and salads. In Ballyvaughan, try the **Larder Deli** (Ballyvaughan Enterprise Centre) for sourdough sandwiches, homemade sausage rolls, and hearty salad plates (lentil and carrot with sesame dressing is a favorite). Locals in Lahinch love the filling breakfasts at **Joe's Café** (Marine Parade), a down-to-earth cafe with friendly service.

Barrtrá Seafood Restaurant ♥♥ SEAFOOD A friendly, family-run place with a good lineup of simple, tasty seafood, this restaurant looks out over Liscannor Bay. Just glance at a map and you'll quickly see why that makes this such a lovely spot in the late evening—the sun sets over the sea on a virtually direct line to the dining room. You can order a la carte or opt for the "surprise" menu. You decide whether you want seafood, meat, vegetarian, or a mixture and specify anything you *don't* want (or can't eat), and the chef prepares a five-course dinner for your table. Otherwise, your a la carte choices might include oysters or fisherman's broth, followed by a juicy steak or pan-fried haddock with caper berries and lime butter.

Miltown Malbay Rd., Lahinch. barrtra.com. ✆ **065/708-1280.** 5-course menus €50–€60; entrees €26–€34. Fri–Sat 5:30–9pm; Sun noon–7pm. Closed Jan–Feb.

Durty Nelly's ♥♥ IRISH/PUB FOOD You don't walk into a pub called Durty Nelly's expecting haute cuisine, especially when it's next door to a tourist attraction like Bunratty Castle (p. 359), but some welcome surprises are to be found here. That includes hearty pub food—fish and chips, steak sandwiches, burgers, and salads. Those who don't mind a bit of cheesy tourist novelty can have their picture taken while pouring their own pint of Guinness. Durty Nelly's is also home to the more refined **Oyster Restaurant,** its menu based around seasonal local produce, with dishes like grilled seabass or slow-cooked pork belly with black pudding mash. If you're wondering about the name, "Durty Nelly" was a somewhat ribald heroine of Irish folklore, said to have invented the magical cure-all (and highly alcoholic) variety of moonshine, *poitín* or *potcheen* (see box on p. 421).

Next to Bunratty Castle, Bunratty. durtynellys.ie. ✆ **061/364-861.** Pub: Entrees €16–€30; daily noon–9:30pm. Oyster Restaurant: Entrees €21–€37; daily noon–9:30pm.

East Clare venison with baked beetroot, stylishly presented at Gregans Castle.

Gregans Castle ♥♥♥ MODERN IRISH The inhouse dining room at **Gregans Castle Hotel** in Ballyvaughan (p. 365), headed up by chef Jonathan Farrell, is the perfect place for an elegant meal with an exquisite view of the wild countryside. Everything is locally sourced and given a creative twist; a four-course menu might include garden pumpkin tortellini, followed by cod with celeriac cream or organic Burren lamb with roast onion and artichoke. The atmosphere is friendly, and the service is excellent.

Ballyvaughan. gregans.ie. ✆ **065/707-7005.** Fixed-price menu €95. Tues–Sun 6–8:30pm. Bar food 12:30–2:30pm. Closed Dec–Jan. Children 6 and under only allowed at 6pm sharp.

Homestead Cottage ♥♥♥ MODERN IRISH Just a stone's throw from Doolin and set in a 200-year-old traditional Irish cottage with stone floors and rustic wooden tables, Homestead is full of atmosphere. The excellent food won it a Michelin star in 2024. Chef Robbie McCauley works with local growers and artisan producers for the seven-course dinner menu, which features the bounty of the Atlantic, just across the field. They also grow most of the vegetables in their own garden. Look for dishes like local Flaggy Shore oysters with dashi and shore herbs; wild Atlantic cod with celeriac, mint, and walnut, or garden blackcurrant with yogurt.

Luogh North, Doolin. homesteadcottagedoolin.com. ✆ **065-679-4133.** 2-course lunch menu €42; 3 courses €50. 7-course dinner menu €109. May–Oct Wed–Sun 6:30–9pm; Sat–Sun 12:30–2:15pm. Nov–Apr Thurs–Sat 6:30–9pm; Sat 12:30–2:15pm; Sun 1–5pm. Closed in Jan.

Vaughan's Anchor Inn ♥♥ SEAFOOD A 10-minute drive from the Cliffs of Moher, this excellent pub specializes in topnotch seafood. Liscannor Bay crab claws come with creamy garlic butter and fresh bread, while the fish and chips are indulgently fried in pure beef drippings. At lunch you'll find a few lighter mains alongside the heartier options. Vaughan's Anchor Inn is on the main street in Liscannor; look for the long white building with the small parking lot on the right, not long after you round the bend and see the small town center ahead of you.

Main St., Liscannor. vaughans.ie. ✆ **065/708-1548.** Entrees €24–€40. Daily noon–8:30pm. Bookings advised.

Wild Honey Inn ♥♥♥ MODERN IRISH This gastropub in tiny Lisdoonvarna was awarded a Michelin star in 2020, and it only takes one meal here to see why. In a 19th-century pub, chef Aidan McGrath and Kate Sweeney are producing extraordinary, unique cuisine, with an emphasis on wild local produce, and they are doing it in an atmosphere as relaxed as your grandmother's kitchen. A wood fire crackles at the hearth while diners sample charred organic salmon with capers and gravlax, or duck and foie gras terrine with wild mushrooms and roasted wild hazelnuts, topped with puree of local apples. Expect whatever is in season, locally sourced, gorgeously cooked with a light touch. The wine list is small but well chosen. To complete the experience, stay over—double rooms cost €220 to €270 (including breakfast), and the ground-floor rooms open onto a little patio.

Kincora Rd., Lisdoonvarna. wildhoneyinn.com. ✆ **065/707-4300.** Set menus €70 and €95. May–Sept Mon–Sat 6–9pm; Mar–Apr and Oct Tues–Sat 6–9pm. Closed Nov–Feb. Reservations essential.

A fire crackles in the bar at the Wild Honey Inn.

Sports & Outdoor Pursuits in County Clare

BIRD-WATCHING The **Bridges of Ross,** on the north side of **Loop Head,** is one of Ireland's prime autumn bird-watching sites, especially during northwest gales, when several rare species have been seen with some consistency. **Loop Head Lighthouse** at the tip of the head is also a popular spot for watching seabirds.

DOLPHIN-WATCHING The **Shannon Estuary** is home to about 70 bottlenose dolphins, one of four such resident groups of dolphins in Europe. **Dolphinwatch** (dolphinwatch.ie; ✆ **086/842-9505**) runs 2- to 3-hour cruises costing €50 adults, €35 children 14 and under. Advance booking is essential.

GOLF One of the region's most famous golf courses is at **Lahinch Golf Club,** Lahinch (lahinchgolf.com; ✆ **065/708-1003**). Of its two 18-hole links courses, the "Old Course"—the longer championship links course—is the one that has given Lahinch its worldwide repute. This course's elevations, especially at the 9th and 13th holes, make for great views, but it also makes wind an integral part of play. Watch the goats, Lahinch's legendary weather forecasters: If they huddle by the clubhouse, it means a storm is approaching. Visitors are welcome to play, especially on weekdays; greens fees are €325 for the Old Course and a more affordable €60 for the newer Castle Course.

The Mass Hole

To say golf is a religious experience in Ireland wouldn't just be hyperbole. Only in Ireland can you experience the unique hazard of the "Mass hole." When the celebration of Mass was outlawed during penal times, secret Masses were often held in hidden dales, culverts, and gorges, out of sight of the British. A few golf links have incorporated such places into their courses. For example, hole 5 at the **Lahinch Golf Course** (above) has a uniquely hidden spot that could easily have served this purpose. Another example is at **Waterville Golf Course** in County Kerry (p. 316), where the 12th hole is still universally known as the Mass hole.

NATURE WALKS The Burren is full of rare plants and flowers and interesting patches of shoreline that make it a wonderful place for a guided walk or tour. Forage for different seaweeds on the rocky shores of the Burren on a 1½-hour tour with **Wild Kitchen** (wildkitchen.ie; tours €40). Or take a Flaggy Shore Oyster Experience tour with **Flaggy Shore Oyster** to see how oysters grow and how to shuck them, following up with **oysters and wine** (flaggyshoreoysters.ie; €55). For something sweeter, the free guided tour at **Burren Perfumery** (burrenperfumery.com; 11:30am and 2:30pm tours daily June–Sept) shows visitors how local flowers and scents are transformed into lovely perfumes, skincare, and soap.

SURFING If you've always wanted to try surfing, here's your chance: **Lahinch Surf School** (lahinchsurfschool.com; ✆ **087/960-9667**), set up in a hut on Lahinch promenade, specializes in getting people suited up and out on the waves—whether you surf every weekend or have never hit a board in your life. They're friendly and know their stuff. Wetsuits and surfboards are included with the lessons, and good thing: Average water temps in late summer are 16°C (61°F), so wetsuits are advised for the length of time you're in the water. Lessons cost €45 adults, €40 students, €35 for children ages 9–15. Private lessons are €130.

COUNTY LIMERICK

Most of County Limerick is peaceful, pleasant farmland. The picture-postcard village of **Adare** is definitely worth a visit (although you'll likely see it amid a row of tourist buses), and the number of good restaurants and hotels nearby make it a good choice for an overnight base. **Limerick City** (see box on p. 371) is not as scenic but has a rich history, and it's worth spending time in the city's medieval quarter and seeing **King John's Castle** (see box on p. 371). If your time is limited, a full day or one overnight in the city should definitely cover the highlights. Elsewhere, **Lough Gur** is also well worth a visit, with its lovely lakeside scenery and intriguing ancient sites.

Visitor Information

The **Limerick Tourist Information Centre** at St. John's Castle, Limerick (limerick.ie; ✆ **1800/230330**), is open daily May through September 9:30am until 5pm. Another office inside the **Adare Heritage Centre,** Main Street, Adare (adareheritagecentre.ie; ✆ **061/396-666**), is open daily year-round from 9am to 5:30pm.

Exploring County Limerick

Adare ♥♥ VILLAGE Looking like a village plucked from a book of fairy tales, Adare has thatched cottages, black-and-white timbered houses, lichen-covered churches, and romantic ruins, all strewn along the banks of the River Maigue. Unfortunately, all of this means that Adare has been seriously discovered by the tour-bus crowds. Even by May, which is still officially off-season, the roads can get clogged at times—but it's absolutely worth a stop, nonetheless. Drop in at the **Adare Heritage Centre** on Main Street, roughly in the middle of the village. Part visitor center, part museum on the history of the town, it also has a small craft store and a

Thatched cottages in the picture-postcard town of Adare.

LIMERICK CITY: step into history

It's synonymous the world over with a type of lively verse, but Limerick itself is a fascinating city with a rich history. With a population of 102,000, it's the Republic of Ireland's third-largest city (only Dublin and Cork are bigger), but the city center itself is tiny and perfectly walkable. Set along the River Shannon, Limerick has had its high and low points over the years—it has been home to Irish kings, a walled medieval city, and a prosperous Georgian town. Bleaker times in the 20th century (some of which were featured in Frank McCourt's memoir *Angela's Ashes*) have given the city a gritty, urban feel usually associated with much bigger cities. Limerick has been undergoing a regeneration in recent years, however, and the atmosphere in the city center is relaxed, vibrant, and safe. There's lots to see and do here. If you are spending a day or two in the city and plan to take in a number of sights, the best way to get your bearings is to take a guided walking tour—see **limerick.ie** for a list of tours and guides.

Start at **King John's Castle ♥♥** (Nicholas St.; kingjohnscastle.com; ✆ **061/370-501**), a magnificent riverside fortress dating from 1210, and the centerpiece of Limerick's historic quarter. A walk through the castle will take you through the history of Ireland via high-tech interactive displays, videos, costumed characters, and fun medieval games, and you can also explore the massive towers. Admission costs €15 adults, €10.50 seniors, €11.50 students, €11 children 4–18 (free for children 3 and under), and €46 to €63 families. It's open daily March to September 9:30am to 6pm, October to March 9:30am to 5pm (last admission 1 hr. before closing).

Also in the medieval quarter, **Saint Mary's Cathedral ♥♥** (Bridge St.; saintmaryscathedral.ie; ✆ **061/310-293**), which dates from 1168, has quirky features like the Leper's Squint (a wall opening from medieval times) and "mercy seats" from the 15th century, which allowed clergy to rest while standing. It has countless small chapels and stained-glass windows, but just stepping through the doors gives you a feel of ancient history. Admission is €5 adults; €3.50 students.

Located in an 18th-century Customs building with a fine Palladian front, the **Hunt Museum ♥♥** (Rutland St.; huntmuseum.com; ✆ **061/312833**) has a magnificent medieval collection, plus exhibits on ancient Greece and Rome and paintings by Picasso and Renoir. Admission costs €12.50 adults, €10 seniors and students, free for age 15 and under. It's open Tuesday to Saturday from 10am to 5pm, Sunday and public holidays from 11am until 5pm. For more modern art, the **Limerick City Gallery of Art ♥♥** (Pery Square; gallery.limerick.ie; ✆ **061/310633**) has contemporary art exhibitions plus a permanent collection with work by the Irish painter Jack B. Yeats. It's open Monday to Saturday from 10am to 5pm and Sunday noon until 5pm (closed on public holidays). Admission is free.

A 1-hour **Treaty City Brewery tour ♥♥** (treatycitybrewery.ie; ✆ **086/453-1400**) in the medieval quarter takes you through the city's history of brewing, which dates back to the 1700s. Tours include tastings and run Friday through Sunday (€23 per person). If you're in town on a weekend, don't miss the **Milk Market Limerick ♥♥** (milkmarketlimerick.ie; ✆ **061/214782**), a lively farmers market offering everything from fruits and veggies to local cheeses, jams, and bread on Saturdays; street food, live music, and vintage shops join the offerings on Fridays and Sundays. It's a great place to sample produce from the rest of the county and collect snacks and treats for day trips. Check website for details; admission is free.

shop selling Irish woolens. In addition, from June to September the center runs bus tours to Desmond Castle (p. 276) (€10 adults; €8 seniors, students, and children; and €22.50 families).

Adare Heritage Centre, Main St., Adare. adareheritagecentre.ie. ✆ **061/396-666.** Free admission. Daily 9am–5:30pm.

Foynes Flying Boat Museum ♥♥ MUSEUM When Shannon Airport was just a remote patch of undeveloped farmland, this was the center of international aviation in Europe. The first commercial flight from the U.S. to Europe touched down at Foynes Airport, one hot July morning in 1937. Five years later, this became one end of the first-ever regular service between the two continents. (In the same year, Foynes was also said to be the birthplace of Irish coffee: After a particularly violent storm turned back a New York–bound flight, the bartender was asked to serve something that would both warm up and calm down the rattled passengers—so he served hot coffee and threw shots of whiskey in for good measure.) At this engaging museum, you can go inside a full-size replica of the original Pan Am "flying boat," which may make you swear never to complain about a modern flight again. Leave lots of time for your visit. There's a Maritime Museum; a Maureen O'Hara exhibition, with fashion and memorabilia from the late star's personal collection; an Irish coffee center; and a fun flying boat flight simulator, plus a restaurant.

Foynes. flyingboatmuseum.com. ✆ **069/65416.** Admission €15 adults; €13 seniors and students; €8 children 5–17; free for children 4 and under; €35 families. Tues–Sun 10am–4:30pm. Last admission 1 hr. before closing.

Lough Gur ♥♥ LAKE/ANCIENT SITES Occupied continuously from the Neolithic period to late medieval times, this lovely lake's shores hold an unusual preponderance of ancient sites, most of which are well-signposted on the R512, the drive that skirts around the lake's edge. Archaeologists have uncovered foundations of a small farmstead built around the year A.D. 900; a lake island dwelling built between A.D. 500 and 1000; a wedge-shaped tomb that was a communal grave around 2500 B.C.; and the extraordinary Grange Stone Circle, a 4,000-year-old site with 113 upright stones forming the largest prehistoric stone circle in Ireland. An interesting visitor center helps put it all into context, with exhibits explaining why Neolithic people chose this area to settle. To find the center, turn east off R512 at Reardons Pub in Holycross, take the first left afterward, and follow Lough Gur Road. The lake itself is a great place to explore and have a picnic.

11km (6¾ miles) SE of Limerick City on R512, Lough Gur. loughgur.com. ✆ **061/385186.** Free access to Lough Gur itself; visitor center €5 adults, €4 seniors and students, €3 children, €15 families. Visitor center June–Aug daily 10am–6pm; Mar–May 10am–5pm; Sept–Feb Tues–Sun 10am–4pm.

Where to Stay in Limerick City & County

Some of the larger hotels and recent builds in Limerick City feel somewhat impersonal, but many real finds are in the rural parts of County

Guest rooms at Adare Manor are traditionally elegant, with views of the landscaped grounds.

Limerick, where you can hide away in a country-house hotel or splurge on a night in a grand manor.

Adare Manor ♥♥♥ This sumptuous place is all about luxury, and it comes as no surprise that in 2023 and 2024, *Condé Nast Traveler* readers named it the best resort in Europe. The beautifully restored and converted Victorian Gothic manor house is set in a whopping 240 hectares (840 acres) of landscaped grounds. Spacious rooms come with king-size beds, Georgian-style furniture, and garden views. It's a golfer's paradise, with a championship-level course set to host the 2027 Ryder Cup, as well as archery, clay pigeon shooting, and horseback riding. The hotel has three restaurants, including the Michelin-starred **Oak Room ♥♥♥** (p. 376). It might break the bank, but you'll have fun on the way.

Adare. adaremanor.com. ✆ **061/605200.** 103 units. €595–€1,300 double; €2,195–€4,175 state room; €3,450–€8,950 suite; €1,600–€3,500 cottage. Breakfast included. Free parking. **Amenities:** 3 restaurants; bar; gym; golf course; pool; room service; spa; Wi-Fi (free).

Courtyard Cottage ♥ A former cowshed may not sound like the height of glamour, but this is a beautifully converted, elegant space, a short drive east of Foynes and 15 minutes' drive from Adare. You really feel away from the herd (no pun intended), with 202 hectares (500 acres) of farmland between you and civilization. This is a self-catering option set on an organic farm—guests can join in whatever farm activities are going at the time, collect eggs, feed the chickens, or play with the dogs. There's no website, but e-mail **donaghogrady@yahoo.com**.

Askeaton. ✆ **087/213-3698.** Self-catering (2 bedrooms). 1 unit. €175 per night, 2-night min., further nights €150 per night. Free parking. **Amenities:** Kitchen; tennis court; Wi-Fi (free).

THERE ONCE WAS A poet FROM LIMERICK . . .

So how exactly did a genre of bawdy pub poetry come to be associated with Limerick? The answer seems buried nearly 300 years in the past. Nobody really knows who wrote the first sharply worded, five-line poem, but the format became popular in the 18th century, thanks to a group of poets who lived in the town of Croom in County Limerick. Known as the *Fili na Maighe*, or "Poets of the Maigue," the poets wrote sardonic, quick-witted poems in Irish that soon became all the rage. Their style was adopted across the region, and within a century, everybody was doing it. Anthologies on the subject list 42 poets and Irish scholars in the county in the 19th century, whose limerick-style compositions covered a range of topics: romance, drinking, personal squabbles, and politics.

But it's possible that the scathing, satiric limerick style we know today rose from an 18th-century battle of wills between poet and pub owner Sean O'Tuama and Andrias MacCraith, his boyhood friend growing up in County Limerick. After a spectacular falling-out (nobody quite remembers over what), they vented their wit in a series of castigating verses about each other. These became enormously popular, thus birthing the modern limerick. In retrospect, they're kind of cute, although the meter sometimes feels a little stretched. As MacCraith once wrote:

O'Tuama! You boast yourself handy,
At selling good ale and bright brandy
But the fact is your liquor
Makes everyone sicker,
I tell you this, I, your good friend, Andy.

Echo Lodge ♥♥ This place was once a convent before being converted into a chic and stylish country-house hotel with a relaxed, homey feel. Guest rooms are relatively small but decorated in old-world style with antiques, vintage-print wallpapers, flowing curtains, and pleasantly eccentric objets d'art such as mini-Ionic columns for bedside tables. Dining is the highlight here—the **Mustard Seed ♥♥♥** restaurant is one of the best in the region (p. 376).

Ballingarry (13km/8 miles S of Adare). mustardseed.ie. ✆ **069/68508.** 18 units. €200–€340 double; €340 suite. Breakfast included. Free parking. **Amenities:** Restaurant; bar; room service; Wi-Fi (free in public areas only). Closed Jan.

Fitzgerald's Woodlands House Hotel ♥♥ The rooms at this pleasant, modern hotel aren't particularly fancy, but they're enormous—rare for a place that charges just €155 a night in low season. The hotel makes a big deal out of how good its beds are, thanks to a full 10cm (4 in.) goose-down mattress topper on each bed. The in-house **Revas Spa** offers relaxation treatments and a thermal suite to while away the last hint of travel fatigue.

Adare. woodlands-hotel.ie. ✆ **061/605100.** 94 units. €155–€295 double; €400–€550 suite. Breakfast included. Dinner, bed-and-breakfast packages, and senior discounts available. Free parking. **Amenities:** Restaurant; bar; room service; spa; Wi-Fi (free).

No. 1 Pery Square ♥♥ This gorgeous restored Georgian town house is on one of the elegant streets of the Georgian part of Limerick City, opposite People's Park and around 10 minutes' walk from the city center. For the full experience, opt for one of the six period bedrooms at the front of the house, which have roll-top and copper bathtubs, sash windows, and views of the park. Don't miss the lovely drawing room for guests in this part of the house. There's also a large underground spa and an excellent restaurant where the chef uses local Limerick produce including gourmet meats, cheeses, and breads from suppliers at the Milk Market.

1 Pery Square, Georgian Quarter, Limerick City. oneperysquare.com. ✆ **061/402-402.** 21 units. €265–€550 double. Check website for dinner and spa packages. Free parking. **Amenities:** 2 restaurants; bar; terrace; room service; spa; Wi-Fi (free).

Where to Eat in Limerick City & County

An exciting food scene in Limerick has emerged in the past few years in both the city and along the rural byways of the county, with places to eat that would be serious contenders on any "best of" lists for the whole of Ireland. In addition to the options listed below, for light bites and coffee in the city, check out **Rift Coffee** (30 Mallow St.; riftcoffee.com; no phone) or **Jack Monday's** (Thomond Bridge House, Thomondgate; jackmondays.com; ✆ **061/279-296**), while **Bean a Tí** (1 Little Catherine St.; facebook.com/beanatibakery; no phone) is the place to go for cakes—the bakery has been run by the same family for three generations.

1826 Adare ♥♥♥ MODERN IRISH It's set in a rustic thatched cottage with plenty of old-world charm (1826 is the year the first Lord of

The ever-changing menu at 1826 Adare may feature seasonal dishes like these ripe heirloom tomatoes paired with creamy local mozzarella.

Dunraven built the cottage), but there's nothing twee or old-fashioned about the cooking here. Chef Wade Murphy has worked in some of the world's top kitchens and was awarded best chef in Limerick, and with a menu that changes every month, he works his culinary magic with the county's best produce. Expect dishes like warm chicken liver salad, served with piccalilli, pickles, and greens, or free-range pork with squash and beer mustard cream, all served in a relaxed setting. Book well in advance.
Main St., Adare. 1826adare.ie. ✆ **061/396-004.** Entrees €27–€43. Thurs–Sat 5–9pm; Sun 3–8pm.

Cornstore ♥♥ MODERN IRISH This is a gorgeous space with a lively atmosphere. For weekend lunches, the menu is bistro-style, with options such as seafood chowder, chicken wings, and steak sandwiches. In the evenings the lights are dimmed, candles are lit, and the menu features dishes like oven-roasted salmon, oven-roasted pork belly, and a selection of local dry-aged beef (tasty sides include truffle mac 'n' cheese with a Parmesan crust or Camembert mash). There's a decent wine and cocktail list, too.
Thomas St., Limerick City. cornstore.ie. ✆ **061/609-000.** Entrees lunch €12–€23, dinner €24–€45; 3-course set menu €40–€50. Tues–Thurs 5–10pm; Fri 4–10pm; Sat–Sun noon–10pm.

Foley's at the Pike ♥ PUB FOOD/GRILL Nearly 16km (9 miles) southwest of Adare, just off the main N21 road, this friendly little bar and grill focuses on hearty, unpretentious comfort food, such as steak, fish, and grilled lamb, alongside a more international selection "from the wok" (stir-fries, fajitas, curries). Heading west from Adare on N21, take the R523 turnoff signposted for Athea.
Reens Pike, Ardagh. foleyspub.ie. ✆ **069/64416.** Entrees €15–€19. Wed–Sat noon–9pm; Sun noon–8pm.

The Mustard Seed ♥♥♥ MODERN EUROPEAN Not so much the in-house restaurant of the excellent **Echo Lodge** ♥♥ (p. 374) as the main attraction with guest rooms upstairs, this is one of the best-loved, and most widely known, restaurants in the region. Dinner is served in the grand reception rooms of this elegant country house, with white table linen and vases of fresh garden flowers completing the scene. Mustard Seed's own kitchen garden supplies many of the ingredients, too. Four-course menus are imaginative and scintillating; after a starter like mussels with sea urchin and radish, you could go for the halibut with *aubergine* (eggplant) and miso, or beef filet with chickpea and black garlic.
Echo Lodge, Ballingarry (13km/8 miles S of Adare). mustardseed.ie. ✆ **069/68508.** Fixed-price 4-course dinner €76. Daily 7–9:30pm.

The Oak Room ♥♥♥ MODERN IRISH The first restaurant to gain a Michelin star in this part of Ireland, the Oak Room is part of **Adare Manor** ♥♥♥ (p. 373). This is a place where you're expected to sit up straight and dress right. The food certainly lives up to the elegant

IF THE story FITZ . . .

"Honey Fitz" was the nickname of John Fitzgerald (1863–1950), maternal grandfather to President John F. Kennedy. Born in America to Irish immigrants (his father was from Limerick), Fitzgerald was twice elected mayor of Boston.

According to the biographer Robert Dallek, Fitz had a reputation for being "the only politician who could sing 'Sweet Adeline' sober and get away with it"—hence the nickname, in praise of his sweet singing voice. Between Adare and Limerick, the small town of Patrickswell is home to the bijou **Honey Fitz Theatre,** which holds performances and comedy nights (run by Lough Gur Dramatic Society; ✆ **087/000-4858**). The theater was opened in 1994 by Fitzgerald's granddaughter Jean Kennedy Smith (then U.S. ambassador). Naturally, "Sweet Adeline" was sung during the ceremony.

surrounds; the six-course tasting menu may include dishes like hand-dived scallop with parsnip, vanilla, and ginger jus, or monkfish with seaweed and lime, with perhaps a passionfruit and chocolate dessert. And if you're enjoying the place too much to leave at meal's end . . . well, you probably should anyway, since an overnight stay here can cost about the same as your transatlantic airfare home.

Adare. adaremanor.com. ✆ **061/605-200.** 6-course tasting menu €160. Wine pairing additional €100. Wed–Sun 5:30–9pm. Smart dress essential. Children must be aged 6 and up.

The Silver Room ♥♥ MODERN Irish This family-run restaurant serves good Irish staples like steaks, chicken, and fish, with an emphasis on quality local produce. As a starter, the Silver Room tasting board is a great way to sample the region's produce, with West Limerick Ham, black pudding, slow-cooked pork belly, farmhouse cheeses, red pepper relish, and sourdough bread, plus a shot of apple liqueur to round it off. For mains, look for slow-cooked lamb shank with mash and roasted root vegetables or pan-seared seabass with tiger prawns and tenderstem broccoli. You definitely won't leave here hungry.

Market Yard, Newcastle West (24km/15 miles SW of Adare). silverroom.ie. ✆ **069/61721.** Fixed-price 3-course dinner €47. Entrees €22–€36. Wed–Thurs and Sun 12:30–8pm; Fri–Sat 12:30–9pm.

Sports & Outdoor Pursuits in County Limerick

CYCLING The **Limerick Greenway** (limerick.ie/greenway) is a 40km (24-mile) walking and cycling trail through bucolic rural Limerick countryside on the old Limerick-to-Kerry railway line. It's gorgeous, but don't expect jaw-dropping, dramatic scenery: This is a gentle jaunt past trees, farms, rivers, and old train stations, soaking up the country feels (and smells), going through a small tunnel, and perhaps stopping off for coffee and cake. It's well set up, with free parking, and a number of bike- and e-bike-hire companies listed on the Greenway website will also take you back to your car or shuttle your luggage; rentals start from €30.

FISHING **Celtic Angling,** in Ballingarry, just south of Adare (celticangling.com; ✆ **069/68202**), offers daylong trout-fishing excursions on the River Maigue or River Deel, including pickup from Limerick City, equipment, and licenses. A day's fishing costs €250 for one person, plus €80 for each additional person, up to a maximum of four. A shorter 3-hour introductory session to river fly-fishing costs €160. (Owner Paddy Dunworth also offers guided sightseeing trips and hillwalking excursions; check the website for details.)

HORSEBACK RIDING The county's fields provide good turf for horseback riding. Rates are around €30 to €40 per hour. The **Clonshire Equestrian Centre** in Adare (clonshire.com; ✆ **061/396770**) has riding holidays for adults and children. It's also one of the only riding schools in Ireland to offer riding for disabled visitors.

COUNTY TIPPERARY

"It's a long way to Tipperary" as the song goes, and it can certainly feel true when you have the map spread out before you, trying to plan your itinerary. Tipperary's big attractions are few and far enough between that they don't always work conveniently as day trips. (Though the one truly essential site, the **Rock of Cashel,** can easily be worked into a road trip on the M8 between Dublin and Cork.) The relative quietness of Tipperary, however, is also part of its appeal. Far from the tour buses and selfie sticks, it just may be the welcoming, unspoiled Ireland everyone is looking for.

Visitor Information

The **Clonmel Tourist Office** at 6 Sarsfield St., Clonmel (✆ **052/612-2960**), is open year-round Monday to Friday from 10am to 5pm. The small **Cashel Tourist Office** at the Heritage Centre, Main Street, Cashel (cashel.ie; ✆ **062/61333**), is open from 9:30am to 5:30pm daily March to October, and Monday through Friday November to February. A **seasonal office** at Castle Street, Cahir (✆ **1850/230-330**), is open April to September only, Tuesday to Saturday from 9am until 5:15pm.

Exploring County Tipperary

Clonmel, the capital of Tipperary, is the unassuming gateway to the region. A working town largely unspoiled by tourism, Clonmel (whose name in Irish, *Cluain Meala,* means "meadow of honey") makes a pleasant strategic touring base. Looking at this sleepy place on the banks of the Suir, it's hard to believe that it once withstood a Cromwellian siege for 3 brutal months.

North of Clonmel and deep in the Tipperary countryside, **Cashel,** with its monastic buildings and dramatic setting, is not to be missed. From

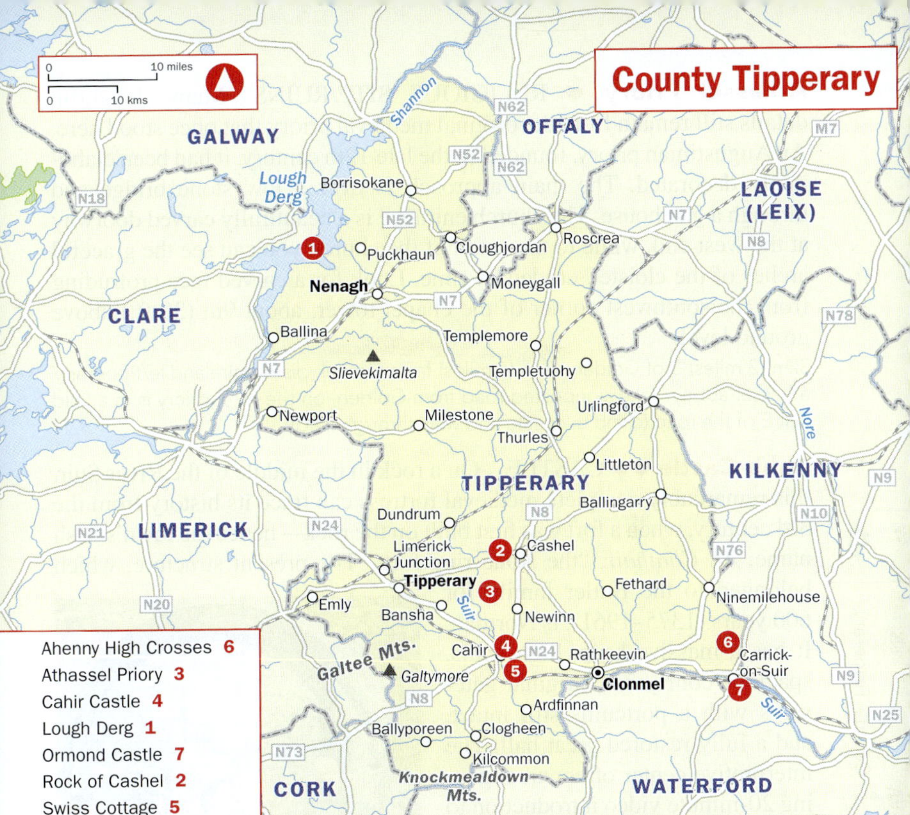

Cahir, there's a gorgeous drive north through the Galtee Mountains to the pristine 11km (7-mile) **Glen of Aherlow,** a secluded and scenic pass between the plains of counties Tipperary and Limerick (see p. 385 for hiking and walking suggestions in this area).

Ahenny High Crosses ♥ RELIGIOUS SITE You're likely to have this little-known and rarely visited site to yourself, except for the cows whose pasture you cross to reach it. On a bright day, the setting is idyllic and gorgeous. The well-preserved Ahenny high crosses date from the 8th or 9th century. Tradition associates them with seven saintly bishops, all brothers said to have been waylaid and murdered. Their unusual stone "caps," thought by some to represent bishops' miters, more likely suggest the transition from wood crosses, which would have had small roofs to shelter them from the rain. Also note their intricate spiral and cable ornamentation in remarkably high relief, which may have been inspired by earlier Celtic metalwork.

Kil Crispeen Churchyard, Ahenny. 8km (5 miles) N of Carrick-on-Suir, signposted off R697. discoverireland.ie/tipperary/ahenny-high-crosses. No phone. Free admission (box for donations).

Athassel Priory ♥ RELIGIOUS SITE/RUINS Many delightful details still remain from the original medieval priory that once stood here. An Augustinian priory, founded in the late 12th century, it had been elaborately decorated. The main approach is over a low stone bridge and through a gatehouse. The church entrance is a beautifully carved doorway at the west end, while to the south of the church you can see the graceful arches of the cloister, eroded by time. Look for a carved face protruding from the southwest corner of the chapel tower, about 9m (30 ft.) above ground level.

3km (2 miles) S of Golden, 7km (4 miles) from Cashel. discoverireland.ie/tipperary/athassel-abbey. Take signposted road from Golden, on the N74; priory is in a field just E of the road (climb over stile and walk through field).

Cahir Castle ♥♥ CASTLE On a rock in the middle of the River Suir, this remarkably complete medieval fortress can trace its history from the 3rd century, when a fort was first built on the rock—hence the town's Irish name, *An Chathair*, "the stone ring-fort." The present structure, which belonged to the Butler family for 600 years (1375–1961), is Norman. It has a massive keep, high walls, spacious courtyards, original gateways with a portcullis still intact, and a fully restored great hall. The interpretive center offers an engaging 20-minute video introduction to the region's major historic sites, and you can take a guided tour of the castle grounds.

Castle St., Cahir. heritageireland.ie. ✆ **052/744-1011.** Admission €5 adults; €4 seniors; €3 students and children; €13 families. Mid-June to Aug daily 9am–6:30pm; Mar to mid-June and Sept to mid-Oct daily 9:30am–5:30pm; mid-Oct to Feb daily 9:30am–4:30pm. Last admission 45 min. before closing.

Guided tours are offered at Cahir Castle.

Ormond Castle ♥♥ CASTLE This mid-15th-century castle built by Sir Edward MacRichard Butler on a strategic bend of the River Suir has lain in ruins for centuries. What still stands, attached to the ancient battlements, is the last surviving Tudor manor house in Ireland. Trusting that "if he built it, she would come," Thomas Butler constructed an extensive manor in honor of his most successful relation (and childhood friend), Queen Elizabeth I. He was to be disappointed, however—Elizabeth never did visit. But many others have, especially since the Heritage Service partially restored this impressive piece of Irish history. The manor's

petticoat loose & OTHER SCENIC DIVERSIONS

Driving up from County Waterford, you might want to travel via the **Vee Gap,** an 18km-long (11-mile) road winding through the Knockmealdown Mountains from Lismore and Cappoquin in County Waterford to Clogheen in County Tipperary. It's a dramatic drive, which peaks at the Tipperary-Waterford border, where the two slopes of the pass converge to frame the patchwork fields of the Galtee Valley far below.

At this point, numerous walking trails lead to the nearby peaks and down to the mountain lake of **Petticoat Loose**—named after a, shall we say, lady of flexible morals. A more edifying local character was Samuel Grubb, who so loved these slopes that he left instructions to be buried upright overlooking them. Look for the rounded stone cairn off the road between Clogheen and the Vee Gap, where Samuel does indeed stand entombed, facing the Golden Vale of Tipperary.

The Vee Gap also has some terrific walking paths. About 2km (1¼ miles) north of R669 and R668, you reach the highest point in the gap; a parking lot is here, as well as a dirt road continuing down to a lake—**Bay Lough**—nestled into the slope below. This dirt road, once the main thoroughfare over the gap, now offers a fine walk to the shores of the lake, with outstanding views of the valley to the north. For a panoramic perspective of the region, start walking due east from the gap parking lot to the summit of **Sugarloaf Hill;** the hike is extremely steep, but well worth the effort—the views from the ridge are superb.

plasterwork, carvings, period furniture, and collection of original 17th- and 18th-century royal charters will make you glad you came and leave you wondering why Queen Bess never did.

Signposted from the center of Carrick-on-Suir. heritageireland.ie. ✆ **051/640787.** Guided tours hourly; prebook by phone. Admission including house tour €5 adults; €4 seniors; €3 students and children; €13 families. Exhibition and courtyard only €3 adults; €2 seniors; €1 students and children; €6 families. Mid-Mar to Oct 10am–6pm; closed Nov to mid-Mar. Last admission 45 min. before closing.

The Rock of Cashel ♥♥♥ RELIGIOUS SITE/RUINS One of Ireland's most iconic medieval ruins, this dramatically craggy abbey atop a hill in the center of Cashel dominates views for miles around. The so-called "Rock"—an outcrop of limestone reaching some 60m (197 ft.) into the sky—tells the tales of 16 centuries. It was the seat of the kings of Munster at least as far back as A.D. 360, and it remained a royal fortress until 1101, when King Murtagh O'Brien granted it to the church. Among Cashel's many great moments was the legendary baptism of King Aengus by St. Patrick in 448. Remaining on the rock are the ruins of a two-towered chapel, a cruciform cathedral, a 28m (92-ft.) round tower, and a cluster of other medieval monuments. Inside the cathedral, extraordinary and detailed ancient carvings survive in excellent condition. The views of and from the Rock are spectacular. Guided tours are available most days and don't need to be pre-booked. You can book admission tickets online, but admission to Cormac's Chapel is by guided tour only and you'll need to buy those tickets on-site. ***Note:*** Check the site's Facebook page for info on upcoming light shows that bathe the ruins in color: It's been green (St. Patrick's Day), purple (International Day of People with Disability), and gold (National Autism Day).

Cashel. heritageireland.ie. ✆ **062/61437.** Admission €8 adults; €6 seniors; €4 children and students; €20 families. Mid-Mar to early Oct daily 9am–5:30pm; mid-Oct to mid-Mar daily 9am–4:30pm; last admission 45 min. before closing.

The Rock of Cashel, County Tipperary's most iconic heritage site.

The Swiss Cottage ♥♥ HISTORIC HOUSE A hunting and fishing lodge for the earls of Glengall from around 1812, the Swiss Cottage is a superb example of *cottage orné:* a rustic house embodying the ideal of simplicity that so appealed to the Romantics of the early 19th century. The thatched-roof cottage has extensive timberwork, usually not seen in Ireland, and is believed to have been designed by royal architect John Nash. The gorgeous interior has some of the first wallpaper commercially produced in Paris. A guided tour (the only way to see the inside of the building) lasts approximately 40 minutes. It can get busy on summer days, so arrive early.

Off R670 Ardfinnan Rd., Cahir. heritageireland.ie. ✆ **052/744-1144.** Guided tour €5 adults; €4 seniors; €3 students and children; €13 families. Mid-Mar to late Oct daily 10am–6pm; last tour 45 min. before closing.

Where to Stay in County Tipperary

Anner Hotel ♥♥ This elegant boutique hotel just outside the bustling town of Thurles has an idyllic location on extensive, manicured grounds. Rooms are bright and spacious if not huge, with comfortable beds, tasteful decor, and views of the gorgeous grounds. It's well located for exploring the Rock of Cashel and Kilkenny, but you may want to stay in for formal afternoon tea in one of the sunny lounges or to try out the swimming pool and steam room. You'll definitely want to stay in for dinner at **Seasons Restaurant,** which relies on Tipperary produce for practically everything it makes; the hotel also has a more casual bar and bistro.

Dublin Rd., Thurles. annerhotel.ie. ✆ **050/421799.** 93 units. €155–€210 double. Breakfast included (room-only rates also available). Free parking. **Amenities:** Restaurant; bar/bistro; gym; indoor pool; Wi-Fi (free).

Bansha House ♥ This vine-covered Georgian manor house in tiny Bansha, in the shadow of the Galtee Mountains, is just a few miles south of Cashel. Guest rooms are simple and old-fashioned—not all have private bathrooms, for instance, so be sure you ask for one if that's important—but it's cheerful, cozy, and you'll get a warm welcome from host Mary. Guests are free to wander the enormous grounds, and a horse-racing stable is just next door—ask and they'll take you to meet the occupants.

Bansha. banshahouse.com. ✆ **062/54194.** 6 units. €125–€130 double. Breakfast included. Free parking. **Amenities:** Wi-Fi (free).

Cashel Palace Hotel ♥♥♥ Recently restored, this historic Palladian manor house dates to 1732. It seems that no luxury was spared during its original construction. Guests can enjoy original features like high ceilings and Corinthian columns with antiques, lounges with open fires, and huge sash windows overlooking 25 acres of grounds. Suites have four-poster beds, marble bathrooms, and features like original fireplaces; some rooms even have a view of the Rock of Cashel. Dinner at the **Bishop's Buttery**

THE lough derg DRIVE

At the meeting point of counties Clare, Limerick, and Tipperary, the Shannon River's largest lake, Lough Derg—virtually an inland sea—creates a stunning waterscape 40km (25 miles) long and almost 16km (10 miles) wide. The road that circles the lake for 153km (95 miles), the **Lough Derg Drive,** is one of Ireland's great scenic drives, a continuous photo op with panoramas of glistening waters, gentle mountains, and hilly farmlands unspoiled by commercialization.

The drive is also a collage of colorful shoreline towns, starting at the lake's south end with **Killaloe,** County Clare, and **Ballina,** County Tipperary. They're so close that they are essentially one community—only a splendid 13-arch bridge over the Shannon separates them. In the summer, their pubs and bars fill with weekend sailors. **Killaloe** is a picturesque town with lakeside views at almost every turn and restaurants and pubs perched on the shore. **Kincora,** on the highest ground at Killaloe, was traditionally said to be the royal settlement of Brian Boru and the other O'Brien kings, although no trace of any buildings survives.

Memorable little towns and harbor-side villages, like **Mountshannon** and **Dromineer,** dot the rest of the Lough Derg Drive. Some towns, like **Terryglass** and **Woodford,** are known for atmospheric old pubs where spontaneous sessions of traditional Irish music are likely to break out. Others, like **Puckane** and **Ballinderry,** offer unique crafts. On the north shore of the lake in County Galway, **Portumna** is worth a visit for its forest park and castle.

The best way to get to Lough Derg is by car or boat. Because the area has limited public transportation, you will need a car to get around the lake. Major roads that lead to Lough Derg are the main Limerick–Dublin road (N7) from points east and south; N6 and N65 from Galway and the west; and N52 from the north. The Lough Derg Drive, which is well signposted, is a combination of R352 on the west bank of the lake and R493, R494, and R495 on the east bank.

celebrates the best of County Tipperary produce, with more casual fare at **Mikey Ryan's**—nab a space on the terrace in good weather.

Main St., Cashel. cashelpalacehotel.ie. ✆ **062/62002.** 42 units. €365–€625 double; €1,009–€1,385 suite. Breakfast included. Free parking. **Amenities:** Restaurant; bar; spa; pool; Wi-Fi (free).

Hotel Minella ♥ The River Suir babbles along in front of this modern hotel in Clonmel, overlooked by a distant mountain range. Guest rooms are properly spacious, with large, comfortable beds and modern (if rather uninspiring) decor. Some rooms even have their own hot tubs. For slightly more space, the hotel also has 10 well-equipped two- and three-bedroom lodges on the grounds that can be rented on a self-catering basis. The hotel has a small spa with a swimming pool; book ahead for treatments. The only real downside to the place is that it's a popular venue for weddings, reunions, and parties, especially in summer.

9 Coleville Rd., Clonmel. hotelminella.com. ✆ **052/612-2388.** 90 units. €185–€220 double. Breakfast included. Check website for special offers. Free parking. **Amenities:** Restaurant; bar; gym; pool; Wi-Fi (free).

Where to Eat in County Tipperary

Befani's ♥ MEDITERRANEAN/TAPAS This cheerful little restaurant in Clonmel is a pleasant surprise in a region where Irish cooking is king. The tapas lunch menu is divided into hot and cold tapas, including *patatas bravas,* prawn salad, and watermelon salad with feta cheese. There are platters of antipasti, and the main courses combine Irish and Mediterranean influences, with oven-roasted spiced salmon and Moroccan vegetarian tagine. Befani's also has simple guest rooms available for from €115 per night, including breakfast.

6 Sarsfield St., Clonmel. befani.com. ✆ **061/617-7893.** Tapas €6.50–€9.50; entrees €18–€34. Thurs–Sat 5–9pm; Sun 12:30–3pm and 5–8pm.

Chez Hans ♥♥ EUROPEAN Located in a beautiful converted church building—which was purchased in the 1860s with a thousand-year lease on terms of 1 shilling per year—Chez Hans is one of the most reliably good restaurants in Cashel. Menus change several times a week, based on what's freshest. Seafood features heavily (smoked fish cakes with prawns, or maybe Dover sole with fennel and red chicory), or you could opt for a roast guinea fowl, served with braised leeks and walnut sauce. Reservations are recommended. The restaurant is a 2-minute walk from the Rock of Cashel.

Rockside, Cashel. chezhans.net. ✆ **062/61177.** Entrees €26–€38. Fri–Sat 5:30–9:30pm; Sun 12:30–3:30pm and 5:30–8pm.

Flanagan's On The Lake ♥♥ GASTROPUB This popular gastropub in the village of Ballina/Killaloe has a lovely location beside Lough Derg. The large menu has a good selection of standard pub-grub fare: steak, duck, burgers, fish and chips, and pizzas, with plenty of vegetarian options. The outside area gets busy in good weather. This is also a pub, so it can get a little lively later in the evening. The kitchen closes at around 8:45pm.

Ballina Quay, Ballina. flanagansonthelake.ie. © **061/622-790.** Fixed price 2-course menu €32; 3 courses €37. Entrees €14–€30. Daily noon–11:30pm (last food orders at 8:30pm).

Queen Bee's Café and Deli ♥♥ CAFE/DELI This cute little cornerside cafe serves tasty snacks, cakes, and brasserie-style lunches. The menu has plenty of traditional favorites—potato and leek soup, Irish stew, deliciously fluffy potato pancakes—or you could opt for a simple chicken salad or toasted sandwich. It also does a great breakfast if you're tired of hotel fare.

98 Irishtown, Clonmel. © **052/618-0255.** Entrees €11–€15. Mon–Sat 9am–3.30pm.

River House Restaurant ♥♥ CAFE Come here for filling cooked breakfasts or good lunchtime sandwiches like Limerick baked ham and brie cheese in a toasted ciabatta, or roast chicken and stuffing. There are more filling options like burgers, steak sandwiches, fish of the day, and lasagna on the menu, too. Grab a table upstairs for glorious views of the castle and river. There's a nice gift shop on the lower level.

1 Castle St., Cahir. © **052/744-1951.** Lunch €6.50–€18. Daily 8:30am–5pm.

Sports & Outdoor Pursuits in Tipperary

BIRD-WATCHING As many as 15 species of Irish water birds—including mute swans, coots, gadwalls, and gray herons—can be seen at the **Marlfield Lake Wildfowl Refuge,** several miles west of Clonmel in Marlfield. On your way, you'll pass signposts for **St. Patrick's Well,** less than 1.6km (1 mile) away, a tranquil spot with an effervescent pool of reputedly healing crystalline water and an ancient Celtic cross rising from the middle of the pool. Legend has it that St. Patrick himself visited here.

CYCLING Centered around the town of Nenagh, the **North Tipperary Cycle Network** consists of three scenic cycling routes around the north Tipperary countryside. Signposted routes pass Lough Derg, small riverside villages, and farmland, before looping back to Nenagh. They vary in length from 30km (18½ miles) to 67km (41½ miles). Maps and other information can be found under "Cycling" at intipperary.ie. **Lough Derg eBike Tours** offers e-bike rentals and guided e-bike tours from Nenagh or Killaloe (loughdergebiketours.ie; © **087/459-3141**).

WALKING In the Clonmel area, you'll find some excellent river and hill walks, some more challenging than others. The most spectacular is the ascent of famed **Slievenamon,** a mountain rich in myth. Inexpensive, detailed trail maps for at least a half-dozen walks are available at the Clonmel Tourist Office on Sarsfield Street, Clonmel.

The **Galtee Mountains,** northwest of the Knockmealdowns, offer some great long and short walks. For trail maps and other assistance, contact the **Glen of Aherlow Fáilte Society,** Coach Road, Newtown (aherlow.com; ✆ **062/56331**). It's open daily June to October from 9am until 6pm (hours vary the rest of the year). One particularly beautiful trail—a 3-hour round-trip—loops around the sparkling waters of **Lake Muskry,** on the north side of the range. (Ask for directions in Rossadrehid, west of Bansha on the R663.)

WATERSPORTS Tipperary is home to two official Blueways (trails that run on and alongside lakes, canals, and rivers). The **Suir Blueway** has 53km (33 miles) of paddling trails and a 21km (13-mile) walking/cycle path along the River Suir; rent bikes from **Blueway Bike Hire** (bluewaybikehire.ie; ✆ **051/640130**) for a pleasant 21km (13-mile) cycle from Clonmel to Carrick-on-Suir. Or check out one of the paddling trails on the **Lough Derg Blueway** (bluewaysireland.org). **My Next Adventure** runs guided paddles from Killaloe including full-moon kayaking (mynextadventure.ie; ✆ **087/395-2777**).

10

COUNTY GALWAY & CONNEMARA

Whether you arrive from the north, south, or east, you will notice the scenery change dramatically once you get to County Galway. Parts of the county have bleak bogs, stone walls, windswept trees, and extraordinary light; you will also find lakes, beaches, and mountains in this wild place. And yet, just near the edge of the windswept, boggy expanse of Connemara, on Galway Bay, is one of Ireland's most vibrant cities. Though small, Galway City has long been a thriving center for the arts—it was even the designated European Capital of Culture for a year. Exploring this lovely city's colorful lanes and taking in its electric atmosphere may be one of the highlights of your trip.

ESSENTIALS

Arriving

BY BUS Buses from all parts of Ireland arrive daily at **Bus Éireann Travel Centre,** Ceannt Station, off Eyre Square in Galway City (bus eireann.ie; ✆ **0818/836-6111**). It also provides daily service to Clifden. Buses to rural areas sometimes run only a handful of times per day, and remote sites may be completely inaccessible without a car. **CityLink** (citylink.ie; ✆ **091/564-164**) runs buses to Galway from Cork, Limerick, Dublin, and Dublin Airport, and it runs services every couple of hours between Galway, Clifden, and Letterfrack.

BY TRAIN Trains from Dublin and Limerick arrive daily at Ceannt Station in Galway City, off Eyre Square (irishrail.ie; ✆ **01/8366- 222**). That's pretty much the end of the line, however; to explore the Galway countryside, you'll need a car.

BY CAR Galway City is on the main M6, M17, M18, and N67 roads. Journey time from Dublin is 2 or 2½ hours; from Killarney it's about 3 hours; and from Cork it's about 2½ hours. Outside of Galway City, your options in this region get pretty limited if you don't have a car. To hire one in Galway, try **Budget,** 12 Eyre Square (budget.ie; ✆ **091/564-570**), or **Europcar** at Motorpark, Headford Road (europcar.ie; ✆ **091/396-555**). For car rental options in Dublin, see p. 91; for Shannon airport, see p. 354.

PREVIOUS PAGE: **Derryclare Lough in Connemara National Park.**

BY PLANE Galway has a small airport, but no scheduled flights or commercial services fly in or out; the nearest active airport is **Shannon** (p. 352), about an hour's drive south of Galway City.

GALWAY CITY

A small but thriving city, Galway still has its winding medieval lanes, but it also has a cosmopolitan core and a young population. The hub of activity is around the pedestrianized streets around Shop Street and High Street, while the more formal **Eyre Square** (pronounced *Air* Square) is a few minutes' walk from here. The **River Corrib** runs through the town, with the city's artsy historic district on its east bank between **St. Nicholas' Church** and the harbor. (Look for the riverside **Spanish Arch** and the **Spanish Parade,** which testify to the city's 16th-century heyday as an international port.) The **Latin Quarter** is a small but vibrant area, filled with lively (read: noisy) bars, nightclubs, and restaurants, while the **Westend** across the river is another creative quarter with bars, restaurants, and small shops.

The best way to experience the city is to stroll around the historic core, picking out a few key sites to visit, but leaving the remainder of your time to explore the many small cafes, quirky shops, pubs, and live music sessions. The area is tiny but tangled, so it's easy to lose your way, but getting lost is half the fun. You certainly won't want a car in Galway City's center—if you've driven here, just park and walk. The historic sites are easily navigated, but if you want to delve further, from June to September the Galway Civic Trust offers free walking tours of medieval Galway, departing from the **Hall of the Red Earl** (p. 392) at 2pm on Tuesdays and Thursdays.

Visitor Information

The **Galway Tourist Information Centre,** at the Galway City Museum on Spanish Parade (discoverireland.ie/galway-city; ✆ **1800/230-330**), is open Monday to Saturday from 9am to 5pm.

GALWAY FESTIVAL OF arts

Held over 2 weeks at the end of July, the prestigious **Galway International Arts Festival** has been an annual fixture on the country's cultural calendar since 1978. It came from somewhat humble beginnings—in its first year, the festival took place in a building that is now a cheesemonger (a very good one too, as it happens; see p. 401). Now around 250,000 people attend every year, with nearly 40% of visitors coming from outside Ireland.

The lively program of music, theater, talks, and visual arts is usually announced in May, although they often tease out many events (and big names) in advance of that. Headline music acts for the 2022 festival included the Pixies and the late Sinead O'Connor; major speakers of recent years have included the former Irish President Mary Robinson.

Ticket prices vary, but many events are free. Check out **giaf.ie** for more information.

Exploring Galway City

Galway is small and best explored on foot. If you start on the waterfront, you might notice an ancient stone arch. Dubbed the **Spanish Arch,** it was built in 1594 near the docks where Spanish galleons used to unload their cargo. It's a popular spot to take in the River Corrib.

Galway Arts Centre ♥♥ CULTURAL CENTER Once the home of W. B. Yeats's patron, Lady Gregory, this attractive town house held local governmental offices for many years. Today it offers an excellent program of concerts, readings, and exhibitions by Irish and international artists—returning the house to a purpose that Lady Gregory would have appreciated. Usually two or three exhibitions run at any one time.

47 Dominick St. galwayartscentre.ie. ✆ **091/565-886.** Free admission. Mon–Fri 10am–5pm; Sat 10am–1pm and 2–5pm.

Galway Cathedral ♥ CATHEDRAL Officially the "Cathedral of Our Lady Assumed into Heaven & St. Nicholas," Galway's cathedral has an impressive domed exterior that looks Romanesque in style, although it was actually built in the 1960s. The striking interior has rows of symmetrical stone archways and dramatic lighting. Contemporary Irish artisans designed the statues, colorful mosaics, and stained-glass windows. The limestone for the walls was cut from local quarries, while the polished floor is made from Connemara marble.

University and Gaol rds. (by W end of Salmon Weir Bridge). galwaycathedral.ie. ✆ **091/563-577** (select option 4). Free admission, suggested donation €3. Daily 8:30am–6:30pm.

Galway City Museum ♥♥ MUSEUM Permanent galleries downstairs relate to Galway's prehistoric and medieval periods, while the upper levels deal with the city's more recent past, including its relationship with the arts. Highlights include a large collection of intricate embroidered textiles, made by a local order of nuns between the 17th and 20th centuries. A lively program of special events includes talks, touring exhibitions, and arts workshops.

Spanish Parade. galwaycitymuseum.ie. ✆ **091/532-460.** Free admission, suggested donation €5. Tues–Sat 10am–5pm.

The Galway City Museum is packed with exhibits explaining the city's unique history, including "Superhuman," a recent exhibit on the country's development as an international hub of medical technology.

ATTRACTIONS

- Aran Islands Ferries ticket office 6
- *Corrib Princess* Cruise 2
- Eyre Square 7
- Galway Arts Centre 24
- Galway Cathedral 1
- Galway City Museum 20
- Galway Fisheries Watchtower Museum 22
- Galway Irish Crystal Heritage Centre 4
- Hall of the Red Earl 14
- Lynch's Castle 9
- Lynch Memorial Window 10
- St. Nicholas' Collegiate Church 11
- Spanish Arch 19

WHERE TO STAY

- The G Hotel 3
- The House Hotel 17
- The Huntsman Inn 3
- Park House Hotel 5
- Petra House 3
- Sea Breeze Lodge 28

WHERE TO EAT

- Aniar 23
- Ard Bia at Nimmo's 18
- Blackrock Cottage 29
- The Dough Bros 13
- Éan 16
- Kai 27
- Little Lane Coffee Company 8
- Oscar's Seafood Bistro 25
- Rúibín 15
- The Seafood Bar @ Kirwan's 21
- Sheridans Cheesemongers 12
- Urban Grind 26

Galway Fisheries Watchtower Museum ♥ MUSEUM This tiny, free museum is worth visiting for the views of the River Corrib alone. The symmetrical yellow tower was built in 1852 as a lookout from which fishing boats on the river could be monitored; it was in use until commercial net fishing died out in the 1970s. Exhibits tell the story of Galway's fishing heritage and the role it played in the city's industry.

Wolfe Tone Bridge, off Father Griffin Rd. galwaycivictrust.ie. No phone. Free admission. Open summer only, generally Mon–Fri 10am–4pm; check opening hours online before visiting.

The Tribes of Galway

By the 15th century, 14 wealthy merchant families ruled Galway Town, giving it a nickname it still bears today—"City of Tribes." These families, mostly of Welsh and Norman origins, ruled as an oligarchy. As you walk around Galway City, look for these names on storefronts and businesses: Athy, Blake, Bodkin, Browne, Darcy, Deane, Font, French, Joyce, Kirwan, Lynch, Martin, Morris, and Skerret.

Galway Market ♥♥ MARKET There has been a regular street market of some kind in Galway for hundreds of years, and its vibrant modern iteration shows no sign of letting the tradition slide. Galway Market is a great place to shop for locally made crafts and homewares, but it's the scent of the food stalls that often brings people in. The market takes place next to St. Nicholas' Church (p. 393), every Saturday from 8am until 6pm and Sundays and bank holidays from noon until 6pm. (In July–Aug, it also runs Wed-Fri noon–6pm, and daily noon–6pm during the Galway Arts Festival [p. 53]). The **Galway Christmas Market** runs daily from 9am to 6pm in Eyre Square mid-November to December 22.

Church Lane. galwaymarket.com.

Hall of the Red Earl ♥♥ ANCIENT SITE This fascinating site is what's left of a baronial hall from the Middle Ages, built by the powerful de Burgh family, Anglo-Norman earls who ruled this region in the 13th century. In the late 1200s, they erected what must have been a lavish hall in which to hold court, receive subjects, settle disputes, and generally live it up in true medieval style. The earls were eventually overthrown by local tribes and the building abandoned. Time slowly covered any trace of the building, until the foundations were found during building work in 1997. You can view the site on glass gangways and see some of the artifacts that were unearthed during the excavation.

Custom House, Druid Lane. galwaycivictrust.ie. ✆ **091/564-946.** Free admission. Mon–Fri 9:30am–4:30pm.

Lynch's Castle ♥ HISTORIC HOUSE Dating from 1490 and renovated in the 19th century, this impressive structure was once home to the Lynch family, who ruled the city for many years. One of the oldest medieval town houses in Ireland, it's now a branch of the Allied Irish Bank.

The Tragic Tale of Lynch's Window

One block away from Eyre Square on Market Street, the **Lynch Memorial Window** sits in a wall above a built-up Gothic doorway. It commemorates the tragic story of the 16th-century Galway mayor James Lynch FitzStephen, who condemned his own son to death for the murder of a Spanish merchant. After finding no one to carry out the deed, he executed the boy himself. The act destroyed him, and he retreated into a life of seclusion.

Gargoyles preside over the exterior, while inside is a small display describing the building's history.

Abbeygate and Shop sts. galwaytourism.ie/lynchs-castle. ✆ **091/567-041.** Free admission. Mon–Fri 10am–4pm.

St. Nicholas' Collegiate Church ♥♥ CHURCH Galway's oldest church, St. Nicholas' was established about 1320. It's claimed that Christopher Columbus prayed here in 1477 before one of his early attempts to reach the New World, although there's no real evidence to suggest it's true. Over the centuries, it has changed from Roman Catholic to Church of Ireland and back again at least four times. Inside are a 12th-century crusader's tomb with a Norman inscription, a carved font from the 16th or 17th century, and a stone lectern with barley-sugar twist columns from the 15th century. You can explore alone (ask for an audio guide or self-guided-tour leaflet) or book a guided tour in advance (check online).

Interior of St. Nicholas' Collegiate Church.

Lombard St. stnicholas.ie. ✆ **086/389-8777.** Admission €5 adults; €4 seniors and students; free for children 11 and under. Guided tours €10. Mon–Sat 10am–5:30pm (opens 11am Wed). Sun 1–5:30pm. Last entry 30 minutes before closing.

Outside the City

Galway Girl Cruises ♥♥ TOUR This fun-filled 90-minute trip around Galway Bay takes in views of the Aran Islands and the Burren, giving the history of different areas in the bay with stories of everything from trading to smuggling, plus the chance to see wildlife. There's a performance of live traditional Irish music on board and sometimes *sean nós* (old-style) dancing.

Departs from Galway Docks. galwaygirlcruises.com. ✆ **087/675-3455.** €40 adults; €25 children 5–16. Sailings daily June–Sept 10:30am and 2pm. Buy tickets online or at the docks.

Corrib Princess Cruise ♥♥ TOUR Sit back and take in the view from this 157-passenger, two-deck boat as it cruises along the River Corrib out of Galway City. The journey along the river takes in castles, historical sites, and wildlife. It's not for those averse to the full tourist treatment, but the 90-minute trip is very picturesque. Buy tickets at the dock or online.

Departs from Woodquay, Galway City. corribprincess.ie. ✆ **087/806-5366.** €21 adults; €17 seniors and students; €10 children 4–12; free for ages 3 and under; €47–€53 families (2 adults, 3 children). Sailings May–Sept Tues–Sun 12:30 and 2:30pm, also at 4:30pm July–Aug.

Galway Irish Crystal Heritage Centre ♥ FACTORY TOUR It might not be as well-known as its feted Waterford rival, but Galway Crystal is just as distinctive and beautiful. At this visitor center, you can observe master craftspeople at work blowing the molten glass and cutting the finished product (Mon–Fri only). But most people just come to browse the factory shop, with its glittering array of crystal and other craft items, such as fragile Belleek pottery.

E of Galway City on main Dublin Rd. (N6), Merlin Park. galwaycrystal.ie. ✆ **091/757-311.** Free admission. Mon–Fri 9am–5:30pm; Sat–Sun and public holidays 9:30am–5:30pm.

Where to Stay in & Around Galway City

Prices have gone up quite a bit in Galway City in recent years, and it's hard to find a bargain. Even B&Bs often run over €200 a night, especially in summer season or during festivals and race week. The hotels listed below are the best options for location and quality.

The G ♥♥ Chic designer flourishes, bright color schemes, and contemporary art grace this modern hotel overlooking the waters of Lough Atalia and Galway Bay, about a 10-minute walk northeast of the city center. Many bedrooms have floor-to-ceiling windows to take full advantage of those views. Beds are big and comfortable, and bathrooms are modern. **Geo** restaurant is a delightful space serving excellent modern Irish cuisine, with plenty of local meats and seafood. Treatments in the hotel spa aren't cheap, but check for special offers online.

Wellpark, Galway City. theghotel.ie. ✆ **091/865-200.** 101 units. €165–€480 double; €600–€1,121 suite. Breakfast included. Free parking. **Amenities:** Restaurant; bar; gym; room service; spa; Wi-Fi (free).

The House Hotel ♥♥ The upbeat, funky hotel is right in the heart of the Latin Quarter. Public areas have stylish design with polished wood floors and retro-style seating, while guest rooms are more muted, with oatmeal, white, or green color schemes. The restaurant is good and surprisingly reasonable for a hotel of this size in the center of the city.

THE aran islands

When you see the ghostly shapes of the Aran Islands floating 48km (30 miles) out at sea like misty Brigadoon, you instantly understand why these sea-battered and wind-whipped isles have been the subject of fable, song, and film for thousands of years.

All three islands—**Inishmore (*Inis Mór*), Inishmaan (*Inis Meáin*),** and **Inisheer (*Inis Oírr*)**—are rather strange looking, with a ring of rocks around their outer edges and, inside, small farms surrounded by soft green grass and wildflowers. Life on the islands is isolated but has been modernized—few of the 1,500 inhabitants still maintain the traditional island lifestyle, fishing from *currachs* (small crafts made of tarred canvas stretched over timber frames), living in stone cottages, and speaking Irish. Some islanders wear the classic, creamy, handmade Aran *baínín* sweaters that originated here and are now popular in Irish gift shops.

Inishmore is the largest island and the easiest to reach from Galway. Most visitors disembark from the ferries at **Kilronan (*Cill Rónáin*),** the island's main town (though it's only the size of a village). From there, it's easy to arrange transportation around the island: Horse-drawn buggies are available for island tours as you step off the boat, minivans stand at the ready, and bicycle-rental shops are within sight. Drop in to **Ionad Fáilte (Tourist Information Centre)** in Kilronan (✆ **1800/230330**) to pick up walking maps, ask questions, and generally get yourself going. It's open daily year-round from 10am to 5pm.

The islands have some excellent geological sights, including the magnificent **Dún Aengus** ♥♥ on Inishmore. A ruined 2,000-year-old stone fortress, on the edge of a cliff that drops 90m (295 ft.) to the sea, Dún Aengus is among the most dramatic ancient ruins in the west. Its original purpose is unknown—some think it had a military purpose, others say it was a ceremonial theater. From the top are spectacular views of Galway Bay, the Burren, and Connemara. Nearby, in what looks like an Irish country cottage, the charming, thatched-roofed cafe/restaurant **Teach Nan Phaidi** ♥♥ (✆ **099/20975**) offers sandwiches, salads, excellent Irish stew, cakes, pies—comfort food, in other words, and incredibly welcome after a blustery day on the island.

Aran Island Ferries (aranislandferries.com; ✆ **091/568-903**) runs daily service to all three islands—Inishmore, Inishmaan, and Inisheer. Boats leave from **Rossaveal (*Ros a' Mhíl*),** 37km (23 miles) west of Galway City. The crossing takes 50 minutes to Inishmore and 1 hour to Inishmaan or Inisheer. For all three islands, there is a crossing daily at 10:30am and another at 6pm daily (6:30pm on Fri); an extra daily 1pm crossing to Inishmore runs from April through September. Always check the schedule, however, and make sure you know the time of the return ferries. The ticket office is at 37 Forster St. in Galway; a shuttle bus goes from nearby Queen's Street to the ferry port (to take the shuttle, you must check in at the booking office at least 90 minutes before sailing time). The round-trip crossing costs €30 adults, €25 seniors and students, €15 children. The shuttle bus costs €10 adults, €9 seniors and students, €7 children, round-trip.

Although visiting the Aran Islands is a thoroughly doable day trip from Galway City, if you're tempted to stay overnight, a handful of good B&Bs and restaurants are available—see listings, p. 397.

That said, you're spoiled for choice when it comes to nightlife in the neighborhood—Galway's buzzing center is literally on your doorstep. Spanish Parade. thehousehotel.ie. ✆ **091/538-900.** 40 units. €116–€299 double; €224–€323 suite. Breakfast not included in lower rates. Parking at nearby lot (€11/24 hr.). **Amenities:** Restaurant; bar; room service; Wi-Fi (free).

The Huntsman Inn ♥♥ This smart, modern inn and restaurant on Lough Atalia, a 20-minute walk from the city center, is a good option. Rooms are surprisingly big—some have super-king beds—and decorated in clean, neutral colors. Bathrooms are modern. A well-rated restaurant and stylish bar, both popular with locals, are located downstairs. There's live music on Saturday evenings, so this may not be one for light sleepers, but the pub quiz on Mondays is good *craic,* as the Irish say. 164 College Rd. huntsmaninn.com. ✆ **091/562-849.** 14 units. €110–€210 double. Breakfast included. Free parking. **Amenities:** Restaurant; bar; Wi-Fi (free).

Park House Hotel ♥♥ This friendly, traditional hotel is just 5 minutes' walk from Eyre Square at the heart of Galway City. The lobby is a bit fussy, with heavy drapes and marble statues, but rooms are simply designed in warm colors with comfortable beds and modern bathrooms. The in-house restaurant does excellent European-influenced Irish food, with an emphasis on fresh seafood. A smaller menu is served all day in **Boss Doyle's Bar**—a relaxed, pub-like space, perfect for a pint. Forster St. parkhousehotel.ie. ✆ **091/564-924.** 99 units. €245–€315 double. Breakfast included. Check website for dinner, bed-and-breakfast packages. Parking included in some room rates. **Amenities:** Restaurant; bar; Wi-Fi (free).

Petra House ♥♥ Just a few minutes' walk from the city center and Eyre Square is this friendly, homestyle B&B, where hosts Amy and Paul give guests a warm welcome and help to arrange tickets or tours to sights in the region. Guest rooms are clean, spacious, and decorated in neutral colors, and there's a quiet back garden to relax in. Treats like homemade cheesecake and filling breakfasts that feature local produce and homemade scones and brown bread, are a big hit with guests. 29 College Rd. petrahousegalway.net. ✆ **0/2717-938.** 9 units. €165–€205 double. Breakfast included. 2-night minimum stay on selected dates. Free parking. **Amenities**: Wi-Fi (free). Closed Dec–Jan.

Sea Breeze Lodge ♥♥ A stylish option in Salthill, just outside Galway City, the Sea Breeze Lodge has a lot to offer. The modern gray exterior gives way to contemporary lounges inside. Guest rooms are spacious, with polished-wood floors and windows looking out over the bay or garden. Beds are king-size and comfortable with memory-foam mattresses. Breakfasts are served in a pleasant conservatory overlooking the garden. The B&B can arrange tours of the area, including an all-day trip to the Aran Islands or to Connemara for €30 to €40 per person (€25–€35 students and seniors). There's no restaurant, and the center of Galway is 5km (3 miles) by car or taxi.

9 Cashelmara, Salthill. seabreezelodge.org. ✆ **091/529-581.** 6 units. €180–€320 double. Breakfast included. 2-night minimum selected dates. Free parking. **Amenities:** Wi-Fi (free). Closed Nov–Mar.

Where to Stay on the Aran Islands

Inis Meáin Island Stays ♥♥♥ This is a special place to stay and a unique way to experience the least-visited of the Aran Islands, Inis Meáin. Formerly a restaurant with suites, it's now two guesthouses— the Currach House, which sleeps up to four, and the Karst House, which can sleep up to eight. Both make the most of the stunning views of Galway Bay with huge windows. Stays are fixed at 4 nights, Wednesday through Sunday, on a self-catering basis with options to have lunch or dinner delivered (if ordered well in advance). There's also a welcome box with honey, eggs, and home baking. Don't expect a TV—they provide "island exploration kits" with bikes and fishing rods instead. Arrive here, breathe in the air, and feel the peace wash over you.

Inis Meáin. inismeain.com. ✆ **086/826-6026.** 2 units. Currach House (sleeps 4) €3,145–€3,490 per 4-night stay; Karst House (sleeps 8) €6,290–€6,950 per 4-night stay. Free parking. **Amenities:** Wi-Fi (free). Closed Sept–Feb.

South Aran House ♥ This whitewashed stone house seems to fit the rugged landscape on Inisheer, the smallest of the Aran Islands. Low and sturdy enough to withstand the windswept winters, inside it's snug, with comfortable, lived-in furniture and a fireplace warming the lounge. Rooms are on the small side but spotless, with modern beds, underfloor heating, and power showers—and each room has its own entrance. The house is owned by Enda, a former lighthouse keeper, and it has plenty of books around for anyone to read. Reserve your space early; with only four rooms, this place gets booked up fast.

Inisheer. southaran.com. ✆ **087/340-5687.** 4 units. €110 double. Breakfast included. No children. **Amenities:** Wi-Fi (free).

Where to Eat in Galway City

This west coast foodie hub offers endless places to eat—you can hardly walk two steps in the city center without passing a cafe or restaurant. In addition to the options listed below, some of the best coffee in Galway is at **Urban Grind** (8 William St. W; urbangrind.ie; ✆ **085/266-1156**), which also serves epic breakfasts (organic bread with grilled sausage and poached egg), or **Little Lane Coffee Company** (10 Abbeygate St. Upper; littlelanecoffee.com; no phone), which takes coffee seriously, with brews from Irish specialty coffee roasters. In the evening, Daróg Wine Bar has an interesting wine list, matched with small plates of local cheeses and charcuterie. If you need help navigating the city's culinary offerings, take a 2½-hour food tour with **Galway Food Tours** (daytime €80, evening €160; galwayfoodtours.com) to sample local artisan products and visit the city's best dining spots.

Tweezing fresh herbs to finish off a perfectly plated dish at Aniar.

Aniar ♥♥♥ MODERN IRISH This Michelin-starred restaurant in the lively Westend of Galway City is one of the best, and most fashionable, places to eat in the region. Chef JP McMahon (who also runs cooking classes) changes the tiny menu constantly around what's best that day, and it's deeply imbued with the produce of the region: smoked cheese with kelp; beef with nasturtium; pork with sorrel and buttermilk. The 24-dish tasting menu doesn't come cheap, but legions of fans (and the people who award Michelin stars) think it's worth it. Needless to say, reservations are essential.
53 Lower Dominick St. aniarrestaurant.ie. ✆ **091/535-947.** Tasting menu €160. Wine pairings €85–€160. Tues–Thurs 5–9pm; Fri–Sat 4:30–9pm.

Ard Bia at Nimmo's ♥♥ SEAFOOD/BISTRO/CAFE The rustic dining room at this fashionable restaurant in Galway City doubles as a popular cafe during the day. At any time, the emphasis is the same: simple cooking using local produce. Stop in for a breakfast or brunch of buttermilk pancakes or a vegan fry-up with mushroom, avocado, spinach, and hummus. At lunch, sample creative salads and sandwiches. In the evening, when the atmosphere gets cozy with candlelight, expect local fish with roasted veggies and lemon yogurt, or a tender rib-eye served with roast potatoes, kale, broccoli, and Crozier Blue butter. The wine list is excellent and reasonably priced, and some tables even have river views.
Spanish Arch, Long Walk. ardbia.com. ✆ **091/561-114.** Breakfast €7.50–€17; lunch €7–€24; dinner entrees €26–€38. Mon–Tues 10am–3pm; Wed–Sun 10am–3pm and 6–9pm.

Blackrock Cottage ♥♥♥ MODERN IRISH This renovated 200-year-old cottage is on the sea at Salthill, a short stroll from the city center and worth the trip. In the morning, the "*alainn* bowl," a breakfast superfood bowl, will set you up for the day, especially if you've taken a dip in the Atlantic. For dinner, look out for pan-roasted hake, roast squash, or plaice Milanese. Specialties include Dooncastle Connemara oysters with shallot and sea truffle dressing, and Achill Island salt-aged beef. They don't take bookings for breakfast or lunch, and it's a popular spot, so be prepared to queue.

Salthill Promenade. blackrockcottage.ie. ✆ **091/399-280.** Entrees €20–€35. Mon–Wed 8am–4:30pm; Thurs–Sat 8am–4:30pm and 6–9:15pm; Sun 8am–7pm.

The Dough Bros ♥♥ PIZZA The young, the trendy, and the just plain hungry stand in line for a table at this popular pizza joint in the middle of Galway City. It's a heartwarming tale: Three local boys, in love with Italian cooking, start a food truck after one of them loses his job. Fast-forward a few years and that truck has become a restaurant, serving wood-baked pizza to hordes of locals. You might go for a classic Neapolitan, with tomato, fresh basil, and mozzarella, but if you're feeling a bit adventurous, how about the "Hail Caesar," with lemon chicken, bacon lardons, and *rocket* (arugula)? They don't take reservations, so you will probably have to stand in line on Friday and Saturday nights. They also serve pizzas in **O'Connells** pub (8 Eyre Sq.; Wed–Sun 5–10pm).

Cathedral Bldgs., 1 Middle St. thedoughbros.ie. ✆ **091/395-238.** Entrees €16–€17. No reservations. Daily noon–10pm.

Éan ♥♥ MODERN IRISH The word éan is the Irish for bird, an appropriate name for the selection of delicate pastries and exquisite savory plates here. This is a bakery by day and a wine bar by night, serving sharing plates like squid toast with blonde miso and bonito, or mackerel with beetroot, fermented blackcurrant, and horseradish. Food is local—if it's not grown in Ireland, you won't find it on the menu. The relaxed setting, in a lovely old stone building on Druid Lane (with a few outdoor tables), is ideal for a pre-theater nibble or a glass of wine (it even has a connecting door to the theater).

Druid Lane. eangalway.com. ✆ **091/447-592.** Entrees €14–€39. Wed–Sun 9:30am–3pm and 5:30–10pm.

Kai ♥♥♥ IRISH Rustic wooden tables and stone walls and floors set a homey atmosphere at this restaurant in Galway's Westend, which has won a Michelin green star—the produce used is local and organic, and waste is either recycled or used to produce energy. There's a casual vibe by day:

The Galway Oyster Festival

On the main road south (N18) of Galway you'll pass two unremarkable small fishing villages, **Clarenbridge** and **Kilcolgan.** If you're here at the end of September, however, these villages become an essential stop, when they host the annual **Galway Oyster Festival** (galwayoysterfest.com; ✆ **091/394-637**). The 5-day festival, held every year since 1954, is packed with traditional music, song, dancing, sports, art exhibits—and, above all, oyster-tasting events.

In this rustic, casual dining room, Kai serves some of Galway City's finest food.

No reservations are needed, and daily dishes are on blackboards. At night things are more formal, with a regularly changing menu emphasizing local ingredients—expect dishes like scallops with burnt butter cauliflower and aioli, or striploin steak with cafe de Kai butter and boozy onions.
22 Sea Rd. kairestaurant.ie. ✆ **091/526-003.** Lunch €16–€19; dinner entrees €28–€36. Tues–Sat noon–3pm and 6:15–9pm.

Rúibín ♥♥ MODERN IRISH Set over two floors, with views out over the Galway docks from the upper level, this relaxed and bright restaurant emphasizes local Irish food—with dishes like smoked black pudding with grilled sweetheart cabbage, or lemon sole with chicken butter, chanterelles, and greens. Lunch is served on both floors by day; in the evening the downstairs becomes a wine bar with sharing plates and upstairs is for fine dining. It's got a great cocktail menu.
1 Dock Rd. ruibin.ie. ✆ **091/563-830.** Lunch €8.50–€16; dinner entrees €27–€40. Mon–Sat noon–2:45pm and 5–9:45pm.

The Seafood Bar @ Kirwan's ♥♥ SEAFOOD The exposed stone walls of this elegant downstairs dining room speak to the building's medieval origins. Open the menu, however, and everything suddenly seems bang up to date—this is one of the most popular and reliable restaurants in Galway City for good seafood, dishes like shrimp and clams with chili, fish and chips, steamed mussels, or a generous cold seafood platter. Tucked down a narrow lane, this place can be hard to find, but it's worth the search. Kirwan's Lane. kirwanslane.ie. ✆ **091/568-266.** Entrees €24–€40. 3-course set dinner menu €55–€60. Mon–Sat 12:30–2:30pm and 6–10pm.

Sheridans Cheesemongers ♥♥ DELI/WINE BAR Here's a delightful idea: an artisan cheese shop and deli, doubling as a bar where you can order a glass of wine and some nibbles. Food comes in the form of cheeseboards and charcuterie, much of it locally produced. So simple, and hugely popular, too—you might struggle to get one of the few tables during busy times. This is a really good alternative to heavy restaurant food when all you want is a chat and a sophisticated snack. Church Yard St. sheridanscheesemongers.com. ✆ **091/564-829** (shop). Entrees €5.50–€29. Shop: Mon–Fri 10am–6pm, Sat 9am–6pm, Sun noon–5pm. Wine bar: Tues–Wed 4–10:30pm, Thurs 4–11:30pm, Fri 2–11:30pm, Sat noon–11:30pm, Sun 4–10:30pm.

Shopping in Galway City

Given its status as both a tourist hub and a vibrant arts community, it's no surprise that Galway has great shopping. Some of the best is in tiny clusters of shops in historic buildings, such as the **Cornstore** on Middle Street or the **Grainstore** on Lower Abbeygate Street, but most stores are concentrated along the aptly named Shop Street, which runs into High Street and Quay Street, and the laneways off these. **Eyre Square Centre,** the downtown area's largest shopping mall, rather incongruously incorporates a section of Galway's medieval town wall into its complex of 50 shops.

Most shops are open Monday to Saturday from 9 or 10am to 5:30 or 6pm. In July and August, many stay open late, usually until 9pm on weekdays, and some also open on Sunday from noon to 5pm.

BOOKS

Bell, Book and Candle ♥♥ You'll find not only a good selection of secondhand books here, but a host of collectible vinyl and CDs, some of them very rare. It's a quirky place (there's even a car inside—long story) and great for a browse. Small Crane, Sea Rd. ✆ **091/589-060.**

Charlie Byrne's Bookshop ♥♥ Packed floor-to-ceiling with books—secondhand, antiquarian, and new—this wonderfully chaotic bookshop has a huge stock, covering just about anything. It's so beloved that the *Irish Times* once named this the best bookshop in Ireland. It also sells very fetching little cotton tote bags. The Cornstore, Middle St. charliebyrne.com. ✆ **091/561-766.**

Kenny's Book Shop and Galleries Ltd ♥ Another long-standing favorite of Galway bibliophiles, Kenny's, which is outside the city, has a great selection of new books on all topics, plus secondhand and

Crammed with books old and new, Charlie Byrne's Bookshop is one of Ireland's best booksellers.

hard-to-find antiquarian titles. (***Tip:*** It delivers anywhere in the world, if you prefer to order online.) The bookstore also has an interesting little art gallery. Liosbán Retail Park, Tuam Rd. kennys.ie. ✆ **091/709-350.**

CRAFTS & DESIGN

Galway Irish Crystal ♥♥ This local brand of fine crystal rivals Waterford Crystal. At the factory on the edge of town, you can watch craftspeople at work and purchase armfuls of the stuff yourself. See p. 394 for more details. Merlin Park, Dublin Rd. galwaycrystal.ie. ✆ **091/757-311.**

Judy Greene Pottery ♥♥ The pottery here captures the essence of Ireland's wild beauty in hand-thrown terra-cotta, with signature floral prints like bluebells, fuchsias, and gentians. The shop itself is a delight, set in an old stone building in the city's medieval quarter. Kirwans Lane. ✆ **091/561-753.**

Mishnóc ♥♥ You can buy beautiful handmade handbags, backpacks, briefcases, and a host of other leather accessories here, many of them unique and Irish-made. 3 Cathedral Buildings, Lower Abbeygate St. mishnoc.com. ✆ **091/563-859.**

My Shop . . . Granny Likes It ♥♥ Irish-made crafts, jewelry, and homewares are for sale at this darling little boutique, run by a nice lady named Rona and her dog. A great place to browse for gifts and high-quality keepsakes. 29–31 Upper Abbeygate St. myshopgranny.com. ✆ **091/534-877.**

JEWELRY

Blacoe ♥♥ This popular jeweler in the Eyre Square Centre sells Claddagh rings, engagement rings, and a large range of jewelry featuring traditional Irish motifs. Plenty of pieces sell for well under €100. 4 Lower Abbeygate St. blacoe.ie. ✆ **091/561-003.**

Claddagh Jewellers ♥♥ In a crowded field, this purveyor of Claddagh rings and other fine Celtic jewelry has something extra: a (free) visitor center next door, the **Legend of the Claddagh Ring,** where you can watch the jewelers at work. 25 Mainguard St. thecladdagh.com. ✆ **091/562-554.**

Cobwebs ♥♥ Located opposite the Spanish Arch, this great little store sells antique and modern jewelry, plus curios, antiques, and objets d'art. 7 Quay Lane. cobwebs.ie. ✆ **091/564-388.**

Fallers of Galway ♥♥ Fallers makes and sells the Claddagh ring, a traditional Galway souvenir that symbolizes love and friendship (see box, below). It also has a large stock of other jewelry with Celtic motifs. Williamsgate St. fallers.com. ✆ **091/561-226.**

Hartmanns of Galway ♥♥ Another maker of Claddagh rings, Hartmanns also specializes in watches and diamonds. This is one of Galway's real high-end jewelry stores. 29 William St. hartmanns.ie. ✆ **091/562-063.**

Thomas Dillon's Claddagh Gold ♥♥ This chirpily colored little store makes two bold claims: to be the original maker of Claddagh rings (they're the only ones allowed to stamp the rings with "ORIGINAL") and to be the oldest jewelry store in all of Ireland. If the date it was

ESSENTIAL SOUVENIR: THE claddagh RING

Known worldwide as a symbol of love and friendship, the delicate **Claddagh** (pronounced *Clad*-uh) ring is probably a design you'll recognize—two hands holding a heart topped with a crown—even if the name is new to you. Over the years this iconic design has also become a symbol for Ireland and its diaspora.

Claddagh rings first appeared sometime in the 17th century, although the design was based on a much older European tradition, dating back to Roman times. The hands are said to represent friendship, the crown loyalty, and the heart love—the three ingredients of a perfect marriage.

Originally, the ring was a wedding band worn facing out for engagement and facing in for marriage. Though no longer widely worn as a symbol of marriage, it is still frequently worn as a friendship ring and makes a lovely memento. The first rings were made in Galway—or more precisely, just over the Father Griffin Bridge, on the west bank of the River Corrib, in the town of Claddagh. It's now a residential satellite to Galway, but in ancient times it was a kingdom with its own laws, fleet, and customs.

established—1750—is anything to go by, it's probably true. The shop has a tiny little museum displaying Claddagh rings from the 1700s. 1 Quay St. claddaghring.ie. ✆ **091/566-365.**

MUSIC & MUSICAL INSTRUMENTS

P. Powell & Sons ♥♥ Usually just called Powell's, this is an excellent source for instruments—including pennywhistles, bodhráns, and the like—as well as a good range of traditional music CDs. 53 William St. powellsmusic.ie. ✆ **091/562-295.**

TWEEDS, WOOLENS & CLOTHING

Galway Woollen Market ♥♥ This colorful store is one of the best for traditional, hand-loomed Aran knits, plus lace and other traditional textiles. Visitors who live outside the European Union don't have to pay sales tax on items bought from here. 21 High St. aranislandsknitwear.com. ✆ **091/562-491.**

Irish Tweeds ♥♥ Although not the oldest tweed maker in town by any means, Irish Tweeds has a great selection of traditionally made garments, including snazzy hats, jackets, and nightwear. They also ship worldwide, free of charge. 51 William St. irishtweeds.com. ✆ **091/539-745.**

O'Máille (O'Malley) ♥♥ Another excellent place to buy Aran knitwear and other Irish knits, this store has a claim to fame of its own—when *The Quiet Man* was filmed near here in 1951 (p. 444), it provided costumes for all the actors, including John Wayne. 16 High St. omaille.com. ✆ **091/562-696.**

Galway City After Dark

THEATER

Druid Theatre ♥♥ THEATER Highly respected across Ireland and beyond for its original, cutting-edge productions, the Druid has been one of the region's foremost arts institutions since the 1970s. It's particularly known for premiering new work from up-and-coming writers, so expect to find challenging, intelligent material staged here. The theater also produces new versions of classic plays by Irish, British, and European dramatists. Shows can sell out some time in advance and are often out on the road (the Druid is a touring company), so it's advisable to check what's on and make bookings as far ahead as possible. Ticket prices range around €15 to €25. Flood St. druid.ie. ✆ **091/568-660.** Performance times vary.

PUBS & BARS

The Crane Bar ♥♥♥ Considered one of the best pubs in the city for traditional music, the Crane Bar has live bands nightly from 9:30pm, and on some weekend afternoons, too. Admission is usually free, but some sessions in the upstairs bar cost anything from a couple euros to €20. 2 Sea Rd. thecranebar.com. ✆ **091/587-419.**

The colorful Crane Bar.

The Front Door ♥♥ Sprawling over two floors, this cheerful pub is a wonderfully social place where you can saunter in at lunchtime for a tasty sandwich and a pint and find yourself staying for hours. It sometimes shows Irish sports on big-screen TVs. 8 Cross St. at High St. frontdoorpub.com. ✆ **091/563-757.**

Murty Rabbitt's ♥♥ Charming and unspoiled, this late-19th-century pub has a delightfully old-school feel. (It's still run by the same family who owned it all the way back then, too. How's that for tradition?) Rabbitt's sometimes has live music in the evening. 23 Forster St. ✆ **091/566-490.**

The Quays ♥♥ Another good place to hear live music, the Quays has the unusual distinction of having interior decor that was reclaimed from a medieval French church. The what's-on list is a real mixed bag—you could find anything from trad to '80s rock, hip-hop to indie. Expect the fun to kick off around 9pm. 11 Quay St. quaysgalway.ie. ✆ **091/568-347.**

Róisín Dubh ♥♥ As much a concert venue as it is a bar, this place gets great acts—expect to see a few famous names crop up among the packed program of live music and standup comedy. 9 Dominick St Upper. roisindubh.net. ✆ **091/586-540.**

Side Trips from Galway City

On the main road inland from Galway City you'll find a number of attractions perfectly geared toward families: the well-preserved medieval town of **Athenry** (p. 409), the giant fish tanks of the **Galway Atlantaquaria**

Galway horse races at the Ballybrit racecourse (see box, below).

(p. 408), and ye-olde-tyme-funne feasting at **Dunguaire Castle** (p. 407). Meanwhile, more literary types may be interested in a string of sites related to one of Ireland's greatest poets, W. B. Yeats (see "A Poetic Soul," p. 462).

Heading west out of Galway City, the R336 coast road makes for a lovely scenic drive, snaking along the edge of Galway Bay. The first stop will be the city suburb and beach resort of **Salthill (*Bóthar na Trá*),** a good respite from the city if you've got kids (as long as you don't mind the crowds). Besides the Galway Atlantaquaria, it has a boardwalk and a fine beach, plus lots of bars, fast food, amusement rides, and game arcades. Farther along the R336, you will also be entering the Gaeltacht, or Irish-speaking area, with some charming historic towns such as Irish-speaking **Spiddal (*An Spidéal*).** The road continues as far as **Inverin (*Indreabhán*),** then turns northward, with signposts for **Rossaveal (*Ros an Mhíl*),**

A DAY AT THE races

"As I went down to Galway Town/To seek for recreation. . . . " So goes the famous folk song "Galway Races," and the **Galway Races** are still a big deal in the Irish horse-racing calendar—and almost as big a social event as a sporting one.

People dress up in posh frocks and big hats, and the crowds cheer enthusiastically as competing racehorses pound the turf. Horse lovers and high rollers pour in from around the country for the race weeks in July, September, and October. The animals are the best around, and the atmosphere is electric.

Since 1869, the action has taken place at the **Galway Racecourse** (galwayraces.com; ✆ **091/700-100**), just outside Galway City in Ballybrit, less than 3km (2 miles) northeast of town. Ticket prices vary depending on the event and day of the week, but expect to pay from around €25 to upwards of €60 for a ticket. Multi-day and season tickets are also available.

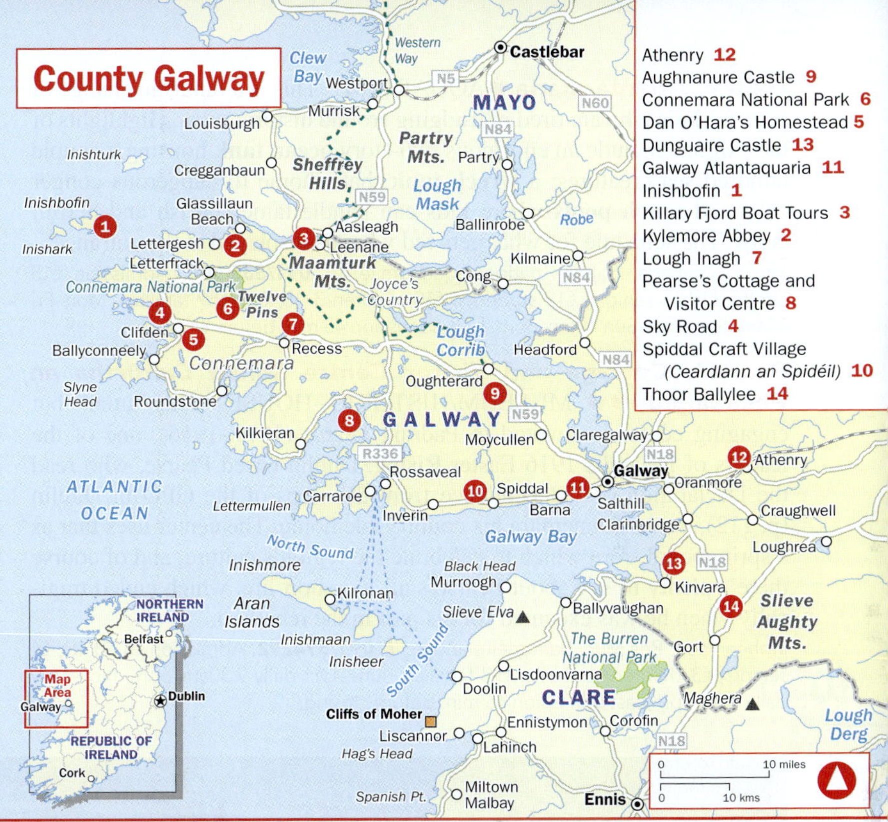

ferry port to the **Aran Islands** (p. 395). Continuing north on R336, you can branch off on R340 to visit **Ros Muc,** site of the **Padraig Pearse Cottage** ♥♥ (p. 408).

Dunguaire Castle ♥ CASTLE This gray and forbidding fortress on the shore of Galway Bay, between Gort and Kilcolgan, was once the royal seat of the 7th-century King Guaire of Connaught. It was at its peak in the 1500s, though, when most of what you see now was constructed. Later, it fell into disrepair, until it was purchased by the Irish writer Oliver St. John Gogarty (1878–1957), who restored it to glory. Today, you can climb the square tower for views of the nearby Burren and Galway Bay. The castle throws a popular **medieval banquet** from April to September—expect mead, a traditional supper, and a show featuring song and poetry. Shows are nightly at 5:30pm, with an additional show at 8:45pm in the summer months. Reservations are essential. Dunguaire is near Kinvara, approximately 26km (16 miles) southeast of Galway.

On N67 (Ballyvaughan Rd.), Dunguaire. dunguairecastle.com. ✆ **061/711-222.** Apr–Sept daily 10am–5pm; last admission 30 min. before closing. **Castle:** €8 adults; €5.50 seniors, students, and children 4–18; free for children 3 and under; €24–€30 families. **Banquet:** €63 adults; €35 children 4–18; free for children 3 and under.

Galway Atlantaquaria ♥ AQUARIUM This is a fantastic change of pace for kids who are tired of trudging around historic ruins. Highlights of the exhibits include an enormous two-story **ocean tank** housing a couple hundred sea creatures; a **wreck tank** that's home to dangerous conger eels; and **touch pools** where kids can handle tame starfish and hermit crabs. The schedule for what gets fed when is displayed at the entrance. The Promenade, Salthill. nationalaquarium.ie. ✆ **091/585-100.** Admission €15 adults; €10.50 seniors; €12 students; €10 children 3–15; €32–€59 families. Mon–Fri 10am–5pm; Sat–Sun 10am–6pm. Last admission 45 min. before closing.

Pearse's Cottage and Visitor Centre *(Ionad Cultúrtha an Phiarsaigh)* ♥♥ MUSEUM/HISTORIC HOUSE This small but engaging center is devoted to Padraig Pearse (1879–1916), one of the leaders of Ireland's 1916 Easter Rising. Dublin-based Pearse, who read the Declaration of Independence from the steps of the GPO in Dublin (p. 112), made Connemara his countryside home. The center uses that as a springboard from which to celebrate the region's culture, and of course there's plenty to say about Pearse's all-too-short life, which ended tragically when he was executed for his part in the rebellion. Inbhear, near Ros Muc. heritageireland.ie. ✆ **091/574292.** Admission €5 adults; €4 seniors; €3 children/students; €13 families. June–Oct daily 9:30am–6pm; Nov–May daily 9:30–4pm; last admission 45 min. before closing.

Jumping off the Blackrock diving board at the Salthill Promenade.

ATHENRY: FADED medieval SPLENDOR

Remarkably intact after more than 6 centuries, the medieval town walls of **Athenry**—about 25 minutes' drive east from Galway—surround a charming small town that feels like a time-warp experience. Those walls are some of the best-preserved in Ireland, constructed in the 1300s, with well over half of the original 2km (1⅓-mile) circuit still surviving—up to 5m (16½ ft.) tall in places.

Start with a visit to the **Athenry Heritage Centre** on the Square, in the town center (athenryheritagecentre.com; ✆ **091/844-661**). As well as providing all the usual orientation—including maps for walking routes—it offers you a choice of a 35-minute guided tour (€6 adults; €5 children, seniors, and students; €30 families) or the lively **Medieval Experience.** Aimed mostly at kids, this has plenty of interactive exhibits, dress-up areas, an archery experience, and re-creations of a torture dungeon and a medieval street. Admission to the Medieval Experience is €10 adults and €9.50 seniors, students, and children. The center is open Monday to Friday from 9.30am to 4:30pm.

Just a 10-minute walk away, on Court Lane, a modest tower keep is most of what's left of medieval **Athenry Castle** (heritageireland.ie); look for interesting carvings on the main doorway and window arches. Admission costs €5 adults, €4 seniors, €3 students and children, and €13 families. From mid-March to October it's open daily 9:30am to 6pm; last admission is at 5:15pm.

Just around the corner from the castle on Bridge Street, check out the ruins of a **Dominican Priory,** built in the mid–13th century and comprehensively destroyed by Cromwell's forces 400 years later. Today it's just a picturesque ruin, incongruously surrounded by modern houses; to medievalists, however, it's of particular interest because of its elaborately carved gravestones.

To reach Athenry from Galway, take the M6 motorway east about 25km (15½ miles) to junction 17, signposted for Athenry and Craughwell. There's also train service hourly from Galway City; the trip takes about 20 minutes and costs around €6 round-trip.

Spiddal Craft Village *(Ceardlann an Spidéil)* ♥♥♥ CULTURAL CENTER On the main road as you enter Spiddal from Galway, this is a fantastic collection of cottage-style crafts stores and workshops. The artists-in-residence here change regularly, but selection is always diverse. Plenty of the work is affordable without stretching the budget too far. Even if you're not buying, it's an inspiring place to browse. The **Builín Blasta Café** sells bakery goods, snacks, and light meals in addition to deli items. You can contact the individual artists via the main website.
About 15km (9 miles) W of Galway on R336, Spiddal. spiddalcrafts.com. No phone. Mon–Sat 10:30am–5:30pm; Sun 11am–5pm (often closes earlier in the winter).

Thoor Ballylee ♥♥ HISTORIC HOUSE Once part of the estate of the Earls of Clanricarde, this restored 15th-century Norman tower house probably still exists today only because it was part of the property owned by the family of Lady Gregory, a close friend and patron of the poet W. B. Yeats. He bought the castle from her family for £35 in 1916 and set about restoring it. The building inspired his poems "The Winding Stair" and

IN THE footsteps OF POETS

In the early 1900s, every summer the area southeast of Galway City became a sort of Bloomsbury Society West, as Dublin's greatest literary minds decamped to a cluster of nearby manor homes. About 36km (22⅓ miles) southeast of Galway City, near the northern border of the Burren (see chapter 9), you'll see signs to the beautiful **Coole Park National Forest** (coolepark.ie; ✆ **091/631-804**). This was once the country home of the dramatist and arts patron Lady Augusta Gregory (1852–1932), who, along with W. B. Yeats and Edward Martyn, founded the **Abbey Theatre** ♥ in Dublin (p. 175). Sadly, her house no longer stands, but her influence is memorialized in a tree on the grounds on which the following people carved their initials while visiting with her: George Bernard Shaw, Sean O'Casey, John Masefield, Oliver St. John Gogarty, W. B. Yeats, and Douglas Hyde, the first president of Ireland. Clearly, she was an exceptional woman, and this is an exceptional place. The visitor center shows a number of films on Lady Gregory and Coole Park and has a tearoom, picnic tables, and some lovely nature trails. The visitor center is open daily 10am to 1pm and 2 to 5pm. Admission is free. The tearooms are open Wednesday through Sunday from 10am until 4pm.

Not too far from the home of his friend, the great poet W. B. Yeats (1865–1939) had his own summer home in Gort at **Thoor Ballylee** (p. 409). The restored 15th-century Norman tower house served as an inspiration for his poetry and is now a museum to Yeats, with exhibitions and events such as poetry readings.

Nearby **Dunguaire Castle** (p. 407) was rescued from ruin by Oliver St. John Gogarty (1878–1957), Irish surgeon, author, poet, and wit. He restored the stone structure to glory and made a home here. His great friends Yeats and Lady Gregory were frequent guests.

"The Tower." It was Yeats who renamed it, from Ballylee Castle to Thoor (or "Tower") Ballylee. Today it serves as a Yeats museum, with displays on his life and a bookshop specializing in Anglo-Irish literature.

Off N18 at Ballylee, Gort. yeatsthoorballylee.org. ✆ **091/631-436.** Tickets €7 adults; €5 seniors; €4 children. April Sat–Sun 11am–4pm; May daily 11am–4pm; June–Sept daily 11am–5pm.

CONNEMARA

If you look for Connemara on road signs, you may be looking forever, because it's not a city or county, but rather a region—and one with a particularly distinct identity. Like the Burren in County Clare, the boundaries are a bit hazy. Most agree that Connemara is west of Galway City, starting at Oughterard and continuing toward the Atlantic. Anyway, you know it when you see it: It's an area of breathtaking barrenness and unique beauty, with dark bogs and tall jagged mountains punctuated by curving lakes dotted with green islands. The desolate landscape is caused, in part, by an absence of trees: Most native stands were felled and dragged off long ago for building ships, houses, and furniture. As Oscar Wilde wrote, "Connemara is a savage beauty."

It's a varied place—in fact, you could say that there are two Connemaras. South of the Galway–Clifden road (N59) is a vast bog-mantled moorland dotted with lakes, with a low, indented, rocky coastline. North of the Galway–Clifden road, tall quartzite domes and cones form the Maumturks and the Twelve Bens (also called the Twelve Pins), rising to Killary Fjord—the only fjord in this part of Europe.

Note: Connemara is part of the **Gaeltacht,** or Irish-speaking area; many signs are in Irish only (p. 47).

Visitor Information

The **Clifden Tourist Office** is on Galway Road, Clifden (© **1800/200300**). Its opening hours are a little unpredictable—generally daily 9am until 5pm in summer, but you might find it closed on spring and fall weekends, and it's closed altogether mid-October to mid-March.

Getting Around

The main road through Connemara—the N59 highway up from Galway City to **Clifden** and **Leenane (*Leenaun*)**—is hardly a crowded superhighway, but you'll still want to branch off from it to explore the region's wild and rugged coast. Loops such as the Sky Road from Clifden (p. 414), the R341 from Ballynahinch to Roundstone, or the Connemara Loop from Letterfrack reward travelers who have time to get off the beaten track. Regular **buses** run from Galway to Clifden; the route takes around half an hour longer than by car. Make sure you check the time of the last return journey—buses tend to stop quite early in the evening.

Exploring Connemara

Much of the attraction of Connemara is the wild countryside, but when you're ready to come in from the cold, the seaside town of **Clifden (*An Clochán*)** has an enviable location at the edge of the blue waters of Clifden Bay, where miles of curving, sandy beaches skirt the rugged coastline. It's an attractive Victorian town with colorful shop fronts and church steeples thrusting skyward, well provided with restaurants, shops, hotels, and pubs, which makes it a handy base for exploring the area. If you prefer a quieter location, seek out one of the many smaller towns and villages in the area, such as the little fishing port of **Roundstone (*Cloch na Rón*)** ♥ on the south coast about 24km (15 miles) away, which also has all the essentials: pristine beaches, comfortable guesthouses, good restaurants, shops, and more than its share of natural charm. North of Clifden, the little community of **Letterfrack (*Leitir Fraic*)** sits at the edge of **Connemara National Park** (p. 412), close to the extraordinary Gothic **Kylemore Abbey** (p. 414). The tiny village, founded by Quakers, has a handful of pubs and B&Bs in a glorious natural setting. It's near the bright white sands of **Glassillaun Beach** and **Lettergesh,** where horses raced across the sand in the film *The Quiet Man* (p. 444). North and east of Letterfrack, on the shore of Killary Fjord, **Leenane (*Leenaun*)** is the starting point for a number of excellent outdoor adventures.

Aughnanure Castle ♥ CASTLE Standing on an outcrop of rock surrounded by forest and pasture, this sturdy fortress is a well-preserved Irish tower castle with an unusual double *bawn* (fortified enclosure) and a still-complete watchtower that you can climb. The castle was built around 1500 as a stronghold of the "Ferocious" O'Flaherty clan, who dominated the region and terrified their neighbors. Aside from the tower the site is mostly a ruin, although you can wander through what remains of the banqueting hall, its fireplaces so big you could fit a double bed in them. The grounds also contain the remnants of a dry harbor.

Dare You Take . . . the Spooky Shortcut?

If you're planning a drive across the Connemara National Park to Clifden, you may want to make a shortcut on the rough but striking "bog road" (to find it, drive south from Clifden on the R341 and turn left at Ballinaboy). Unless you're traveling at night, that is. A hotel manager in these parts once told us that some locals consider the road to be haunted and won't take it after dark. Spooks or not, that's probably good advice at night, especially in bad weather.

Oughterard. heritageireland.ie. ✆ **091/552-214.** Admission €5 adults; €4 seniors; €3 children; €13 families. Mar to mid-Nov daily 9:30am–6pm. Last admission 45 min. before closing.

Connemara National Park ♥♥♥ NATURE SITE This gorgeous national park encompasses more than 2,000 hectares (4,940 acres) of mountains, bogs, grasslands, and hiking trails. Some of the best trails lead through the peaceful ***Gleann Mór*** (which means "Big Glen"), through which flows the **River Polladirk,** or up to the **Twelve Bens** (also called the "Twelve Pins"), a small, quartzite mountain range north of the Galway–Clifden road. None of the Twelve Bens rises above 730m (2,392 ft.), which makes their summits quite accessible to those who don't mind walking at a steep incline. Nearby are the lesser-known, equally lovely **Maumturk** range and the breathtaking **Killary Fjord**—the only fjord in Ireland, indeed this entire region of Europe. Frequent rainfall produces dozens of tiny streams and waterfalls, and the views are spectacular. The excellent visitor center south of the crossroads in **Letterfrack** dispenses general information on the park, as well as providing sustenance in the form of tea, sandwiches, and fresh baked goods.

Visitor center signposted from N59, Letterfrack. connemaranationalpark.ie. ✆ **076/100-2528.** Free admission. Visitor center daily 9am–5:30pm.

Dan O'Hara's Homestead ♥♥ HERITAGE SITE This open-air museum tells the story of Connemara, its people, and how they worked this rocky and inhospitable land. Dan O'Hara was a real person who farmed the land for his family, until the potato famine destroyed their livelihood. The reconstructed farmstead is set up exactly as it would have been in the years before the Famine, complete with farm dwellings. Also on the grounds of the museum is a dolmen and prehistoric tomb.

About 6.5km (4 miles) E of Clifden off N59 in Lettershea. connemaraheritage.com. ✆ **095/21808.** Admission €9 adults; €8.50 seniors and students; €4.50 children; €25 families. Apr–Nov daily 10am–6pm; last admission 1 hr. before closing.

Inishbofin ♥♥ ISLAND A place of seclusion and spectacular beauty, this small emerald-green gem lies 11km (6¾ miles) off the northwest coast of Connemara. Try to come here on a day when the skies are clear enough to deliver the unforgettable views. Once the domain of monks, then the lair of pirate queen Grace O'Malley (p. 447), later Cromwell's infamous priest prison—you can still see his original, star-shaped barracks—Inishbofin is currently home to just 180 year-round human residents, a seal colony, and a seabird sanctuary. Numerous ferries to the island operate from the port of Cleggan (13km/8 miles northwest of Clifden off N59). **Inishbofin Ferry** (inishbofinferry.ie; ✆ **095/37228**) sails three times a day (twice daily mid-Oct to mid-Mar). Round-trip fares are €25 adults, €15 students, €10 children 6-17, and €5 children 3-5; children 2 and under are free. ***Note:*** Reservations are essential, and evening sailing times can change in bad weather.

Inishbofin. Ferries from Cleggan.

Killary Fjord in Connemara National Park.

Killary Fjord Boat Tours ♥♥ CRUISE This pleasant 90-minute cruise gives you ample time to enjoy the gorgeous views across smooth waters to where green hills seem to cascade down to the shoreline. Weather permitting, you should be able to see three major mountain ranges: the Maumturk and Twelve Bens to the south, and the Mweelreas in County Mayo to the north. The boat—designed, they claim, to avoid seasickness, or your money back—has viewing decks inside and out, so the tour can be taken in all weather. Boats depart from Nancy's Point, about 2.7km (1½ miles) west of Leenane (*Leenaun*).

Signposted on N59, Leenane. killaryfjord.com. ✆ **087/235-9136.** Tickets €26 adults; €22 seniors and students; €14 children 11–17; free for children 10 and under; €52–€66 families. Departures daily June–Aug 10:30am, 12:30, 2:30, and 4pm; May and Sept 10:30am, 12:30 and 2:30pm; Mar–Apr and Oct 12:30 and 2:30pm. Closed Nov–Feb.

Kylemore Abbey ♥♥ RELIGIOUS SITE As you round yet another bend on the particularly wild stretch of country road around Kylemore, this extraordinary neo-Gothic abbey looms into view, at the base of a wooded hill across mirror-like Kylemore Lake. The vast, crenelated 19th-century house was donated to the Benedictine nuns in 1920, and the sisters have run a convent boarding school here ever since. You can see a little of the interior, but it's surprisingly plain; the exterior and the grounds are the real reason to visit, especially that breathtaking view across the lake. The highlight is the restored Gothic chapel, an exquisite cathedral in miniature with a plain, somber cemetery to one side; don't miss the lavish Victorian walled garden. Short history talks take place inside the abbey at 11am, noon, 2, and 3pm daily. From June to August guides lead a tour of the walled gardens daily at noon. The complex includes a restaurant that serves produce grown on the nuns' farm, a very well-stocked shop, and a visitor center. The abbey is most atmospheric when the bells are rung for midday office or for 6pm vespers.

The neo-Gothic Kylemore Abbey perches on its lakeside site.

Kylemore (follow signs from N59). kylemoreabbey.ie. ✆ **095/52001.** Admission €17 adults; €13.50 seniors and students; €8 children 13–16; children 12 and under free; €40 families. Daily 10am–6pm (last admission 1 hr. before closing).

The Sky Road ♥♥ SCENIC ROUTE One of the most picturesque drives in the west, the Sky Road is the name given to a mountain pass that

walk this way: THE WESTERN WAY

Nestled between the Maumturk and the Twelve Bens mountains in the heart of Connemara, the waters of **Lough Inagh** lie cupped in a spectacularly beautiful valley, where mountain slopes rise precipitously from the valley floor and small streams cascade into the lake in a series of sparkling waterfalls. The **Western Way,** a walking route that traverses the high country of Galway and Mayo, follows a quiet country road above the R344 through the Lough Inagh Valley.

To reach the beginning of the walk, drive north on the R344, turning right on a side road—look for the sign for Maum Ean—about 200m (656 ft.) before the Lough Inagh Lodge Hotel. Continue on this side road for about 6km (3¾ miles) to a large gravel parking lot on the left. Park here and follow the well-worn trail 2km (1.25 miles) to the top of the pass, through glorious mountain scenery.

At the top of the pass, which has long been associated with St. Patrick, a small oratory has been built. There's a hollow in the rock known as **Patrick's Bed,** a life-size statue of the saint, and a series of cairns marking the Stations of the Cross. Together, these monuments make a striking ensemble, strangely eerie when the mists descend and conceal the far slopes in their shifting haze. A clear day offers great views, with the Atlantic Ocean and Bertraghboy Bay to the southwest and more mountains to the northeast. The round-trip walking time is about 1 hour.

rises from Clifden and loops around the Kingstown Peninsula. There are spectacular vistas over the hills and cliffs to the wide Atlantic Ocean, with plenty of viewpoints where you can pull over to take it all in. The Sky Road starts and ends just off the N59 highway. The route is signposted (perhaps a little too discreetly), and you can go in either direction, but we suggest counterclockwise. Starting in the center of Clifden, turn down Church Hill (second left after the tourism office, facing north). Stay left at the fork and you're on the Sky Road. About 2.5km (1½ miles) later, you'll pass the remains of **Clifden Castle,** a Gothic folly dating from 1818. It's completely derelict, but you can visit for free by passing through the marked gate and walking across the pasture. The whole Sky Road takes about 40 minutes to drive, but you may double that with stopping time. ***Be warned:*** It is very narrow, little more than a paved track in places, so we don't recommend it in bad weather, and always be prepared to meet oncoming cars traveling in the other direction.

Clifden.

Where to Stay in Connemara

EXPENSIVE

Abbeyglen Castle ♥♥ This is how a stay in a castle should be. The gray stone fortress perched on a low hill might look stern and unforgiving from a distance, but inside it's all welcoming charm. Abbeyglen has an ambience of slightly faded nobility, with roomy lounges where chairs are grouped around warming fireplaces and huge windows overlook the grounds. At night, guests gather in the piano bar to chat over brandies. Rooms are spacious, with four-poster beds. The staff can arrange fishing trips and packed lunches and give you tips on local sights. Dinners are convivial and chatty, and the food is delicious.

Sky Rd., Clifden. abbeyglen.ie. ✆ **095/21201.** 45 units. €181–€447 double; €226–€492 suite. Breakfast included. Free parking (if booked online). **Amenities:** Restaurant; bar; Jacuzzi; outdoor pool; sauna; spa; tennis court; Wi-Fi (free). Closed Jan.

Ballynahinch Castle ♥♥ At the side of Owenmore River, near the foot of Ben Lettery, this gabled manor house looks too good to be true. It's a postcard setting, perfect in almost every way. The 16th-century building, once the seat of the O'Flaherty chieftains, is now a casually elegant hotel. Lounges have towering ceilings and warming fireplaces. Guest rooms are just modern enough, in muted shades of cream and toast, and all have orthopedic mattresses. The river is known for its trout and salmon; your catch can be weighed up each evening in the wood-paneled **Fishermen's Pub.** Dinner in the beautiful **Owenmore Restaurant** is a highlight of any stay.

Hunts Room, a guest lounge at the Ballynahinch Castle Hotel & Estate.

Recess. ballynahinch-castle.com. ✆ **095/31006.** 40 units. €305–€525 double; €515–€830 suite. Breakfast included. 2-night minimum stay on certain dates. **Amenities:** Restaurant; bar; limited room service; tennis courts; Wi-Fi (free).

Currarevagh Country House ♥♥ This elegant Italianate manor house, built in 1842, sits just outside tiny Oughterard, in the middle of a huge private park, at the edge of the clear blue waters of Lough Corrib. The house is a perfect retreat—its spacious lounges have fires crackling at the hearth, ideal for relaxing on a rainy day. There's also a lakeside sauna. Rooms are large, with floral curtains, and beds are comfortable. The guesthouse can help you plan activities, from pony trekking and hiking to fishing on the Lough (you can even borrow one of the house's traditionally made boats). Meals in the pink-hued dining room are excellent, often featuring the day's catch or specials like Connemara lamb or wild venison.

Oughterard. currarevagh.com. ✆ **091/552-312.** 9 units. €375 double. 2-night minimum stay. Breakfast and dinner included. **Amenities:** Restaurant; bar; sauna; Wi-Fi (free). Closed Dec–Feb.

THE BEST smell IN ALL OF IRELAND?

"Níl aon tinteán mar do thinteán féin (there is no fireside like your own fireside)."
—Irish proverb

You might experience the strong, smoky, slightly sweet smell of burning turf—dried bricks of peat taken from bogs—on your travels in the west of Ireland. There are plenty who don't care for this quintessentially Irish smell, and for sure it can be quite overpowering. But for the rest of us, there's nothing else like it. In fact, if there's another smell so instantly redolent of this land—of cozy evenings by smoky hearths, of tales told and faraway friends—well, we've yet to find it.

A full third of the Connemara countryside is classified as bog, and these stark and beautiful boglands—formed over 2,500 years ago—have long been an important source of fuel. (During the Iron Age, the Celts also found another use for the bogs, using them to store perishable foods such as butter.) Although no longer the lifeline it once was, cutting and drying turf is still an integral part of the rhythm of the seasons in Connemara.

Cutting requires a special tool, a spade called a *slane*, which slices the turf into bricks about 46cm (18 in.) long. The bricks are first spread out flat to dry, and then stacked in pyramids for further drying—you might see stacks of turf as you pass.

The climate crisis means that, along with other smoky fuels, turf burning is gradually being reduced. While some households still cut and burn turf domestically, it is no longer allowed to be sold commercially.

Delphi Lodge ♥♥ This vine-covered 18th-century country house dwarfed by mountains on a 1,000-acre lakefront estate was made for Instagram. Calling this place a "lodge" isn't just cute nomenclature; it is very much an actual hunting lodge, and a veritable paradise for fishing. Everything is arranged to make fishing easy—boats, *ghillies* (guides), and licenses are all taken care of. If you don't fish, you can just enjoy the utterly splendid countryside, spending the day hiking the enormous grounds, where filling your lungs with the fresh air is like a balm for the soul. Afterward, relax by the fire in the cozy library with a sherry from the honor bar, or try your hand at a game of snooker. Guest rooms are comfortable and generously proportioned (though note that the doors don't have locks). The pricier rooms have views of the lake. The

Delphi Lodge is a thousand-acre country estate.

excellent dinners here are an event, eaten at a long dining table to encourage conversation.

The Delphi Estate and Fishery, Leenane. delphilodge.ie. ✆ **095/42222.** 13 units. €345–€395 double. Breakfast included. **Amenities:** Restaurant (guests only); honor bar; Wi-Fi (free). Closed Nov–Mar (except for private hire only).

MODERATE

The Anglers Return ♥♥ Surrounded by beautiful gardens, this lovely, artsy retreat was built as a hunting lodge in the 19th century; today it's a quiet and relaxed B&B run with great charm by Lynn Hill. Bedrooms are simple and modestly sized, furnished in traditional style. Two of the rooms are en-suite; the others have the use of one of two bathrooms located down the corridor—robes are thoughtfully provided. You can cook your own dinner in the fully equipped kitchen or on the grills outside. There are log fires and pleasant river or garden views from bedrooms—guests are free to wander the gardens, which are practically an attraction by themselves. ***Note:*** The Anglers Return doesn't accept credit cards.

Toombeola, Roundstone. anglersreturn.com. ✆ **095/31091.** 4 units. €190 double. 3-night minimum stay. Breakfast included. Free parking. No credit cards. No children 13 and under. **Amenities:** Guest lounge and kitchen; Wi-Fi (free).

Murray's Doonmore Hotel ♥♥ This waterfront hotel on Inishbofin Island might not be fancy, but the views are extraordinary—from every window you see stunning vistas of the sea and High Island. Guest rooms are quite basic, but families will be pleased to find spacious units with children's bunk beds. Rooms in the modern extension are furnished with pine furniture and flooded with light. Older rooms in the main house are a little worn but still pleasant. Staff are cheerful, and the restaurant offers good, unpretentious cooking.

Inishbofin Island. doonmorehotel.com. ✆ **095/45804.** 25 units. €170–€190 double. Breakfast included. 2-night minimum stay on weekends. **Amenities:** Restaurant; bar; Wi-Fi (free). Closed Oct–Apr.

Renvyle House Hotel ♥♥ The poet W. B. Yeats honeymooned here when it was a family home; Winston Churchill was also a regular guest. This grand old house on the rocky edge of the Atlantic Ocean seems to be in the middle of nowhere, although it's close to Connemara National Park. Still, it's worth the journey, and not just for the breathtaking sea views and warm hospitality. You'll have miles of pristine Irish wilderness to explore; there's a lake you can go boating on, an outdoor pool, and an outdoor hot tub overlooking the beach. Decor is old-school, with sprawling, wood-floored lounges warmed by open fires. Guest rooms vary in size and decor—some are grand and spacious, others small and cozy. The in-house restaurant offers divine European-inspired Irish cooking.

Renvyle. renvyle.com. ✆ **095/46100.** 70 units. €190–€300 double. Breakfast included. **Amenities:** Restaurant; bar; hot tub; outdoor pool; 2 tennis courts; Wi-Fi (free). Closed Jan to mid-Feb.

INEXPENSIVE

Rockmount House ♥♥ It should come as no surprise that the views from this cozy little B&B are pretty amazing, given its location on the Sky Road (p. 414). Rooms are basic but cheerful, with comfortable beds. Hosts Anne and Paddy are filled with knowledge about the region. The grounds contain a private cliff-top path with spectacular views across the bay. Rockmount House is on the Lower Sky Road, which branches off the main Sky Road about 5km (3 miles) west of Clifden.

Lower Sky Rd., Clifden. rockmounthouse.com. ✆ **095/21763.** 4 units. €100–€140 double. Breakfast included. **Amenities:** Wi-Fi (free). Closed Sept–Apr.

Where to Eat in Connemara

In addition to the area's great restaurants, some of the tastiest finds in Connemara are from food trucks. The **Misunderstood Heron** (Derrynacleigh, Leenane; misunderstoodheron.com; no phone) has won awards for its creative menu of fresh seafood, local lamb, and foraged foods assembled in wraps, flatbreads, and savory pastries, all served in an amazing setting overlooking the fjord at Killary Harbour. For coffee with views of Diamond Hill—and of some friendly neighboring donkeys—check out **Diamond View Coffee,** on the Baunoge Road (turn off the N59, 2km/1¼ miles south of Letterfrack).

The Misunderstood Heron food truck serves surprisingly creative food from its Killary Harbour parking spot.

The Carriage Restaurant ♥♥ MODERN CONTINENTAL Locals flock to this restaurant, hidden away in the courtyard at the rear of the Clifden Station House Hotel. The draw is imaginative cooking that manages to infuse even the simplest dish with zest and originality. Look for dishes like braised pork belly, Connemara smoked salmon with crab meat, and seabass served with wild rice and asparagus. For more casual dining, grab a cozy window seat in the adjacent **Signal Bar,** a charming spot set in the original railway station, with many vintage features to admire.
Clifden Station House Hotel, on the N59, Clifden. clifdenstationhouse.com. ✆ **095/21699.** Entrees €17–€36. Reservations essential. Daily 6–8:30pm (occasionally closed Nov–Mar).

O'Dowd's of Roundstone ♥♥ SEAFOOD There's not much room in this tiny pub in Roundstone, which means you'll be fighting for space with dozens of hungry locals. But trust them, for they know exactly what they're here for: extremely good, fresh seafood, simple and beautifully prepared. Start with some Roundstone crab claws with garlic butter, followed by a local catch of the day, served in classic style with lemon and tartar sauce. The creamy seafood chowder is always a crowd-pleaser. A simpler bar menu is also available. Needless to say, booking for dinner is advisable.
R341, on the harbor, Roundstone. odowdsseafoodbar.com. ✆ **095/35809.** Entrees €15–€29. Breakfast 10am–noon; bar food noon–9:30pm; restaurant 5–9:30pm. No reservations before 5pm.

Paddy Coyne's Pub ♥♥♥ IRISH It can be hard to find this lovely pub in tiny, blink-and-you'll-miss-it Renvyle—just outside blink-just-a-little-bit-longer-and-you'll-miss-it-too Tullycross—but it's worth the trek. Aside from the postcard-worthy frontage, dating from 1811, this doesn't *look* like the kind of place that's going to wow you with its cooking. But the numbers of people making their way here for dinner should provide a clue. There's nothing pretentious about the cooking—it's just wonderful, classic Irish fare, done extremely well. Seafood is a specialty—the daily specials are chalked up outside, but expect hake, salmon, mussels, and maybe some Clew Bay oysters, served as they come. Wash it all down with a pint of Guinness (of course). Desserts are avowedly traditional (try the homemade trifle). ***Note:*** They don't take reservations, so arrive early or expect to wait.
Tullycross, Renvyle. paddycoynespub.com. ✆ **095/43499.** Entrees €16–€30. Daily 5–9pm (but times vary—call to check).

Steam Cafe ♥♥ CAFE This cute and simple little cafe is one of the best places in Clifden for lunch. The menu isn't fancy, but it's all good: wraps, sandwiches, light meals, and daily specials, everything made with quality ingredients. The cakes and desserts are great to wash down with the excellent coffee.
Station House Courtyard, off N59 (Galway Rd.), Clifden. facebook.com/SteamCafe Clifden. ✆ **095/30600.** Entrees €5–€12. Wed–Fri 10am–5:30pm; Tues and Sat 9:30am–5:30pm. Closed Sun–Mon.

TAKING A (moon) SHINE TO *POITÍN*

"Keep your eyes well peeled today, the excise men are on their way, searching for the mountain tay, in the hills of Connemara. . . . "

Poitín (sometimes written as *poteen*) is a potent form of Irish moonshine, traditionally brewed from grain or potatoes. It was banned by the English crown in 1661, in an act that effectively criminalized thousands of distillers overnight. That didn't stop people from making the stuff, however, and after 336 years on the wrong side of the law, *poitín* was finally made legal again in 1997.

One 17th-century writer said of *poitín* that "it enlighteneth ye heart, casts off melancholy, keeps back old age and breaketh ye wind." Its usefulness didn't stop there, evidently, as history records the drink being used as everything from a bath tonic to a substitute for dynamite.

Poitín has long been used in fiction as a symbol of Irish nationalism, its contraband status rich with rebellious overtones. The traditional folk song "The Hills of Connemara" describes *poitín* being secretly distributed right under the noses of excise men.

In 2008, the European Union awarded the drink "Geographical Indicative" protection. This means that only the genuine Irish product is allowed to carry the name (the same status enjoyed by Champagne and Parma ham).

There are many commercial or "legal" versions of *poitín* on the market now, although these versions are less potent than the moonshine version. Like most liquors, it can be drunk straight, on the rocks, or with a mixer, but at anything from 80 to a massive 180 proof, *poitín* packs a mean punch, so enjoy . . . cautiously.

Veldon's Seafarer ♥♥ SEAFOOD The fishermen's nets, captain's wheels, and assorted sailing paraphernalia plastered across the polished wooden walls of this friendly bar and restaurant leave no doubt as to the house specialty. You can eat from a fairly simple bar menu—traditional fish and chips, hamburgers, Irish stew—or retreat to the restaurant area. Local crab is a specialty, although if you want to go all out, the seafood platter has a bit of everything. Try the cheesecake of the day for dessert.
On the N59, Letterfrack. veldons.ie. ✆ **095/41046.** Entrees €16–€34. Bar daily noon–9pm; restaurant daily 6–9pm (Fri–Sat only in off-season).

Sports & Outdoor Pursuits in Connemara

WALKING **Connemara National Park ♥♥♥** (p. 412) has excellent walking trails, some of which lead up the sides of the Twelve Bens. You can get maps at the park's visitor center. From the town of **Leenane (*Leenaun*),** there's an exhilarating 4km (2.4-mile) walk to the picturesque Aasleagh Waterfall (*Eas Liath*) northeast of the Killary Fjord harbor. A 2- to 3-hour walk around the fjord follows the Green Road, a sheep track that was once the primary route from the Renvyle Peninsula to Leenane; along the way you'll even pass a ghost town (a village abandoned after the Famine), where the fields rise at a devilishly steep slope from ruined cottages clustered at the water's edge. Trails are rocky, so wear proper shoes.

CONNEMARA pony TREKKING

The sturdy yet elegant Connemara pony is the only horse breed native to Ireland, though it has received an infusion of Spanish blood over the centuries. Often raised in tiny fields with limestone pastures, the ponies are known for their stamina and gentleness, which make them ideal for amateur riders and young people. Born and bred to traverse the region's rugged terrain, they are adept at scaling short, steep hills and delicately picking their way along rocky shores.

Because much of the countryside is well off the beaten track, pony trekking is actually a fantastic way to cover ground. It gets you off the busy roads and out into the countryside, even onto the white-sand beaches near Roundstone and elsewhere along the coast. **Diamonds Equestrian Centre** in Renvyle (diamonds-of-renvyle.com; ✆ **095/434-86**) has beach and mountain rides including a 3-hour coastal trek and picnic to Grace O'Malley's Castle in Renvyle. In Ballyconneely, the **Point Pony Trekking & Horse Riding Centre** (thepointponytrekkingcentre.com; ✆ **087/246-8294**) can set you up with guided treks for all levels of ability.

WATERSPORTS & ADVENTURE SPORTS One-stop shopping for outdoorsy activities—kayaking, waterskiing, hill and coastal walking, rock climbing, archery, you name it—can be found at the **Killary Adventure Company** in Leenane (killary.com; ✆ **095/43411**). Rates start at around €47 per session. The **Delphi Adventure Resort** in Leenane (delphi adventureresort.com; ✆ **095/42208**) offers courses in kayaking, windsurfing, and raft building, as well as mountaineering, abseiling, hiking, and archery. Everything is reasonably priced, and the atmosphere is laid-back and friendly. **Roundstone Outdoors** at Gurteen Beach (roundstone outdoors.ie; ✆ **085/139-7174**) offers various water-based activities including windsurfing, kayaking, and SUP. Rates start at €45.

11
THE MIDLANDS

Promoted as the "Hidden Heartlands," the middle parts of Ireland are all too often overlooked by visitors. On the one hand, we can guess why. You get less bang for your buck here when it comes to must-see attractions (and if you don't have the freedom of a car, you may as well forget it). But great discoveries await those willing to head . . . not off the beaten path exactly, but certainly *against* the flow of traffic. When we think of the Midlands, we picture green grass and rolling fields, veined with long, winding rivers and picturesque, slow-moving streams. And nestled among them are a few real gems, such as the romantic medieval castles at Charleville and Birr, the atmospheric ancient monastic site at Clonmacnoise, and the surprisingly little-known (and *very* old indeed) Corlea Trackway.

The most significant history here dates to the late 17th century, with the fateful battle for supremacy between two English kings: the Protestant William III and the Catholic James II. After William won at the bloody Battle of Aughrim in 1691, he cemented the Protestant establishment's hold in Ireland for centuries to come. The lavishly high-tech museum at Athlone Castle is the best of several in the region that tell this important story.

ESSENTIALS

Arriving

BY CAR By far the best way to get to and around the Midlands is by car. Although Athlone is easy to reach by public transportation from Galway or Dublin, you'll need a car to see the smaller towns and remote sites. Major roads that lead to this area are the main Galway–Dublin road (M6) from points east and west, N62 from the south, and N55 and N61 from the north. For car rentals in Dublin, see p. 91; for rentals from Shannon Airport, see p. 354.

BY BUS **Bus Éireann** (buseireann.ie; ✆ **01/703-4111**) runs buses every half-hour to 90 minutes from Galway City to Athlone (journey time 80–100 min.). From the main bus station in Dublin, buses go to Athlone about every hour (journey time 2–3 hr.) and a handful of times a day to Birr (3–4 hr.).

PREVIOUS PAGE: **Hiking Slieve Bloom Way.**

BY TRAIN **Irish Rail** operates direct trains from Dublin to Athlone Station, Southern Station Road (irishrail.ie; ✆ **090/647-3300**), about every hour; most journeys take just over an hour. From Galway City, trains go to Athlone every 1 to 2 hours; the trip takes 90 minutes.

A Note on Listings

Officially the Midlands region covers the counties of Laois, Longford, Offaly, and Westmeath; we've also included a couple of sights in County Roscommon and in the far eastern part of County Galway, because of their close proximity. Attractions in this region are widely spread out—hiring a car is the only practical way to see the Midlands' best sights without spending excessive amounts of time on public transport, which is scarce in rural areas. Therefore, we present the sights as one list, not split up by county, allowing travelers to pick and choose according to their interests.

EXPLORING THE MIDLANDS

The area's most appealing town of any size—although it's hardly a teeming metropolis, with a population of just over 22,000—is **Athlone (*Baile***

***Átha Luain*),** on the River Shannon. It's a vibrant place where brightly painted buildings house craft stores and cool boutiques. It's also a perfect spot to base yourself for exploring the area, with excellent small hotels, charming restaurants, and pubs. Heading south from Athlone, the Shannon winds past the early Christian settlement of **Clonmacnoise (*Cluain Mhic Nóis*),** with its stone chapels and mysterious round towers; **Banagher (*Beannchar na Sionna*),** a sleepy working town with a picturesque river harbor; and eventually **Portumna Castle** (p. 431), artfully set where the Shannon flows into Lough Derg.

The town of **Birr (*Biorra*),** known for its magnificent historic gardens, is south of Banagher, with the Slieve Bloom Mountains rising to its east; the N52 angles northeast from Birr, passing through the county towns of **Tullamore** (Co. Offaly) and **Mullingar** (Co. Westmeath).

Athlone Castle ♥♥ CASTLE Built in 1210 for King John of England, this mighty stone fortress sits on the edge of the Shannon, atop the ruins of an earlier fort built in 1129 as the seat of the chiefs of Connaught. Besieged for almost 6 months in 1641, the castle was attacked again in 1690 and finally fell in 1691 after an intense bombardment by forces sent by William of Orange. The fall of Athlone was a key event in the war that would cement the Protestant establishment in Ireland and ensure British rule, all the way up to the War of Independence in the 1920s. (The Dutch military commander who took the town, Godard van Glinkel, was rewarded for his efforts with the earldom of Athlone.) Three centuries later, in 2012, the castle underwent a multimillion-euro renovation; it now houses eight separate galleries on the history of Athlone, particularly the 1690–91

Exhibit showcasing key figures from the 1690–91 Siege of Athlone at Athlone Castle.

siege, using plenty of high-tech wizardry. The castle's original medieval walls have been preserved, as have two large cannons dating from the reign of George II, and a pair of 25cm (10-inch) mortars cast in 1856.

Athlone, Co. Westmeath. athlonecastle.ie. ✆ **090/644-2130.** Admission €12 adults; €8 seniors and students; €5.50 children 14 and under; free for children 3 and under; €30–€38 families. June–Aug Tues–Sat 9:30am–6pm, Sun 10:30am–6pm; Sept–Nov and Mar–May Tues–Sat 10am–5:30pm (5pm Nov), Sun 11am–5:30pm; Dec–Feb Wed–Sat 10:30am–5pm, Sun 11:30am–5pm. Last admission 1 hr. before closing.

Battle of Aughrim Interpretative Centre ♥♥ BATTLEFIELD About midway between Galway City and Athlone, just off the M6 motorway, lies this interesting little museum, dedicated to a battle between two kings that took place here in 1691. When James II became king of England in 1685, his days on the throne were already numbered. He had a "flaw" that the Protestant establishment simply couldn't live with: He was a convert to Catholicism. In 1688, James was deposed by Parliament in favor of his own son-in-law—the Protestant William III. Retreating to Ireland, James led a rebellion that was to have far-reaching consequences for Irish history. Aughrim wasn't the most famous nor arguably the most important battle of that war, but it was the last. With the defeat of the so-called Jacobite forces loyal to James, the prospect of a Catholic Ireland was crushed for almost 2½ centuries. The center does a competent job of telling the story through displays and exhibits, plus the obligatory visitor-center film.

R446, Aughrim, near Ballinasloe, Co. Galway. ✆ **090/967-3939.** Admission €5 adults; €4 seniors and students; €3 children 11 and under; €15 families. May–Sept Tues–Sat 10:30am–4:30pm, Sun 2–5pm. Last admission 30 min. before closing. Closed early Oct–April.

Birr Castle ♥♥ GARDENS This magnificent 90-room, 17th-century castle stands amid gorgeous sprawling gardens, beautifully crafted as a kind of wonderland. The great house is still lived in by the same family that has owned it for centuries. It is only open to the public from May to September, 6 days a week—and even then for just a handful of pricey guided tours, limited to 15 adults, so advance booking is essential. But the real reason to come to Birr is to see the extraordinary grounds, which are open year-round. The *demesne* (estate) of the Parsons family, now the earls of Rosse, wraps around a peaceful lake and stretches over miles of pastures and wild woodland. There's much to discover: beautiful topiaries, huge box hedges, a lovely wrought-iron bridge, a newly renovated science exhibition, and even a steampunk-esque, 19th-century Great Telescope (see box on p. 428). The 60-minute outdoor tour visits the telescope and delves into the Parsons family's achievements in science, astronomy, and botany. There's also a tea shop and a kids' play area.

Birr, Co. Offaly. birrcastle.com. ✆ **057/912-0336.** Admission to grounds €12 adults; €7 children 4–17; free for children 3 and under; €34 families. Castle tour €20 per person, no children under age 12; outdoor tour €14; garden tour €14.50. Grounds open daily 9am–5:30pm, last admission 1 hr. before closing. Castle tours May–Sept Mon–Sat 10 and 11:30am, 1pm; outdoor tour Sat noon.

THE GREAT telescope

At noble **Birr Castle** ♥♥ (p. 427), one of the key attractions is not the historic castle itself, nor the beautiful grounds, but a fascinating exhibition on 19th-century science. William Parsons, the 3rd Earl of Birr, was a scientist and astronomer, obsessed with discovering all he could about the night sky. Under his leadership, Birr Castle became an unlikely hub of research into astronomy, photography, and botany. One of his inventions—now known as the Great Telescope—was built in 1845 and soon nicknamed (somewhat sarcastically) the "Leviathan of Parsonstown." Until the 20th century, it was the largest telescope in the world.

The huge astronomical machine may resemble a medieval siege engine, but the key thing about it was that it worked. Using it, Parsons discovered and documented numerous nebulae, some of which were later determined to be hitherto unknown galaxies. He found and named the Crab Nebula, among others. He also discovered that certain galaxies were shaped like spirals. Birr Castle was the only place in the world where the phenomenon could be observed until 1914, when new, more advanced telescopes were developed.

To this day, the Great Telescope is kept in full working order, and demonstrations of its power are held regularly in summer. If you want to witness one of these displays for yourself, call ahead to check times.

Charleville Castle ♥♥♥ CASTLE Now, *this* is a castle. Designed in 1798 by Francis Johnston, the crenellated Gothic Revival masterpiece took 12 years to build. Today it's considered one of the best of Ireland's early-19th-century castles, with fine limestone walls and plenty of towers, turrets, and battlements. Those who believe in such things say it is haunted (it has even been featured on the TV shows *Ghost Hunters* and *Most Haunted*). Inside you'll find spectacular plasterwork and hand-carved stairways, as well as secret passageways and dungeons. The castle is open year-round (the land is grazed by horses, but visitors must wait at the gate to be escorted in). Hourly tours are offered daily April to September; the rest of the year, tours are by appointment, booked in advance by e-mail at info@charlevillecastle.com. Charleville is run by volunteers, who are as accommodating as possible—keep in mind that they're running it out of love rather than for profit. The money from the tours is used for restoration of the castle. Check hours before visiting; a shortage of volunteers can affect times.

Off Birr Rd. (N52), Tullamore, Co. Offaly. charlevillecastle.ie. ✆ **057/932-3040.** Guided tour €15 adults; €12 students ages 17–18; €6 children 6–16; free for children 5 and under. Castle open year-round; Apr–Sept tours daily 11–4pm; Oct–Mar tours by appointment.

Clonmacnoise ♥♥♥ RELIGIOUS SITE/RUINS Resting somberly on the east bank of the Shannon, this is one of Ireland's most profound ancient sites. St. Ciaran founded the monastic community of Clonmacnoise in A.D. 548 at the crucial intersection of the Shannon and the

Dublin–Galway land route, and it soon became one of Europe's great centers of learning and culture. For nearly 1,000 years, Clonmacnoise flourished under the patronage of Irish chiefs; the last high king, Rory O'Connor, was buried here in 1198. Though it was raided repeatedly by native chiefs, Danes, and Anglo-Normans, there was always something left with which to rebuild—until English troops destroyed it in 1552. In a report written by a monk from that time, "There was not left a bell, small or large, an image or an altar, or a book, or a gem, or even glass in a window, from the wall of the church out, which was not carried off." Today you can see remnants of the cathedral, a castle, eight churches, two round towers, three sculpted high crosses, and more than 200 monumental slabs. On some stones, the old carvings can still be seen with thoughtful messages in ancient Irish, such as "A PRAYER FOR DANIEL."

On R357, 6.5km (4 miles) N of Shannonbridge, Co. Offaly. heritageireland.ie. ✆ **090/967-4195.** Admission €8 adults; €6 seniors; €4 students and children; €20 families. June–Aug daily 9am–6:30pm; Sept–Oct and mid-March to May daily 10am–6pm; Nov–Jan daily 10am–5pm; Feb to mid-March 10am–5:30pm. Last admission 30 min. before closing.

Corlea Iron Age Roadway ♥♥ ANCIENT SITE This is one of those places that makes you stand back, scratch your head, and marvel at just how *old* Ireland is. The fairly unassuming, modern interpretive center, situated in a bog, contains what at first glance looks like an elevated platform of planks nailed onto rails, like a boardwalk through a marsh or swamp. It is, in fact, an excavated wooden trackway that has been carbon dated to the year 148 B.C. Roughly 18m (59 ft.) of original track has been

Exploring the mystical ruins of Clonmacnoise, once one of Ireland's greatest centers of monastic learning and culture.

uncovered so far and can be seen on a (free) guided tour. The center also contains an exhibition and a film to put the whole thing into context. A replica version crosses a starkly beautiful section of bog, roughly where the rest of the track is believed to be buried. The weird thing is that the modern version really doesn't look all that different. Was the track built merely as a bridge over the bog, or did it have some religious significance—perhaps enabling people to reach a part of the bog considered sacred for some long-forgotten reason? Archaeologists disagree, but it's fascinating to contemplate the possibility.

Kenagh, Co. Longford. heritageireland.ie. ✆ **043/332-2386.** Free admission. Mid-March to Oct daily 10am–6pm. Last admission 1 hr. before closing.

Derryglad Folk & Heritage Museum ♥♥ MUSEUM For a highly concentrated dose of mid-20th-century nostalgia, visit this sweet little museum just outside Athlone. You walk through a series of re-created businesses, each little building jam-packed with memorabilia and antiques—a "medical hall" (drugstore), grocery store, hardware store—and a few farmer's crofts. The intriguing **McCormack Photography Room** preserves the collection of a real photography studio that operated in Athlone from 1948 until 2002. As well as antique cameras and developing equipment, it displays photographs from the decades the shop was in operation. Museum guides could hardly be keener to impart their encyclopedic knowledge.

Curraghboy, Co. Roscommon (13.8km/8½ miles NW of Athlone on R362). derrygladfolkmuseum.com. ✆ **090/648-8192.** Admission €8 adults; €4 children; €20 families. May–Oct Mon–Sat 10am–6pm.

Kilbeggan Distillery ♥♥ FACTORY TOUR The oldest licensed distillery in Ireland, Kilbeggan has been producing whiskey here since 1757. Well, almost—it closed in 1957 and was virtually derelict for 25 years, until locals revived it as a small-time distillery and museum. Full production resumed in the early 2000s, in part using traditional methods and equipment, including oak mash *tuns* (vats) and a 2-century-old copper still—thought to be the oldest still in day-to-day use anywhere in the world. (The distillery also has a working waterwheel and a steam-powered engine, although these are mostly for show.) Unlike most distilleries, you can wander around some of it yourself, or choose a guided tour. The daily **Distillery Experience** (€30 per person; Apr–Oct 10 and 11:30am, 1, 2:30, and 3:45pm; Nov–Mar 10 and 11:30am, and 2pm; 12 or older only) starts with a cocktail taster and includes a master-class tasting of four whiskeys and a dram glass to take home. The **Irish Coffee Masterclass** (€25 per person; 18 or older only) includes a guided distillery tour and a lesson in making an Irish coffee with Kilbeggan whiskey; and the 30-minute **Distillers Cask Bottling Experience** (€115 per person) gives you a chance to draw whiskey from the cask and bottle it yourself. Check website for tour times.

On M6 (Junction 5), Kilbeggan, Co. Westmeath. kilbegganwhiskey.com. ✆ **057/933-2134.** Mid-Mar to Oct daily 10am–5:30pm; Nov to mid-Mar daily 10am–3:30pm.

Sampling whiskeys at the Kilbeggan Distillery.

Portumna Castle and Forest Park ♥♥ CASTLE/PARK Built in 1609 by Earl Richard Burke, this massive, noble structure on the northern shores of Lough Derg is a particularly fine manor house. Had it not been gutted by fire in 1826, who knows what billionaire might own it now? The fire spared much of the impressive exterior, including its decorative Dutch-style gables and rows of stone-mullioned windows; the ground floor is open to the public and contains exhibits on the history of the castle, particularly the so-called "Flight of the Wild Geese," when James II's Jacobite supporters fled Ireland in defeat. The grounds contain a restored walled kitchen garden and a willow maze. Surrounding the castle, the beautiful 560-hectare (1,383-acre) expanse of **Portumna Forest Park** offers trails and signposted walks, plus viewing points, picnic areas, and the remains of a 13th-century Cistercian abbey.

Off N65, Portumna, Co. Galway. ✆ **090/974-1658.** Castle €5 adults; €4 seniors; €3 children and students; €13 families. Free admission to gardens and Forest Park. Castle: Mid-Mar to late Oct daily 10am–6pm. Last admission 45 min. before closing.

Rathcroghan Visitor Centre ♥♥ ANCIENT SITE Rathcroghan is one of Europe's oldest royal sites, with more than 240 archaeological monuments including prehistoric burial mounds, ringforts, standing stones, and linear earthworks. The visitor center has a fantastic exhibition, with stories about the warrior Queen Medb and the epic tale, the Táin,

A somber SORT OF GRANDEUR: STROKESTOWN & ITS FAMINE MUSEUM

For nearly 4 centuries, from 1600 to 1979, **Strokestown Park House** (strokestownpark.ie; ✆ **071/963-3013**) in County Roscommon was the seat of the Pakenham-Mahon family. After the Restoration, King Charles II granted the vast estate, which stretches for miles in every direction, to Nicholas Mahon in appreciation for supporting the House of Stewart during the bloody English Civil War. (Quite a reward indeed!) Nicholas's grandson, Thomas, considered the original house, completed in 1697, too small and unimposing, so he upped the ante by hiring Richard Cassels—aka "Richard Castle," the architect behind Russborough House (p. 204) and Powerscourt House (p. 160)—to build him something more impressive. The result? This stunning 45-room Palladian mansion, a monument to upper-class privilege. In the north wing, note Ireland's last existing galleried kitchen (where the lady of the house could observe the culinary activity without being part of it), and in the south wing you'll find a vaulted stable so magnificent it has been described as an "equine cathedral."

These days Strokestown is also the permanent home of the **National Famine Museum,** one of the country's very best museums devoted to that tragic period in Irish history. It dramatically sets forth not only the natural disaster, but also the shocking cruelty of the British establishment's response. Exhibits include letters penned by some of the tenants of Strokestown during the Famine years.

The pairing of these two historic attractions may seem incongruous, until you learn a little more of Strokestown Park's history—particularly the behavior of Major Denis Mahon, the landlord at Strokestown during the 1840s. When the potato blight struck and famine started to spread, Mahon and his land agents could have done many things to help the hundreds of starving people who lived and worked on the property. Instead, they evicted them as soon as it became clear they couldn't pay their rent; callously, Mahon even chartered ships to send his own tenants away from Ireland. In 1847, Major Mahon was shot to death near Strokestown. Two men were hastily (and dubiously) convicted of the crime, but it seems clear that many hungry people had motives.

Strokestown Park is on the main Dublin–Castlebar Road (N5). A self-guided visit to the National Famine Museum, estate gardens, and woodland gardens costs €14.50 adults, €12 seniors

while a guided walk visits Rathcroghan Mound itself and surrounding sites. The 2pm summer tour includes the Oweynagat Cave, which was said to connect to the "Otherworld" (the underground cave is wet and muddy, so dress appropriately).

Co. Roscommon. rathcroghan.ie. ✆ **071/963-9268.** Admission €21 adults; €7 children 10–17; €4 children 9 and under; €19 seniors and students. Mon–Sat 9am–5pm. Last admission to visitor center 30 min. before closing. Guided tours May–Aug Mon–Fri noon and 2pm (2pm tour includes cave); Sept–Apr Mon–Fri noon; weekends by appointment.

The Rock of Dunamase ♥ RUINS There isn't much left of the castle that once stood atop this rocky outcrop overlooking a valley near the town and students, €7 children, free for children 4 and under, and €31 families. Admission to the above plus a guided visit to Strokestown Park House costs €18.50 adults, €14.50 seniors and students, €10 children, free for children 4 and under, and €39 families. It's open daily June to August 10am to 6pm; March to May and September to October 10:30am until 5pm; November to February 10:30am until 4pm. The house can only be seen on a 45-minute guided tour, at noon, 2, and 4pm (noon only Nov-Feb).

A lady's bedroom inside Strokestown Park House.

of Portlaoise; what remains, however, is quite an impressive sight. The ruins were once **Dunamase Castle** (though nobody calls it that anymore), built during the 12th century. It clearly didn't last long; records indicate that it was a total ruin by as early as 1350. A much earlier fort is believed to have once stood on the same site. A few arched gateways survive intact, and the scattered remains of walls and turrets give a good idea of how large it must have once been. The stunning view from among the ruins, over rolling green fields toward the Slieve Mountains in the distance, is worth the visit alone. The Rock is signposted from the main road, but it's very easy to get lost. So to get there, follow these directions: Leave Portlaoise on N80, heading southeast toward Carlow. Shortly after crossing

leprechauns: YOU'RE DOING IT ALL WRONG

For better or worse, leprechauns have long been known around the world as a symbol of Ireland. Usually portrayed as little green creatures, grinning broadly, they are absurd, cartoonish figures, with which we've all grown up.

Originally, though, they were something much different. The word "leprechaun" comes from the Irish *leath bhrógan*, meaning "shoemaker." And in early folklore, leprechauns were often depicted as cobblers by trade. Though they were elven, mischievous creatures, they weren't evil exactly—just prone to the occasional malicious practical joke.

In those days, different regions of Ireland had their own versions of the leprechaun folklore. Back then, all leprechauns were portrayed as wearing *red* coats, not the green you see today. The green coats came much later in the 20th century, probably invented by foreigners to denote their Irishness.

Where that pot of gold came from is anybody's guess, but many people believe that some of the modern image of leprechauns was created by Disney for the movie *Darby O'Gill and the Little People* in 1959.

Nowadays, Irish people view leprechauns as a tourist concept rather than something authentic, and indeed, the description is sometimes used by the Irish to describe the crass side of the tourism industry. So bear all this in mind when you consider buying that little leprechaun figurine wearing an Irish flag.

over the M7 motorway, just outside the town limits, you'll pass some large green industrial sheds. Approximately 1.8km (just over 1 mile) after this you will come to some scattered houses, with a turning on the left, next to a triangular patch of lawn and a telegraph pole. Take this turning; you will start to see the Rock on the hill to your left in about .5km (550 yards).

Off N80 (Portlaoise-Carlow Rd.), about 9km (5½ miles) E of Portlaoise, Co. Laois. Free admission. Daily dawn–dusk.

Tullynally Castle Gardens ♥♥ CASTLE/GARDENS A turreted and towered Gothic Revival manor, this creamy white castle is dazzling. It has been the home of the Pakenham family, the earls of Longford, since 1655. The 12-hectare (30-acre) grounds are an attraction in themselves: Highlights include a large kitchen garden, where the grass is kept short by grazing llamas; forest trails and a riverside walk; and an idyllic path leading to a Victorian grotto. Tullynally is near Lough Derravaragh, a tranquil spot featured in the legendary Irish tale *The Children of Lir.* Castle tours run three times a day—book in advance, as numbers are limited (children 10 and over only).

About 32km (20 miles) E of Longford and 21km (13 miles) N of Mullingar, off the Dublin-Sligo Rd. (N4), Pakenham Hall Rd., Castlepollard, Co. Westmeath. tullynally castle.ie. ✆ **044/966-1856.** Gardens €8.50 adults, €4 children, €23 families. Castle tours €16.50 adults, €8.50 children 11 and over; May–Sept Thurs–Sun 11am, 12:30 and 2pm. Gardens open Apr–Sept Thurs–Sun and public holidays 11am–5pm. Open daily during Heritage Week in Aug.

WHERE TO STAY IN THE MIDLANDS

Athlone, on the southern tip of Lough Ree and almost halfway between Galway and Dublin, makes a natural base from which to explore the Midlands region. It's a colorful waterside town, small enough to explore on foot, with good hotels and eateries and some gorgeous old pubs.

Athlone

Bastion ♥♥ This delightful B&B is run by the lovely Anthony and Vinny McCay, who have converted an old Athlone town house into a chic, rather bohemian getaway. The decor fills the place with light and cheer, from the whitewashed walls and polished-wood floors in the bedrooms to the sophisticated furniture and Eastern-influenced accent pieces strewn here and there. Breakfasts (not included) are available across the street at the **Bastion Kitchen** (p. 438). Two minor downsides: Two of the bedrooms have shared bathrooms, and visitors with mobility problems should be sure to ask for a room on a lower floor—there are quite a few stairs to climb.

2 Bastion St., Athlone. thebastion.net. ✆ **090/649-4954.** 7 units. €75–€120 double. No parking (street parking nearby). **Amenities:** Wi-Fi (free).

Bastion, in Athlone, is a cheery B&B with contemporary, light-filled guest rooms.

Hodson Bay Hotel ♥♥ The deep blue waters of Lough Ree stretch out before this modern spa hotel just outside Athlone. Views of the lake are stunning, which somewhat makes up for what the guest rooms lack in character, with their rather plain, corporate look. (Needless to say, you should ask for a room on the lake side.) Rooms in the "Retreat" wing are better designed but more expensive. The spa is excellent, with a huge list of treatments. The hotel has two good restaurants and a pub, and the center of Athlone is only a 10-minute drive away.

Signposted off N61, 7km (4½ miles) NW of Athlone. hodsonbayhotel.com. ✆ **090/644-2004.** 176 units. €110–€270 double. Breakfast not included in lower rates. Check website for special offers. Free parking. **Amenities:** 2 restaurants; bar; pool; room service; spa; Wi-Fi (free).

Wineport Lodge ♥♥ This romantic, modern hotel overlooking Lough Ree is a truly relaxing getaway. The contemporary bedrooms have plenty of space, and balconies offer glorious views of the lake—perfect for watching the clear waters turn to amber as the sun goes down. The hotel has a spa if you're worn out from exploring. The restaurant is highly rated and offers a modern take on Irish/French cuisine, with an emphasis on seafood—this is one of best eateries in the region.

Glasson, Athlone. wineport.ie. ✆ **090/643-9010.** 29 units. €230–€535 double; €305–€610 suite. Breakfast included. Free parking. **Amenities:** Restaurant; bar; room service; spa; Wi-Fi (free).

Birr

Townsend House ♥ This family-run Georgian town house B&B in the center of the heritage town of Birr has plenty of character. Rooms are decorated in a classic style keeping to the Georgian theme, with antique furniture and some four-poster beds. There's also a tapas restaurant and wine bar (open evenings Thurs–Sat), plus a garden to relax in, and the house is just a short walk from the castle.

Townsend St., Townparks, Birr, Co. Offaly. townsendhouse.ie. ✆ **057/912-1276.** 10 units. €100 double. Reductions for children, and discounts for longer stays. Breakfast included. Limited parking. **Amenities:** Restaurant; wine bar; Wi-Fi (free).

Longford

Viewmount House ♥♥ Tranquil, elegant gardens await at this country-house B&B just outside Longford. Guest rooms are done in a pleasingly old-fashioned style, with antique wood furniture and plenty of space. Some have little sitting areas and roll-top tubs in the bathrooms. Viewmount also has a deserved reputation as one of the best places to eat in the area; the **VM Restaurant** in the old stables serves superb modern Irish meals, and it also does Sunday lunch. The house was under restoration at the time of writing so check the website.

Dublin Rd., Longford, Co. Longford. viewmounthouse.com. ✆ **043/334-1919.** 12 units. €160–€190 double. Breakfast included. Free parking. **Amenities:** Restaurant; Wi-Fi (free).

THE OLDEST pub IN IRELAND

Who can lay claim to the title of Ireland's oldest pub? It's a vexing question, with several contenders battling it out. **The Brazen Head ♥♥♥** in Dublin (p. 172) has been serving customers since 1198, making it an oft-cited candidate for the honor—although detractors would scoff that most of the building was replaced in the 17th century, thus disqualifying it. The other big contender is **Sean's Bar ♥♥**, Main Street in Athlone (seansbar.ie; ✆ **090/649-2358**). Records show that a drinking establishment of some kind or another has been on this site since the astonishingly faraway date of A.D. 900. The fact that a section of wall is believed to be original further strengthens the claim—but again, the extent to which it can be considered *the same pub* is debatable.

The dispute was finally settled when the *Guinness Book of Records* ruled in favor of Sean's. Presumably this means that it's now acceptable to call it officially Ireland's oldest pub. And, although some of the decor is modern, the fact that you still have to duck low to get in the door gives it an *olde* feel. All the same, to look at the place you'd certainly never guess that it's been serving customers since half a millennium before Columbus sailed to America.

WHERE TO EAT IN THE MIDLANDS

Most small towns in this area have little in the way of restaurant life. In some villages, the only place serving food at all is the pub. But **Athlone** has some good restaurants, plus a couple of quality coffee shops. Along with the choices below, most of the hotels listed above have excellent restaurants.

Abbeyleix

Bramley ♥♥♥ LUNCH/DINNER At this relaxed neighborhood restaurant in the historic Bramley building in Abbeyleix, talented chef Sam Moody celebrates the best of County Laois's larder, with dishes like Portarlington mushrooms served with sourdough and egg yolk, cured Goat's Bridge trout with gherkin and radish, and organic Laois pork served with caramelized apples. Art pieces based on local flora by Irish artist Erica Devine suit the building's Georgian heritage (and are for sale if you have room in your baggage). A very good supper menu is served on Wednesdays and Thursdays from 6 to 7pm (two courses €29.50, three courses €34.50), but if you really want to sample the chef's full range, go for the full seven-course tasting menu.

10 Main St., Knocknamoe, Abbeyleix, Co. Laois. bramleyabbeyleix.com. ✆ **057/875-7749.** Lunch entrees €10–€18; dinner entrees €35–€39; 7-course tasting menu €75. Wed 6–9:30pm; Thurs–Sat noon–2:30pm and 6–9:30pm.

Athlone

Al Mezza ♥♥ MIDDLE EASTERN/MEDITERRANEAN Athlone is an unlikely location in which to find a topnotch Lebanese restaurant, but Al Mezza has fast become one of the best places to eat in the area. After seating you at one of the nicely shabby-chic tables (ours was an old sewing table), the staff helpfully takes you through the options—especially useful if you're not familiar with Middle Eastern food. Order off the menu for healthy, delicious meat and fish dishes (try the chicken shawarma, or the sea bream, simply served with cilantro and garlic), or go for the *mezza* plate, filled with tasty small servings of traditional Lebanese dishes (the hummus is a must, of course). Plenty of vegetarian options are available. Round the meal off with some sweet baklava and ice cream. There's a good wine list, too.

6 Bastion St., Athlone. almezza.ie. ✆ **090/649-8765.** Entrees €17–€29. *Mezza* plates (for 2 people) €72–€84. Wed–Sun 5–9pm.

Bastion Kitchen ♥♥ CAFE Delicious, healthy meals are the main focus at this charming little cafe and deli. Its specialty is organic pita sandwiches, served in a variety of interesting ways (turkey and cranberry; chicken with fresh hummus; organic yams with pepper and pesto). You can also make your own combinations with "No hassle!" as the menu says. There are also salads and excellent daily soups—try the pea, kale, and coconut broth served with spelt bread, if it's on offer. Lots of vegetarian options, too. Most items can be ordered to go.

1 Bastion St., Athlone. bastionkitchen.com. ✆ **090/649-8369.** Lunch entrees €7.30–€14. Mon–Sat 9am–4:30pm.

Beans & Leaves ♥♥ CAFE This cheerful cafe/deli is another great place for a quick, healthy lunch in Athlone. In addition to excellent sandwiches, it offers tasty pancakes and waffles, soups, salads, and an all-day breakfast menu. Desserts are well worth checking out.

23 Lloyds Lane, Athlone. facebook.com/beans.leaves. ✆ **090/643-3534.** Lunch entrees €7–€16. Thurs–Mon 9am–4pm.

The Cellar Bistro ♥♥ BISTRO Black-and-white portraits of movie stars adorn the walls of this friendly little bistro in the center of Athlone. The menu doesn't present too many surprises, but it's all done very well: sirloin or rib-eye steak, lamb shank with basil mashed potatoes, or perhaps roast duck with seasonal greens. For dessert, try the Toblerone cheesecake—it's made with the Swiss chocolate-bar brand, popular here since the '70s. The "early bird" set menu is a pretty good deal at €30 for three courses (it's served all night Thurs and Sun, until 6:45pm Fri–Sat).

1-2 Strand St., Athlone. facebook.com/HattersLaneBistro. ✆ **085/868-5058.** Entrees €21–€34. Thurs–Sat 5–9pm; Sun noon–8pm.

The Fatted Calf ♥♥ MODERN IRISH The latest upscale restaurant to gain attention in Athlone, the Fatted Calf is an attractive place with a sustainable, local approach. Run by a husband-and-wife team, the restaurant has a glossy, modern look, with rows of tables lined up against dark gray walls—it's elegant without being fussy. The cooking is just the same. Expect inventive appetizers like remoulade of mango and kohlrabi, or Dublin Bay prawn wontons with spiced pineapple jam. For the main event, try the seared Irish duck breast with anise-poached pear—tender and sweet. The lovely desserts are an Instagram post waiting to happen. Reservations for dinner are recommended.
Church St., Athlone. thefattedcalf.ie. ✆ **090/643-3371.** Entrees €24–€29. Tues–Thurs 5–9pm; Fri 5–9:30pm; Sat 2–3:30pm and 4–9:30pm; Sun 2:30–7pm.

Thyme ♥♥♥ MODERN IRISH Offering fine dining without being overly fussy or formal, this excellent bistro is one of the best places to eat in Athlone—or anywhere in the Midlands, come to that. Local ingredients feature heavily on the imaginative menu; to start, you may be offered young buck cheese mousse with candied walnuts, then maybe a loin of Wagyu beef, cooked to perfection, with smoked Gubeen cheese, or wild venison served with *cavolo nero* (Tuscan kale) salsa and elderberry ketchup. The "value menu," served all night Thursday and Sunday and from 5 until 5:45pm Friday and Saturday, offers similar dishes at €40 for three courses. Be sure to make reservations, especially on weekends.
Custom Place, Athlone. thyme restaurant.ie. ✆ **090/647-8850.** Set dinner menu €68; Sun lunch entrees €26–€35. Wed–Sat 5–9pm; Sun 1–7pm.

Dry aged beef, smoked Gubbeen gougère, braised onion, and broccoli at Thyme.

Tullamore

The Blue Apron ♥♥♥ IRISH This great little bistro is in Tullamore, about 3.4km (2 miles) northeast of **Charleville Castle** (p. 428). Start with a plate of tender king scallops with prawn toast or a spiced pear and Cashel blue cheese salad, before choosing from honey-and-thyme-glazed duck breast or slow-roasted lamb with garlic potatoes and rosemary jus. A

walk this way: THE SLIEVE BLOOM WAY

Linking counties Laois and Offaly, the lush and gentle Slieve Bloom mountain range is great hillwalking territory—its tallest peak is just 527m (1,729 ft.), which clocks in at about the same as the 44th tallest in the Wicklow Mountains (p. 205). The Slieve Blooms also have the great advantage of being decidedly undervisited, so peace and solitude are easy to come by.

The Slieve Bloom Mountains Nature Reserve—Ireland's largest state-owned nature reserve—has several looped hiking trails, including several around **Lough (Lake) Boora;** one of them has its own sculpture trail. Another takes you through the tiny but charming village of **Clonaslee,** and up to the **Rickets Rock waterfall.** For a touch of scenic wilderness, walk a portion of the **Slieve Bloom Way,** a circular 34km (21-mile) signposted trail that begins and ends in Glenbarrow, County Laois; see **slieve bloom.ie** for details. Several trained guides live locally and will offer their services if you'd prefer to be taken around by an expert; a list with contact details is available at **slievebloom.ie** (click "Walking").

The terrain also lends itself particularly well to horseback riding; the **Birr Equestrian Centre,** Kingsborough House, Birr, Co. Offaly (birrequestrian.ie; ✆ **087/244-5545**), organizes regular treks and special trips.

Several castles lie within the boundaries of the Slieves, including **Charleville ♥♥** (p. 428) and **Portumna ♥♥** (p. 431).

For more information, visit **slievebloom.ie**.

full vegetarian menu is always available (try the sweet roast vegetable and honey log with goat cheese). There's a set menu for dinner on Wednesday and Thursday (two courses €30, three courses €36) and a set menu for Sunday lunch (two courses €29, three courses €35)—it's a great but very filling choice, so don't expect to get much done afterward.

Harbour St., Tullamore, Co. Offaly. theblueapronrestaurant.ie. ✆ **057/936-0106.** Entrees €24–€38. Wed–Thurs 5:30–9pm; Fri–Sat 5:30–10pm; Sun 12:30–6:30pm.

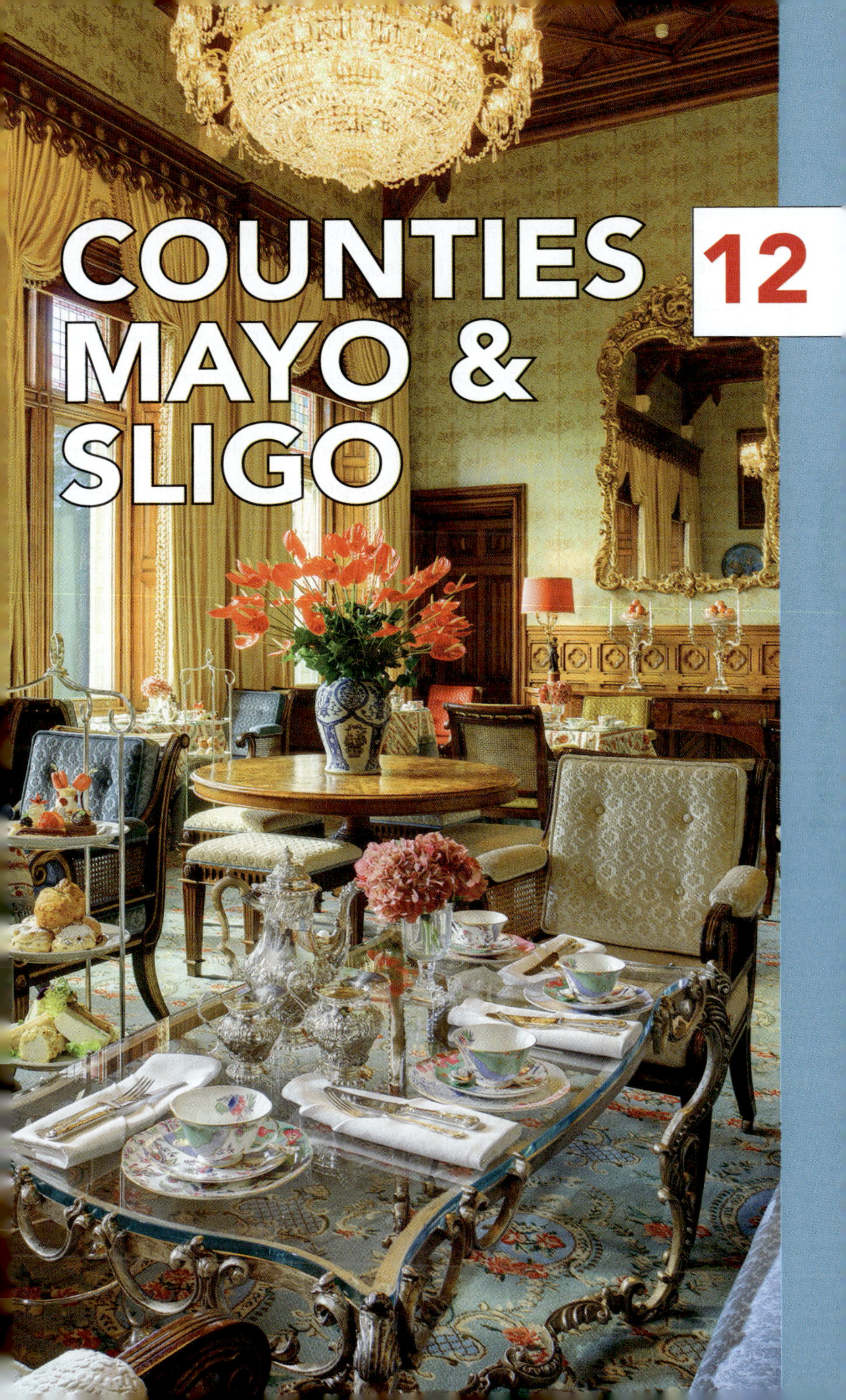

COUNTIES MAYO & SLIGO

12

The strikingly beautiful landscapes of northern Galway become even more rugged and mountainous as you segue into County Mayo. This is a land of dramatic scenery, with stark, craggy hills, ancient woodlands, boglands, and rocky cliffs plunging down into the opaque blue waters of the icy sea. Picture-postcard villages lie nestled among lush valleys and the kind of mountainous vistas that make your soul soar. Northeast of Mayo, County Sligo offers an altogether gentler sort of landscape, still very much associated with the great Irish poet William Butler Yeats, who drew much of his inspiration from its unique character. Though Sligo is dotted with fairy-tale castles and mysterious prehistoric sites, its biggest gift to the visitor is tranquility.

ESSENTIALS

Arriving

BY BUS **Bus Éireann** (buseireann.ie; ✆ **071-916-0066**) runs daily bus service to Sligo Town from Dublin, Galway, and other points including Derry in Northern Ireland. It provides daily service to major towns in Mayo. The bus station in Sligo is on Lord Edward Street.

BY CAR County Mayo can be reached by four major highways: N84 from the south; N59 from the south and north; and N5 and N60 from the east. Four other major roads lead to Sligo: N4/M4 from Dublin and the east, N17 from Galway and the south, N15 from Donegal to the north, and N16 from Northern Ireland.

BY PLANE **Ireland West Airport Knock (NOC)** in Charlestown, County Mayo (knockairport.com; ✆ **094/936-8100**), is becoming quite a popular hub for budget airlines from the U.K. and mainland Europe. **Ryanair** (ryanair.com; ✆ **0871/246-0000**) is the main airline operating from the airport. Year-round, at least a handful of scheduled flights travel per week to and from London, Edinburgh, Manchester, and Liverpool in the U.K.; Barcelona in Spain; and Cologne in Germany. Additional routes open up between April and October. As befits Knock's own status (p. 451), you can also catch occasional flights to other major pilgrimage sites in Europe, such as Lourdes, Cadiz, Fátima, and Medjugorje.

BY TRAIN Trains from Dublin and other major points arrive daily at **Westport** in Mayo, and **Sligo Town** in Sligo. The train station in Westport

PREVIOUS PAGE: **Connaught Room, Ashford Castle.**

is on Altamont Street, about a 10-minute walk from the town center; in Sligo it's on Lord Edward Street, next to the bus station.

COUNTY MAYO

For experienced Ireland travelers, Mayo is the place they escape to after visiting Galway—its rugged coastal scenery is similar, but it has less of the traffic and tourist overload from which Galway suffers in the summer. It's a delightfully unpredictable place, where the terrain changes at the turn of a steering wheel, from lush and green to stark, desert-like, boggy, and mountainous. This region was hit so hard by the Great Famine that, in certain ways, it has never quite recovered. Starvation and emigration emptied it then, and that emptiness is still palpable.

In 1951, the tiny village of **Cong** became the setting for the John Ford film *The Quiet Man,* starring John Wayne and Maureen O'Hara (see box on p. 444). Surprisingly, the county still vigorously celebrates this 70-year-old connection to cinematic stardust—the townsfolk of Cong even paid for a bronze statue of the film's stars in 2013. More recently, Mayo had another brush with movie fame when **Achill Island** (p. 448) stood in for the fictional Inisherin in the 2022 film *The Banshees of Inisherin.*

Among Mayo's other attractions are the mysterious 5,000-year-old settlement at **Céide Fields,** the religious shrine at **Knock,** and some of Europe's best fishing waters at **Lough Conn, Lough Mask,** and the **River Moy** (p. 457). It's such a storied angler's destination that **Ballina (*Béal an Átha*),** Mayo's largest town, calls itself the home of the Irish salmon.

Visitor Information

The main tourist information center for County Mayo is the **Westport Tourist Office,** Bridge Street, Westport (mayo.ie; ✆ **098/28459**). Other offices are on Pearse Street, **Ballina** (✆ **096/72800**), and in the Old Courthouse on Abbey Street in **Cong** (✆ **094/954-6542**).

Exploring County Mayo

Because it's a rural county with no major cities or many large towns, County Mayo feels a bit like a place without a center. Towns such as Castlebar, Claremorris, and Ballinrobe in the southern part of the county, and Ballina in the northern reaches, make good places to stop, refill the tank, and have lunch, but they offer little to make you linger. The county's attractions lie in the countryside, and in smaller communities like Foxford, Ballycastle, and Louisburgh.

County Mayo's loveliest town, **Westport (*Cathair na Mairt*) ♥♥**, nestled on the shore of Clew Bay, makes an excellent touring base. Once a major port, it was designed by the famed architect Richard Cassels (he of Leinster House [p. 113] and Powerscourt House [p. 160]) with a tree-lined mall, rows of Georgian buildings, and an octagonal central mall. From here, you can take a scenic drive west to **Achill Island** (p. 448),

WHEN THE GOLDEN AGE OF hollywood CAME TO MAYO

When director John Ford descended on the sweet village of **Cong,** County Mayo, to make his 1952 film *The Quiet Man,* starring John Wayne and Maureen O'Hara, the town's profile skyrocketed. Thousands of tourists were soon visiting, and Cong was transformed.

But what's surprising is that visitors still flock here on Quiet Man pilgrimages, and Cong continues to hang its hat on its association with a film that's nearly 75 years old. **The Quiet Man Museum,** Circular Road (quietmanmuseum.com; ✆ **094/954-6089**), is a charming thatched cottage that's an exact replica of John Wayne's house in the movie, right down to the furniture. (The actual cottage used in the film was long ago reduced to rubble by souvenir hunters.) From April to October, it's open daily from 10am until 4pm; admission is €5.50 adults, €5 seniors and students, €4 ages 12–18, €3 children 11 and under. The museum runs daily tours of the village at noon (Apr–Oct). Tours cost €18 adults, €17 seniors and students, €13 ages 12–18, and €5 children 11 and under.

Just around the corner on Abbey Street are the ruins of **Cong Abbey.** Founded in 623, it was rebuilt in the 12th century, then comprehensively destroyed by Henry VIII in the 1540s. The ruins are an open site that you can wander at leisure—but even here there's a Hollywood tie-in: **The Quiet Man Statue,** a full-size bronze of Maureen O'Hara being whisked off her feet by John Wayne, just outside the abbey.

Aside from *The Quiet Man,* Cong is also famous as the location of the 13th-century **Ashford Castle ♥♥♥**, one of Ireland's biggest medieval castles, now a super-exclusive hotel and resort (p. 452). A bit more budget-friendly is **The Lodge** (thelodgeac.com), a former estate keeper's house on the castle grounds, with its outstanding restaurant, **Wilde's ♥♥♥** (p. 457).

Cong is roughly halfway between Galway and Westport, on R344, R345, and R346.

A statue in Cong commemorates a scene from *The Quiet Man.*

walk in **Wild Nephin National Park** (p. 452), or catch a ferry to the bay's **Clare Island,** once the home of Mayo's legendary "Pirate Queen," Grace O'Malley (p. 447). Southeast of Westport, **Croagh Patrick,** a 750m (2,460-ft.) mountain, dominates the views of western Mayo for miles. St. Patrick is said to have spent the 40 days of Lent praying here in the year 441. To commemorate that, on the last Sunday of July, thousands of Irish

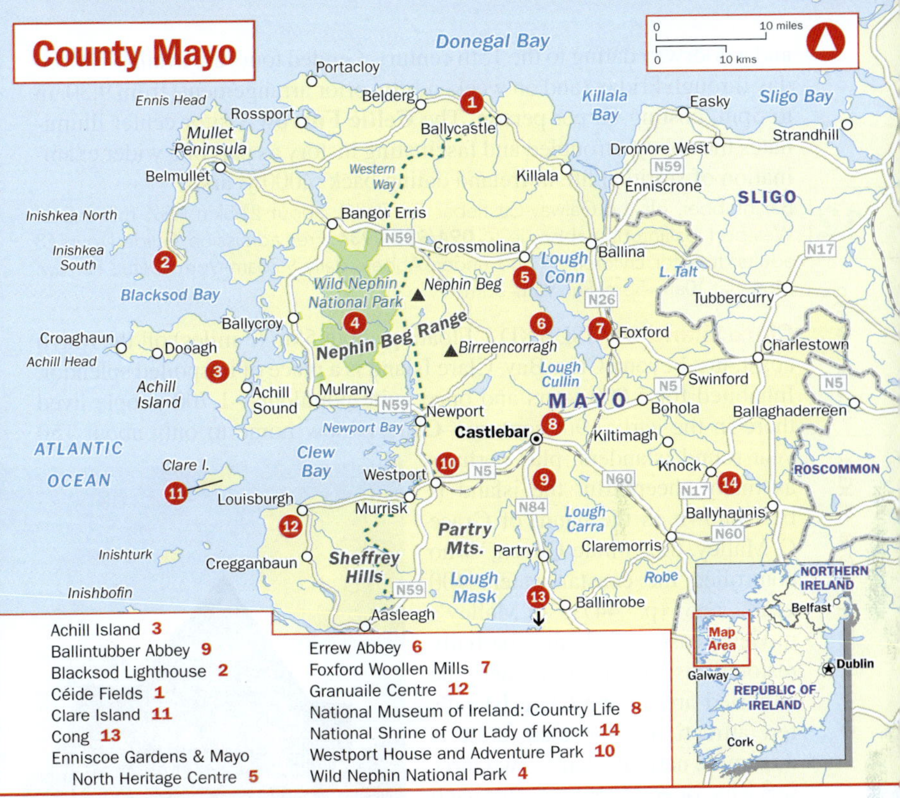

people make a pilgrimage to the site, which has become known as St. Patrick's Holy Mountain.

A short drive inland from Westport, in **Castlebar,** you can pick up the R310 road, which swings north past the clear, mountain-ringed waters of **Lough Cullin** and **Lough Conn** and eventually to **Ballina (*Béal an Átha*).** A dramatic coastal drive runs along the R314 from Ballina to Downpatrick Head, passing through the secluded harbor village of **Killala (*Cill Ala*)** and on to **Céide Fields** (p. 450). Farther along the coast is the windswept **Mullet Peninsula** (p. 449), with cliff walks, beaches, and island views.

IN & AROUND WESTPORT

Ballintubber Abbey ♥♥ CHURCH This abbey is a real survivor—one of only a few Irish churches in continuous use for almost 800 years. Founded in 1216 by Cathal O'Connor, king of Connaught, it has endured fires, numerous attacks, pestilences, and anti-Catholic pogroms. Although Oliver Cromwell's forces thoroughly dismantled the abbey—they even carried off its roof in 1653 in an effort to finally suppress it—clerics continued discreetly conducting religious rites. Today it's an impressively restored church, with 13th-century windows on the right side of the nave and a doorway dating to the 15th century. Guided tours are available Monday through Friday (and on weekends by prior arrangement) from 9:30am to 5pm, costing €8 per person. The **Celtic Furrow** visitor center illuminates the abbey's troubled and fascinating history as part of a wider examination of spiritual life in Ireland dating back 5,000 years.

Ballintubber, off the Galway-Castlebar Rd. (N84), about 21.5km (13½ miles) E of Westport. ballintubberabbey.ie. ✆ **094/903-0934.** Free admission. Guided tours €8 adults; free for children 15 and under. Abbey: daily 9:30am–9pm. Celtic Furrow: Mon–Sat 10am–5pm; Sun 9am–3pm.

Clare Island ♥♥ ISLAND Floating about 5km (3 miles) off the Mayo coast, just beyond Clew Bay, Clare Island is a place of unspoiled splendor. Inhabited for 5,000 years and once quite populous—1,700 people lived there in the early 19th century—Clare is now home to only about 150 year-round islanders, plus perhaps as many sheep. But the island is best known as the haunt of Grace O'Malley, the "Pirate Queen," who controlled the coastal waters 400 years ago (p. 447). O'Malley's modest castle and the partially restored Cistercian abbey where she is buried are among Clare Island's few attractions—the main draw is its remote natural beauty. Two ferry services operate out of Roonagh Harbour, 29km (18 miles) south of Westport: **O'Malley Ferries** (omalleyferries.com; ✆ **098/25045**) and **Clare Island Ferries** (clareislandferry.com; ✆ **098/23737** or 086/851-5003). The round-trip fare for the 15-minute journey is €18 adults, €11 children and students 5–18, and free for children 4 and under.

Clare Island. clareisland.info.

It's believed that the pirate queen Grace O'Malley (p. 447) was buried at this ruined abbey on Clare Island.

Granuaile Centre ♥ MUSEUM This small but rather charming museum is devoted to a particularly cool local hero: Grace O'Malley, also known as "the Pirate Queen" (p. 447). Today she is feted as a defender of the rights of the people of Mayo as much as for being a ruthless pirate—but the pirate stuff is more fun. The center, set in a former church building, is a little dated but offers a historical film, some engaging exhibits about O'Malley's life, and displays on the area's wider history, particularly during the Great Famine. A short drive from the Roonagh Harbour ferry to Clare Island (see above), it makes a worthwhile introduction to O'Malley's

local hero: GRACE O'MALLEY, THE PIRATE QUEEN

By all accounts, Grace O'Malley—aka the "Pirate Queen"—was a woman ahead of her time. Born in 1530 on **Clare Island** (p. 446), she grew up to be an adventurer, pirate, gambler, mercenary, traitor, chieftain, noblewoman, and general badass. And while she is remembered now with affection, at the time she was feared and despised in equal measure.

Even as a child, Grace was fiercely independent. When her mother refused to let her sail with her father, she cut off her hair and dressed in boys' clothing. Her father called her *"Grainne Mhaol,"* or "Bald Grace," later shortened to Granuaile (pronounced Graw-nya-*wayl*), a nickname she'd carry all her life.

At 16, Grace married Donal O'Flaherty, second in line to the O'Flaherty clan chieftain, who ruled all of Connacht. Her career as a pirate began a few years later when the city of Galway, one of the largest trading posts in northern Europe, refused to do business with the O'Flahertys. Grace used her fleet of fast galleys to waylay slower vessels on their way into Galway Harbour. She then offered safe passage for a fee in lieu of pillaging the ships.

She is most fondly remembered for refusing to trade her lands in return for an English title, a common practice of the day.

When the English captured her sons in 1593, she went to London to try to win their release. In an extraordinary turn of events, she actually secured a meeting with Queen Elizabeth I herself. History records that the two women got on quite well (although legend has it that Grace initially tried to smuggle a knife in with her, in case things went differently). A deal was struck: Elizabeth agreed to release Grace's sons and to return some captured lands if Grace would agree to renounce piracy. This she did and returned to Ireland triumphantly.

The truce did not last, however. Grace got her sons back, but not her property—so she took up piracy again and continued her legendary seafaring career until her death from natural causes in 1603.

life and times, but call ahead first—opening times can be a little unpredictable, especially in winter.

Church St., Louisburgh, 21km (13 miles) W of Westport on R334. ✆ **098/66341.** Admission €7.50 adults; €5 seniors and students; €4 children; €20 families. Tues–Fri 10:30am–2:30pm. Call ahead to check times, particularly in winter.

The National Museum of Ireland: Country Life ♥♥ MUSEUM

The countryside outpost of Ireland's multi-site national museum (the others are all in Dublin—see chapter 4), this one specializes in Irish life, trade, culture, and tradition since the mid–19th century. Absorbing exhibits deal with folklore; the natural environment and how local communities have relied on it for survival; political and social upheaval, particularly in the years preceding the Great Famine; traditional trades and crafts; and the changing life of the Irish people at home and at work. You could easily spend 3 hours wandering around here, especially if you include the grounds. The museum also has a thoughtful program of changing

A TRIP TO achill island

The rugged, bog-filled, sparsely populated coast of counties Mayo and Sligo makes for scenic drives to secluded outposts. Leading the list is **Achill Island,** a heather-filled slip of land with sandy beaches and spectacular views of waves crashing against rocky cliffs.

Once you've crossed the bridge from the mainland, follow a winding road across the island to the little village of **Keel,** a trip that requires patience but rewards you with lots of photo opportunities. About 5.7km (3½ miles) west of Keel, you'll find the secluded Blue Flag beach of **Keem Bay** (it was once a major fishing ground—basking shark were caught here commercially up until the 1950s—but no more). You can reach the bay along a small cliff-top road, which passes by cliff faces containing rich seams of glittering amethyst. You might recognize this area from the film *The Banshees of Inisherin*, which was filmed on the island.

At the foot of the slopes of **Mount Slievemore,** Achill's tallest mountain, are a hundred or so crumbling stone cottages, the remains of an **abandoned village.** Dating back to sometime around the 12th century, it was deserted during the Great Famine, although some cottages were in occasional use until the very early years of the 20th century, a traditional practice known as "booleying"—seasonal occupation by farming communities, which continued here long after it had died out in the rest of Ireland. Mount Slievemore is between Keel and Doogort, in the central northeastern part of Achill Island.

At Kildavnet, between Derreen and Cloughmore, in the southeastern corner of the island, you'll find **Granuaile's Tower,** an impressive 15th-century tower house once owned by Grace O'Malley, the "Pirate Queen" (see box on p. 447). There's not a great deal to see, but it's a stunning spot to admire. Nearby **Kildavnet Church** is thought by some archaeologists to date from the 8th century. From here, the Atlantic Drive north, overlooking the cliffs, is spectacular.

To get to the Achill Island bridge, take N59 heading northwest out of Westport, then join R319, signposted to Achill. The drive from Westport to the crossing is about 42km (26 miles) and should take around 40 minutes. Once you're on Achill Island, Keel is about another 14km (8⅔ miles) down the same road.

exhibitions. As at all the National Museum sites, entry is completely free. On the grounds opposite the museum is **Turlough Park House,** a moderately sized country house built for the wealthy Fitzgerald family in the 1860s. The two rooms on view have been kept much as they would have been in the house's Victorian heyday, complete with original furniture.

Signposted from N5, Turlough Park, about 8km (5 miles) E of Castlebar. museum.ie/Country-Life. ✆ **094/903-1755.** Free admission. Tues–Sat 10am–5pm; Sun–Mon 1–5pm.

Westport House and Adventure Park ♥♥ HISTORIC HOUSE/THEME PARK This is the sort of family-friendly attraction that requires a deep breath before listing everything there is to do here. It's all centered around an elegant late-18th-century residence—the home of Lord Altamont, the Marquess of Sligo and a descendant, it is said, of Pirate Queen Grace O'Malley (hence the bronze statue of her on the grounds). The work of Richard Cassels and James Wyatt, the house has a graceful staircase of ornate white Sicilian marble, unusual Art Nouveau glass and carvings, family heirlooms, and silver. The residence is undeniably grand, yet in summer most visitors come here without even setting foot in the building, heading instead for the recently revamped **Westport Adventure Park,** with its range of zip lines, giant swings, slides, rock climbing, a net park, and other high-adrenaline activities. There's also an interactive **Gaming Zone** in the farmyard area. The house turns into a festive Winter Wonderland in November/December. The estate grounds are open to walkers during daylight hours year-round.

The Westport Demense, Westport. westporthouse.ie. ✆ **098/27766. House and Gardens:** €14.50 adults; €11.50 seniors and students; €7 children. **Adventure Park:** €27–€37 per person, depending on activity, combo tickets available; €12 children 3 and under. **House:** May–Oct daily 10am–4pm (until 5pm Jul–Aug); Mar–Apr Wed–Sun 10am–4pm; Nov–Dec open for Winter Wonderland event only. **Grounds:** June–Aug 8am–11pm; Sept 8am–9pm; Oct–May 8am–7pm. **Adventure Park:** Sept–Dec and Feb–May Sat–Sun and bank holidays 11am–4pm; June–Aug daily 11am–8pm.

IN & AROUND BALLINA

Blacksod Lighthouse and the Mullet Peninsula ♥♥ LIGHTHOUSE Beyond the town of Belmullet at the northwest corner of Mayo, the windswept Mullet Peninsula, surrounded on three sides by the Atlantic, is an atmospheric place for walks and relaxed exploring. The best walks are along the cliff paths from Erris Head, Benwee Head, or Portacloy (p. 458), while there are beaches on both shores at Elly Bay. The peninsula is also home to an Irish-speaking community, with heritage sites like St. Deirbhile's Church in Aghleam (*An Eachléan*). At the foot of the peninsula, **Blacksod Lighthouse** tells the story of the role of the area's lighthouses and the people who lived in them before they were automated. Boat trips from the pier here travel to the uninhabited Inishkea Islands. Also worth a stop is the **Solas Visitor Centre,** with exhibits on the area's history and heritage.

Mist rising at Blacksod Lighthouse.

Blacksod. visitblacksodlighthouse.ie. ✆ **097/85-727. Blacksod Lighthouse tours:** €10 adults; €7 seniors and students; €5 children; €25 families. June–Sept daily 11am–5pm (opens 10am in Aug); Mar–May and Oct Sat–Sun 11am–5pm. Book in advance. **Solas, Aghleam:** visitsolas.ie. ✆ **097/65-035**. Admission €10 adults; € 7 seniors and students; €5 children. June–Sept daily 10am–6pm.

Exhibit at the Céide Fields Visitor Centre, where installations interpret the megalithic relics and Stone Age fields found on this remote cliff-top site.

Céide Fields ♥♥ ANCIENT SITE In a breathtaking setting above huge chalk cliffs that plunge hundreds of feet down into a deep blue sea, an ancient people once lived, worked, and buried their dead. But nobody knew this until the 1930s, when a local farmer noticed that the stones in his fields were piled in strange patterns. More than 40 years later, his archaeologist son discovered Stone Age fields, megalithic tombs, and the foundations of a village. Standing amid it now, you can see a pattern of farm fields as they were laid out 5,000 years ago (predating the Egyptian pyramids). Preserved for millennia beneath the bog, the site is both fascinating and inscrutable. To a casual observer, it's little more than piles of stones, but the visitor center makes it meaningful in a series of displays, films, and tours. It also contains a cafeteria, which comes as a relief since this hilly, rocky site is miles of winding roads from anywhere.

On R314, 8km (5 miles) W of Ballycastle. heritageireland.ie. ✆ **096/43325.** Admission €5 adults; €4 seniors; €3 students and children; €13 families. Mid-Mar to mid-Nov daily 10am–5pm (until 6pm June–Sept); last admission 45 min. before closing.

Enniscoe Gardens & Mayo North Heritage Centre ♥ GARDENS/GENEALOGY CENTER Part of the huge Enniscoe estate—where you can stay in the charming manor house (**Enniscoe House ♥♥**, p. 454)—these beautiful gardens comprise woods, parkland, and part of Lough Conn. One of the highlights is an 18th-century walled garden, restored to its layout from the estate's Victorian heyday. A little museum displays a somewhat random collection of historic farm equipment and household items from the early to mid–20th century. The on-site **Mayo North Heritage Centre** (northmayoheritagecentre.ie; free admission; Mon–Fri 9:30am–4pm year-round) is the ideal place to start if you're checking out your roots. It offers extensive records such as church registers (Catholic, Presbyterian, Methodist, and others); registers of births, marriages, and deaths; estate and probate records; property leases and rent rolls; school registers; emigrant rolls; and census records. Research fees, which give you access to expert genealogists, range from €45 for 1 hour up to €350 for 10 hours.

On Lough Conn, about 3.2km (2 miles) S of Crossmolina, off R315, Enniscoe, Castlehill, Ballina. enniscoe.com. ✆ **096/31809.** Free admission to Heritage Centre and gardens. Tours of house and gardens available. Apr–Oct Tues–Sat 10am–4pm, Sun noon–4pm.

Errew Abbey ♥ RELIGIOUS SITE This atmospheric ruined 13th-century Augustinian church sits on a tiny peninsula in Lough Conn. The cloister is well-preserved, as is the chancel with altar and *piscina,* a stone basin used for disposing of the water used during Mass. An oratory of massive stone walls in fields adjacent to the abbey stands on the site of a church founded in the 6th century. It's known locally by the marvelous tongue-twisting name *Templenagalliaghdoo,* which means "Church of the Black Nun."

Signposted about 3.2km (2 miles) S of Crossmolina on the Castlebar Rd., then 5km (3 miles) down a side road. No phone. Free admission (open site).

Foxford Woollen Mills Visitor Centre ♥♥ FACTORY TOUR Mother Agnes Morragh Bernard founded this popular Irish brand of knitwear and tweed in the late 19th century, hoping to build a new local industry to try to ameliorate the effects of the Great Famine. Not only did her scheme help to stave off poverty for the local workforce, but the brand became hugely successful in Ireland and beyond, producing rugs, clothing, and the like. You can tour the mills to hear the story on free half-hour guided tours (book in advance, Mon–Fri at 10:30 and 11:30am; note that the mill is not working on Fri tours). Also on-site is a jewelry workshop, a cafe, and a full store where you can buy everything from woolen scarves and clothing to homewares and gifts.

Providence Rd., Foxford. foxford.com. ✆ **094/925-6104.** Free admission. Mon–Sat 10am–5.30pm; Sun noon–5pm (cafe closes 4pm).

National Shrine of Our Lady of Knock and the Church of the Apparition ♥♥ SHRINE Ireland's version of Lourdes, Our Lady of Knock draws pilgrims, mostly Irish Catholic, in droves. It all stems from a day in August 1879 when two young local girls said they saw Joseph, Mary, and St. John standing in bright light in front of the southern tower of the parish church. Soon, 13 other witnesses claimed to have seen the same thing. Before long, miracles were occurring fast and furious, as sick

and lame visitors to the church pronounced themselves healed. In 1979, Pope John Paul II visited the shrine, bringing it to the world's attention. More than 10,000 pilgrims visit every year, and during Novena week in August (marking the anniversary of the miracle), the shrine holds special twice-daily ceremonies and other commemorative events. The grounds also hold a folk museum (with a few letters relating to the original testimonies) and a religious bookshop. There's not much to the town of Knock on the whole—it sits unspectacularly at the intersection of the N17 and R323 roads—but it's filled with increasingly large, modern religious structures, including a huge, circular basilica that seats 7,000 and contains artifacts or furnishings from every county in Ireland.
On the N17 Galway Rd., Knock. knockshrine.ie. ✆ **094/938-8100.** Free admission. Daily 8am–9pm, museum 10am–5pm.

Wild Nephin National Park ♥♥ NATIONAL PARK Home to some of the wildest scenery in Mayo—and indeed Ireland—with 15,000 hectares (37,000 acres) of vast boglands, rivers, mountains, and forests, this is probably the least-known of Ireland's seven national parks, which means it is rarely overrun with tourists. Start your visit at the visitor center at Ballycroy (on the N59 between Mulranny and Bangor Erris), which has views over to the Nephin Beg Mountain range and Achill Island and a fantastic exhibition about the area, its nature, and its history. It also has a cafe and a 2km (1.25-mile) looped walking trail. In the main park you'll find the main walking trails, such as the marked looped walking trails at Letterkeen, ranging from 6km (3.7 miles) to 12km (7.5 miles). This is around 40 minutes' drive from the visitor center, off the N59 just outside the village of Newport. It's worth making the drive, where the reward from hikes is views for miles in each direction. Parts of the park are being rewilded—keep an eye out for sheep, deer, and eagles. Because it has so little light pollution, Wild Nephin is also a designated **Dark Sky Park** (mayodarkskypark.ie). The 2km (1.25-mile) **Claggan Mountain Coastal Trail,** just south of the Ballycroy Visitor Centre, has a boardwalk over peat bog along a gorgeous coastal route.
Visitor center at Ballycroy Village. wildnephinnationalpark.ie. ✆ **098/49-888.** Free admission to park. Visitor center daily 10am–5pm.

Where to Stay in County Mayo

This region of Ireland is not the most abundant ground for topnotch lodgings. Even the major towns have only a smattering of decent B&Bs and small hotels. However, some gems are to be found in the deepest reaches of the countryside. It takes effort to get to these places, but the journey will be worth it.

Ashford Castle ♥♥♥ This extraordinary, fairy-tale-like castle has entertained plenty of famous guests over the years—Grace Kelly, Ronald Reagan, Brad Pitt, and Pierce Brosnan, to name just a few. Ashford Castle was built in the 13th century and still looks and feels every inch the palatial

The richly paneled Oak Hall of Ashford Castle, a medieval castle transformed into an exclusive luxury hotel.

abode, with suits of armor and old portraits lining the hallways, plus antiques and four-poster beds in some guest rooms. You can walk or cycle the stunning grounds—it overlooks Lough Corrib, with acres of forest and landscaped gardens. The drawing room is the place for an elegant afternoon tea, and the **George V** dining room is worth dressing up for at dinnertime, but you'll find a couple of less formal eateries on the grounds, too. On R346, on the eastern approach to Cong. ashfordcastle.com. ✆ **094/954-6003.** 83 units. €535–€1,375 double; €1,045–€2,655 state room; €2,145–€7,500 suite. Breakfast included. Free parking. **Amenities:** 3 restaurants; 2 bars; cigar terrace; gym; massage treatments; swimming pool; 9-hole golf course; fishing; clay pigeon shooting; Wi-Fi (free).

The Bervie ♥♥♥ Overlooking the Atlantic Ocean on **Achill Island** (p. 448), the Bervie is an inspiring place to stay. Husband-and-wife hosts John and Elizabeth Barrett spent years lovingly restoring the sturdy building. Elizabeth actually grew up in this house; it's been a B&B since the 1930s, although today it's a far more sophisticated place than she remembers from her childhood. Guest rooms are large and spacious, with well-chosen furniture, much of it made locally. Most rooms directly overlook the sea—and what a view! You can see islands dotted around the bay from certain rooms, while others have a dramatic view of cliffs. Light pours in from huge windows, and the whispering of the waves soothes you to sleep. The garden has direct access to the beach. Elizabeth's home-cooked breakfasts are to die for, and evening menus might offer black sole or Clare Island salmon. Worth staying in for.

The Strand, Keel, Achill Island. bervieachill.com. ✆ **098/43114.** 14 units. €185–€195 double. 2-night minimum stay some dates. Breakfast included. Free parking. 3-course dinner menu €55. **Amenities:** Restaurant; garden; Wi-Fi (free). Closed Nov to mid-Apr.

Enniscoe House ♥♥ Flanked by Mount Nephin on one side and the shimmering waters of Lough Conn on the other, Enniscoe is a stunningly restored 18th-century mansion. Little has been altered from the original structure, so the place is overflowing with period detail (one room even has original silk wallpaper). Bedrooms are spacious, with big windows and half-tester beds. Make sure you book in for evening dinner in the dining room (€50). There are sitting rooms to relax in, and you could spend a day exploring the lovely grounds (see **Enniscoe Gardens & Mayo North Heritage Centre,** p. 450). Book one of the self-catering cottages if you want more privacy.

Castlehill, Ballina. enniscoe.com. ✆ **096/31112.** 6 units. €200–€280 double. Breakfast included. Free parking. **Amenities:** Guest lounge; Wi-Fi (free) in public areas. Closed Nov–Mar.

The Ice House ♥♥ At the edge of Ballina, this boutique hotel offers a tantalizing mixture of old and new: The main building is over a hundred years old and was once used for storing salmon, and the modern extensions are bright and warm, with panoramic views of the Moy River. Rooms are good-size and quiet, with gorgeous views and comfy beds. You can choose a traditional room in the old building or a modern room, but all come with eiderdown bedcovers and Voya toiletries. The in-house spa is luxury personified (outdoor hot tubs overlook the river), and the restaurant is a destination eatery that brings people from miles around for European/Irish cuisine served in an airy room overlooking the river.

Quay Rd., Ballina. icehousehotel.ie. ✆ **096/23500.** 32 units. €250–€450 double. Breakfast included. Free parking. Access to thermal suite and outdoor hot tubs €30 for hotel residents. **Amenities:** Restaurant; bar; spa; hot tubs; Wi-Fi (free).

Knockranny House ♥♥ This modern hotel less than 15 minutes by foot from the town of Westport is a great place to base yourself while exploring the region. Decor is minimal, but guest rooms are sizable, with firm beds and up-to-date bathrooms. The more expensive rooms and suites are more elegant than the cheaper rooms, but both are perfectly serviceable. Relax with a cup of tea or a pint of beer in one of the pleasant lounges. The **Fern Grill** restaurant is highly rated for its local Irish produce and offers gorgeous views over the verdant countryside. The pool and spa are lovely, and the thermal suite will work all the knots out of your aching muscles. Check website for offers.

Castlebar Rd., Westport. knockrannyhousehotel.ie. ✆ **098/28600.** 97 units. €125–€350 double; €155–€420 suite. Free parking. **Amenities:** Restaurant; pool; spa; Wi-Fi (free).

Westport Coast Hotel ♥♥ This pleasant, modern hotel on the Quay in Westport overlooks the smooth, dreamy waters of Clew Bay and the mountains beyond. It's worth paying a little extra for a room with a view or a spacious suite. The **Veda spa** has plenty of invigorating and affordable treatments. The top-floor restaurant, which looks out over the bay, serves tasty, crowd-pleasing fare (leg of lamb, roast chicken, steaks—you get the picture).

The Quay, Westport. westportcoasthotel.ie. ✆ **098/29000.** 85 units. €80–€388 double; €170–€428 suite. Breakfast included. Dinner, bed-and-breakfast deals available. Free parking. **Amenities:** Restaurant; bar; pool; spa; Wi-Fi (free).

Where to Eat in County Mayo

While the west coast is not one of Ireland's main foodie regions, innovative chefs are using the Wild Atlantic Way's freshest seafood and produce to create topnotch dishes. In addition to the restaurants listed below, **This Must Be The Place** in Westport (High St.) serves gorgeous sourdough toasties, vegan curries, and sweet potato cakes, while **Christy's Harvest** (Shop St.) is a tiny, charming cafe for tea and cake. At **Mocha Beans** in Ballina (Pearse St.; mochabeans.com), you can get salads, wraps, soups, and good coffee. In Castlebar, **Café Rua** (New Antrim St.; caferua.com) is an award-winning deli that specializes in breakfast with locally sourced eggs and meats.

This Must Be The Place coffee shop and cafe.

An Port Mór ♥♥ SEAFOOD/MODERN IRISH At this multi-award-winning seafood restaurant in Westport, local catches dominate the menu—from Connemara smoked salmon to grilled Clew Bay scallops. The seafood is excellent, but it's not all that's on the menu; expect juicy steaks served with something fresh and tasty like apple treacle, as well as local chicken and lamb. There are two three-course set menus, everything is impeccably presented, and the atmosphere in the cheerful dining room is relaxed. Service is excellent, too.

1 Brewery Place, Westport. anportmor.com. ✆ **098/26730.** Entrees €22–€38. 3-course fixed-price menu €39 or €68. Tues–Sat 5–9pm.

The Beehive ♥♥ CAFE There aren't that many places to eat on Achill Island, and this cafe is one of the best. (Technically, this is what they call a "Craft Coffee Shop," since it sells lovely knickknacks and homewares, too.) Stop and refuel on excellent sandwiches and cakes, or a bowl of homemade soup—the chowder is particularly good. The craft store isn't bad, either. The Beehive overlooks the beach at Keel, and you can sit outside with your food on a warm day.

Keel, Achill Island. ✆ **086/854-2009.** Items €5–€11. Daily 11am–4pm. Closed Dec–Jan.

The Poacher ♥♥♥ MODERN IRISH Fish from the Atlantic, meat and poultry from local farms, foraged finds, and daily specials: The seasonal menu here features the best of local produce from land and sea. But it is the tiny, delicate surprises in each dish, like the forest berries infused with sweet port served over lamb, a flat-leaf-parsley risotto with beef, or the popcorn-fried globe artichoke with roast chicken, that take the food here to the next level. It's all set in a cozy dining space above a bakery and deli, and the wine list is reasonably priced to boot.

First Floor, 4 Market Sq., Ballina. facebook.com/p/Poacher-Restaurant-100053947103765. ✆ **096/77982.** Entrees €24–€36. Wed–Fri 5–9pm; Sat 4–9:30pm; Sun 1–8pm.

Savoir Fare ♥♥♥ IRISH/FRENCH Take the best of Irish cheese and charcuterie, and mix it with French style and a little wine, and you have Savoir Fare (a play on the French phrase *savoir faire,* which means "knowing the right thing to do"). Specialties at this charming bistro and wine bar include pork mushroom and hazelnut terrine; port-infused Young Buck blue cheese, and a weekly pâté *en croute* (made with pastry), such as duck and fig. The selections of Irish cheeses are fantastic; to share, go for the board with four cheeses, four cured meats, pickle chutney, roast nuts, and sourdough (from €55 for four people).

Bridge St., Westport. facebook.com/SavoirFareWestport. ✆ **098/60095.** Sharing plates €6–€42. Tues–Thurs noon–5pm; Fri noon–6pm; Sat 11am–5pm.

take the GREENWAY

The dedicated walking and cycle trail the **Great Western Greenway** traverses a 44km (26-mile) route between Westport and Achill Island, taking in some stunning scenery, particularly around Clew Bay. The trail, which completely avoids public roads, roughly follows the line of an old railway that closed in the 1930s. It naturally divides into three stages: Westport to Newport, Newport to Mulranny, and Mulranny to Achill—you can either do the route in stages or all in one go (***Tip:*** The last two stages are the most scenic if you don't plan to do it all). Bike-hire companies will shuttle your luggage or deliver you back to your car. Hills are gentle, but if you need a little help, e-bikes are available to rent. For maps and further details, see **greenway.ie**.

Wilde's at the Lodge ♥♥♥ MODERN IRISH If, like the other 99% of us, you can't quite swing a night at **Ashford Castle ♥♥♥** (p. 452), then you might find this lodge on the castle grounds a viable alternative for a slice of upper-crust Irish glamour. Wilde's is overseen by Jonathan Keane, an up-and-coming star of the Irish culinary world. A lot of his ingredients come from the castle's own garden, with menus deeply rooted in the flavors of the season. Vegans are catered to with a full separate menu. The wine list is curated to be paired with the seasonal menus, with plenty of choices available by the glass. The somewhat more straightforward children's menu should please the junior palate (entrees €8). The dining room has a fantastic view of Lough Corrib, and you can also stay overnight (double rooms €221–€640).

On the grounds of Ashford Castle, Cong. thelodgeac.com. ✆ **094/954-5400.** Entrees €27–€65. 3-course fixed-price Sun lunch €55. Mon–Sat 6–9:30pm; Sun 1–3:30pm and 6–9:30pm.

Sports & Outdoor Pursuits in County Mayo

CYCLING Get up close and personal with the Wild Atlantic Way on two wheels with the **Clew Bay Bike Trail** (clewbaybiketrail.ie), which takes in a loop around Clew Bay and includes Clare Island (by ferry) and Achill Island. The total distance is 105km (65 miles), but you can do as much or as little as you like—an overnight stay on Clare Island (p. 446) is a nice way to break up the journey. Keep in mind that some of the trail is on main roads (with traffic), but it also links up with the off-road **Great Western Greenway** (p. 456). There are bike-hire companies in Westport, Newport, Mulranny, and Achill; rentals start from €25 per day or €50 for an e-bike.

FISHING The waters of the River Moy and loughs Carrowmore, Conn, and Cullin are renowned fishing destinations, particularly for salmon and trout. To arrange a day's fishing, contact **Cloonamoyne Fishery,** Castlehill, near Crossmolina, Ballina (✆ **096/31928**). The fishery rents fully equipped boats and tackle, teaches fly-casting, and provides local transport to and from fishing: for brown trout on loughs Conn, Cullin, and Talt; and for salmon and sea trout on the rivers Moy and Deel. Daily rates are around €40 for a rowboat, €80 for a boat with engine, and €130 for a boat with engine and *ghillie* (guide).

Obtain a permit and state fishing license at the **Mayo Angling Advice Centre,** at the Tiernan Bros. fishing tackle shop, Upper Main Street, Foxford (themoy.com; ✆ **094/925-6731**). It also offers a range of services, including boat hire and *ghillies.*

For fishing tackle, try **Kingfisher Bates,** Pier Road, Enniscrone, County Sligo (✆ **096/36733**), or the **Ballina Angling Centre,** Unit 55, Ridge Pool Road, Ballina (✆ **096/21850**). On Achill Island, get fishing tackle at **Supervalu Supermarket,** Achill Sound (✆ **098/45211**). Also a good place to stock up on supplies, it's the smallish white-and-red building on the right, immediately after the bridge crossing from the mainland.

walk this way: PORTACLOY

The region to the east of the Mullet Peninsula (p. 449) has a spectacular array of sheer sea cliffs and rugged, craggy islands. The small, secluded beach at **Portacloy,** 14km (8⅔ miles) north of Glenamoy on the R314, is a good starting point for a dramatic walk. On a sunny day, its aquamarine waters and fine-grained white sand recall the Mediterranean more than the North Atlantic.

From the concrete quay at the beach's western edge, head north up the steep green slopes of the nearest hill. The sea views from here are breathtaking. Don't be too distracted by the fantastic vista or adorable little sheep—the boggy slopes on which you are walking end precipitously at an unmarked cliff edge. The walk is therefore ***not*** recommended for children and should not be undertaken in bad weather. Resist the urge to get a better view of the mysterious sea caves, or to reach the outermost edges of the coast's promontories. Instead, using the farmer's fence as a guide, head west toward the striking profile of **Benwee Head,** about 2.4km (1½ miles) away. This will give you gorgeous views of blue sea and rocky countryside. Return the same way to finish with a swim in the chilly, tranquil waters of Portacloy.

HORSEBACK RIDING One of the best riding centers in the west is **Drummindoo Stud & Equestrian Centre,** Knockranny, Westport (drummindoo.com; ✆ **087/271-3974**).

WINDSURFING & OTHER WATERSPORTS With constant winds off the Atlantic Ocean, Achill Island is ideal for breeze-dependent sports like windsurfing, surfing, and kitesurfing. The **Achill Outdoor Education Centre** on R319, between Cashel and Bunacurry (achilloutdoor.com; ✆ **098/47253**), can outfit you for windsurfing and surfing as well as other water activities like kayaking and sailing. Adrenalin junkies can take kitesurfing lessons and set up wing-boarding or gentler stand-up paddleboarding sessions on Keel Lake, Achill Island, with **Pure Magic** (puremagic.ie; ✆ **098/43859**).

COUNTY SLIGO

Inland, bucolic, rural County Sligo is blessed with an extraordinary concentration of ancient burial grounds and pre-Christian sites, most of them within easy reach of the county capital, **Sligo Town.** Remnants of a distant past feel like they're everywhere here, whether or not you can visit them. Driving down the country lanes on your way to the Stone Age cemeteries at **Carrowmore** and **Carrowkeel,** you can't help spotting a standing stone or ***dolmen*** (ancient stone table) in some farmer's pasture or another, with sheep or ponies grazing casually around it. The countryside has been labeled "Yeats Country" in honor of the great Irish poet W. B. Yeats, who was born in Dublin but spent so much time in County Sligo that it became a part of him, and he a part of it—literally, as he is buried here.

County Sligo
Carrowkeel Passage Tomb Cemetery 8
Carrowmore Megalithic Cemetery 4
Drumcliffe Church & Yeats's Grave 2
Eagles Flying 7
Inishmurray 1
Knocknarea 3
Lough Gill Drive 5
Parke's Castle 6
NORTHERN IRELAND
Map Area
Belfast
Galway
Dublin
REPUBLIC OF IRELAND
Cork
Donegal Bay
Inver Bay
Killybegs
Ballintra
DONEGAL
Ballyshannon
Tullaghan
Bundoran
Lower Lough Erne
Lough Melvin
Inishmurray
Cliffoney
Dartry Mts.
Benbulben
Glencar L.
Enniskillen
NORTHERN IRELAND
Drumcliffe
Rosses Point
Sligo Bay
Manorhamilton
L. Macnean
Belcoo
Upper Lough Erne
Easky
Ballycastle
Strandhill
Sligo
Killala Bay
Dromore West
Lough Gill
Dromahair
Killala
Enniscrone
Knockalongy
Ballysadare
Collooney
Glengavlen
Slieve Gamph (Ox Mts.)
Drumkeeran
LEITRIM
CAVAN
SLIGO
Riverstown
Crossmolina
Ballina
Lough Allen
Ballyconnell
L. Talt
Ballymote
Lough Arrow
Iron Mts.
MAYO
Castlebaldwin
Ballyfarnon
Tubbercurry
Drumshanbo
Ballinamore
Lough Key
Lough Oughter
Lough Conn
Ballinafad
Curlew Mts.
Foxford
Birreencorragh
Carrick-on-Shannon
Charlestown
Lough Gara
Boyle
Lough Cullin
Swinford
Drumsna
Arva
Mohill
Brosna
Bohola
Ballaghaderreen
ROSCOMMON
Lough Boderg
LONGFORD
N15
A47
A46
N16
A4
A32
N4
N59
A509
N87
N17
N26
N5
N61
0 10 miles
0 10 kms

Sligo is also a coastal county along the Wild Atlantic Way with long, golden beaches—you may have one all to yourself on a walk or share the sand with surfers. The village of Strandhill is a popular surf spot; you can also watch pro surfers go for big-wave action on windy days farther north at Mullaghmore.

Visitor Information

The **Sligo Tourist Office** is on the ground floor of the Old Bank Building, O'Connell Street, Sligo Town (sligotourism.ie; ✆ **071/916-1201**). It's open Monday to Saturday from 9am until 5pm (closed Sun).

Exploring Sligo Town

It goes to show just how rural this part of Ireland is that a small port and farming town with a population of just 20,000 is the largest urban center in the northwest—but welcome to Sligo Town! Bisected by the River Garavogue and surrounded on three sides by mountains (the most famous are Ben Bulben to the north and Knocknarea to the south), Sligo is a gray and solid place, with a mix of historic and less interesting modern architecture. Though few would name Sligo their favorite of Ireland's major towns, it has undergone something of a renaissance in recent years. From a visitor's perspective, the focus of this has been Sligo's "Left Bank," where cafes and restaurants spill onto the waterfront promenade whenever weather permits, while the new Queen Maeve Square is a hub for festivals and events. Most of its commercial district is on the river's south bank. **O'Connell Street** is the main north-south artery, while the main east-west thoroughfare is **Stephen Street,** which becomes Wine Street and then Lord Edward Street. Three bridges span the river; the **Douglas Hyde Bridge,** named for Ireland's first president, is the main link between the two sides.

The Model ♥♥ MUSEUM/CULTURAL CENTER One of Ireland's most renowned contemporary art museums, the Model houses an impressive collection of paintings and other visual art. It includes probably the best collection of works by Jack B. Yeats (1871–1957) outside the National Gallery in Dublin (p. 99). Brother of William, Jack was one of the foremost Irish painters of the 20th century, painting landscapes and figures in a bold expressionist style. Other luminaries of the Irish art world represented here include Louis le Brocquy (1916–2012), an extraordinary figurative painter; and the portraitist Estella Solomons (1882–1968). The Model is also a venue for live music and film screenings. Check the website for listings.

The Mall, Sligo Town. themodel.ie. ✆ **071/914-1405.** Free admission to exhibitions (suggested donation €5); event tickets vary from free to around €25. Tues–Sat 11am–5pm.

Sligo Abbey ♥ RELIGIOUS SITE/RUIN Founded as a Dominican house in 1252 by Maurice Fitzgerald, Earl of Kildare, Sligo Abbey was the center of early Sligo Town. It thrived for centuries and flourished in

medieval times when it was the burial place of the chiefs and earls of Sligo. But, as with other affluent religious settlements, the abbey was under constant attack, and it was finally destroyed in 1641. Much restoration work has been done in recent years; the fine cloisters contain outstanding examples of stone carving, and the 15th-century altar is one of the few intact medieval altars in Ireland.

Abbey St., Sligo Town. heritageireland.ie. ✆ **071/914-6406.** Admission €5 adults; €4 seniors; €3 students and children; €13 families. Mid-Mar to Oct daily 10am–6pm; last admission 45 min. before closing.

Sligo County Museum ♥♥ MUSEUM This museum in the center of Sligo Town presents a good overview of the county's history from ancient times to the present day. The most interesting sections cover the region's extraordinary prehistoric heritage, including a couple of ancient artifacts. Other standout sections are devoted to two of Sligo's most famous residents: the poet W. B. Yeats (see below), whose Sligo childhood permeates his poetry, and Constance Markievicz (see box on p. 465), an aristocrat who grew up in Sligo and went on to become a prominent Irish revolutionary.

Stephen St., Sligo Town. sligolibrary.ie/museum. ✆ **071/911-1679.** Free admission. May–Sept Tues–Sat 9:30am–12:45pm and 2–4:45pm; Oct–Apr Tues–Sat 9:30am–12:45pm.

Yeats Society and Hyde Bridge Gallery ♥♥ MUSEUM Located in a distinctive red-and-white town house building beside the Douglas Hyde Bridge, this engaging little museum, art gallery, and heritage center acts as a kind of focal point for the W. B. Yeats–related attractions in County Sligo. Exhibits focus on the life and work of the great poet, including some recently rediscovered color film footage of his funeral. The center is also home to the **Hyde Bridge Gallery,** which showcases work by contemporary Irish artists. Stop in for coffee and scones at **Penny Café.** For more on Yeats, see "A Poetic Soul," below.

Douglas Hyde Bridge, Sligo Town. yeatssociety.com. ✆ **071/914-2693.** Admission to Yeats exhibit €6; free for children 11 and under; €18 families. Free admission to gallery. Yeats exhibit Thurs–Sat 11am–3pm; gallery Tues–Sat 10am–3pm.

Farther Afield in County Sligo

The area around Sligo Town is known for its ancient burial grounds and pagan sites, some dating from the Stone Age. These include the vast

a poetic soul: W. B. YEATS

One of Ireland's greatest and most beloved writers, **William Butler Yeats** (1865–1939) had Sligo in his soul.

The first of Ireland's four Nobel laureates, Yeats (pronounced "Yates") was a poet, playwright, and politician. He was at the forefront of the Celtic Revival, which celebrated and championed native Irish culture and heritage. Drawing heavily upon the traditional folklore of Ireland, his work was steeped in myth and imagination.

Yeats grew up amid Sligo's verdant hills and dales, which figure so prominently in his poetry that the area has come to be known as "Yeats Country." You can cruise Lough Gill while listening to a live recital of Yeats's poetry, follow Yeats trails, buy a hundred items of Yeats memorabilia, and visit dozens of his purported haunts—some reputedly still spooked by his ghost, though others have only tenuous connections with the man.

Yeats died in Menton, on the French Riviera, in 1939. Knowing he was ill, he stated, "If I die here, bury me up there on the mountain, and then after a year or so, dig me up and bring me privately to Sligo." True to his wishes, in 1948 his body was moved to Sligo and reinterred at **Drumcliffe Church** (p. 464).

Views of Carrowkeel Passage Tomb Cemetery from surrounding hills.

Neolithic cemetery **Carrowmore,** the atmospheric hilltop cairn grave of **Knocknarea,** and the haunting Neolithic mountaintop cemetery of **Carrowkeel.** Some lesser sites are also open to the public, but most are not. The Irish are passionate about property rights (and fields often have livestock), so don't go clambering over a fence for a better photo without getting permission first.

At the foot of Knocknarea is the delightful resort area of **Strandhill,** 8km (5 miles) from Sligo Town. Stretching into Sligo Bay, Strandhill has a sand dune beach that's popular for surfing (it's not possible to swim because of the strong currents) and a small island nearby called Coney Island, usually credited as the namesake of New York's amusement park. Across the bay is **Rosses Point,** popular for golf and sailing.

Carrowkeel Passage Tomb Cemetery ♥♥ ANCIENT SITE Atop a hill overlooking Lough Arrow, this ancient passage-tomb cemetery is impressive, isolated, and frequently empty. Its 14 cairns, dolmens, and stone circles date from the Stone Age (ca. 5000 B.C.), and it's easy to feel a mystical connection to that history, standing among the cold, ageless rocks. The tombs face **Carrowmore** ♥♥♥ (see below) in the far distance below and are aligned with the summer solstice. The walk uphill from the parking lot takes about 20 minutes, but the exercise is worth the effort. This is a simple site—no visitor center, no tea shop, no admission fee—nothing but ancient mystery.
Signposted on N4 btw. Sligo Town and Boyle. No phone. Free admission (open site).

Carrowmore Megalithic Cemetery ♥♥♥ ANCIENT SITE This is one of the great sacred landscapes of the ancient world. At the center of the Coolera Peninsula sits a massive passage grave that once had a Stonehenge-like stone circle of its own. Around that were as many as 200 additional stone circles and passage graves arranged in an intricate and mysterious design. Over the years, some of the stones have been moved; more than 60 circles and passage graves still exist, although the site spreads out so far that many of them lie in adjacent farmland. Look for your first dolmen in a paddock next to the road about a mile before you reach the site. The dolmens were the actual graves, once covered in stones and earth. Some of these sites are open to visitors, and you can get a map to them from the visitor center, which has good exhibits and guided tours (Not all are open, however; so be careful not to trespass on private land.) On the main site, the oldest tomb is thought to date from around 3700 B.C.—making it one of the oldest pieces of freestanding stone architecture in the world. From Carrowmore, you can see the hilltop cairn grave of **Knocknarea ♥** (p. 466), which is about 4km (2½ miles) away. Follow signs from Woodville Road heading west out of Sligo Town, or from R292 at Ransboro.

Carrowmore. heritageireland.ie. ✆ **071/916-1534.** Admission €5 adults; €4 seniors; €3 students and children; €13 families. Mid-Mar to Oct daily 10am–6pm; last admission 1 hr. before closing.

Drumcliffe Church ♥♥ CHURCH/GRAVESITE An essential stop for Yeats fans, this square-towered village church, where Yeats's great-grandfather was once rector, was the poet's chosen burial site. (See "A Poetic Soul," p. 462.) His grave is marked with a dark, modest stone just left of the church, alongside his young wife, Georgie Hyde-Lee (when they married in 1917, he was 52 and she was 23). His epitaph, "CAST A COLD EYE ON LIFE, ON DEATH. . . . " comes from his poem "Under Ben Bulben." While you're here, check out the churchyard's 11th-century high cross—its faded eastern side shows Christ, Daniel in the lions' den, Adam and Eve, and Cain murdering Abel. The site also has a little visitor center, craft shop, and the **Pink Clover** cafe, which serves light lunches.

Drumcliffe. 10km (6½ miles) N of Sligo Town, on the N15 road. discoverdrumcliffe.com. ✆ **071/914-3815.** Free admission.

Eagles Flying ♥♥ AVIARY Some of the biggest birds of prey in the world are displayed at this aviary and educational center near Ballymote. Eagles, vultures, owls, and falcons take part in an hour-long flying show daily at 11am and 3pm. Most of the awe-inspiring birds that live at the center can be handled by visitors. The center also has a "touch zoo" with lambs, goats, donkeys, and rabbits. It has two 2-hour programs daily, including a guided tour, bird show, and visit to the touch zoo.

Ballymote. eaglesflying.com. ✆ **085/269-0717.** Admission €20 adults; €17 students; €11 children 3–16; free for children 2 and under; €55 families. Apr to early Nov daily, programs 10:30am–12:30pm and 2:30–4:30pm. Bird shows 11am and 3pm.

local hero: CONSTANCE MARKIEVICZ

Aristocrat, suffragette, revolutionary, politician, and all-round badass, Constance Markievicz (1868–1927) was one of the most influential Irish women of the 20th century and a key figure in the country's struggle for independence from Britain.

Born in London to Anglo-Irish gentry, at an early age Constance became aware of the realities of life for the poor in Ireland. Her father, Sir Henry Gore-Booth, owned Lissadell House, a great estate in County Sligo. Unlike many landowners of the time, he was widely loved by his tenants; during an outbreak of famine when Constance was eleven, he provided them with lifesaving food relief.

In 1900 Constance married a Polish count, Casimir Markievicz (1874–1932), and the two settled in Dublin. Actively involved in the fight for women's suffrage, she soon began to move in revolutionary circles, too. In 1914 she joined the Irish Citizens Army and became known for her leading role in gun-running missions, alongside Douglas Hyde (1860–1949), who'd later become the first president of Ireland.

During the Easter Rising of 1916 she manned barricades in St. Stephen's Green, Dublin, engaging in gunfights with British soldiers. After the Rising was put down, Markievicz was among the many revolutionaries sentenced to death. When the court commuted her sentence to life in prison because she was a woman, she shot back from the dock, "I wish you had the decency to shoot me."

In the end Markievicz served only a year in prison, including solitary confinement at **Kilmainham Gaol** ♥♥♥ (p. 98), although she'd later be jailed again for sedition. While serving a sentence in 1918, she learned she'd become the first woman elected to the British Parliament. She refused to take her seat and was later elected to the Irish Dáil. Following the War of Independence, Markievicz achieved another political first when she was appointed Minister for Labor in the new Irish government—the first woman in Europe to serve at cabinet level.

Inishmurray ♥♥ ISLAND/RUINS Northwest of Sligo Bay, this tiny, uninhabited island shelters an ancient past. The haunting ruins of St. Molaise, a 6th-century monastic settlement that was destroyed by the Vikings in 807, stands within its circular walls. You can still see the remains of several churches, beehive cells, altars, and an assemblage of "cursing stones" once used to bring ruin on those who presumably deserved it. In the 19th and early 20th centuries, however, Inishmurray harbored a different identity: a thriving illicit trade in the distilling of moonshine whiskey. The last permanent residents left the island in 1948; their ruined houses can still be seen, battered by the elements. Boat trips to the island are operated by **Inishmurray Island Trips** (inishmurray islandtrips.com; ✆ **087/254-0190**), which also runs charters, and **Ewing's Sea Angling and Boat Charters** (sligoboatcharters.com; ✆ **086/891-3618**). ***Note:*** At the time of writing, the island was closed to visitors, so check in advance.

Inishmurray. NW of Sligo Bay, 6km (3¾ miles) offshore. Ferries leave from Mullaghmore or Killybegs.

Knocknarea ♥♥ ANCIENT SITE From the low vantage point of **Carrowmore ♥♥♥** (p. 464), if you study the mountain ranges that ring the surrounding valley, you'll notice a stone cairn in the center of each. One of these is the unexcavated **Knocknarea.** Local legend has it that this is the grave of the warrior Queen Maeve or Medb—the legendary queen of Connacht, who is said to have led armies into Ulster on the Cattle Raid of Cooley. If you have the time to make the relatively gentle 30-minute climb to the top, the views are extraordinary.

Knocknarea, about 6.4km (4 miles) W of Sligo Town. gostrandhill.com/explore/places-of-interest/knocknarea. No phone. Free admission (open site). Signposted from small farm road btw. Cullenduff and Knocknarea, and from R292 heading S from Strandhill. Follow signs for MESCAN MEADHBHA CHAMBERED CAIRN.

Parke's Castle ♥♥ CASTLE If you happen to be on the north side of the Lough Gill Drive (p. 467), just over the County Leitrim border, you'll see Parke's Castle standing out as a lone outpost amid the natural tableau of lake views and woodland scenery. Named after an English family that gained possession of it during the 1620 plantation of Leitrim (when land was confiscated from the Irish and given to favored English families), this castle was originally the stronghold of the O'Rourke clan, rulers of the Kingdom of Bréifne. Beautifully restored using Irish oak and traditional craftsmanship, it exemplifies the 17th-century fortified manor house. In the visitor center, informative exhibits and a splendid audiovisual show illustrate the history of the castle and the surrounding area.

On R286, 11.2km (7 miles) E of Sligo Town, Co. Leitrim. heritageireland.ie. ✆ **086/071-6968.** Admission €5 adults; €4 seniors; €3 students and children; €13 families. Mid-Mar to Nov daily 10am–6pm; last admission 45 min. before closing.

Where to Stay in County Sligo

As with County Mayo, many of the best places to stay in County Sligo are hidden in the countryside.

Castle Dargan ♥♥ Set on 170 acres of rolling countryside just 10 minutes' drive from Sligo Town, this country estate offers a peaceful, rural escape. Castle Dargan itself is an 18th-century manor house rather than a castle, and most of the accommodation is in modern buildings to the rear,

THE lough gill DRIVE

An essential stop on Yeats Country pilgrimages is this beautiful lake, featured prominently in the writings of W. B. Yeats. A well-signposted drive-yourself tour around the lake's perimeter covers 42km (26 miles) and takes less than an hour.

To start, head 1.6km (1 mile) south of Sligo Town and follow the signs for Lough Gill. Within 3.2km (2 miles) you'll be on the lower edge of the shoreline. Among the sites are **Parke's Castle** (p. 466); **Dooney Rock,** with its own nature trail and lakeside walk (inspiration for the poem "Fiddler of Dooney"); the **Lake Isle of Innisfree,** made famous in poetry and song; and the **Hazelwood Sculpture Trail,** a unique forest walk along the lakeshore, with 13 wood sculptures. At the lake's east end, branch off to visit **Dromahair,** a delightful village on the River Bonet.

The road along Lough Gill's upper shore brings you back to the northern end of Sligo Town. Continue north on the main road (N15), and you'll see the graceful profile of **Ben Bulben** (519m/1,702 ft.), one of the Dartry Mountains, rising off to your right. One of Yeats's last poems, "Under Ben Bulben," alludes to this majestic rock formation as a silent sentinel looming over Irish history.

If you prefer to see all this beautiful scenery from the water itself, **Lough Gill Cruises** take you around Lough Gill and the Garavogue River aboard the 72-passenger *Wild Rose* waterbus as you listen to the poetry of Yeats. The boat departs from Parke's Castle daily at 12:30pm between Easter and September; tours last around an hour. In July and August there are also 1-hour trips daily from Doorly Park in Sligo Town at 1:30pm. Tickets for the hour-long tour are €25 adults, €20 seniors and students, and €10 children. Trips to Innisfree, sunset cruises, and dinner cruises are also scheduled. Visit roseofinnisfree.com or call ✆ **087/259-8869** for details and booking.

so a stay here is more about comfort than luxury, which is reflected in the prices. Golfers will love the 18-hole course and driving range, designed by Darren Clarke, and there's also an in-house spa.

Ballygawley. castledargan.com. ✆ **071/911-8080.** 39 units. €149–€249 double. Breakfast included. Check online for special offers. Free parking. **Amenities:** Restaurant; bar; golf course, spa; Wi-Fi (free).

The Glasshouse ♥♥ A solid, modern option in Sligo Town, the Glasshouse overlooks the River Garavogue, and from the outside resembles a gleaming, modern ship. The public areas inside either look bold and funky or like an explosion in a kitsch factory, depending on your point of view: multicolored circles on the carpet, misshapen blue sofas, and a bright orange signature color in the towering atrium. Bedrooms are a little more refined, with muted tones and modern art on the walls. There is an in-house restaurant, although you could eat more cheaply in town. The appropriately named **View Bar** looks out over Sligo Town and has live music (if you are sensitive to noise, ask for a room away from the bar when you book). A few years ago, places like this were all but unheard-of in Sligo, and the Glasshouse offers a good alternative for those who want a decently priced, convenient, and contemporary place to stay.

Swan Point, Sligo Town. theglasshouse.ie. ✆ **071/919-4300.** 116 units. €130–€330 double; €170–€380 suite. 2-night minimum stay some weekends. Breakfast not included in lower rates. Parking €6/night. **Amenities:** Restaurant; 2 bars; room service; Wi-Fi (free).

Ross Farmhouse ♥♥ Not far from Carrowkeel (p. 463), Ross Farmhouse is a restored 1880s cottage, surrounded by acres and acres of rolling farmland. The owner, Gemma Hill-Wilkinson, took over the place from her parents in 2019 (they had been running it for a mere 60 years). Bedrooms are reasonably sized, with simple, unfussy furnishings. One is a family room, and another is fully accessible to wheelchairs. Downstairs are two lovely guest lounges, filled with antiques. An open peat fire warms the hearth in winter. Breakfasts are varied and delicious—porridge is served either "nice" (plain) or "naughty" (with a shot of Baileys Irish cream liqueur).

Riverstown. Follow signs from Drumfin on N4 or Coola on R284. rossfarmhousesligo.com. ✆ **071/916-5140.** 5 units. €150 double. Breakfast included. Free parking. **Amenities:** Wi-Fi (free).

Sligo Park Hotel ♥♥ A pleasant little park surrounds this convenient, cheap-ish hotel in Sligo Town. Guest rooms are simply furnished in a contemporary style, with muted color schemes of gray and brown and good-size bathrooms. It won't win any awards for heart-of-Ireland atmosphere, but as a clean, modern base, it's a good option in a region that's short on choice. Families are especially well catered for, with treasure hunts, kids' pool obstacle courses, and movie nights. There's regular live entertainment, and the hotel is also a popular venue for weddings, so noise can sometimes be a problem on weekends. You might want to ask for a room as far away from the bar as possible.

Pearse Rd., Sligo Town. sligoparkhotel.com. ✆ **071/919-0400.** 136 units. €139–€259 double. Free parking. **Amenities:** Restaurant; bar; pool; room service; sauna; Wi-Fi (free).

Temple House ♥♥♥ This is one of *the* best places to stay in the northwest if you're after a unique and historic B&B experience. Make no mistake: Temple House is not a hotel, and it's not packed with five-star extras—but it is full of

Getting into Hot Water

The minerals and nutrients from seaweed are thought to have therapeutic properties—it's said to moisturize the skin and help with circulation, healing, and detoxing—so bathing in hot water with added wild seaweed from the Atlantic is a popular tradition on Ireland's west coast. **Kilcullen Seaweed Baths** in Enniscrone (kilcullenseaweedbaths.com; ✆ **096/36238**) is a gorgeous traditional bathhouse dating back to 1912; it still has the original baths. Start with a few minutes in the steam cabinet before relaxing in the hot water. A bath costs €30. **Voya** in Strandhill (voyaseaweedbaths.ie; ✆ **071/916-8686**) has a 50-minute detox seaweed bath for €45, as well as other organic treatments like wraps and facials.

Antique furnishings set a gracious tone in the guest rooms at Temple House.

historical authenticity, beautiful surroundings, and sheer, unforgettable charm. The delightful custodians of the estate, Roderick and Helena Perceval, are now more than a decade into their painstaking restoration of the 1665 manor house. Once a thriving country estate, it had fallen slowly into near-ruin during the turbulent years of the 20th century. (When we first stayed, the 18th-century silk curtains in one room, now fully restored, would literally crumble to the touch.) Now the huge guest rooms are packed with interesting antiques but have completely modern, recently renovated bathrooms. Nightly dinners are more akin to parties, with all guests seated around an enormous old table enjoying outstanding food. Breakfasts hit the spot, too, with plenty of homemade treats. The beautiful grounds include a boating lake, a walled garden, and even a ruined Knights Templar castle—hence the name. Supposedly a couple of resident ghosts are roaming around, although they must be of a very Bacchanalian kind, amid such a welcoming and convivial atmosphere as this. A self-catering cottage is also on the grounds.

Ballymote, Ballinacarrow. templehouse.ie. ✆ **087/997-6045.** 6 units. €215–€255 double. 3-course dinner from €64 (no dinner Sun) or ask about light suppers. Breakfast included. Free parking. **Amenities:** Wi-Fi (free). Closed Mid-Nov to Apr.

Where to Eat in County Sligo

The food scene in Sligo has transformed in recent years, with so many excellent food producers and culinary experiences that it has its own **Sligo Food Trail** (sligofoodtrail.ie), which links together everything from food workshops, foraging, and tastings to farmers markets and cafes. In Sligo

Town, a 2½-hour **Taste of Sligo Foodie Tour** (tasteofsligo.ie; ✆ **071/913-8591**) with restaurateur Anthony Gray of Hooked (see below) will show off some of the culinary highlights, taking in oyster, beer, and whiskey tastings as well as restaurant visits. Tours cost €85 and run at noon and 3pm, Wednesday through Saturday.

Coach Lane at Donaghy's ♥♥ IRISH/INTERNATIONAL A very popular spot with Sligo residents, Coach Lane has two dining rooms: a bar serving easy crowd-pleasers such as chowder, burgers, fish and chips, and fisherman's pie; and a more upmarket, gastropub-style restaurant. Most ingredients are regionally sourced, and the seafood is particularly good. Try the pork belly with scallops and ample compote, or dive into a dry-aged striploin steak. Coach Lane also makes its own craft beer.
1–2 Lord Edward St., Sligo Town. coachlanesligo.com. ✆ **071/916-2417.** Entrees €28–€36. Bar food Thurs–Mon 2–9pm, restaurant Thurs–Sun 5:30–9pm.

Eala Bhán ♥♥♥ INTERNATIONAL This popular brasserie has been awarded best restaurant in Connaught by the Irish Restaurant Awards many times. The menu takes traditional brasserie classics and adds a light touch of creative flair—tender rack of local lamb comes with *courgette* (zucchini) purée and shallot mash, while the trio of fish combines buttered scallops, pistachio-crumb hake, and a sea trout lemon risotto. Three-course set menus are a good value and feature many dishes from the main menus. The early-bird menu (served 5–6:20pm daily) is €45 for three courses. The lunch menu is almost as extensive as dinner, with a few lighter options such as poached chicken salad and seafood chowder.
Rockwood Parade, Sligo Town. ealabhan.ie. ✆ **071/914-5823.** 3-course fixed-price menu €65 or €70. 8-course tasting menu €89. Entrees €24–€43. Mon–Wed 5–9pm; Thurs–Sat noon–3pm and 5–9pm; Sun noon–4:30pm and 5–9pm.

Eala Bhán (Gaelic for "white swan") offers creative takes on brasserie classics.

Hooked ♥♥ IRISH Despite the name and the upturned boat on the ceiling, the menu in this informal bistro-style restaurant is not all about seafood. The family has owned butcher shops, so expect great meat dishes like tempura beef strips and 12-hour slow-cooked pork belly, as well as fish and chips and crispy squid tacos, plus decent vegetarian and vegan

Fruit-topped dessert at Hooked, a riverside restaurant in Sligo Town.

options. This is all about comfort food made with good produce from local artisan producers from County Sligo or just beyond, at reasonable prices in a family-friendly setting.
3–4 Rockwood Parade, Sligo Town. hookedsligo.ie. ✆ **071/913-8591.** Brunch €15–€20; dinner entrees €17–€20. Mon–Thurs noon–9pm; Fri–Sun 9:30am–9pm.

Kate's Kitchen ♥♥ DELI This great delicatessen has a large stock of gourmet foods, Irish cheese, fresh bread, salads, chutneys, and other tasty items that just beg to be put together to make an elegant picnic or lunch on the go. It also has a small shop selling bath products and a particularly nice range of handmade chocolates—perfect for gifts, if you can keep yourself from raiding them before the journey home.
3 Castle St., Sligo Town. kateskitchen.ie. ✆ **071/914-3022.** Most items €5–€12. Tues–Sat 8am–4:30pm.

Osta Café & Wine Bar ♥♥ CAFE The owners of this sweet cafe overlooking the river in Sligo are big believers in the slow-food and organic movements, and their delicious, healthful food makes superb use of ingredients from small local producers. There are usually only a few dishes on offer every day, but you're guaranteed to find something properly, authentically Irish. Even the sandwiches qualify as local—they're made with deliciously fresh bread from a nearby bakery. There are tasty brunches every day until 3pm, and in the early evenings Thursday to Saturday, the food switches to a simple but delicious tapas menu. Live music is on tap every Thursday evening. ***Tip:*** An Irish-speaking group meets here every Friday evening, which makes it a good time to drop by if you fancy hearing the language being spoken.
Garavogue Weir, off Stephen St., Sligo Town. osta.ie. ✆ **071/914-4639.** Entrees €8–€12. Mon–Wed 8:30am–5pm; Thurs–Fri 8:30am–7pm; Sat 8:30am–5pm; Sun 9am–4pm.

Shell's Café ♥♥ What started out as a small cafe on the seafront in Strandhill has earned legions of fans for its hearty, healthy food, eventually inspiring cookbooks and a gift store. Nevertheless, breakfasts with names like "the simple" (two poached eggs, two slices of bacon, on buttered toast) have stayed true to their roots. Small but perfectly designed (and perfect for Instagram), this darling cafe offers good, freshly made food (with lots of options for vegetarians) and excellent coffee. There's an outdoor terrace too, plus a shop so you can take home treats and cookbooks.
Strandhill. shellscafe.com. ✆ **071/912-2938.** Breakfast €9–€13; lunch entrees €10–€18. Daily 9am–6pm.

Shopping in Sligo Town

Sligo Town has some great little boutiques and independent local businesses. Most shops are open Monday to Saturday from 9am until 6pm; some may have extended hours in July and August.

The Cat & the Moon ♥♥ Named after a Yeats poem, this is a great place to shop for Irish crafts and jewelry. They design their own silver rings and pendants with Celtic motifs. In addition, the shop stocks an interesting range of art, ceramics, candles, and other handicrafts, and always seems to offer something in the way of unique finds and souvenirs. 4 Castle St., Sligo Town. thecatandthemoon.ie. ✆ **071/914-3686.**

Made in Sligo ♥♥♥ This is a chance to buy some of the work of 10 skilled crafters in County Sligo, with art, baskets, ceramics, jewelry, wood turning, and wool craft on sale. One of the crafters is usually on-site. 4 Wine St., Sligo Town. madeinsligo.com. ✆ **087/210-9020.**

Artisan wares at the craft collective Made in Sligo.

Michael Quirke ♥♥ Michael Quirke is a real Sligo character. He used to be a butcher but got bored with it and decided to follow his real passion: woodcarving. Out went the meat and in came the artisan tools, and his shop became a studio. Now he spends his time carving and selling exquisite statues, ornaments, and objets d'art out of Irish wood, with a particular focus on figures from Irish mythology. His carvings are quite affordable for the quality. Wine St., Sligo Town. ✆ **071/914-2624.**

Wehrly Bros. Ltd ♥♥ The granddaddy of Sligo jewelry stores, this firm has been trading from behind its elegant black-and-gold storefront since 1875. It specializes in diamond rings, watches, and pearls, with a wide range of designer jewelry. It also sells Waterford Crystal. 3 O'Connell St., Sligo Town. wehrlybros.ie. ✆ **071/914-2252.**

Sports & Outdoor Pursuits in County Sligo

HORSEBACK RIDING Arrange an hour or a day of horseback riding on the beach, in the countryside, or over mountain trails through **Sligo Riding Centre,** Carrowmore (sligoridingcentre.com; ✆ **087/230-4828**). Rates are €33 per hour. **Island View Riding Stables** (islandviewridingstables.com; ✆ **071/916-6156**) near Grange offers horse-riding holidays, starting from 2 nights with B&B and 5 hours of riding for €480 adults and €430 children.

SEA SAFARI **Enniscrone Boat Tours** (enniscroneboattours.ie; ✆ **087/354-7359**) runs 2-hour tours taking in the **Dún Briste** sea stack, **Céide Fields** sea cliffs, and coastal wildlife. Tours are €60 per person and run daily June through August and on request September through May, weather depending. There's also a 1-hour tour (€30), plus customized half- and full-day sea safaris.

SURFING The beaches of County Sligo are the home of surf, with excellent waves for all levels at **Strandhill,** reef breaks for the more experienced at **Easkey,** and big waves for pros only at **Mullaghmore.** For lessons that provide all the gear including wetsuits, try **Sligo Surf Experience** at Strandhill (sligosurfexperience.com; ✆ **087/747-1915;** lessons €45 adults, €40 children 9–16).

WALKING & HIKING **Sligo Walks** (sligowalks.ie) has details of 60 different trails around the county, giving useful information like terrain type and walk length. Explore the hills and peaks of County Sligo with **Northwest Adventure Tours** (northwestadventuretours.ie; ✆ **087/125-9594**). Hikes to mountains like Ben Bulben or Knocknarea start at €35; Northwest also runs biking, free-diving, and SUP (stand-up paddleboarding) tours along gorgeous waterways like Lough Gill.

13

COUNTY DONEGAL

When the landscape opens up into great sweeping views of rocky hills and barren shores, and a freezing mist blows off the sea, you know you've reached Donegal. The beauty of this county is both austere and bleak—but it is also unforgettable. On a clear day, you can stand on a cliff facing the sea at Malin Head at the very top of Ireland, and, despite the sun, the sea spray will blow a chill right through you. It feels as if you're standing at the edge of the world. If you've reached this far—congratulations! You can truly say that you've seen Ireland now, in all its wild, exhilarating beauty.

County Donegal's natural wonders include the magnificent *Sliabh Liag* (Slieve League) cliffs and remote beaches tucked into the bays and inlets of its sharply indented coast. While Donegal is one of Ireland's least touristy counties, it does have some truly fantastic places to stay, but they tend to be hidden away amid mountainous roads and tiny seaside towns. Buildings are made of cold stone; villages sit near tiny harbors or at the foot of hills; road signs sometimes vary from cryptic to nonexistent. When you stop to take a wander, you can't help but worry whether the car's brakes will hold. But take the chance. You will spend half your time lost, but wherever you're headed, you'll get there eventually, most likely with a few adventures along the way. And the people in Donegal are as nice as can be—meeting them is worth the trip in itself.

ESSENTIALS

Arriving

BY BUS **Bus Éireann** (buseireann.ie; ✆ **074/912-1309**) operates daily bus service to Donegal Town from Dublin, Derry, Sligo, Galway, and other points, and runs a daily service from Dublin to Letterkenny. Buy tickets in advance online for the best price.

BY CAR The only practical way to get around the remote attractions of County Donegal is by car. Donegal is reached on the N15 from Sligo or the A5 or A6 (connecting to the N15) from Northern Ireland. N56 is the main road from Donegal Town circling around the rest of the county.

BY PLANE **Donegal Airport (CFN),** in Carrickfinn in northwest Donegal (donegalairport.ie; ✆ **074/954-8284**), also known as Carrickfinn Airport, is a small budget airline hub and has been voted one of the world's

FACING PAGE: Glenveagh Castle in Glenveagh National Park.

most scenic landings. Currently a couple of scheduled flights connect per day with Dublin, operated by **Aer Lingus** (aerlingus.com; ✆ **1890/800-600**), and up to four flights per week with Glasgow in Scotland, operated by **Loganair** (loganair.co.uk; ✆ **0344/800-2855**).

BY TRAIN There are no trains to Donegal. You can catch a train as far as Sligo and then switch to bus, but it's easiest to take a bus all the way.

DONEGAL TOWN & DONEGAL BAY

Overseen by a low, gloomy castle at the edge of the picturesque estuary of the River Eske on Donegal Bay, Donegal Town is a tiny burg, with just 2,600 residents. As recently as the 1940s, the town's triangular central mall (called "the Diamond"), set at the meeting point of roads from Killybegs, Ballyshannon, and Ballybofey, was used as a market for trading livestock and goods. Today the marketing takes the form of tweeds and tourist goods, as the Diamond is surrounded by little crafts shops and small hotels of variable quality. In the center stands an obelisk erected in memory of four 17th-century Irish clerics from the local abbey (p. 477) who wrote *The Annals of the Four Masters,* the first recorded history of Gaelic Ireland.

Visitor Information

The **Donegal Tourist Information Centre** is on the Quay, Donegal Town (govisitdonegal.com; ✆ **1800/230-330**), and is open Tuesday to Saturday

Donegal's colorful cityscape.

from 9am to 5pm (also Sun June–Sept). The **Ardara Heritage Centre** (✆ **087/242-4590**) is on the main road through Ardara and is open Monday to Saturday 11am until 4pm.

Exploring Donegal Town

Donegal Abbey ♥ RELIGIOUS SITE/RUINS Sitting in a peaceful spot on the Quay in Donegal Town, where the River Eske meets Donegal Bay, this ruined Franciscan monastery was founded in 1474 by the first Red Hugh O'Donnell and his wife, Nuala O'Brien of Munster. It was generously endowed by the O'Donnell family and became an important center of religion and learning; records show that there was a great gathering of clergy and lay leaders here in 1539. It was from this friary that some scholars undertook to salvage old Irish manuscripts and compile *The Annals of the Four Masters* (1632–36). Enough remains of the abbey's glory—ruins of a church and a cloister—to give you an idea of how magnificent it once was.

The Quay. Free admission (open site).

Donegal Bay Waterbus ♥♥ BOAT TOUR These guided 75-minute tours of Donegal Bay take place daily on a modern, two-deck boat. Points of interest along the way include the **Old Abbey** ♥ (see above); the aptly named **Seal Island,** home to a colony of about 200 noisy seals; and **The Hassans,** a port from which many emigrants from the northern part of the country left for the New World. The guides are enthusiastic and knowledgeable; unfortunately, their commentary is nonstop (guides have even been known to play the keyboard to fill in moments of silence). The views, however, are wonderful. There's a bar on board, plus seniors get free tea, coffee, and bottled water (ask for a voucher when picking up your tickets). Sailing times are usually morning and afternoon or evening but are dependent on tides and weather, so check online or call ahead. Buy tickets online or from the office on Quay Street—it's the white-and-blue building next to Dom's Pier 1 Bar.

The Pier. donegalbaywaterbus.com. ✆ **074/972-3666.** Tour €25 adults; €15 students 17–23 (must have student ID); €8 children 5–16; free for children 4 and under; €60 families. Closed Nov–Feb.

Summer Festival in Donegal Town

If you're heading this way in late June or early July, check out Donegal Town's laid-back annual **Summer Festival.** The program is an enthusiastic mixture of free concerts (from local bands that, in all probability, you've never heard of) and family-friendly fun and games. The festival lasts 4 days, with the biggest events scheduled over a weekend. See **govisitdonegal.com** for more event details.

Donegal Castle ♥ CASTLE Built in the 15th century on the banks of the River Eske, this solid gray stone castle was once the chief stronghold for the O'Donnells, a powerful Donegal clan. In the 17th century, during the Plantation period, it was taken over by Sir Basil Brook, who added an extension with 10 gables, a large bay window, and smaller mullioned windows in Jacobean style. Much of the building has survived the centuries, and both the interior and exterior of the castle were beautifully restored in the 1990s. Guided tours run hourly and are included in the admission price.

Castle St. heritageireland.ie. ✆ **074/972-2405.** Admission €5 adults; €4 seniors; €3 students and children; €13 families. Mid-Mar to early Nov daily 10am–6pm; Nov to mid-Mar daily 9:30am–4pm; last admission 45 min. before closing.

Exploring Around Donegal Bay

The coastline around Donegal Bay is wild and beautiful. Speeds much above 55kmph (35 mph) are dangerous, but that's just as well, because the

County Donegal
The Abbey Mill 14
Ardara Heritage Center 10
Ballyshannon 14
Doagh Famine Village 2
Doe Castle 7
Dunfanaghy Workhouse 6
Fort Dunree Military Museum 4
Glebe House & Gallery 9
Glencolumbkille Folk Village 11
Glenveagh National Park & Castle 8
Grianan of Aileach 5
Inishowen Maritime Museum & Planetarium 3
Lough Derg 13
Malin Head 1
Sliabh Liag (Slieve League) 12
ATLANTIC OCEAN
DONEGAL
NORTHERN IRELAND
Inishowen
Fanad
Derryveagh Mts.
Blue Stack Mts.
Sperrin Mts.
Dartry Mts.
SLIGO
LEITRIM
Inishtrahull
Malin Head
Ballygorman
Malin
Culdaff Bay
Culdaff
Kinnagoe Bay
Ballyliffin
Drumfree
Moville
Buncrana
L. Swilly
Carrowkeel
Lough Foyle
Rathmullan
Milford
Ramelton
Kilmacrenan
Letterkenny
Derry (Londonderry)
Eglinton
Ballykelly
Limavady
Portstewart
Castlerock
Coleraine
Tory I.
Tory Sound
Horn Head
Rosguill
Dunfanaghy
Creeslough
Bloody Foreland
Magheroarty
Gortahork
Gola I.
Derrybeg
Owey I.
Cruit I.
Arranmore I.
Burtonport
Ballintra
Dungloe
Lough Beagh
Glenveagh National Park
Gartan Lough
Fintown
Gweebarra Bay
Portnoo
Naran
L. Finn
Finn
Raphoe
Lifford
Strabane
Stranorlar
Ballybofey
Sion Mills
Loughros More Bay
Glenties
Ardara
Glencolumbkille
Sliabh Liag
Teelin
Kilcar
Killybegs
Mountcharles
Donegal
L. Eske
Inver Bay
Rossnowlagh
Ballintra
Lough Derg
Derg
Ballyshannon
Donegal Bay
Tullaghan
Bundoran
Inishmurray
Lough Melvin
Lower Lough Erne
Enniskillen
Pettigo
Ederny
Dromore
Fivemiletown
Ballygawley
Newtownstewart
Castlederg
Mourne
Foyle
Omagh
Sixmilecross
Beragh
Pomeroy
Donaghmore
Dungannon
Cookstown
Moneymore
Magherafelt
Draperstown
Plumb Bridge
Sawel Mtn.
Maghera
Dungiven
Lough Neagh
N13
N14
N15
N56
A2
A4
A5
A6
A29
A32
A35
A37
A46
M1
0 10 miles
0 10 kms
Map Area
NORTHERN IRELAND
Belfast
Galway
Dublin
REPUBLIC OF IRELAND
Cork

spectacular views will cause you to stop again and again to take in the rolling hills, jagged mountains, bright green fields, and crashing seas.

Heading south from Donegal Town, there are few attractions besides the historic village of **Ballyshannon** (***Béal Átha Seanaidh;*** below) and, inland, the pilgrimage site on the shore of **Lough Derg** (p. 482). But this area's a magnet for sporty types, with fine beaches, outstanding golf courses, and some of the best surfing in Ireland (p. 486).

To the north of Donegal Town, however, the coastal scenery is breathtaking. Follow the main road (N56) west out of Donegal Town for a slow, winding, but spectacularly scenic drive along the bay. You may see some of the distinctive thatched-roof cottages typical of this area, with rounded roofs held down by ropes (called *sugans*) fastened beneath the eaves to help the thatch resist the strong sea winds.

Just before the fishing village of **Killybegs (*Na Ceala Beaga*),** where the main N56 road swings inland, continue on the coastal road R263 through Killybegs to **Kilcar (*Cill Chártha*),** where you can pick up Donegal tweeds at a bargain at **Studio Donegal** (the Glebe Mill; studiodonegal.ie). Truly spectacular photo ops await at **Sliabh Liag** (p. 482), with its perilously high sea cliffs crashing down into the waters below. (Take the turnoff for the Bunglas viewing point at Carrick.) The traditional end of the west coast drive is the heritage site of **Glencolumbkille (*Gleann Cholm Cille*),** 48km (30 miles) from Donegal Town (p. 481).

To continue touring from Glencolumbkille, follow the signs directing you on the R230 to Ardara (*Árd an Rátha*). This is a breathtaking drive through **Glengesh Pass,** a narrow, sinuous, scenic roadway that rises to a height of 270m (886 ft.) before plunging in hairpin curves into the valley below to reach the village of **Ardara (*Árd an Rátha*)**—ready to take on the rest of the county.

Ballyshannon *(Béal Átha Seanaidh)* ♥♥ VILLAGE The first proper town you'll come to on a drive south of Donegal Town is this busy, pretty little place, built on a hill, with a 15th-century town center. Some claim that Ballyshannon is the oldest town in Ireland, in part because traces have been found of permanent settlements dating as far back as 4000 B.C. The small **Ballyshannon and District Museum,** on the second floor of Slevin's Department Store, has artifacts and information on local history. It's open Monday to Saturday from 10am until 6pm, and admission is free. Ballyshannon is also the location of the **Abbey Mill** (**© 071/985-1260**), a heritage center and crafts store. Part of a ruined Cistercian abbey, the mill still has a working waterwheel (opening hours vary—generally Mon–Sat 10am–5pm, summer months only; entry is free, but leave a few coins in the collection box by the waterwheel to help pay for its upkeep). While you're here, check out tiny **Catsby Cave,** about 50m (164 ft.) along the riverbank. During the years of British occupation, when Catholicism was outlawed (from the 16th century until the mid–19th century), priests would give Mass here in secret. You can still see the remains of an altar, chiseled from the rock. Admission is free. Ballyshannon is known for its lively pubs, many of which have reliably good traditional music—never more so than during a weekend in late July or early August, when the streets come alive for the **Ballyshannon Folk & Traditional Music Festival** (ballyshannonfolkfestival.com).

Tourism office: The Bridge, Ballyshannon. About 22km (13½ miles) S of Donegal Town on N15.

Glencolumbkille *(Gleann Cholm Cille)* ♥♥ HERITAGE SITE An extraordinarily beautiful outpost overlooking the Atlantic Ocean, the village of Glencolumbkille is sited in a lush green valley, west of the dark boglands. It is said that St. Columba established a monastery here in the 6th century and gave his name to the glen (its Irish language name—*Gleann Cholm Cille*—means "Glen of Columba's Church"). Today it's home to the **Glencolumbkille Folk Village,** a wonderful "living history" park and craft center, set up and maintained entirely by local people. In a series of small traditional cottages, the park tells the story of this remote community and of traditional life in Ireland in the 19th century, in an engaging way. Guided tours are available, or you can take it at your own pace. Don't leave without browsing the craft shop selling local products,

walk this way: CLIMBING *SLIABH LIAG* (SLIEVE LEAGUE)

There are two ways to see *Sliabh Liag* (Slieve League)—and rarely has the phrase "the easy way or the hard way" been more appropriate.

The walking path is a truly spectacular hike across stunning countryside, about 10km (6¼ miles) in length, which takes between 4 and 5 hours. The summits of *Sliabh Liag*, rising almost 600m (1,968 ft.) above the sea, are often capped in clouds, and you shouldn't undertake the walk if there are high winds or any danger at all of losing visibility along the way. In any case, this is only for the fearless and fit. And we *really* mean fearless; the high point (literally) is the frankly terrifying **One Man's Pass,** a footpath so narrow that it can only take one person at a time—and it's *on top of* the cliff, with a 450m (1,500-ft.) drop on one side and a perilously steep incline on the other. Your starting point will be the Bunglas lookout point, and you end up at Trabane Strand in Malin Beg, a few miles southwest of Glencolumbkille. Be sure to arrange a pickup at the end.

So where does "the easy way" come into all this? The less intrepid (or possibly just "sane") can walk or take a shuttle bus from the visitor center up to the best viewing point. You won't be able to see the vista from the cliffs, but you'll get a great view *of* them.

Sliabh Liag Tours (sliabhliagtours.ie; ✆ **087/671-1944**) runs a tour from Carrick and can arrange to drop you off at the best (and more manageable) walking points on the way back. Tours are all customized; call for information.

Hikers taking in the scenery along the Sliabh Liag trail.

while the tearoom serves traditional Irish stews, soups, and brown bread. Tea *brack* (a fruity cake) is a house specialty.

On R263, about 26km (16 miles) NW of Killybegs. glenfolkvillage.com. ✆ **074/973-0017.** Admission €7 adults; €6 seniors and students; €3 children 7–16; free for children 6 and under; €18 families. Easter–Sept daily 10am–6pm; Oct 10am–4:30pm.

Lough Derg ♥♥ NATURE SITE Sharing a name with the much larger Lough Derg on the River Shannon (p. 383), this beautiful island-dotted lake lies about 16km (10 miles) east of Donegal Town. Legend has it that St. Patrick spent 40 days and 40 nights fasting in a cavern at this secluded spot, and since then it has been revered as a place of penance and pilgrimage. From June 1 to August 15, thousands of Irish Catholics take turns coming to Lough Derg to do penance for 3 days at a time, remaining awake and eating nothing but tea and toast. It's considered one of the most rigorous pilgrimages in all of Christendom.

Take R232 to Pettigo, then R233 for 8km (5 miles). loughderg.org.

***Sliabh Liag* (Slieve League)** ♥♥ NATURE SITE It's surprising that these towering sea cliffs aren't better known, because at 601m (1,972 ft.), they're almost three times the height of their far more feted southern cousins, the **Cliffs of Moher** (p. 360), and arguably even more spectacular. Needless to say, given the remote location, they also get a tiny fraction of the visitors that the Cliffs of Moher attract. During peak summer season, around July and August, you can park (free) in the lower car park and either walk up to the main viewing point (a lovely walk of around 45 min.) or take a shuttle bus up (€6 adults; €5 seniors and students; €4 children; €20 families). There's also parking halfway up (€5/2 hr. or €15/day), and the walk from there is about 25 minutes. In the off-season, you may be able to drive all the way to the upper viewing point, but walking is the nicest way to appreciate the surroundings. When you reach the viewpoint, you can fully take in the wild, ominous beauty of this rugged, far-flung outpost. If you really want to test yourself against the terrain, try the hike right to the top of the cliff (see box on p. 481). The lower car park at Bunglas has a visitor center and cafe. You can also see the cliffs from the water with **Sliabh Liag Boat Trips** (sliabhleagueboattrips.com; ✆ **087/628-4688**; €25 adults, €15 ages 13–17, and €10 ages 5–12). Meanwhile the **Slieve League Cliffs Centre** (slieveleague.com; ✆ **074/973-9077**) in Teelin, about 3km (1⅔ miles) southwest of Carrick, is a friendly little visitor center, run by an archaeologist and an artist, with a great cafe and a gorgeous crafts store. Admission is free, and it's open daily 9am to 6pm.

Carrick (signposted from R263). sliabhliag.com. ✆ **074/973-9620.** Free admission. Open year-round.

Where to Stay in Donegal Town & Donegal Bay

Ard Na Breátha ♥♥ Though it's only a 10-minute walk from the center of Donegal Town, the peaceful surroundings and mountain views of this B&B give the feeling of rural seclusion. Bedrooms are summery and spacious, with bright colors, polished-wood floors, and antique-style iron-frame beds in some rooms. The lounge has a cozy fireplace and a small honesty bar, and guests have the use of a small kitchen.

Railway Park, Middle Drumrooske. ardnabreatha.com. ✆ **074/972-2288.** 6 units. €109–€139 double. Breakfast included. Free parking. **Amenities:** Kitchen; Wi-Fi (free). Closed Nov–Easter.

The Gateway Lodge ♥♥ This stylish and contemporary lodging, just a few minutes' walk from the town center, incorporates a 19th-century house and two modern wings. Good-size bedrooms make the most of the space, with modern furniture and just enough quirky touches to be characterful and functional at the same time. Bathrooms have what may be described as a "utilitarian chic" air to them, with white-tiled walls and satisfyingly powerful showers. A little restaurant and cafe called **Blas** is located in the old house, where you can get delicious and healthful bistro-style lunches featuring plenty of local produce—or just a cup of fresh coffee.

Killybegs Rd., Donegal Town. thegatewaydonegal.ie. ✆ **074/974-0405.** 26 units. €99–€139 double. Breakfast not included in lower rates. Free parking. **Amenities:** Wi-Fi (free).

Harvey's Point Hotel ♥♥♥ There are few more romantic views in Donegal than the glassy expanse of Lough Eske, and this wonderful lakeside resort takes full advantage of the location. Rooms and bathrooms are spacious, modern, and very comfortable. The decor is traditional throughout, with marble bathrooms, striped wallpaper, and antique reproduction beds. All guest rooms are suites, with seating areas and plenty of space to relax. Downstairs, the restaurant serves rich meals along with exquisite views of the lake, and afternoon tea here is absolutely decadent, offering up fresh-baked scones, cakes, and homemade jam. The wood-paneled bar has the feel of a private club, with a good selection of wine and whiskey. This place has the ambience of an exclusive getaway, as if you're hiding from the world. No wonder it's won so many awards.

Deluxe suite at Harvey's Point Hotel.

At Lough Eske, about 7km (4½ miles) from Donegal Town, off N15. harveyspoint.com. ✆ **074/972-2208.** 101 units. €258–€470 double. 2-night minimum some weekends. Breakfast included. Free parking. **Amenities:** Restaurant; bar; room service; Wi-Fi (free).

Where to Eat in Donegal Town & Donegal Bay

Blueberry Tea Room and Restaurant ♥♥ CAFE A buttermilk-colored shopfront, adorned with little baskets of azaleas, twinkling fairy lights, and walls filled with knickknacks—and the friendliest owner in Donegal—what more could you want from a small-town cafe? If the answer is "tasty, simple lunches in huge portions," guess what, you're in luck there, too! The homemade soups are a specialty (served with or without a toasted sandwich), or you could fill up on a hearty plate of steak fajitas or breaded chicken with pasta and the house special sauce. The cafe also has a little deli selling Irish cheese, breads, muffins, and other tasty treats to go.

Castle St., Donegal Town. theblueberrytearooms.ie. ✆ **074/972-3663.** Entrees €10–€12. Mon–Sat 9am–6pm.

Quay West ♥♥ IRISH Romantic, contemporary food is served up in this delightful place overlooking Donegal Bay. The food is modern without a hint of pretension. Start with a plate of local shellfish with fresh sourdough toast, then for your main course try a chargrilled steak (cooked

on hot lava stones) or stick with the local seafood and opt for a creamy fish pie with a comet cheese crust. Desserts are mostly of the indulgent, comfort-food variety. If you can resist the profiteroles with dark chocolate ganache sauce, you are a better person than either of us.
Quay St., Donegal Town. quaywestdonegal.ie. ✆ **074/972-1590.** Entrees €19–€30. Wed–Sun 5–9pm.

Classic fish and chips (and mushy peas) at Smugglers Creek.

Smugglers Creek Inn ♥♥ SEAFOOD With a breathtakingly beautiful cliff-top view of Donegal Bay, this mid-19th-century inn is a fantastic place to come and watch the sun setting over the Atlantic Ocean. See if you can get a table outside or in the conservatory. Although you can order steaks and other meaty dishes, the seafood is what's best here: chowder, smoked mackerel, scampi, crab claws, or the ever-reliable fish and chips. Vegetarians and vegans are better catered to than you might expect at a little restaurant in the back of beyond; try the delicious penne with roasted vegetables. Wash it all down with a pint of local ale.
Cliff Rd., Rossnowlagh. smugglerscreekinn.com. ✆ **071/985-2366.** Entrees €17–€32. Mid-May to Sept daily 12:30–10:30pm; Oct and Jan to mid-May Fri–Sun 12:30–10:30pm. Closed Nov–Dec.

Sports & Outdoor Pursuits Around Donegal Bay

BEACHES Donegal Bay's beaches are wide, sandy, clean, and flat—ideal for walking. **Ballyshannon** has a good beach, but it gets crowded; **Rossnowlagh** and **Bundoran** are better options, and both are popular for surfing (see below). On the North Donegal Bay drive, **Glencolumbkille** has two fine beaches: one a flat, sandy beach at the end of Glencolumbkille village, where the R263 swings left, the other a tiny gem of a beach surrounded by a horseshoe of cliffs, accessible from the small road signposted to Malin More (off the R263) about 1.6km (1 mile) southwest of town.

CYCLING If you're very fit, the north side of Donegal Bay has great cycling roads—tremendously scenic but with some demanding climbs. One good but arduous route from Donegal Town follows the coast roads west to Glencolumbkille (day 1), continues north to Ardara and Dawros Head via Glengesh Pass (day 2), and then returns to Donegal (day 3). It takes in some of the most spectacular coastal scenery in Ireland along the way, but follows small, winding roads that must sometimes be shared with fast-moving cars.

GOLF The coast around Donegal Bay is home to two outstanding 18-hole championship seaside golf courses. **Donegal Golf Club,** Murvagh, Ballintra (donegalgolfclub.ie; ✆ **074/973-4054**), is 5km (3 miles) north of Rossnowlagh and 11km (6¾ miles) south of Donegal Town. It's a par-73 course with greens fees of €210 April to October, €60 November to March. The **Bundoran Golf Club,** off the Sligo–Ballyshannon road (N15) in Bundoran (bundorangolfclub.com; ✆ **071/984-1302**), is a par-69 course designed by Harry Vardon. Greens fees are €100, or €35 before 10am or after 3pm.

SURFING **Bundoran** is popular with surfers for its steady waves; it has hosted the European Surfing Championships. **Rossnowlagh** also has excellent surf. You can rent boards and wetsuits locally from around €25 each per day or take a lesson from around €45 per person, which includes all equipment. Try **Bundoran Surf Co.** (bundoransurfco.com; ✆ **071/984-1968**) in Bundoran, which offers lessons year-round at Tullan Strand in Bundoran or Rossnowlagh. For surf and SUP in Donegal Bay and South Donegal, try **Wild and Free** (wildandfree.ie; ✆ **089/608-6693**), with surf lessons from €42.

WALKING The peninsula to the west of Killybegs offers some of the most spectacular coastal scenery in Ireland, much of it accessible only from the sea or on foot. Besides the ***Sliabh Liag* (Slieve League)** hike (p. 481), there's a spectacular coastal walk between Glencolumbkille and the townland of **Maghera** (a small cluster of houses). Begin by hiking up to the Martello tower on Glen Head, which overlooks Glencolumbkille to the north, then continue along the cliff face for 24km (15 miles), passing only one remote outpost of human habitation along the way, the tiny town of **Port.** For isolated sea splendor, this is one of the finest walks in Ireland, but only experienced walkers with adequate provisions should undertake it, and only in fine weather. For other routes and trails, see **hikingdonegal.com**.

AROUND COUNTY DONEGAL

Donegal is the most isolated county in Ireland. It doesn't get much more rugged and exhilarating, and, well . . . *isolated* than this. At a certain point when you're driving through the Gaeltacht area (p. 47), the signs switch entirely to Irish. It's disorienting—one minute you know exactly where you are and the next you haven't a clue. And at that moment—which almost always occurs on a mountainside by a rushing stream amid rocky terrain—you're in the true Donegal.

Traditional weaver at work in Ardara.

The best place to start a tour of County Donegal is at **Ardara (*Árd an Rátha*),** an adorable village about 40km (25 miles) northwest of Donegal Town. From there, weave your way up the coast. This drive can take 4 hours or 4 days, depending on your schedule and interests. Our advice is to take your time. You may never come this way again, and you will want to remember every moment.

Exploring County Donegal

Looking as if it were carved from stone, charming little **Ardara** is known for its exceptional tweed and wool creations. Astride a narrow river in a steep gulch, it is a pleasant place to stop, chat with the locals, and do a bit of shopping or maybe have a cup of tea in its small but useful **Heritage Centre** on the N56 main road through the village. You will also be able to see weavers at work in some of the shops—ask at the Heritage Centre.

Heading north from Ardara, the N26 passes through the neat-as-a-pin little town of **Glenties (*Na Gleanta*),** where playwright Brian Friel set his play *Dancing at Lughnasa,* and eventually curves inland to gorgeous **Glenveagh National Park ♥♥♥** (p. 489) and **Mount Errigal,** Donegal's highest mountain. Just east of the park, the surprisingly good **Glebe House and Gallery ♥♥** (p. 489) sits on lovely Lough Gartan.

It would be a shame, however, not to sample some scenic coastal detours along the way. The southernmost is on R261, taking in **Naran (*An Fhearthainn*)** and **Portnoo**—beaches that are favorites with Irish families in the summer. Your next option is at Dungloe, where you can split off on coastal R259 to visit **the Rosses,** a rock-strewn land punctuated by mountains, rivers, and glassy lakes (and vacation homes). On this loop you'll pass the tiny port of **Burtonport (*Ailt an Chorráin*),** where, it's said, more salmon and lobster are landed than at any other port in the country. The next coastal loop heading north is on R257, swinging through Derrybeg and Gortahork. This is known as the **Bloody Foreland,** from the fact that its rocks take on a ruddy color when lit by the setting sun. For a remote area, it is surprisingly built-up, but if you can arrange to be driving through here at sunset on a clear day, you are in for some rewarding views.

If you follow N56 to the top rim of Donegal, you'll find a series of small peninsulas like fingers jabbing out into the sea. West to east, they are **Horn Head (*Corrán Binne*),** where spectacular cliffs tower 180m (590 ft.) above the ocean; **Rosguill (*Ros Goill*);** and **Fanad,** jutting out between Mulroy Bay and the glassy waters of Lough Swilly. Each peninsula has its own driving circuit. Horn Head's clifftop drive is the most spectacular but also rather perilous; you may want to opt instead for Rosguill's scenic 16km (10-mile) Atlantic Drive, or, if you have more time, the Fanad's 73km (45-mile) circuit, which takes in the beautiful **Fanad Head Lighthouse.** There is a bridge between Rosguill and Fanad on the R245 just beyond Carrickart, and the **Mulroy Drive** circles Mulroy Bay, between the Fanad and Rosguill peninsulas. At the base of the Horn Head Peninsula, pretty **Dunfanaghy (*Dún Fionnachaidh*)** can be a good option for an overnight stay, with a fine beach and an intriguing heritage center, the **Dunfanaghy Workhouse** (see below). Between Horn Head and Rosguill, **Doe Castle** (see below) is also well worth a stop. At the base of the Fanad Peninsula, the tiny village of **Rathmelton (*Ráth Mealtain*)** is eminently photographic, with its gray Georgian warehouses reflected in the mirrorlike water of the lake.

About 10 minutes' drive north of Rathmelton, on the coast of Lough Swilly, the village of **Rathmullan (*Ráth Maoláin*)** is an excellent stopping point, with an evocative ruined abbey, a beautiful stretch of flat, sandy beach, and a couple of good hotels (splurge on **Rathmullan House** ♥♥♥ if you can swing it—see p. 491).

Doe Castle (*Caisleán na dTuath*) ♥ CASTLE This little 600-year-old castle at the edge of a mirrorlike lake is so perfect it's hard to believe it's real. A battlement wall with round towers at the corners encloses the central tower house, which was once the stronghold of Clan Sweeney. Built in the early 16th century, the castle was extensively restored in the 18th century and was used as a home until 1843. Uninhabited since then, it's now maintained by Heritage Ireland. It's a lovely little place, surrounded on three sides by the waters of Sheephaven Bay, and on the fourth by a moat carved into the bedrock that forms its foundation. Admission to the grounds is free (castle access is limited).

5.6km (3½ miles) off N56; turnoff signposted just S of Creeslough. heritageireland.ie/visit/places-to-visit/doe-castle. Free admission to the grounds.

Dunfanaghy Workhouse ♥♥ MUSEUM This rather unassuming gray stone building was the scene of great hardship and fear in the 19th century, when it was one of around 100,000 workhouses set up to feed and house the poor during the Great Famine. Their approach was hardly altruistic, however; fearing that merely feeding people would engender a "something-for-nothing" culture in the poor, the authorities decreed that the destitute should perform backbreaking labor in return for their bread. It's estimated that workhouses killed around a million people in Ireland. This particular one housed about 300 inmates. The museum does a good job of describing their daily lives, as well as providing a history of the Famine in this area. One exhibit focuses particularly on a local girl, "Wee Hannah" Herrity, who lived here and survived to tell the tale—which she did, in extensive conversation with a local biographer. Guided tours are available on request (these do not need to be prebooked except in high season).

Just W of Dunfanaghy on N56. dunfanaghyworkhouse.com. ✆ **074/913-6540.** Admission €6 adults; €5 seniors, students, and teens; €20 families. Daily Mar–Dec 10am–5pm. Closed Jan–Feb.

Glebe House & Gallery ♥♥ ART MUSEUM What a pleasant surprise, in such a remote location, to find an art gallery as good as this. This early-19th-century house on the shores of Lake Gartan was once home to noted English painter Derek Hill (1916–2000), who donated the house, along with his personal art collection, to the Irish state in the 1980s. And what a collection—highlights include paintings by Picasso, Renoir, Jack Yeats, and Oskar Kokoschka, along with rare Islamic and Far Eastern art and original William Morris prints. About 300 works are on display from the permanent collection, plus temporary and special exhibitions. The house itself is worth seeing, too—a handsome Regency building, surrounded by pretty woods and gardens, stretching down to the lough. It can only be visited on a guided tour, and space is limited to 15 people at a time.

Signposted from R251, 17km (10½ miles) NE of Letterkenny, Church Hill. glebegallery.ie. ✆ **074/913-7071.** Free gallery admission; house admission €5 adults, €4 seniors, €3 students and children, €13 families. Gallery and house: May–Sept daily 10am–6pm; Oct 11am–5pm; Nov–Mar 9am–4:30pm; last tour 1 hr. before closing. House and gallery closed Fri June, Sept, and Oct. Grounds open year-round.

Glenveagh National Park and Castle ♥♥♥ NATURE SITE/CASTLE This thickly wooded valley is peaceful now, but its history is dark. Nestling at its heart, **Glenveagh Castle** was originally the home of the infamously cruel landlord John George Adair, who evicted scores of struggling tenant farmers in the freezing winter of 1861, leaving many to die, ostensibly because their presence on his estate was ruining his view. If the tale is true, it's divine justice that this estate now belongs to all the people of Ireland. Today the fairy-tale setting includes woodlands, herds of red deer, alpine gardens, a crystal-clear lake, and the highest mountain in Donegal, Mount Errigal. There's a visitor center with a little shop, and

Red deer roam the parklands of Glenveagh National Park.

a charming tearoom in the castle. You can see the castle interior on a self-guided tour. You can also explore the gardens at the castle, take walking trails along the lake, or go on ranger-led walks of the park for €10. Cars must be parked at the entrance, and a shuttle bus can take you up to the castle for €3 round-trip (€2 seniors, students, and children)—but it's also a lovely walk in nice weather.

Church Hill (signposted from R251, 24.4km/15 miles NE of Letterkenny). glenveagh nationalpark.ie. ✆ **01/539-3232.** Free park admission. Castle admission €7 adults; €5 seniors, students and children; €15 families. Visitor center and castle: Mid-Mar to Oct daily 9:15am–5:15pm; Nov–Mar daily 10am–5:15pm; last admission 1 hr. before closing.

Where to Stay in County Donegal

Arnold's Hotel ♥♥ Near the harbor in Dunfanaghy, this simple but pleasant hotel overlooks Sheephaven Bay. Rooms are tastefully decorated, and some have views of the bay and beach, while others overlook the garden. There is also a horseback-riding stable on the hotel grounds. Food options include **Arnolds Restaurant** and **Arnou Café.**

On N56, Dunfanaghy. arnoldshotel.com. ✆ **074/913-6208.** 30 units. €110–€374 double. Breakfast included. Free parking. **Amenities:** Restaurant; bar; Wi-Fi (free). Open April 1–Nov 1; Nov–March weekends only.

Castle Grove House ♥♥ Lancelot "Capability" Brown, the famous English landscaper who virtually invented landscape gardening in the 18th century, laid out the elegant grounds at this inviting white manor house. Inside the decor is avowedly traditional in style, with plenty of period detail and heritage hues. Rooms have antique furnishings (including a four-poster bed in one). All have views of the grounds. Breakfasts are outstanding, and the **Castle Grove restaurant** (see below) is one of the best in the region.

Ballymaleel, off Ramelton Rd., Letterkenny. castlegrove.com. ✆ **074/915-1118.** 15 units. €185–€210 double; €210–€260 suite. Breakfast included. Check website for dinner, bed-and-breakfast packages. Free parking. **Amenities:** Restaurant; bar; room service; Wi-Fi (free).

Rathmullan House ♥♥♥ Right on the edge of Lough Swilly, this delightful mid-18th-century mansion is one of our favorite places to stay in the northwest. The guest lounges are warm and hospitable, with sumptuous period decor and fires crackling in the hearth on cold days. Bedrooms are spacious and extremely comfortable; rooms in the modern extension lose nothing in terms of style and charm to the rooms in the older section of the house. Some have fireplaces and deep roll-top bathtubs. Superior rooms have even more space. Family rooms can work out to be only slightly more expensive than standard doubles. The house has a swimming pool, but you can also take a short stroll down to the beautiful beach. The **Cook & Gardener restaurant ♥♥♥** (see below) is outstanding, deserving its reputation as one of the top places to eat in Donegal; alternatively, in summer months the **Pavilion** serves tasty stone-baked pizza and craft beers outside under a traditional king pole canvas tent in the garden—while the **Cellar Bar** offers seafood dishes in winter months.

On R247 (Chapel Rd.), Rathmullan. rathmullanhouse.com. ✆ **074/915-8188.** 31 units. €200–€330 double. 2-night minimum stay. Breakfast included. Free parking. **Amenities:** 2 restaurants; bar; pool; Wi-Fi (free). Open Wed–Sun only Oct–May.

Where to Eat in County Donegal

Castle Grove ♥♥♥ IRISH This place has won plenty of awards over the years, and it's easy to see why—the food is superb and a top recommendation if you're staying here or nearby. Seasonal menus present classic Irish flavors with a modern edge: asparagus with blood-orange hollandaise, followed by beef filet with onion jam or Barbary duck prepared with honey and clove. **Castle Grove House ♥♥** is also a lovely option for an overnight stay—see above.

Ballymaleel, off Ramelton Rd., Letterkenny. castlegrove.com. ✆ **074/915-1118.** Entrees €24–€36. 3-course set menu €55. Daily 6–9pm; Sun noon–2:30pm.

The Cook & Gardener ♥♥♥ IRISH It's entirely befitting that, as one of the best hotels in Donegal, **Rathmullan House ♥♥♥** (see above) would also have one of its best restaurants. Many of the ingredients have come no greater distance than the house's own gardens, and most of the rest haven't traveled all that much farther. The menu changes daily, but expect delights such as seared Greencastle hake with chargrilled vegetables or free-range Glin Valley roast chicken with shallot puree, cabbage, and bacon.

Rathmullan House hotel, R247 (Chapel Rd.), Rathmullan. rathmullanhouse.com. ✆ **074/915-8188.** Set menu 2 courses €50, 3 courses €60. Daily 6–8:30pm.

Fisk @ the Harbour Bar ♥♥ SEAFOOD This cozy seafood bar next to the Harbour Bar, a country pub in Downings, is a buzzing spot in summer. Owners Tony and Lina are passionate about seafood, and the menu changes regularly. Expect to find dishes like tasty smoked mackerel pate with sourdough crisps, crab mac 'n' cheese, or Atlantic scampi with fries (there's usually a meat and a vegetarian option, too). The seafood bar has just five tables inside, but there's lots of space outside in good weather, and they also serve food in the Harbour Bar's lounge and outdoor area.

At the Harbour Bar, Downings, Co. Donegal. fiskseafoodbar.com. No phone. Entrees €10–€25. July–Aug Tues 5–8pm, Wed–Sat 1–8pm, Sun 1–5pm; Sept–June Thurs 5–8pm, Fri–Sat 1–8pm, Sun 1–5pm.

The Rusty Oven ♥♥ PIZZA Locals love this place, hidden in a courtyard behind Patsy Dan's Pub, for delicious sourdough pizza. The atmosphere is very casual—it's a bit like eating in someone's living room, in a good way. In the summer, dining happens outside, on the bohemian courtyard, beneath the trees. It's best to not be in a hurry, for the pizzas are made at a leisurely pace. But sometimes someone's playing guitar, and everyone sings, and the mood is chill.

Off Market Sq., behind Patsy Dan's Pub, Dunfanaghy. therustyoven.ie. No phone. Pizzas €10–€13. July–Aug daily 5–9:30pm; mid-Mar to Dec Fri–Sun 5–9:30pm. Closed Jan to mid-Mar.

Sports & Outdoor Pursuits in County Donegal

BEACHES **Portnoo** and **Navan** have Blue Flag beaches. **Magheroarty,** near Falcarragh on the northern coast, has a breathtaking beach, unspoiled by crowds or development. The same goes for **Tramore** beach on the western side of Horn Head near Dunfanaghy; you have to hike a short distance, but the rewards are seclusion and miles of creamy sand.

WALKING **Ards Forest Park,** on a peninsula jutting into Sheep Haven Bay about 5.6km (3½ miles) south of Dunfanaghy on N56, has coastal boardwalks running between the beach and sand dunes, with gorgeous sea views, plus inland forest trails.

For a bit more of a challenge, try some scenic hiking on **Horn Head,** signposted off N56 just west of Dunfanaghy. From the concrete lookout point, a trail leads out to a ruined castle on the headland and continues south along a line of impressive quartzite sea cliffs that glitter in the sun.

THE INISHOWEN PENINSULA

Driving around the northernmost point of Ireland is worth doing just so you can say you did. You stood on Malin Head and felt the icy mist come in on a wind that hit you like a fist. You have felt the satisfaction that comes from knowing there is no farther to go.

There is, however, so much more to this land than that. Around the edges are ancient sites, beautiful beaches, and charming villages. At its center are gorgeous views, mountains, and quiet, vivid green pastures. If you are looking to get lost, this is a great place to do it—although the Inishowen Peninsula circuit is very well signposted, with all directions clearly printed in English and Irish.

Exploring the Inishowen Peninsula

The Inishowen (*Inis Eoghain*) Peninsula reaches out from Lough Foyle to the east and Lough Swilly to the west toward **Malin Head ♥♥** (p. 495), its farthest point.

From Donegal Town, take N15 through the scenic Barnesmore Gap—a vast, open stretch through the Blue Stack Mountains—to N13 and on to Letterkenny (*Leitir Ceanainn*), the largest town in County Donegal, set on a hillside overlooking Lough Swilly. From there, head north on N13, then east on R238, to Buncrana, an excellent place to rest and have a meal. Near Buncrana are a couple of worthwhile stops—**Fort Dunree Military Museum ♥♥** (see below) to the north, and the much more ancient hilltop fort known as **Grianan of Aileach ♥** (see below), a short drive south of Buncrana.

Ascend a corkscrew road (R238) from Buncrana through the Gap of Mamore, a mountain pass that rises 240m (787 ft.). Head east to the beach town of Ballyliffin for golf and surfing, and from here, take a detour for the fascinating **Doagh Famine Village ♥♥♥** (see below). Passing the cute village of Malin (*Málainn*), with its picturesque stone bridge and village green, it's another 20-minute drive north on R242 to Malin Head (*Cionn Mhélanna*), for stunning coastal views from Ireland's most northerly point (p. 495).

From Malin Head, head back on R242/238 to **Culdaff (*Cúil Dabhcha*),** a sleepy waterfront village with a pretty beach. On its main street, the Clonca Church is a solid 17th-century structure with a fine carved high cross. The coastal road leads from here to picturesque **Inishowen Head** (follow signs off the R241 onto a side road, follow that to its end, and walk the rest of the way to the headland). It's eerily isolated, but the views are stupendous—on clear days, you can see all the way to the Antrim Coast.

Continuing around the peninsula, follow coastal road R241 southwest to **Greencastle (*An Cáisleá Nua*),** site of the quirky **Inishowen Maritime Museum & Planetarium ♥♥** (see below).

Doagh Famine Village ♥♥♥ MUSEUM A visit here takes you on a fascinating and sometimes humorous journey through Irish history and culture. The village comprises original Irish thatched cottages as they would have looked during the 1840s and includes everything from an Irish wake and eviction scene to a hedge school and haunted rooms. It's all the creation of Pat Doherty, who built this village around his own family history. It's a fantastic way to understand the different periods of Irish history and worth the drive—even the views are stunning. A short, guided tour includes tea and scones and a shot of *poitín* (p. 421) and then free time to explore (allow 2 hr. for the visit). At Christmas (Nov 26–Dec 22, daily 5–9pm), Pat transforms the village into "Donegal Lapland," with all sorts of magical characters, Santa's Castle, and a toy factory (tickets €18.50).

Doagh Island, Ballyliffin, Inishowen, Co. Donegal. doaghfaminevillage.com. ✆ **086/846-4749.** Admission €13.50 adults; €7 children 4–16; free for children 3 and under. Mid-Mar to mid-Oct daily 10am–5pm; guided tours from 10:30am. Last admission 4pm.

Fort Dunree Military Museum ♥♥ MUSEUM Rising precipitously from the cliffs beside Lough Swilly, this impressive-looking fort was constructed as a defensive lookout in the event of a French invasion during the Napoleonic Wars. It later became part of Irish sea defenses against German invasion during World War I. Neither came, and today Dunree serves as an informative museum. Spread partly through subsurface bunkers, the exhibitions tell the history of the fort, and of the local

Cannon photo op at Fort Dunree, built during the Napoleonic Wars.

area as a whole. It also serves as the starting point for scenic walks around Dunree Point along three recommended walking paths. The museum has a handy coffee shop overlooking Lough Swilly.

Signposted on the coast road, about 11km (7 miles) N of Buncrana, Co. Donegal. fortdunree.com. ✆ **074/936-1817.** Admission €8 adults; €6 seniors and children; €16 families. Daily 10:30am–4:30pm.

Grianan of Aileach ♥ ANCIENT SITE Built high atop a hill outside the village of Burt, this beautifully preserved ring fort can be seen from miles away, a crown made of stone. Experts think the existing structure was built in the 6th or 7th century A.D., although the site had already been used for many centuries by then. There's evidence it may have originally been a temple of the sun as long ago as 1700 B.C. From the mid–5th century A.D. to the early 12th century, this was the seat of the kingdom of Aileach, home to the O'Neills, the chieftains of this area. The view from the top is spectacular. The waters of the two sea inlets—Lough Swilly and Lough Foyle—sparkle in the distance, and you can make out the shape of the entire peninsula. The round fort is made of stone without mortar; the walls are terraced, giving access to the top.

Signposted on N13, behind the town of Burt, about 16km (10 miles) S of Buncrana. discoverireland.ie/donegal/grianan-of-aileach. No phone. Free admission. Mid-June to Sept daily 9am–9pm; Oct to mid-June daily 9am–7pm.

Inishowen Maritime Museum & Planetarium ♥♥ MUSEUM/PLANETARIUM Overlooking Lough Foyle, this small but engaging museum packs all it can into the Old Coastguard building in the harbor town of Greencastle. It follows the town's maritime history from the armadas of the 16th century through emigration to the modern-day lifeboat crews and their selflessly heroic work. Inside the planetarium is a full-dome digital theater presenting more or less hourly shows such as "Sea Monsters—A Prehistoric Adventure" and "Dynamic Earth." The museum also has a small shop and cafe.

The Harbour, Greencastle. inishowenmaritime.com. ✆ **074/938-1363.** Museum only: €6 adults; €5 seniors and students; €4 children. Museum plus planetarium: €12 adults; €10 seniors and students; €8 children. May–Aug Mon–Sat 10am–5:30pm, Sun noon–5pm, last show 3pm, last admission 4:30pm; Sept–Apr Mon–Fri 10:30am–4pm, last admission 3:30pm.

Malin Head *(Cionn Mhélanna)* ♥♥ NATURE SITE On this stunning promontory, the road goes no farther. This is Ireland's most northerly point. Even on a sunny day, the wind often howls, and temperatures can be a few degrees colder than just a few miles south. To reach Malin Head, take R242 north until it turns into a small, unnamed road. Following the few signs, meander past a small cluster of houses until you reach rocky **Banba's Crown (*Fíorcheann Éireann*),** the farthest point of the headland. Winds permitting, you can even wander down to the edge of the land and catch a glimpse of some old concrete huts built in World War II as

Hell's Hole at Malin Head.

lookout points. To the west of them is the dramatically named **Hell's Hole,** a natural land formation where waves crash deafeningly against the craggy shore. To the east, a path leads to a hermit's cave known as the **Wee House of Malin.** A little information board explains all this—but you may be too busy gazing at the incredible view to notice. discoverireland.ie/donegal/malin-head.

Where to Stay on the Inishowen Peninsula

Ballyliffin Lodge ♥♥ With impressive views of **Malin Head** (see above), this hotel is a relaxing place to stay. Bedrooms, which take full advantage of the gorgeous views, are nice and spacious, with muted, autumnal decor. The hotel can help organize plenty of activities, from horseback riding to surfing and golf. The in-house spa, **Rock Crystal,** provides a welcome respite at the end of a long day's travel, with prices that are a lot more reasonable than they would be in an equivalent place in a more visited part of the country.

Shore Rd., Ballyliffin. ballyliffinlodge.com. ✆ **074/937-8200.** 40 units. €140–€305 double. **Amenities:** Restaurant; bar; gym; pool; room service; spa; Wi-Fi (free).

Inishowen Gateway ♥ This large, modern hotel is a particularly appealing choice for families. It overlooks Lough Swilly—a dramatic view that's either glorious in sunshine or stark and moody in the rain. Guest rooms are basic and quite small, but they tick enough boxes as long as you're not craving anything too fancy. This place has excellent facilities for kids—a supervised play area, Planet Active, and plenty to keep the little ones busy, including game tables, video games, and soft play for younger kids. If you book a family room package, you even get perks such as a free children's craft workshop for each child, movie nights, and so on. ***Tip:*** Just make sure you ask for a room away from the bar, as it can get a little noisy.

Railway Rd., Buncrana. inishowengateway.com. ✆ **074/936-1144.** 80 units. €95–€216 double. Breakfast included. Free parking. **Amenities:** Restaurant; bar; gym; pool; spa; Wi-Fi (free).

Riversdale Country House ♥♥ This gorgeously restored farmhouse B&B 2km (1¼ miles) from Carndonagh has a peaceful country setting and a family-friendly atmosphere. The B&B is on a working farm so you can get a taste of farm life with a pond of ducks and geese, plus donkeys, cows, and sometimes calves in the fields. Rooms are spacious and comfortable, breakfasts are filling, and the hosts will help you plan what to see and do in the area.

Carndonagh. riversdalecountryhouse.ie. ✆ **074/937-4017.** 3 units. €85 double. Breakfast included. Free parking. **Amenities:** Wi-Fi (free).

Where to Eat on the Inishowen Peninsula

Nancy's Barn ♥♥♥ CAFE With its red shutters and gray stone walls, this old barn looks so pretty from the outside that on a sunny day, you may stop to take a picture and end up having lunch. You'll be glad you did. Nancy's serves delicious sandwiches, organic salads, and other light meals. Don't miss their chowder, which is famous for miles—chef Kieran Doherty was crowned World Seafood Chowder Champion in 2017. They also bake all their own breads, cakes, and scones, and sell pottery and other bits and pieces to take home.

On the main road through Ballyliffin. nancysbarn.ie. ✆ **074/937-6556.** Entrees €11–€18. Mon–Fri 9am–4pm; Sat–Sun 9am–5pm.

The Rusty Nail ♥♥ GASTROPUB This is one of those pubs out in the middle of nowhere, where, when you open the door, you are greeted with an open fire and maybe even a live music session. The rear part is the gastropub with tasty favorites like steaks, 6-ounce beef burgers, beer-battered cod with caper mayo, and cornfed chicken. They also do pizzas with ingredients like Fivemiletown goat's cheese.

Crossconnell, Clonmany. facebook.com/p/The-Rusty-Nail-Crossconnell-100057551045833. ✆ **0374/937-6116.** Entrees €17–€23 Thurs–Mon 5–9pm.

Ubiquitous ♥♥ IRISH If you're looking for a filling dinner and a friendly welcome, the "Ubiq" on the main street in Buncrana does both well. Dishes are the standard Irish fare, with plenty of meat and seafood options—look for entrees like braised lamb shank with celeriac and thyme mash; pan-fried hake with chickpeas and chorizo; or a 10-ounce rib-eye steak, with tasty sides like truffle and Parmesan fries. Prices are reasonable, and there's a good-value early-bird menu Wednesday through Friday (€21.50 two courses, €25.50 three).

47 Main St Upper, Buncrana. ubiqrestaurant.com. ✆ **074/932-2320.** Main courses €16–€24. Mon–Fri 4–8:45pm; Sat noon–9pm; Sun noon–8pm.

A round of seaside golf at the Ballyliffin Golf Club.

Sports & Outdoor Pursuits in the Inishowen Peninsula

GOLF A definite center for golf in Ireland, the Inishowen Peninsula has four 18-hole golf courses. Two are at **Ballyliffin Golf Club,** Ballyliffin (ballyliffingolfclub.com; ✆ **074/937-6119**). Greens fees are €240 to €260. The **North West Golf Club,** Fahan, Buncrana (northwestgolfclub.com; ✆ **074/936-1715**), founded in 1890, is a par-69 seaside course with greens fees of €75 (Nov–Mar) and €150 (Apr–Oct). **Greencastle Golf Course** in Greencastle (greencastlegolfclub.com; ✆ **074/938-1013**) is a par-69 parkland course with greens fees of around €50 (Mon–Fri) and €60 (Sat–Sun).

KAYAKING If you're feeling adventurous, **Inish Adventures** (inishad ventures.com; ✆ **074/938-5903**) will take you kayaking along some of Inishowen's most scenic coastline around Moville or under Fort Dunree at Dunree Head, where you get to see sea caves and bird life. The 3-hour trips take place Wednesday to Saturday between Easter and the end of September at 9:30am or 1:30pm and cost €50.

SURFING The Inishowen Peninsula's northwest coast presents some of Europe's most challenging surfing conditions. For information and classes, contact the **Inishowen Surf School,** Hill Road, Buncrana (inishowen surfschool.ie; ✆ **086/358-8824**).

BELFAST

14

The beautiful and vibrant six counties of Northern Ireland, which are part of the United Kingdom, are all the more fascinating for their complex history. At the epicenter is Belfast, the capital of Northern Ireland—a curious combination of faded grandeur and forward-looking optimism. Belfast boomed in the 19th century as prosperity flowed from its vast textile and shipbuilding industries. The 20th century was not so kind to the city, which spent decades in decline, riven with political divisions and terrorism. But an entire generation has grown up since those troubled years ended in the 1990s, and with them, Belfast has forged a new identity, complete with an energetic art and food scene.

The old Belfast is still here—both in its grand Victorian buildings and some old-school, never-the-twain-shall-meet Protestant and Catholic neighborhoods. But new developments signal change and renewal, such as the Titanic Quarter, with its sleek museums and modern visitor attractions, and the opening of two distilleries in historic buildings. This is a lively, funky, youthful, and complicated city. Come and let it surprise you.

ESSENTIALS

Arriving

BY BUS **Ulsterbus** (translink.co.uk; ✆ **028/9066-6630**) runs buses from Dublin to Belfast and towns across Northern Ireland. In Belfast, the main bus station is **Europa Bus Centre** on Glengall Street.

BY CAR Driving from Dublin to Belfast is easy; just go north up the M1 motorway. From Dublin Airport, the journey takes about 90 minutes in good traffic. From Sligo Town, take N16 and A4 west; from there it's 200km (124 miles), about 2½ hours.

BY PLANE Belfast has two airports: **Belfast International (BFS;** belfast airport.com; ✆ **028/9448-4848**) and **George Best Belfast City Airport (BHD;** belfastcityairport.com; ✆ **028/9093-9093**). **Aer Lingus** (aer lingus.com; ✆ **01/761-7834**), **British Airways** (ba.com; ✆ **0344/493-0787** in the U.K.), and **easyJet** (easyjet.com; ✆ **0330/551-5151** in the U.K.) operate regular scheduled flights from Britain to Belfast. Most intercontinental routes require a change in London or Manchester. You can also fly direct to Belfast from several European cities. If you fly into

PREVIOUS PAGE: **Belfast City Hall, testament to the city's grand industrial past.**

Dublin Airport (p. 81), you can take an express bus to Belfast run by either **Dublin Express** (dublinexpress.ie; ✆ **01/903-9508**) or **AirCoach** (aircoach.ie; ✆ **01/844-7118**). The trip takes just under 2 hours.

BY TRAIN The main station is **Belfast Grand Central Station** and the city is also served by Lanyon Place Station on East Bridge Street. Contact **Translink** (translink.co.uk; ✆ **028/9066-6630**) for tickets. The journey from Dublin takes about 2 hours, 10 minutes; book on translink.co.uk or irishrail.ie.

[Fast FACTS] BELFAST

ATMs/Banks ATMs are easy to find in central Belfast. Several banks around Donegall Square include **Ulster Bank** (✆ **0345/948-2222**) and **Bank of Ireland** (✆ **028/9024-4901**).

Currency As part of the United Kingdom, Northern Ireland uses the **pound sterling,** not the euro. The cheapest way to get local currency is to use an ATM. The pound/euro exchange rate fluctuates, but it currently hovers between €1.14 and €1.18.

Dentists For dental emergencies, your hotel can contact a dentist for you. Otherwise, you could try **Paste Dental,** 23 Dublin Rd. (✆ **028/9032-5345**), or **Lisburn Road Dental Clinic,** 424 Lisburn Rd. (✆ **028/9038-2262**).

Doctors For medical emergencies, dial ✆ **999.** For non-emergencies, your hotel can call you a doctor. Otherwise, there's **Ormeau Health Centre,** 120 Ormeau Rd. (✆ **028/9032-6030**), or the **Crumlin Road Health Centre,** 94–100 Crumlin Rd. (✆ **028/9074-1188**).

Emergencies For police, fire, or other emergencies, dial ✆ **999.**

Pharmacies Belfast has branches of **Boots the Chemist** at 35–47 Donegall Place (✆ **028/9024-2332**) and 17–21 Great Northern Mall (✆ **028/9031-0530**).

Post Offices Main branches in Belfast include 16 Howard St. and 12–16 Bridge St.

Taxis You can catch a taxi at the stand in front of City Hall. Alternatively, try phoning **Value Cabs** (✆ **028/9080-9080**), **Courtesy Cabs** (✆ **028/9032-9988**), or **Gransha Taxis** (✆ **028/9060-2092**).

Visitor Information

The main tourist information center for the city is the **Visit Belfast Welcome Centre** at 9 Donegall Square, BT1 5GJ (visitbelfast.com; ✆ **028/9024-6609**). It's open Monday to Saturday from 9am until 5:30pm (until 6:30pm July–Aug) and Sunday from 11am to 4pm. The staff can help book accommodations, tours, and tickets in the city; they also have free Wi-Fi and a left-luggage facility. A smaller visitor information point at Belfast International Airport can assist with onward transport and tour tickets (✆ **028/9448-4677**).

City Layout

Small and easily traversed, central Belfast is best explored by walking. The main tourist districts are as follows.

VISITING NORTHERN IRELAND: f.a.q.

What is Northern Ireland? It's still part of Ireland, right?

Yes—and no. It's a part of the island of Ireland, but not the Republic of Ireland.

I'm confused. Is it a different country or not?

Bear with us—this is complicated. Northern Ireland is part of the United Kingdom. It has been a separate entity from the rest of Ireland since 1921. If "entity" sounds a little vague, that's because—get this—there isn't even an official term to describe what Northern Ireland is. (Trust us, we checked.) It's referred to, variously, as a country, a nation, a region, and a province. Note, however, that your mobile phone company will treat Northern Ireland as the U.K., so you may find yourself hit with extra roaming charges. Also, check that your travel insurance and any car-rental agreements are equally valid in Northern Ireland.

Will I need to show my passport at the border crossing?

No, because there really isn't a border crossing. In fact, it can be hard to tell when you've entered Northern Ireland—except that the road signs change from miles to kilometers (signs around the border usually show both) and your phone network or roaming network may change.

What are those letters and numbers at the end of Northern Irish addresses?

They're British-style postal codes, and almost every address in Northern Ireland has one. This is actually a big advantage if you're driving, as it makes GPS navigation much easier.

Does Northern Ireland use the euro?

No. The currency in Northern Ireland is the **British pound (sterling).** In practice, euros are accepted in some border areas, at tourist attractions and hotels; however, you may be given change in pounds. (And just try using those pounds in the rest of Ireland!) And if you're traveling on to Britain, be aware that Northern Irish pounds look completely different, and many British businesses won't accept them. Any bank in England, however, will change Northern Irish pounds to English pounds for free.

What about Brexit? Has that changed anything?

Everything and nothing. The U.K. left the E.U. in January 2020, and because it is part of the United Kingdom, Northern Ireland had to leave the E.U. as well. To avoid a hard border between Northern Ireland and the Republic of Ireland, however, Northern Ireland still adheres to E.U. Customs rules—an economic arrangement that has caused tension politically, but should not affect tourists or visitors.

CATHEDRAL QUARTER North of Donegall Square, surrounding Donegall Street, **St. Anne's Cathedral** (p. 512) presides over this area with a mix of vast Victorian warehouses and more modern buildings. The district has quite a lively feel, with plenty of interesting restaurants, cafes, and shops.

CITY CENTER Dominated by the impressive, domed City Hall (p. 506), the bustling **Donegall Square** area is the best place for shopping, particularly along **Donegall Place,** which extends north from the square, onto **Royal Avenue. Bedford Street,** which travels south from Donegall Square, becomes **Dublin Road,** which leads to:

GOLDEN MILE Southwest of Donegall Square, the stretch of **Great Victoria Street** leading to Bradbury Place is the city's best address for restaurants and pubs, although it's a bit hyperbolically named. As one local said to us, "It's not a mile and it's not golden. But it's nice enough."

TITANIC QUARTER Northeast of the city center, the entire Belfast Harbour area has been redeveloped as the Titanic Quarter. Attractions include **Titanic Belfast** (p. 510), the **SS *Nomadic*** (p. 510), **Titanic Distillers at Thompson Dock** (p. 511), and the **HMS *Caroline*** (p. 510).

UNIVERSITY QUARTER The leafy area around **Queen's University** (p. 513), also known as the Queen's Quarter, contains the **Botanic Gardens** (p. 504), Ulster Museum (p. 509), and art galleries as well as a buzzing nightlife scene.

Getting Around

BY BIKE Belfast has a public bike-sharing system. "Belfast Bikes" are available at 50 unmanned rental stations around the city. You can set up an account at the station's terminal, or by downloading the **Nextbike** app for your phone. When you're done, simply return the bike to any station. Prices start at £1 per half-hour. See **belfastbikes.co.uk** for details.

BY BUS **Metro** (translink.co.uk; ✆ **028/9066-6630**) city buses depart from Donegall Square East, West, and North, plus Upper Queen Street, Wellington Place, Chichester Street, and Castle Street, and from bus stops throughout the city. The cheapest way to use the buses/gliders is to use the **mLink** app, which allows unlimited travel all day for £4 for adults or £2 for children. You can also buy a **Metro/Glider dayLink** ticket on board or from the Visit Belfast Welcome Centre (p. 501), which costs £5 adults or £3 children.

BY CAR If you've brought a **car** into Belfast, it's best to leave it parked and take public transport or walk. If you must drive and want to park downtown, look for a blue P sign that shows a parking lot, or buy a pay-and-display ticket if you are parking in a designated street parking zone. You can buy a ticket with cash at a machine or via the **JustPark.com** website or app. No parking is allowed in "control zones," marked by pink-and-yellow signs.

BY TAXI **Taxis** are available at all main rail stations, ports, and airports, and in front of City Hall. You can hail a taxi on the street, although it rarely takes long for a cab to arrive if you call (see "Taxis" in Fast Facts, p. 501).

EXPLORING BELFAST

Belfast's wealthy past has left the city with some handsome industrial remnants. However, it's the more troubled, 20th-century Belfast that many visitors find most intriguing, and a **Black Taxi Tour** ♥♥♥ (p. 506) is a unique way to explore that history. Meanwhile, there's a whole mini-industry of attractions related to the most famous shipwreck in history. Because the SS *Titanic* was built in Belfast—a curious symbol of pride for natives of this city—shipwreck aficionados (aka "Titanoraks") are drawn to the bold **Titanic Belfast** museum (p. 510) and the **Titanic's Dock & Pumphouse** (p. 511) in the newly regenerated harbor district.

Top Attractions

Belfast Botanic Gardens & Palm House ♥♥ GARDENS Dating from 1828, these gardens were first laid out by the Belfast Botanic and Horticultural Society, but their most important feature came along 10 years later, when noted Belfast architect Charles Lanyon designed the beautiful glass-and-cast-iron conservatory. Now known as the Palm House, this curvilinear Victorian glasshouse contains an excellent variety of tropical plants, including sugarcane, coffee, cinnamon, banana, aloe, ivory nut, rubber, bamboo, guava, and birds of paradise. The Tropical Ravine, which first opened in 1889, has everything from ferns to giant waterlilies. If the weather's fine, stroll in the outdoor rose gardens, which date back to 1927. The **Ulster Museum** (p. 509) is also on the grounds. College Park, Botanic Ave., BT7 1LP. belfastcity.gov.uk/botanicgardens. ✆ **028/9031-4762.** Free admission. Palm House daily 10am–4:30pm; Tropical Ravine daily 10am–5pm; gardens 7:30am–dusk (hours vary; call ahead or check online).

The Victorian-era Palm House, centerpiece of the Belfast Botanic Gardens.

Belfast Attractions
To Carrickfergus
The Great Light, Maritime Mile
Slipways
Hamilton Dock Caisson
Belfast Harbour Marina
River Lagan
Queens Rd.
Hamilton Rd.
Sydenham Rd.
Antrim Rd.
Westlink
A12
North Queen St.
York St.
Nelson St.
Corporation St.
Donegall St.
Gt. Patrick St.
Carrick Hill
Kent St.
Peter's Hill
Univ. of Ulster
St. Anne's Cathedral
Smithfield Market
Castle Court Center
Lagan Bridge
M3
Queen Elizabeth II Bridge
Queen's Bridge
Ann St.
High St.
Castle St.
Victoria Square
Chichester St.
Wellington Pl.
City Hall
Donegall Sq. S.
May St.
Waterfront Hall
East Bridge St.
Central Station
Hamilton St.
Gt. Victoria Street Station
Ormeau Ave.
McAuley St.
Donegall Pass
Botanic Station
Vernon St.
McClure St.
Cromwell Rd.
Cooke St.
University St.
Fitzroy Ave.
Rugby Ave.
Agincourt Ave.
Ormeau Rd.
Ormeau Rd. Bridge
Ormeau Embankment
Ormeau Park
Botanic Gardens
NORTHERN IRELAND
Belfast
Galway
Dublin
REPUBLIC OF IRELAND
Cork
To Cultra
Information
0 300 yds
0 300 m
Belfast Botanic Gardens & Palm House 15
Belfast Castle 6
Belfast Cathedral 8
Belfast Zoo 6
Cave Hill Country Park 6
City Hall 9
Crown Liquor Saloon 11
Crumlin Road Gaol 7
Cultúrlann McAdam Ó Flaich 12
HMS Caroline 2
McConnell's Distillery 7
Queen's University 13
St. George's Market 10
SS Nomadic 4
Titanic Belfast 3
Titanic Distillers at Thompson Dock 1
Ulster Museum 14
W5/Odyssey Complex 5

Belfast street murals can be viewed via open-top bus tours or Black Taxi Tours.

Black Taxi Tour ♥♥♥ TOUR For many years, Belfast was best known for its most conflicted neighborhoods, where in the 1970s and '80s protest and violence occurred daily. Peace has held on the Catholic Falls Road and its nearby parallel, the Protestant Shankill Road, since the Good Friday Agreement of 1998, and now locals from both communities tell of their past experiences via tours conducted in black taxicabs. The Black Taxi Tour company's **Belfast Political & Mural** tour is by far the best option. Tours take you through the neighborhoods, past the barbed wire, towering "peace walls" dividing communities, and partisan murals, as guides explain their significance. Drivers, who are all locals, are relaxed, patient, and unbiased, with a talent for explaining this complicated history to outsiders in an easy and engaging way. Tours aren't just limited to politics; the guides will also take you to see the *Titanic* shipyard or on a day-long tour to see the locations where *Game of Thrones* was filmed (one of many such tours that have sprung up; see box on p. 546). The standard tour lasts about 90 minutes, and guides will pick you up and drop you off anywhere in the city.

belfasttours.com. ✆ **028/9064-2264.** Political and Mural Tour £70 for up to 2 passengers, then £35 for each additional passenger, up to 8 people.

City Hall ♥♥ ARCHITECTURAL SITE The clearest remaining testament to the city's grand industrial past, this domed building of granite, marble, and stained glass dominates central Belfast. Built in classical Renaissance style in 1906, it has white Portland stone walls and a soft green copper dome. Several statues dot the grounds, including a

the art of conflict: **BELFAST'S STREET MURALS**

Painted by amateur artists—albeit very talented ones—the huge street murals in West Belfast tell tales of history, strife, anger, or peace. The densest concentration is around the **Falls and Shankill roads**—the epicenter of the conflict during the Troubles, from the late 1960s to the mid-1990s. The Falls Road is staunchly Catholic and Republican (largely those who want Ireland united as a single country). Shankill, just half a mile away, is resolutely Protestant and Loyalist (those who want Northern Ireland to remain part of the United Kingdom).

While all are deeply political, there is a noticeable difference in the tone of these murals. Those on the Falls Road tend to be about solidarity with the downtrodden (and not just in Ireland—you'll see murals about war and oppression in other parts of the world, too). By contrast, the Shankill murals are more strident, featuring more violent and threatening imagery, although some of the most offensive examples were removed a few years ago.

Perhaps the most famous political mural in Ireland, if not the world, is on the corner of Falls Road and Sevastopol Street: a mural of the late hunger striker **Bobby Sands** (1954–81).

Locals in all districts are very proud of their murals and are fine with visitors taking photos. Still, you should exercise the usual caution you would in any rough city neighborhood. It's best to steer clear of these parts of town on **parade days**—ostensibly celebratory events, they tend toward displays of nationalism, erupting into street violence. The biggest, and most controversial, is the Protestant "Orange Order" parade on July 12 (marking the Battle of the Boyne in 1690, which was basically Year Zero for the big sectarian divide in Ireland; see p. 30). Any parades likely to cause trouble are well covered by the local media, so it's easy to know when one is coming up. From time to time there are P.R.–led attempts to sanitize these events, promoting them as inclusive and celebratory, but don't buy it. They remain contentious and should be avoided—plan your visit so that it does not coincide with parade dates.

The best, safest, and certainly most informative way to see the murals is to take a **Black Taxi Tour** ♥♥♥ (p. 506). The tours are a real Belfast highlight and could hardly be more convenient—the drivers will pick you up at your hotel and drop you off anywhere you like in the city.

Street art of a less political nature has also begun popping up in the city in recent years, particularly around the Cathedral Quarter. Two-hour **Seedhead Street Art Walking Tours** (seedheadarts.com) are led by local artists who will show you the latest masterpieces; tours run Sundays at noon and cost £12.

grim-faced Queen Victoria, who stands out front looking as if she wished she were anywhere else. Bronze figures around her represent the textile and shipbuilding industries that powered Belfast's success. There's also a memorial to the victims of the *Titanic* disaster. Inside the building, the elaborate entry hall is heavy with marble but lightened by stained glass and a rotunda with a painted ceiling. A 16-room exhibition center hosts displays on the city and its history and guided tours offer a surprisingly absorbing insight into the building's history.

Donegall Sq. North, BT1 5GS. belfastcity.gov.uk/cityhall. ✆ **028/9032-0202.** Free admission. City Hall building Mon–Fri 9:30am–5pm, Sat–Sun 10am–5pm; grounds May–Sept 7am–9pm, Oct–Apr 7am–7pm. Closed mid-Nov to mid-Jan for Christmas market. Guided tours £6 adults, free for children; Mon–Fri 11am, 2 and 3pm; Sat–Sun noon, 2, 3, and 4pm.

Crown Liquor Saloon ♥♥♥ ARCHITECTURAL SITE/PUB Easily the most impressive Victorian pub in the city, and possibly the best building in Belfast, the Crown Liquor Saloon piles on the atmosphere. The old "gin palace" owes its ornate appearance to Italian workers who came to Ireland in the late 19th century to work on churches but ended up building this, in 1873. Some of the finer features definitely have something ecclesiastical about them, from the stained glass in the windows to the pewlike "snugs," their elaborately carved doors designed to shield the more refined class of Victorians from their fellow drinkers. Floors are intricately tiled, and the ceiling is gorgeous hammered copper. This place was considered so important to the iconography of Belfast that it was actually bought for the nation by the National Trust in the 1970s, ensuring its impeccable upkeep while it continues to run as a working pub.

46 Great Victoria St., BT2 7BA. nicholsonspubs.co.uk/thecrownliquorsaloonbelfast. ✆ **028/9024-3187.** Mon–Sat 11:30am–midnight; Sun 12:30pm–midnight.

Crumlin Road Gaol ♥♥ HISTORIC SITE From 1846 until its closure 150 years later, Crumlin Road Gaol (known as "The Crum") was one of the most notorious prisons in Northern Ireland. Improbable though it sounds, the Crum is now used as a conference center and wedding venue (festive!) and is also home to a distillery (see below), although the original structure has been excellently preserved. The building brings to mind the popular image of a Victorian-era prison, with its forbidding, fortresslike exterior and row upon row of cells. An informative 90-minute tour takes you around the building, filling in some fascinating details about prison life. It would take a hard person indeed not to shudder as you walk down the claustrophobic underground tunnel connecting to the old courthouse across the street, or stand inside the condemned cell from which prisoners made their final journeys until 1961.

53–55 Crumlin Rd., BT14 6ST. crumlinroadgaol.com. ✆ **028/9074-1500.** Admission £14.50 adults; £13 seniors and students; £8 children 5–15; free for children 4 and under; £40 families. Book online for discounts. Daily 10am–6pm (last admission 4pm).

McConnell's Distillery ♥♥ DISTILLERY You don't usually find three huge copper stills in an old prison (the roof was taken off to lower them in), but on a tour of this distillery in the A-wing of Crumlin Road Gaol, you can see the stills in action and learn about the recent revival of distilling in Belfast. The original McConnell's whisky (with no "e") dates back to 1776, but the distillery closed down in 1938. The brand was revived in 2016, and production moved here in 2024. The guided tour focuses on the whisky, so it's best to take a separate tour of the Gaol (see above) if you are interested in the prison's history. A 1-hour distillery tour ends with a tasting of three whiskies. The Connoisseur tour includes tastings of a cask-strength and 20-year-old whisky, and the cocktail-making experience is a fun hands-on class where you get to make two cocktails.

Crumlin Road Gaol, 53–55 Crumlin Rd., BT14 6ST. intl.mcconnellsirishwhisky.com. ✆ **028/9590-2929.** Tues–Sun 9:30am–5pm. Guided tour £25 adults, £20 alcohol-free, £15 children 10–18; tours hourly noon–6pm. Connoisseur tour £49; Thurs–Sat 4pm. Cocktail experience £45 (minimum 4 people); Fri–Sat 1 and 6pm. Times may change so check when booking.

Shopping bustle under the arches of St. George's Market.

St. George's Market ♥♥ INDOOR MARKET Built in 1896, the iron-and-glass **St. George's Market** has a number of different street markets with live music and food and craft stalls. It's a fun, vibrant place to visit on weekends. On Friday, the **Variety Market** (8am–2pm) is packed with 200 stalls of fresh produce, antiques, clothing, and bric-a-brac. On Saturdays, the **City Food & Craft Market** (9am–3pm) specializes in artisan foods, with plenty of tempting fresh snacks on offer, plus an assortment of local crafts. The **Sunday Market** (10am–4pm) is a happy combination of the two, although the balance tends to be in favor of crafts. It's a great place for coffee, good eats, and local atmosphere.

12–20 E. Bridge St., BT1 3NQ. belfastcity.gov.uk/things-to-do/markets/st-george-s-market. ✆ **028/9043-5704.**

Ulster Museum ♥♥♥ MUSEUM One of Ireland's best museums, the Ulster Museum has a comprehensive collection of everything from dinosaur bones and prehistoric artifacts to art and other treasures from Ireland and around the world. Highlights include 16th- to 18th-century Dutch and Italian paintings; a hoard of priceless 16th-century Spanish jewelry, recovered off the coast near Belfast in the 1960s; and clothes, textiles, and ceramics from Asia and Africa. The "Life and Death in Ancient Egypt" permanent exhibit has about 2,000 artifacts from Pharaonic times, as well as items from ancient Mesopotamia, Rome, and Greece.

At the Botanic Gardens, BT9 5AB. nmni.com/um. ✆ **028/9044-0000.** Free admission. Tues–Sun 10am–5pm.

Top Attractions in the Titanic Quarter

HMS *Caroline* ♥♥ SHIP The last surviving ship of the Battle of Jutland (1916), this World War I–era ship is now permanently moored in Belfast's Titanic Quarter. It has been carefully restored and offers a glimpse into what life was like onboard. You can take a tour to see the captain's quarters, the cabins where the crew slept and ate, and the engine room, as well as learning all about the ship's roles over the years. In the Drill Hall, a movie about the Battle of Jutland explains the events of the famous battle between Britain and Germany for control of the North Sea. **Titanic Distillers at Thompson Dock** (p. 511) is next door.

Alexandra Dock, Queens Rd., BT3 9DT. hmscaroline.co.uk. ✆ **023/9289-1370.** Admission £11 adults; £10 seniors; £9 children 5–15; free for children 4 and under; £22–£26 families. Tours at 10 and 11:30am, and 1:30 and 3pm. Fri–Sun 10am–4:30pm (daily July–Aug). Last admission 1 hr. before closing.

SS *Nomadic* ♥♥ SHIP The last working ship in the White Star Line fleet, the *Nomadic* was built in Belfast as a tender to the most famous ocean liner in history—the ill-fated SS *Titanic.* (Tenders were small steamships that ferried passengers and supplies to and from the oceangoing behemoths.) After seeing action in both world wars—first press-ganged into service by the French navy, then used by the British to evacuate—*Nomadic* was given a decade-long restoration and returned to her original 1911 glory. You can tour the vessel, from the cramped and claustrophobic crew quarters to the bridge and upper deck. Daily ticket numbers are limited due to space and are timed—book in advance.

Hamilton Dock, Queens Rd., BT3 9DT. nomadicbelfast.com. ✆ **028/9076-6386.** Admission (includes entry to Titanic Belfast) £25 adults; £19 seniors and students (Mon–Fri only); £11 children 5–15; free for children 4 and under; £62 families. Daily June 10am–6:30pm; July–Aug 10am–7pm; Apr–May and Sept–Oct 10am–5:30pm; Nov–Dec 11am–4:30pm; Jan 11am–4pm; mid-Feb to Mar 11am–5pm. Last admission 30 min. before closing.

Titanic Belfast ♥♥♥ MUSEUM This ambitious and impressive museum, which opened to huge fanfare in 2012 and was upgraded in 2022, tells the story of the *Titanic* in revelatory detail. Located next to the site where the doomed vessel was built, the angular aluminum-clad frontage juts out in four directions at the height of the ship's actual bow. You can explore the museum yourself or take an hour-long "Discovery Tour" of its innovative galleries.

Titanic Belfast discovery tour.

Exhibitions cover everything from the *Titanic*'s construction to her triumphant launch, disastrous sinking, and the lasting cultural phenomenon that rose in her wake. A ride takes you on a virtual tour of the shipyard to see how *Titanic* and her sister ship, *Olympic,* were built. In a split-level gallery you can even "visit" the wreck. The last few galleries deal with the aftermath of the sinking, the survivors, and the science behind Robert Ballard's undersea search for the wreck. Needless to say, an extremely well-stocked gift shop is at the end. Crowds can swell at busy times, so book ahead in summer.
1 Olympic Way, BT3 9DP. titanicbelfast.com. ✆ **028/9076-6386.** Admission (includes entry to SS *Nomadic*) £25 adults; £19 seniors and students (Mon–Fri only); £11 children 5–15; free for children 4 and under; £62 families. **Discovery Tour:** £15 adults; £10 children. Parking £2 for 1st hr., £1 per hr. afterward. Daily Apr–Oct 9am–6pm (until 7pm June, 7:30pm July–Aug); Nov–Mar 10am–5pm. Last admission 1 hr. 40 min. before closing.

Titanic Distillers at Thompson Dock ♥♥♥ DISTILLERY Another of Belfast's ship-related attractions, this fascinating tour takes you around Titanic Distillers in the pumphouse and the Thompson Dry Dock at the old Harland & Wolff shipyard, where *Titanic* was fitted out after she was built from 1909–11. It's a unique way to learn what it was like to work here at the turn of the last century, when Belfast was a great industrial city, and to see how the enormous Edwardian pumphouse, which could drain a staggering 21 million gallons of water in just over 90 minutes, has been given a new lease on life as a distillery. Visits are by guided tour—a 60-minute Signature tour will take you around the distillery and pumphouse, ending with a tasting of whiskey (spelled with an "e" here) and vodka; the 2-hour Premium tour includes these and a visit down into the Thompson Dry Dock outside; the Legacy tour also visits the original Gwynne pumps; and a 60-minute dock tour just visits the Thompson Dry Dock (not the distillery or pumphouse). There is also a small shop to purchase whiskey and paraphernalia.

Titanic Distillers have given new life to this Edwardian pumphouse in a historic Belfast shipyard.

Queen's Rd., Queen's Island, BT3 9DT. titanicdistillers.com. ✆ **028/9099-2992.** Signature tour £25 adults; £20 seniors and students (Mon–Fri); £12.50 children 5–18; free for ages 4 and under; £62.50 families. Dock tour £10; free for children 4 and under. Premium tour £35 adults; £30 seniors and students (Mon–Fri only); £22.50 children 5–18; free for children 4 and under. Legacy tour £100. Daily 10am–7pm, last admission 5:30pm. Parking £1.50 per hr.

Other Attractions

Belfast Castle ♥ CASTLE Northwest of downtown and 120m (394 ft.) above sea level stands Belfast Castle, its 80-hectare (198-acre) estate spreading down the slopes of what is now **Cave Hill Country Park** ♥ (see below). Dating from 1870, this was the family residence of the third marquis of Donegall, and it was built in the style of Balmoral Castle, the Scottish residence of the British monarch. The outside is more interesting than the inside, which has been modernized and is now a popular wedding venue. The estate is a lovely place to visit, offering sweeping views of Belfast and the lough. Its cellars contain a Victorian arcade, a cafe, and a shop selling antiques and crafts. According to legend, a white cat brought the castle residents luck, so look around for carvings featuring cats.

Signposted off Antrim Rd., 4km (2½ miles) N of city center, BT15 5GR. belfastcastle.co.uk. ✆ **028/9077-6925.** Free admission and parking. Sun–Mon 9am–6pm; Tues–Sat 9am–9pm. Tavern coffee shop open daily 10am–5pm.

Belfast Cathedral (St. Anne's) ♥ CATHEDRAL Although the foundation stone on this monumental cathedral, also known as **St. Anne's,** was laid in 1899, it remained incomplete for more than a century; even now it still awaits a steeple. Blending architectural genres from Romanesque to Victorian to modern, the huge structure is more attractive inside than out. In the nave, the ceiling soars above black-and-white marble walls and stone floors, and stained-glass windows flood it with color. Carvings representing life in Belfast top the 10 pillars. The cathedral's most impressive features are the delicate mosaic ceilings of the tympanum, and a baptistery made of thousands of pieces of glass.

Donegall St., BT1 2HB. belfastcathedral.org. ✆ **028/9032-8332.** Admission £3 adults; free for children 15 and under. Guidebook £1. Audio guides or guided tours £7. Mon–Sat 10:30am–4pm; Sun 12:30–3pm. Last admission 45 min. before closing.

Cave Hill Country Park ♥♥ PARK Atop a 360m (1,181-ft.) basalt cliff, this park offers panoramic views, walking trails, and archaeological and historical sights (including **Belfast Castle** ♥, above). Its name derives from five small caves thought to have been Neolithic iron mines; several other ancient sites are scattered about the place, often unmarked. These include stone cairns, dolmens, and **McArt's Fort**—the remains of an ancient defensive hill fort in which Wolfe Tone and his fellow United Irishmen planned the 1798 rebellion. It's mostly gone now, but you can explore the ruins, which sit atop the park's most famous viewpoint. The **Cave Hill Visitor Centre,** on the second floor of Belfast Castle, contains information on the history of the park and the castle plus a leaflet with maps of the park's three walks, which range from a 0.8-mile trail to 4.5 miles.

Visitor center: Belfast Castle, off Antrim Rd., 6.5km (4 miles) N of city center, BT15 5GR. belfastcity.gov.uk/cavehill. ✆ **028/9077-6925.** Free admission. Park 7:30am–dusk; visitor center daily 9am–6pm.

Cultúrlann McAdam Ó Fiaich ♥ CULTURAL CENTER Located in a former church building on the notorious Falls Road (a Republican stronghold during the Troubles), this cultural and arts center is a friendly, inclusive place. It has a handy cafe, a tourist information point, and a well-stocked shop full of Irish interest books, traditional crafts, and music CDs. The **Dillon Gallery,** West Belfast's only public art gallery, showcases work by Irish artists and those from farther afield. The center's theater has a varied program of traditional music, plays, spoken word events, and films. Check website for listings.

216 Falls Rd., BT12 6AH. culturlann.ie/en. ✆ **028/9096-4180.** Free admission. Mon–Thurs 9am–6pm; Fri–Sat 9am–9pm; Sun 11am–4pm.

Queen's University ♥♥ UNIVERSITY Founded in 1845 during the reign of Queen Victoria to provide nondenominational higher education, this is Northern Ireland's most prestigious university. The turreted main building, an imposing example of 19th-century Tudor Revival, may remind you of England's Oxford; its design was based on the Founder's Tower at Magdalen College. But there's much more to this university, which sprawls through 250 buildings and where around 28,000 students are studying at any given time. The surrounding neighborhood is a quiet, attractive place to wander, and University Square on the north side of campus is simply beautiful. At one end of the square, Union Theological College, dating from 1853, housed Northern Ireland's Parliament after the partition of Ireland in 1921 until its abolition in 1972. Tours of the campus can be arranged on request; contact the university's welcome center for details. Note that access to parts of the campus may be restricted during exam times.

Queen's University, founded in 1845.

Queen's Welcome Centre, Queen's University, University Rd., BT7 1NN. qub.ac.uk/home/welcome-centre. ✆ **028/9024-5133.** Free admission. Mon–Fri 8:30am–5pm.

Especially for Kids

Belfast Zoo ♥ ZOO On the northern slopes of Cave Hill, near **Cave Hill Country Park** ♥♥ (p. 512), this zoo emphasizes conservation and education. Many rare species are bred here, including Hawaiian geese, lowland gorillas, red lechwe (a kind of antelope), sea bears, Barbary lions, and golden lion tamarins. The **Rainforest House** is a tropical environment filled with birds and jungle creatures. Most activity days are quite kid-oriented, although some more grown-up events include all-day photography competitions. Special tours and events run all year. Check the website for up-to-date listings.

Antrim Rd., BT36 7PN. belfastzoo.co.uk. ✆ **028/9077-6277.** Admission £15.50 adults; £7.75 seniors, students, and children 4–16; free for children 3 and under; £44.50 families. Book online for discounts. Apr–Sept daily 10am–6pm (last admission 4:30pm); Oct–Mar daily 10am–4pm (last admission 2:30pm).

W5 ♥♥ SCIENCE CENTER This great science play center for kids is part of the Odyssey Complex, a huge modern entertainment center in the Titanic District. Properly known as "Whowhatwhenwherewhy"—you can see why they abbreviate it to W5—this high-tech, interactive learning environment lets kids try out over 250 individual activities, all in the spirit of science-based fun. They can create animated cartoons, try to beat a lie detector test, and present the weather on TV. The Odyssey also contains a cinema, bowling alley, shops, restaurants, and a sports arena.

2 Queen's Quay, BT3 9QQ. w5online.co.uk. ✆ **028/9046-7790.** Prebooking is essential. Admission £7.70; free for children 2 and under; £31–£33 families. Wed–Thurs 10am–4pm; Fri–Sun 10am–6pm. Last admission 1 hr. before closing.

Outlying Attractions: Belfast Lough

Belfast built up around the mouth of this coastal inlet; today the city's outer suburbs stretch along its north and south shores. There are a few worthwhile sights here. A dozen miles or so to the northeast, just off the M3 motorway, the castle town of **Carrickfergus** offers a nice break from the hustle and bustle of the city. Locals like to say that Carrickfergus was thriving when Belfast was a sandbank, and looking around its winding medieval streets, it's easy to believe. On the other side of the lough, **Cultra** is home to the excellent **Ulster Folk & Transport Museum** ♥♥♥ (p. 515).

Andrew Jackson Cottage and U.S. Rangers Museum ♥ HISTORIC HOUSE This re-created 18th-century dwelling is built in the style of cottages once lived in by Scotch-Irish settlers—including the ancestors of Andrew Jackson (1767–1845), the seventh president of the United States and the first president of Irish heritage. The cottage is decorated as it would have looked in the 1750s; also here is an exhibition devoted to Jackson's life. Although it's a faithful reproduction, the house isn't the actual home of the Jacksons—that was demolished in the 19th century. Next door is a very small museum devoted to the U.S. Rangers, who were stationed in Carrickfergus during World War II.

2 Boneybefore, Carrickfergus, BT38 7EQ. nimc.co.uk/members/andrew-jackson-and-us-rangers-centre. ✆ **028/9335-8262.** Free admission. Wed–Sun 11am–3pm.

Carrickfergus Castle ♥ CASTLE Built in 1180 by John de Courcy, this massive Norman keep was Ireland's first real castle, designed to loom darkly over the entrance to Belfast Lough. Centuries later, its defensive location would prove prophetic, as William of Orange landed here on June 14, 1690, en route to the Battle of the Boyne. The central part dates to the 12th century, the thick outer walls were completed 100 years later, and the gun ports are a comparatively new addition (only 400 years old). The outside is more impressive than the inside, which has been largely outfitted to trigger kids' interests, with waxwork figures riding horses, threatening to shoot people over the walls, and so on. Sometimes actors in medieval costume add a touch of hammy fun. The castle has a visitor center and a small museum. In the summer, medieval banquets, a medieval fair, and a crafts market all add a touch of play and pageantry.

Marine Hwy., Carrickfergus, BT38 7BG. antrimcoastandglensaonb.ccght.org/carrickfergus-castle. ✆ **028/9335-1273.** Admission £6 adults; £4.50 seniors and students; £4 children 5–17; free for children 4 and under; £18 families. Tues–Sun 9am–4pm. Last admission 30 min. before closing.

Ulster Folk Museum ♥♥ MUSEUM/HERITAGE SITE One of Northern Ireland's best living-history museums, the Ulster Folk & Transport Museum is made up of buildings rescued from demolition and reconstructed, piece by piece. Mostly dating from the 19th century, they include houses, schools, a chemist's shop, a pub, and even a working farm. The level of detail is impressive—the shops are fully decked out as they would have been in Victorian times, complete with shelves overflowing with authentic bottles, jars, and items of clothing. As you wander about, you may encounter a Victorian housewife engaged in day-to-day domestic drudgery or watch a village blacksmith working away in a forge using authentic period methods. Across the street, the **Ulster Transport Museum** (see below) should not be missed.

Titanic exhibition at the Ulster Folk & Transport Museum.

Signposted off A2, 153 Bangor Rd., Cultra, Holywood, BT18 0EU. ulsterfolkmuseum.org. ✆ **028/9042-8428.** Admission £11.50 adults; £9 seniors and students; £7 children 5–17; free for children 4 and under; £25–£32 families. Tues–Sun 10am–5pm. Last admission 2pm. Free parking.

A brief HISTORY OF NORTHERN IRELAND

Shelves upon shelves of books have been written in an attempt to unravel the complicated history and politics of Northern Ireland. Only a fool would expect to be able to do it clearly and concisely, in just a few short paragraphs. So here goes.

In 1921, after nearly a thousand years of British occupation and more rebellions and civil wars than you could count, Ireland won its independence from Great Britain. At least, *most* of it did. Britain didn't want to give it all up, nor did the Protestant, pro-British majority in parts of the north. So, a compromise was reached: The northern counties of Antrim, Armagh, Down, Fermanagh, Londonderry, and Tyrone (which are part of the province of "Ulster") were split off to form a new country called Northern Ireland. This, in turn, would be part of the United Kingdom—a U.K. state, effectively. It was a messy deal, but the violence would end. That, at least, was the plan.

It didn't work out well. The Catholic minority in Northern Ireland was treated appallingly, discriminated against in almost every aspect of life, from work and housing to elections and policing. Not unreasonably, they wondered if they would be better off in the Republic of Ireland, too. Things came to a head in the late 1960s, when the Catholic population began an intense civil rights campaign. Their marches and demonstrations were crushed by the authorities, sometimes with brute violence—which spurred the reemergence of the Irish Republican Army (IRA), a paramilitary group that had first appeared early in the 20th century.

In 1972, things reached a fever pitch in the "Bloody Sunday" massacre, when the British army opened fire on a peaceful protest in Derry (p. 563). After that, the IRA launched a terror campaign aimed at civilians, both in Northern Ireland and on the British mainland. Bombs were planted in bus stops, cafes, schools, pubs, and shopping malls, killing many innocent people. Politicians were assassinated. (In 1985, Prime Minister Margaret Thatcher was inches away from being killed by a bomb.) The British army, meanwhile, patrolled Northern Irish streets and colluded with pro–U.K. terrorist groups. People were thrown in jail for crimes they didn't commit. Those in jail went on hunger strikes to protest their treatment. There were shootings and bombings almost weekly, far too many to list here. Over 3,000 died, both here and in Britain, and tens of thousands were injured—mostly just ordinary folks who were in the wrong place at the wrong time.

The struggle—known as the Troubles—continued for decades, until the "Good Friday Agreement" was negotiated, with the help of U.S. President Bill Clinton, and signed in 1998. While it didn't end all political and religious violence, it did change the atmosphere considerably. A massive constitutional overhaul, the agreement ended institutional discrimination against the Catholic minority, installed power sharing between the unionist and nationalist parties, and devolved government. Paramilitary groups such as the IRA agreed to disarm. Mortal enemies agreed to share power together, peacefully.

Skip forward 24 years, and the region is still at peace. Sporadic flare-ups of violence do happen, the "Orange" marches still stir up bad feelings, but nothing remotely approaching what it was.

More recently, however, Brexit opened a whole new can of worms politically. Northern Ireland voted heavily to remain in the E.U. but was forced to leave along with the rest of the U.K. in 2020—leading some speculation at the time about a vote on Irish reunification in the near future. Unionist refusal to accept the post-Brexit agreement led to the collapse of power sharing from 2022 to early 2024, when it was reinstated.

Ulster Transport Museum ♥♥ MUSEUM/HERITAGE SITE This museum, opposite the **Ulster Folk Museum** (above) tells the story of transport in this region, covering everything from road, rail, and shipping to space exploration. There's a wealth of historic vehicles to see, from old cars and small planes to buses and trams, as well as a trove of rare *Titanic* artifacts. There's also a surfing museum called **Celtic Wave.**

Signposted off A2 (Bangor Rd.), Cultra, Holywood, BT18 0EU. ulstertransport museum.org. ✆ **028/9042-8428.** Admission £11.50 adults; £9 seniors and students; £7 children 5–17; free for children 4 and under; £25–£32 families. Mon–Sun 10am–5pm. Free parking.

WHERE TO STAY IN BELFAST

Belfast's hotel scene increasingly rivals Dublin's, but at a significantly lower price. There are good hotels in every price range—the farther you go from the city center, the better the bargain. ***A good money-saving tip:*** Several hotels offer packages that include entry to some of the city's biggest attractions. We've included a few offers below.

Expensive

Europa Hotel ♥♥ For some time this has been the lodging of choice for politicians, diplomats, and celebrities visiting Belfast, partly thanks to its great location. While it was targeted heavily during the Troubles, you wouldn't know it to look at it now. The decor is subtly masculine; the lobby has marble floors and a modern gas fireplace. The large guest rooms are contemporary in style, with comfortable beds, sizable bathrooms, and air-conditioning. Views from some of the upper floors stretch as far as Cave Hill. Downstairs is a piano bar and the laid-back—if slightly generic—**The Causerie** restaurant. Book yourself in for the afternoon tea, complete with sandwiches, scones, and cake. Check the website for packages that include entry to Titanic Belfast.

Great Victoria St., BT2 7AP. europahotelbelfast.com. ✆ **028/9027-1066.** 272 units. £142–£404 double; £491–£1,490 suite. Breakfast not included in lower rates. Dinner, bed-and-breakfast packages available. Valet parking £25 per day or £14 at a nearby lot. **Amenities:** Restaurant; 2 bars; room service; Wi-Fi (free).

The Fitzwilliam Hotel ♥♥♥ You can't beat the location of this luxury hotel on Great Victoria Street, right next to the Grand Opera House and just steps from restaurants, pubs, and shops. Inside, the rooms are super stylish, with geometric carpets, warm colors, king-size beds, spacious bathrooms, and floor-to-ceiling windows for views over the surrounding rooftops (ask for a room on the 8th or 9th floor). The hotel's modern design carries through to the restaurant and cozy bar. Afternoon tea is popular, or check out the "Crafternoon Tea" with craft beers and filling sliders and pies.

Great Victoria St., BT2 7BQ. fitzwilliamhotelbelfast.com. ✆ **028/9044-2080.** 146 units. £183–£389. Breakfast included. See the website for packages and offers. Valet parking £28 or discount at nearby parking lot. **Amenities:** Restaurant; bar; Wi-Fi (free).

Grand Central Hotel ♥♥ This hotel in the city center is the tallest in Belfast, offering panoramic views from the upper floors. Rooms are a good size, with sophisticated, neutral decor and orthopedic beds. Bathrooms are not huge, but they are big enough and feature rainfall showers. In the end, though, the views are the thing here—sweeping, bird's-eye vistas of the City Hall dome, the city center, and the hills beyond from all the upper-floor rooms. The restaurants and bars have high ceilings and enormous windows, letting in a flood of light. The ground-floor **Grand Café** is open in the morning for breakfast and coffee, and the **Seahorse Bar and Restaurant** offers upscale French-influenced cuisine and local craft gins. The trendy, 23rd-story **Observatory Bar** offers the best views in the house and pricey cocktails.

9–15 Bedford St., BT2 7FF. grandcentralhotelbelfast.com. ✆ **028/9023-1066.** 300 units. £225–£296 double. Breakfast not included in lower rates. Valet parking £30 or discount at nearby car park. **Amenities:** Restaurant; bar; cafe; gym; Wi-Fi (free).

The Merchant Hotel ♥♥♥ One of Ireland's most luxurious hotels, the Merchant is a real treat. The Victorian building was once a bank, and the conversion is stunning, from the grand dining room (lacquered and gilded Corinthian columns, marble floors, ceiling friezes) to an elegant cocktail lounge (chandeliers and a gently curved, dark wood bar). There are two styles of guest rooms: traditional Victorian-style rooms in the old part of the building, or more modern rooms with Art Deco–style decor,

Guest room in the Grand Central Hotel.

Where to Stay & Eat in Belfast
WHERE TO STAY
Bullitt 4
Europa Hotel 16
The Fitzwilliam Hotel 17
Grand Central Hotel 12
The Harrison Chambers of Distinction 23
Malmaison Belfast 5
The Merchant Hotel 3
Ravenhill Guesthouse 24
Regency House 20
Tara Lodge 19
Ten Square 13
WHERE TO EAT
Coco 14
Common Market Belfast 1
Ginger Bistro 18
Harlem Cafe 15
Holohans Pantry 21
James Street & Co 11
John Long's Fish & Chips 9
Molly's Yard 22
Mourne Seafood Bar 7
MrDeanes 10
The Muddlers Club 2
Ox 6
Roam 8
Saga 23
Univ. of Ulster
St. Anne's Cathedral
Smithfield Market
Castle Court Centre
City Hall
Waterfront Hall
St. George's Market
Victoria Square
Queen Elizabeth Bridge
Queen's Bridge
Central Station
Gt. Victoria Street Station
Botanic Station
Queen's University
Botanic Gardens
Ormeau Park
Ormeau Rd. Bridge
River Lagan
NORTHERN IRELAND
Belfast
Dublin
Galway
Cork
REPUBLIC OF IRELAND
Information
0 300 yds
0 300 m

which are larger and better designed. The excellent **spa** comes complete with hydrotherapy pool and treatment rooms, and a rooftop gym has an eight-person hot tub with lovely city views. The **Great Room Restaurant** is located in the beautiful banking hall. Afternoon tea is a bit of an event here, and popular, so book ahead if you want to indulge.

16 Skipper St., BT1 2DZ. themerchanthotel.com. ✆ **028/9023-4888.** 62 units. £279–£379 double; £390–£599 suite. Breakfast included. Dinner, bed-and-breakfast packages available. Valet parking £39 or discount at nearby parking lot. **Amenities:** Restaurant; bar; gym; spa; Wi-Fi (free).

Regency House ♥♥♥ When you arrive at this white Georgian terrace with its tall houses and Corinthian columns, facing a small square, you might think you were in Bath or London, England, rather than Belfast. The rooms and suites in this upmarket boutique hotel, set in fully renovated Georgian town houses, are a blend of historic style with modern luxury. Suites come with a record player and vinyl, a cocktail-making kit, and a kitchen so well supplied you could even bake a cake (to accompany the coffee from the De'Longhi machine)—not to mention a 24-hour butler—while the brand-new executive rooms promise a restful night's sleep in king-size beds. Set in a quiet corner of the Queen's Quarter, Regency House is within walking distance of the area's restaurants, venues, and cafes—that is, if you can drag yourself away.

12 Upper Crescent, BT7 1NT. regencyhouse.co.uk. ✆ **028/9588-1846.** 12 units. £300–£375 double; £350–£1,250 suite. On-street parking, subject to availability. **Amenities:** Restaurant; bar; gym; wellness suite; Wi-Fi (free).

Moderate

The Harrison Chambers of Distinction ♥♥♥ This bohemian Victorian residence in the Queen's Quarter is jam-packed full of character and quirks. The heritage "chambers" (aka rooms) come with interesting features like bay windows, original fireplaces, freestanding bathtubs, brass beds, and art and antiques collected by host Melanie over the years. Each room is unique—live out your literary fantasies in the C.S. Lewis Suite (the *Chronicles of Narnia* author was born in Belfast), complete with a mini-library and an antique typewriter; or sink into a four-poster

Eclectic decor at the Harrison Chambers of Distinction.

bed or freestanding bathtub accompanied by jazz records in the Ruby Murray suite, named for the popular Northern Irish singer. There's a small downstairs bar for a nightcap, and a light breakfast can be served in the room. It's also right next to **Saga Restaurant** (p. 526). Check online for packages such as free theater tickets or Black Taxi Tour with a 3-night stay.

45 Malone Rd., BT9 6RX. chambersofdistinction.com. ✆ **028/9460-0123.** 16 units. £160–£394 double. Free parking. **Amenities:** Bar; room service; Wi-Fi (free).

Malmaison Belfast ♥♥ This is the only Irish outpost of Malmaison, a British mini-chain that specializes in turning unusual historic buildings into hip boutique hotels. This four-story building used to be a seed warehouse, and it's gorgeous, with weathered stone walls and tall, arched windows. Inside, the chic, playful design retains original industrial touches. Bedrooms are large, quiet, and comfortable, with low lighting, huge beds, and modern bathrooms; most have deep bathtubs and walk-in showers. Breakfasts are large and varied—we love the homemade granola. **Malmaison Bar & Grill** is the good, in-house brasserie, and the plush **Mal-Bar** is lively.

34–38 Victoria St., BT1 3GH. malmaison.com/locations/belfast. ✆ **028/9600-1405.** 62 units. £99–£600 double; £300–£900 suite. Breakfast not included in lower rates. Discount parking at nearby lot (£17.50/24 hr.). **Amenities:** Restaurant; bar; gym; room service; Wi-Fi (free).

Ten Square ♥♥ Set in a historic building right behind City Hall, this boutique hotel aims to emulate five-star luxury hotels at a fraction of the cost. Its decor deliberately contrasts styles—exposed stone and tall, arched windows in public areas; bedrooms treading the line between chic and kitsch, with polka-dotted carpet and blue velvet fabrics. The king-size beds, draped in pure white linens, are very firm. **Jospers** restaurant specializes in Irish meats, particularly steak, and the **Loft** bar has a great cocktail menu. The penthouse has a huge rooftop terrace with views across the city. Check the website for deals, including a *Titanic*-themed package.

Yorkshire House, 10 Donegall Sq., BT1 5JD. tensquare.co.uk. ✆ **028/9024-1001.** 131 units. £140–£240 double; £770–£840 suite. Breakfast not included in lower rates. Street parking at nearby lot (£17/24 hr.). **Amenities:** Restaurant; bar; Wi-Fi (free).

Inexpensive

Bullitt ♥ Positioned between the Titanic Quarter and the historic downtown, this hip, modern hotel has a chic industrial design, starting in the downstairs cafe with its exposed metal beams, polished concrete floor, and exposed support columns beneath moody lighting. Soundproofed bedrooms also have an industrial edge, replacing closets with brightly painted metal racks for hanging clothes. Beds are comfortable, and bathrooms are small but modern. A breakfast of granola and fruit is left outside your door every morning, or you can pop downstairs for a latte from

Cheery accommodations at Ravenhill Guesthouse.

the espresso bar or seek out a hot breakfast in the restaurant. Very cheap deals are offered on the smallest hotel rooms.

40a Church Lane, BT2 7GE. bullitthotel.com. ✆ **028/9590-0600.** 74 units. £95–£159 double. Breakfast not included in lower rates. **Amenities:** Restaurant; bar; Wi-Fi (free).

Ravenhill Guesthouse ♥♥ A friendly welcome awaits from hosts Roger and Olive, whose handsome Victorian corner house has been converted into one of the best B&Bs in Belfast. Rooms are simple but neat as a pin. You're in a residential area but not far from the action; the city center is about a 10-minute cab or bus ride away. Roger cooks delicious breakfasts, and guests can expect the full Ulster fry, in addition to options such as kippers with parsley butter and scrambled eggs. They bake their own traditional Irish wheaten bread from scratch, right down to milling their own flour.

690 Ravenhill Rd., BT6 0BZ. ravenhillhouse.com. ✆ **028/9028-2590.** 5 units. £115–£180 double. 2-night minimum stay. Breakfast included. Free parking. **Amenities:** Wi-Fi (free). Closed Mid-Dec to Mar.

Tara Lodge ♥♥ This popular boutique hotel is well positioned for exploring the city—the **Botanic Gardens** ♥ (p. 504) and **Ulster Museum** ♥♥♥ (p. 509) are 10 minutes away on foot. The contemporary guest rooms are not big, but they're well designed and quiet, with large, comfortable beds. Instead of a closet, there's a metal rack for clothes in the corner—a U.K. hotel trend. The breakfast selection is excellent, with everything cooked to order. The hotel has no in-house restaurant or bar, but staff can guide you to good eateries nearby. Check online for packages that include the **Titanic Experience** (p. 510) or discounts on *Game of Thrones* location tours.

36 Cromwell Rd., BT7 1JW. taralodge.com. ✆ **028/9059-0900.** 34 units. £100–£155 double. Breakfast included. Free parking. **Amenities:** Wi-Fi (free).

WHERE TO EAT IN BELFAST

Belfast has an expansive foodie scene that's growing all the time. With a university and a booming business sector, there's demand for variety and affordability. In addition to the restaurants listed below, you can find plenty of options for light meals at places like **Harlem** (34 Bedford St.; harlemcafebelfast.com; ✆ **028/9024-4860**), where locals come for breakfast or lunch in a trendy antiques-filled dining room near City Hall. At weekends, drop into **St. George's Market** (p. 509) for tasty offerings from the food stalls, or visit the street food market at **Common Market Belfast** in the Cathedral Quarter (16–20 Dunbar St.; commonmarket belfast.com; no phone) for Mexican food, Filipino fusion, or pizzas.

Expensive

The Muddlers Club ♥♥♥ MODERN IRISH It's located down a laneway and named after a secret society that used to meet here 200 years ago, but there's nothing secret about the food in this gem in the Cathedral Quarter—the restaurant has earned many awards since it opened in 2015, including a Michelin star. The atmosphere is casual rather than fine-dining formal, with wood furniture, lively tunes, and an open kitchen. Chef Gareth McCaughey creates a six-course seasonal tasting menu using the best local ingredients he can find—look for dishes like venison carpaccio with hazelnut and black garlic, or scallops with roe beurre blanc and Iberico ham. There's also a vegetarian or vegan version. Book well in advance—reservations open 6 weeks ahead of available dates.

1 Warehouse Lane, BT1 2DX. themuddlersclubbelfast.com. ✆ **028/9031-3199.** Tasting menu £90. Paired wines add £65. Wed–Thurs 5–9:30pm; Fri–Sat 12:30–1pm and 5–9:30pm.

Ox ♥♥♥ MODERN EUROPEAN Contemporary, seasonal, well-balanced flavors form the small but sumptuous menus at this Michelin-starred restaurant. The tasting menus change constantly, with local and seasonal availability a constant priority, but expect dishes such as halibut bisque with artichoke and sea fennel, or Skeaghanore duck with salsify, buckwheat, and elderberries. The service strikes precisely the right balance between professionalism and friendliness—the waitstaff really know their stuff—and the modern dining room provides a sophisticated backdrop. Needless to say, reservations are essential. If, however, you can't quite stretch to dinner here, you can sample the restaurant's excellent wine list in the entirely informal **Ox Cave,** the adjacent wine bar, while enjoying cheese and light bites.

1 Oxford St., BT1 3LA. oxbelfast.com. ✆ **028/9031-4121.** 6-course tasting menu £90. Wine pairing additional £65. Wed 6–9:30pm; Thurs–Sat noon–2:30pm and 6–9:30pm. Closed Sun–Tues.

Local Mourne lamb and mushrooms at Ox.

Moderate

Coco ♥♥ MODERN EUROPEAN/INTERNATIONAL Coco's stylishly whimsical dining room is plastered in modern art along with posters and photo collages that set the tone. The contemporary menu is full of welcome surprises that innovate without overcrowding the more traditional ingredients; squid is cooked with salt and chili and served with Napa slaw, aioli, and chili jam, for example, and halibut comes with roast cauliflower and shrimp butter. For dessert, try the rich buttermilk panna cotta served with strawberries and shortbread. A pre-theater menu (served until 7:30pm) is just £23 for two courses and £29.50 for three courses.

7–11 Linenhall St., BT2 8AA. cocobelfast.com. ✆ **028/9031-1150.** Entrees £18.50–£32.50. Wed–Fri noon–3pm and 5:30–9:30pm; Sat 5–9:30pm; Sun 1–7pm.

Ginger Bistro ♥♥ MODERN IRISH Lively food and atmosphere keep the regulars coming back to this city-center favorite. This bistro wins rave reviews for dishes like seabass with broccoli, cannellini beans, nduja butter, hazelnuts, and dauphinoise potatoes, or slow-cooked featherblade of beef matched with green beans, roast potatoes, mash, and bourguignon gravy. Staff are friendly yet professional, and the overall vibe is good food in a relaxed atmosphere. The restaurant is near both the Grand Opera House (p. 529) and the Crown Liquor Saloon (p. 508), so you could put together a great night out featuring all three.

68/72 Great Victoria St., BT2 7AF. gingerbistro.com. ✆ **028/9024-4421.** 3-course set menu £43.50, 2-course menu £20.50–£33.50. Wed 5–9:15pm; Thurs 4–9:15pm; Fri–Sat noon–9:30pm.

James Street & Co ♥♥ MODERN IRISH One of Belfast's most popular restaurants, James Street & Co has built a great reputation on its creative modern Irish cuisine. With exposed brick walls and an industrial-chic vibe, the place may look unpretentious, but the food is reliably excellent—expect dishes like local pheasant with onion and creamed chestnuts, or a perfect rib-eye with blue cheese sauce. Kids are catered to with a surprisingly good menu that is a little more, well, grown-up than most places. There's an all-day menu on weekends.

19–21 James St. S, BT2 7GA. jamesst.co.uk. ✆ **028/9560-0700.** Entrees £20.50–£39. Mon and Thurs 5–9:30pm; Fri–Sat 1–9:30pm; Sun 1–8pm.

Molly's Yard ♥♥ IRISH Tucked away in the University Quarter in restored Victorian stables, this place is as justifiably popular for its relaxed atmosphere as for the delicious food. Appetizers such as fresh bread with tapenade go well with a glass of whatever you fancy. You could follow that up with some lamb with horseradish and potato gnocchi, cod with chili jam, or vegetable curry. The six-course tasting menu also comes as a vegetarian or vegan option, and the craft-beer selection is extensive.

1 College Green Mews, BT1 1LW. mollysyard.co.uk. ✆ **028/9032-2600.** Entrees £20–£32. Mon–Sat noon–8:30pm.

Mourne Seafood Bar ♥♥ SEAFOOD This is one of the best places in Belfast for top-quality seafood. The dining room has a casual air—this is a seafood *bar* after all—but the food speaks for itself. Oysters are a specialty, served traditionally or Japanese-style with pickled ginger and soy dressing. Alternatively, you could go for some spicy piri-piri prawns with fresh focaccia bread to start, followed by one of the fresh daily specials like seared scallops with butternut squash risotto. The atmosphere is relaxed and convivial, and the prices thoroughly reasonable for food this good. The restaurant doesn't take reservations at lunchtime, but evening booking is essential. A second branch is on Main Street in Dundrum, just outside Newcastle, County Down (✆ **028/4375-1377;** p. 553).

34–36 Bank St., BT1 1HL. mourneseafood.com. ✆ **028/9024-8544.** Entrees £17–£25. Mon–Thurs 5–9:30pm; Fri–Sat noon–3:15pm and 5–10pm; Sun noon–6pm.

MrDeanes ♥♥ MODERN IRISH Local celebrity chef Michael Deane has opened a few different restaurants in Belfast over the years, and his latest offering, **MrDeanes,** is a hit for its great Irish produce served in a mix of world cuisines. Here you'll find plates such as salmon with Moroccan couscous, romesco, mint yogurt, and almond, or Portavogie prawn risotto with fennel salad and gremolata. Next door is the excellent **Meat Locker** (✆ **028/9033-1134**), a laid-back grill where you can choose among around eight different cuts of steak, with a long list of sauces. Both restaurants have an impressive wine list that includes a private cellar selection. Deane also runs the informal bistro **Deanes at Queens** (1 College Gardens; ✆ **028/9038-2111**) in the University Quarter, where you can go for sharing plates or opt for mains like chargrilled steak or cod filet with crab and chili noodles.

36–40 Howard St., BT1 6PF. michaeldeane.co.uk/mrdeanes. ✆ **028/9033-1134.** Entrees £16–£34. Tues–Fri noon–2:45pm and 5–9:30pm; Sat noon–9:30pm.

Roam ♥♥♥ IRISH The dining room here may have a minimalist feel, with bare walls and industrial-type pipes overhead, but the food on the plate is an explosion of color and flavor. Skilled young chef Ryan Jenkins originally started this as a series of pop-ups in 2018, and the bricks-and-mortar version serves food of fine-dining-standard in a relaxed, laid-back atmosphere. The menu changes regularly, using the best local ingredients available. Start with tasty openers like Portavogie langoustines with lemon butter, or Kilkeel scallops with squash, lardo, and hazelnut, before moving into mains like Mourne lamb rump with braised potato, cauliflower, and merlot, or coley with shiitake and white miso beurre blanc. The cocktail list is creative, too—look for the house special Honeytrap (vodka, honey, egg white, and yellaman, a candy from the north coast).

Whiskey sour cocktail at Roam.

6a Callendar St., BT1 5HX. roambelfast.com. ✆ **07917/957-162.** Entrees £22–£26. Wed–Sat noon–2:30pm and 5–9:30pm. Closed Sun–Tues.

Saga ♥♥♥ IRISH This gem in the Queen's Quarter is where to come for unfussy food, good wine, and surroundings that encourage good conversation (we especially love the curved booths). Plates might include pan-fried trout with romesco, broccoli, spinach purée, and herb-crushed potatoes; or venison loin with bitter chocolate, Jerusalem artichoke purée, artichoke crisps, and game jus. There's a retro playlist for tunes, and don't miss the Sunday roast, which comes with all the trimmings (potatoes, vegetables, gravy, and even Yorkshire pudding).

43 Malone Rd., BT9 6RX. sagabelfast.com. ✆ **028/9040-6399**. Entrees £23–£30. Thurs–Fri 5–9pm; Sat noon–9:30pm; Sun 1–8pm.

Inexpensive

Holohans Pantry ♥♥ IRISH This homey, old-style restaurant near Queen's University is away from the city center buzz so the vibe is relaxed and low-key. Like the decor of antiques, old mirrors, and old plates, the menu is slightly old-fashioned, but it's full of filling, comfort-style food

like roast lamb with potatoes, vegetables, and mint jus, or Sunday roasts served with all the trimmings like mashed potatoes and gravy. The house specialty is *boxty* pancakes, filled with ingredients like seafood and dill white wine cream, or ham with cabbage and mustard cream. Service is friendly, and a good pre-theater menu (5–6:30pm) offers two courses for £28 and three courses for £34. Leave room for the sticky toffee pudding for dessert.
43 University Rd., BT7 1ND. holohanspantry.co.uk. ✆ **028/9029-1103.** Entrees £16.50–£22. Tues–Sat noon–2:30pm and 5–9pm (until 9:30pm Fri–Sat); Sun 1–7:15pm.

John Long's Fish & Chips ♥ SEAFOOD Widely acclaimed as the best fish and chips spot in Belfast, John Long's has certainly been around a long time—the first one opened in 1914—and its fans are legion and loyal. It offers nothing fancy, just fresh fish in a light batter, quickly fried and served immediately, along with fries (called chips here) and mushy peas or, if you must, baked beans. "Good food and lots of it" is the motto. It also provides gluten-free alternative batter for those who need it, so everyone can have some fish. The menu is short and sweet; the fish is fresh and cheap. But get here early, it closes at 6:30pm (6pm Sat).
39 Athol St., BT12 4GX. johnlongs.com. ✆ **028/9032-1848.** Entrees £7–£11. Tues–Fri noon–6:30pm; Sat noon–6pm.

SHOPPING

Belfast is a surprisingly good place to shop. Start at Donegall Place, where the streets are lined with shops and the Victorian arcades are filled with gift and jewelry stores. Good buys are to be had on Belleek china, linen, and crystal from County Tyrone.

The main shopping street is **Royal Avenue,** home of several well-known chain stores, while the **Westfield Castlecourt Shopping Centre** on Royal Avenue and the glass-domed **Victoria Square** shopping center are Belfast's main downtown multi-story shopping malls. There are some good fashion shops on the pedestrianized streets around Arthur Street. Shops are typically open Monday to Saturday from 9:30 or 10am to 5:30 or 6pm—some also open on Sundays from 1 to 5 or 6pm.

Antiques

Archive's Antiques Centre ♥ Several dealers sell their wares at this sprawling center, with specialists in everything from silverware to pub memorabilia and militaria. 88 Donegall Pass, BT7 1BX. ✆ **028/9023-2383.**

Oakland Antiques ♥♥ This enormous antiques emporium specializes in furniture, glassware, and other household items from the 18th to early 20th centuries. 137 Donegall Pass, BT7 1DS. oaklandantiques.co.uk. ✆ **028/9023-0176.**

Books & Stationery

No Alibis ♥♥ This excellent bookshop specializes in crime fiction from all over the world. It's a lovely place to linger. 83 Botanic Ave., BT7 1JL. noalibis.com. ✆ **028/9031-9601.**

Crafts and Gifts

Born and Bred ♥♥♥ A treasure trove of gifts and art, all sourced from talented Irish artists. Look for the mugs, socks, and prints with amusing colloquial sayings on them. 60–62 Ann St., BT1 4EG. wearebornandbred.com. ✆**028/9023-0475.**

The Norn Irish Gift Shop ♥♥ Most of the gifts and souvenirs here are made in Northern ("Norn") Ireland, with everything from mugs with humorous slogans to colorful art, jigsaw puzzles of the Belfast shipyards, and Belleek fine china. 48–50 Fountain St., BT1 5EE. ✆ **07715/344-873.**

14

Food

Sawers ♥♥♥ A treasure trove of all types of food, with a lively deli counter and more than 200 cheeses alone, this shop is so historic (it dates back to 1897) it even supplied nibbles to the *Titanic*. 5–6 College St., BT1 6ES. sawersbelfast.com. ✆ **028/9032 2021.**

Jewelry

Steensons ♥♥♥ Behind Belfast City Hall, this long-established jewelry shop is known for its beautiful pieces inspired by *Game of Thrones* (see box on p. 546); other popular lines include limited-edition pieces commemorating the *Titanic*. There's also a branch on Seaview Hall, New Road, in Glenarm, County Antrim (✆ **028/2884-1445**). Bedford St., BT2 7FD. thesteensons.com. ✆ **028/9024-8269.**

BELFAST AFTER DARK

Belfast has a plethora of historic pubs serving friendly local crowds, along with a fast-growing scene of late-night bars for the young and trendy, mostly clustered in the University Quarter. If you're looking for a traditional pub, several of the best are tucked away in the pedestrian lanes off Donegall Place.

The **licensing laws** in Northern Ireland aren't as notoriously strict as they used to be. Pub hours are generally Monday to Saturday from 11:30am until 11pm and Sunday 12:30 to 2:30pm and 7 until 10pm; bars stay open later. Nightclubs tend not to get busy until after the pubs close; admission ranges from a few pounds to about £15.

Bars & Clubs

Hell Cat Maggies ♥ This fun bar is named for an infamous member of the Dead Rabbit gang who terrorized New York in the 19th century. A varied program of nightly live music keeps things lively, and the food is good. 2 Donegall Sq. W, BT1 6JA. hellcat-maggies.com. ✆ **028/9099-4120.**

Performing Arts

Belfast Empire ♥ This former music hall is now one of the city's busiest live venues, with acts a few times a week and standup comedy every Tuesday. It's also a busy bar and nightclub, open until 1am every night except Sunday. 42 Botanic Ave., BT1 1JQ. thebelfastempire.com. ✆ **028/9024-9276.**

Black Box ♥♥ This eclectic venue has a great program of theater, spoken word, cabaret, film, and other live events, as well as exhibition spaces featuring whatever's interesting in the worlds of photography and visual arts. From Wednesday to Saturday nights, the Green Room bar has DJs and live music, usually free. 18–22 Hill St., BT1 2LA. blackboxbelfast.com. ✆ **028/9024-4400.**

Grand Opera House ♥♥ One of the main landmarks of Belfast's Golden Mile, the Grand Opera House opened in 1895. The interior is full of late-Victorian detail, including an elaborately painted frieze on the high ceiling. Severely damaged twice by IRA bombs, it's a cornerstone of the Belfast live arts scene, hosting touring plays, ballet, and opera. Ticket prices vary, but expect to pay between £18 and £47. 2–4 Great Victoria St., BT2 7HR. goh.co.uk. ✆ **028/9024-1919.**

Lyric Theatre ♥♥ The Lyric is a highly respected repertory theater producing original work and hosting touring plays. Ticket prices are generally between £15 and £35. 55 Ridgeway St., BT9 5FP. lyrictheatre.co.uk. ✆ **028/9038-1081.**

The Mac ♥♥ This cultural hub in the Cathedral Quarter has three art galleries, two theaters, a dance studio, and workshop rooms plus a bar and restaurant. Theater tickets cost £16 to £27.50. 10 Exchange St. West, BT1 2NJ. themaclive.com. ✆ **028/9023-5053.**

Pubs

Crown Liquor Saloon ♥♥♥ There's a very real possibility that this impeccably restored Victorian gin palace is the handsomest pub in the world. See full review on p. 508. 46 Great Victoria St., BT2 7BA. nicholsonspubs.co.uk/thecrownliquorsaloonbelfast. ✆ **028/9024-3187.**

Kelly's Cellars ♥♥ One of a couple pubs claiming to be Belfast's oldest, Kelly's Cellars certainly looks the part, with low doorways and a high-beamed ceiling. It's considered one of the best pubs in town for live traditional music; sessions are usually held on Tuesdays, Wednesdays, and Thursdays from 8:30pm on and Saturdays from 4:30pm. 30–32 Bank St., BT1 1HL. kellyscellars.co.uk. ✆ **028/9024-6058.**

Intricate woodcarving, tilework, and stained glass at the Crown Liquor Saloon.

The Morning Star ♥ Another lovely traditional pub, the Morning Star has been in business since at least 1810. Originally it was next to a stagecoach terminus, providing sunrise pick-me-ups for overnight passengers—hence the name. The pub is famously hard to find: Pottinger's Entry is a small, pedestrian-only alleyway off High Street, across from the post office; look for the iron arch over the entrance. 17–19 Pottinger's Entry, BT1 4DT. themorningstarbar.com. ✆ **028/9023-5986.**

White's Tavern ♥♥ White's Tavern has been serving liquor since 1630, which makes it even older than all of the above (though technically not the oldest pub; it began life as a wine shop). The decor is all old whiskey bottles and vintage photos around a fireplace. There's live music nightly. The **Beer Hall** has lots of cozy snugs. Upstairs, the **Oyster Room** serves up a small menu of hearty comfort food. Enter between Rosemary and High streets. 2–4 Winecellar Entry, BT1 1QN. whitestavernbelfast.com. ✆ **028/9031-2582.**

DAY TRIPS FROM BELFAST

15

Medieval castles, mountain ranges, coastal drives, and one of the most spectacular (and certainly unique) landscapes you'll find anywhere—all are within easy reach of Belfast. That is, if you don't mind driving down tiny, winding roads that take at least twice as long as they should to get anywhere. Though the destinations covered in this chapter are no more than about 60 miles in any direction from Northern Ireland's capital, it could take you up to 90 minutes to drive there—more if you take the scenic way. And frankly, why wouldn't you, when it's this beautiful?

As if that wasn't enough, the countryside these winding roads lead to is simply breathtaking—the verdant greens of the **Glens of Antrim,** the rugged **Mourne Mountains,** and the famously craggy coastline to the **Giant's Causeway,** surely one of the world's great natural wonders. Take the time to get out of your car and explore what this region has to offer—it may even turn out to be the highlight of your trip.

ESSENTIALS

Arriving

BY BUS **Ulsterbus** (translink.co.uk; ✆ **028/9066-6630**) runs buses from Belfast to Downpatrick, Carrickfergus, and Ballymena. While several other towns are reachable by bus, routes are long and circuitous—you're better off driving, or joining an organized tour.

BY CAR Most of the attractions listed in this chapter are easily accessible by car, with a journey time of between 1 and 2 hours (at most) from Belfast. Roads are good in the regions around the city, although traffic can be a problem, particularly during rush hour. In reasonable traffic, Comber is about a half-hour drive from the city; Strangford and Armagh, about an hour; Newcastle, 1¼ hours; Bushmills and the Giant's Causeway, 1½ hours.

BY TRAIN **Translink** (translink.co.uk; ✆ **028/9066-6630**) has train connections with several towns in the region, including Lisburn, Armagh, Bangor, and Portrush, although journey times can be long. The Translink website and the **mLink** app both have great journey planners.

PREVIOUS PAGE: **Visiting the 200-year-old avenue of beech trees known as Dark Hedges.**

THE CAUSEWAY COAST

The most extraordinary stretch of countryside in Northern Ireland, the glorious Causeway Coast stretches north and west from Belfast, curving around the County Antrim coast toward Donegal. This beautiful rocky shoreline includes the North's most striking sights: the awe-inspiring **Giant's Causeway** (p. 537) and the picturesque **Carrick-a-Rede Rope Bridge** (see below). The spectacular Causeway Coastal Route drive meanders along under bridges and stone arches, with the green Glens of Antrim on one side, and the crescent bays, sandy beaches, harbors, and huge rock formations on the other. The ocean gleams beside you as you curve along its craggy shores, and the light creates intense colors. In the spring and autumn, you often have the road all to yourself.

The drive is more or less equidistant from Belfast and Derry. It's possible to see all the sights in 1 day, staying in either city, although most travelers prefer to get a room on the coast and take their time.

Visitor Information

The principal visitor information centers in North Antrim are at 96b Main St., Larne (© **028/2826-2450**); Portnagree House, 14 Bayview Rd., Ballycastle (© **028/2076-2024**); and the **Giant's Causeway Information Centre,** 44 Causeway Rd., Bushmills (© **028/2073-1855**). All offices are open daily in summer; the Larne and Ballycastle offices are closed Sundays the rest of the year. The Giant's Causeway office stays open until 6pm in July and August.

Exploring the Causeway Coast

Carnlough ♥♥ VILLAGE The first major stop along the Antrim Coast Drive, this quiet village is known for its glassy harbor bobbing with sailboats. It's a lovely place to wander about, sampling interesting little shops and restaurants. Just outside Carnlough is a peaceful yet little-known waterfall called **Cranny Falls.** To get there, look for a marked 1-mile walking trail beginning on the waterfront. After crossing the white-stone bridge, the route traverses idyllic countryside, following an abandoned railway bed, past a disused quarry, until it reaches the falls. Along the way, occasional markers tell you about the history of the area.

Carnlough.

Carrick-a-Rede Rope Bridge ♥♥♥ BRIDGE We'll start with some advice: *Don't look down.* This rope bridge stretches across a chasm 18m (59 ft.) wide and 24m (79 ft.) deep, swinging over the sea between the mainland and a small island. The bridge once had a practical purpose, allowing access to the island's salmon fishery, which has been here since 1755 (don't worry, they do regular maintenance on the bridge). Now it also gives visitors a thrilling walk, but if you're afraid of heights, don't even think about it—like, seriously, what are you even doing here? And if

THE causeway coastal ROUTE

One of the most memorable drives in Ireland, the 130km (80-mile) Causeway Coastal Route in County Antrim, from Belfast to the Giant's Causeway, offers sweeping views of midnight-blue seas against gray, unforgiving cliffs and deep green hillsides. The whole coastal route runs as far as Derry, but the most scenic section goes as far as the Giant's Causeway. You could do the whole journey in a few hours, but allow much longer if you can—it's the sort of drive you want to savor.

Once you leave Belfast and join the coast road (A2), about 26km (16 miles) north of Carrickfergus, the first town is **Glenarm,** decked out with castle walls and a barbican gate; you can tour the castle and gardens. In the picturesque seaside village of **Carnlough ♥** (p. 533), you can take a pleasant hike to a waterfall. On up the coast, you'll find the National Trust village of **Cushendun ♥** (p. 536), known for its tea shops and whitewashed cottages.

For the most spectacular views, detour off the main A2 road at Cushendun onto the **Torr Head Scenic Road ♥♥** (p. 539). Just note that this narrow, rugged, cliffside road can induce vertigo as it climbs in seemingly perilous fashion to the tops of hills that are higher than you might think. On a clear day, you can see all the way to Scotland.

Crossing the Carrick-a-Rede Rope Bridge.

In the late spring and summer, you can take a ferry from the bustling town of **Ballycastle** to **Rathlin Island** (p. 536), where seals and nesting birds make their homes at the **Kebble National Reserve.** Or take a 15-minute detour south on the A22 from Ballycastle to see the picturesque **Dark Hedges,** a beautiful avenue of 200-year-old beech trees that intertwine overhead and were featured in an episode of *Game of Thrones.* (It's just past the Gracehill Golf Club on Bregah Rd.)

Farther west, the heart-stopping **Carrick-a-Rede Rope Bridge ♥♥♥** (p. 533) allows the brave to cross on foot over to a small island just off the coast. Others may prefer to press straight on to the postcard-perfect little town of **Ballintoy,** filled with charming stone cottages and flowery gardens. Ballintoy is stretched out at the edge of **Whitepark Bay,** a wide, crystalline curve of sandy beach at the foot of rocky hills surrounded by green farms. On a sunny day, you might find it hard to venture farther.

The last major stop is the eerily lunar **Giant's Causeway ♥♥♥** (p. 537), one of the world's true natural wonders. And after all that adventure, don't you think you've earned yourself a tipple—to enjoy later, if you're the one driving—at the **Old Bushmills Distillery ♥♥** (p. 538)?

Day Trips from Belfast
Inishowen
Giant's Causeway
Rathlin I.
Fair Head
Torr Head
Ballintoy
Portrush
Bushmills
Ballycastle
Moville
Portstewart
Castlerock
Coleraine
Armoy
Cushendun
Lough Foyle
Ballymoney
Cushendall
Red Bay
North Channel
To Troon
Limavady
Trostan
Ballykelly
Antrim Mts.
Carnlough Bay
To Cairnryan
LONDONDERRY (DERRY)
Garvagh
Bann
Carnlough
Glenarm
Kilrea
ANTRIM
Dungiven
Broughshane
To Stranraer
Sperrin Mts.
Sawel Mtn.
Maghera
Ballymena
Larne
Island Magee
Draperstown
Magherafelt
Ballyclare
Whitehead
Cranagh
Randalstown
Carrickfergus
To Douglas, Heysham, Liverpool
Moneymore
Antrim
Greenisland
Belfast Lough
Newtownabbey
Belfast Int'l
Bangor
Donaghadee
Cookstown
Glengormley
TYRONE
Lough Neagh
Crumlin
BELFAST
Newtownards
Pomeroy
Sixmilecross
Comber
Ards Peninsula
Strangford Lough
Coal Island
Lisburn
Lagan
Dungannon
Killinchy
Portavogie
Craigavon
Lurgan
Saintfield
Ballygawley
Augher
Portadown
Dromore
Ballynahinch
Killyleagh
Aughnacloy
DOWN
Portaferry
Strangford
Tandragee
Banbridge
Downpatrick
Armagh
Scarva
Middletown
Markethill
Castlewellan
Dundrum
Ardglass
Monaghan
ARMAGH
Rathfriland
Newcastle
IRISH SEA
Keady
Newry
Mourne Mts.
Dundrum Bay
MONAGHAN
Slieve Gullion
Ballybay
Warrenpoint
Annalong
Castleblayney
Forkhill
Omeath
0 10 miles
0 10 kms
Cootehill
Carlingford
Kilkeel
Dundalk
Greenore
Carlingford Lough
NORTHERN IRELAND
Belfast
Map Area
Galway
Dublin
REPUBLIC OF IRELAND
Cork
Armagh County Museum 25
Armagh Observatory and Planetarium 26
Benburb Valley Park & Castle 27
Carnlough 8
Carrick-a-Rede Rope Bridge 4
Castle Espie Wetlands Centre 12
Castle Ward 15
Castlewellan Forest Park 19
Cushendun 7
Downpatrick 16
Drumena Cashel 20
Dundrum Castle 18
Dunluce Castle 1
Giant's Causeway & Visitor Centre 2
Game of Thrones Studio Tour 29
Giant's Ring 9
Greencastle Royal Castle 23
Grey Abbey 11
Legananny Dolmen 17
Mount Stewart House 10
Navan Fort 24
Nendrum Monastic Site 13
Old Bushmills Distillery 3
Peatlands Park 28
Portaferry Castle 14
Rathlin Island 5
St. Patrick's Church of Ireland Cathedral 25
St. Patrick's Roman Catholic Cathedral 26
Silent Valley Mountain Park 22
Tollymore Forest Park 21
Torr Head Scenic Road 6

GOING TO THE birds: A TRIP TO RATHLIN ISLAND

Want to get close to nature? Plan a trip to **Rathlin Island,** 10km (6 miles) off the coast north of Ballycastle. The tiny island is 6km (3¾ miles) long, less than 1.5km (1 mile) wide, and almost completely treeless, with rugged coastal cliffs, a small beach, and crowds of seals and seabirds in spring and summer. Once you get there, you'll realize that it's not quite as isolated as it seems—there's a resident population of about 100 people, plus a pub, a hostel, and a guesthouse, should you miss the last boat to shore.

Start with a visit to the **Rathlin Island Boathouse Visitor Centre,** near the ferry landing at Church Bay (✆ **028/2076-0054**). The center contains an exhibit on the history of the islands, as well as plenty of handy visitor information. It's usually open from April to September daily 9am to 1pm and 1:30 until 5pm (check before visiting). Admission is free.

Rathlin is a favorite bird-watching spot, especially in spring and early summer when the birds are nesting. Given that there's little else to do here, it's no surprise that the island's biggest draw is bird-watching at the **Kebble National Nature Reserve** (✆ **028/7035-9963**) on the western side of the island, and the **RSPB Rathlin West Light Seabird Centre** (rspb.org.uk; ✆ **028/2076-0062**), located in Rathlin's unique "upside-down" lighthouse. Entry costs £8 adults, £5.50 students, and £4 children; free for ages 16–24 and kids 4 and under. From here you can watch colorful puffins, guillemots, kittiwakes, fulmars, razorbills, and other birds. It's open Monday through Saturday 9:30am until 5pm (last entry 4pm).

Boat trips operate daily from Ballycastle pier; the crossing takes 50 minutes. Boat schedules vary and are always subject to weather conditions, but there are usually several crossings a day. (Do check for cancellations in bad weather, though.) To check times and book tickets, call **Rathlin Island Ferry** (rathlin-ferry.com; ✆ **028/2076-9299**). One-way tickets cost £8 adults and £4 children 5–15, and are free for children 4 and under; it's advisable to book in advance.

If you find yourself wanting to stay a little longer, **Manor House Rathlin** (manorhouserathlin.com; ✆ **028/2076-0046**), which overlooks the harbor, costs £140 to £160 for a double.

For more information about Rathlin, visit **rathlin-island.co.uk**.

you don't know whether you suffer from vertigo, this may not be the best place to find out. ***Note:*** A 19km (12-mile) coastal cliff path leads between the Giant's Causeway (p. 537) and the rope bridge. It is always open and worth the exhaustion.

8km (5 miles) W of Ballycastle off the A2, 119A Whitepark Rd., Ballintoy, BT54 6LS. nationaltrust.org.uk/carrick-a-rede. ✆ **028/2076-9839.** Admission £13.50–£15.50 adults; £6.75–£7.75 children; £34–£39 families. Mar–Oct daily 9am–4:30pm; Nov–Feb daily 10am–2:30pm. Double-check opening hours before visiting.

Cushendun ♥♥ VILLAGE Back in the 1950s, the National Trust bought most of this charming seaside village to preserve it from overdevelopment. Today, the seafront is lined with an elegant sweep of perfect white Cornish-style cottages, and the quaint teashops do a bustling trade. The Glendun River winds through the village, crossed by an old stone

bridge, while down on the beach atmospheric sea caves line the shore. Just north of here, in a field overlooking the coast, stand the scant remains of **Curra Castle.** Cushendun is a good place to stop and take pictures before heading on down the main A2 road—or, if you want the most amazing views, the **Torr Head Scenic Road ♥♥** (p. 539).
Cushendun.

Dunluce Castle ♥♥ CASTLE Between the Giant's Causeway and the busy harbor town of Portrush, the coastline is dominated by the hulking skeletal outline of what must have once been a glorious castle. This was the main fort of the Irish MacDonnells, chiefs of Antrim. From the 14th to the 17th century, it was the largest and most sophisticated castle in the North, with a series of fortifications built on rocky outcrops extending into the sea. In 1639, part of the castle fell into the sea, taking some of the servants with it; soon after that, it was allowed to fall into a beautiful ruin. The 17th-century courtyard survives, including a few buildings. The site incorporates two of the original Norman towers dating from 1305. ***An enticing footnote:*** In 2011, an archaeological dig uncovered the remains of a town thought to have been destroyed during a rebellion in 1641. Only a tiny fraction of what is now believed to exist has so far been excavated.
87 Dunluce Rd., Bushmills, BT57 8UY. ✆ **028/2073-1938.** Admission £6 adults; £4.50 seniors and students; £4 children 5–17; free for children 4 and under; £18 families. Daily 9:30am–5pm (until 4pm Dec–Jan); last admission 30 min. before closing.

Giant's Causeway ♥♥♥ NATURE SITE A UNESCO World Heritage Site, this is an extraordinary sight indeed. Sitting at the foot of steep

The extraordinary basalt formations of the Giant's Causeway.

cliffs and stretching out into the sea, it is a natural formation of thousands of tightly packed basalt columns. The tops of the columns form flat steppingstones, all of which are perfectly hexagonal. They measure about 30cm (12 in.) in diameter; some are very short, others are as tall as 12m (39 ft.). Scientists believe they were formed 60 or 70 million years ago by volcanic eruptions and cooling lava. The ancients, on the other hand, believed the rock formation to be the work of giants. To reach the causeway, you walk from the parking area down a steep path for nearly 1.6km (1 mile), past amphitheaters of stone columns and formations with fanciful names like Honeycomb, Wishing Well, Giant's Granny, King and his Nobles, and Lover's Leap. If you wish, you can then climb up a wooden staircase to Benbane Head to take in the views, and then walk back along the cliff top. Regular shuttle service from the visitor center is available for those who can't face the hike. ***Note:*** The visitor center has a cafe, shop, interpretive center, and hugely expensive parking, justifying the fairly steep admission price. However, the Causeway itself is a free, open site, so if you can find safe and legal parking, there's nothing to stop you from walking down on your own.

44 Causeway Rd., Bushmills, BT57 8SU. nationaltrust.org.uk/giants-causeway. ✆ **028/2073-1855.** Visitor center and parking £14–£15 adults; £7–£7.50 children 5–17; free for children 4 and under; £35–£38 families. Visitor center Mar–Nov daily 9am–5pm; Nov–Feb daily 10am–4pm.

The Old Bushmills Distillery ♥♥ FACTORY TOUR Licensed to distill spirits in 1608, but with historical references dating from as far back as 1276, this distillery is endlessly popular. Visitors can tour the working sections and watch the whiskey-making process. At the end of

THE GIANT'S CAUSEWAY: A poet's-eye VIEW

With what tremendous force, aerial powers,
Once did ye rage in subterraneous bowers.
When roused by torturing fires from all your cayes.
Ye swept the glowing lava's sulphurous wayes;
Ye then beheld the thundering waters pass
Through wide rent gulfs, and changed to instant gas;
Struggling for vent again they upward roll.
And burst their narrow bounds from pole to pole.
'Twas nature's throe, and from the labouring frame
The solid strata, midst encircling flame
Severed and torn, their serried peaks upreared
And o'er the foamy surge the new-formed land appeared.

—From "The Giant's Causeway" by William Hamilton Drummond (1778–1865)

the tour, you can sample the wares in the **1608 Bar.** Tours last about an hour. The Bushmills coffee shop serves tea, coffee, snacks, and lunch. ***Tip:*** Although tours take place on weekends, the distillery itself is only in operation from Monday to Friday.

2 Distillery Rd., Bushmills, BT57 8XH. bushmills.com. ✆ **028/2073-3218.** Distillery tour £15 adults, £12 seniors and students, £6 children 8–17. No children 7 and under on tour. Tours every hour 10am–3pm. Mon–Sat 10am–5pm (Sun Mar–Oct 11am–5pm). Check times before visiting.

Whiskey-making tour at the Bushmills Distillery.

Torr Head Scenic Road ♥♥ SCENIC DRIVE This diversion is spectacular, but it's not for those with a fear of heights or narrow dirt roads; nor is it a good idea to drive in bad weather. But on a sunny, dry day, the brave can follow signs from **Cushendun ♥♥** (p. 536) up a very steep hill at the edge of town onto the Torr Head Scenic Road. After a precipitous climb, the road narrows further and inches its way along the edge of the cliff overlooking the sea. Arguably the best views are to be had at Murlough Bay (follow the signs).

Torr Rd., heading N out of Cushendun.

Where to Stay on the Causeway Coast

EXPENSIVE

The Bushmills Inn ♥♥ This very popular inn close to the Giant's Causeway makes a handy place to base yourself while exploring the area. It's been welcoming guests in one way or another since the 1600s, and it has centuries of charm. Lounges are warmed by wood fires, and there are little snugs and side rooms where you can settle down with a book. Rooms are modestly sized but have large, comfortable beds and modern bathrooms. The **restaurant** (p. 542) is among the best in the region for locally sourced seafood and sturdy Irish cooking. There's casual dining in the bar, and high tea in the afternoon. Book early—this place fills up well in advance.

9 Dunluce Rd., Giant's Causeway, Bushmills, BT57 8QG. bushmillsinn.com. ✆ **028/2073-3000.** 41 units. £170–£350 double. Breakfast included. Free parking. **Amenities:** Restaurant; bar; Wi-Fi (free).

Galgorm Resort ♥♥ With its creamy-white buildings and vast green grounds, this riverside resort makes an impact from the moment you pull up outside. The reception rooms and lounges are in the original 19th-century house, where you'll find fires crackling at the hearth and polished oak paneling. Most guest rooms are in well-designed modern extensions, which blend seamlessly with the old. Guest rooms have a masculine edge, with dark leather couches. There are also cottage suites, log cabins, forest dens, and shepherd's huts on the grounds. The hotel has *three* restaurants, so you won't lack for food. **Gillies Grill** serves brasserie and Asian-inspired dishes; **Fratelli** is a casual Italian in a vaulted space; **Castle Kitchen** has a gastropub vibe. You can also get lunch and afternoon tea in the conservatory, plus there are two bars: a "gin library" and **McKendry's** pub with nightly music. The **Thermal Spa Village** is huge, with pools, woodland paths, and hot tubs. Most guests flock to the spa village in the afternoon, so be prepared for it to be busy at peak times.

Guests enjoying the extensive spa facilities at the Galgorm Resort.

Fenaghy Rd., Ballymena, BT42 1EA. galgorm.com. ✆ **028/2588-1001.** 196 units. £190–£420 double. Breakfast included. Free parking. **Amenities:** 3 restaurants; 2 bars; golf course; pool; spa; Wi-Fi (free).

MODERATE

The Harbour View Hotel ♥♥ A pleasant Georgian inn in Carnlough, the Harbour View is a well-run, traditional kind of place on the Causeway Coast. It was built in 1847, so the building has its quirks—but having changed hands in 2024 (it was formerly the Londonderry Arms Hotel), it was given much needed revamp. Bedrooms have a homey feel, and a couple have views of the nearby sea. Part of the hotel's new identity is a focus on whiskey, featuring more than 400 whiskeys from all around the world, plus events and tastings. An unexpected piece of historical trivia about this place: Winston Churchill was once (briefly) the landlord. He inherited it and sold it soon afterward.

Harbour Rd., Carnlough, BT44 0EU. theharbourviewhotel.com. ✆ **028/2888-5255.** 35 units. £144–£244 double. Breakfast included. Free parking (limited). **Amenities:** Restaurant; bar; room service; Wi-Fi (free).

The Salthouse ♥♥ This lovely hotel in Ballycastle is a bright, welcoming space with a cozy feel. The gardens and courtyard have lots of peaceful areas to soak up the sea views of the Atlantic and Rathlin Island.

Outdoor hot tub with sea views at the Salthouse.

Rooms have all the touches of luxury, and there are individual lodges on the grounds, too. A spa has two outdoor hot tubs and an outdoor sauna. Enjoy fine dining in the **Salthouse Bar and Restaurant,** casual bites in the **Lookout** bar, and afternoon tea beside the fire.

39 Dunamallaght Rd., Ballycastle, BT54 6PF. thesalthousehotel.com. ✆ **028/2051-0000.** 24 units. £203–£307 double. Breakfast included. Free parking. **Amenities:** Wi-Fi (free).

INEXPENSIVE

Ballylagan Organic Farm ♥♥♥ Ballylagan is a working organic farm (the first in Northern Ireland), and at the center of it all is this welcoming little 1840s farmhouse. Owners Patricia and Tom Gilbert are passionate about what they do, and that passion shines through. This is an ideal rural escape. The guest apartment sleeps four and is in a separate building from the owners' home, while the main farmhouse has four bedrooms. There's a private garden, woodland walks, on-site horseback riding, and bicycles for hire—and of course lots happening around the farm at different times (just ask), plus a farm shop to stock up on delicious produce.

12 Ballylagan Rd., Straid, Ballyclare, BT39 9NF. ballylagan.com. ✆ **028/9332-2129.** Apartment from £90 per night; farmhouse from £450. 2-night minimum. Free parking. **Amenities:** Farm shop; Wi-Fi (free).

Trail riding at Ballylagan Organic Farm.

Inn on the Coast ♥♥ This family-friendly seaside hotel lies between the harbor towns of Portrush and Portstewart, and some of the rooms have uninterrupted sea views. Rooms are basic but comfortable and spacious, and most double rooms have an extra single bed. Triple and family rooms sleep up to four people. For food, you won't have to go far for atmosphere: The hotel has a traditional pub and restaurant that sometimes offers live entertainment. Check website for special offers.

50 Ballyreagh Rd., Portrush, BT56 8LT. innonthecoastportrush.com. ✆ **028/7082-3509.** 30 units. £89–£169 double. Breakfast included. Free parking. **Amenities:** Restaurant; Wi-Fi (free).

Where to Eat on the Causeway Coast

MODERATE

Bushmills Inn ♥♥ IRISH This popular restaurant in the Bushmills Inn (p. 539) has all the ambience you'd expect in a 17th-century building. Tables are arranged around warming fireplaces, and the food is classic Irish—creamy seafood pie, slow-braised ham hock with cabbage, poached smoked haddock with sautéed potatoes. Sandwiches are on offer during the day. At night the menu becomes more elaborate. Light bites are available in the **Gas Bar,** and high tea can be taken in the afternoon. Booking is recommended.

9 Dunluce Rd., Giant's Causeway, Bushmills, BT57 8QG. bushmillsinn.com. ✆ **028/2073-3000.** Entrees £18–£42. Daily noon–4pm and 5–9:30pm.

Harry's Shack ♥♥♥ SEAFOOD You won't get closer to the sea than this windswept restaurant right on Portstewart Strand beach. It's widely considered the best restaurant in the area, so don't let the casual vibe fool you. Inside is a sizable dining room, with rustic wooden seating, and people book well in advance so they can dig into dishes like the garlicky fresh mussels with homemade bread, pan-fried hake with chorizo and chickpeas, or cockles with capers and parsley. Desserts are fabulous here, so try to save room. Have a cocktail before dinner at the bar at the side of the shack. Breakfasts here are memorable. Don't forget to walk the beach first (or swim in the sea, if the temperature allows).

118 Strand Rd., Portstewart, BT55 7PG. facebook.com/HarrysShack. ✆ **028/7083-1783.** Entrees £16–£32. Mar–Oct daily 12:30–3pm and 5–8pm (to 8:30pm Fri–Sat); Nov–Feb Mon–Tue 12:30–3pm, Wed–Thurs 12:30–3pm and 5–7pm, Fri–Sat 12:30–3pm and 5–8:30pm, Sun 12:30–3pm and 5–7pm.

Tartine at the Distillers Arms ♥♥ IRISH There's no shortage of choice at this popular brasserie, which serves all the classics as well as its own sauces. Starters might include honey-baked Camembert with toasted bread and Distillers Pickle Sauce. For mains, there's usually a choice of chicken, steak, lamb, or pork, while a salmon plate might come with salmon sausage and "North-coast smokehouse" gratin with pea puree, roast parsnips, wine velouté, and sweet potato wedges. The early-bird dinner menu (5-6:30pm) is good value, with two courses and a glass of house

> **The Red Hand of Ulster**
>
> Around Belfast and Northern Ireland, you'll frequently come across representations of a red hand. It's carved in door frames, painted on walls and ceilings, and even planted in red flowers in gardens. Known as the Red Hand of Ulster, it is one of the symbols of the region. According to one version of the old tale, the hand can trace its history from a battle between two men competing to be king of Ulster. They held a race (some say by boat; others say it took place on horseback) and agreed that the first man to touch Ulster soil would win. As one man fell behind, he pulled out his sword and cut off his right hand, then with his left, flung the bloody hand ahead of his competitor, winning the right to rule.

wine or half pint of beer for £25 (you can "upgrade" your glass of wine to something fancier for £1 or £2).

140 Main St., Bushmills, BT57 8QE. distillersarms.com. ✆ **028/2073-1044.** Entrees £16–£32. Wed–Sun 5–8pm; Sun 12:15–2:15pm.

INEXPENSIVE

Thyme & Co. ♥♥ MODERN IRISH A great little cafe on the Causeway Coast Drive, Thyme & Co. serves tasty, healthy lunches. Ingredients are locally sourced, and the short menu is thoughtfully put together, featuring freshly baked pies, fishcakes made from salmon and smoked haddock, and gourmet sandwiches and wraps. In the summer, it stays open into the evenings on Fridays and Saturdays and serves thin-crust pizzas—a popular choice with locals.

5 Quay Rd., Ballycastle, BT54 6BJ. facebook.com/thymeandcocafe. ✆ **028/2076-9851.** Entrees £9–£14. Mon–Tue and Thurs–Fri 9:30am–4pm; Sat 9am–4pm and 5–8:30pm. Closed Wed and Sun.

Sports & Outdoor Pursuits

GOLF North Antrim has several notable courses, including champion pro golfer Darren Clarke's home course, the **Royal Portrush Golf Club,** Dunluce Road, Portrush (royalportrushgolfclub.com; ✆ **028/7082-2311**). Royal Portrush has two links courses; its celebrated Dunluce Course has been ranked number 3 in the United Kingdom. Greens fees here range from £140 (Valley Links) to £340 (Dunluce).

PONY TREKKING In the Portrush area, contact **Maddybenny Riding Centre,** Loguestown Road, Portrush (maddybenny.com; ✆ **028/7082-3394**); Maddybenny also has some self-catering cottages. For a trek in the hills or on the beach, try **Sheans Horse Farm** in Armoy, Ballymoney (sheanshorsefarm.com; ✆ **0775/9320-434**).

WALKING **The Gobbins** is a 3-hour guided cliff path walk with caves and sea views near Larne (thegobbinscliffpath.com; ✆ **028/9337-2318**). A section of the **Ulster Way,** 904km (560 miles) of marked trail, follows the North Antrim Coast from Glenarm to Portstewart. The **Moyle Way** offers a spectacular inland detour from Ballycastle south for 37km (26 miles) to Glenariff Forest Park. Last, but far from least, the **Causeway Coast Path** stretches for 47km (33 miles) from Ballintoy Harbour to Bushfoot Strand, near Bushmills. Short of sprouting wings, this is the best way to take in the full splendor of the North Antrim Coast. For a taster, **Away A Wee Walk** (awayaweewalk.com; ✆ **078-3770-3643**) will take you on a 5-mile tour of the Causeway cliffs. There are comprehensive guides to each route, including downloadable maps, on the excellent Northern Ireland walker's website **walkni.com.**

THE ARDS PENINSULA & MOURNE MOUNTAINS

The **Ards Peninsula,** beginning on the County Down coast about 16km (10 miles) east of Belfast, curls around **Strangford Lough.** A wildlife reserve of great natural beauty, it's also lined with historic buildings and ancient sites, from the austere **Castle Ward** (p. 545) and the elegant **Mount Stewart House** (p. 547) to the mysterious, megalithic **Giant's Ring** (p. 546). All are an easy drive from Belfast city center—you can reach most sights in half an hour, perfect for a day trip.

More outdoorsy types will want to press on south to explore the **Mourne Mountains,** the highest mountains in Northern Ireland. The rocky landscape here is breathtaking—all gray granite, yellow gorse, purple heather, and white stone cottages. The ancestral home of the Brontës is here, in ruins. But the region is not desolate: You have forest parks, sandy beaches, lush gardens, and, of course, pubs to explore.

Visitor Information

The **Downpatrick Visitor Information Centre** at the St. Patrick Centre, Market Street (✆ **028/4461-9000**), is open daily. You can also get information at the **Newcastle Visitor Information Centre** at 10–14 Central Promenade, Newcastle (✆ **0330/137-4046**), and the **Kilkeel Visitor Information Centre** at the Nautilus Centre, The Harbour, Kilkeel (✆ **028/4176-2525**).

Exploring the Ards Peninsula

Two roads traverse the **Ards Peninsula:** the A20 (the lough road) and the A2 (the coast road). The lough road is the more scenic. At the southern tip of the peninsula in Portaferry, you'll need to take a 10-minute car ferry ride (nidirect.gov.uk/articles/strangford-ferry-timetable) across the Narrows to the village of Strangford on the other side. Ferries run twice an hour on weekdays more or less from 7:30am (8am Sat, 9:30am Sun) to 10:30pm (11pm Sat).

Castle Espie Wetland Centre ♥ NATURE SITE This wildlife center, named for a castle that has long since ceased to be, is home to rare migratory geese, ducks, and swans. Some birds are so accustomed to visitors that they will eat grain from their hands. Guided trails are designed for children and families, and the center sponsors activities and events year-round. Every summer, the "duckery" becomes home to dozens of

Castle Ward was the film location for Winterfell in *Game of Thrones.*

adorable newly hatched goslings, ducklings, and cygnets. The **Kingfisher Café** serves breakfast, light lunches (no duck on the menu . . .), and cakes. 78 Ballydrain Rd., Comber, BT23 6EA. wwt.org.uk/wetland-centres/castle-espie. ✆ **028/9187-4146.** Admission £9.45 adults; £8.05 seniors and students; £6.15 children 4–17; free for children 3 and under; £26.50 families. Visitor center daily 10am–5pm (5:30pm on summer weekends); cafe 10am–4pm; nature reserve 10am–4:30pm. In winter, last admission 3:30pm.

Castle Ward ♥♥ HISTORIC HOUSE About 2km (1¼ miles) west of Strangford village, this grand manor house dates from 1760. A hybrid of architectural styles melding Gothic with neoclassical, it sits on a 280-hectare (692-acre) country estate. Inside, kids can dress up in period clothes and play with period toys, while outside they can roam formal gardens, woodlands, lakes, and seashore and even ride a tractor-trailer out to see the farm animals. A theater in the stable yard hosts operatic performances in summer. Castle Ward achieved a degree of latter-day fame as Winterfell, one of the key locations for HBO's *Game of Thrones* (see box on p. 546)—albeit heavily disguised.

Park Rd., Strangford, BT30 7LS. nationaltrust.org.uk/castle-ward. ✆ **028/4488-1204.** Admission £13 adults; £6.50 children; £32.50 families. Grounds daily 10am–6pm; house Mar–Oct daily 11am–4pm.

khaleesi DOES IT

Unless you've been living beyond the Wall, you'll have heard of a little TV show called *Game of Thrones.* For nearly a decade, the HBO super-hit was the most popular show in the world—and much of it was filmed right here, in Northern Ireland.

Although *Game of Thrones* ended in 2019, it's still raking in big bucks for the local tourism industry. In many places you'll even find the kind of permanent information boards more usually associated with real-life history, instead describing what was filmed there. Major locations included **Cushendun ♥♥** (p. 536) and **Ballintoy** (p. 534) on the Antrim Coast Drive, and **Castle Ward ♥♥** (p. 545) and the **Tollymore Forest Park ♥♥** (p. 551) in County Down.

Many companies offer locations tours, but perhaps the best, and longest-running, come from **Brit Movie Tours** (britmovietours.com; ✆ **0844/247-1007** in Northern Ireland and Britain, 44/207-118-1007 in the rest of the world). The epic, 8½-hour **Game of Thrones Tour from Belfast with Giant's Causeway** takes in many scenic places used in the show, with various fan-related fun along the way, such as a quiz (dressing up is not unheard of). It includes a 90-minute visit to the Causeway (p. 537), which hasn't actually appeared in the show, but why pass by such an evocative site? Tours depart daily at 9am from the Irish Tour Tickets Office at 10 Great Victoria St., Belfast, and return roughly 8½ hours later (in July–Aug there's a second tour at noon). Tickets cost £28 and reservations are absolutely essential. Due to the content, the tour is not suitable for kids 15 and under; disabled travelers should also note that, because of the historic and sometimes remote locations visited, the tour is not wheelchair-accessible. Private tours can also be booked from £625, depending on the number of people (maximum six).

The self-guided 2½-hour **Game of Thrones Cycle Tour** (winterfell-tours.com/locationscycletour) takes in around 10 locations in Castle Ward, covering around 4km (2.5 miles) on a flat route, from Winterfell Castle along the shoreline of Strangford Lough to Robb's camp and Audley's Castle, where Jamie Lannister was captured. You can also see the crooked tree where Brienne found the hanging bodies, the castle window that Bran "fell" from, and the field of Baelor Battle. The tour starts at Castle Ward and costs £38.50 per person (£23.50 children 11 and under).

The excellent **Game of Thrones Studio Tour** at the Linen Mills studio in Banbridge (gameofthronesstudiotour.com; ✆ **028/4046-4777**) lets you delve into behind-the-scenes details of the show, from its early concepts and designs to all the art and craftsmanship that went into creating its sets, props, costumes, and special effects. The self-guided tour takes 2 to 3 hours. Book in advance; tickets cost £29.50 adults, £24 seniors and students, £12 teens ages 13 to 15, £5 children ages 5 to 12, free for children 4 and under, and £67 families.

Giant's Ring ♥♥ ANCIENT SITE This massive and mysterious prehistoric earthwork, 180m (590 ft.) in diameter, has at its center a megalithic chamber with a single capstone. Ancient burial rings like this were thought to be protected by fairies and were left untouched, but this one is quite an exception. In the 19th century, it was used as a racetrack, with the high embankment around it serving as grandstands. Today, its dignity has been restored, and it is a place of wonder for the few travelers who make the journey. It's 6km (3¾ miles) southwest of Belfast center, west off A24. Near Shaw's Bridge, off Ballynahatty Rd., Ballynahatty, BT8 8LE. No phone. Free admission (open site).

Grey Abbey ♥ RELIGIOUS SITE On the eastern shore of Strangford Lough, the striking ruins of Grey Abbey sit amid a beautifully landscaped setting, perfect for a picnic. Founded in 1193 by the Cistercians, it contained one of the earliest Gothic churches in Ireland. Many Cistercian ruins were quite elaborate, but this one is surprisingly plain. Amid the ruined choirs is a fragmented stone effigy of a knight in armor, possibly a likeness of John de Courcy, husband of the abbey's founder, Affreca of Cumbria. There's a reconstructed medieval herb garden, and a small visitor center has exhibits on the abbey's history.
Main St., Greyabbey, BT22 2NQ. ✆ **028/9082-3207.** Free admission. Visitor center Sat 1–4pm, Sun 2:30–4pm.

Legananny Dolmen ♥ ANCIENT SITE This mysterious granite *dolmen* (Neolithic tomb) on the southern slope of Slieve Croob is huge, and yet its massive capstone seems weightlessly poised on the uprights. It's halfway between Dromara and Castlewellan on the lower slopes of Slieve Croob Mountain, 40km (25 miles) south of Belfast.
Signposted off Legananny Rd., Leitrim, BT32 3QR. No phone. Free admission (open site).

The lovely formal gardens at Mount Stewart House.

Mount Stewart House, Garden, and Temple of the Winds ♥♥ HISTORIC HOUSE/GARDENS Once the home of Lord Castlereagh, this 18th-century house with lush gardens sits on the eastern shore of Strangford Lough. An impressive array of unusual plants flourishes here, thanks to a rare mild microclimate. Inside the house, the excellent art collection includes the *Hambletonian* by George Stubbs and portraits by Pompeo Batoni and Anton Raphael Mengs. The Temple of the Winds, a fine 18th-century banqueting house, is also on the estate, but it's only

DOWNPATRICK: sainted TOWN

Legend has it that when St. Patrick came to Ireland in A.D. 432 to begin his missionary work, strong winds blew his boat to the ancient fortified town of Downpatrick, at the south end of Strangford Lough. He'd meant to sail up the coast to County Antrim, where as a young slave he had tended flocks on Slemish Mountain. Instead, as fate would have it, he settled here and converted the local chieftain Dichu and his followers to Christianity. Over the next 30 years, Patrick roamed through Ireland carrying out his work, but this is where he died. Some believe he is buried in the graveyard of Downpatrick Cathedral, although there's no proof. Because of all of this, the town tends to be crowded, largely with Catholic pilgrims, around St. Patrick's Day.

Stop in first at the **Down County Museum** (downcountymuseum.com; ✆ **033/0137-4049**), The Mall, English Street, BT30 6AH. Set in a converted jail, the museum tells the story of Down from the Stone Age to the present day. It also has a handy tearoom. The museum is open Tuesday to Saturday from 10am until 4:30pm. Entry is free.

Almost next door to the museum, at the end of the English Street cul-du-sac, is **Down Cathedral** (downcathedral.org; ✆ **028/4461-4922**). Excavations show that Downpatrick was a *dún* (fort), perhaps from the Bronze Age, and its earliest structures were built on the site where this church now sits. Ancient fortifications ultimately gave way to a series of churches, each built atop the ruins of the previous incarnation, over 1,800 years. The current cathedral is an 18th- and 19th-century reconstruction of its 13th- and 16th-century predecessors. Just south of the cathedral stands a relatively recent monolith inscribed with the name "PATRIC." By some accounts, it roughly marks the grave of the saint, who is said to have died at Saul, 3km (2 miles) northeast. The tradition identifying this site as Patrick's grave seems to go back no further than the 12th century, though, when John de Courcy reputedly transferred the bones of saints Columba and Brigid to lie beside those of St. Patrick. The cathedral is open to visitors Monday to Saturday from 10am to 3:30pm. Entry is free.

A 5-minute walk away, the modern glass-and-steel **The Saint Patrick Centre,** 53A Market St., BT30 6LZ (saintpatrickcentre.com; ✆ **028/4461-9000**), tells the story of Ireland's patron saint through a new exhibition. It also has an exhibition devoted to the legacy of Irish missionaries who helped spread Christianity in Europe in the latter half of the first millennium. The center is open Monday to Saturday 9am until 5pm (last admission 4pm) and also on Sunday 9am to 5pm in July and August. Entry to the exhibition costs £9.75 adults, £8.75 seniors and students, £7.75 children, and £29.75 for families.

Downpatrick is about 34km (21 miles) southeast of Belfast. To get there from the city by car, take A24 then A7; the drive takes just under 40 minutes. You can also get there by bus (a 1-hr. trip) from the Europa Bus Station on Great Victoria Street.

open Sunday afternoons (and not in winter). Admission to the house is by guided tour only.

Portaferry Rd., Newtownards, BT22 2AD. nationaltrust.org.uk/mount-stewart. ✆ **028/4278-8387.** House and lakeside garden: £14 adults; £7 children; £35 families. House Apr–Oct daily 11am–5pm, Nov–Feb 11am–4pm; gardens daily 10am–5pm. Last admission 1 hr. before closing.

Nendrum Monastic Site ♥ RELIGIOUS SITE Hidden away on an isolated island, this site dates from the 5th century. It's much older than Grey Abbey across the water, and the remains of the ancient community founded by St. Mochaoi (St. Mahee) are fascinating. Foundations show the outline of ancient churches, a round tower, and beehive cells. Other interesting details are concentric stone ramparts and a sundial, reconstructed from long-broken pieces. Its visitor center shows informative videos and has insightful exhibits. The road to Mahee Island crosses a causeway to Reagh Island and a bridge still protected by the 15th-century Mahee Castle.

Mahee Island, Ringneill Rd., Comber, BT23 6EP. ✆ **028/9082-3207.** Free admission (open site). Visitor center: Apr–Sept Wed–Sun 10am–5pm; last admission 4:30pm.

Portaferry Castle ♥ CASTLE Though it's little more than a small 16th-century tower house, at one time Portaferry Castle, together with another tower house in Strangford, controlled all the ship traffic through the Narrows. This piece of history stands right beside the harbor. ***Note:*** The castle was closed for repairs at press time; check discovernorthern ireland.com for updates.

Castle St., Portaferry. No phone. Free admission.

Exploring the Mourne Mountains

Below the Ards Peninsula, the A2 continues to the southern part of County Down, the **Mourne Mountains** area. If you're going there directly from Belfast, the A24 is a good shortcut—the drive from Belfast directly to Newcastle should take just under an hour. If you're driving up from Dublin, turn east off the Dublin–Belfast Road at Newry and take A2, following the north shore of Carlingford Lough, between the mountains and the sea. It's a drive you won't soon forget.

This outdoorsy region is dominated by the massive barren peak of **Slieve Donard** (839m/2,752 ft.). From the top, the view takes in the full length of Strangford Lough, Lough Neagh, the Isle of Man, and, on a crystalline day, the west coasts of Wales and Scotland. (The recommended ascent of Slieve Donard is from Donard Park on the south side of Newcastle.) If that's too high for you, head to the heart of the Mournes, to the exquisite **Silent Valley Reservoir** (p. 551). Recreational opportunities abound (p. 554), but it also has some intriguing old ruins to explore. **Newcastle,** a lively traditional seaside resort with a golden sand beach and one of the finest golf courses in Ireland, makes a good base for exploring the area; several small coastal towns strung along the A2 road—**Kilkeel, Rostrevor,** and **Warrenpoint**—offer their own low-key charms.

Castlewellan Forest Park ♥♥ NATURE SITE Surrounding a fine trout lake and watched over by the stately mid-19th-century Castlewellan Castle (sadly, closed to the public), this forest park is ideal for picnics and outdoor activities. Woodland walks, a formal walled garden, and an interesting lakeside sculpture trail are among its attractions. Anglers can fish for trout (brown and rainbow) in the lake. You can get lost in the **Peace Maze,** an enormous hedge maze designed to represent the path to peace in Northern Ireland. The main draw is the **National Arboretum,** opened in 1740 and now 10 times its original size. The largest of its three greenhouses features aquatic plants and a collection of free-flying tropical birds. The town of Castlewellan, elegantly laid out around two squares, is a short distance away, as is the ancient fort of **Drumena Cashel** (see below).

Forest Office: The Grange, Castlewellan Forest Park, Castlewellan, BT31 9BU. visitmournemountains.co.uk. ✆ **0330/137-4046.** Admission and parking £5 per car. Daily May–Aug 9am–9pm; Apr and Sept 9am–8pm; Mar and Oct 9am–6pm; Nov–Feb 9am–5pm.

The Peace Maze in Castlewellan Forest Park.

Drumena Cashel ♥ ANCIENT SITE Ireland once had thousands of fortifications like this irregularly shaped stone-ring fort, a farmstead dating from the early Christian period. This is one of the better-preserved examples. During the age of the Viking invasions, it likely provided protection for the local population. Its walls, partially rebuilt in the mid-1920s, measure 2.7m (9 ft.) to 3.6m (12 ft.) thick. The *souterrain* (underground stone tunnel) is T-shaped and was likely used in ancient times for cold storage.

Signposted from A25, 3km (2 miles) SW of Castlewellan. No phone. Free admission (open site).

Dundrum Castle ♥ CASTLE The oldest visible portions of this castle's extensive ruins date from the 12th century. Once one of the mightiest of the Norman castles in Northern Ireland (second only to Carrickfergus), it still commands the imagination. The enormous keep was built in the 13th century, as was the gatehouse. It was the home of the Maginnis family until the 17th century, when it was captured by Oliver Cromwell's army, who destroyed it in 1652. The hilltop setting is lovely, with panoramic views.

6.5km (4 miles) E of Newcastle, off A2, Dundrum, BT33 0NF. ✆ **028/9082-3207.** Free admission. Castle June–Aug daily 10am–5pm, rest of year Tues–Sun 9am–4pm; grounds open daily year-round. Last admission 30 min. before closing.

Greencastle Royal Castle ♥ CASTLE The first castle on this site, built in 1261, was a two-story rectangular tower surrounded by a curtain wall with corner towers; it faced its companion, Carlingford Castle, across the mouth of the lough. Very little of that survives, however; most of what you see is from the 14th century, a royal garrison that was destroyed by Cromwell's forces in 1652. Opening times are somewhat unpredictable, so call before visiting.

6.5km (4 miles) SW of Kilkeel, Greencastle, Cranfield Point, BT34 4LR. ✆ **028/9082-3207.** Free admission.

Silent Valley Mountain Park ♥♥ NATURE SITE This park surrounds the Silent Valley Reservoir, the major source of water for County Down. Easy, well-marked paths wind around the lake, and there's a coffee shop near the information center. A shuttle bus takes visitors from the center to the top of nearby Ben Crom; it runs on weekends in May, June, and September and daily in July and August.

Information center: Head Rd., Kilkeel, Newry, BT34 4HU. niwater.com/silent-valley. ✆ **084/5744-0088.** Free admission. Parking £5; pedestrians £1.60 or 60p per child. Daily Apr–Oct 10am–6pm; Nov–Mar 10am–4pm.

Tollymore Forest Park ♥♥ NATURE SITE All that's left of the once-glorious Tollymore House is this delightful 480-hectare (1,186-acre) wildlife and forest park. The park offers a number of walks up into the north slopes of the Mourne Mountains or along the Shimna River (known for its exceptionally fine salmon). The Shimna walk has several beguiling caves and grottos. The park is scattered with follies, such as faux-medieval castle gatehouses and other fanciful fakes. The forest is also a nature preserve inhabited by local wildlife like badgers, foxes, otters, and pine martens. And don't miss the trees for the forest—exotic species include magnificent Himalayan cedars and a 30m (98-ft.) sequoia in the arboretum.

Off B180, 3.2km (2 miles) NW of Newcastle, Tullybrannigan Rd., BT33 0PX. nidirect.gov.uk/articles/tollymore-forest-park. ✆ **028/4372-2428.** Free admission. Parking £5. Daily 10am–dusk.

walk this way: THE MOURNE WALL TREK

Between 1904 and 1922, the 36km (22-mile) dry-stone Mourne Wall and dam was built to enclose Silent Valley. The **Mourne Wall Trek** follows the wall in a circuit that climbs over 15 of the Mourne Mountains' main peaks. The steep path is more than most hikers want to take on, and probably shouldn't be attempted in a single day (though some serious hikers have done it in a day). But it is a fine, long walk for experienced ramblers and offers wonderful views. You can join the pathway at several different places, and you can hike either clockwise or counterclockwise. For more information about the route, including maps and a photo log of every stage, go to **mournewall.co.uk**.

Where to Stay & Eat in the Mourne Mountains

Ards Peninsula sights are close enough to Belfast to allow you to get back to your Belfast hotel for the night, but if you're venturing out to the Mourne Mountains—particularly if you're engaging in the outdoor activities for which the area is famed—you'll need a place to lay your head overnight.

Brunel's ♥♥♥ IRISH Local flavors are prepared with imaginative flair at this excellent restaurant just a mile from the Slieve Donard Spa and Resort (p. 553). Mussels fresh from Strangford Lough are a simple but delicious lead-in to a dish of coley (a fish similar to cod) cooked with smoked egg-yolk puree, or rigatoni with hay-baked celeriac. This is the kind of place where you'll witness a sea of cellphones taking photos of each course before demolition of the artful arrangements. The early-evening menu (Thurs-Fri 5-6:30pm) offers two courses for £27, or three for £34.

32 Downs Rd., Newcastle, BT33 0HJ. brunelsrestaurant.co.uk. ✆ **028/4379-8277.** Entrees £21–£34. Thurs 5–9pm; Fri 5–9:30pm; Sat noon–2:30pm and 5–9:30pm; Sun 12:30–8pm.

The Carriage House ♥♥ With a view of Dundrum Castle on one side, and a shimmering bay dotted with sailboats on the other, it's little wonder that this lovely little B&B inspires artistic sentiment. Owner Maureen Griffith is a collector of unique art, and her creative eye has furnished almost every corner of her terraced house with something wonderful to look at. She's also a great cook; breakfasts here are special, including produce picked fresh from the garden. She doesn't cook evening meals but will recommend places to eat within walking distance.

71 Main St., Dundrum, BT33 0LU. carriagehousedundrum.com. ✆ **028/4375-1635.** 3 units. £150 double. Breakfast included. Free parking (on street). **Amenities:** Garden; Wi-Fi (free).

The Daily Grind ♥♥ CAFE A great place to know about for a quick lunch in Downpatrick, this funky local favorite cafe specializes in creative and tasty sandwiches, which go down nicely with a cup of fresh coffee (if you can forgive the atrociously punning names—"Buy One Get One Brie," "Pitta Pocket or Two," you get the idea). The Daily Grind Special is a delicious salad served with toast and chili jam. There are also vegan options, not to mention a host of tempting cakes.

St. Patrick's Ave., Downpatrick, BT30 6DW. facebook.com/TheDailyGrindDownpatrick. ✆ **028/4461-7173.** Entrees £5–£8.50. Mon–Sat 10am–3:30pm.

Dunnanelly Country House ♥♥♥ Just outside Downpatrick, this delightful country mansion is a truly idyllic retreat, set on beautiful grounds that stretch for miles. The decor inside mixes a feeling of history with a playful edge: traditional, Regency-style color schemes and furnishings offset by pieces of modern art, an interesting sculpture, and (memorably)

J.J. Farrall's restaurant in the Slieve Donard Resort has views of the Mourne Mountains.

an antique rocking horse, complete with mouth open in an oh-so-happy-to-see-you grin. The guest rooms are thoughtfully designed with large, modern bathrooms and have lovely views of the estate, tempting you to take a gentle stroll or invigorating hike. And you may need that exercise to help work off the hearty and delicious breakfasts. Guests have the use of a conservatory, a sitting room, and a separate game room. There's no dinner, but the owners can cheerfully point you in the direction of the best local pubs.

26 Rocks Chapel Rd., Downpatrick, BT30 9BA. dunnanellycountryhouse.com. ✆ **077/1277-9085.** 6 units. £130 double. Breakfast included. No children 11 and under unless all rooms booked by same group. Free parking. **Amenities:** Wi-Fi (free).

Mourne Seafood Bar ♥♥ SEAFOOD Situated just a street back from the quay in Dundrum, this seaside outpost of one of Belfast's best restaurants (p. 525) is worth traveling for if you're staying in the country-side—or worth a detour for a leisurely lunch. The menu is strictly oriented around whatever's good and fresh that day, but you may well be offered salt and pepper prawns with cucumber and soy, crispy whitebait (tiny, bite-size fish, deep-fried), or a plate of oysters from Carlingford Lough. The only real snag is that it's hardly an undiscovered gem—you'll be lucky to get a table for dinner without a reservation on weekends, especially in summer.

10 Main St., Dundrum, BT33 0LU. mourneseafood.com. ✆ **028/4375-1377.** Entrees £17–£30. Thurs 12:30–3pm and 5–9pm; Fri 12:30–3pm and 5–9:30pm; Sat 12:30–9:30pm; Sun 12:30–6pm.

The Slieve Donard Spa and Resort ♥♥ The spindly, neo-Gothic turret of this 1897 hotel stands like a beacon overlooking Dundrum Bay.

The surroundings are certainly dramatic, but inside this is a relaxing, luxurious place. Cozy bedrooms are decorated in Victorian style with lots of frills (literally) and antique-style furnishings; many have views of the bay and Mourne Mountains. The excellent spa has a long list of treatments, from Ayurvedic regimens to hot stone massages and full-body salt scrubs. The restaurants are the formal **J.J. Farrall's,** the more relaxed **Lighthouse Lounge** for light meals, and the **Percy French** for pub classics. Check the website for offers and spa packages.

Downs Rd., Newcastle, BT33 0AH. marineandlawn.com/slievedonard. ✆ **028/4372-1066.** 180 units. £181–£505 double. Breakfast included. Free parking. **Amenities:** 2 restaurants; bar; gym; pool; room service; spa; Wi-Fi (free).

Sports & Outdoor Pursuits

ADVENTURE SPORTS For canoeing, rock climbing, bushcraft, watersports, and a variety of other intrepid activities in the Mourne Mountains, contact **One Great Adventure,** the Grange Yard, Castlewellan Forest Park, Castlewellan (onegreatadventure.com; ✆ **028/4377-0714**).

CYCLING The foothills of the Mournes around Castlewellan are ideal for cycling, with panoramic vistas and very little traffic. In these parts, the perfect year-round outfitter is **Ross Cycles,** 44 Clarkhill Rd., Castlewellan (✆ **028/4377-8029**), signposted from the Clough–Castlewellan Road, .8km (½ mile) out of Castlewellan. The shop carries mountain bikes for the whole family, including children's seats. You can park and ride or request local delivery. Daily rates start at around £20, with family and weekly rates available.

DIVING The Ards Peninsula's lakes and offshore waters are a diver's dream—remarkably clear and littered with wrecks. One of Europe's finest training centers, **DV Diving,** 138 Mount Stewart Rd., Newtownards (dvdiving.co.uk; ✆ **028/9186-1686**), offers diving courses.

GOLF Nestled in huge sand dunes with the Mourne Mountains in the background, the **Royal County Down** ♥ in Newcastle (royalcountydown.org; ✆ **028/4372-3314**) is an 18-hole, par-71 championship course created in 1889 and still considered among the best. Greens fees are £425 to £575, depending on the time of year. Not too far away, the **Kilkeel Golf Club,** Mourne Park, Ballyardle, Kilkeel (kilkeelgolfclub.org; ✆ **028/4176-5095**), is a beautiful parkland course on the historic Kilmorey Estate. Greens fees are £35 weekdays and £50 on weekends and bank holidays.

COUNTY ARMAGH

A green, rolling stretch of gentle hills and small villages, County Armagh is also one of Northern Ireland's most rebellious Republican regions—you'll notice police watchtowers atop some hills, as well as the occasional barracks (mostly empty these days).

The handsome cathedral town of **Armagh City** makes a good touring base. A short distance outside the city, the small town of **Bessbrook** has historic cottages, the forests of Slieve Gullion, and ancient **Navan Fort** (p. 556), Ulster's most important archaeological site. The area's greatest natural attraction is a 40-minute drive north of Armagh City: **Lough Neagh,** Ireland's largest lake (see box on p. 558).

Visitor Information

Tourist information is available at the **Armagh County Museum,** The Mall East, Armagh City (visitarmagh.com; ✆ **028/3752-3070**). The museum (see below) is open all year, Monday to Friday from 10am until 5pm, Saturday 10am to 4pm.

Exploring County Armagh

Armagh City's name, from the Irish *ard Mhacha* (Macha's height), refers to the pagan queen Macha, who is said to have built a fortress here. It's no coincidence that St. Patrick also chose to base himself here—it was a bold challenge to the native paganism. The simple stone church he built in the 5th century is now the stately **St. Patrick's Church of Ireland Cathedral** (p. 557). (Not to be outdone, Armagh City's Roman Catholic cathedral is also called St. Patrick's—see p. 558.) East of the town center, the city also boasts the Mall, a lush park lined with handsome Georgian town houses built of the colorful local limestone. To get to Armagh City from Belfast, take M1 and A3 southwest for 64km (40 miles); the journey takes a little less than an hour.

Armagh County Museum ♥ MUSEUM Intriguing Armagh-related artifacts going back to the Neolithic Age fill this history museum on the Mall. Highlights include a collection of 19th-century Irish bog oak jewelry; Irish police uniforms from the 1820s up to the mid–20th century; and a collection of elaborate fans from around the world, from as far back as the 1700s. Chillingly, the museum also has a genuine scold's bridle, an iron torture instrument and "correctional" device that was placed over a woman's head, with a spike inside her mouth to prevent her from talking.

The Mall East, Armagh City, BT61 9BE. visitarmagh.com. ✆ **028/3752-3070.** Free admission. Mon–Fri 10am–5pm; Sat 10am–4pm.

Armagh Observatory and Planetarium ♥♥ PLANETARIUM A perfect place for kids with an interest in science, this state-of-the-art planetarium has an impressive digital projection system with 3D elements. During the summer there's usually a full program every day. Outside the planetarium, take a stroll around the **Astropark,** filled with scale models of planets. You'll pass the 200-year-old **Armagh Observatory** (still a working observatory, not open to the public). The planetarium can get

Interactive displays chart the universe at the Armagh Planetarium.

busy with school groups on weekdays during term time, so best to visit after noon or on weekends.

College Hill, Armagh City, BT61 9DB. armagh.space. ✆ **028/3752-3689.** Admission to show and exhibition area £10 adults; £8 seniors and students; £7 children 4–15; free for children 3 and under; £32 families. Tues–Sun 10am–5pm.

Benburb Valley Park ♥ NATURE SITE This sylvan park 11km (7 miles) northeast of Armagh on the River Blackwater contains the ruins of **Benburb Castle,** a squat, fortresslike ruin dating from the Plantation of Ulster in the early 1600s. It occupies an impressive cliffside spot overlooking a gorge. In 1646, an Irish army defeated an Anglo-Scottish invasion force at Benburb, thus ending the brief Scottish bid to rule Ireland. The castle is on the grounds of a Servite priory; admission is free, but you have to arrange in advance if you want to do more than see it from the outside. Call the priory at ✆ **028/3754-8241** to inquire.

89 Milltown Rd., Benburb (take B128 off A29), BT71 7LY. walkni.com/walks/benburb-valley-park. No phone. Free admission.

Navan Fort ♥♥ ANCIENT SITE Believed to have been the royal and religious capital of Ulster from 1150 B.C. until the spread of Christianity, Navan Fort is a mysterious place. Its central circular earthwork enclosure holds a smaller circular structure, and it all encloses an Iron Age burial mound. Even today, scientists do not really understand what it was used for, although they know that it was all set on fire around 95 B.C., possibly as part of a ritual.

On A28, signposted from Armagh City center, 81 Killylea Rd., BT60 4LD. armagh.co.uk/navan-centre-fort. ✆ **028/3752-9644.** Admission £11 adults; £9.25 seniors and students; £7.50 children 4–16; £32.50 families. Tues–Sun 11am–5pm.

Peatlands Park ♥ NATURE SITE A surprisingly lovely 240 hectares (593 acres) of lakes and peat bogs, this park effectively forms one giant nature reserve. You wander through it on a well-designed system of walking paths, or (slightly more fun on rainy days) ride through it on a narrow-gauge railway. Nature walks and events are offered throughout the year. The park is southwest of Lough Neagh, just across the border into County Tyrone.

33 Derryhubbert Rd. 11km (6¾ miles) SE of Dungannon, at exit 13 off M1, Co. Tyrone, BT71 6NW. nidirect.gov.uk/articles/peatlands-park-dungannon. ✆ **028/3839-9195.** Free admission to park; rail ride £2 adults; £1 seniors and children 2–16; £5 families. Park open daily May–Aug 9am–9pm; Apr and Sept 9am–8pm; Mar and Oct 9am–7pm; Nov–Feb 9am–4:30pm. ***Note:*** Railway was not open at press time, so check before visiting.

St. Patrick's Church of Ireland Cathedral ♥ CATHEDRAL Built on the site of St. Patrick's 5th-century church, Armagh's Anglican cathedral

Iron Age re-enactors probe the mysteries of Navan Fort.

LOUGH neagh

Now here's a great creation story: Irish lore maintains that Lough Neagh—the largest lake in Ireland—was created by the mighty giant Fionn MacCumhail (Finn McCool) when he dug up a chunk of earth to fling into the sea to create the Isle of Man. It must have been a sizeable chunk indeed to gouge out this 396-sq.-km (153-sq.-mile) lake.

The **Lough Neagh Discovery Centre,** Oxford Island, Craigavon (oxfordisland.com; ✆ **028/3832-2205**), is open Monday to Friday 9am to 5pm and Saturday and Sunday 10am to 5pm (6pm Apr–Sept). Admission is free. Part of the enormous, lush Oxford Island Nature Reserve, the center has an exhibition on the lough and its history, plus information about the best walking trails. It also hosts occasional guided walks (aka "rambles") through the reserve; prices and times of any upcoming tours are advertised on the website. There's also a cafe, craft shop, and tourist information center—where, handily, you can rent a pair of binoculars.

Interestingly, the lake's claim to fame is its massive population of eels. Yep, the waters are positively infested with the slimy creatures. Hundreds of tons of eels are taken from Lough Neagh and exported each year, mainly to Germany and Holland. The ages-old eel-extraction method involves "long lines" baited with up to 100 hooks. As many as 200 boats trailing these lines are on the lake each night (the best time to go fishing for eels).

If you want to take a **boat trip** on the lake, boats depart regularly from the nearby **Kinnego Marina** (✆ **028/3832-7573**), signposted from the main road. The trip lasts about 45 minutes and costs about £10 for adults, £7 for children. It's advisable to call in advance to book. For a **cultural tour** of Lough Neagh with some history of the area and a trip with a local fisherman, arrange a 4-hour tour with **Lough Neagh Tours** (loughneaghtours.com; ✆ **028/7941-7941**). Tours start from £45 and leave from Cranfield Church at 36 Cranfield Rd., Randalstown BT41 3ND.

dates from the 13th century, although much of the current square-towered brown stone church was built in the 1830s. Inside the church are the remains of an 11th-century Celtic cross and a strange granite-carved figure known as the Tandragee Idol, which dates from the Iron Age. A stone slab on the exterior wall of the north transept marks the spot where Brian Boru, the high king of Ireland who died in the last great battle with the Vikings in 1014, is buried.

43 Abbey St., Armagh City, BT61 7DY. stpatricks-cathedral.org. ✆ **028/3752-3142.** Admission £4 adults; £3.50 seniors and students; free for children. Apr–Sept Mon–Sat 9am–5pm; Oct–Mar Mon–Sat 9am–1:30pm.

St. Patrick's Roman Catholic Cathedral ♥ CATHEDRAL Built in the mid-1800s, this grand Gothic Revival building commands a hilltop, its slim twin spires dominating its portion of the town. Outside the church is monochromatic gray, but inside is another story, as vividly painted mosaics bathe the interior in color. Unfortunately, a 1980s renovation added some modern touches that stand out starkly against its otherwise perfect 19th-century authenticity. Book guided tours 2 weeks in advance.

Cathedral Rd., Armagh City, BT61 7QX. armaghparish.net. ✆ **028/3752-2813.** Free admission; guided tours £5, self-guided tours £2. Daily 9am–5pm; guided tours daily 2, 3, and 4pm.

Where to Stay & Eat in County Armagh

Embers ♥♥ CAFE/GRILL For a reviving snack or meal in Armagh City, check out this casual spot, a 3-minute walk from St. Patrick's Church of Ireland Cathedral (see above). Embers serves great coffee and sandwiches, plus a full menu of crowd-pleasing bar-food favorites. It's very much "something for everyone" territory: fish and chips, fajitas, ribs, steaks, salads, and so on. Chase it all down with a comforting plate of deep-dish apple pie, served with a scoop of ice cream. The early-bird special—available Monday to Saturday from 4 to 6pm—is a bargain at £17 for two courses, £20 for three.

7 Market St., Armagh City, BT61 7BW. embersrestaurant.co.uk. ✆ **028/3751-8544.** Entrees £16–£27. Mon–Tues 9am–3:30pm; Wed 9am–3pm; Thurs 9am–8pm; Fri–Sat 9am–8:30pm. Closed Sun.

Newforge House ♥♥♥ What's not to love? Great food, warm hosts, and a restful night's sleep in a four-poster bed await you in this idyllic

Guest room at Newforge House.

country mansion, only a half-hour's drive southwest of Belfast. Host John Mathers, whose family has owned the house since it was built in the early 18th century, is a trained chef, and his gourmet dinners (£65) are a real treat. (It's also open to non-guests, so be sure to make dinner reservations by noon on the day.) Seasonal menus, prepared with many ingredients from the house's own garden, feature local meats and seafood. Guest rooms are spacious and light-filled, with floor-to-ceiling windows; one room has a four-poster, while another has a king-size canopy bed. Check the website for special offers, including romantic weekend breaks.

58 Newforge Rd., Magheralin (halfway btw. Lisburn and Craigavon), BT67 0QL. newforgehouse.com. ✆ **028/9261-1255.** 6 units. £233–£328 double. 2-night minimum certain dates. Breakfast included. Free parking. **Amenities:** Wi-Fi (free). Closed Jan.

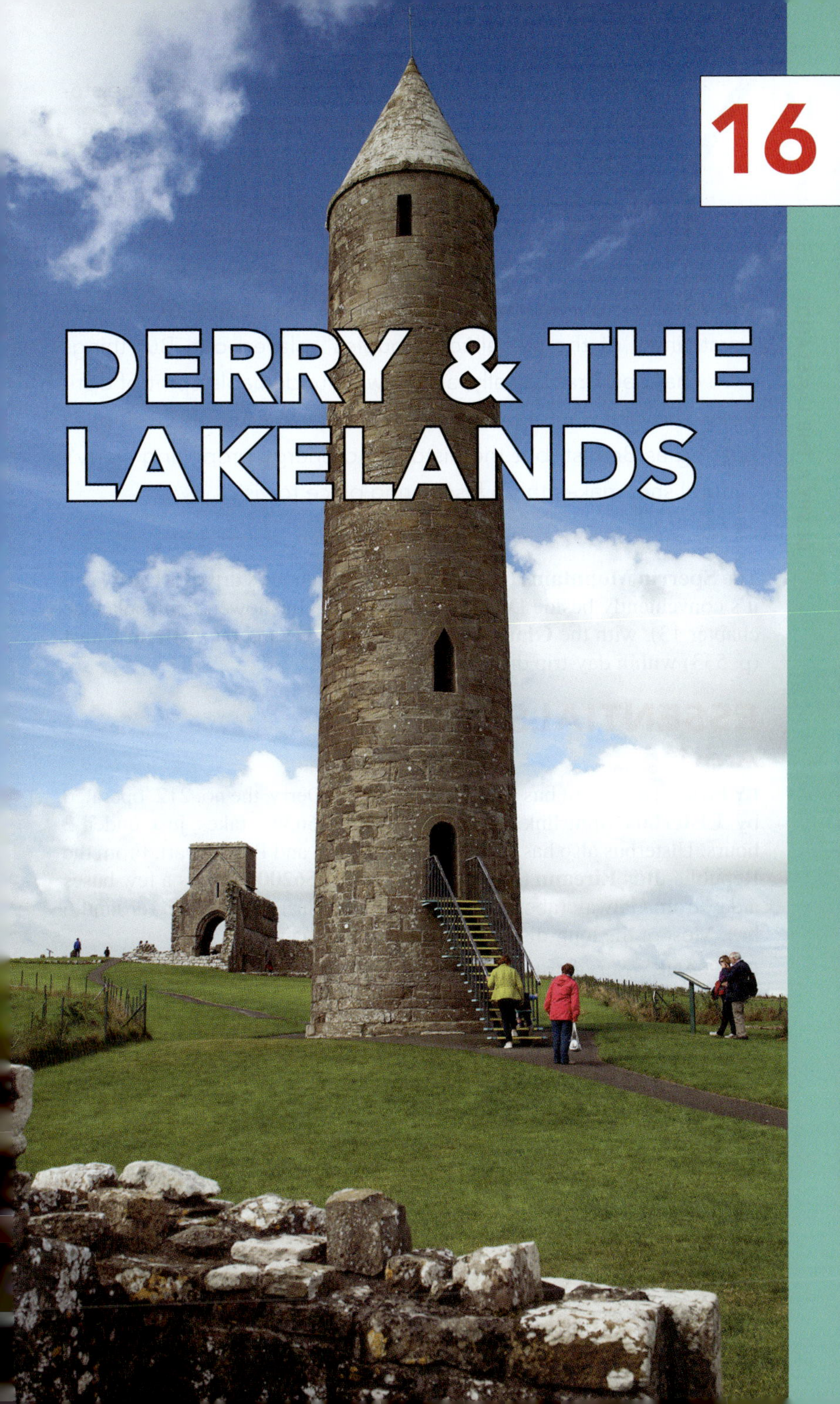

16

DERRY & THE LAKELANDS

You'd expect a city with two names to have some stories to tell. And sure enough, Northern Ireland's second city is full of surprises. Derry is *officially* called Londonderry—but trust us when we tell you that this is a thorny issue (see box on p. 563 for more on the fraught question of what to call Northern Ireland's second city). The 20th century was unkind to Derry, where some of the very worst times of the so-called "Troubles" played out. But things have changed dramatically, and now an undeniable spirit of optimism and renewal reigns. There are still problems, and it's not as buzzing as Belfast, but the history and energy propelling Derry's cultural shift makes this a fascinating place to visit.

The **Sperrin Mountains** (p. 574) are within an hour's drive of Derry, and it's conveniently beside Donegal's picturesque Inishowen Peninsula (see chapter 13), with the **Giant's Causeway** (p. 537) and the **Antrim Coast** (p. 533) within day-trip distance.

ESSENTIALS

Arriving

BY BUS The fastest bus between Belfast and Derry, the no. 212, operated by **Ulsterbus** (translink.co.uk; ✆ **028/9066-6630**), takes just under 2 hours. Ulsterbus also has service from Portrush and Portstewart. From the Republic, **Bus Éireann** (buseireann.ie; ✆ **091/562000**) offers a few buses a day from Galway (about 5½ hr.), Cork (7–9 hr.), and Dublin (around 6 hr.). Most of the long-distance routes involve changes.

BY PLANE Service to **Derry Airport (LDY;** cityofderryairport.com; ✆ **028/7181-0784**) is provided by **Ryanair** (ryanair.com; ✆ **0818/303030** in Ireland, 0871/246-0000 in the U.K.) from Manchester and Birmingham; **Loganair** (loganair.co.uk; ✆ **0344/800-2855**) from Glasgow and London Heathrow; and **EasyJet** (easyjet.com; ✆ **0330/5515-151** in the U.K.) from Edinburgh and Liverpool.

BY TRAIN **Northern Ireland Railways** (translink.co.uk; ✆ **028/9066-6630**) operates frequent trains from Belfast, which arrive at the Londonderry/Derry Station—known by everyone as **Waterside Railway**

PREVIOUS PAGE: **The remarkably intact 12th-century tower at Devenish Island.**

Station (✆ **028/7134-2228**), on Duke Street, on the east side of the Foyle River. The journey takes about 2 hours. Regular buses run from the train station to the city center.

DERRY CITY

Northern Ireland's second city is a vibrant place, combining a medieval center with sprawling Georgian and Victorian neighborhoods. It's made for walking, surrounded by 17th-century walls that you can climb, following the ramparts all the way around the city center (the route is around 1 mile). Although they were the focus of attacks and sieges for centuries, the 5-foot-thick fortifications are solid and unbroken to this day.

Within Ireland, though, Derry is not known for its architecture, but for the fact that, in the 1960s and '70s, the North's civil rights movement was born here, and baptized in blood on the streets. The "Bloody Sunday"

DERRY OR LONDONDERRY: what's in a name?

The short answer is: quite a lot.

Depending on which side of the border you're on, Northern Ireland's second city is called two different things. Road signs and maps in the Republic say **Derry;** in Northern Ireland they point to **Londonderry.**

This stubborn dispute dates to the Plantation of Ulster in the 1600s, when English settlers were given land in Ireland as an attempt to entrench Protestant rule. A new city was founded by the City of London trade guilds and named Londonderry in their honor. Nationalists have always objected to the term, preferring Derry, an Anglicization of *Daire Calgaich (oak-wood of Calgach),* the name of the much older settlement that once stood on the same site.

During the Troubles, the dispute was a cause célèbre. Many attempts have been made to find a solution, including several unsuccessful court cases. Loyalists fiercely defend the name. But having a city with two names poses a knotty problem for residents and visitors alike—what to call it?

The best advice is just to be tactful. If you're drinking in a pub with a big Irish tricolor on the side, it's probably best to use Derry; but if they're flying the British flag, opt for Londonderry. Of the two, Derry is probably more commonly used in town, and certainly throughout the Republic, so we've chosen to call it Derry in this book.

Fed up with having to make a political statement whenever they talk about their own city, residents have long since tried to find an acceptable solution to the Derry/Londonderry dilemma. In the 1990s, local radio DJ Gerry Anderson suggested the wry compromise "Stroke City." (American readers: Stroke is a slash in the U.K.) Quick-witted locals swiftly nicknamed the DJ "Gerry/Londongerry."

To see more evidence of how far back this titular dispute goes, look no further than a United States road atlas. Near Manchester, New Hampshire, is a small old town called Derry. In the early 19th century there was a dispute over its name, so a group of residents set up a new town just to the south called—you guessed it—Londonderry.

The sculpture *Hands Across the Divide* symbolizes an end to sectarian strife.

massacre in 1972, in which British troops killed 14 peaceful civil rights protesters in Derry, shocked the world and led to years of violent unrest. In the **Bogside,** the neighborhood at the bottom of the hill west of the walled section, the famed mural reading "YOU ARE NOW ENTERING FREE DERRY" remains as a symbol of those times.

Happily, much of that sectarian strife seems to be behind Derry now, as it reinvents itself as a center of culture and commerce. Symbolic of the changes in Derry are the **Peace Bridge** footbridge across the River Foyle and ***Hands Across the Divide,*** a 1992 bronze sculpture of two men reaching out toward one another on the Craigavon Bridge into town. The lighthearted comedy TV show ***Derry Girls,*** set during the Troubles in the 1990s, has been a huge hit in recent years.

Visitor Information

The **Visit Derry Visitor Information Centre** at 1–3 Waterloo Place, B48 6BT (visitderry.com; ✆ **028/7126-7284**), is open year-round Monday to Friday 9:30am to 5:30pm and Saturday and Sunday 10am to 5pm. The **Visit Derry Pass** (visitderrypass.com; £25 adults, £20 children for 1 day or £30 adults, £25 children for 2 days), available online or at the visitor center, gives access to 10 attractions including walking tours and museums.

ATTRACTIONS

Bloody Sunday Monument & Bogside Murals **5**

Centre for Contemporary Art **12**

Guildhall **9**

Museum of Free Derry **4**

St. Columb's Cathedral **13**

St. Eugene's Cathedral **1**

Tower Museum **8**

WHERE TO STAY

Bishop's Gate Hotel **14**

Ebrington Hotel **17**

The Saddler's House **2**

WHERE TO EAT

Artis Restaurant By Phelim O'Hagan **7**

Badgers **11**

Blackbird **10**

Browns Bonds Hill **15**

Castle Bistro **6**

Pyke 'N' Pommes **3**

Walled City Brewery **16**

THE bogside: THE PEOPLE'S GALLERY

In many ways, Derry's recent history is embodied in the district known as the Bogside. In the 1960s and '70s, the neighborhood bore witness to violent scenes that shocked the world. Today, it's known as much for its powerful street art, chronicling those troubled decades of the late 20th century.

Located just outside the walled city center, the Bogside was developed in the 19th and early 20th centuries as a home for Catholic workers. In the late 1960s, civil rights protests became regular here, and the residents declared their neighborhood as "Free Derry," independent of local and British government. The situation came to a head on January 30, 1972, later to be known as "Bloody Sunday," when British troops opened fire on a peaceful demonstration, killing 14 civilians. The soldiers said they'd been fired upon first; eventually, in 2010, after a 12-year inquiry costing more than £200 million, the British government finally accepted this was completely untrue and apologized.

The Free Derry corner remains, near a house painted with the mural reading "YOU ARE NOW ENTERING FREE DERRY," and since the 1990s, local artists known as the **Bogside Artists** have painted more murals around the district, similar to those on the Falls Road in Belfast (p. 507). Some are overtly political in nature, but many depict simple yet powerful messages of peace. Together the murals have become known as the **People's Gallery.** For a local insight into the area and what the murals mean, take one of the excellent **Bogside History Tours** (p. 568).

City Layout

The focal point of Derry is the **Diamond,** a large square holding a war memorial in the center of the city. Four streets radiate out from the Diamond: Bishop, Ferryquay, Shipquay, and Butcher. Each extends for several blocks and ends at a gateway (Bishop's Gate, Ferryquay Gate, Shipquay Gate, and Butcher's Gate) cut into the thick city walls.

The original walled city was built on the west bank of the River Foyle, but as Derry has spread across to the east bank, three bridges connect the two sides. The **Craigavon Bridge,** built in 1933, is one of only a few double-decker bridges in the British Isles. The **Foyle Bridge,** Ireland's longest bridge, opened in 1984 and provides a dual-lane highway about 3.2km (2 miles) north of the Craigavon Bridge. The sleek, modern **Peace Bridge** footbridge links Ebrington Square and Waterside with the rest of the city's central area. Its name refers to the fact that it joined two traditionally warring districts, the mostly Catholic **Cityside** and the largely Protestant **Waterside.**

On the city side of the river there are two major areas: the walled **inner city** and, outside the walls to the west, the area known as the **Bogside.** Across the River Foyle on **Waterside** is a small grassy viewing point called the **Top of the Hill,** where you can enjoy spectacular eagle's-eye views of the city. You'll never find your own way here, so take a taxi and bring your map. Short of a helicopter tour, this is the best way to get your initial bearings.

Exploring Derry City

Centre for Contemporary Art ♥♥ ART MUSEUM Drop in to see new and touring works by contemporary artists from Ireland and farther afield. Themed seasons include visual art, film screenings, performances, and public debates. In recent years, these have included a fascinating (but rather gruesome) immersive installation centered around the concept of microbes and decay, and a performance-based project linking LGBTQ issues with climate change. It's all serious and fascinating stuff for grown-up minds. With strong international links, the center often hosts residencies for artists from across the globe. Admission to most events is free, but you may pay a small charge for some; check website for up-to-date listings.

10–12 Artillery St., BT48 6RG. ccadld.org. ✆ **028/7137-3538.** Free admission. Tues–Sat noon–6pm.

Guildhall ♥♥ ARCHITECTURAL SITE Just beside the city walls, between Shipquay Place and the River Foyle, this landmark Tudor Gothic–style building is sometimes mistaken for a church. The site's original structure was constructed in 1887, but it was rebuilt after a fire in 1908 and again after two bomb attacks in 1972. The hall is distinguished by its huge, four-faced clock (designed to resemble London's Big Ben)

Guildhall and the Peace Bridge.

and 23 stained-glass windows made by Ulster craftsmen, which illustrate almost every episode of note in the city's history. The wood-paneled Main Hall is for the site of concerts, plays, and exhibitions; its organ, which dates to 1891, is used for performances. ***A nice bit of historical trivia:*** The Guildhall clock is designed not to strike between midnight and sunrise—at the time it was finished in 1890, the management of an expensive hotel nearby protested that a clock striking hourly through the night would disturb sleeping guests.

Guildhall Square, BT48 6DQ. guildhallderry.com. ✆ **028/7137-6510.** Free admission. Mon–Fri 9am–8pm; Sat–Sun 9am–6pm.

Museum of Free Derry ♥♥ MUSEUM Outside this small museum is an extraordinary piece of art, which may at first glance look like a long, rusty iron wall. But look again—it's a model of the actual sound waves from the 21 seconds in which the crowd on Bloody Sunday sang the civil rights anthem "We Shall Overcome," shortly before 26 of them were shot, and 14 killed, by the British army. Such a thought-provoking statement nicely frames the story told inside the museum, which was established by the Bloody Sunday Trust. Thousands of documents and artifacts related to the Irish Catholic civil rights movement of the mid– and late 20th century are housed here, while displays tell the story of Bloody Sunday and other key events in the "Troubles" of the 1960s to '90s. The timeline is clearly laid out and easy to understand; the calm, level tone makes the impact all the more powerful. The **Bogside** (p. 566) naturally becomes the focus for much of this history—take one of the excellent walking tours of the district, such as **Bogside History Tours** (bogsidehistorytours.com; ✆ **077/3145-0088;** daily 11am and 1pm; £10 adults), for a local perspective on the events and the area.

55 Glenfada Park, BT48 9DR. museumoffreederry.org. ✆ **028/7136-0880.** Admission £8 adults; £7 seniors, students, and children. Mon–Sat 10am–4pm (to 6pm May–Sept); Sun 10am–4pm May–Oct. Last admission 30 min. before closing.

St. Columb's Cathedral ♥ CATHEDRAL Within the city walls, near the Bishop's Gate, this Protestant cathedral was built by the Church of Ireland between 1628 and 1633. A prime example of the so-called "Planters Gothic" style of architecture, it was the first cathedral built in Europe after the Reformation, although several sections were added afterward, including the impressive spire and stained-glass windows depicting scenes from the siege of 1688–89. The chapter house contains a display of city relics such as four massive original padlocks for the city gates. On the porch, a small stone inscribed "IN TEMPLO VERUS DEUS EST VEREO COLENDUS" ("The true God is in His temple and is to be truly worshipped") is a relic of an earlier 1164 church. An old mortar shell on the porch was fired into the churchyard during the great siege of 1689; in its hollow core it held the proposed terms of surrender. Flags around the chancel window were captured during the siege, a pivotal moment in William of Orange's war against James II. The war was ultimately decided at the Battle of the

CLIMBING THE walls

One of the best ways to explore Derry is via its 17th-century stone walls, about 1.6km (1 mile) in circumference and more than 5m (16 ft.) thick. Climb the stairs to the top and you can circle the entire walled city in about 30 minutes. There are a number of stairways off of the parapets, so you'll never get stuck up there. If you start at the **Diamond,** as the square in the center of the walled section is called, walk down Butcher Street to climb the steps at **Butcher's Gate,** a security checkpoint between the Bogside and the city during the Troubles. Walk to the right across **Castle Gate,** opened in 1802, and on to **Magazine Gate,** which was once near a powder magazine. Shortly after, you'll pass **O'Doherty's Tower,** which houses the worthwhile Tower Museum (p. 570). From there you can see the brick walls of the Guildhall (p. 567).

Farther along, you'll pass **Shipquay Gate,** once located very near the port, back when the waters passed closer to the town center. The walls turn uphill from there, past the Millennium Forum concert hall, and up to **Ferryquay Gate.** Here in 1688, local apprentice boys saved the town from attacking Catholic forces by locking the city gates—thus saving the town from attack, but launching the Great Siege of Derry, which lasted for months. (By the time it ended, nearly a quarter of the town's population was dead.) A little farther along, you can access the serene churchyard of **St. Columb's Cathedral** (p. 568).

Next, you'll pass **Bishop's Gate,** where a tall brick tower just outside the gate is all that remains of the **Old Gaol.** The rebel Wolfe Tone was imprisoned here after the unsuccessful uprising in 1798. Farther along, the **Double Bastion** holds a military tower with elaborate equipment used to keep an eye on the Bogside—it's usually splashed with paint hurled at it by Republicans. From the next stretch of wall, you have a good view over the political murals of the Bogside down the hill.

A bit farther along the wall, an empty plinth stands where once there was a statue of Rev. George Walker, a governor of the city during the siege of 1689. It was blown up by the IRA in 1973. Nearby is **St. Augustine's Church** (1872), and the building across the street from it is the **Apprentice Boys' Memorial Hall,** commemorating the boys from the Siege of Derry. Walk a short way farther, and you're back to Butcher's Gate.

City **walking tours** which include the walls leave from 11 Carlisle Rd. (Foyleside Shopping Centre) at 10am, noon, 2, and 4pm (derrycitytours.com; £6); no need to book, just turn up. They also run a **Derry Girls Walking Tour,** which goes around the walls, on Saturdays at noon (£10, book this one in advance).

Boyne (p. 30), still commemorated annually in Northern Ireland with controversial parades, led by the Protestant Orange Order, on and around July 12.

17 London St., BT48 6RQ. stcolumbscathedral.org. ✆ **028/7126-7313.** Requested donation £2. Mar–Oct Mon–Sat 9am–5pm; Nov–Feb Mon–Sat 10am–2pm; Sun for services only.

St. Eugene's Cathedral ♥♥ CATHEDRAL Designed in the Gothic Revival style, Derry's Roman Catholic cathedral is appropriately located in the heart of the Bogside district, just beyond the city walls. The foundation was laid in 1851, but work continued until 1873. The spire was added

Fans of the TV series *Derry Girls* pose at the Tower Museum's Derry Girls Experience.

in 1902. It's built of local sandstone and known for its stained-glass windows depicting the Crucifixion, designed by famed stained-glass makers Meyer and Company of Munich.

Francis St., BT48 9AP. steugenescathedral.com. ✆ **028/7126-2894.** Free admission. Mon–Sat 8am–8pm; Sun 8am–6:30pm.

The Tower Museum ♥♥ MUSEUM This engaging museum chronicles the history of Derry from the earliest times to the 21st century. It's located in **O'Doherty Tower,** a reconstructed medieval fortress originally built in the early 17th century (rather wonderfully to pay off a tax debt, rather than for any specific defensive purpose). The **Story of Derry** exhibition presents a chronology of life in the city from the first monastic settlers through the Plantation era, up to the turbulent 20th century, when the city was a focus of the civil rights movement. Even if you don't take in all the information (there is a lot), don't miss the 15-minute video at the end, which provides a great synopsis. The fun **Derry Girls Experience** has memorabilia from the sitcom, including the sets of the Quinns' kitchen and living room, plus costumes and virtual tours of some of the rooms. In the old tower, the multi-floor exhibition **An Armada Shipwreck** tells the story of *La Trinidad Valencera,* part of the massive Spanish Armada that attempted to invade England in 1588. The ship sank during a storm; 400 years later, the wreck was salvaged, together with a hoard of treasure including clothes, pottery, cannons, and goblets that reveal tantalizing glimpses of life on board. A viewing point at the top of the tower offers nice views of the city.

Union Hall Place, BT48 6LU. towermuseumcollections.com. ✆ **028/7137-2411.** Admission £6 adults; £4 seniors and students; £3 children; £16 families. Mon–Sat 9am–5:30pm. Last admission 4pm.

Where to Stay in Derry

Bishop's Gate Hotel ♥♥ First opened in 1899, this hotel is something of a local landmark. The Victorian-era decor is sympathetically preserved without being trapped in the past; guest rooms, for example, are chic and businesslike, with silver-gray and chocolate color schemes. A few rooms are fully accessible, for those with limited mobility. **The Wig and Gown** restaurant is popular with locals for a special night out. There's also a champagne bar, and a library in which you can take afternoon tea. The hotel also has one- and two-bedroom self-catering apartments at **London Street** in the building adjacent and **Palace Street,** opposite the hotel.

24 Bishop St., BT48 7DB. bishopsgatehotelderry.com. ✆ **028/7114-0300.** 31 units. £145–£255 double; £235–£395 suite. Limited free parking (on street); otherwise, paid lot parking nearby. **Amenities:** Restaurant; bar; gym; Wi-Fi (free).

The Ebrington Hotel and Spa ♥♥ First opened in 2023, this hotel on the quiet Waterside of the River Foyle is a 10-minute walk to the city center over the Peace Bridge footbridge. The hotel is on Ebrington Square, site of a former barracks. Parts of the hotel (such as the lobby, dining room, and spa) are in a modern wing, while most of the bedrooms are in the former barracks' clock tower. The hotel faces the old parade grounds and River Foyle beyond (the best views are from riverview rooms on the second floor). Rooms are cozy, if businesslike, and the spa has a hydropool with therapeutic jets. Choose from the fine-dining **Oak Room** restaurant or the more casual **Corner House Pub & Lounge** gastropub.

Ebrington Square, BT47 6FA. theebringtonhotel.com. ✆ **028/7122-0700.** 89 units. £149–£258 double. Breakfast not included in lower rates. Parking £6 per night in open-air parking lot. **Amenities:** 2 restaurants; bar; gym; spa; Wi-Fi (free).

The Saddler's House ♥♥ A charming building full of character, this lovely B&B is among the best accommodations in Derry. The Saddler's House was built in 1870 and is a great example of a mid-19th-century Victorian house (it was originally built for a saddle-maker). It has been beautifully maintained and renovated over the years, with design-magazine interiors and antiques scattered about. There's a cozy sitting room and a nice city garden to the rear—look for resident dog Bruno. The owners Peter and Joan also have three self-catering places in Derry, including two small, terraced cottages opposite the cathedral; and three apartments on nearby Pump Street, within the walled part of the city.

36 Great James St., BT48 7DB. thesaddlershouse.com. ✆ **028/7126-9691.** 6 units. £100–£120 double. Breakfast included. Limited free parking (on street). **Amenities:** Wi-Fi (free).

Where to Eat in Derry

EXPENSIVE

Artis by Phelim O'Hagan ♥♥♥ MODERN IRISH *Artis* is the Latin word for "craft"—an appropriate name for this restaurant, not only because it's located in the Craft Village (p. 574), but also because chef Phelim O'Hagan so carefully designs his tasty combinations of local ingredients. Look for mains like roast cod with *courgette* (zucchini), broccoli, burnt tomato, and avruga caviar, or Achill Island lamb rack with polenta, carrot, and goats' curd. It's a relaxing space with cool colors and clean lines, and there's only one dinner seating, so your table is yours for the night. Go for the full seven-course tasting menu if you can.

28 Craft Village, Shipquay St., BT48 6AR. artisatcraftvillagederry.com. ✆ **028/7137-1635.** Entrees £28–£39. Set menu 2-course £32, 3-course £38; both available Fri–Sat noon–2:30pm, Wed–Thurs 5–7:30pm. Dinner 7-course tasting menu £75 (wine pairing add £55); available Wed–Sat 5–9:30pm.

Browns Bonds Hill ♥♥ BRASSERIE One of Derry's best restaurants, Browns serves excellent Irish food with international influences. The menu uses plenty of local and regional ingredients, embracing traditional flavors with a touch of well-judged, modern innovation. Menus change frequently, but you're likely to encounter local seafood, steaks, wild wood pigeon, or honey-glazed duck. Vegetarians and vegans will be delighted with the full menu of non-meaty options. A more casual sister branch, **Browns in Town** (✆ **028/7136-2889**), on Strand Road in the city center, serves up tasty burgers, fish, and steaks, with a two-course menu for £34.50.

1 Bonds Hill, BT47 6DW. brownsbondshill.com. ✆ **028/7134-5180.** Entrees £24–£38. Tasting menu £80; wine pairing £40. Tues 5–9pm; Wed–Thurs noon–2:30pm and 5–9pm; Fri–Sat noon–2:30pm and 5–10pm.

MODERATE

Castle Bistro ♥♥ IRISH This lively restaurant and cocktail bar, formerly Castle St Social, recently moved from inside the city walls to the Craft Village. The menu remains largely similar, with a strong emphasis on vegan and allergy-friendly food, particularly gluten-free. One of the most popular dishes is the vegan lentil cottage pie, a lentil stew with a crispy potato topping made with Broighter Gold rosemary rapeseed oil. The delicious Guinness and black treacle wheaten bread is also vegan-friendly. There's an interesting cocktail list—try one of the house specials, such as the "Rooh," made with local Rooh vodka, chai tea, and chili syrup.

13–15 Craft Village, Shipquay St., BT48 6AR. castlebistro.co.uk. ✆ **028/7137-2888.** Entrees £14–£26. Mon–Sat 10am–4pm; Thurs–Sat 5–10pm; Sun 9am–4pm.

Walled City Brewery ♥♥ IRISH A short walk across the Peace Bridge from the city center to Ebrington Square brings you to this delightful heritage building in the corner of the parade ground (with outside tables in summer), where you can tuck into gastro delights while sampling fresh craft beers, brewed on-site. Menu highlights include flatiron steak with carrot, black garlic, miso butter, pepper sauce, and hand-cut chips; or Donegal pan-roasted cod with chorizo, avocado, tomato, chili peas, and burnt onion powder. Sunday roasts (1–5pm) are another specialty. Craft beers include lager, pale ale, oyster stout, wheat beers, and the "Rock the Boat" hard seltzer, which changes regularly. Between 5 and 6:30pm Monday to Friday, save on the early-bird fixed-price menus (£22 for two courses and £26 for three). You can also sign up for craft beer tastings and master classes.

70 Ebrington Sq., BT47 6FA. walledcitybrewery.com. ✆ **028/7134-3336.** Fixed-price menu 2–course £28, 3-course £32. Wed–Thurs 4:30–8:30pm; Fri–Sat 1–3pm and 5–9:30pm; Sun 1–5pm.

INEXPENSIVE

Badgers Bar ♥♥ IRISH A friendly local pub right in the center of Derry, Badgers serves hearty traditional grub—stews, fish and chips, steak and Guinness pie, burgers, and the like—plus a few lighter options such as hot sandwiches and wraps. Plates are generous, and of course, you can wash it all down with a pint of the black stuff. The dining room is appealingly unreconstructed, with plenty of polished wood. No matter what the time of day, there always seem to be a few locals propping up the bar, which helps keep the atmosphere authentic. Fans of the TV show *Derry Girls* should look for the huge mural on the rear gable wall.

16–18 Orchard St., BT48 6EG. ✆ **028/7136-3306.** Entrees £12–£17. Food served Mon–Thurs noon–7pm; Fri–Sat noon–8pm; Sun noon–5pm. No children after 9pm.

Blackbird ♥♥ GASTROPUB The menu at this busy gastropub has something for everyone, with plenty of chicken, fish, meat, and vegetarian options. Look for the half-roast chicken with sausage and herb stuffing and red wine jus; the open steak ciabatta with chili beef strips; or the cauliflower steak with hummus and chimichurri. A house special is Blackbird tagliatelle with smoked bacon, Parma ham, chorizo, shiitake mushrooms, spinach, pine nuts, and Parmesan. This is a lively spot—enjoy your food with a side of craft beers from local breweries like Rough Brothers or Northbound, as well as live music from local bands.

24 Foyle St., BT48 6AL. blackbirdderry.com. ✆ **028/7136-2111.** Entrees £14–£25. Mon–Fri noon–8pm; Sat–Sun noon–6pm.

Pyke 'N' Pommes 53–55 ♥♥ INTERNATIONAL Once a hugely popular food truck, this place now has two permanent restaurants in Derry. The main outlet is at 53–55 Strand Rd., near the River Foyle; the other, called **POD,** is nearby (124 Strand Rd.) in a converted shipping container on the riverfront. Both have similar menus and the same ethos: fresh local food cooked incredibly well with no fuss. At both you can get burgers of all kinds, including tender, melting Wagyu beef burgers or chickpea and sweetcorn "vegenderry" burgers. A taco menu features fried squid tacos,

Baja fish tacos, and sweet potato tacos with chipotle cashew salsa. It's casual, innovative, light, and affordable.
53–55 Strand Rd., BT48 7BN. pykenpommes.ie. ✆ **028/7167-2691.** Entrees restaurant £7.50–£28, POD £6–£12. Wed–Thurs noon–3pm and 5–9pm; Fri noon–3pm and 5–10pm; Sat noon–10pm; Sun 1–8pm.

Shopping

The Craft Village ♥♥♥ A little oasis from the busy city streets, this delightful courtyard off Shipquay Street has a selection of artisan craft shops with colorful art, ceramics, jewelry, and gifts made by local and Irish designers. Check out **Number 19, Walled City Crafters,** and **Derry Designer Makers.** Shipquay St., BT48 6AR. derrycraftvillage.com. ✆ **028/7126-0329.**

Derry After Dark

Derry pubs are an important part of the local fabric. They are tied into the local music scene, and some even host debating contests, in the midst of which you'll hear Irish eloquence at its well-lubricated best. **Waterloo Street** is where you'll find some of Derry's most traditional and popular pubs.

Bennigans Bar ♥♥ Bennigans is known for its fantastic live jazz, which attracts performers from all over Ireland (and beyond). Sessions usually start around 9pm. 13 John St., BT48 6JY. facebook.com/bennigansbar. ✆ **028/7126-9127.**

Peadar O'Donnells ♥♥ One of the best places for traditional live music, with a buzzing atmosphere and music sessions every night except Monday. Sessions run from Monday to Thursday 8pm to closing, and from 5:30pm on Saturday and Sunday—although spontaneous sessions can start up any time. 59–63 Waterloo St., BT48 6HD. facebook.com/peadarsderry. ✆ **028/7126-7295.**

River Inn ♥♥ Allegedly Derry's oldest pub (the city walls form part of the building), the River Inn opened its doors in the 17th century. It also serves food, but people generally come for the atmosphere. 34–38 Shipquay St., BT48 6DW. riverinn1684.com. ✆ **028/7137-1965.**

DAY TRIP TO THE SPERRIN MOUNTAINS

The beautiful Sperrin Mountains, a short drive southeast of Derry in County Tyrone, are filled with scenic walks, national parks, and extraordinary views, plus one really must-see site: the **Ulster American Folk Park** (p. 577). This is splendid, wide-open walking country, home to golden plover, red grouse, and thousands upon thousands of fluffy white sheep. There's no shortage of ancient sites, including standing stones

(about a thousand have been counted in these hills), high crosses, dolmens, and hill forts. Whether you're traveling on foot, wheels, or horseback, be sure to traverse the **Glenshane Pass** between Mullaghmore (545m/1,788 ft.) and Carntogher (455m/1,492 ft.), and the **Sawel Mountain Drive** along the east face of the mountain. The vistas along these routes through the Sperrins will remind you why you've gone out of your way to spend time in Tyrone.

Visitor Information

The **An Creagán Visitors Centre,** on the A505 road just outside Creggan (see below), is a good place to start, with tourist information and an interesting exhibition on the history of the area. Other area sites include the **Cookstown Tourist Information Centre,** Burn Road, Cookstown (✆ **028/8676-9949**); the **Dungannon Visitor Information Centre,** 26 Market Sq., Dungannon (✆ **028/8776-7259**); the **Omagh Visitor Information Centre** at the Strule Arts Centre, Townhall Square, Omagh (✆ **028/8224-7831**); and the **Strabane Visitor Information Centre,** at the Alley Arts and Conference Centre, 1A Railway St., Strabane (✆ **028/7138-4444**). Generally, these are open Monday to Saturday year-round from about 10am to 4:30 or 5pm; the Dungannon and Cookstown centers also open on Sunday afternoons in summer.

Exploring the Sperrins

An Creagán Visitors Centre ♥♥ INTERPRETIVE CENTER Beautifully designed to fit in with the craggy countryside around, this modern center is an excellent place to get your bearings when you first arrive in the Sperrins. A small gallery has an interactive exhibit about the mountains and the area; a few Bronze Age artifacts excavated from nearby sites are also on display. The helpful staff will give you all the information you need on walking and cycling routes, as well as maps and bicycle rentals. The center has a restaurant and craft shop, and even owns a few self-catering properties if you're interested in staying longer (prices start at £170 per night for a one-bedroom cottage in low season).

A505, Creggan (about 60km/37 miles SE of Derry), Omagh, BT79 9AB. an-creagan.com. ✆ **028/8076-1112.** Free admission. Daily 10am–4pm.

Beaghmore Stone Circles ♥ ANCIENT SITE In 1945, seven stone circles and a complex assembly of cairns and alignments were uncovered here, in remote moorland north of Evishbrack Mountain and near Davagh Forest Park on the southern edge of the Sperrins. Arranged inside the largest circle are around 800 small stones, christened the "Dragon's Teeth." No one knows what this intriguing bit of Bronze Age stonework was built for, but it may have involved astronomical observation and calculation. The layout has also led archaeologists to believe that the stones surround unexcavated megalithic tombs.

17km (11 miles) NW of Cookstown, signposted from A505, BT80 9PA. No phone. Free admission (open site).

Drum Manor Forest Park ♥ NATURE SITE Once a private estate, this extensive park and woodland has numerous trails and three old walled gardens, one of them designed as a butterfly garden. Also on the grounds are a visitor center, a heronry, and a pond that attracts a variety of wildfowl.

4km (2½ miles) W of Cookstown on A505, BT80 8UN. ✆ **028/6634-3165.** Admission £3 per car; pedestrians £1 adults, 50p children. Daily 10am–dusk.

Gortin Glen Forest Park ♥ NATURE SITE Nearly 400 hectares (988 acres) of conifers make up this serene nature park. The woodlands provide habitat for a variety of wildlife, including a herd of Japanese sika deer. A forest drive offers splendid views of the Sperrins. Here you'll also find a nature center, wildlife enclosures, trails, and a cafe. The park has three separate marked walking trails; details can be found at the visitor center on the B48 road just south of Gortin. The long-distance **Ulster Way** hiking trail also passes through the park; for more information on the Ulster Way, visit **walkni.com/ulsterway**.

Visitor center: On B48 (Glenpark Rd.), about 4km (2½ miles) S of Gortin, BT79 7SU. ✆ **0300/303-1777.** Free admission. Apr–Sept 6:30am–9pm; Oct–Mar 6:30am–6pm.

Seamus Heaney HomePlace ♥♥ MUSEUM East of the Sperrins, Nobel Prize–winning poet Seamus Heaney took inspiration for his work from the landscape and local people he grew up among in rural County Derry. The Seamus Heaney HomePlace in Bellaghy, near the family farm where he lived, tells the story of Heaney's life and work through an interactive exhibition plus books, archive material, and audio recordings with the voice of the poet himself. The exhibition is thoughtfully put together with lots of personal stories and photos. It's a lovely way to access Heaney's moving poetry, whether you are a Heaney fan or a first-timer. There's also a library, digital archive, a cafe, and a fun creative zone for kids of all ages.

45 Main St., Bellaghy, Co. Derry, BT45 8HT. seamusheaneyhome.com. ✆ **028/7938-7444.** Admission £12 adults; £8 seniors and students; £7.50 children; free for children 7 and under; £29 families. Free parking. Mon–Sat 10am–4pm; Sun 1–4pm.

Ulster American Folk Park ♥♥♥ HERITAGE SITE Another of the region's excellent "living history" outdoor museums, this one celebrates and commemorates the links between Ulster and the New World. It chronicles the story of those 18th- and 19th-century emigrants who left their homes in the north of Ireland to seek a new life overseas. The park contains authentic structures from the period—some of them actual dwellings reconstructed from elsewhere—to give an idea of the life they left behind. After looking around the humble thatched cottages, you can explore a period street with convincingly decked-out shops, manned by costumed actors. There's a full-size replica emigrant ship as well. The park has an active schedule of

The Ulster American Folk Park is a living-history museum.

special events, including a respected bluegrass festival in the autumn. Check the website for listings.

2 Mellon Rd., Castletown, BT78 5QU. nmni.com. ✆ **028/8224-3292.** Admission £12.50 adults; £9.75 seniors and students; £7.65 children 5–17; £27–£35 families. Prices rise by a few pounds on major event days. Tues–Sun 10am–4pm. Last admission 3:30pm.

THE FERMANAGH LAKELANDS

In the extreme southwest corner of Northern Ireland, County Fermanagh is a lakeland area dominated by **Lough Erne,** a long, narrow lake with 154 islands and countless coves and inlets. The **Shannon-Erne Waterway** links the lake to the Shannon River system through the Republic of Ireland. Were you to cruise the whole length of the waterway between the village of Leitrim and Lough Erne, you'd travel 63km (39 miles), past 16 locks (gates), three lakes, and the Woodford River. At the south end of Lough Erne, **Enniskillen** is a good touring base for the region, with many overnight options if you intend to spend much time here.

In medieval times, a chain of island monasteries stretched across the waters of Lough Erne, establishing it as a haven for those seeking peace and contemplation. Traces of those monasteries can still be found on those unspoiled islands—and the Fermanagh Lakelands remains a peaceful place to get away from it all.

Visitor Information

The **Fermanagh Visitor Information Centre,** Enniskillen Castle, Enniskillen, BT74 7HL (✆ **028/6632-5000**), is open year-round, Monday to Friday from 9:30am until 5pm and Saturday 11am to 5pm (also Sun 11am–5pm June–Sept). For an introduction to the Fermanagh Lakelands on the web, check out **fermanaghlakelands.com**.

Exploring the Lakelands

The hub of this lakeland paradise—wedged between Upper Lough Erne to the south and Lower Lough Erne to the north—is **Enniskillen,** a delightful town that was the medieval seat of the Maguire clan and a major crossroads between Ulster and Connaught. Both Oscar Wilde and Samuel Beckett were once students here at the royal school. A handful of lovely historic homes are dotted around the midsection of the lake as well, including **Castle Coole** ♥ (see below), the **Crom Estate** ♥♥ (see below), and **Florence Court** ♥♥ (p. 581). At the northern tip of the lake, near the Republic of Ireland border, **Belleek** (see box on p. 579) is known the world over for its trademark delicate bone chinaware.

Castle Coole ♥♥ HISTORIC HOUSE Not really a castle at all, Coole is in fact a lavish stately home on the east bank of Lower Lough Erne. This quintessential neoclassical mansion was designed by James Wyatt

BUYING belleek

Perhaps the most famous Irish homeware brand in the world after Waterford Crystal, Belleek Pottery has been making fine china since 1864. The **Belleek Pottery Visitor Centre,** 3 Main St., Belleek (belleek.com; ✆ **028/6865-8501**), is the world headquarters of the brand. You can visit their museum—which displays unique objects of Belleek pottery, such as the extraordinary International Centre Piece vase created for the 1900 Paris Expo—and also take factory tours. But of course, the reason most people come is to visit the enormous gift shop. It has a large selection of patterns from which to choose, in a wide price range. If you're not a china expert but still want to bring back some Belleek pieces from your trip, here are a few tips to ensure that your purchases become heirlooms:

- At the center, the china is displayed around the room. Look at all the pieces, and then note the item numbers of those pieces you like. Take the numbers to the central counter, and the boxed china pieces are brought to you.
- Ask to see the pieces in the boxes to ensure they are what you want. Take the pieces from the sales assistant and look at them closely. This is delicate china, and it can have tiny imperfections that you can only see by getting up close and personal. We bought a lovely Belleek vase once that looked perfect but leaked through a nearly invisible crack.
- The center will ship internationally if you don't want to risk taking your purchases on a plane.
- If it looks good to you and you love it—buy it! You may not get the chance again.

The Belleek Visitor Centre is open Monday through Friday from 9am until 4pm, Saturday 10am to 4pm, and Sunday 1 to 4pm (Oct–Dec Mon–Sat 10am–3pm; Jan–Mar Mon–Fri 10am–3pm). Free admission. Thirty-minute guided tours run on weekdays between 10am and 3pm (tour times vary). Guided tour £6.

for the Earl of Belmore and completed in 1796. Its rooms include a state bedroom hung with crimson silk, said to have been prepared for George IV (1762–1830). A sprawling woodland estate surrounds the house. A classical music series runs from May to October. You can book a guided house tour when you arrive.

2.4km (1½ miles) SE of Enniskillen on A4, BT74 6JY. nationaltrust.org.uk/castle-coole. ✆ **028/6632-2690.** Guided house tour: £12 adults; £6 children; £30 families. Grounds only: £5.50 adults; £2.75 children; £13.75 families. House May–Sept daily 11am–4pm. Grounds daily 10am–6pm (closes 5pm Nov–Feb). Last admission 30 min. before closing; last house tour 1 hr. before closing.

Crom Estate ♥♥ NATURE SITE On the east bank of Upper Lough Erne, this nearly 800-hectare (1,976-acre) nature reserve is a splendid National Trust–owned estate, with forest, parks, wetlands, fen-meadows (peatlands), and an award-winning lakeshore visitor center. The numerous trails have concealed places for observing birds and wildlife. You can rent a rowboat and row out to the islands. A 19th-century castle is also located on the grounds, though it's not open to visitors. The estate is a great place to fish for bream and roach; permits and day tickets are available at the gate lodge. During the summer, weekends frequently feature special programs and guided nature walks. The estate also has several cottages available for rent by the week (about £320–£630). Call or check the National Trust website for more information.

34km (21 miles) S of Enniskillen via A4 and A34, then take signposted right turn. Upper Lough Erne, Newtownbutler, BT92 8AP. nationaltrust.org.uk/crom. ✆ **028/6773-8118.** Admission £8 adults; £4 children; £20 families. Grounds daily 10am–6pm. Visitor center Mar–Sept daily 11am–5pm. Last admission 1 hr. before closing.

Devenish Island ♥♥ NATURE SITE The most extensive of the ancient Christian sites in Lough Erne, Devenish Island is a marvelous mélange of remnants and ruins, providing a glimpse into the lake's mystical past. In the 6th century, St. Molaise founded a monastic community here, to which the Augustinian Abbey of St. Mary was added in the 12th century. In other words, this is hallowed ground, even more so for the legend that the Old Testament prophet Jeremiah is buried somewhere nearby—if you can figure that one out. The jewel of Devenish is the perfectly intact 12th-century round tower, which was erected with Vikings in mind. You can take an organized tour to the island on the Lough Erne cruise offered by **Erne Tours** (p. 582) or a private water taxi tour with **Erne Water Taxi** (ernewatertaxi.com; ✆ **077/1977-0588**). Or hire a boat from **Erne Boat Hire** (erneboathireltd.com; ✆ **075/2342-3232**) if you want to navigate the route to the island yourself; the boats can hold six adults, and 4-hour rentals start at £65.

Ruins of St. Mary's Augustinian Priory, Devenish Island.

2.4km (1½ miles) downstream from Enniskillen, BT94 2FE. ✆ **028/6632-3110.** Free admission.

Enniskillen Castle ♥♥ CASTLE/MUSEUM On the banks of Lower Lough Erne in Enniskillen, this impressive castle was built sometime around the first half of the 14th century and significantly remodeled in the

17th. It's unusual in that the design owes more to the Scottish Baronial style of castle—note the small round turrets, redolent of Gothic motifs—than the fortresslike English-French style that predominates throughout Ireland. The castle is home to two museums, included in the ticket price, which were recently reopened after a major renovation. **Fermanagh County Museum** illuminates the region's colorful history, with interesting sections on local crafts and the development of the castle from medieval times onward. The **Inniskillings Museum** houses the castle's large collection of militaria, historic weapons, uniforms, and other artifacts dating back to the 1600s.

Castle Barracks, Enniskillen, BT74 7HL. enniskillencastle.co.uk. ✆ **028/6632-5000.** Admission £5.80 adults; £4.20 seniors, students, and children; free for children 4 and under; £16 families. Mon–Fri 9:30am–5pm; Sat–Sun 11am–5pm (Oct–May closed Sun).

Florence Court ♥♥ HISTORIC HOUSE Set among dramatic hills, 13km (8 miles) southwest of Lower Lough Erne and Enniskillen, this 18th-century Palladian mansion was originally the seat of the earls of Enniskillen. Its interior is rich in rococo plasterwork and antique Irish furniture, while outside are a fine walled garden, an icehouse, and a water-wheel-driven sawmill. You can book a house tour at the visitor center. The forest park offers a number of trails, one leading to the top of Mount Cuilcagh (nearly 660m/2,165 ft.). Florence Court is the sister property to Castle Coole (p. 578).

Florence Court, off A32, Enniskillen, BT92 1DB. nationaltrust.org.uk/florence-court. ✆ **028/6634-8249.** Admission house and grounds £13 adults, £6.50 children, £32.50 families; grounds only £7.50 adults, £3.75 children, £18.75 families. House: May–Aug daily 11am–5pm; Oct–Apr Sat–Sun 11am–5pm. Gardens and park: Mar–Oct daily 10am–6pm; Nov–Feb daily 10am–4pm. Last admission 1 hr. before closing.

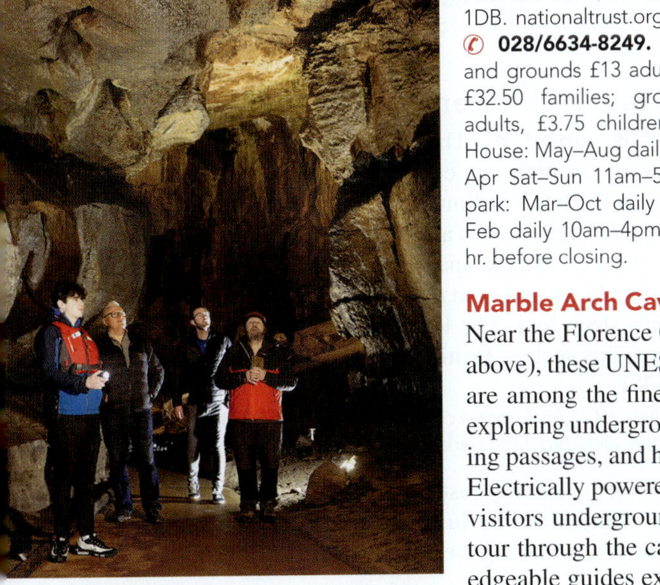

Marble Arch Caves.

Marble Arch Caves ♥♥ CAVES Near the Florence Court estate (see above), these UNESCO-listed caves are among the finest in Europe for exploring underground rivers, winding passages, and hidden chambers. Electrically powered boat tours take visitors underground for a walking tour through the caves, and knowledgeable guides explain the origins

CRUISING LOUGH ERNE by boat

One of the best ways to explore Lough Erne is by boat. **Erne Tours,** Enniskillen (ernetours.com; ✆ **028/6632-2882**), operates 2-hour cruises on Lower Lough Erne aboard the *MV Kestrel,* departing daily May through September from the delightfully named Round "O" Jetty, Brook Park, Enniskillen. Tours include a 45-minute stop on **Devenish Island ♥♥** (p. 580). Erne Tours also runs sunset and dinner cruises.

Independent boatmen offer ferry crossings to some of the many islands in Lough Erne, or you can book a tour with **Erne Water Taxi** (ernewatertaxi.com; ✆ **077/1977-0588**), which also runs the electric passenger boat *Island Discovery* and can organize bespoke tours. Besides Devenish Island, **White Island** and **Boa Island** are rich in archaeological and early Christian remains. On White Island, seven stone figures remain from a vanished 10th-century monastery inside a ruined 12th-century church. Boa Island is connected to the shore by bridges; poke around the cemetery at the island's west end to find two ancient idols of the god Janus (with faces looking both ways), thought to date from the 1st century.

of the amazing stalactites and stalagmites. Tours last 75 minutes and leave at 15-minute intervals. The caves are occasionally closed after heavy rains, so phone ahead before making the trip during times of particularly bad weather.

Marlbank Rd., off A32, Enniskillen, BT92 1EW. marblearchcaves.co.uk. ✆ **028/6632-8855.** Admission £15.50 adults; £12 seniors and students; £7.80 children; £39–£47 families. Reservations recommended. July–Aug daily 10am–5pm (last tour); Mar–June and Sept daily 10am–4:30pm (last tour); Oct–Feb daily 10:30am–3.30pm (last tour).

Where to Stay in the Fermanagh Lakelands

Belmore Court & Motel ♥ The humble motel is so unknown in Europe that its few incarnations are considered quite exotic. At this quality budget option on the edge of Enniskillen, basic rooms are clean and modern, with compact kitchen areas and free Wi-Fi. Pay just a little more, however, and you get a lot of extra space, plus nice little touches like Nespresso machines, breakfast, and even (in the executive rooms) little balconies. Family rooms sleep four. The location isn't too far from the town center and nearby sights such as **Enniskillen Castle ♥♥** (p. 580) or **Castle Coole ♥** (p. 578).

Tempo Rd., Enniskillen, BT74 6HX. motel.co.uk. ✆ **028/6632-6633.** 60 units. £120–£210 double. Breakfast included. Free parking. **Amenities:** Wi-Fi (free).

Castle Leslie ♥♥♥ Actually just across the border in the Republic, this historic estate surrounded by lush grounds is one of the very best places to stay in the North, having welcomed a dazzling list of luminaries

An elegant guest room at Castle Leslie.

over the years (W. B. Yeats was a houseguest, Winston Churchill was a cousin of the Leslie family, and Paul McCartney and Heather Mills were married here in 2002). Strolling around the house, you'll wander past Wordsworth's harp and the Bechstein grand piano on which Wagner composed *Tristan and Isolde.* Guest rooms are individually designed to varying degrees of grandeur; most are located in the converted hunting lodge. The outstanding in-house restaurant offers sophisticated dishes prepared with local ingredients, such as filet of seabass with red pepper drops and baby carrots, or roast chicken with garlic and citrus dressing. You can also opt for a more casual meal at **Conor's Bar.** There are also guest rooms at **The Lodge** (£195–£325 double) at the estate entrance, which has been restored in country-house style and overlooks the equestrian center. On the several hundred acres of grounds, horseback riding, clay pigeon shooting, and other outdoor activities can be arranged, and an elegant spa will smooth away the few cares you have left.

Glaslough, Co. Monaghan (Republic of Ireland). castleleslie.com. ✆ **047/88100.** 21 units. £315–£600 double. 2-night minimum on summer weekends. Breakfast included. Dinner, bed-and-breakfast packages available. Free parking. **Amenities:** 2 restaurants; bar; room service; spa; Wi-Fi (free).

Finn Lough ♥♥ This surely qualifies as one of the most unusual places to stay in Ireland. The five-star lakeside compound at Finn Lough has a unique feature: so-called bubble domes, individual plastic dome cottages from which you can see the wide sky and verdant countryside all around you, all the time (although you're surrounded by foliage for privacy). If such an open environment isn't for you, more traditional cottages are tucked away around the compound. Most have three bedrooms, a kitchen, and a living room, as well as good Wi-Fi. You can dine in the on-site restaurant (inclusive packages are available), hire kayaks to paddle out on the pristine lake, or rent a mountain bike and explore the forests.

Bubble Dome room at Finn Lough.

On the other hand, you could just hide yourself away in your own cottage and enjoy the peace.

Letter Rd., Enniskillen, BT93 2BB. finnlough.com. ✆ **028/6838-0360.** 15 units. £270–£525 double; £300–£450 bubble dome. Free parking. **Amenities:** Wi-Fi (free).

Lough Erne Resort ♥♥♥ With a glorious location overlooking Lough Erne, this hotel positively exudes old-school charm. It's one of Ireland's top golfing resorts, though you certainly don't have to be a golfer to enjoy what it has to offer. Guest rooms are comfortable and spacious; lake-facing rooms are definitely worth the extra cost to take in the view. It offers three dining options: the **Loughside Grill** steakhouse; the more casual **Blaney Bar,** which serves favorites like soups and stews; and the **Catalina Restaurant** (see below) for fine dining and seasonal produce. Book a treatment in the award-winning **Thai Spa,** then afterwards prepare to float away in the Lap Sabai ("deep sleep") relaxation room.

Belleek Rd., Enniskillen, BT93 7ED. lougherneresort.com. ✆ **028/6632-3230.** 120 units. £170–£284 double; £399–£354 suite. Check online for special offers. Free parking. **Amenities:** 2 restaurants; 2 bars; golf course; spa; Wi-Fi (free).

Where to Eat in the Fermanagh Lakelands

The Catalina Restaurant ♥♥♥ MODERN IRISH The main restaurant at the excellent **Lough Erne Resort** (see above) has been recognized for its seasonal flavors. Chef Stephen Holland makes elegant meals with plenty of locally sourced ingredients. Depending on the time of year, expect dishes like seared Irish stone bass with red cabbage gel, or Thornhill duck breast with roasted beetroot and orange terrine. The vegetarian menu is small but good—try the roasted pumpkin and sweet onion tart with forest mushroom marmalade.

At the Lough Erne Resort, Belleek Rd., Enniskillen, BT93 7ED. lougherneresort.com. ✆ **028/6632-3230.** Entrees £26–£37; fixed-price menu £70; Sun lunch £45. Mon–Sat 6:30–9:30pm; Sun 1–3pm.

The Jolly Sandwich ♥ CAFE This bright, light sandwich shop is a cheery place to grab a quick lunch or breakfast or create a picnic to go. As the name suggests, the specialty is freshly made sandwiches of all kinds, but there's more to this place than that. Towering stacks of American-style pancakes are often available, as well as homemade scones, elaborate cakes, gorgeous layered coffees, and steaming pots of tea.

3 Darling St., Enniskillen, BT74 7DP. ✆ **028/6632-2277.** All items £5–£15. Tues–Sat 9am–3pm.

The Taphouse ♥♥ IRISH/INTERNATIONAL Converted into a gastropub, this handsome old stone building is a good-looking place, with exposed stone walls, rugged wood floors, and leather furniture. The front bar is sleek and modern, contrasting beautifully with the aged setting. Dishes are smart reinterpretations of traditional pub food. You might start with some goat cheese fritters, or soup with treacle bread. Main courses might include a creamy Thai curry or Cajun chicken tagliatelle. There's a separate menu for vegetarians and pescatarians.

46 Old Tempo Rd., Enniskillen, BT74 4RR. thetaphouseenniskillen.com. ✆ **028/6634-6800.** Entrees £14–£27. Daily 11am–11pm (food served until about 9pm).

Tully Mill ♥♥ IRISH Relaxed and sophisticated, this bistro on the edge of the Florence Court estate (p. 581) is located inside an old watermill. Plenty of local flavors find their way onto the three-course set menus, including some from the mill's own walled garden. Start with some wild mushrooms with bearnaise sauce, then go for the Silverhill duck with black cherry sauce, or delicious curry-crusted monkfish. A vegan menu has almost as much choice as the main offerings. Sunday lunches are popular here, with plenty of interesting fish and vegetarian options alongside traditional plates of roast meats. The quiet grounds also contain a few self-catering cottages; prices in summer start at around £260 for the weekend, £590 for a full week.

On the Florence Court estate, Enniskillen, BT92 1FN. tullymill.com. ✆ **028/6634-9879.** 3-course dinner £40; Sun lunch £35. Fri–Sat 5–8pm; Sun noon–5pm.

Sports & Outdoor Pursuits in the Lakelands

BOATING Lough Erne is an explorer's dream, and you can take that dream all the way to the Atlantic if you want. The price range for fully equipped, four- to eight-berth cruisers is around £1,100–£3,000 per week, including tax, depending on the season and the size of the boat. The many local cruiser-hire companies include **Erne Marine,** Bellanaleck (ernemarine.com; ✆ **077/0812-7700**), and **Carrickcraft,** Lurgan (cruise-ireland.com; ✆ **028/3834-4993**). On Lower Lough Erne, you can hire motorboats from **Manor House Marine,** Killadeas (manormarine.com; ✆ **028/6862-8100**). Charges average £80 to £110 for a half-day and £110 to £150 for a full day, depending on the size of the boat (max. 8 people). You'll have to pay a refundable deposit before heading out.

WALKING The southwestern branch of the **Ulster Way** follows the western shores of Lough Erne, between the lake and the border. The area is full of other great walks as well. One excellent 11km (6.75-mile; 3–7 hr.) hike leads from a starting point near Florence Court and the Marble Arch Caves (p. 581) along a boardwalk to the summit of **Mount Cuilcagh** (656m/2,152 ft.). For a detailed description of the route and a downloadable map, visit **walkni.com/walks/cuilcagh-boardwalk-trail**.

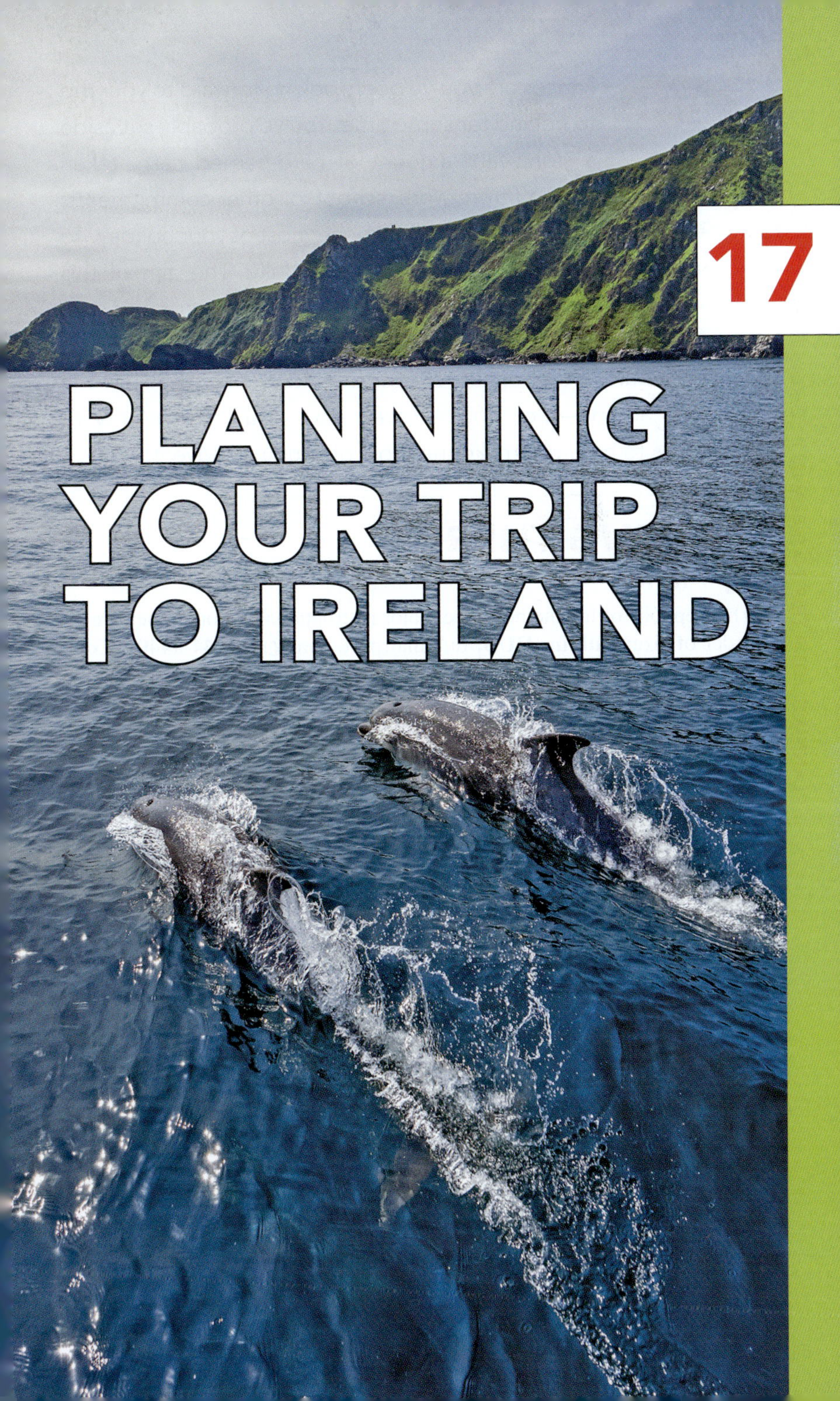

17

PLANNING YOUR TRIP TO IRELAND

Chances are you've been looking forward to your trip to Ireland for some time. You've probably set aside a significant amount of hard-earned cash, taken time off from work, school, or other commitments, and now want to make the most of your holiday. To accomplish that, you'll need to plan carefully. The aim of this chapter is to provide you with the information you need and answer any questions you might have, including: How to get there? Should you book a tour or travel independently? How will you get around once you're here? Here you'll find plenty of resources to help you make the most of your Irish adventure.

GETTING THERE

By Plane

The Republic of Ireland has three major international airports. They are, in order of size: **Dublin (DUB;** dublinairport.com; ✆ **01/944-0440**); **Cork (ORK;** corkairport.com; ✆ **021/431-3131**); and **Shannon (SNN;** shannonairport.ie; ✆ **061/712-000**). Northern Ireland's main airport is **Belfast International Airport (BFS;** belfastairport.com; ✆ **028/9448-4848**).

The Republic of Ireland has several smaller regional airports. The airports at Donegal and Kerry offer service to Dublin; in addition, the airports at Donegal, Kerry, Knock, and County Mayo (Ireland West Airport) receive some (limited) European traffic. In Northern Ireland, the secondary airports are George Best Belfast City Airport and Derry City Airport. Airline service to these smaller airports changes frequently, so be sure to consult your preferred airline or travel agent as soon as you begin to sketch out your itinerary.

By Ferry

If you're traveling to Ireland from Britain or the Continent, traveling by ferry is a good alternative to flying. Several car and passenger ferries offer reasonably comfortable furnishings, cabin berths (for longer crossings), restaurants, duty-free shopping, and lounges. You may be surprised, however, by how long it takes, even from super-near neighbor Britain; the U.K.-to-Ireland ferry route from Holyhead, in Wales, to Dublin can take 3½ hours (there's also a fast ferry, which takes just over 2 hours; see below); the sailing from Fishguard, Wales, to Rosslare also takes 3½ hours. From Cherbourg in France, it's a surprisingly long 17½ hours.

PREVIOUS PAGE: **Dolphins at Malin Head.**

Prices fluctuate seasonally and depend on your route, time of travel, and whether you are on foot or in a car. Check with your travel agent for up-to-date details, but the lowest one-way adult fare on the Holyhead–Dublin ferry starts at around £44. A car usually costs from £200 including one adult passenger, plus £30 per extra adult, £15 extra child.

Irish Ferries (irishferries.ie; ✆ **0818/300-400** in the Republic of Ireland or 353/818-300-400 in Northern Ireland/U.K.) operates between Holyhead and Dublin, with sailings taking either 3½ hours or 2 hours on the Dublin Swift fast ferry. There are also ferries from Pembroke, Wales, to Rosslare, County Wexford, and from Cherbourg in France.

Stena Line (stenaline.ie; ✆ **01/907-5388**) sails from Fishguard, Wales, to Rosslare; from Holyhead to Dublin; and from Cairnryan, Scotland, and Liverpool, England, to Belfast, Northern Ireland.

P&O Irish Sea Ferries (poferries.com; ✆ **0871/664-2121** in Britain, 01/407-3434 in Ireland, or 0044/1304-448-888 in the rest of the world) operates from from Cairnryan, Scotland, to Larne, County Antrim, Northern Ireland.

TRIPS & TOURS

Package Tours

Package tours are simply a way to buy the airfare, accommodations, and other elements of your trip (such as car rentals, airport transfers, and even activities) at the same time and often at discounted prices.

Most major **airlines** offer air/land packages, with surprisingly cheap hotel deals. Several big online travel agencies, such as **Expedia** (expedia.com), **Travelocity** (travelocity.com), **Orbitz** (orbitz.com), and **Lastminute** (lastminute.com), also do a brisk business in packages.

Fully escorted tours mean a travel company takes care of absolutely everything, including airfare, hotels, meals, tours, admission costs, and local transportation. Although we hope this book will help you plan your trip independently and safely, many travelers still prefer the convenience and peace of mind that a fully escorted tour offers. These are particularly good for inexperienced travelers or people with limited mobility. They can also be a great way to make new friends. On the downside, you'll have little opportunity for serendipitous interactions with locals. The tours can be jam-packed with activities, leaving little room for individual sightseeing, whim, or adventure. They often focus on heavily trafficked sites, and large tour buses have to stick to main roads, so you may miss out on lesser-known gems.

C.I.E. Tours (cietours.com; ✆ **1800/243-8687**) offers fully escorted tours, self-guided tours, and individual chauffeur-driven tours. **Hidden Ireland Tours** (hiddenirelandtours.com; ✆ **087/221-4002** or 251/751-3087 in the U.S.) specializes in off-the-beaten-path tours of Kerry, Galway, and Donegal. **Vagabond** (vagabondtoursofireland.com; ✆ **01/563-4358**) runs fun small-group tours around Ireland, which are 5 to 12 days long and blend culture with adventure. **Independent Ireland** (independent ireland.com; ✆ **207/221-0737** in the U.S.) offers custom tours for small or special-interest groups. Those wanting to combine their trip with learning opportunities might be interested in the **International Summer School** program at the National University of Ireland, Galway (University Rd., Galway; nuigalway.ie/international-summer-school), which includes courses on Irish language and history. Contact the course administrator at ✆ **091/495-442** for more information.

Special-Interest Tours

CYCLING

All-inclusive bicycle trips in Ireland can be booked from the United States with either **Backroads** (backroads.com; ✆ **800/462-2848**) or **VBT** (vbt.com; ✆ **844/999-0310**), both well-regarded companies. Tour packages include bikes, gear, luggage transportation via a support van, good food, and rooms in local inns and hotels of character—everything bundled into one price. In Ireland, **Irish Cycling Safaris,** Belfield Bike Shop, Belfield House, University College Dublin (cyclingsafaris.com; ✆ **01/260-0749**), offers cycling trips to practically every part of Ireland, including B&B stays and some meals, as does **Cycle Tours Ireland** (cycletoursireland.ie; ✆ **085/112-5411**). For self-guided tours in the southwest, with luggage transfers and 24-hour phone support, contact **Ireland Walk Hike Bike** (irelandwalkhikebike.com; ✆ **066/718-6181**).

GOLF

A host of U.S. companies offer package golf tours. Among them is **Premier Golf** (premiergolf.com; ✆ **866/260-4409**).

HIKING

For a full walking holiday package to County Kerry or County Clare and Connemara, the U.S.–based **Backroads** (backroads.com; ✆ **800/462-2848**) is one highly recommended operator. **Footfalls Walking Holidays** (walkinghikingireland.com; ✆ **0404/451-52**) offers guided and self-guided walking holidays with accommodation, maps, and luggage transfers. For guided walks in the southwest, contact **Ireland Walk Hike Bike** (ireland walkhikebike.com; ✆ **066/718-6181**). We've included walking-path suggestions in most chapters.

HORSEBACK RIDING

Hidden Trails (hiddentrails.com; ✆ **888/987-2457** in the U.S.) offers 7-day guided riding tours in several regions in Ireland, including the Wicklow Mountains, West Cork, and Connemara. We've included horseback-riding options in each chapter where we were able to find good providers.

GETTING AROUND

By Car

Although Ireland has a reasonably extensive network of public transportation, it will only be useful if you don't mind being confined to the major towns and cities, or using organized tours for attractions farther afield. Trains tend not to go to charming small towns and villages, and great houses and castles are usually miles from any major town. Bus service to places off the beaten track can be infrequent.

Renting a car is not for everyone—particularly if you're not used to driving on small, winding European country roads (and on the ***left*** side of the road). But if you're intrepid enough to do it, this is by far the best way to get around. It will give you the most freedom and open up more choices to you than any other way of getting around. Put simply: Rent a car, and you'll see more of Ireland.

In the summer, weekly rental rates on a manual-transmission compact vehicle begin at around €350 and ascend steeply. Rates are much cheaper out of season. (Also bear in mind that in Europe, when a car is described as "compact," they really mean it.)

Unless your stay in Ireland extends beyond 6 months, your own valid driver's license (provided you've had it for at least 6 months) is all you need to drive in Ireland. Rules and restrictions for car rentals correspond roughly to those in other European nations and the U.S., with two important distinctions: Most rental-car agencies in the Republic won't rent to you (1) if you're under 25 or over 74 (or they may have additional requirements for over 74s. There's no upper age limit in the North) or (2) if your license has been valid for less than a year.

DRIVING LAWS, TIPS & WARNINGS

Highway safety has become a critical issue in Ireland during the past several years. The number of highway fatalities is high for such a small nation—Ireland regularly comes out near the bottom of European league tables for accident rates. In an effort to rein in Irish drivers, the Republic uses a penalty "points" system similar to that in the U.K. and the U.S. Although visitors won't have points added to their licenses, they may still be fined if they speed or commit driving infractions.

All distances and speed limits on road signs in the Republic of Ireland are in **kilometers,** while in Northern Ireland they are in **miles.** Take care if you're driving around the borderlands—the border is unmarked, so you can cross over from one side to the other without knowing it. It's easy to get confused and speed accidentally.

Getting used to left-side driving, left-handed stick shift, narrow roads, and a new landscape all present a challenge, especially if you're driving solo—it's helpful if you have somebody along to navigate. Some

road rules **IN A NUTSHELL**

1. Drive on the **left** side of the road.
2. Road signs are in kilometers, except in Northern Ireland, where they are in miles.
3. On motorways, the left lane is the traveling lane. The right lane is for passing.
4. Everyone must wear a seat belt by law. Young children must be in age-appropriate child seats.
5. Children 11 and under are not allowed to sit in the front seat.
6. When entering a roundabout (traffic circle), give way to traffic coming from the right.
7. Another roundabout rule: Always go *left* (clockwise) around the circle.
8. Speed limits are 50kmph (31 mph) in urban areas; 80kmph (50 mph) on regional and local roads; 100kmph (62 mph) on national roads, including divided highways (called dual carriageways); and 120kmph (75 mph) on freeways (called motorways).

people even use tricks such as sticking a big arrow to the dashboard reminding you that the left is your default lane.

A GPS navigation device (ask if your rental firm offers them) or a good mapping app on your phone (if you have service) can be invaluable in finding your way around, especially in the remote countryside.

Roundabouts (what Americans call traffic circles or rotaries) are found on most major roads and take a little getting used to. Always yield to traffic coming from the right as you approach a roundabout and follow the traffic to the left, signaling before you exit the circle.

One signal that could be misleading to U.S. drivers is a flashing amber light at a pedestrian traffic light. This almost always follows a red light, and it means yield to pedestrians but proceed when the crossing is clear.

The Republic has relatively few types of roads. **Motorways (M)** are major highways, the equivalent of interstates in the U.S. **National (N)** roads, which link major cities, are rarely more than two lanes in each direction (and are sometimes as small as one American-size lane). Most pass directly through towns, making cross-country trips longer than you'd expect. **Regional (R)** roads have one lane of traffic traveling in each direction and generally link smaller cities and towns. **Local roads (L)** are often the most scenic back roads. These can be poorly signposted, very narrow, and a bit rough, but they usually travel through beautiful countryside.

Both the Republic and Northern Ireland have severe laws against **drink-driving.** The legal limit is 22 micrograms of alcohol per 100 milliliters of breath in the Republic of Ireland and 35 micrograms in Northern Ireland. What that equates to varies by person, but even one drink can be enough to put you over the limit and affect your ability to drive. The general rule is: **Do not drink and drive.**

RENTING A CAR

Most rental companies offer their best prices to customers who reserve in advance from their home country. Ireland is a small country, and in high season it can virtually run out of rental cars—but long before it does, it runs out of *affordable* rental cars. Note that weekly rentals are almost always less expensive than day rentals, and the vast majority of available rental cars have **manual transmissions** (stick shifts). Automatics are available, but for a premium.

Prepare for a shock at the pump! Fuel is very expensive in Ireland. At first, those numbers may seem pleasantly small . . . until you realize that over here, fuel is sold in liters, not gallons. Expect to pay around €1.80 per liter (which works out to around €6.80 per gallon—roughly $7.30).

By law, you must be older than 21 to rent a car in Ireland, but many companies will not rent to those younger than 25 or older than 75. The only documentation you should need is your driver's license and photo ID, such as a passport, plus a printout of your reservation if you have one.

When you reserve a car, be sure to ask if the price includes: all taxes including value-added tax (VAT); breakdown assistance; unlimited mileage; personal accident or liability insurance (PAI); collision-damage waiver (CDW); theft waiver; and any other insurance options. If not, ask what these extras cost, because they can make a big dent in your bottom line. The CDW and other insurance might be covered by your credit card if you use the card to pay for the rental; check with your card issuer to be sure there are no restrictions on that coverage in Ireland. (Not all cards do offer insurance protection for car rentals in Ireland.) Some travelers like to live dangerously and waive optional insurance. But when no CDW is purchased, many rental agencies will make you pay for any damages on the spot when you return the car—making even the smallest dent or scratch a potentially costly experience. To avoid any issues, take cellphone photos of your car with a time stamp, so that you have any dents and dings recorded beforehand and won't be charged for it. Also ask the car rental company to record any of these flaws on their own system before you take the vehicle.

If your credit card doesn't cover the CDW, consider buying car rental collision coverage from a third party such as **Travel Guard** (travelguard.com; ✆ **844/404-5477** in the U.S. and Canada). In the U.K., **Insurance 4 Car Hire** (insurance4carhire.com) offers similar coverage.

By Train

Train travel is generally the fastest way to get around the country. **Iarnród Éireann (Irish Rail;** irishrail.ie; ✆ **1850/366222** or 01/836-6222) operates the train services in Ireland. Most lines radiate from Dublin to other principal cities and towns. From Dublin, the journey time to Cork is about 2½ hours; to Belfast, just over 2 hours; to Galway, just under 2½ hours; to Killarney, 3¼ hours; to Sligo, 3 hours; and to Waterford, about 2¼ hours.

Irish Rail Routes
North Channel
ATLANTIC OCEAN
Portrush
Ballycastle
Coleraine
Derry
Ballymoney
Larne Harbour
Larne
Whitehead
Carrickfergus
Antrim
Bangor
Belfast York Road
BELFAST CENTRAL
Lurgan
Portadown
Lisburn
Enniskillen
Newry
Dundalk
Ballina
Sligo
Collooney
Boyle
Carrick-on-Shannon
Ballymote
Foxford
MANULLA JUNCTION
Dromod
Castlebar
Westport
Claremorris
Ballyhaunis
Longford
Castlerea
Roscommon
Mostrim
Drogheda
Irish Sea
Mosney
Balbriggan
Skerries
Malahide
Dublin Connolly
DUBLIN
Dublin Pearse
Tuam
Woodlawn
Athenry
Galway
Attymon
Ballinasloe
Athlone
Mullingar
Enfield
Maynooth
Clara
Kildare
Tullamore
Dublin Heuston
PORTARLINGTON
Newbridge
Dun Laoghaire
Bray
Greystones
ARAN ISLANDS
Ennistymon
Portlaoise
Roscrea
Athy
Cloughjordan
Wicklow
Rathdrum
Ennis
Nenagh
Carlow
BALLYBROPHY
Birdhill
Temple-more
Arklow
Castle-connell
Kilkenny
Muine Bheag
Limerick
Thurles
Gorey
Thomastown
Mouth of the Shannon
LIMERICK JUNCTION
Listowel
Clonmel
Enniscorthy
Charleville
Tipperary
Campile
Wexford
Tralee
Cahir
Rosslare Strand
Carrick-on-Suir
Farranfore
Rathmore
MALLOW
WATERFORD
Rosslare Harbour
Killarney
Banteer
Millstreet
Ballycullane
Bridgetown
Fota
Cork
Wellington Bridge
Cobh
St. George's Channel
ATLANTIC OCEAN
0 30 mi
0 30 km

In addition to Irish Rail service between Dublin and Belfast, **Translink** (translink.co.uk; ✆ **028/9066-6630**) operates routes from Belfast that include Coleraine, Derry, and 21 other localities in Northern Ireland.

One useful piece of lingo: When buying any sort of travel tickets—air, ferry, train, or bus—a "single" means one-way, a "return" is round-trip.

RAIL PASSES

The greatest value in European travel has traditionally been the **rail pass,** a single ticket allowing you unlimited travel (or travel on a certain number of days) within a set time period. The granddaddy of passes, the **Eurail Pass** (eurail.com) covers some 33 countries, including Ireland (both the Republic and Northern Ireland). Prices can be very reasonable for Ireland-only passes. However, if you're a citizen of the European Union (or a long-term resident), you'll need to purchase the equivalent **Interrail Pass** instead. See the box on p. 68 for details.

By Bus

Bus Éireann (buseireann.ie; ✆ **01/836-6111**) operates an extensive system of express bus services, as well as local service, to nearly every town in Ireland. The Bus Éireann website provides timetables and fares for bus service throughout the country. Similarly, **Translink** provides details on services in Northern Ireland (translink.co.uk; ✆ **028/9066-6630**). Bus travel in both countries is affordable, reliable, and comfortable—but also slow. See map on p. 596 for major Irish bus routes.

By Plane

Ireland is such a small country that there is very little point in flying from one end to the other. Plus, the options for internal flights seem to get more limited every year, partly because of improved roads and faster rail journey times. **Aer Lingus** (aerlingus.com) offers daily flights from Dublin to Kerry and Donegal; **Ryanair** (ryanair.com) also operates daily Dublin–Kerry flights.

By Bike

Cycling is an option for exploring the Irish landscape. Distances are quite manageable, and many hostels, B&Bs, and hotels offer bike storage and luggage transfers for touring cyclists. In this guide, we've listed **bike-rental agencies** in every county where we could find one. For a list of recommended operators offering **all-inclusive cycling trips** in Ireland, see "Special-Interest Tours," earlier in this chapter.

There are, however, a few things to consider. As mentioned earlier, roads in Ireland are categorized as **M** (Motorway), **N** (National), **R** (Regional), or **L** (Local). It is illegal to cycle on motorways, and while R roads are always suitable for cycling, as are the N roads in outlying areas

Major Irish Bus Routes

North Channel
ATLANTIC OCEAN
Portrush
Coleraine
Magherafelt
DERRY
Letterkenny
Larne
Strabane
Ballybofey
BELFAST
Donegal
Lough Derg
Cookstown
Omagh
Ballyshannon
Dungannon
Bundoran
Portadown
Enniskillen
SLIGO
Monaghan
Armagh
BALLINA
Newry
Ballinamore
Clones
C'Blayney
Dooagh
Charlestown
Carrick-on-Shannon
Cavan
Dundalk
Boyle
Achill
Castlebar
Knock
Virginia
Carrickmacross
Westport
Strokestown
Mohill
Kells
Ardee
Claremorris
Ballyhaunis
Drogheda
Navan
LONGFORD
Irish Sea
Leenane
Roscommon
Slane
Mullingar
Tuam
Moylough
Kinnegad
Clifden
ATHLONE
Roundstone
Oughterard
Ballinasloe
Rhode
DUBLIN
Moate
GALWAY
Edenderry
Bray
Loughrea
Dr. Nua
Portumna
Kildare
Naas
Gort
Lahinch
Birr
Wicklow
Portlaoise
ROSCREA
Miltown Malbay
Ennis
Athy
Shannon Airport
Nenagh
Durrow
Arklow
Kilkee
Carlow
Tullow
Thurles
Mouth of the Shannon
Kilrush
LIMERICK
Kilkenny
Gorey
Adare
Cashel
Ballybunion
Listowel
Callan
Enniscorthy
Tipperary
Clonmel
New Ross
WEXFORD
Rathluirc
Cahir
Carrick-on-Suir
Rosslare Harbour
Dingle
Tralee
Mitchelstown
WATERFORD
Killarney
Mallow
Fermoy
Cappoquin
Dungarvan
St. George's Channel
Kenmare
Youghal
CORK
Bandon
Glengarriff
Clonakilty
Bantry
Skibbereen
ATLANTIC OCEAN

with little traffic, high vehicle speeds and limited space for maneuvering can lead to vulnerabilities for cyclists. Also be prepared for two inevitable obstacles: wind and hills. Outside the Midlands, hills are just about everywhere, and those on the back roads can have thigh-burning grades. (***Tip:*** If you're biking in the west, plan your route from south to north—the same direction as the prevailing winds.) Finally, be prepared for rain and for uneven or wet road surfaces, and have a plan B if weather is inclement—there's nothing more miserable than a week on a bicycle in driving rain. Note that you can bring your bike on all passenger ferries to Ireland's islands, often for no extra charge.

[Fast FACTS] IRELAND

Area Codes Area codes in Ireland range from one number (the Dublin area code is "1") to three. Area codes are included in all listings in this guide. Within Ireland, you dial 0 before the area code. Outside of Ireland, however, you do not dial 0 before the area code.

Business Hours **Banks** are generally open 10am to 4pm Monday to Friday. **Post offices** (also known as An Post) are generally open 9am to 5:30pm Monday to Friday and 9am to 1:30pm Saturday. Some take an hour for lunch from 1 to 2pm, and small or rural branches may close on Saturday. **Museums and sights** are generally open 10am to 5pm Tuesday to Saturday and 2 to 5pm on Sunday. **Shops** generally open 10am to 5:30 or 6pm Monday to Saturday with some staying open late on Thursday until 7 or 8pm. Most shops in larger towns and cities will also open on Sundays (typically from late morning or noon to late afternoon). Major shops, such as department stores, often stay open much later than other businesses.

Cellphones See "Mobile Phones," later in this section.

Doctors Healthcare in Ireland is comparable to that in other European nations. In the Irish system, private doctors and hospitals provide care and patients purchase healthcare insurance. See individual listings under "Fast Facts" in chapters 4 and 14.

Drinking Laws The minimum legal age to buy alcohol in Ireland is 18. Children under age 15 are allowed in pubs until 9pm (10pm May–Sept), so long as they're with parents or guardians. Pubs serving food often have separate function areas, which can accommodate children age 15 to 18 later, as long as a meal is being served. Pubs are open 10:30am to 11:30pm Monday to Thursday; until 12:30am Friday and Saturday (some have licenses that allow them to stay open later); and 12:30–11pm Sunday. These times are roughly comparable in Northern Ireland.

A restaurant can serve alcohol to diners if it has a liquor license (restaurants with no liquor license may allow you to bring your own alcoholic beverages; however, these are rare). Alcohol is for sale at dedicated liquor stores (or "Off Licenses"), in addition to supermarkets and convenience stores. ***Important note:*** Drink-driving laws in Ireland are very strict. A single drink could be enough to put you over the limit. If you're arrested for drink-driving, penalties range from a hefty fine to jail time. Rules in Northern Ireland are even more severe. The safest approach is simply not to drink and drive.

Electricity The Irish electric system operates on 220 volts with a large plug bearing three rectangular prongs. The Northern Irish system operates on 250 volts with a similar plug. To use standard American 110-volt appliances, you'll need both a transformer and a plug adapter. Most new laptops have built-in transformers, but some do not, so beware. Also check if hair tools and hair dryers are compatible before using.

Embassies & Consulates The **American Embassy** is at 42 Elgin Rd., Ballsbridge (ie.usembassy.gov; ✆ **01/668-8777**); the **Canadian Embassy** is at 7–8 Wilton Terrace, 3rd floor (international.gc.ca/country-pays/ireland-irlande; ✆ **01/234-4000**); the **British Embassy** is at 29 Merrion Rd. (gov.uk/government/world/organisations/british-embassy-dublin; ✆ **01/205-3700**); and the **Australian Embassy** is at Fitzwilton House, 7 floor, Wilton Terrace (ireland.embassy.gov.au; ✆ **01/664-5300**). In Northern Ireland, there's an **American Consulate** at Danesfort House, 223 Stranmillis Rd., Belfast BT9 5GR (uk.usembassy.gov/embassy-consulates/belfast/; ✆ **028/9038-6100**).

Emergencies For the **Garda (police),** fire, ambulance, or other emergencies, dial ✆ **999** or **112.**

Family Travel Recommended family travel websites include **Family Travel Forum** (myfamilytravels.com) and **Family Travel Files** (thefamilytravelfiles.com).

Internet & Wi-Fi Wi-Fi is widespread in Irish hotels and B&Bs, even in rural areas. Most B&Bs and hotels provide it free.

Language Ireland has two official languages: English and Irish (which is sometimes called Gaelic outside Ireland). All native Irish people can speak English. There is a strong national movement to preserve and expand the language, and the areas of the country where Irish is protected and promoted are known as **The Gaeltacht.** Irish is a complex and ancient language that you will not be able to figure out on your own; ask for help (in English) if you get lost. Also, everybody in the Gaeltacht regions speaks English.

LGBTQ Travelers Homosexuality was legalized in Ireland in 1993 (1982 in the North), and same-sex marriages were ratified in the Republic in 2015. Nevertheless, gay and lesbian visitors should be aware that this is still a conservative country. Cities like Dublin and Galway are far more liberal in attitudes (particularly among the younger generation), but it's a good idea to proceed with caution when traveling in rural areas. Recommended websites for gay and lesbian travelers include **Gay Ireland** (gay-ireland.com) and **Outhouse** (outhouse.ie).

Lost Property If your passport is lost or stolen, contact your country's embassy immediately. Be sure to tell all of your credit card companies the minute you discover that your wallet is gone and file a report at the nearest Garda (police) station.

Mobile Phones Before you leave your home country, check directly with your mobile phone provider to find out about using your phone overseas. You may have to ask for the "international roaming" capability to be switched on **before** you're overseas.

Unfortunately, using your own phone in Ireland can prove very expensive. Most mobile phone companies charge very large premiums on call charges made while abroad; check before traveling to see whether your provider offers a good roaming package. Be sure to turn off features such as location services and push notifications on your smartphone, or you could face **enormous** data roaming charges. Always use Wi-Fi if you need to download anything.

Some travelers prefer to **buy an Irish prepaid SIM card** for their phone for their trip to Ireland. You can buy SIM cards in any phone shop, plus some grocery stores and at Dublin Airport, and add it to your own phone—make sure your phone is "unlocked" before you travel.

Money The Republic of Ireland uses the European currency known as the **euro (€).** Euro notes come in denominations of €5, €10, €20, €50, €100, €200, and €500. The euro is divided into 100 cents; coins come in denominations of €2, €1, 50¢, 20¢, 10¢, 5¢, 2¢, and 1¢. The 1¢ and 2¢ coins are being phased out, so increasingly prices are rounded to the nearest 5¢.

As part of the United Kingdom, Northern Ireland uses the **British pound sterling (£).** Notes come in denominations of £5, £10, £20, £50, and £100. Coins are issued in £2, £1, 50p, 20p, 10p, 5p, 2p, and 1p denominations.

The British pound is not accepted in the Republic, and the euro is not accepted in the North—if you're traveling in both parts of Ireland you'll need some of both currencies, although shops on the border do tend to accept both. Note that pounds issued in Northern Ireland, while legal tender in Great Britain, actually **look** different. You may find that cabdrivers and small business owners in the North won't accept bills issued in Great Britain, and vice versa. In that case, you can change money into locally issued currency at any large central bank, free of charge.

Note for international travelers: Exchange rates can fluctuate wildly in the space of just a few weeks. Before departing, consult a currency exchange website such as **xe.com** to check up-to-the-minute rates.

When it comes to obtaining foreign currency, please **skip the currency exchange kiosks** in airports, train stations, and elsewhere. These give the poorest rates and charge exorbitant fees. Instead, order a small amount of foreign currency from your bank before leaving home, and then use your **debit card** for the duration of your trip. ATMs (in Ireland also called "cash machines" or "cash points") will give you a favorable rate, and you can withdraw however much cash you need for a day or so. Before you leave home, be sure you know your personal identification number (PIN) and daily withdrawal limit. Confirm with your bank that your PIN will work in Europe and be sure to let them know the dates and destinations to which you're traveling—you don't want to find your card frozen while you're abroad!

Another option is to open an international currency transfer account with a service such as **Wise** (wise.com) or **Revolut** (revolut.com), which allow you to hold multiple currencies and order a physical debit card to use for payments.

Credit cards are accepted just about everywhere, save street markets, small independent retailers, street-food vendors, and occasional small businesses. North American visitors should note that American Express is accepted far less widely than at home. Bring along a Visa or MasterCard to cover your bases.

In common with most of Europe, shops and restaurants now use "contactless" payment options for small amounts (under €50) simply by holding your card above the reader. Only certain cards have this capability, which is indicated with a logo similar to the Wi-Fi symbol. For amounts over €50, or to use chip-and-pin payment, you will need to enter your PIN code. Some machines don't like foreign cards, so always carry some cash with you, just in case.

Pharmacies Drugstores are called "chemists" and are found in every city and town and most villages of any size. You'll find individual listings under "Fast Facts" in chapters 4 and 14.

Police In the Republic of Ireland, a law enforcement officer is called a **Garda,** a member of the Garda Síochána ("Guardian of the Peace"); in the plural, it's **Gardaí** (pronounced **Gar-**dee) or simply "the Guards." Dial ✆ **999** or **112** to reach the Gardaí in an emergency. Except for special detachments, Irish police are unarmed and wear dark blue uniforms, with soft-shell jackets with hi-vis panels. In Northern Ireland you can also reach the police by dialing ✆ **999** or **112**.

Safety By U.S. standards, Ireland is safe, but—particularly in the cities—not safe enough to warrant carelessness. Be wary of the usual tourist plagues: pickpockets, purse snatchers, and car thieves. Do not leave cars unlocked or cameras and other expensive equipment unattended, and by all means do not leave valuables in a car. Ask at your hotel which areas are safe and which are not. Take a taxi back to your hotel if you're out very late.

Senior Travel In Ireland, seniors are sometimes referred to as "O.A.P.'s" (short for "Old Age Pensioners"). People over age 60 often qualify for reduced admission to museums and other attractions. Always ask about an O.A.P. discount if special rates aren't posted. **Discover Ireland** (p. 85) can offer advice on how to find the best discounts.

Smoking Ireland and Northern Ireland both have broad antismoking laws that ban smoking in all public places, including bars, restaurants, and hotel lobbies. However, many restaurants and most pubs have covered outdoor smoking areas.

Taxes Sales tax (VAT, or value-added tax) is always included in the price shown on price tags. In the Republic, VAT rates vary—for hotels, restaurants, and car rentals, it is 13.5%; for souvenirs and gifts, it is 23%. In Northern Ireland, the VAT is 20% across the board. VAT charged on services such as hotel stays, meals, car rentals, and entertainment cannot be refunded to visitors, but the VAT on products such as souvenirs is refundable. Save your receipts and present them at the Global Refund Desk when you get to the airport (they're located airside in the main terminals at Dublin and Shannon; in Dublin the desk is now an automated kiosk, located on the left just after you pass the Starbucks on the way to the departure gates). They can usually issue you a refund there and then. Some larger stores can issue you a Global Refund form and refund your VAT themselves, although you'll need to know your passport number, flight number, and departure time. In practice, this is usually much more fuss than it's worth.

Telephones In both the Republic and the North, there are multiple operators of landline and cell networks, Every effort has been made to ensure that the numbers and information in this guide were accurate at the time of writing.

To call Ireland from home:

1. **Dial the international access code:** 011 from the U.S., 00 from the U.K., 0011 from Australia, or 0170 from New Zealand.
2. **Dial the country code:** 353 for the Republic, 44 for the North.
3. **Dial the local number, remembering to omit the initial 0,** which is for use only within Ireland (for example, to call the County Kerry number ✆ 066/12345 from the United States, you'd dial ✆ 011-353-66/12345).

To make international calls from Ireland: First dial 00, then the country code (U.S. or Canada 1, U.K. 44, Australia 61, New Zealand 64). Next you dial the area code and local number. For example, to call the U.S. number ✆ 212/000-0000 you'd dial ✆ 00-1-212/000-0000. The toll-free international access code for **AT&T** is ✆ **1-800/550-000;** for **T-Mobile** it's ✆ **1-800/937-8997.**

To make local calls: To dial a local number within the same area code, drop the initial 0. To dial a number within Ireland but in a different area code, use the initial 0.

Time Ireland follows Greenwich Mean Time November to March, and British Summer Time April to October. Ireland is 5 hours ahead of the eastern United States. Ireland's latitude makes for longer days and shorter nights in the summer and the reverse in the winter. In June, the sun doesn't fully set until around 11pm, but in December, it is dark by 4pm.

Tipping For taxi drivers, hairdressers, and other providers of service, tip an average 10% to 15%. For restaurants, a gratuity of 10% to 15% is usually customary; if a restaurant has an automatic service charge (for a group, for example), it will be specified on the menu. As a rule, bartenders do not expect a tip, except when table service is provided.

Toilets Public toilets are usually simply called "toilets" or are marked with international symbols. In the Republic of Ireland, some of the older ones carry the

Irish words FIR (men) and MNA (women). Free restrooms are usually available to customers at sightseeing attractions, museums, hotels, restaurants, pubs, shops, and theaters. Many gas stations (called "petrol stations" in Ireland) have public toilets, and a few even have baby-changing facilities. The website **pee.ie** is a good resource for finding the nearest public toilets.

Travelers with Disabilities For travelers with disabilities, Ireland is a mixed bag. Its modern buildings and cities are generally accessible, but many of its historic buildings lack wheelchair access. Trains can be accessed by wheelchairs but only with assistance. If you plan to travel by train in Ireland, check out **Iarnród Éireann**'s website (irishrail.ie), which includes services for travelers with disabilities.

Finding accessible lodging can be tricky in Ireland. Many buildings here are hundreds of years old, and older hotels, small guesthouses, and landmark buildings still have steps outside and in. The rule of thumb should be: Never assume that a B&B, hotel, or restaurant has accessible facilities—ask about your requirements before booking. To research options prior to your trip, there is some information on **ireland.com**. For advice on travel to Northern Ireland, contact **Disability Action** (disabilityaction.org; ✆ **028/9029-7880**). The website **accessable.co.uk** has a search tool for restaurants, hotels, hospitals, and universities by area, while **Euan's Guide** (EuansGuide.com) has reviews of disabled access. For more resources, see **Tourism Northern Ireland**'s website (tourismni.com).

Visas Citizens of the United States, Canada, Australia, and New Zealand entering the Republic of Ireland or Northern Ireland for a stay of up to 3 months do not need a visa, but a valid **passport** is required.

Water Tap water throughout the island of Ireland is safe to drink, but make sure you are taking water from a "mains" tap in a kitchen; it is not advised to drink water from a bathroom tap; the water is stored in a separate tank. If you're in a hotel or B&B, ask them to refill your water bottle from the kitchen or bar.

Wi-Fi See "Internet & Wi-Fi," earlier in this section.

Women Travelers Women should expect few problems traveling in Ireland. In small towns, you may attract a little attention if you eat alone in a restaurant at night, but you won't be hassled. If you drink in a pub on your own, though, expect all kinds of attention—even if you're reading a book, talking on your cellphone, or doing a crossword puzzle. (Irish men almost always respond well to polite rejection, though.) Take a cab home at night and follow all the usual precautions you use when you travel anywhere, especially at night. Essentially, don't do anything in Ireland that you wouldn't do at home.

Index

See also Accommodations and Restaurants indexes, below.

3Arena (Dublin), 169
14 Henrietta Street (Dublin), 113
37 Dawson Street (Dublin), 169
1798 Rebellion, 31–32
1916 Rebellion Walking Tour (Dublin), 101

A

Abbey Theatre (Dublin), 175
Accessibility, 601
Accommodations. *See* Accommodations index; Hotels
Achill Island (Co. Mayo), 448
Adare (Co. Limerick), 6, 370, 372
Adventure sports. *See* Outdoor activities
Aghadoe Cathedral (Co. Kerry), 305
Ahenny High Crosses (Co. Tipperary), 379
Aillwee Burren Experience (Co. Clare), 354, 356
Air travel, 588, 595
All-Inclusive Pass (Dublin), 93
An Bodhrán (Cork City), 267
An Creagán Visitors Centre (Co. Tyrone), 576
Andrew Jackson Cottage (Belfast), 514
An Gailearai Beag (Co. Kerry), 348
Anglo-Irish Compromise, 37–38
An Spailpín Fánac (Cork City), 266, 267
Anti-Catholic laws, 30–31
Aran Islands (Co. Galway), 8, 395, 397
Aran Sweater Market (Co. Kerry), 314
Áras an Uachtaráin (The President's House) (Dublin), 110
Archive's Antiques Centre (Belfast), 527
Ardara (*Árd an Rátha*) (Co. Donegal), 487
Ardara (Co. Donegal), 7
Ardmore High Cross (Co. Waterford), 221
Ards Forest Park (Co. Donegal), 492
Ards Peninsula (Co. Down) , 544–549
Area codes, 597
The Ark: A Cultural Centre for Children (Dublin), 121–122
Armagh County Museum, 555
Armagh Observatory and Planetarium, 555–556
Arnotts (Dublin), 161
Athassel Priory (Co. Tipperary), 380
Athenry (Co. Galway), 409
Athlone Castle (Co. Westmeath), 426–427
ATMs, 92, 501
Attractions passes. *See* Tickets
Aughnanure Castle (Co. Galway), 412
Authentic experiences, best of, 17, 20–21
Avoca (Dublin), 159–160, 164
Avoca at Moll's Gap (Co. Kerry), 322
Avoca Handweavers (Co. Wicklow), 205
Avondale House (Co. Wicklow), 200

B

Baboró International Arts Festival for Children (Co. Galway), 54
Ballinskelligs (Co. Kerry), 327–328
Ballintubber Abbey (Co. Mayo), 445–446
Ballymaloe Cookery School (Co. Cork), 271
Ballyshannon *(Béal Átha Seanaidh)* (Co. Donegal), 480–481
Bank holidays, 51–52, 91
Bank of Ireland (Dublin), 110
The Bank on College Green (Dublin), 172
Banks, 92, 501
Bantry House (Co. Cork), 5, 284–285
Bars
- Belfast, 528–529
- Dublin, 169–170

Battle of Aughrom Interpretative Centre (Co. Galway), 427
Bay Lough (Co. Tipperary), 381
Beaches. *See* Outdoor activities
Beaghmore Stone Circles (Co. Tyrone), 576
Beatty, Alfred Chester, 97
Beckett, Samuel, 42
Behan, Brendan, 43
Belfast, 499–530
- arrival information, 500–501
- attractions, 503–517
- city layout, 501–503
- day trips from
  - Ards Peninsula & Mourne Mountains (Co. Down), 544–554
  - Causeway Coast (Co. Antrim), 533–544
  - County Armagh, 554–560
  - transportation options, 532
- family-friendly activities, 513–514
- fast facts, 501
- hotels, 517–523
- itineraries, 76
- nightlife, 528–530
- restaurants, 523–527
- shopping, 527–528
- transportation in, 503
- visitor information, 501

Belfast Botanic Gardens & Palm House, 504
Belfast Castle, 512
Belfast Cathedral (St. Anne's), 512
Belfast City Marathon, 52
Belfast Empire, 529
Belfast Political & Mural tour, 506
Belfast Zoo, 513–514
Bell, Book and Candle (Co. Galway), 401
Belleek china (Co. Fermanagh), 17, 579
Ben Bulben (Co. Sligo), 467
Benburb Valley Park (Co. Armagh), 556
Bennigans Bar (Derry), 574
Best of Ireland
- authentic experiences, 17, 20–21
- castles & historic houses, 4–5
- driving tours, 11–12
- early Christian ruins, 9–10
- family-friendly activities, 10–11
- hotels, 13–14
- for literature lovers, 7–8
- museums, 3–4
- natural wonders, 2–3
- picture-postcard towns, 6–7
- prehistoric sites, 8
- restaurants, 15–17
- shopping, 17

Beyond the Trees (Co. Wicklow), 11, 200
Biking. *See* Cycling
Bird-watching
- Bull Island (Dublin), 167
- County Clare, 369
- County Tipperary, 385
- County Wexford, 232, 238
- Rathlin Island (Co. Antrim), 536

Birr Castle (Co. Offaly), 427–428
Bishop's Palace (Co. Waterford), 215
Black Abbey (Co. Kilkenny), 239–240
Black Box (Belfast), 529
Black Taxi Tour (Belfast), 506
Blacksod Lighthouse (Co. Mayo), 449
Blacoe (Co. Galway), 403
Blarney Castle (Co. Cork), 258–259
Blarney Woollen Mills (Cork City), 266
Blasket Island Eco Marine Tours (Co. Kerry), 10

The Blasket Islands (Co. Kerry), 342–343
Blennerville Windmill (Co. Kerry), 334–335
Bloomsday Festival (Dublin), 53
Boat tours
Connemara (Co. Galway), 414
County Sligo, 473
Dingle Bay (Co. Kerry), 340
Dingle Peninsula (Co. Kerry), 340
Donegal Bay, 478
Dursey Island (Co. Cork), 286
The Fermanagh Lakelands, 580, 582
Galway City, 393–394
Inishmurray (Co. Sligo), 465–466
Kenmare (Co. Kerry), 316–317
Killarney (Co. Kerry), 305
Lough Gill (Co. Sligo), 467
Lough Neagh (Co. Armagh), 558
Skellig Islands (Co. Kerry), 327
Sliabh Liag (Slieve League) (Co. Donegal), 483
Boat Tours of Dingle Bay (Co. Kerry), 340
Boating on Lough Erne (Co. Fermanagh), 585–586
The Bogside (Derry), 566
Bogside History Tours (Derry), 568
Book Market (Dublin), 165
Book of Kells Experience (Dublin), 93, 96
Born and Bred (Belfast), 528
Boxty, 146
Boyne Valley. *See* Brú na Bóinne (Co. Meath)
Bram Stoker Festival (Dublin), 54
Bray Head (Co. Wicklow), 200
The Brazen Head (Dublin), 172–173, 437
Breweries. *See* Distilleries & breweries
Brian de Staic Jewellery Workshop (Co. Kerry), 348
Bricín (Co. Kerry), 314
Brigid (saint), 195
Brit Movie Tours, 546
Brown Thomas (Cork City), 265–266
Brown Thomas (Dublin), 17, 161
Brownshill Dolmen (Co. Carlow), 201
Brú na Bóinne (Co. Meath), 73, 181–183
Bull Island (Dublin), 167
The Bull Ring (Co. Wexford), 228
Bunratty Castle & Folk Park (Co. Clare), 5, 11, 72, 359–360
The Burren (Co. Clare), 2, 20
attractions, 354–359
itineraries, 64–65, 69–70, 72, 74
nature walks, 369
Burren Birds of Prey Centre (Co. Clare), 356
Burren National Park (Co. Clare), 357
The Burren Way (Co. Clare), 359
Bus tours, 122, 180
Bus travel, 595
Business hours, 597
Butlers Chocolate Café (Dublin), 162

C

Café en Seine (Dublin), 170
Caherconnell Stone Fort (Co. Clare), 356–357, 361
Cahir Castle (Co. Tipperary), 380
Calendar of events, 52–55
Cape Clear Island (*Oileán Chléire*) (Co. Cork), 286
Car rental, 593
Carlow Arts Festival, 53
Carnlough (Co. Antrim), 533
Carrick-a-Rede Rope Bridge (Co. Antrim), 533, 536
Carrickfergus Castle (Belfast), 515
Carrowkeel Passage Tomb Cemetery (Co. Sligo), 8, 463
Carrowmore Megalithic Cemetery (Co. Sligo), 8, 464
Castle Coole (Co. Fermanagh), 578–579
Castle Espie Wetland Centre (Co. Down), 544–545
Castle Ward (Co. Down), 545
Castles & historic houses, best of, 4–5
Castletown House (Co. Kildare), 192–193
Castlewellan Forest Park (Co. Down), 549–550
The Cat & the Moon (Co. Sligo), 472
The Cat Laughs Comedy Festival (Co. Kilkenny), 53
Causeway Coast (Co. Antrim), 533–544
attractions, 533–539
hotels, 539–542
outdoor activities, 543–544
restaurants, 542–543
visitor information, 533
Causeway Coastal Route driving tour (Co. Antrim), 12, 534
Cave HIll Country Park (Belfast), 512
Caxton (Dublin), 158
Céide Fields (Co. Mayo), 8, 73, 450
Celtic Wave (Belfast), 517
Cemeteries in Dublin, 115
Centre for Contemporary Art (Derry), 567
Charles Fort (Co. Cork), 274–276
Charleville Castle (Co. Offaly), 428
Charlie Byrne's Bookshop (Co. Galway), 401
Charlie Foley's (Co. Kerry), 314
Chester Beatty Library (Dublin), 3, 96
Christ Church Cathedral (Co. Waterford), 216
Christ Church Cathedral (Dublin), 97, 98
Christmas Markets, 55
Christy Bird (Dublin), 158
Church of St. Begnet (Dublin), 124
Church of the Assumption (Co. Wexford), 229
Church of the Immaculate Conception (Co. Wexford), 229
City Hall (Belfast), 506–508
Claddagh Jewellers (Co. Galway), 403
Claddagh rings, 403
Clare Island (Co. Mayo), 446
Clifden Castle (Co. Galway), 415
Cliffs of Moher (Co. Clare), 359, 360–361
Clonmacnoise (Co. Offaly), 10, 428–429
The Cobblestone (Dublin), 173
Cobh (Co. Cork), 270
Cobh: The Queenstown Story (Co. Cork), 270
Cobwebs (Co. Galway), 403
College Green (Dublin), 110
Collins, Michael, 282–283
Comedy clubs in Dublin, 170–171
Comeragh Mountains (Co. Waterford), 221
Cong (Co. Mayo), 444
Connacht, counties in, 58
Connemara (Co. Galway), 410–422
attractions, 411–415
boat tours, 414
hotels, 415–419
itineraries, 68–69
outdoor activities, 421–422
restaurants, 419–421
transportation in, 411
visitor information, 411
Connemara National Park (Co. Galway), 412
Consulates, 598
Coole Park National Forest, 410
Corcomroe Abbey (Co. Clare), 358
Cork Butter Museum, 254
Cork City, 58–59, 251–268
attractions, 254–260
city layout, 252–254
history of, 252
hotels, 260–263
nightlife, 266–268
outdoor activities, 268
restaurants, 263–265
shopping, 265–266
Cork City Gaol, 254
Cork City Tours, 259–260
Cork Craft & Design (Cork City), 266
Cork International Film Festival, 55
Cork Midsummer Arts Festival, 53
Cork Opera House, 267
Cork Public Museum, 254–255
Corlea Iron Age Roadway (Co. Longford), 429–430
Cornmarket (Co. Wexford), 228
Corrib Princess Cruise (Co. Galway), 394

Costelloe & Costelloe (Dublin), 161
County Antrim, 76–77. *See also* Belfast; Causeway Coast (Co. Antrim)
County Armagh, 554–560
attractions, 555–559
hotels, 559–560
restaurants, 559–560
visitor information, 555
County Carlow, 199–210
attractions, 200–206
hotels, 206–207
restaurants, 208–210
visitor information, 200
County Clare, 59, 354–370
arrival information, 352, 354
attractions, 359–364
The Burren, 354–359
hotels, 364–366
itineraries, 69–70
outdoor activities, 369–370
restaurants, 366–368
visitor information, 354
County Cork, 58–59, 249–294
arrival information, 250–251
Cork City, 251–268
East Cork, 268–274
itineraries, 64, 71
Kinsale, 274–284
visitor information, 251
West Cork, 284–294
County Donegal, 59, 474–498
arrival information, 475–476
attractions, 486–490
Donegal Town & Donegal Bay, 476–486
driving tours, 487–488
hotels, 490–491
Inishowen Peninsula, 493–498
itineraries, 78
outdoor activities, 492
restaurants, 491–492
County Down. *See* Ards Peninsula (Co. Down); Mourne Mountains (Co. Down)
County Fermanagh. *See* The Fermanagh Lakelands
County Galway, 59, 387–422
arrival information, 388–389
Connemara, 410–422
day trips from Galway City, 405–410
Galway City, 389–405
itineraries, 65, 68–69
County Kerry, 20, 59, 295–350
arrival information, 296–297
Dingle Peninsula, 338–350
itineraries, 71–72
Ring of Kerry, 298–334
tours, 298
Tralee, 334–338
visitor information, 298
County Kildare, 192–199
attractions, 192–195
hotels, 195–197
outdoor activities, 199
restaurants, 197–199
visitor information, 192
walking tours, 192
County Kilkenny, 239–248
arrival information, 212
attractions, 239–244
hotels, 245–246
itineraries, 62, 64
outdoor activities, 248
restaurants, 247–248
transportation in, 214–215
visitor information, 239
walking tours, 240, 242
County Laois. *See* The Midlands (Co. Laois, Longford, Offaly, Westmeath)
County Limerick, 370–378
arrival information, 352, 354
attractions, 370–372
hotels, 372–375
outdoor activities, 377–378
restaurants, 375–377
visitor information, 370
County Longford. *See* The Midlands (Co. Laois, Longford, Offaly, Westmeath)
County Louth, 180–191
attractions, 181–188
hotels, 188–190
restaurants, 190–191
visitor information, 181
County Mayo, 59, 443–458
arrival information, 442–443
attractions, 443–452
hotels, 452–455
itineraries, 65
outdoor activities, 457–458
restaurants, 455–457
visitor information, 443
County Meath, 180–191
attractions, 181–188
hotels, 188–190
restaurants, 190–191
visitor information, 181
County Offaly. *See* The Midlands (Co. Laois, Longford, Offaly, Westmeath)
County Roscommon. *See* The Midlands (Co. Laois, Longford, Offaly, Westmeath)
County Sligo, 59, 458–473
arrival information, 442–443
attractions, 460–466
hotels, 466–469
itineraries, 66–68, 73–74, 78–79
outdoor activities, 473
restaurants, 469–472
shopping, 472–473
visitor information, 460
Yeats, W. B., 7, 462
County Tipperary, 378–386
arrival information, 352, 354
attractions, 378–382
hotels, 382–384
outdoor activities, 385–386
restaurants, 384–385
visitor information, 378
County Waterford, 215–227
arrival information, 212
attractions, 215–222
hotels, 222–224
itineraries, 64
outdoor activities, 226–227
restaurants, 224–226
transportation in, 214–215
visitor information, 215
walking tours, 216, 220–221
County Westmeath. *See* The Midlands (Co. Laois, Longford, Offaly, Westmeath)
County Wexford, 227–239
arrival information, 212
attractions, 228–235
hotels, 235–236
outdoor activities, 238
restaurants, 236–238
transportation in, 214–215
visitor information, 227
walking tours, 230
Yola language, 214
County Wicklow, 199–210
attractions, 200–206
hiking, 209
hotels, 206–207
itineraries, 62, 64
outdoor activities, 210
restaurants, 208–210
visitor information, 200
The Craft Village (Derry), 574
Crag Cave (Co. Kerry), 335
Craggaunowen (Co. Clare), 361–362
The Crane Bar (Co. Galway), 404
Cranny Falls (Co. Antrim), 533
Crawford Art Gallery (Co. Cork), 255
Croagh Patrick (Co. Mayo), 444
Croke Park Stadium (Dublin), 113–114
Crom Estate (Co. Fermanagh), 579–580
Cromwell, Oliver, 29–30
Crown Liquor Saloon (Belfast), 508, 529
Crumlion Road Gaol (Belfast), 508
Cúirt International Festival of Literature (Co. Galway), 52
Cultúrlann McAdam Ó Fiaich (Belfast), 513
Cummeengeera (Co. Cork), 285
Curra Castle (Co. Antrim), 537
The Curragh (Co. Kildare), 193
Currency exchange, 92, 501, 598–599
Cushendun (Co. Antrim), 536–537
The Custom House (Dublin), 110–111
Cycling, 590, 595, 597. *See also* Outdoor activities

D

Dakota (Dublin), 170
Dalkey (Co. Dublin), 6–7
Dalkey Castle & Heritage Centre (Dublin), 124
Dan O'Hara's Homestead (Co. Galway), 412–413
DART trains (Dublin), 90
Davy Byrnes (Dublin), 7, 173
Dentists, 92, 501
Derry, 562–574

arrival information, 562–563
attractions, 567–571
city layout, 566
hotels, 571
itineraries, 77–78
nightlife, 574
origin of name, 563
restaurants, 572–574
shopping, 574
visitor information, 564
walls of, 569
Derry Girls Experience, 570
Derryglad Folk & Heritage Museum (Co. Roscommon), 430
Derrynane House National Historic Park (Co. Kerry), 328
The Design Tower (Dublin), 160
Designer Mart (Dublin), 165
DESIGNyard (Dublin), 163
Desmond Castle (Co. Cork), 276
Devenish Island (Co. Fermanagh), 580
Dillon Gallery (Belfast), 513
Dingle (Co. Kerry), 6
Dingle Oceanworld Aquarium (Co. Kerry), 340
Dingle Peninsula (Co. Kerry), 338–350
attractions, 338–345
hotels, 345–346
outdoor activities, 349–350
restaurants, 346–348
shopping, 348–349
spectator sports, 349
Dingle Regatta (Co. Kerry), 349
Dingle Way (Co. Kerry), 348
Dining. *See* Restaurants; Restaurants index
Distilleries & breweries
Belfast, 508–509, 511
Causeway Coast (Co. Antrim), 538–539
County Limerick, 371
Dublin, 108–109
East Cork, 272–273
Kenmare (Co. Kerry), 318
The Midlands, 430
Diving, 293, 350, 554
Doagh Famine Village (Co. Donegal), 494
Doctors, 92, 501, 597
DoDublin bus tours, 122
DoDublin Days Out cards, 93
Doe Castle *(Caisleán na dTuath)* (Co. Donegal), 488
Doheny and Nesbitt (Dublin), 173
Dolphin-watching tours, 10, 369
Donegal Abbey, 477–478
Donegal Bay Waterbus, 478
Donegal Castle, 478
Donegal Town & Donegal Bay, 476–486
attractions, 477–483
boat tours, 478
driving tour, 480
hotels, 483–484
outdoor activities, 485–486
restaurants, 484–485
visitor information, 476–477
Doolin (Co. Clare), 362–363
The Doorway Gallery (Dublin), 159
Down Cathedral, 548
Down County Museum, 548
Downpatrick (Co. Down), 548
Drinking laws, 597
Drinking water, 601
Driving, 591–593
Driving tours
Belfast, 506
best of, 11–12
Causeway Coastal Route (Co. Antrim), 534
County Donegal, 487–488
County Tipperary, 381
Dingle Peninsula (Co. Kerry), 344–345
Donegal Bay, 480
Inishowen Peninsula (Co. Donegal), 493
Killarney to Kenmare (Co. Kerry), 315
Lough Derg Drive (Co. Clare, Limerick, Tipperary), 383
Lough Gill (Co. Sligo), 467
The Ring of Kerry, 323–329
Sheep's Head Loop (Co. Cork), 292
The Sky Road (Co. Galway), 414–415
Slea Head Drive (Co. Kerry), 341–344
Torr Head Scenic Road (Co. Antrim), 539
Wild Atlantic Way (Co. Cork to Co. Donegal), 275
Drogheda (Co. Louth), 183
Drombeg Stone Circle (Co. Cork), 286
Druid Theatre (Co. Galway), 404
Drum Manor Forest Park (Co. Tyrone), 576
Drumcliffe Church (Co. Sligo), 464
Drumena Cashel (Co. Down), 550
Dublin, 58, 80–176
arrival information, 81, 84–85
attractions, 92–125
bus tours, 122
city layout, 86–87
day trips from
Counties Meath & Louth, 180–191
Counties Wicklow & Carlow, 199–210
County Kildare, 192–199
transportation options, 178, 180
family-friendly activities, 121–124
fast facts, 92
horse-drawn carriage tours, 120
hotels, 125–141
itineraries, 62, 70–71
neighborhoods in brief, 87–89
nightlife, 168–176
outdoor activities, 165–167
restaurants, 141–157
shopping, 157–165
souvenirs, 164
spectator sports, 167–168
statue nicknames, 99
street markets, 165
transportation in, 89–91
visitor information, 85–86
walking tours, 101
Dublin Castle, 111–112
Dublin Dance Festival, 53
Dublin Fringe Festival, 54
Dublin Ghost Bus, 122
Dublin International Film Festival, 52
Dublin LGBTQ+ Pride Festival, 53
Dublin Liberties Distillery, 108
Dublin Portal, 99
Dublin Theatre Festival, 54
Dublin Zoo, 123
Dublinia (Dublin), 123–124
Duiske Abbey (Co. Kilkenny), 242–243
Duke Pub (Dublin), 101
Dún Aengus (Aran Islands), 8, 395
Dunamase Castle (Co. Laois), 433
Dunbeg Fort (*Dún Beag*) (Co. Kerry), 343
Dunbrody Abbey (Co. Wexford), 232
Dundrum Castle (Co. Down), 550
Dunfanaghy Workhouse (Co. Donegal), 488–489
The Dungeon Bookshop (Co. Kerry), 314
Dunguaire Castle (Co. Galway), 407, 410
Dunluce Castle (Co. Antrim), 5, 537
Dunmore Cave (Co. Kilkenny), 243
Dursey Island (Co. Cork), 286

E

Eagles Flying (Co. Sligo), 464
Early Christian ruins
best of, 9–10
high crosses, 185
history of Ireland, 25–26
Eask Tower (Co. Kerry), 340–341
Eason (Cork City), 266
Eason (Dublin), 159
East Cork, 268–274
arrival information, 271
attractions, 271–273
hotels, 273–274
restaurants, 273–274
Easter Rising, 36
Elective Picnic (Co. Laois), 54
Electricity, 597–598
Embassies, 598
Emergencies, 92, 501, 598
English Market (Co. Cork), 21, 256
Ennis Friary (Co. Clare), 363
Enniscoe Gardens (Co. Mayo), 450–451
Enniskillen Castle (Co. Fermanagh), 580–581
EPIC The Irish Emigration Museum (Dublin), 4, 114
Epic Tour of the Viking Triangle (Co. Waterford), 216

Errew Abbey (Co. Mayo), 451
Eurail Pass, 68
An Evening of Food, Folklore & Fairies (Dublin), 175
Experience Glasnevin (Dublin), 115
Explorer Pass (Dublin), 93

F

Fallers of Galway (Co. Galway), 403
Fallon & Byrne Food Hall (Dublin), 163
Family-friendly activities
  best of, 10–11
  Dublin, 121–124
  itineraries, 70–73
  travel tips, 598
Fermanagh County Museum, 581
The Fermanagh Lakelands, 578–586
  attractions, 578–582
  boat tours, 580, 582
  hotels, 582–584
  outdoor activities, 585–586
  restaurants, 584–585
  visitor information, 578
Ferries, 588–589
  Aran Islands (Co. Galway), 395
  Cape Clear Island (*Oileán Chléire*) (Co. Cork), 285–286
  Clare Island (Co. Mayo), 446
  Counties Waterford, Wexford, Kilkenny, 212, 215
  County Cork, 251
  Dublin, 85, 125
  Great Saltee Island (Co. Wexford), 238
  Ilnacullin (Garinish Island) (Co. Cork), 288
  Inishbofin (Co. Galway), 413
  Rathlin Island (Co. Antrim), 536
The Firkin Crane Cultural Centre (Cork City), 267–268
First Fortnight, 52
Fishing. *See* Outdoor activities
Fitzgerald, John "Honey Fitz," 377
Flanagans Bar & Restaurant (Dublin), 101
Flapjacks, 164
Fleadh Cheoil na hÉireann, 54
Flight of the Earls, 29
Florence Court (Co. Fermanagh), 581
Food & drink. *See also* Restaurants
  boxty, 146
  flapjacks, 164
  hedgerow jam, 164
  poitín, 421
Food Market (Dublin), 165
Forbidden Planet (Dublin), 165
Fort Dunree Military Museum (Co. Donegal), 494–495
Fota House & Gardens (Co. Cork), 271
Fota Wildlife Park (Co. Cork), 10, 272
The Four Courts (Dublin), 112
Foxford Woollen Mills Visitor Centre (Co. Mayo), 451
Foynes Flying Boat Museum (Co. Limerick), 372
Free Derry, 566
Freedom of Waterford tickets, 216
Freedom Tickets (Dublin), 89
The Front Door (Co. Galway), 405

G

GAA Museum (Dublin), 113–114
Gaelic games, 167–168, 268
The Gaeltacht, 47, 598
Gaiety Theatre (Dublin), 175
Gallarus Oratory (Co. Kerry), 343–344
Galway Arts Centre, 390
Galway Atlantaquaria, 408
Galway Cathedral, 390
Galway Christmas Market, 392
Galway City, 59, 389–405
  attractions, 390–394
  boat tours, 393–394
  day trips from, 405–410
  hotels, 394–397
  nightlife, 404–405
  restaurants, 397–401
  shopping, 401–404
  visitor information, 389
Galway City Museum, 390
Galway Fisheries Watchtower Museum, 392
Galway Girl Cruises, 393
Galway International Arts Festival, 53, 389
Galway International Oyster and Seafood Festival, 54
Galway Irish Crystal, 402
Galway Irish Crystal Heritage Centre, 394
Galway Market, 392
Galway Oyster Festival, 399
Galway Racecourse, 406
Galway Races, 406
Galway Woollen Market, 404
Game of Thrones Cycle Tour, 546
Game of Thrones Studio Tour, 546
Game of Thrones (television program), 546
Game of Thrones Tour from Belfast with Giant's Causeway, 546
Gap of Dunloe (Co. Kerry), 301–302
Gardens. *See* Parks & gardens
Garter Lane Arts Centre (Co. Waterford), 216
The Gate Theatre (Dublin), 176
Geneaology, 450–451
General Post Office (GPO) (Dublin), 112
Giant's Causeway (Co. Antrim), 3, 21, 537–538
"The Giant's Causeway" (Drummond), 538
Giant's Ring (Co. Down), 546–547
Glasnevin Cemetery & Visitor Center (Dublin), 115
Glebe House & Gallery (Co. Donegal), 489
Glencolumbkille *(Gleann Cholm Cille)* (Co. Donegal), 481–482
Glendalough (Co. Wicklow), 9, 76, 201
Glendalough Bus (Dublin day trips), 180
Glenmacnass Waterfall (Co. Wicklow), 202
Glenveagh National Park and Castle (Co. Donegal), 489–490
Glucksman Gallery (Co. Cork), 257–258
Golf, 590. *See also* Outdoor activities
Gollum's Precious (Dublin), 163
Gortin Glen Forest Park (Co. Tyrone), 576–577
Gougane Barra (Co. Cork), 287
GPO Museum (Dublin), 112, 116
Grand Canal Way (Co. Kildare), 199
Grand Opera House (Belfast), 529
Granuaile Centre (Co. Mayo), 446–447
Grave robbing, 98
Gravedigger Ghost Tour (Dublin), 122
Great Irish Famine, 34–35
Great Saltee Island (Co. Wexford), 238
Great Telescope (Co. Offaly), 428
Great Western Greenway (Co. Mayo), 11, 456
Green on Red (Dublin), 159
Greencastle Royal Castle (Co. Down), 551
Grey Abbey (Co. Down), 547
Greyhound racing, 168
Grianan of Aileach (Co. Donegal), 495
Grogan's Castle Lounge (Dublin), 173–174
Guildhall (Derry), 567–568
Guinness Cork Jazz Festival, 54, 268
Guinness Storehouse (Dublin), 108–109
Gus O'Connor's Pub (Co. Clare), 362

H

Hall of the Red Earl (Co. Galway), 392
Ha'penny Bridge (Dublin), 112–113
Hartmanns of Galway (Co. Galway), 403
Heaney, Seamus, 43
Hedgerow jam, 164
Hell Cat Maggies (Belfast), 528–529
High crosses, 185, 221, 379
Hiking. *See also* Walking
  County Sligo, 473
  County Wicklow, 209

Dingle Way (Co. Kerry), 348
Horn Head (Co. Donegal), 492
Kerry Way, 332
Killarney National Park (Co. Kerry), 300
Sliabh Liag (Slieve League) (Co. Donegal), 481
tours, 590

Hill of Tara (Co. Meath), 8, 183–184
Hinterland Festival (Co. Meath), 53
Historical Walking Tours of Dublin, 101
History
of Cork City, 252
of Ireland, 24–40
of Northern Ireland, 516
HMS *Caroline* (Belfast), 510
Hodges Figgis (Dublin), 159
Holidays, 51–52, 91
Holy Trinity Cathedral (Co. Waterford), 218
Home Rule, 35–36
Honey Fitz Theatre (Co. Limerick), 377
Hook Lighthouse & Heritage Centre (Co. Wexford), 230–231
Hook Peninsula (Co. Wexford), 232
Horn Head (Co. Donegal), 12, 492
Horse racing, 168, 193, 349, 406
Horseback riding, 590. *See also* Outdoor activities
Horse-drawn carriage tours in Dublin, 120
Hospitals (Dublin), 92
Hotels, 49–51. *See also* Accommodations index
Belfast, 517–523
best of, 13–14
Causeway Coast (Co. Antrim), 539–542
Connemara (Co. Galway), 415–419
Cork City, 260–263
Counties Meath & Louth, 188–190
Counties Wicklow & Carlow, 206–207
County Armagh, 559–560
County Clare, 364–366
County Donegal, 490–491
County Kildare, 195–197
County Kilkenny, 245–246
County Limerick, 372–375
County Mayo, 452–455
County Sligo, 466–469
County Tipperary, 382–384
County Waterford, 222–224
County Wexford, 235–236
Derry, 571
Dingle Peninsula (Co. Kerry), 345–346
Donegal Town & Donegal Bay, 483–484
Dublin, 125–141
East Cork, 273–274
The Fermanagh Lakelands, 582–584
Galway City, 394–397
Inishowen Peninsula (Co. Donegal), 496–497
Kenmare (Co. Kerry), 318–320
Killarney (Co. Kerry), 306–311
Kinsale (Co. Cork), 277–278
The Midlands, 435–436
Mourne Mountains (Co. Down), 552–554
The Ring of Kerry, 330–331
Tralee (Co. Kerry), 336–337
West Cork, 288–290

House of Waterford Crystal (Co. Waterford), 218
Howth (N of Dublin), 125
Hugh Lane Gallery (Dublin), 97–98
Hunt Museum (Co. Limerick), 371
Huntington Castle and Gardens (Co. Carlow), 202
Hyde Bridge Gallery (Co. Sligo), 462

I

The Idle Hour (Cork City), 266
Ilnacullin (Garinish Island) (Co. Cork), 287–288
Indigo & Cloth (Dublin), 161
Inishbofin (Co. Galway), 413
Inishmurray (Co. Sligo), 10, 74, 465–466
Inishowen Maritime Museum & Planetarium (Co. Donegal), 495
Inishowen Peninsula (Co. Donegal), 493–498
attractions, 493–496
driving tours, 12, 493
hotels, 496–497
outdoor activities, 498
restaurants, 497
Innisfallen (Co. Kerry), 302
Inniskillings Museum (Co. Fermanagh), 581
The International Bar & Comedy Cellar (Dublin), 170–171
International Bar (Dublin), 101
International Literature Festival Dublin, 53
International Pan Celtic Festival, 52
Internet service, 598
Interrail Pass, 68
Ireland. *See also* Northern Ireland
arrival information, 588–589
authors & poets from, 41–43
bank holidays, 51–52, 91
best of
authentic experiences, 17, 20–21
castles & historic houses, 4–5
driving tours, 11–12
early Christian ruins, 9–10
family-friendly activities, 10–11
hotels, 13–14
for literature lovers, 7–8
museums, 3–4
natural wonders, 2–3
picture-postcard towns, 6–7
prehistoric sites, 8
restaurants, 15–17
shopping, 17
books about, 33
calendar of events, 52–55
driving in, 591–593
fast facts, 597–601
in film & television, 44–46
history of, 24–40
itineraries, 61-79
music of, 46–48
political climate, 23
regions in brief, 57–60
smell of, 417
tours, 589–590
transportation in, 60–61, 591–597
when to visit, 51–52

Ireland's Eye Ferries (Dublin), 125
Irish Agricultural Museum and Famine Exhibition (Co. Wexford), 232–233
Irish Antique & Fine Art Fair (Dublin), 54
Irish Derby (Co. Kildare), 53
Irish Design Shop (Dublin), 160
Irish Famine Cottage (Co. Kerry), 344
Irish Film Institute (Dublin), 106
Irish Museum of Modern Art (IMMA) (Dublin), 106
Irish Museum of Time (Co. Waterford), 219
Irish National Heritage Park (Co. Wexford), 11, 228
Irish National Stud and Japanese Gardens (Co. Kildare), 193–194
Irish Rock 'n' Roll Museum Experience and Wall of Fame (Dublin), 116
Irish Silver Museum (Co. Waterford), 219
Irish Tweeds (Co. Galway), 404
Itineraries
ancient sites, 73–76
best adventures, 66–70
east to southwest, 61–64
family-friendly activities, 70–73
north & northwest, 76–79
2-week, 64–65

J

Jam Art Factory (Dublin), 158–159
James Fort (Co. Cork), 275
James Joyce Centre (Dublin), 7, 116–117
Jameson Bow St. Distillery (Dublin), 109
Jarveys (jaunting cars), 300
***Jeanie Johnston* (Dublin), 117**
Jerpoint Abbey (Co. Kilkenny), 9, 243–244
Jerpoint Glass Studio (Co. Kilkenny), 244

John Barry Monument (Co. Wexford), 228
John F. Kennedy Arboretum (Co. Wexford), 234
John Henchy & Sons (Cork City), 267
Joyce, James, 42, 116–117
Judy Greene Pottery (Co. Galway), 402

K

Kebble National Nature Reserve (Rathlin Island), 536
Kehoe's (Dublin), 174
Kells Priory (Co. Kilkenny), 244
Kelly's Cellars (Belfast), 529
Kenmare (Co. Kerry), 6, 316–323
- attractions, 316–318
- boat tours, 316–317
- hotels, 318–320
- outdoor activities, 323
- restaurants, 320–322
- shopping, 322

Kenmare Bay Boat Tours (Co. Kerry), 316–317
Kenmare Druid Circle (Co. Kerry), 317
Kenmare Farmer's Market (Co. Kerry), 317
Kennedy, John F., 234, 377
Kennedy Homestead (Co. Wexford), 234
Kenny's Book Shop and Galleries Ltd (Co. Galway), 401–402
Kerry County Museum, 335
Kerry Interational Dark Sky Reserve, 316
Kerry Seas National Park, 344
Kerry Way, 332
Kevin & Howlin (Dublin), 161
Kevin's Bed (Co. Wicklow), 201
Kilbeggan Distillery (Co. Westmeath), 430
Kilcullen Seaweed Baths (Co. Sligo), 468
Kildare Town Historic Guided Walking Tour, 192
Kilfenora Cathedral (Co. Clare), 357
Kilkenny (store in Dublin), 17, 160
Kilkenny Arts Festival, 54
Kilkenny Castle, 4–5, 240
Kilkenny Walking Tours, 240, 242
Killarney (Co. Kerry), 299–316
- attractions, 301–306
- boat tours, 305
- hotels, 306–311
- nightlife, 314–315
- outdoor activities, 315–316
- restaurants, 311–313
- shopping, 313–314
- spas, 310
- tours, 299
- town layout, 300–301

Killarney Art Gallery (Co. Kerry), 314
Killarney Grand (Co. Kerry), 314
Killarney National Park (Co. Kerry), 300–305
Killarney Water Bus (Co. Kerry), 305
Killary Fjord Boat Tours (Co. Galway), 414
Killiney Hill (Dublin), 124
Killorglin (Co. Kerry), 324
Kilmainham Gaol (Dublin), 98–99
King John's Castle (Co. Limerick), 4, 371
Kinsale (Co. Cork), 6, 274–284
- attractions, 274–277
- hotels, 277–278
- outdoor activities, 283–284
- restaurants, 278–282
- walking tours, 276

Kinsale Historic Stroll (Co. Cork), 276
Kinsale Mad Hatters festival (Co. Cork), 279
Kinsale Pottery and Arts Centre (Co. Cork), 277
Kinsale Restaurant Week (Co. Cork), 279
Knocknarea (Co. Sligo), 466
Knockreer Estate (Co. Kerry), 306
Knowth (Co. Meath), 8, 73, 181–183
Kylemore Abbey (Co. Galway), 414

L

Ladies View (Co. Kerry), 315
The Lakelands. *See* The Fermanagh Lakelands
Languages, official, 47, 598
Laughter Lines (Dublin), 171
The Laurels (Co. Kerry), 315
Leap Cards (Dublin), 89
Legananny Dolmen (Co. Down), 547
Legends of Kildare virtual reality experience, 192
Leinster, counties in, 58
Leinster House (Dublin), 113
Leprechauns, 119, 434
LGBTQ travelers, 598
Libraries (Dublin), 93, 96, 113–120
Limerick City
- attractions, 371
- hotels, 372–375
- restaurants, 375–377

Limerick City Gallery of Art, 371
Limerick Greenway, 377–378
Limerick-style poetry, 374
Lisdoonvarna Matchmaking Festival (Co. Clare), 363
Lismore Castle Gardens and Arts (Co. Waterford), 222
Listowel Castle (Co. Kerry), 336
Literary Pub Crawl (Dublin), 101
Literature lovers, best of Ireland for, 7–8
Little Museum of Dublin, 117–118
Live music in pubs, 17, 20, 267, 362
Londonderry. *See* Derry
The Long Hall (Dublin), 174
Long Valley Bar (Cork City), 267
Lorge Chocolatier (Co. Kerry), 322
Lost property, 598
Lough Derg (Co. Donegal), 482
Lough Derg Drive (Co. Clare, Limerick, Tipperary), 383
Lough Erne (Co. Fermanagh), 582, 585–586
Lough Gill (Co. Sligo), 467
Lough Gur (Co. Limerick), 372
Lough Neagh (Co. Armagh), 558
Loughcrew Cairns and Gardens (Co. Meath), 184
Louis Mulcahy Pottery (Co. Kerry), 17, 348–349
Louise Kennedy (Dublin), 161–162
Luggage storage in Dublin, 92
Lusitania Memorial (Co. Cork), 270
Lynch Memorial Window (Co. Galway), 393
Lynch's Castle (Co. Galway), 392–393
Lyric Theatre (Belfast), 529

M

The Mac (Belfast), 529
MacGillycuddy's Reeks (Co. Kerry), 2, 304
Made in Sligo, 472
Mahon Falls (Co. Waterford), 221
Mail, 92, 501
Malin Head *(Cionn Mhélanna)* (Co. Donegal), 2, 495–496
Marble Arch Caves (Co. Fermanagh), 581–582
Markievicz, Constance, 465
Marsh's Library (Dublin), 118
Mass hole, 369
Mayo Dark Sky Festival, 55
Mayo North Heritage Centre, 450–451
McArt's Fort (Belfast), 512
McConnell's Distillery (Belfast), 508–509
McGann's (Co. Clare), 362
Medieval Museum (Co. Waterford), 220
The Meeting of the Waters (Co. Kerry), 306
Michael Collins Centre (Co. Cork), 283
Michael Quirke (Co. Sligo), 472–473
The Midlands (Co. Laois, Longford, Offaly, Westmeath), 59, 423–440
- arrival information, 424–425
- attractions, 425–434
- hotels, 435–436
- restaurants, 437–440

Midleton Distillery Experience (Co. Cork), 272–273
Milk Market Limerick, 371
Millmount Fort (Co. Louth), 183
Mishnóc (Co. Galway), 402
Mizen Head (Co. Cork), 2, 288
Mobile phones, 598
The Model (Co. Sligo), 460
MoLI (Museum of Literature Ireland) (Dublin), 7, 118–119
Monasterboice (Co. Louth), 184–185

Monasteries in history of Ireland, 27
Monreal (Cork City), 266
Moone High Cross (Co. Kildare), 194
The Morning Star (Belfast), 530
Mount Stewart House, Garden, and Temple of the Winds (Co. Down), 547–548
Mount Usher Gardens (Co. Wicklow), 202–203
Mourne Mountains (Co. Down)
attractions, 549–551
hotels, 552–554
outdoor activities, 554
restaurants, 552–554
visitor information, 544
Mourne Wall Trek (Co. Down), 551
Mr. McGuire's Olde Sweet Shop (Co. Kerry), 314
Muckross Craft Shop (Co. Kerry), 314
Muckross Creamery (Co. Kerry), 304
Muckross House & Gardens (Co. Kerry), 11, 302–303
Muckross Traditional Farms (Co. Kerry), 303–304
Muiredeach's High Cross (Co. Louth), 185
Mullet Peninsula (Co. Mayo), 449
Munster, counties in, 58
Murals
Belfast, 507
Cork City, 256
Derry, 566
Murty Rabbitt's (Co. Galway), 405
Museum of Free Derry, 568
Museums, best of, 3–4
Music
of Ireland, 46–48
live music in pubs, 17, 20, 267, 362
Mutton Lane Mural (Co. Cork), 256
My Shop . . . Granny Likes It (Co. Galway), 402

N

National Arboretum (Co. Down), 550
National Bird of Prey Centre (Co. Wicklow), 204
National Concert Hall (Dublin), 169
National Famine Museum (Co. Roscommon), 432–433
National Gallery of Ireland (Dublin), 99–100
National Heritage Week, 54
National Leprechaun Museum (Dublin), 119
National Library of Ireland (Dublin), 119–120
National Museum of Ireland: Archaeology (Dublin), 4, 100–102
National Museum of Ireland: Country Life (Co. Mayo), 447–448
National Museum of Ireland: Decorative Arts & History, Collins Barracks (Dublin), 102
National Museum of Ireland: Natural History (Dublin), 103
National Opera House (Co. Wexford), 228–229
National Shrine of Our Lady of Knock and the Church of the Apparition (Co. Mayo), 451–452
Natural wonders, best of, 2–3
Nature walks, 369
Navan Fort (Co. Armagh), 556–557
Neary's (Dublin), 174
Ned's Carriage Tours (Dublin), 120
Nendrum Monastic Site (Co. Down), 549
Newbridge House and Farm (Dublin), 124
Newgrange (Co. Meath), 8, 21, 73, 181–183
Newgrange Farm (Co. Meath), 185–186
Newgrange Tours by Mary Gibbons (Dublin day trips), 180
Nightclubs, 171, 528–529
Nightlife
Belfast, 528–530
Cork City, 266–268
Derry, 574
Dublin, 168–176
Killarney (Co. Kerry), 314–315
No Alibis (Belfast), 528
Norman invasion, 28–29
The Norn Irish Gift Shop (Belfast), 528
Northern Ireland. *See also* Belfast
Derry, 562–574
The Fermanagh Lakelands, 578–586
frequently asked questions (FAQs), 502
history of, 516
itineraries, 76–79
regions in brief, 57, 59–60
safety tips, 60
Sperrin Mountains (Co. Tyrone), 574–578
The Troubles, 39–40

O

O2. *See* 3Arena (Dublin)
Oakland Antiques (Belfast), 527
O'Brien's Tower (Co. Clare), 361
O'Connell, Daniel, 33–34
O'Connors (Co. Kerry), 315
O'Doherty Tower (Derry), 570
The Old Bushmills Distillery (Co. Antrim), 538–539
Old Library (Trinity College, Dublin), 93, 96, 104
Old Mellifont Abbey (Co. Louth), 186
Oliver St. John Gogarty pub, 101
Om Diva (Dublin), 162
O'Máille (O'Malley) (Co. Galway), 404
O'Malley, Grace, 447
Original Kerry, 349
Ormond Castle (Co. Tipperary), 380–381
Outdoor activities
best adventures itinerary, 66–70
Causeway Coast (Co. Antrim), 543–544
Connemara (Co. Galway), 421–422
Cork City, 268
County Clare, 369–370
County Donegal, 492
County Kildare, 199
County Kilkenny, 248
County Limerick, 377–378
County Mayo, 457–458
County Sligo, 473
County Tipperary, 385–386
County Waterford, 226–227
County Wexford, 238
County Wicklow, 210
Dingle Peninsula (Co. Kerry), 349–350
Donegal Town & Donegal Bay, 485–486
Dublin, 165–167
The Fermanagh Lakelands, 585–586
Inishowen Peninsula (Co. Donegal), 498
Kenmare (Co. Kerry), 323
Killarney (Co. Kerry), 315–316
Kinsale (Co. Cork), 283–284
Mourne Mountains (Co. Down), 554
Tralee (Co. Kerry), 338
West Cork, 293–294

P

P. Powell & Sons (Co. Galway), 404
Paddy Wagon Tours (Dublin day trips), 180
Panti Bar (Dublin), 171
Parade days (Belfast), 507
Parke's Castle (Co. Sligo), 466
Passes. *See* Tickets
Peace Maze (Co. Down), 550
Peadar O'Donnells (Derry), 574
Pearse Lyons Distillery (Dublin), 108
Pearse's Cottage and Visitor Centre (*Ionad Cultúrtha an Phiarsaigh*) (Co. Galway), 408
Peatlands Park (Co. Armagh), 557
Pennywhistles, 164
People's Gallery (Derry), 566
Performing arts
Belfast, 529
Cork City, 267–268
Dublin, 169, 175–176
Petticoat Loose (Co. Tipperary), 381
Pharmacies, 92, 501, 599
Phoenix Park (Dublin), 121
Picture-postcard towns, best of, 6–7

Poets, 374, 410
***Poitín*, 421**
Police, 599
Pony trekking, 422, 543
Portacloy (Co. Mayo), 458
Portaferry Castle (Co. Down), 549
The Porterhouse (Dublin), 175
Portumna Castle and Forest Park (Co. Galway), 431
Post offices, 92, 501
Potato famine, 34–35
Poulnabrone Dolmen (Co. Clare), 358
Powerscourt Estate (Co. Wicklow), 203–204
Powerscourt Townhouse Centre (Dublin), 160–161
Powerscourt Waterfall (Co. Wicklow), 204
Prehistoric sites
- best of, 8
- history of Ireland, 24–25
- itineraries, 73–76

Proleek Dolmen (Co. Louth), 186–187
Pub crawls (Dublin), 101
Pubs
- Belfast, 529–530
- Cork City, 266–267
- County Clare, 362
- Derry, 574
- Dublin, 171–175
- Galway City, 404–405
- hours of operation, 49
- Killarney (Co. Kerry), 314–315
- oldest, 437
- traditional music in, 17, 20, 267, 362

Púca Festival (Co. Meath), 55
Puck Fair (Co. Kerry), 54, 324

Q

The Quays (Co. Galway), 405
Queen's University (Belfast), 513
***The Quiet Man* (film, 1952), 444**
Quills Woollen Market (Co. Kerry), 322

R

The R.A.G.E. (Dublin), 165
Rail passes, 68, 595
Rathcroghan Vistor Centre (Co. Roscommon), 431–432
Rathlin Island (Co. Antrim), 536
Raven Nature Reserve (Co. Wexford), 239
Red Hand of Ulster, 543
Reginald's Tower (Co. Waterford), 220
Republic of Ireland. *See also* Ireland
- formation of, 38
- regions in brief, 57–60

Restaurants. *See also* Restaurants index
- Belfast, 523–527
- best of, 15–17
- Causeway Coast (Co. Antrim), 542–543
- Connemara (Co. Galway), 419–421
- Cork City, 263–265
- Counties Meath & Louth, 190–191
- Counties Wicklow & Carlow, 208–210
- County Armagh, 559–560
- County Clare, 366–368
- County Donegal, 491–492
- County Kildare, 197–199
- County Kilkenny, 247–248
- County Limerick, 375–377
- County Mayo, 455–457
- County Sligo, 469–472
- County Tipperary, 384–385
- County Waterford, 224–226
- County Wexford, 236–238
- Derry, 572–574
- Dingle Peninsula (Co. Kerry), 346–348
- dining tips, 48–49
- Donegal Town & Donegal Bay, 484–485
- Dublin, 141–157
- East Cork, 273–274
- The Fermanagh Lakelands, 584–585
- Galway City, 397–401
- Inishowen Peninsula (Co. Donegal), 497
- Kenmare (Co. Kerry), 320–322
- Killarney (Co. Kerry), 311–313
- Kinsale (Co. Cork), 278–282
- The Midlands, 437–440
- Mourne Mountains (Co. Down), 552–554
- pricing, 48
- reservations, 48
- The Ring of Kerry, 332–334
- Tralee (Co. Kerry), 336–337
- West Cork, 290–292

Rhinestones (Dublin), 164
The Ring of Hook (Co. Wexford), 232
The Ring of Kerry, 298–334
- driving tours, 11–12, 323–329
- hotels, 330–331
- itineraries, 64
- Kenmare, 316–323
- Killarney, 299–316
- restaurants, 332–334

River Inn (Derry), 574
The Rock of Cashel (Co. Tipperary), 9–10, 381–382
The Rock of Dunamase (Co. Laois), 432–434
Roe & Co (Dublin), 108
Róisín Dubh (Co. Galway), 405
Rose of Tralee (Co. Kerry), 336
Rose of Tralee International Festival (Co. Kerry), 54
Ross Castle (Co. Kerry), 5, 304
Rowing, 349
RSPB Rathlin West Light Seabird Centre (Rathlin Island), 536
Rugby, 168
Russborough House (Co. Wicklow), 204

S

Safety, 60, 599–600, 601
Sailing, 284
Saint Mary's Cathedral (Co. Limerick), 371
The Saint Patrick Centre (Co. Down), 548
Sawers (Belfast), 528
Scattery Island (Co. Clare), 363–364
Scenic drives. *See* Driving tours
Scilly (Co. Cork), 277
Sciúird Archaeological Adventures (Co. Kerry), 341
Seamus Heaney HomePlace (Co. Derry), 7, 577
The Seanchaí: Kerry Writers' Museum (Co. Kerry), 7, 336
Sean's Bar (Co. Westmeath), 437
Seaweed baths, 20–21, 468
Seedhead Street Art Walking Tours (Belfast), 507
Selskar Abbey (Co. Wexford), 230
Senior travel, 600
Shandon Tower (Co. Cork), 256–257
Shane's Howth Adventures (N of Dublin), 125
Shaw, George Bernard, 42
Sheep's Head Loop (Co. Cork), 292
Sheep's Head Way (Co. Cork), 292
Sheridans Cheesemongers (Dublin), 163
Shopping
- Belfast, 527–528
- best of, 17
- Cork City, 265–266
- County Sligo, 472–473
- Derry, 574
- Dingle Peninsula (Co. Kerry), 348–349
- Dublin, 157–165
- Galway City, 401–404
- Kenmare (Co. Kerry), 322
- Killarney (Co. Kerry), 313–314

Siamsa Tíre (National Folk Theatre of Ireland) (Co. Kerry), 334
Silent Valley Mountain Park (Co. Down), 551
Silken Thomas (Thomas FitzGerald, 10th Earl of Kildare), 198
Sin é (Cork City), 267
The Skellig Experience (Co. Kerry), 329
Skellig Islands (Co. Kerry), 326–327
Skellig Michael (Co. Kerry), 9, 75–76, 326–327
Skellig Ring (Co. Kerry), 327–328
The Sky Road (Co. Galway), 414–415
Slea Head Drive (Co. Kerry), 12, 341–344
***Sliabh Liag* (Slieve League) (Co. Donegal), 2, 481, 482–483**

The Slieve Bloom Way (Co. Laois & Offaly), 440
Slieve Donard (Co. Down), 549
Sligo Abbey, 460–461
Sligo County Museum, 461–462
Sligo Town shopping, 472–473
Smoking, 600
Soccer, 168
The Southeast. *See* County Kilkenny; County Waterford; County Wexford
Souvenirs in Dublin, 164
Spas, 310
Spectator sports, 167–168. 349
Sperrin Mountains (Co. Tyrone), 574–578
Spiddal Craft Village (*Ceardlann an Spidéil*) (Co. Galway), 409
SS *Dunbrody* Famine Ship Experience (Co. Wexford), 233–234
SS *Nomadic* (Belfast), 510
St. Anne's (Belfast Cathedral), 512
St. Anne's Church (Co. Cork), 256–257
St. Brigid's Cathedral (Co. Kildare), 194–195
St. Canice's Cathedral (Co. Kilkenny), 242
St. Carthage Hall (Co. Waterford), 222
St. Colman's Cathedral (Co. Cork), 270
St. Colmcille's House (Co. Meath), 187
St. Columb's Cathedral (Derry), 568–569
St. Eugene's Cathedral (Derry), 569–570
St. Fin Barre's Cathedral (Co. Cork), 257
St. George's Market (Belfast), 17, 509
St. Iberius Church (Co. Wexford), 229
St. Kevin's Kitchen (Co. Wicklow), 201
St. Kevin's Way (Co. Wicklow), 209
St. Mary's Cathedral (Co. Kerry), 306
St. Michan's Church (Dublin), 98, 107
St. Mullin's Monastery (Co. Carlow), 205
St. Nicholas' Collegiate Church (Co. Galway), 393
St. Patrick's Cathedral (Dublin), 103–104
St. Patrick's Church of Ireland Cathedral (Co. Armagh), 557–558
St. Patrick's Day parades, 52
St. Patrick's Festival Dublin, 52
St. Patrick's Roman Catholic Cathedral (Co. Armagh), 558–559
St. Peter's Church of Ireland (Co. Louth), 183
St. Peter's Roman Catholic Church (Co. Louth), 183
St. Stephen's Green (Dublin), 121
Stable (Dublin), 162
The Stag's Head (Dublin), 175
Staigue Fort (Co. Kerry), 329
Stargazing, 316, 428
Statue nicknames (Dublin), 99
Steensons (Belfast), 528
Storage services in Dublin, 92
Storytelling, 175
Street markets in Dublin, 165
Strokestown Park House (Co. Roscommon), 432–433
Sugerloaf Hill (Co. Tipperary), 381
Surfing, 369–370, 473, 486, 498
Swift, Jonathan, 41, 102
The Swiss Cottage (Co. Tipperary), 382

T

Taste of Dublin, 53
Tatler Jack (Co. Kerry), 315
Taxes, 600
Taxis
  Belfast, 501, 503
  Dublin, 91, 92
Teampall na Skellig (Co. Wicklow), 201
Teeling Whiskey Distillery (Dublin), 108, 109
Telephone numbers, 600
Temperatures, 51
Temple Bar (Dublin) street markets, 165
Temple Bar Gallery + Studios (Dublin), 106–107
Theater
  Belfast, 529
  Dublin, 175–176
  Galway City, 404
Thomas Dillon's Claddagh Gold (Co. Galway), 403–404
Thoor Ballylee (Co. Galway), 409–410
Tickets
  Dublin attractions passes, 93
  Dublin nightlife, 168–169
  Freedom of Waterford, 216
  rail passes, 68, 595
Time zones, 600
Tintern Abbey (Co. Wexford), 234–235
Tipping, 600
Titanic Belfast, 3–4, 510–511
Titanic Distillers at Thompson Dock (Belfast), 511
Titanic Experience (Co. Cork), 270
Titanic Trail walking tour (Co. Cork), 270
Toilets, 600–601
Tollymore Forest Park (Co. Down), 551
Tom Crean Brewery (Co. Kerry), 318
Iorc Waterfall (Co. Kerry), 304–305
Torr Head Scenic Road (Co. Antrim), 539
Tours, 589–590
  Cork City, 259–260
  County Kerry, 298
  Derry, 568
  Dingle Peninsula (Co. Kerry), 341
  Game of Throness, 546
  Killarney (Co. Kerry), 299
The Tower Museum (Derry), 570–571
Tradfest (Dublin), 52
Traditional Irish Music Pub Crawl (Dublin), 101
Traditional music in pubs, 17, 20, 267, 362
Train travel, 68, 593–595
Tralee (Co. Kerry), 334–338
  attractions, 334–336
  hotels, 336–337
  outdoor activities, 338
  restaurants, 336–337
Tralee to Finit Greenway (Co. Kerry), 338
Trams in Dublin, 90–91
Transportation, 60–61, 591–597
Tread Softly (Co. Sligo), 53
Treaty City Brewery (Co. Limerick), 371
Trim Castle (Co. Meath), 187–188
Trinity College (Dublin), 104–105
Trinity Trails tour (Trinity College, Dublin), 105
The Troubles, 39–40
Tullynally Castle Gardens (Co. Westmeath), 434
Turlough Park House (Co. Mayo), 448
Twelve Bens (Co. Galway), 3, 412

U

Ulster, counties in, 57
Ulster American Folk Park (Co. Tyrone), 577–578
Ulster Folk Museum (Belfast), 515
Ulster Museum (Belfast), 504, 509
Ulster Transport Museum (Belfast), 517
Ulster Way (Co. Fermanagh), 586
Ulysses Rare Books (Dublin), 159
United Irishmen, 31–32
University College Cork, 257–258
Urban Brewing (Dublin), 108
U.S. Rangers Museum (Belfast), 514

V

Vale of Avoca (Co. Wicklow), 205
Valentia Lighthouse (Co. Kerry), 329
Vee Gap (Co. Tipperary), 381
Vibes and Scribes (Cork City), 266
Vicar Street (Dublin), 169
Viking invasions, 27–28
Viking Triangle tours (Co. Waterford), 216
The Vintage Cocktail Club (Dublin), 170
Visas, 601

W

W5 (Belfast), 514
Walking. *See also* Hiking
- Bray Head (Co. Wicklow), 200
- The Burren Way (Co. Clare), 359
- Causeway Coast (Co. Antrim), 543–544
- Connemara (Co. Galway), 421
- County Donegal, 492
- County Sligo, 473
- County Tipperary, 385–386
- Cummeengeera (Co. Cork), 285
- Derry city walls, 569
- Donegal Town & Donegal Bay, 486
- in Dublin, 91
- Grand Canal Way (Co. Kildare), 199
- Great Western Greenway (Co. Mayo), 456
- Mourne Wall Trek (Co. Down), 551
- Portacloy (Co. Mayo), 458
- Sheep's Head Way (Co. Cork), 292
- The Slieve Bloom Way (Co. Laois & Offaly), 440
- Ulster Way (Co. Fermanagh), 586
- Waterford Greenway, 227
- West Cork, 293–294
- Western Way (Co. Galway), 415
- Wexford Coastal Pathway, 239

Walking tours
- Belfast street murals, 507
- County Kildare, 192
- County Kilkenny, 240, 242
- County Wexford, 230
- Derry, 569
- Dublin, 101
- Kinsale (Co. Cork), 276
- Scilly (Co. Cork), 277
- Titanic Trail (Co. Cork), 270
- Trinity College (Dublin), 104, 105
- Viking Triangle (Co. Waterford), 216
- Waterford City, 220–221

Waterford City Walking Tours, 220–221
Waterford crystal, 218
Waterford Greenway, 227
Waterford Treasures, 3, 215
Watersports. *See* Outdoor activities
Weather, 51
Wehrly Bros. Ltd (Co. Sligo), 473
Weir & Sons (Dublin), 164
West Cork, 284–294
- arrival information, 284
- attractions, 284–288
- hotels, 288–290
- outdoor activities, 293–294
- restaurants, 290–292

West Cork Chamber Music Festival, 53
Western Way (Co. Galway), 415
Westgate Heritage Centre (Co. Wexford), 230
Westport (*Cathair na Mairt*) (Co. Mayo), 443
Westport House and Adventure Park (Co. Mayo), 448–449
Wex Walks (Co. Wexford), 230
Wexford Coastal Pathway, 239
Wexford Festival Opera, 55, 228–229
Wexford Wildfowl Reserve, 238
Whale-watching tours, 10, 294
Whelans (Dublin), 171
Whitefriar Street Carmelite Church (Dublin), 107
White's Tavern (Belfast), 530
Wicklow Mountains National Park, 62, 205–206
Wicklow Way, 209
Wi-Fi, 598
Wild Atlantic Way (Co. Cork to Co. Donegal), 11, 275
Wild Nephin National Park (Co. Mayo), 452
Wild Wicklow Tour (Dublin day trips), 180
Wilde, Oscar, 41–42
Wine Cellar (Dublin), 170
Women travelers, 601
The Wool Shed (Dublin), 170
World Irish Dancing Championships, 52

X–Y–Z

Yeats, W. B., 7, 42, 462
Yeats Society (Co. Sligo), 462
Yola language, 214

Zoos
- Belfast, 513–514
- Dublin, 123
- East Cork, 272

Accommodations

Abbeyglen Castle (Co. Galway), 415–416
Aberdeen Lodge (Dublin), 140
Actons Hotel (Co. Cork), 277–278
Adare Manor (Co. Limerick), 13, 373
The Address (Co. Cork), 262
Aghadoe Heights (Co. Kerry), 306–307
The Alex (Dublin), 131–132
Aloft Dublin City, 132
Anantara The Marker (Dublin), 135–136
The Anglers Reture (Co. Galway), 418
Anner Hotel (Co. Tipperary), 382
Ard Na Breátha (Co. Donegal), 483
Ard na Sidhe Country House (Co. Kerry), 330
Ariel House (Dublin), 140
Armada House (Co. Clare), 364–365
Arnold's Hotel (Co. Donegal), 490
Ashford Castle (Co. Mayo), 13, 452–453
Ashling Hotel (Dublin), 138
Ballygarry Estate Hotel (Co. Kerry), 336–337
Ballylagan Organic Farm (Co. Antrim), 541
Ballyliffin Lodge (Inishowen Peninsula), 496
Ballymaloe House Hotel (Co. Cork), 273
Ballymascanlon House Hotel (Co. Louth), 187
Ballynahinch Castle (Co. Galway), 416
Ballyseede Castle (Co. Kerry), 337
Bansha House (Co. Tipperary), 383
Barberstown Castle (Co. Kildare), 195–196
Bastion (Co. Westmeath), 435
Bayview Hotel (Co. Cork), 273
Bellinter House (Co. Meath), 188
Belmore Court & Motel (Co. Fermanagh), 582
Benner's Hotel (Co. Kerry), 345
The Bervie (Co. Mayo), 453–454
Bishop's Gate Hotel (Derry), 571
Blue Haven Hotel (Co. Cork), 278
Brook Lane Hotel (Co. Kerry), 319
BrookLodge & Macreddin Village (Co. Wicklow), 206
Brooks Hotel (Dublin), 132–133
Bullitt (Belfast), 521–522
The Bushmills Inn (Co. Antrim), 539
Buswells (Dublin), 133
Butler House (Co. Kilkenny), 245
Cahernane House (Co. Kerry), 307
The Carriage House (Co. Down), 552
Cashel Palace Hotel (Co. Tipperary), 13, 383–384
Castle Dargan (Co. Sligo), 466–467
Castle Grove House (Co. Donegal), 491
Castle Leslie (Co. Fermanagh), 582–583
Castlewood House (Co. Kerry), 345
Ceann Sibéal Hotel (Co. Kerry), 346
Chléire Haven (Co. Cork), 285
Cliff at Lyons (Co. Kildare), 196
Cliff House Hotel (Co. Waterford), 13–14, 222
The College Green Hotel (Dublin), 128
Conrad Dublin, 128
The Cottages (Co. Meath), 188
Courtyard Cottage (Co. Limerick), 373
Currarevagh Country House (Co. Galway), 416
The Dean (Co. Cork), 262
Delphi Lodge (Co. Galway), 417–418
Desmond House (Co. Cork), 278
The Devlin (Dublin), 140–141
Dingle Skellig Hotel (Co. Kerry), 346
Dromoland Castle (Co. Clare), 14, 365

Dunmore House (Co. Cork), 289
Dunnanelly Country House (Co. Down), 552–553
Earls Court House (Co. Kerry), 308–309
The Ebrington Hotel and Spa (Derry), 571
Eccles Hotel & Spa (Co. Cork), 288–289
Echo Lodge (Co. Limerick), 374
Enniscoe House (Co. Mayo), 454
Europa Hotel (Belfast), 517
The Europe (Co. Kerry), 14, 307–308
Fergus View (Co. Clare), 365
Finn Lough (Co. Fermanagh), 583–584
Fitzgerald's Woodlands House Hotel (Co. Limerick), 374
The Fitzwilliam Hotel (Belfast), 517
Fota Island Resort (Co. Cork), 271
The G (Co. Galway), 394
Galgorm Resort (Co. Antrim), 540
The Gateway Lodge (Co. Donegal), 483
Ghan House (Co., Louth), 188–189
The Glasshouse (Co. Sligo), 467–468
The Grafton (Dublin), 130–131
Grand Canal Hotel (Dublin), 136
Grand Central Hotel (Belfast), 518
Granville Hotel (Co. Waterford), 222–223
Gregans Castle Hotel (Co. Clare), 365–366
The Happy Pig (Co. Kerry), 319–320
The Harbour View Hotel (Co. Antrim), 540
Harding Hotel (Dublin), 134
The Harrison Chambers of Distinction (Belfast), 520–521
Harvey's Point Hotel (Co. Donegal), 484
Hayfield Manor (Co. Cork), 260–261
Headfort Arms Hotel (Co. Meath), 189
Hodson Bay Hotel (Co. Westmeath), 436
Hotel Minella (Co. Tipperary), 384
The House Hotel (Co. Galway), 394, 396
The Huntsman Inn (Co. Galway), 396
The Ice House (Co. Mayo), 454
Imperial Hotel (Co. Cork), 262
Inchydoney Lodge & Spa (Co. Cork), 289–290
Inis Meáin Island Stays (Aran Islands), 397
Inishowen Gateway (Inishowen Peninsula), 496–497
Inn on the Coast (Co. Antrim), 542
InterContinental Dublin, 139–140
Kells Bay House & Gardens (Co. Kerry), 330–331
Killarney Park (Co. Kerry), 308
Killarney Plaza (Co. Kerry), 309
Killeen House Hotel (Co. Kerry), 309
Knockranny House (Co. Mayo), 454
Lagom Restaurant & Townhouse (Co. Kerry), 319
Larkinley Lodge (Co. Kerry), 311
Lawcus Farm Guesthouse (Co. Kilkenny), 245
The Lord Bagenal (Co. Carlow), 206–207
Lough Erne Resort (Co. Fermanagh), 584
Maldron Hotel Smithfield (Dublin), 138
Malmaison Belfast, 521
Manor House Rathlin (Rathlin Island), 536
Martinstown House (Co. Kildare), 196–197
The Mayson (Dublin), 136–137
The Merchant (Belfast), 14, 518, 520
The Merrion (Dublin), 14, 129
Mespil Hotel (Dublin), 134–135
The Metropole (Co. Cork), 262–263
Monart Spa (Co. Wexford), 235
The Mont (Dublin), 133
The Montenotte (Co. Cork), 261
The Moorings (Co. Kerry), 331
The Morrison (Dublin), 137–138
Mount Juliet Estate (Co. Kilkenny), 245–246
Murray's Doonmore Hotel (Co. Galway), 418
Newforge House (Co. Armagh), 559–560
No. 1 Pery Square (Co. Limerick), 375
Number 31 (Dublin), 133–134
Park Hotel Kenmare (Co. Kerry), 318
Park House Hotel (Co. Galway), 396
Parknasilla Resort (Co. Kerry), 331
Pembroke Kilkenny, 246
Petra House (Co. Galway), 396
Pier House (Co. Cork), 278
Powerscourt Hotel (Co. Wicklow), 207
Quinlan & Cooke (Co. Kerry), 331
Rathmullan House (Co. Donegal), 491
Ravenhill Gusthouse (Belfast), 522
Regency House (Belfast), 520
Renvyle House Hotel (Co. Galway), 418
The River Lee (Co. Cork), 261
Riverbank House Hotel (Co. Wexford), 235
Riversdale Country House (Inishowen Peninsula), 497
Rockcrest House (Co. Kerry), 320
Rockmount House (Co. Galway), 419
The Ross (Co. Kerry), 309
Ross Farmhouse (Co. Sligo), 468
The Saddler's House (Derry), 571
The Salthouse (Co. Antrim), 540–541
Samuel's Heritage (Co. Waterford), 223
Sea Breeze Lodge (Co. Galway), 396–397
Sheedy's (Co. Clare), 366
Sheen Falls Lodge (Co. Kerry), 14, 319
The Shelbourne (Dublin), 129
The Slieve Donard Spa and Resort (Co. Down), 553–554
Sligo Park Hotel (Co. Sligo), 468
South Aran House (Aran Islands), 397
The Spencer (Dublin), 136
The Station House (Co. Meath), 189–190
Tara Lodge (Belfast), 522–523
Temple House (Co. Sligo), 468–469
Ten Square (Belfast), 521
Townsend House (Co. Offaly), 436
Trim Castle Hotel (Co. Meath), 190
Trinity City Hotel (Dublin), 131
Trinity Townhouse (Dublin), 134
Viewmount House (Co. Longford), 436
Waterford Marina Hotel, 223–224
The Westbury (Dublin), 13, 129–130
Westport Coast Hotel (Co. Mayo), 455
Whitford House Hotel (Co. Wexford), 235–236
Wicklow Way Lodge (Co. Wicklow), 207
The Wilder Townhouse (Dublin), 131
Wineport Lodge (Co. Westmeath), 436
Woodbrook House B&B (Co. Wexford), 236
Wren Urban Nest (Dublin), 135

Restaurants

5Points Café (Co. Cork), 263
101 Talbot (Dublin), 152
147 Deli (Dublin), 152
1826 Adare (Co. Limerick), 375–376
Agape (Co. Kildare), 197
Al Mezza (Co. Westmeath), 438
Aniar (Co. Galway), 398
An Port Mór (Co. Mayo), 455
Ard Bia at Nimmo's (Co. Galway), 398
Ard na Sidhe Country House (Co. Kerry), 332
Ariosa Café (Co. Louth), 190
Artis by Phelim O'Hagan (Derry), 15, 572
Badgers Bar (Derry), 573
Bang (Dublin), 153
The Bank on College Green (Dublin), 141
Bare Food Company (Co. Louth), 190

Barrtrá Seafood Restaurant (Co. Clare), 366
Bastion (Co. Cork), 279
Bastion Kitchen (Co. Westmeath), 438
The Bay Tree (Co. Louth), 191
Bean & Berry (Co. Cork), 290
Bean a Tí (Co. Limerick), 375
Bean in Dingle (Co. Kerry), 346
Beans & Leaves (Co. Westmeath), 438
Beara Barista (Co. Cork), 290
The Beehive (Co. Mayo), 456
Befani's (Co. Tipperary), 384
Bewley's (Dublin), 154–155
Bianconi (Co. Kerry), 332–333
The Black Pig (Co. Cork), 16, 279
Blackbird (Derry), 573
Blackrock Cottage (Co. Galway), 398–399
Blairscove (Co. Cork), 290
The Blind Piper (Co. Kerry), 332
The Blue Apron (Co. Offaly), 439–440
Blueberry Tea Room and Restaurant (Co. Donegal), 484
The Boathouse Bistro (Co. Kerry), 320–321
Bodega! (Co. Waterford), 225
Bramley (Co. Laois), 437
Bread 41 (Dublin), 141
Bricín (Co. Kerry), 312
Bridge Café & Bistro (Co. Kerry), 333–334
The Brown Bear (Co. Kildare), 197
Browns Bonds Hill (Derry), 572
Brunel's (Co. Down), 552
Bunsen (Dublin), 147
Burke's Restaurant (Co. Louth), 191
Bushmills Inn (Co. Antrim), 542
Cafe Paradiso (Co. Cork), 263–264
Café Rua (Co. Mayo), 455
Campagne (Co. Kilkenny), 247
The Carriage Restaurant (Co. Galway), 420
Cask (Co. Cork), 263
Castle Bistro (Derry), 572
Castle Grove (Co. Donegal), 491
The Catalina Restaurant (Co. Fermanagh), 584–585
The Cellar Bistro (Co. Westmeath), 438
Chakra by Jaipur (Co. Wicklow), 208
Chapter One (Dublin), 15–16, 150–151
Chez Hans (Co. Tipperary), 384
Christy's Harvest (Co. Mayo), 455
Cleaver East (Dublin), 144
Coach House Coffee (Co. Waterford), 224
Coach Lane at Donaghy's (Co. Sligo), 470
Coco (Belfast), 524
Common Market Belfast, 523
The Cook & Gardener (Co. Donegal), 16, 491–492
Cornstore (Co. Limerick), 376
Cunningham's (Co. Kildare), 197
The Daily Grind (Co. Down), 552
Dede at the Customs House (Co. Cork), 15, 291
Diamond View Coffee (Co. Galway), 419
D'Lush Café (Co. Wexford), 236–237
D'Olier Street (Dublin), 148
The Dough Bros (Co. Galway), 399
Doyle's Seafood Restaurant (Co. Kerry), 346
Durty Nelly's (Co. Clare), 366–367
Eala Bhán (Co. Sligo), 470
Éan (Co. Galway), 399
Ecofish (Co. Cork), 263
Embers (Co. Armagh), 559
Everett's (Co. Waterford), 225
Fallon & Byrne (Dublin), 149
The Fatted Calf (Co. Westmeath), 439
Fenton's (Co. Kerry), 347
Ferrit & Lee (Co. Cork), 273
Finns' Farmcut (Co. Cork), 280
Fire and Feast (Co. Cork), 290
Firehouse Bakery (Co. Wicklow), 208
Fish Shop (Dublin), 152–153
The Fisherman's Bar (Co. Kerry), 333
Fishy Fishy (Co. Cork), 280
Fisk @ the Harbour Bar (Co. Donegal), 492
Flanagan's On The Lake (Co. Tipperary), 384–385
Flying Poet (Co. Cork), 278
Foley's at the Pike (Co. Limerick), 376
Foodworks (Co. Kilkenny), 247
Forbes Street by Gareth Mullins (Dublin), 156
Frank's Place (Co. Wexford), 237
Fresh (Dublin), 153
Gallagher's Boxty House (Dublin), 144, 146
Ginger Bistro (Belfast), 524
The Glass Curtain (Co. Cork), 264
The Glyde Inn (Co. Louth), 191
Goldie (Co. Cork), 15, 264
Gourmet Burger Kitchen (Dublin), 147
Gourmet Store (Co. Kilkenny), 247
Green Acres (Co. Wexford), 237
Green Barn (Co. Kildare), 197
Greene's (Co. Cork), 264
Gregans Castle (Co. Clare), 367
Harbour Kitchen (Co. Wicklow), 208–209
Harlem (Belfast), 523
Harrow (Co. Kerry), 312
Harry's Shack (Co. Antrim), 542
Hartes (Co. Kildare), 198
The Harvest Room Restaurant at Dunbrody House (Co. Wexford), 237–238
The Heron's Cove (Co. Cork), 291
Holohans Pantry (Belfast), 526–527
Homestead Cottage (Co. Clare), 367
Hooked (Co. Sligo), 470–471
Hunter's Hotel (Co. Wicklow), 209
Il Valentino (Dublin), 147
Jack Monday's (Co. Limerick), 375
Jack's Coastguard Restaurant (Co. Kerry), 333
James Street & Co (Belfast), 524–525
John Long's Fish & Chips (Belfast), 527
The Jolly Sandwich (Co. Fermanagh), 585
Kai (Co. Galway), 399–400
Kate Brown's (Co. Kerry), 337
Kate Kearney's Cottage (Co. Kerry), 312
Kate's Kitchen (Co. Sligo), 471
Kelly's Café (Co. Wexford), 237
Kingdom 1795 (Co. Kerry), 333
Kingfisher Café (Co. Down), 545
Kyteler's Inn (Co. Kilkenny), 247
Lady Helen (Co. Kilkenny), 247
Larder Deli (Co. Clare), 366
Lemon Crepe & Coffee Co. (Dublin), 155
Lemon Leaf Café Bar and Townhouse (Co. Cork), 279
Leo Burdock's (Dublin), 150
Leona's (Co. Cork), 279
Library Street (Dublin), 154
The Lime Tree (Co. Kerry), 321
Lir Café (Co. Kerry), 311
Little Lane Coffee Company (Co. Galway), 397
Loose Canon (Dublin), 155–156
Lotus Eaters by the Pig's Ear (Dublin), 148
Maison Gourmet (Co. Kerry), 321
Mamó (Dublin), 156
Man Friday (Co. Cork), 281
Market Lane (Co. Cork), 264–265
Mary Ann's (Co. Cork), 291
Max's (Co. Cork), 281
The Merry Ploughboy (Dublin), 157
Misunderstood Heron (Co. Galway), 419
Mocha Beans (Co. Mayo), 455
Molly's Yard (Belfast), 525
Momo (Co. Waterford), 225
The Moorings (Co. Kerry), 332
Mourne Seafood Bar (Belfast), 525
Mourne Seafood Bar (Co. Down), 553
Mr Fox (Dublin), 151
MrDeanes (Belfast), 525
The Muddlers Club (Belfast), 523
Mulcahys (Co. Kerry), 321
Murphy's Ice Cream (Co. Kerry), 312
The Mustard Seed (Co. Limerick), 376
Nancy's Barn (Inishowen Peninsula), 497
Neighbourhood (Co. Kildare), 198–199
Network Café (Dublin), 141

No. 35 (Co. Kerry), 321
The Oak Room (Co. Limerick), 376–377
O'Dowd's of Roundstone (Co. Galway), 420
The Old Storehouse (Dublin), 146
Orso (Co. Cork), 265
Osta Café & Wine Bar (Co. Sligo), 471
Out of the Blue (Co. Kerry), 347
Ox (Belfast), 17, 523–524
The Oyster Tavern (Co. Kerry), 337
Paddy Coyne's Pub (Co. Galway), 420
Paladar (Co. Cork), 263
Pho Viet (Dublin), 152
The Pigeon House (Co. Wicklow), 210
Pizza Base (Co. Cork), 290
The Poacher (Co. Mayo), 456
Poffs (Co. Kerry), 320
Poppies (Co. Wicklow), 208
Pyke 'N' Pommes 53–55 (Derry), 573–574
QC's (Co. Kerry), 332
Quay West (Co. Donegal), 484–485
Queen Bee's Café and Deli (Co. Tipperary), 385
Quills (Co. Cork), 290
Quinlan's Seafood Bar (Co. Kerry), 312–313
Reel Dingle Fish (Co. Kerry), 347–348
Restaurant Chestnut (Co. Cork), 292
Richmond House (Co. Waterford), 225–226
Rift Coffee (Co. Limerick), 375
Ristorante Rinuccini (Co. Kilkenny), 248
River House Restaurant (Co. Tipperary), 385
Roam (Belfast), 15, 526
Roberta's (Dublin), 146
Rookery Lane (Co. Kerry), 320
Rozzers (Co. Kerry), 313
Ruby Ellen's Tea Rooms (Co. Louth), 190
Rúibín (Co. Galway), 400
The Rusty Nail (Inishowen Peninsula), 497
The Rusty Oven (Co. Donegal), 492
Saga (Belfast), 526
Savoir Fare (Co. Mayo), 456
The Seafood Bar @ Kirwan's (Co. Galway), 400–401
Seagull Bakery (Co. Waterford), 224
Seed Café (Co. Wicklow), 200
Shell's Café (Co. Sligo), 472
Sheridans Cheesemongers (Co. Galway), 401
Silken Thomas (Co. Kildare), 199
The Silver Room (Co. Limerick), 377
Smugglers Creek Inn (Co. Donegal), 485
Sole Seafood & Grill (Dublin), 149–150
The Spaniard (Co. Cork), 281–282
St. George's Market (Belfast), 523
Stage Door Café (Dublin), 141
Statham's (Co. Kilkenny), 247
Steam Cafe (Co. Galway), 420
Stonechat (Co. Kerry), 313
Strandfield House (Co. Louth), 190
The Strawberry Field (Co. Kerry), 321–322
The Strawberry Tree (Co. Wicklow), 210
The Supper Club (Co. Cork), 282
Table Forty ONe (Co. Wexford), 238
The Tannery (Co. Waterford), 226
The Taphouse (Co. Fermanagh), 585
Tartine at the Distillers Arms (Co. Antrim), 542–543
Teach Nan Phaidi (Aran Islands), 395
Terre (Co. Cork), 15, 274
This Must Be The Place (Co. Mayo), 455
Thyme (Co. Westmeath), 439
Thyme & Co. (Co. Antrim), 543
Tully Mill (Co. Fermanagh), 585
Ubiquitous (Inishowen Peninsula), 497
Umi Falafel (Dublin), 147–148
Urban Grind (Co. Galway), 397
Vanilla Pod (Co. Meath), 191
Vaughan's Anchor Inn (Co. Clare), 368
Veldon's Seafarer (Co. Galway), 421
The Village Kitchen (Co. Kerry), 334
The Vintage Kitchen (Dublin), 149
Walled City Brewery (Derry), 572–573
Wharton's Traditional Fish & Chips (Co. Kerry), 334
Wild Honey Inn (Co. Clare), 16, 368
Wilde's at the Lodge (Co. Mayo), 457
The Winding Stair (Dublin), 151
Wooden Spoon (Co. Clare), 366

PHOTO CREDITS

Front cover: © Arcad / Shutterstock.com; p. i: © ENCPhotography / Shutterstock; p. iii: © Tourism Ireland / Richard Watson; p. 1: Courtesy of EPIC The Irish Emigration Museum / © Peter Varga; p. 3: Courtesy of Tourism Ireland / Bren Whelan; p. 4: © Peter Krocka / Shutterstock; p. 5: Courtesy of Tourism Ireland / Chris Hill; p. 6: © Patryk Kosmider / Shutterstock; p. 7: Courtesy of Fáilte Ireland / Outlier; p. 9: Courtesy of Fáilte Ireland; p. 10: © Wicker Imaging / Shutterstock; p. 11: Courtesy of Fáilte Ireland / 1IMAGE / Bryan Brophy; p. 12: © MNStudio / Shutterstock; p. 13: Courtesy of Adare Manor / Jack Hardy; p. 14: Courtesy of Fáilte Ireland / The Merrion Hotel; p. 15: Courtesy of Fáilte Ireland / Dromoland Castle Hotel; p. 16, left: Courtesy of Cook & Gardener / PAUL MCGUCKIN; p. 16, right: Courtesy of OX / Elaine Hill Photography; p. 17: Courtesy of Belfast City Council / www.belfastcity.gov.uk / markets; p. 20: Courtesy of Tourism Ireland; p. 22: Courtesy of Fáilte Ireland / GIAF_Galway International Arts Festival; p. 24: © Maciek A; p. 26: Courtesy of Fáilte Ireland / Sonder Visuals; p. 28: © chrisdorney / Shutterstock; p. 29: Courtesy of Fáilte Ireland / Martin Fleming; p. 31: © Alex_Mastro / Shutterstock; p. 32: © David Soanes / Shutterstock; p. 34: © Nick Fox / Shutterstock; p. 37: Courtesy of Fáilte Ireland / Ruth Medjber; p. 39: © glynnis2009; p. 41: Courtesy of Tourism Ireland / Dave Walsh; p. 42: © YingHui Liu / Shutterstock; p. 45: © Tourism Northern Ireland / Finn Richards; p. 46: © Fáilte

Ireland; p. 55: Courtesy of Fáilte Ireland / Courtesy Harris PR / Barry Cronin; p. 56: © Cenz07 / Shutterstock; p. 58: © Kirk Fisher / Shutterstock; p. 61: Courtesy of Fáilte Ireland / Rob Durston; p. 66: Courtesy of Fáilte Ireland / Christian McLeod; p. 69: © Bernd Meissner / Shutterstock; p. 70: Courtesy of Fáilte Ireland / Dylan Vaughan; p. 72: © meunierd / Shutterstock; p. 74: © MNStudio / Shutterstock; p. 78: © Gvictoria / Shutterstock.com; p. 79, top: Courtesy Fáilte Ireland / Johnny Frazer for Islander; p. 79, bottom: © dies-irae / Shutterstock; p. 80: Courtesy of Fáilte Ireland / Liana Modonova; p. 86: © Alyssa Mattei; p. 88: © Alyssa Mattei; p. 90: © Meunierd / Shutterstock; p. 96: Courtesy Failte Ireland / Sonder Visuals; p. 99: Courtesy of Fáilte Ireland / Chris Hill; p. 100: Courtesy of Fáilte Ireland; p. 103: © David Soanes / Shutterstock; p. 106: Courtesy of Fáilte Ireland; p. 108: Courtesy Fáilte Ireland / Guinness Storehouse / Naoise Culhane; p. 111: © Steve Travelguide / Shutterstock; p. 114: Courtesy of Fáilte Ireland; p. 115: © jksz.photography / Shutterstock; p. 117: Courtesy of Fáilte Ireland; p. 119: Courtesy of Fáilte Ireland / Tourism Ireland / Antoinette Reilly; p. 123: © Irina Wilhauk / Shutterstock; p. 125: Courtesy of Tourism Ireland / John Fahy; p. 129: Courtesy of The Merrion Hotel; p. 130: Courtesy of The Shelbourne / Barry Murphy Photography; p. 132: Courtesy of Brooks Hotel; p. 137: Courtesy of The Morrison / David Cantwell Photography; p. 144: Courtesy of Gallagher's Boxty House / Pedro Giaquinto; p. 148: Courtesy of D'Olier / David McClelland Photography; p. 149: © Courtesy of Fáilte Ireland / Sole Seafood and Grill_Corporate.ie; p. 150: © Alyssa Mattei; p. 151: Courtesy of Tourism Ireland; p. 154: Courtesy of Library Street; p. 155: Courtesy of Fáilte Ireland / Courtesy Pól Ó Conghaile; p. 158: Courtesy of Jam Art Factory; p. 162: Courtesy of Stable / Aisling McCoy; p. 163: Courtesy of Sheridan's Cheesemongers; p. 166: © Smokestack Co / Shutterstock; p. 169: Courtesy of Failte Ireland / Sonder Visuals; p. 172: © Chad and Steph; p. 174: Courtesy of Tourism Ireland / Theresa Aherne; p. 177: Courtesy Fáilte Ireland / Sonder Visuals; p. 181: © MNStudio / Shutterstock; p. 186: © Bjoern Alberts; p. 189: Courtesy of The Cottages; p. 194: © Irish National Stud / Fáilte Ireland; p. 196: Courtesy of Martinstown House / Olga Hogan; p. 202: Courtesy of Tourism Ireland; p. 203: © Fáilte Ireland / Courtesy Celtic Routes; p. 206: Courtesy of Tourism Ireland / Chris Hill; p. 208: Courtesy of Chakra by Jaipur / Richard Stokes; p. 211: Courtesy of Failte Ireland / Áine O'Connor; p. 218: Courtesy of Fáilte Ireland / Andrew Bradley; p. 219, top: © shawnwil23 / Shutterstock; p. 219, bottom: Courtesy Fáilte Ireland / Patrick Browne for Waterford Treasures; p. 220: © Fáilte Ireland / Courtesy Waterford Museum of Treasures; p. 221: © Osadchaya Olga; p. 223: © Courtest of Granville Hotel / David Cantwell; p. 224: Courtesy of Bodega; p. 230: © Michal Wlodarczyk / Shutterstock; p. 233: Courtesy Fáilte Ireland / Roamer; p. 236: Courtesy of Frank's Place / Greenacres Wexford / Ger Lawlor Photo; p. 237: Courtesy of Dunbrody Country House; p. 240: © BOULENGER Xavier / Shutterstock.com; p. 242: © Betofoto / Shutterstock; p. 243: © MNStudio / Shutterstock; p. 246: Courtesy Failte Ireland / Glasseye; p. 249: © Fáilte Ireland / Courtesy Blarney Castle and Gardens; p. 255: Courtesy of Tourism Ireland / Brian Morrison; p. 256: © INTREEGUE Photography / Shutterstock; p. 257: © INTREEGUE Photography / Shutterstock; p. 258: © AlexUm5 / Shutterstock; p. 260: Courtesy of Hayfield Manor; p. 265: Courtesy of Market Lane / Ruth Calder Potts; p. 270: © Riekelt Hakvoort / Shutterstock; p. 272: Courtesy of Midleton Distillery Experience / Cathal Noonan; p. 274: Courtesy of Terre / Barry Murphy Photography; p. 275: Courtesy Failte Ireland / Sonder Visuals; p. 276: © Kirk Fisher / Shutterstock; p. 280: Courtesy of Finns' Farmcut / Joleen Cronin; p. 281: Courtesy of The Spaniard; p. 287: © Tourism Ireland / Arthur Ward; p. 288: Courtesy of Tourism Ireland / Joshua McMichael; p. 289: Courtesy of Inchydoney Lodge & Spa / Barry Murphy Photography; p. 291: Courtesy of Dede / Clare Keogh; p. 295: © essevu / Shutterstock; p. 299: Courtesy of Tourism Ireland / Valerie O'Sullivan; p. 302: Courtesy of Tourism Ireland; p. 305: Courtesy of Tourism Ireland / © David Rocaberti; p. 307: Courtesy of Aghadoe Heights Hotel & Spa / Barry Murphy; p. 308: Courtesy of The Europe; p. 311: Courtesy of Agdahoe Heights / © Barry Murphy Photography; p. 313: Courtesy of Rozzers; p. 317: © Gabriel12 / Shutterstock; p. 318: Courtesy of Park Hotel Kenmare; p. 320: Courtesy of The Boathouse; p. 322: © Judith Lienert / Shutterstock; p. 328: © jksz.photography / Shutterstock; p. 329: Courtesy of Valentia Lighthouse; p. 330: Courtesy of Ard na Sidhe Country House; p. 335: © gabriel12 / Shutterstock; p. 341: Courtesy of Fáilte Ireland / Gareth McCormack; p. 343: Courtesy of Tourism Ireland / Kim Leuenberger; p. 347: Courtesy of Tourism Ireland / Therese Ahern; p. 351: © Arcady / Shutterstock; p. 356: © Michael Mc Lughlin; p. 358: © Mark Carthy / Shutterstock; p. 360: © Anton_Ivanov / Shutterstock; p. 361: © Elzbieta

Sekowska / Shutterstock; p. 362: © Kwiatek7 / Shutterstock; p. 364: Courtesy of Armada House / Awake and Dreaming Photography; p. 367: Courtesy of Gregans Castle Hotel; p. 368: Courtesy of Wild Honey; p. 370: Courtesy Fáilte Ireland / Tourism Ireland / Chris Hill Photographic; p. 373: Courtesy of Adare Manor / Jack Hardy; p. 375: Courtesy of 1826 Adare; p. 380: Courtesy Failte Ireland / Outlier; p. 382: © Thomas Bresenhuber / Shutterstock; p. 387: © Karlo Curis / Shutterstock; p. 390: © © Galway City Museum / Marta Barcikowska; p. 393: Courtesy of St. Nicholas' Collegiate Church; p. 398: Courtesy of Aniar / Anita Murphy; p. 400: Courtesy of Kai Galway / Mark Conlon; p. 402: Courtesy of Charlie Byrne's Bookshop; p. 405: Courtesy of Faite Ireland / Fionn Davenport; p. 406: Courtesy of Tourism Ireland; p. 408: Courtesy of Tourism Ireland; p. 413: © MNStudio / Shutterstock; p. 414: © Gimas / Shutterstock; p. 416: Courtesy of Ballynahinch Castle / Barry Murphy Photography; p. 417: Courtesy of Tourism Ireland / Big Smoke Studio; p. 419: Courtesy of Misunderstood Heron / Nathalie Marquez Courtney; p. 423: Courtesy of Slieve Bloom Way; p. 426: Courtesy of Failte Ireland / Sonder Visuals; p. 429: Courtesy of Tourism Ireland / Tristan Hutchinson; p. 431: Courtesy of Failte Ireland / Simon Crowe; p. 433: Courtesy of Irish Heritage Trust; p. 435: Courtesy of Bastion / Mark Duffy; p. 439: Courtesy of Failte Ireland / Westmeath County Council / Corin Bishop; p. 441: Courtesy of Ashford Castle / Kelvin Gillmor; p. 444: © Andrei Nekrassov / Shutterstock; p. 446: Courtesy of Clare Island; p. 449: © makasana photo / Shutterstock; p. 450: © Maria_Janus / Shutterstock.com; p. 453: Courtesy of The Red Carnation Hotel Collection; p. 455: © Wozzie / Shutterstock; p. 463: © jon sullivan / Shutterstock; p. 465: © Brendan Howard / Shutterstock.com; p. 469: Courtesy of Temple House / Steve Rogers; p. 470: Courtesy of Eala Bhan; p. 471: Courtesy of Hooked; p. 472: Courtesy of Sligo Craft Shop / John Mee; p. 474: Courtesy of Glenveagh National Park and Castle / © GARETH WRAY; p. 476: © Madrugada Verde; p. 482: Courtesy Fáilte Ireland / Big Style Media; p. 484: Courtesy of Harvey's Point Hotel; p. 485: Courtesy of Smuggler's Creek; p. 487: © Pack-Shot / Shutterstock; p. 490: Courtesy of Glenveagh National Park and Castle / Paul McGuckin; p. 494: Courtesy of Fáilte Ireland / Gareth Wray Photography; p. 496: © CA Irene Lorenz / Shutterstock; p. 498: Courtesy of Tourism Ireland / Chris Hill Photographic; p. 499: © Cynthia Shirk / Shutterstock; p. 504: © dvlcom / Shutterstock.com; p. 506: Courtesy of Tourism Ireland / Paul Lindsay; p. 509: Courtesy of Belfast City Council / Hype Factory / www.belfastcity.gov.uk / markets; p. 510: Courtesy of Tourism Ireland / Chris Hill; p. 511: Courtesy of Titanic Distillers at Thompson Dock; p. 513: © NorthLight PhotoArt / Shutterstock; p. 515: Courtesy of Tourism Ireland; p. 518: Courtesy of Grand Central / JACK HARDY; p. 520: Courtesy of The Harrison Chambers of Distinction; p. 522: Courtesy of Ravenshill Guesthouse; p. 524: Courtesy of The OX / Elaine Hill Photography; p. 526: Courtesy of Roam; p. 530: Courtesy of Crown Liquor Saloon / Lorenzo Mosica / Archivolatino / Red; p. 531: © Alyssa Mattei; p. 534: Courtesy of Tourism Ireland / Chris Hill; p. 537: © Umomos / Shutterstock; p. 539: Courtesy of Tourism Ireland / Christopher Heaney; p. 540: Courtesy of Tourism Ireland / Christopher Heaney; p. 541, top: Courtesy of The Salthouse Hotel / Alexandra Barfoot Photography; p. 541, bottom: Courtesy of Ballylagan Organic Farm; p. 545: © 4kclips / Shutterstock; p. 547: Courtesy of Tourism Ireland / Art Ward; p. 550: © Navorolphotography / Shutterstock.com; p. 553: Courtesy of Tourism Ireland; p. 556: Courtesy of Tourism Ireland; p. 557: Courtesy of Tourism Ireland; p. 559: Courtesy of Newforge House / Geoff Telford Photography; p. 561: Courtesy of Tourism Ireland / Gardiner Mitchell; p. 564: Courtesy of Tourism Ireland / Chris Hill; p. 567: © Susanne Pommer; p. 570: Courtesy of Tourism Ireland; p. 577: © Courtesy of Tourism Northern Ireland / Donal Maloney; p. 580: © Laura S G / Shutterstock; p. 581: Courtesy of Fermanagh Lakelands / Paul Lindsay; p. 583: Courtesy of Castle Leslie; p. 584: Courtesy of Finn Lough; p. 587: © Fáilte Ireland / Gareth Wray Photography; back cover: © Mike Shaw / Shutterstock.com.

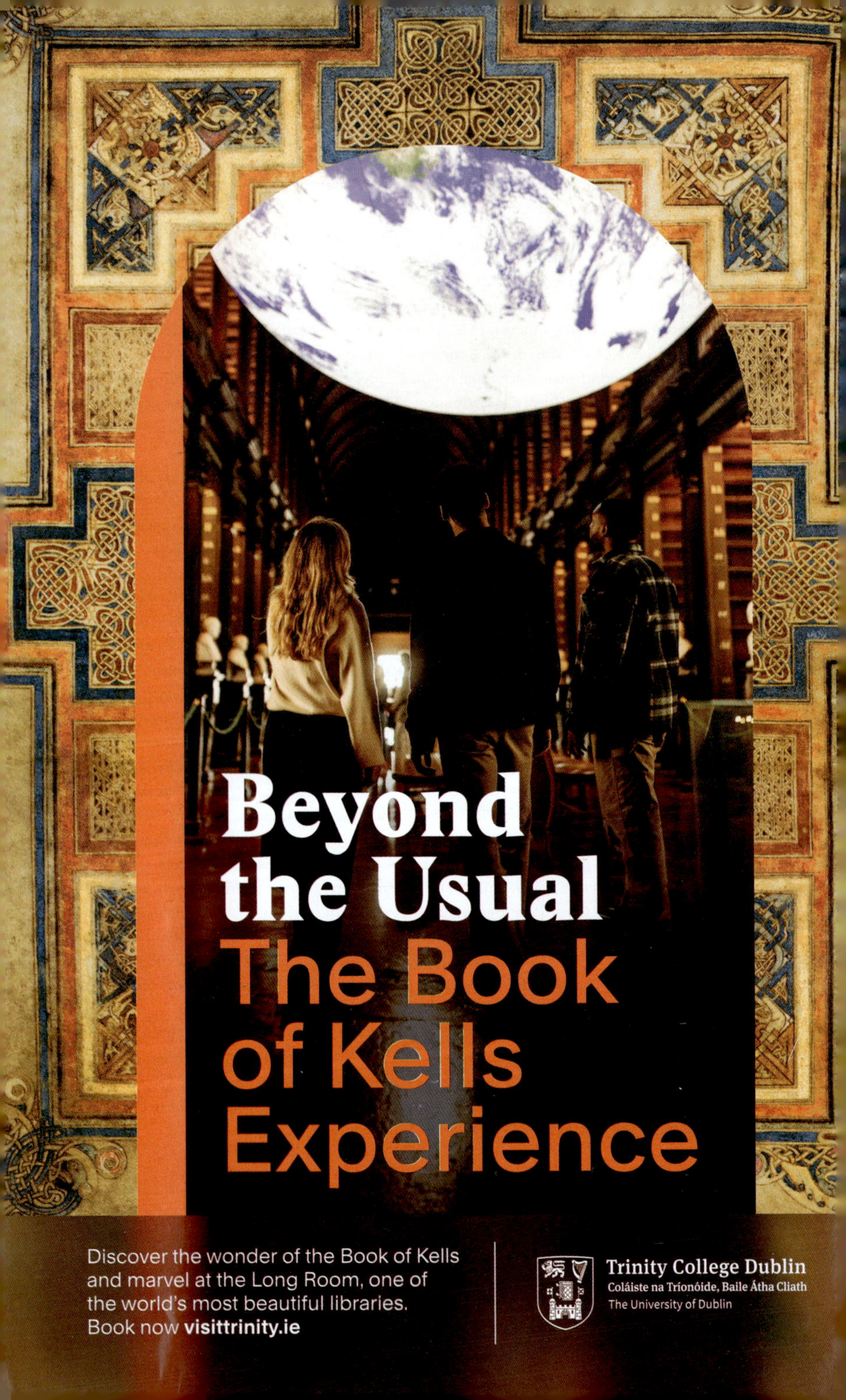